Fodor
Affordable
Florida

PRAISE FOR FODOR'S GUIDES

"Fodor's guides . . . are an admirable blend of the cultural and the practical."
—The Washington Post

"Researched by people chosen because they live or have lived in the country, well-written, and with good historical sections . . . Obligatory reading for millions of tourists."
—The Independent, *London*

"Usable, sophisticated restaurant coverage, with an emphasis on good value."
—*Andy Birsh*, Gourmet *restaurant columnist, quoted by Gannett News Service*

"Packed with dependable information."
—Atlanta Journal Constitution

"Fodor's always delivers high quality . . . thoughtfully presented . . . thorough."
—Houston Post

"Valuable because of their comprehensiveness."
—Minneapolis Star-Tribune

Portions of this book appear in *Fodor's Florida*

Fodor's Travel Publications, Inc.
New York • Toronto • London • Sydney • Auckland

Second Edition

ISBN 0–679–02965–6

Fodor's Affordable Florida

Editor: Andrea E. Lehman
Area Editor: Herb Hiller
Editorial Contributors: Pamela Acheson, Robert Andrews, Robert Blake, Jennifer Burgess, Marianne Camas, Robert Fisher, Janet Foley, Catherine Fredman, Barbara Freitag, Janet and Gordon Groene, Anto Howard, Ann Hughes, George and Rosalie Leposkey, Mary Meehan, Rebecca Miller, Mary Ellen Schultz, M. T. Schwartzman, G. Stuart Smith, Karen Feldman Smith, Dinah Spritzer, Rowland Stiteler
Creative Director: Fabrizio La Rocca
Cartographer: David Lindroth
Illustrator: Karl Tanner
Cover Photograph: Barbara Doernbach/WaterHouse, Inc.

Design: Vignelli Associates

Special Sales

Contents

Maps

How These Guides Will Save You Money

If you're on a truly rock-bottom budget and you want information on really low-end accommodations and restaurants with names like "Eats," then look to another guidebook for your travel information.

But if you want to find crisp sheets, a firm bed, and a soft pillow at night and to enjoy a good meal in a nice atmosphere, read on. It's for you that Fodor's team of savvy, budget-conscious writers and editors have prepared this book.

Saving money is all about making choices. Some of us do it by sticking to public transportation and picnic lunches. Others spend more on a hotel with amenities but don't care about fancy meals. Still others take the hostel route in order to go on a shopping spree. Fitting some of the finer things into your travel doesn't mean you have to blow your budget.

In this guide, we've tried to include enough options so that all of you spend time and money in the ways you most enjoy. The hotels we suggest are good values, and there are no dives, thank you—only clean, friendly places with an acceptable level of comfort, convenience, and charm. We also recommend a range of inexpensive and moderately priced restaurants where you can eat well in pleasant surroundings. We've even included a few splurges in case you want to spend a little more for that extra-special dining or lodging experience. And you can read about the best budget shopping, how to make the arts-and-nightlife scene in major cities without breaking the bank, and how to get around in the most economical fashion.

As for planning what to see and do, you'll find the same lively writing and authoritative background information available in Fodor's renowned Gold Guides.

Please Write to Us

Everyone who has contributed to *Fodor's Affordable Florida* has worked hard to make the text accurate. All prices and opening times are based on material supplied to us at press time, and Fodor's cannot accept responsibility for any errors that may have occurred. The passage of time always brings changes, so it's a good idea to call ahead to confirm information when it matters—particularly if you're making a detour to visit specific sights or attractions. When making reservations at a hotel or inn, be sure to mention if you have a disability or are traveling with children, if you prefer a private bath or a certain type of bed, or if you have specific dietary needs or any other concerns.

Do let us know about your trip. Did you enjoy the restaurants we recommended? Was your hotel comfortable and were the museums you visited worthwhile? Did you happen upon a treasure that we haven't included? We would love to have your feedback, positive and negative. If you have suggestions or complaints, we'll look into them and revise our entries when it's the right thing to do. So please send us a letter or postcard (we're at 201 East 50th Street, New York, New York 10022). We look forward to hearing from you. In the meantime, have a wonderful trip!

Karen Cure
Editorial Director

Fodor's Choice for Budget Travelers

No two people will agree on what makes a perfect vacation, but it's fun—and can be helpful—to know what others think. We hope you'll have a chance to experience some of Fodor's Choices yourself while you're visiting Florida. For detailed information about each entry, refer to the appropriate chapters within this guidebook.

Lodging

Bluewater Bay Resort, Niceville, *$$*

Carriage Way Bed and Breakfast, St. Augustine, *$$*

Crown Hotel, Inverness, *$$*

Hibiscus House, West Palm Beach, *$$*

Orlando Heritage Inn, Orlando, *$$*

Blue Seas, Lauderdale-by-the-Sea, *$*

Sagamore Hotel, Miami Beach, *$*

Bonefish Resort, Grassy Key, *¢–$*

Dining

Columbia, Tampa, *$$*

Darbar, Coral Gables, *$$*

11 Maple Street, Jensen Beach, *$$*

Le Coq au Vin, Orlando, *$$*

Mangia Mangia, Key West, *$–$$*

Richard Acursio's Capri Restaurant and King Richard's Room, Florida City, *$–$$*

Bud & Alley's, Seaside, *$*

Mangiere Ristorante, Daytona Beach, *$*

Studio One French Bistro, Fort Lauderdale, *$*

Beehive Diner, Miami Beach, *¢*

Florida

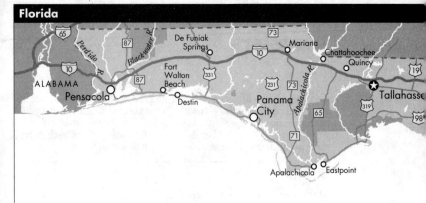

Gulf of Mexico

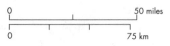

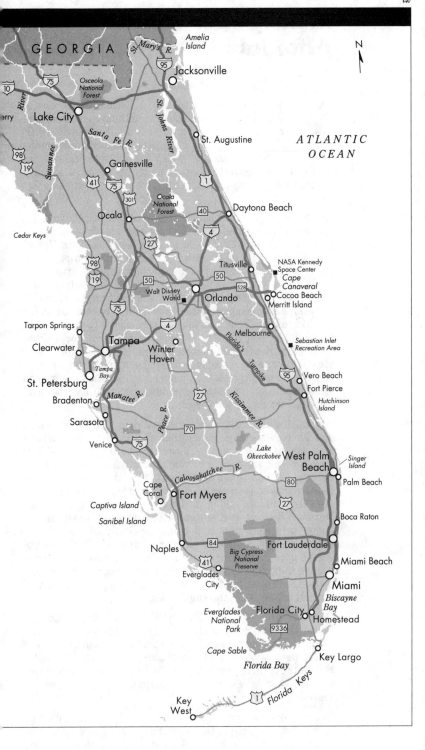

Making Your Vacation Affordable

Vacationers have been coming to Florida for 125 years, so you can bet this state knows something about looking after its visitors. Florida's tourism officials invented the concept of welcome stations; Florida resort operators invented modified American plan (in which a room rate includes two meals); Florida rewrote the book on mega–theme parks, turning the central part of the state into a mecca for vacationing families.

And for every rich vacationer who ever danced in a gilded hall by the sea, 10 have come down the back roads to sit by a lake and just watch the sunset. For every luxury hotel like Palm Beach's the Breakers, there has always been a mom-and-pop motel ready to take in a traveler. For every hoity-toity Restaurant de Paris, there has always been a Sam's or a Three Sisters Coffee Shop featuring early-bird specials and the tangiest citrus pie you ever ate. Once upon a time, if you wanted to vacation for less you had to head for certain areas—say, north of St. Petersburg or around Jacksonville. But nowadays even Miami, Fort Lauderdale, Palm Beach, and Naples—resort areas that once were strictly for the rich—are affordable if you know where to look. Since tourism is the state's number-one industry, there's endless competition for whatever vacationers want, and the result can be a bargain hunter's dream.

And during all those years that vacationers have been coming down here, some have gotten that glint in their eye that says, Hey, maybe I can figure out how to live here all the time! They do come back, and to earn a living they do what comes naturally: hosting and feeding the next batch of tourists. As a result, your innkeepers and restaurant owners are often more enthusiastic than they are schooled in the lodging and restaurant business. But such do-it-yourselfers are willing to bend, twist, and reshape their prices to meet demand, especially off-season, when they're just trying to stay in business until it's profitable high season once more. Florida is one of those places where prices change radically depending on the time of year you come (summer is the cheap time in south Florida, late spring and early fall in Orlando, winter in the Panhandle).

Of course Florida has plenty of professional hoteliers and restaurateurs, too, many of them graduates of hotel management schools. But most managers in the travel business never forget how to deal, never forget to do whatever it takes to fill that last bed for the night or get that last chicken breast on a plate for one more check. So don't be afraid to bargain, especially in the off-season.

To save money on your trip to Florida, it helps to remember that there's nothing almighty about brand names. There are no hotel chains that can top the Breakers in Palm Beach or the Boca Raton Resort in Boca Raton. There are no restaurants better than Chef Allen in North Miami Beach or Didier's in Coral Gables. Some of the best places to stay are Florida's astonishing bed-and-breakfasts—there are more than 200 of them, and not one is affiliated with a chain. This book lists plenty of these independent hotels, motels, and restaurants, many of them just a bit off the beaten tourist track. As a general rule, the more out-of-the-way a place is, the less it'll cost. "Out-of-the-way" generally means far from the biggest concentrations of people, around the lakes and rivers and on the quieter seashores. You may even be able to shave a couple of hundred dollars off your vacation expenditures just by staying one or two blocks away from the beach—well worth a few minutes' walk.

To avoid overspending, think about what you really like to do rather than what some mega-resort tells you it has to offer. Florida's prime attraction has always been the glorious outdoors, where you can enjoy sunbathing, swimming, snorkeling, diving, canoeing in streams, hiking along backwoods trails, and cycling on the back roads. These sorts of things are easy to do for little money. For everything you need to know about nature vacations in Florida, one agency or another in Tallahassee, the state capital, has an informative booklet. We describe these sources of information in Important Contacts (*see* Chapter 1, Essential Information).

When it comes to Disney and the other big attractions, prepare to spend. There's no way around it—the more man-made anything is in Florida, the more it's going to cost. But we'll tell you the most affordable way to tour Disney, Universal Studios, and the rest of the mega-attractions.

You can get to Florida pretty cheaply, too. Though the least expensive way is to come with your own car, there are several other affordable options. Plentiful air traffic breeds lots of competition, keeping prices well below what you pay to fly elsewhere. Amtrak provides good service into Florida, and Greyhound serves most major towns.

But no matter how you arrive, you'll still probably want a car to get around, unless you only want to go to the beach and back or are staying at a self-contained resort and don't wish to leave the property. (The largest and most notable of these is Walt Disney World; if you stay on Disney property, transportation to the various Disney theme parks is included in your room rate.) But attractions are generally spread out over large areas, and parks and some of the better restaurants are often far from the beach. What's more, cabs are expensive, and buses and rapid-transit trains, designed more for commuters than for vacationers, don't always go where you want when you want. With a car you can usually be close to someplace natural and still accessible to cities and sights. Luckily, rental-car rates are at least half what they are up north. Remember when comparing transportation prices always to factor in the local costs of getting around at your destination.

So sure there are hundreds of ways to spend your money in Florida, but there are as many ways to save it. We've collected a slew of additional ideas for keeping your vacation economical; you'll find them and other suggestions for getting the most out of your trip in Smart Budget Travel Tips (*see* Chapter 1, Essential Information). Above all, keep this in mind: Florida lives or dies by its tourist trade. That really puts you in the catbird seat. As long as you can be flexible about when you come, where you stay, what time of day you'll eat, and how you enjoy yourself, there are bargains to be found everywhere. And we'll help you find them.

Budget Hotel and Restaurant Information

The affordable restaurants and lodging places in this guide were chosen with a view to giving you the cream of the crop in each location at each price range. Price categories are as follows. For hotels:

Category	Cost*
$$	$60–$90
$	$40–$60
¢	under $40
Splurge	over $90

*All prices are for a standard double room in high season, excluding 6% state sales tax (some counties also have a local sales tax) and nominal (1%–4%) tourist tax.

For restaurants:

Category	Cost*
$$	$20–$35
$	$12–$20
¢	under $12
Splurge	over $35

*per person for a three-course meal, excluding drinks, service, and 6% sales tax

Stars Stars in the margin are used to denote highly recommended hotels and restaurants (as well as sights and attractions).

Hotel Facilities Note that in general you incur charges when you use many hotel facilities. We wanted to let you know what facilities are available, but we don't always specify whether or not there's a charge, so when planning a vacation of several days, it's wise to ask what's included in the rate.

Restaurant Open Hours The restaurants reviewed generally serve lunch and dinner unless otherwise noted.

Credit Cards Throughout the book, credit card abbreviations refer to the following: **AE**, American Express; **D**, Discover; **DC**, Diners Club; **MC**, MasterCard; and **V**, Visa.

1 Essential Information

Important Contacts

No single travel resource can give you every detail about every topic that might interest or concern you at the various stages of your journey—when you're planning your trip, while you're on the road, and after you get back home. The following organizations, books, and brochures will supplement the information in Fodor's *Affordable Florida*. For related information, including both basic tips on visiting Florida and background information on many of the topics below, study Smart Budget Travel Tips, the section that follows Important Contacts.

Air Travel

The major gateways to Florida include Miami International Airport; Orlando International; Tampa International, each year voted as one of America's most user-friendly; and Palm Beach International, which offers a striking collection of art in public places. If you're destined for the north side of Dade (metro Miami), consider flying into Fort Lauderdale–Hollywood International; it's much easier to use than Miami International and has less expensive ground transportation. Several airlines also serve smaller Florida cities, including Jacksonville, Daytona Beach, Melbourne, Fort Myers, Tallahassee, Gainesville, Key West, Sarasota, Naples, Panama City, and Pensacola. Flying time is just over three hours from New York, about three hours from Chicago, and not quite five hours from Los Angeles.

Carriers Most major U.S. airlines schedule regular flights into Florida, and some, such as Delta and USAir, serve Florida airports extensively. Delta (and its commuter affiliate, Comair) and USAir have regular service into Jacksonville, Daytona Beach, Orlando, Melbourne, West Palm Beach, Fort Lauderdale, Miami, Fort Myers, Tampa, Tallahassee, Gainesville, and Key West. Delta also flies into Sarasota, Naples, Panama City, and Pensacola.

Other major airlines that serve the Florida airports include American, American Trans Air, Continental, Northwest, TWA, and United. Many foreign airlines also fly into some of the major airports in Florida; the smaller, out-of-the-way airports are usually accessible through the commuter flights of major domestic carriers.

Packages that combine airfare and vacation activities at special rates are often available through the airlines. For a list of recommended carriers, *see* Packages and Tours, *below*.

For inexpensive, no-frills flights, contact **Carnival Air Lines** (tel. 800/824–7386), which serves Fort Lauderdale, Miami, Tampa, and West Palm Beach; **Kiwi International** (tel. 800/538–5494), serving Orlando, Tampa, and West Palm Beach; **Midwest Express** (tel. 800/452–2022), which serves Fort Lauderdale, Fort Myers, and Tampa; **Private Jet** (tel. 404/231–7571, 800/546–7571, or 800/949–9400), serving Miami and Orlando; and **ValuJet** (tel. 404/994–8258 or 800/825–8538), serving Fort Myers, Tampa, and West Palm Beach.

Complaints To register complaints about charter and scheduled airlines, contact the U.S. Department of Transportation's **Office of Consumer Affairs** (400 7th St. NW, Washington, DC 20590, tel. 202/366–2220 or 800/322–7873).

Publications For general information about charter carriers, ask for the Office of Consumer Affairs' brochure **"Plane Talk: Public Charter Flights."** The Department of Transportation also publishes a 58-page booklet, **"Fly Rights"** ($1.75; Consumer Information Center, Dept. 133B, Pueblo, CO 81009).

For other tips and hints, consult the Consumers Union's monthly **"Consumer Reports Travel Letter"** ($39 a year; Box 53629, Boulder, CO 80322, tel. 800/234–1970); the newsletter **"Travel Smart"** ($37 a year; 40 Beechdale Rd., Dobbs Ferry, NY 10522, tel. 800/327–3633); *The Official Frequent Flyer Guidebook,* by Randy Petersen ($14.99 plus $3 shipping; 4715-C Town Center Dr., Colorado Springs, CO 80916, tel. 719/597–8899 or 800/487–8893); *Airfare Secrets Exposed,* by Sharon Tyler and Matthew Wonder (Universal Information Publishing; $16.95 plus $3.75 shipping from Sandcastle Publishing, Box 3070-A, South Pasadena, CA 91031, tel. 213/255–3616 or 800/655–0053); and *202 Tips Even the Best Business Travelers May Not Know,* by Christopher McGinnis ($10 plus $3 shipping; Irwin Professional Publishing, 1333 Burr Ridge Pkwy., Burr Ridge, IL 60521, tel. 800/634–3966).

Better Business Bureau

For local contacts, consult the **Council of Better Business Bureaus** (4200 Wilson Blvd., Arlington, VA 22203, tel. 703/276–0100).

Bus Travel

For information and schedules contact **Greyhound Lines** (tel. 800/231–2222), which passes through practically every major Florida city.

Car Rental

All major car-rental companies are represented in Florida, including **Alamo** (tel. 800/327–9633), **Avis** (tel. 800/831–2847), **Budget** (tel. 800/527–0700), **Dollar** (tel. 800/800–4000), **Hertz** (tel. 800/654–3131), **National** (tel. 800/227–7368), and **Thrifty** (tel. 800/367–2277). **Value** (tel. 800/468–2583) offers some of the state's lowest rates. Rates in Miami range from $25 to $40 a day and $130 to $165 a week with unlimited mileage. In Jacksonville, rates range from $23 to $40 a day and $110 to $158 a week.

Besides the national rental companies, several local firms offer good deals in major Florida cities. In Fort Lauderdale, local companies include **Aapex Rent A Car** (tel. 305/782–3400) and **Florida Auto Rental** (tel. 305/764–1008 or 800/327–3791). In Orlando, try **Snappy Car Rental** (tel. 407/859–8808). In Tampa–St. Petersburg call **Pinellas Rent-A-Car** (tel. 813/287–1872 or 800/526–5499). In Miami, **Pass** (tel. 305/444–3923) and **InterAmerican Car Rental** (tel. 305/871–3030) sometimes beat the competition. Down in Key West, try **Tropical Rent-a-Car** (tel. 305/294–8136). **Rent-A-Wreck** (tel. 800/535–1391) and **Ugly Duckling** (tel. 800/843–3825) rent used cars, mostly outside major destinations, usually with more stringent mileage restrictions.

Children and Travel

Flying Look into **"Flying With Baby"** ($5.95 plus $1 shipping; Third Street Press, Box 261250, Littleton, CO 80126, tel. 303/595–5959), cowritten by a flight attendant. **"Kids and Teens in Flight,"** free from the U.S. Department of Transportation's Office of Consumer Affairs, offers tips for children flying alone. Every two years the February issue of *Family Travel Times* (*see* Know-How, *below*) details children's services on three dozen airlines.

Games The gamemeister, Milton Bradley, has games to help keep little (and not so little) children from getting fidgety while riding in planes, trains, and automobiles. Try packing the *Travel Battleship* sea battle game ($7); *Travel Connect Four,* a vertical strategy game ($8); the *Travel Yahtzee* dice game ($6); the *Travel Trouble* dice and board game ($7); and the *Travel Guess Who* mystery game ($8).

Know-How *Family Travel Times,* published four times a year by Travel with Your Children ($40 a year; TWYCH, 45 W. 18th St., New York, NY 10011, tel. 212/206–0688), covers destinations, types of vacations, and modes of travel.

The *Family Travel Guides* catalogue ($1 postage; Box 6061, Albany, CA 94706, tel. 510/527–5849) lists about 200 books and articles on family travel. From Globe Pequot Press (Box 833, 6 Business Park Rd., Old Saybrook, CT 06475, tel. 203/395–0440 or 800/243–0495) are *The 100 Best Family Resorts in North America,* by Jane Wilford with Janet Tice ($12.95), and the two-volume (eastern and western editions) set of *50 Great Family Vacations in North America* ($18.95 each plus $3 shipping).

Tour Operators Contact **Rascals in Paradise** (650 5th St., Suite 505, San Francisco, CA 94107, tel. 415/978–9800 or 800/872–7225).

Customs

Canadians Contact **Revenue Canada** (2265 St. Laurent Blvd. S, Ottawa, Ontario K1G 4K3, tel. 613/993–0534) for a copy of the free brochure "I Declare/Je Déclare" and for details on duties that exceed the standard duty-free limit.

U.K. Citizens **HM Customs and Excise** (Dorset House, Stamford St., London SE1 9NG, tel. 0171/202–4227) can answer questions about U.K. customs regulations and publishes "A Guide for Travellers," detailing standard procedures and import rules.

For Travelers with Disabilities

Complaints To register complaints under the provisions of the Americans with Disabilities Act, contact the U.S. Department of Justice's **Public Access Section** (Box 66738, Washington, DC 20035, tel. 202/514–0301, fax 202/307–1198, TTY 202/514–0383).

Organizations
For Travelers with Mobility Impairments Contact the **Information Center for Individuals with Disabilities** (Fort Point Pl., 27–43 Wormwood St., Boston, MA 02210, tel. 617/727–5540, 800/462–5015 in MA, TTY 617/345–9743); **Mobility International USA** (Box 10767, Eugene, OR 97440, tel. and TTY 503/343–1284, fax 503/343–6812), the U.S. branch of an international organization based in Belgium (*see below*) that has affiliates in 30 countries; **MossRehab Hospital Travel Information Service** (1200 W. Tabor Rd., Philadelphia, PA 19141, tel. 215/456–9603, TTY 215/456–9602); the **Society for the Advancement of Travel for the Handicapped** (347 5th Ave., Suite 610, New York, NY 10016, tel. 212/447–7284, fax 212/725–8253); the **Travel Industry and Disabled Exchange** (TIDE, 5435 Donna Ave., Tarzana, CA 91356, tel. 818/344–3640, fax 818/344–0078); and **Travelin' Talk** (Box 3534, Clarksville, TN 37043, tel. 615/552–6670, fax 615/552–1182).

For Travelers with Hearing Impairments Contact the **American Academy of Otolaryngology** (1 Prince St., Alexandria, VA 22314, tel. 703/836–4444, fax 703/683–5100, TTY 703/519–1585).

For Travelers with Vision Impairments Contact the **American Council of the Blind** (1155 15th St. NW, Suite 720, Washington, DC 20005, tel. 202/467–5081, fax 202/467–5085) or the **American Foundation for the Blind** (15 W. 16th St., New York, NY 10011, tel. 212/620–2000, TTY 212/620–2158).

In the U.K. Contact the **Royal Association for Disability and Rehabilitation** (RADAR, 12 City Forum, 250 City Rd., London EC1V 8AF, tel. 0171/250–3222) or **Mobility International** (Rue de Manchester 25, B1070 Brussels, Belgium, tel. 00–322–410–6297), an international clearinghouse of travel information for people with disabilities.

Publications Several free publications are available from the U.S. Information Center (Box 100, Pueblo, CO 81009, tel. 719/948–3334): **"New Horizons for the Air Traveler with a Disability"** (address to Dept. 355A), describing legally mandated changes; the pocket-size **"Fly Smart"** (Dept. 575B), good on flight safety; and the Airport Operators Council's worldwide **"Access Travel: Airports"** (Dept. 575A).

Fodor's *Great American Vacations for Travelers with Disabilities* ($18; available in bookstores, or call 800/533–6478) details accessible attractions, restaurants, and hotels in U.S. destinations. The 500-page *Travelin' Talk Directory* ($35; Box 3534, Clarksville, TN 37043, tel. 615/552–6670) lists people and organizations who help travelers with disabilities. For specialist travel agents worldwide, consult the *Directory of Travel Agencies for the Disabled* ($19.95 plus $2 shipping; Twin Peaks Press, Box 129, Vancouver, WA 98666, tel. 206/694–2462 or 800/637–2256). The Sierra Club publishes *Easy Access to National Parks* ($16 plus $3 shipping; 730 Polk St., San Francisco, CA 94109, tel. 415/776–2211 or 800/935–1056).

You can request a free copy of **"Florida: Planning Companion For Travelers with Disabilities"** from the Florida Governor's Alliance (345 S. Magnolia Dr., Suite D-11, Tallahassee 32301, tel. 904/487–2222, fax 904/922–9619, TTY 904/487–2223), which lists by region agencies and organizations that offer resources and referrals.

Travel Agencies and Tour Operators The Americans with Disabilities Act requires that travel firms serve the needs of all travelers. However, some agencies and operators specialize in making group and individual arrangements for travelers with disabilities, among them **Access Adventures** (206 Chestnut Ridge Rd., Rochester, NY 14624, tel. 716/889–9096), run by a former physical-rehab counselor; **Sprout, Inc.** (893 Amsterdam Ave., New York, NY 10025, tel. 212/222–9575), which specializes in custom-designed itineraries; and **Tailored Tours** (Box 797687, Dallas, TX 75379, tel. 214/612–1168 or 800/628–8542). In addition, many operators and agencies (*see* Tour Operators, *below*) can also arrange vacations for travelers with disabilities.

For Travelers with Mobility Impairments A number of operators specialize in working with travelers with mobility impairments, including **Hinsdale Travel Service** (201 E. Ogden Ave., Suite 100, Hinsdale, IL 60521, tel. 708/325–1335 or 800/303–5521), a travel agency that will give you access to the services of wheelchair traveler Janice Perkins, and **Wheelchair Journeys** (16979 Redmond Way, Redmond, WA 98052, tel. 206/885–2210), which can handle arrangements worldwide.

For Travelers with Hearing Impairments One agency is **International Express** (7319-B Baltimore Ave., College Park, MD 20740, tel. and TTY 301/699–8836, fax 301/699–8836), which arranges group and independent trips.

For Travelers with Developmental Disabilities Travelers with developmental disabilities and their families can contact the nonprofit **New Directions** (5276 Hollister Ave., Suite 207, Santa Barbara, CA 93111, tel. 805/967–2841) as well as the general-interest operations above.

Discount Clubs

Options include **Entertainment Travel Editions** (fee $28–$53, depending on destination; Box 1068, Trumbull, CT 06611, tel. 800/445–4137), **Great American Traveler** ($49.95 annually; Box 27965, Salt

Lake City, UT 84127, tel. 800/548–2812), **Moment's Notice Discount Travel Club** ($25 annually, single or family; 163 Amsterdam Ave., Suite 137, New York, NY 10023, tel. 212/486–0500), **Privilege Card** ($74.95 annually; 3391 Peachtree Rd. NE, Suite 110, Atlanta, GA 30326, tel. 404/262–0222 or 800/236–9732), **Travelers Advantage** ($49 annually, single or family; CUC Travel Service, 49 Music Sq. W, Nashville, TN 37203, tel. 800/548–1116 or 800/648–4037), and **Worldwide Discount Travel Club** ($50 annually for family, $40 single; 1674 Meridian Ave., Miami Beach, FL 33139, tel. 305/534–2082).

Driving

For current information on tolls and other services, try the **Florida's Turnpike** public information number (tel. 800/749–7453).

Gay and Lesbian Travel

Organizations The **International Gay Travel Association** (Box 4974, Key West, FL 33041, tel. 800/448–8550), a consortium of 800 businesses, can supply names of travel agents and tour operators.

Publications The premier international travel magazine for gays and lesbians is *Our World* ($35 for 10 issues; 1104 N. Nova Rd., Suite 251, Daytona Beach, FL 32117, tel. 904/441–5367). The 16-page monthly *Out & About* ($49 for 10 issues; tel. 212/645–6922 or 800/929–2268) covers gay-friendly resorts, hotels, cruise lines, and airlines.

Tour Operators Cruises and resort vacations are handled by **Toto Tours** (1326 W. Albion, Suite 3W, Chicago, IL 60626, tel. 312/274–8686 or 800/565–1241), which has group tours worldwide.

Travel Agencies The largest agencies serving gay travelers are **Advance Travel** (10700 Northwest Fwy., Suite 160, Houston, TX 77092, tel. 713/682–2002 or 800/695–0880), **Islanders/Kennedy Travel** (183 W. 10th St., New York, NY 10014, tel. 212/242–3222 or 800/988–1181), **Now Voyager** (4406 18th St., San Francisco, CA 94114, tel. 415/626–1169 or 800/255–6951), and **Yellowbrick Road** (1500 W. Balmoral Ave., Chicago, IL 60640, tel. 312/561–1800 or 800/642–2488). **Skylink Women's Travel** (746 Ashland Ave., Santa Monica, CA 90405, tel. 310/452–0506 or 800/225–5759) works with lesbians.

Insurance

Travel insurance covering baggage, health, and trip cancellation or interruptions is available from **Access America** (Box 90315, Richmond, VA 23286, tel. 804/285–3300 or 800/284–8300), **Carefree Travel Insurance** (Box 9366, 100 Garden City Plaza, Garden City, NY 11530, tel. 516/294–0220 or 800/323–3149), **Near Travel Services** (Box 1339, Calumet City, IL 60409, tel. 708/868–6700 or 800/654–6700), **Tele-Trip** (Mutual of Omaha Plaza, Box 31716, Omaha, NE 68131, tel. 800/228–9792), **Travel Insured International** (Box 280568, East Hartford, CT 06128-0568, tel. 203/528–7663 or 800/243–3174), **Travel Guard International** (1145 Clark St., Stevens Point, WI 54481, tel. 715/345–0505 or 800/826–1300), and **Wallach & Company** (107 W. Federal St., Box 480, Middleburg, VA 22117, tel. 703/687–3166 or 800/237–6615).

In the U.K. The **Association of British Insurers** (51 Gresham St., London EC2V 7HQ, tel. 0171/600–3333; 30 Gordon St., Glasgow G1 3PU, tel. 0141/226–3905; Scottish Provident Bldg., Donegall Sq. W, Belfast BT1 6JE, tel. 01232/249176; and other locations) gives advice by phone and publishes the free "Holiday Insurance."

Lodging

The **Florida Hotel & Motel Association** (200 W. College Ave., Box 1529, Tallahassee 32301-1529, tel. 904/224–2888) publishes an "Annual Travel Directory," which you can obtain from the association if you send a No. 10 SASE and $2 for handling ($4 outside the U.S.), or without charge from the Florida Division of Tourism (*see* Visitor Information, *below*).

Apartment and Villa Rental Among the companies to contact are **Hometours International** (Box 11503, Knoxville, TN 37939, tel. 615/588–8722 or 800/367–4668), **Rent-a-Home International** (7200 34th Ave. NW, Seattle, WA 98117, tel. 206/789–9377 or 800/488–7368), **Vacation Home Rentals Worldwide** (235 Kensington Ave., Norwood, NJ 07648, tel. 201/767–9393 or 800/633–3284), and **Villas and Apartments Abroad** (420 Madison Ave., Suite 1105, New York, NY 10017, tel. 212/759–1025 or 800/433–3020). Members of the travel club **Hideaways International** ($99 annually; 767 Islington St., Portsmouth, NH 03801, tel. 603/430–4433 or 800/843–4433) receive two annual guides plus quarterly newsletters and arrange rentals among themselves.

B&Bs and Inns Bed-and-breakfast referral and reservation agencies in Florida include: **Bed & Breakfast Co., Tropical Florida** (Box 262, Miami 33243, tel. and fax 305/661–3270), **Bed & Breakfast Scenic Florida** (Box 3385, Tallahassee 32315-3385, tel. 904/386–8196), **RSVP Florida & St. Augustine** (Box 3603, St. Augustine 32085, tel. 904/471–0600), and **Suncoast Accommodations of Florida** (8690 Gulf Blvd., St. Pete Beach 33706, tel. 813/360–1753).

Inn Route, Inc. (Box 6187, Palm Harbor 34684, tel. and fax 813/786–9792 or 800/524–1880), a statewide association of small, architecturally distinctive historic inns, will send you a free brochure. *Florida's Country Inns* (Buchan Publications, Box 7218, St. Petersburg 33734, tel. 813/526–9121) describes 100 favorites of author Robert Tolf.

Camping and RV Facilities For information on camping facilities, contact the national parks and forests you plan to visit directly or, for state parks, contact the Department of Environmental Protection (*see* Parks and Preserves, *below*, for both).

The free annual "Florida Camping Directory," published each December, lists 220 commercial campgrounds in Florida with 66,000 sites. It's available at Florida welcome centers, from the Florida Division of Tourism (*see* Visitor Information, *below*), and from the **Florida Association of RV Parks & Campgrounds** (1340 Vickers Dr., Tallahassee 32303-3041, tel. 904/562–7151, fax 904/562–7179).

Home Exchange Principal clearinghouses include **Intervac International** ($65 annually; Box 590504, San Francisco, CA 94159, tel. 415/435–3497), which has three annual directories, and **Loan-a-Home** ($35–$45 annually; 2 Park La., Apt. 6E, Mount Vernon, NY 10552-3443, tel. 914/664–7640), which specializes in long-term exchanges.

Marine Charts

A packet of charts to the Keys (and elsewhere in Florida) helpful to boaters, divers, and fisherfolk is available for $7.95 ($3.60 each individual chart) from **Teall's, Inc.** (111 Saguaro La., Marathon 33050, tel. 305/743–3942, fax 305/743–3942). A directory of available charts is free.

Money Matters

ATMs For specific **Cirrus** locations in the United States and Canada, call 800/424–7787. For U.S. **Plus** locations, call 800/843–7587 and enter the area code and first three digits of the number you're calling from (or of the calling area where you want an ATM).

Wiring Funds Funds can be wired via **American Express MoneyGram**^{SM} (tel. 800/926–9400 from the U.S. and Canada for locations and information) or **Western Union** (tel. 800/325–6000 for agent locations or to send using MasterCard or Visa, 800/321–2923 in Canada).

Parks and Preserves

Although Florida is the fourth-most-populous state in the nation, more than 10 million acres of public and private recreation facilities are set aside in national forests, parks, monuments, reserves, and seashores; state forests and parks; county parks; and nature preserves owned and managed by private conservation groups.

National Parks, Forests, and Refuges The federal government maintains no centralized information service for its natural and historic sites in Florida. Consult the **"Guide and Map of National Parks of the U.S."** (GPO No. 024005008527; $1.25 from the U.S. Government Printing Office, Washington, DC 20402) for park addresses and facilities. For further details, contact each site directly.

In 1993 Fort Jefferson National Monument in the Dry Tortugas was declared a national park. Everglades National Park was established in 1947, Biscayne National Park in 1980. Other natural and historic sites in Florida under federal management include Big Cypress National Preserve in the Everglades, Canaveral National Seashore in central Florida, Castillo De San Marcos National Monument in north Florida, De Soto National Memorial in Bradenton, the 46,000-acre Timucuan Ecological & Historic Preserve on the St. Johns River in Jacksonville, Fort Matanzas National Monument south of St. Augustine, and Gulf Islands National Seashore in north Florida.

The federal government operates three national forests in Florida. The Apalachicola National Forest encompasses 557,000 acres of pine and hardwoods across the northern coastal plain. The 336,000-acre Ocala National Forest includes the sandhills of the Big Scrub. Cypress swamps and numerous sinkhole lakes patch the 157,000-acre Osceola National Forest.

National wildlife refuges in Florida include the Great White Heron National Wildlife Refuge and National Key Deer Refuge in the Keys, Pelican Island National Wildlife Refuge (America's first) in Indian River County, Loxahatchee National Wildlife Refuge near Palm Beach, J. N. "Ding" Darling National Wildlife Refuge in southwest Florida, and Merritt Island National Wildlife Refuge. The federal government also operates the Key Largo National Marine Sanctuary, Looe Key National Marine Sanctuary, and the Florida Keys National Marine Sanctuary, largest in the national system.

State Parks The **Florida Department of Environmental Protection** (Marjory Stoneman Douglas Bldg., MS 535, 3900 Commonwealth Blvd., Tallahassee 32399-3000, tel. 904/488–2850, fax 904/488–3947) is responsible for hundreds of historic buildings, landmarks, nature preserves, and an expanding state park system. When you request a free copy of the *Florida State Park Guide*, mention which parts of the state you plan to visit. For information on camping facilities at the state parks, ask for the free "Florida State Parks, Fees and Facilities" and "Florida State Parks Camping Reservation Procedures" brochures. Delivery takes 10–14 days.

Responding to cutbacks in its budget, the DEP has established a citizen support organization called **Friends of Florida State Parks.** Membership information is available from tel. 904/488–8243.

Private Preserves Contact the **National Audubon Society** (Sanctuary Director, Miles Wildlife Sanctuary, R.R. 1, Box 294, W. Cornwall Rd., Sharon, CT

06069, tel. 203/364–0048) for information on the Corkscrew Swamp Sanctuary near Naples and its other 65 or so Florida properties, including islands, prairies, forests, and swamps. Visitation at these sites is limited, although at the National Audubon Wildlife Sanctuary on Lake Okeechobee you can tour on boats operated by concessionaire **Swampland Tours, Inc.** (10300 Rte. 78 W, Okeechobee 34974, tel. 941/467–4411).

The **Nature Conservancy** (Florida Chapter, 2699 Lee Rd., Suite 500, Winter Park 32789, tel. 407/628–5887) admits the public to five of its preserves: the 6,267-acre Apalachicola Bluffs & Ravines Preserve in Liberty County, Blowing Rocks Preserve with its unique anastasia limestone rock formations, the 970-acre Cummer Sanctuary in Levy County, the 4,500-acre Tiger Creek Preserve near Lake Wales in Polk County, and the 150-acre Spruce Creek Preserve, with its restored historic buildings, in Volusia County. Visitors are welcome at the Winter Park office and at offices in Tequesta (250 Tequesta Dr., Suite 301, 33469, tel. 407/575–2297), Key West (201 Front St., Suite 222, 33040, tel. 305/296–3880), Lake Wales (225 E. Stuart Ave., 33853, tel. 941/678–1551), Tallahassee (625 N. Adams St., 32301, tel. 904/222–0199), and West Palm Beach (Comeau Building, 319 Clematis St., Suite 611, 33401, tel. 407/833–4226). All offices are open weekdays 9–5.

Passports and Visas

U.K. Citizens For fees, documentation requirements, and to get an emergency passport, call the **London passport office** (tel. 0171/271–3000). For visa information, call the **U.S. Embassy Visa Information Line** (tel. 0891/200–290; calls cost 48p per minute or 36p per minute cheap rate) or write the **U.S. Embassy Visa Branch** (5 Upper Grosvenor St., London W1A 2JB). If you live in Northern Ireland, write the **U.S. Consulate General** (Queen's House, 4 Queen St., Belfast BT1 6EQ).

Photo Help

The **Kodak Information Center** (tel. 800/242–2424) answers consumer questions about film and photography.

Rail Travel

Amtrak (tel. 800/872–7245) provides north–south service on two routes to the major cities of Jacksonville, Orlando, Tampa, West Palm Beach, Fort Lauderdale, and Miami, and, since 1993, east–west service through Jacksonville, Tallahassee, and Pensacola, with many stops in between on all routes.

Senior Citizens

Educational Travel The nonprofit **Elderhostel** (75 Federal St., 3rd Floor, Boston, MA 02110, tel. 617/426–7788), for people 60 and older, has offered inexpensive study programs since 1975. The nearly 2,000 courses cover everything from marine science to Greek myths and cowboy poetry. Fees for programs in the United States and Canada, which usually last one week, run about $300, not including transportation.

Organizations Contact the **American Association of Retired Persons** (AARP; $8 per person or couple annually; 601 E St. NW, Washington, DC 20049, tel. 202/434–2277). Its Purchase Privilege Program gets members discounts on lodging, car rentals, and sightseeing, and the AARP Motoring Plan furnishes domestic trip-routing information and emergency road-service aid for an annual fee of $39.95 per person or couple ($59.95 for a premium version).

For other discounts on lodgings, car rentals, and other travel products, along with magazines and newsletters, contact the **National Council of Senior Citizens** (membership $12 annually; 1331 F St. NW, Washington, DC 20004, tel. 202/347–8800) and **Mature Outlook** (subscription $9.95 annually; 6001 N. Clark St., Chicago, IL 60660, tel. 312/465–6466 or 800/336–6330).

Publications *The 50+ Traveler's Guidebook: Where to Go, Where to Stay, What to Do,* by Anita Williams and Merrimac Dillon ($12.95; St. Martin's Press, 175 5th Ave., New York, NY 10010, tel. 212/674–5151 or 800/288–2131), offers many useful tips. "**The Mature Traveler**" ($29.95; Box 50400, Reno, NV 89513, tel. 702/786–7419), a monthly newsletter, covers travel deals.

Sports The **Governor's Council on Physical Fitness and Sports** (1330 N.W. 6th St., Suite D, Gainesville 32601, tel. 904/955–2120, fax 904/373–8879) puts on the annual Senior Games each December.

Sports and Outdoor Activities

All told, Florida now has some 3,500 miles of trails, which encompass 1,500 miles of canoe and kayak trails, about 670 miles for bicycling and other uses, 900 miles exclusively for hiking, about 350 exclusively for equestrian use, plus some 30 miles of purely interpretive trails chiefly in state parks. An active greenways development plan that seeks to protect wildlife habitat as much as foster recreation identified 150 greenways in use or under development. More information is available from the **Florida Department of Environmental Protection** (Office of Greenways, Mail Station 585, 3900 Commonwealth Blvd., Tallahassee 32399-3000, tel. 904/487–4784).

Florida steadily makes it easier for visitors to get in touch with its natural attractions. The *Florida Wildlife Viewing Guide* ($7.95 plus $2.95 shipping; Falcon Press, Box 1718, Helena, MT 59624, tel. 800/582–2665), by Susan Cerulean and Ann Morrow, lists 96 wildlife-watching sites identified by Florida Department of Transportation signs. The Florida Division of Tourism (*see* Visitor Information, *below*) publishes "**Florida Trails: A Guide to Florida's Natural Habitats**," a 102-page review of bicycling, canoeing, horseback-riding, and walking trails, with additional information on camping, snorkeling and diving, and Florida ecosystems, and a good set of sources for finding out still more. You can request a free trails-oriented "**Recreational Guide**" from the Southwest Florida Water Management District (tel. 800/423–1476) or the free "**Recreation Guide to District Lands**," with detailed descriptions of 32 marine, wetland, and upland recreational areas, from the St. Johns River Water Management District (Box 1429, Palatka 32178-1429). (Most of the large state-owned lands are managed by the five water management districts.)

The **Governor's Council on Physical Fitness and Sports** (*see* Senior Citizens, *above*) puts on the Sunshine State Games each July in a different part of the state and promotes the business of sports. The **Florida Sports Foundation** (107 W. Gaines St., Suite 466, Tallahassee 32399-2000, tel. 904/488–8347) publishes guides on Florida boating, diving, fishing, golf, and baseball spring training.

Biking The **Florida Department of Environmental Protection** (*see above*) has developed three overnight bicycle tours of different areas of the state. The tours vary in length from 100 to 450 miles (for two–six days of cycling) and use state parks for rest stops and overnight camping. The office can also provide information on recreational cycling trails, rail-trails, and the rim trail atop the levee around Lake Okeechobee.

Florida's **Department of Transportation (DOT)** publishes free bicycle trail guides, which you can request from the state bicycle-pedestrian coordinator (605 Suwannee St., Mail Station 82, Tallahassee 32399-0450, tel. 904/487–1200); you can also request a free touring information packet. Also contact the DOT for names of bike coordinators around the state. In Greater Miami, contact **Dade County's bicycle-pedestrian coordinator** (Office of County Manager, Metro-Dade Government Center, 111 N.W. 1st St., Suite 910, Miami 33128, tel. 305/375–4507).

Canoeing A free guide issued by the Florida Department of Environmental Protection (*see above*), *Florida Recreational Trails System Canoe Trails* describes nearly 950 miles of designated canoe trails. The DEP guide lists support services along 36 Florida creeks, rivers, and springs. Two additional guides are *Canoe Liveries and Outfitters Directory,* which lists organizations that offer livery and rental services for canoe trails in the system, and *Canoe Information Resources Guide,* which lists canoe clubs and organizations and gives a bibliography of maps, books, films, etc., about canoeing. Contact individual national forests, parks, monuments, reserves, and seashores for information on their canoe trails. Local chambers of commerce have information on canoe trails in county parks.

Two Florida canoe-outfitter organizations publish free lists of canoe outfitters who organize canoe trips, rent canoes and canoeing equipment, and help shuttle canoeists' boats and cars. The **Florida Association of Canoe Liveries and Outfitters** (Box 1764, Arcadia 33821) publishes a free list of 22 canoe outfitters who organize trips on 47 creeks, rivers, and bays. The not-for-profit **Florida Canoeing and Kayaking Association** (Box 20892, West Palm Beach 33416, tel. 407/575–4530) publishes a quarterly newsletter, sponsors events, and can provide up-to-date information on many trail conditions. **"Canoe Outpost System"** is a brochure listing five independent outfitters serving eight Florida rivers (2816 N.W. Rte. 661, Arcadia 33821, tel. 941/494–1215).

Fishing For a free copy of the annual *Florida Fishing Handbook,* write to the **Florida Game and Fresh Water Fish Commission** (620 S. Meridian St., Tallahassee 32399-1600, tel. 904/488–1960). You can also request fishing guides for five Florida regions as well as educational bulletins on catch-and-release fishing and on largemouth and striped bass.

Write the **Florida Sea Grant Extension Program** (Bldg. 803, University of Florida, Gainesville 32611, tel. 904/392–5870) for a free list of publications on saltwater fishing, pier fishing, Florida varieties of fish, and much more.

Hiking The best source of information is the **Florida Trail Association** (FTA; Box 13708, Gainesville 32604, tel. 904/378–8823 or 800/343–1882 in FL). FTA is the principal sponsor of the Florida Trail, which before the end of the decade is expected to stretch 1,300 miles—most of it through wilderness—across Florida from the Big Cypress Swamp in the far south to the Alabama border. At present approximately 900 miles are complete, not all contiguous. The most popular stretches run through the Apalachicola National Forest and St. Marks Wildlife Refuge in the Panhandle, in the vicinity of Lake Tohopekaliga just southeast of Orlando, and atop the dike around Lake Okeechobee in the southeast. FTA sponsors hikes through all parts of the state through its 12 local chapters and publishes various trail guides and a bimonthly newspaper called "Footprint." Memberships begin at $23 per year.

Horseback Riding Trail and endurance riding are popular throughout the state. Sixteen Florida parks and recreational trails include horse trails, while five parks have overnight facilities for campers and their horses. **Sea Horse Stable** (7500 First Coast Hwy., Amelia Island 32034, tel. 904/

261–4878) offers horseback riding on the beach at the foot of Amelia Island. Equestrians meet twice a year, in fall in Altoona in the Ocala National Forest, and in spring at an annually changing location. For more information, contact the **Sunshine State Horse Council** (temporary tel. 800/792–3833) or *Horse & Pony* (6229 Virginia La., Seffner 33584, tel. 813/621–2510).

Hunting Each year in June, the **Florida Game and Fresh Water Fish Commission** (620 S. Meridian St., Tallahassee 32399-1600, tel. 904/488–4676) announces the dates and hours of the fall hunting seasons for public and private wildlife-management areas. Hunting seasons vary across the state. Where hunting is allowed on private property, you need the landowner's written permission—and you must carry that letter with your hunting license in the field. Trespassing with a weapon is a felony. Contact the commission for a free copy of the annual *Florida Hunting Handbook.*

Jogging, Running, and Walking Local running clubs all over the state sponsor weekly public events for joggers, runners, and walkers. For a list of local clubs and events, call or send a SASE to **USA Track & Field–Florida** (Attn. Event Marketing & Management Int'l., 1322 N. Mills Ave., Orlando 32803, tel. 407/895–6323, fax 407/897–3243), the Florida affiliate for the governing body of the sport and a complete source of information. For information about events in south Florida, contact the 1,600-member **Miami Runners Club** (7920 S.W. 40th St., Miami 33155, tel. 305/227–1500, fax 305/220–2450).

Pari-Mutuel Sports Florida runs a big year-round variety of sports you can lawfully bet on. These include 18 greyhound race tracks, six tracks for harness and Thoroughbred racing, and eight jai-alai frontons. You can request a schedule, updated every six months, from the **Department of Business & Professional Regulations, Division of Pari-Mutuel Wagering** (8405 N.W. 53rd St., Suite C-250, Miami 33166, tel. 305/470–5675, fax 305/470–5686).

Scuba Diving and Snorkeling **Ginnie Springs** (7300 N.E. Ginnie Springs Rd., High Springs 32643, tel. 904/454–2202 or 800/874–8571), near Branford, is one of Florida's most famous springs for diving. **Crystal Lodge Dive Center** (525 N.W. 7th Ave., Crystal River 34428, tel. 904/795–6798) is a popular gateway to river diving in central Florida's Crystal River.

Tennis For a schedule of tournaments and other tennis events in Florida, you can order the yearbook of the **United States Tennis Association Florida Section** (1280 S.W. 36th Ave., Suite 305, Pompano Beach 33069, tel. 305/968–3434, fax 305/968–3986). It's $11 by credit card including postage and handling.

Students

Groups Major tour operators include **Contiki Holidays** (300 Plaza Alicante, Suite 900, Garden Grove, CA 92640, tel. 714/740–0808 or 800/466–0610).

Hosteling Contact **Hostelling International–American Youth Hostels** (733 15th St. NW, Suite 840, Washington, DC 20005, tel. 202/783–6161) in the United States, **Hostelling International–Canada** (205 Catherine St., Suite 400, Ottawa, Ontario K2P 1C3, tel. 613/237–7884) in Canada, and the **Youth Hostel Association of England and Wales** (Trevelyan House, 8 St. Stephen's Hill, St. Albans, Hertfordshire AL1 2DY, tel. 01727/855215 or 01727/845047) in the United Kingdom. Membership ($25 in the U.S., C$26.75 in Canada, and £9 in the U.K.) gets you access to 5,000 hostels worldwide that charge $7–$20 nightly per person.

I.D. Cards To get discounts on transportation and admissions, get the **International Student Identity Card** (ISIC) if you're a bona fide student or the **International Youth Card** (IYC) if you're under 26. In the United

States, the ISIC and IYC cards cost $16 each and include basic travel accident and illness coverage, plus a toll-free travel hot line. Apply through the Council on International Educational Exchange (*see* Organizations, *below*). Cards are available for $15 each in Canada from **Travel Cuts** (187 College St., Toronto, Ontario M5T 1P7, tel. 416/979–2406 or 800/667–2887) and in the United Kingdom for £5 each at student unions and student travel companies.

Organizations   A major contact is the **Council on International Educational Exchange** (CIEE, 205 E. 42nd St., 16th Floor, New York, NY 10017, tel. 212/661–1450), with locations in Boston (729 Boylston St., 02116, tel. 617/266–1926), Miami (9100 S. Dadeland Blvd., 33156, tel. 305/670–9261), Los Angeles (1093 Broxton Ave., 90024, tel. 310/208–3551), 43 other college towns nationwide, and the United Kingdom (28A Poland St., London W1V 3DB, tel. 0171/437–7767). Twice a year, it publishes *Student Travels* magazine. The CIEE's Council Travel Service offers domestic air passes for bargain travel within the United States and is the exclusive U.S. agent for several student-discount cards.

Campus Connections (325 Chestnut St., Suite 1101, Philadelphia, PA 19106, tel. 215/625–8585 or 800/428–3235) specializes in discounted accommodations and airfares for students. The **Educational Travel Centre** (438 N. Frances St., Madison, WI 53703, tel. 608/256–5551) offers rail passes and low-cost airline tickets, mostly for flights departing from Chicago.

In Canada, also contact **Travel Cuts** (*see above*).

Tour Operators

Among the companies selling tours and packages to Florida, the following have a proven reputation, are nationally known, and offer plenty of options.

Group Tours   In the first-class and tourist range, try **Collette Tours** (162 Middle St., Pawtucket, RI 02860, tel. 401/728–3805 or 800/832–4656) or **Domenico Tours** (750 Broadway, Bayonne, NJ 07002, tel. 201/823–8687 or 800/554–8687). For budget and tourist-class programs, try **Cosmos** (5301 S. Federal Circle, Littleton, CO 80123, tel. 303/797–2800 or 800/221–0090).

Packages   Independent vacation packages are available from major tour operators and airlines. Contact **American Airlines Fly AAway Vacations** (tel. 800/321–2121), **Continental Airlines' Grand Destinations** (tel. 800/634–5555), **Delta Dream Vacations** (tel. 800/872–7786), **Globetrotters** (139 Main St., Cambridge, MA 02142, tel. 617/621–9911 or 800/999–9696), **Kingdom Tours** (300 Market St., Kingston, PA 18704, tel. 717/283–4241 or 800/872–8857), **United Vacations** (tel. 800/328–6877), and **USAir Vacations** (tel. 800/455–0123). **Funjet Vacations**, based in Milwaukee, Wisconsin, and Gogo Tours, based in Ramsey, New Jersey, sell Florida packages only through travel agents.

Regional operators specialize in putting together Florida packages for travelers in their local area. Arrangements may include charter or scheduled air travel. Contact **Apple Vacations** (25 Northwest Point Blvd., Elk Grove Village, IL 60007, tel. 708/640–1150 or 800/365–2775) and **Travel Impressions** (465 Smith St., Farmingdale, NY 11735, tel. 516/845–7000 or 800/224–0022).

From the U.K.   Tour operators offering packages to Florida include **British Airways Holidays** (Astral Towers, Betts Way, London Rd., Crawley, West Sussex RH10 2XA, tel. 01293/518–022), **Jetsave Travel Ltd.** (Sussex House, London Rd., East Grinstead, West Sussex RH19 1LD, tel. 01342/312–033), **Key to America** (1–3 Station Rd., Ashford Middlesex TW15 2UW, tel. 01784/248–777), and **Virgin Holidays Ltd.** (The

Galleria, Station Rd., Crawley, West Sussex RH10 1WW, tel. 01293/562–944).

Travel agencies that offer cheap fares to Florida include **Trailfinders** (42–50 Earl's Court Rd., London W8 6FT, tel. 0171/937–5400), **Travel Cuts** (295a Regent St., London W1R 7YA, tel. 0171/637–3161), and **Flightfile** (49 Tottenham Court Rd., London W1P 9RE, tel. 0171/700–2722).

Theme Trips

Adventure **Outdoor Adventures** (6110-7 Powers Ave., Jacksonville, FL 32217, tel. 904/739–1960) runs kayaking, backpacking, bicycling, and tubing vacations in the wilderness of northeastern Florida. **Wilderness Inquiry** (1313 5th St. SE, Box 84, Minneapolis, MN 55414, tel. 612/379–3858 or 800/728–0719) runs canoeing trips through the Florida Everglades.

Fishing **Cutting Loose Expeditions** (Box 447, Winter Park, FL 32790, tel. 407/629–4700) can arrange a charter yacht or resort fishing vacation.

Golf **Golfpac** (Box 162366, Altamonte Springs, FL 32716-2366, tel. 800/327–0878) and **Great Florida Golf** (Box 590, Palm Beach, FL 33480, tel. 407/820–9336 or 800/544–8687) sell golf packages at resorts throughout the state.

Health **Spa-Finders** (91 5th Ave., New York, NY 10003, tel. 800/255–7727) represents several spas in Florida.

Learning Vacations The **Smithsonian Institution's Study Tours and Seminars** (1100 Jefferson Dr. SW, Room 3045, Washington, DC 20560, tel. 202/357–4700) and the **National Wildlife Federation** (1400 S. 16th St. NW, Washington, DC 20036, tel. 703/790–4363 or 800/245–5484) operate natural-history programs. **Earthwatch** (680 Mount Auburn St., Box 403SI, Watertown, MA 02272, tel. 617/926–8000 or 800/776–0188) recruits volunteers to serve in its EarthCorps as short-term assistants to scientists on research expeditions.

Sailing **Annapolis Sailing School** (Box 3334 STI, Annapolis, MD 21403, tel. 800/638–9191) has vacation packages to the Florida Keys that include sailing instruction. **Offshore Sailing School** (16731-110 McGregor Blvd., Fort Myers, FL 33908, tel. 800/221–4326) offers similar packages in St. Petersburg.

Yacht Charters For crewed or uncrewed yachts, try **Sail Away** (15605 S.W. 92nd Ave., Miami, FL 33157, tel. 305/253–7245 or 800/724–5292).

Organizations The **National Tour Association** (546 E. Main St., Lexington, KY 40508, tel. 606/226–4444 or 800/755–8687) and **United States Tour Operators Association** (USTOA, 211 E. 51st St., Suite 12B, New York, NY 10022, tel. 212/750–7371) can provide lists of member operators and information on booking tours.

Publications Consult the brochure **"Worldwide Tour & Vacation Package Finder"** from the National Tour Association (*see* Organizations, *above*) and the Better Business Bureau's **"Tips on Travel Packages"** (publication No. 24-195, $2; 4200 Wilson Blvd., Arlington, VA 22203).

Travel Agencies

For names of reputable agencies in your area, contact the **American Society of Travel Agents** (1101 King St., Suite 200, Alexandria, VA 22314, tel. 703/739–2782).

Visitor Information

Contact the **Florida Division of Tourism** (Department of Commerce, 126 Van Buren St., Tallahassee 32399, tel. 904/487–1462, fax 904/487–0132) for information and publications on Florida, including the very useful "Florida Value Activities Guide." Canadian travelers can get assistance from **Travel, U.S.A.** (tel. 900/451–4050, US$2 per minute).

In the U.K. Contact the **United States Travel and Tourism Administration** (Box 1EN, London W1A 1EN, tel. 0171/495–4466). For a free USA pack, write the USTTA at Box 170, Ashford, Kent TN24 0ZX). Enclose stamps worth £1.50.

Weather

For current conditions and forecasts, plus the local time and helpful travel tips, call the **Weather Channel Connection** (tel. 900/932–8437, 95¢ per minute) from a touch-tone phone.

Smart Budget Travel Tips

The more you travel, the more you know about how to make trips run like clockwork. To help make your travels hassle-free, Fodor's editors have rounded up dozens of tips from our contributors and travel experts all over the world, as well as basic information on visiting Florida. For names of organizations to contact and publications that can give you more information, *see* Important Contacts, *above.*

Air Travel

If time is an issue, **always look for nonstop flights,** which require no change of plane. If possible, **avoid connecting flights,** which stop at least once and can involve a change of plane, although the flight number remains the same; if the first leg is late, the second waits.

Cutting Costs For good deals, **look for ads in the Sunday travel section of most newspapers.** Major airlines might be running specials; the newer, lower-overhead airlines often advertise cheap rates; and you might learn of a charter flight that's going where you want when you want.

Major Airlines The least-expensive airfares from the major airlines are priced for round-trip travel and are subject to restrictions. You must usually **book in advance and buy the ticket within 24 hours** to get cheaper fares, and you may have to **stay over a Saturday night.** The lowest fare is subject to availability, and only a small percentage of the plane's total seats are sold at that price. It's good to **call a number of airlines, and when you are quoted a good price, book it on the spot—** the same fare on the same flight may not be available the next day. Airlines generally allow you to change your return date for a $25 to $50 fee, but most low-fare tickets are nonrefundable. However, if you don't use it, you can apply the cost toward the purchase price of a new ticket, again for a small charge.

Consolidators Consolidators, who buy tickets at reduced rates from scheduled airlines, sell them at prices below the lowest available from the airlines directly—usually without advance restrictions. Sometimes you can even get your money back if you need to return the ticket. Carefully read the fine print detailing penalties for changes and cancellations. If you doubt the reliability of a consolidator, **confirm your reservation with the airline.**

Aloft If you hate airline food, **ask for special meals when booking.** These
Airline Food can be vegetarian, low cholesterol, or kosher, for example; commonly prepared to order in smaller quantities than standard catered fare, they can be tastier.

Smoking Smoking is banned on all flights within the United States of less than six hours' duration and on all Canadian flights; the ban also applies to domestic segments of international flights aboard U.S. and foreign carriers. Delta has banned smoking system-wide.

Beaches

The wonderful thing about Florida is that beaches are everywhere, and everywhere, except at designated parks, they're free. Florida rates 12 of the top 20 U.S. beaches, while no point in the state is more than 60 miles from salt water. The long, lean peninsula is bordered by a 526-mile Atlantic coast from Fernandina Beach to Key West and a 792-mile coast along the Gulf of Mexico and Florida Bay from Pensacola to Key West. If you were to stretch Florida's convoluted coast in a straight line, it would extend for about 1,800 miles.

What's more, if you add in the perimeter of every island surrounded by salt water, Florida has about 8,500 miles of tidal shoreline—more than any other state except Alaska. Florida's coastline comprises about 1,016 miles of sand beaches.

Along the Atlantic Coast from the Georgia border south through the Daytona Beach area the beaches are broad and firm. In Daytona Beach you can **drive on them** (though the number of cars is restricted). Some beachfront communities in this area charge for the privilege; others provide free beach access for vehicles.

From Daytona Beach south, Hurricane Gordon caused considerable erosion of beaches late in 1994, and the usual cycle of seasonal tides and winds has so far been slow to rebuild those beaches. Major beach rehabilitation projects have been completed in Fort Lauderdale, the Sunny Isles area of north Dade County, Miami Beach, and Key Biscayne. By 1996, the experimental renourishing of beaches in metro Miami's Surfside and at John U. Lloyd Beach State Recreation Area will be complete.

In the Florida Keys, coral reefs and prevailing currents prevent sand from building up to form beaches. The few Keys beaches are small, narrow, and generally have little or no sandy bottom. A happy exception is the beach at Bahia Honda State Park.

The waters of the Gulf of Mexico are somewhat murky, and Tampa Bay is polluted though improving, but the Gulf Coast beaches are beautiful. The Panhandle is known for its sugarlike white sand; around Sarasota the sand is soft and white. The barrier islands off Fort Myers are known for the excellent shelling on their beaches, particularly Sanibel Island.

Although the state owns all beaches below the mean high-tide line, even in front of hotels and private resorts, gaining access to the public beach can be a problem along much of Florida's coastline. You must pay to enter and/or park at most state, county, and local beachfront parks. Where hotels dominate the beach frontage, public parking may be limited or nonexistent.

If you are unaccustomed to strong subtropical sun, you run a risk of sunburn and heat prostration, even in winter. The natives go to the beach early in the day or in the late afternoon, and like them, if you must be out in direct sun at midday, **limit your sun exposure and strenuous exercise, drink plenty of liquids, and wear a hat.** Wherever you plan to swim, **ask if the water has a dangerous undertow.**

To avoid jacked-up prices, **buy sunscreen and other sundries at shops away from the beach.**

Bus Travel

Greyhound is still the cheapest way to travel if you're not in a hurry and if you're willing to put up with often unclean bathrooms. To get the best fare, **travel during the summer,** when 21-day advance purchase options are usually available. These fares can cut standard fares by up to half. Greyhound, which changes routes frequently, links more cities during summer (after Easter to Labor Day) than in the rest of year. The line's buses pass through practically every major city in Florida, including Jacksonville, Daytona, Orlando, West Palm Beach, Fort Lauderdale, Miami, Sarasota, Tampa, Tallahassee, and Key West.

Indicative of Greyhound fares, round-trip between Miami and New York City was recently $149 in the high season (winter), $126.65 for senior citizens (55 and up). A late-winter nonrefundable "special" brought the senior fare to $119. Senior citizens generally save about 15%. Within Florida, specials (usually Easter to Labor Day) can lower fares by some 30%, though tickets are nonrefundable, advance purchase is usually required, and there's a surcharge for changing dates. The standard round-trip between Miami and Orlando is $66 ($56.10 for senior citizens).

Cameras, Camcorders, and Computers

Laptops Before you depart, **check your portable computer's battery,** because you may be asked at security to turn on the computer to prove that it is what it appears to be. At the airport, you may prefer to **request a manual inspection,** although security X-rays do not harm hard-disk or floppy-disk storage.

Photography If your camera is new or if you haven't used it for a while, **shoot and develop a few rolls of film** before you leave. Always **store film in a cool, dry place**—never in the car's glove compartment or on the shelf under the rear window.

Every pass of film through an X-ray machine increases the chance of clouding. To protect it, carry it in a clear plastic bag and **ask for hand inspection at security.** Such requests are virtually always honored at U.S. airports. Don't depend on a lead-lined bag to protect film in checked luggage—the airline may increase the radiation to see what's inside.

Video Before your trip, **test your camcorder, invest in a skylight filter to protect the lens, and charge the batteries.** (Airport security personnel may ask you to turn on the camcorder to prove that it's what it appears to be.)

Videotape is not damaged by X-rays, but it may be harmed by the magnetic field of a walk-through metal detector, so **ask that videotapes be hand-checked.**

Children and Travel

Baby-Sitting To find a local sitter, **check with your hotel desk for recommendations.**

Driving If you are renting a car, **arrange for a car seat when you reserve.** Sometimes they're free.

Flying On domestic flights, children under two not occupying a seat travel free, and older children currently travel on the lowest applicable adult fare.

Baggage In general, the adult baggage allowance applies for children paying half or more of the adult fare.

Safety Seats According to the Federal Aviation Administration, it's a good idea to **use safety seats aloft.** Airline policy varies. U.S. carriers allow FAA-approved models, but airlines usually require that you buy a ticket, even if your child would otherwise ride free, because the seats must be strapped into regular passenger seats. If you choose not to buy a seat for your child, many airlines will allow you to use a vacant seat (if there is one) free of charge and will often rearrange seating to accommodate you. When reserving seat assignments, **ask to have an empty seat in the middle of your traveling party.** Often it will remain vacant, and you can use it for your child, so bring your safety seat just in case. If the flight is full, you can check the safety seat at the gate.

Facilities When making your reservation, **ask for children's meals or free-standing bassinets** if you need them; the latter are available only to those with seats at the bulkhead, where there's enough legroom. If you don't need a bassinet, **think twice before requesting bulkhead seats**—the only storage for in-flight necessities is in the inconveniently distant overhead bins.

Lodging Most hotels allow children under a certain age to stay in their parents' room at no extra charge, while others charge them as extra adults; be sure to **ask about the cut-off age.**

Often the best bet for traveling with children is to **book space that comes with a kitchen and more than one bedroom.** Such properties are especially plentiful around Orlando, where hoteliers expect steady family trade. Children are welcome generally everywhere in Florida.

Florida may have the highest concentration of hotels with organized children's programs in the United States; sometimes they are complimentary and sometimes there's a charge. Not all accept children who are still in diapers, and programs may not be available all year or all days of the week. If a central reservations service doesn't know what exactly is available, **call the hotel directly.**

Crime Prevention

Before setting out, **make sure you know where you're going.** If you think you're getting lost, **stop while you're still in a safe neighborhood and ask for directions**—there have been instances of lost tourists being attacked. To **guard against theft,** always put your wallet in the same place, lock your car and hotel doors, don't carry anything in your car (even the trunk) that you can better leave where you're staying, and put valuables in the hotel's safe if necessary.

Customs and Duties

In Florida British visitors age 21 or over may import the following into the United States: 200 cigarettes or 50 cigars or 2 kilograms of tobacco; 1 liter of alcohol; gifts to the value of $100. Restricted items include meat products, seeds, plants, and fruits. Never carry illegal drugs.

Back Home Once per calendar year, when you've been out of Canada for at least
In Canada seven days, you may bring in C$300 worth of goods duty-free. If you've been away less than seven days but more than 48 hours, the duty-free exemption drops to C$100 but can be claimed any number of times (as can a C$20 duty-free exemption for absences of 24 hours or more). You cannot combine the yearly and 48-hour exemptions, use the C$300 exemption only partially (to save the balance for a later trip), or pool exemptions with family members. Goods claimed under the C$300 exemption may follow you by mail; those claimed under the lesser exemptions must accompany you.

Alcohol and tobacco products may be included in the yearly and 48-hour exemptions but not in the 24-hour exemption. If you meet the age requirements of the province through which you reenter Canada, you may bring in, duty-free, 1.14 liters (40 imperial ounces) of wine or liquor *or* 24 12-ounce cans or bottles of beer or ale. If you are 16 or older, you may bring in, duty-free, 200 cigarettes, 50 cigars or cigarillos, and 400 tobacco sticks or 400 grams of manufactured tobacco. Alcohol and tobacco must accompany you on your return.

An unlimited number of gifts valued up to C$60 each may be mailed to Canada duty-free. These do not count as part of your exemption. Label the package "Unsolicited Gift—Value under $60." Alcohol and tobacco are excluded.

In the U.K. From countries outside the EU, including the United States, you may import duty-free 200 cigarettes, 100 cigarillos, 50 cigars or 250 grams of tobacco; 1 liter of spirits or 2 liters of fortified or sparkling wine; 2 liters of still table wine; 60 milliliters of perfume; 250 milliliters of toilet water; plus £136 worth of other goods, including gifts and souvenirs.

Dining

Florida's cuisine changes as you move across the state, based on who settled the area and who now operates the restaurants. You can **expect seafood to be a staple on nearly every menu,** however, with greater variety on the coasts, and catfish, frogs' legs, and gator tail popular around inland lakes and at Miccosukee restaurants along the Tamiami Trail. Florida has launched some big-league culinary stars. Restaurateurs like Fort Lauderdale's Mark Militello are nationally acclaimed, while others who got their start here, such as Douglas Rodriguez, formerly of Yuca in Coral Gables, have gone on to glory in Manhattan.

South Florida's diverse assortment of Latin American restaurants offers the distinctive national fare of Argentina, Brazil, Colombia, Cuba, El Salvador, Mexico, Nicaragua, and Puerto Rico, and it's also easy to find island specialties born of the Bahamas, Haiti, and Jamaica. A new fusion of tropical, Continental, and nouvelle cuisine—some call it Floribbean—has gained widespread popularity. It draws on exotic fruits, spices, and fresh seafood. The influence of earlier Hispanic settlements remains in Key West and Tampa's Ybor City.

All over Florida, Asian cuisine no longer means just Chinese. Indian, Japanese, Pakistani, Thai, and Vietnamese specialties are now available. Continental cuisine (French, German, Italian, Spanish, and Swiss) is also well represented all over Florida.

Every Florida restaurant claims to make the best Key lime pie. Pastry chefs and restaurant managers take the matter very seriously—they discuss the problems of getting good lime juice and maintaining top quality every day. Traditional Key lime pie is yellow, not green, with an old-fashioned graham cracker crust and meringue top. The filling should be tart and chilled but not frozen. Some restaurants serve their Key lime pie with a pastry crust; most substitute whipped cream for the more temperamental meringue. Since each pie is a little different, **try several and make your own decision.**

Cutting Costs When it comes to saving on meals, you can help yourself in many ways. If you don't mind eating early, **ask about early-bird or sunset specials.** These usually offer limited choices, maybe only a third or a half of the regular entrées; smaller portions of regular entrées; or different entrées altogether. Generally the hours for early birds are between 4:30 and 6:30 PM. Alternatively, **look into light eaters' menus,** with lesser portions at lower cost. If you do get a full meal, **don't be ashamed to ask for a doggy bag,** especially if your room has a fridge.

Another cost-saver is to **forego coffee and dessert**—big-markup items that add disproportionately to your total bill (and to your tip!). Instead, get something scrumptious from a bakery or deli and bring it to the beach. Or take it one step further and skip the restaurant altogether. Many Publix and other supermarkets now feature complete salad bars. With a loaf of fresh bread, you can **enjoy an affordable picnic almost anywhere.** If you have a kitchenette, you can **fix a meal or two each day in your room.**

Health Concerns One cautionary word: **be careful about ordering raw oysters,** which have been identified as a problem for people with chronic illness of the liver, stomach, or blood, or who have immune disorders. All Florida restaurants serving raw oysters are required to post a notice in plain view of all patrons warning of risks associated with consuming the product.

For Travelers with Disabilities

When discussing accessibility with an operator or reservationist, **ask hard questions.** Are there any stairs, inside *or* out? Are there grab bars next to the toilet *and* in the shower/tub? How wide is the doorway to the room? To the bathroom? For the most extensive facilities, meeting the latest legal specifications, **opt for newer facilities,** which more often have been designed with access in mind. Older properties or ships must usually be retrofitted and may offer more limited facilities as a result. Be sure to **discuss your needs before booking.**

Discount Clubs

Travel clubs offer members unsold space on airplanes, cruise ships, and package tours at as much as 50% below regular prices. Membership may include a regular bulletin or access to a toll-free hot line giving details of available trips departing from three or four days to several months in the future. Most also offer 50% discounts off hotel rack rates. Before booking with a club, **make sure the hotel or other supplier isn't offering a better deal.**

Driving

Cars rival buses as the cheapest way to get around the state, but cars are much more convenient. And even if you don't bring your own, you can rent one quite inexpensively. Three major interstates lead to Florida from various parts of the country. I–95 begins in Maine, runs south through New England and the Mid-Atlantic states, and enters Florida just north of Jacksonville. It continues south past Daytona Beach, the Space Coast, Vero Beach, Palm Beach, and Fort Lauderdale, eventually ending in Miami.

I–75 begins at the Canadian border in Michigan and runs south through Ohio, Kentucky, Tennessee, and Georgia before entering Florida. The interstate moves through the center of the state before veering west into Tampa. It follows the west coast south to Naples, then crosses the state, and ends in Fort Lauderdale. The toll between Naples and Fort Lauderdale is $1.50.

California and all the most southern states are connected to Florida by I–10. This interstate originates in Los Angeles and moves east through Arizona, New Mexico, Texas, Louisiana, Mississippi, and Alabama before entering Florida at Pensacola on the west coast. I–10 continues straight across the northern part of the state until it terminates in Jacksonville.

Travelers heading from the Midwest or other points west for the lower east coast of Florida can use Florida's Turnpike from Wildwood, which crosses the state for 304 miles and terminates in Florida City. Coin service plazas have replaced the use of toll cards through the urban southern sections of the turnpike, and the total from Orlando to Miami runs about $9.30 (varying maybe a dollar depending on which exits you use). To save money, **take I–95 instead between Fort Pierce and North Miami.** Another long stretch that can save money while not adding a lot of extra time is between Kissimmee–St. Cloud and Fort Pierce. Driving south, take U.S. 441 to Route 68 in Okeechobee County, and head east to Fort Pierce and I–95. The alternate route is about 120 miles and saves $5.50.

In Florida the speed limits are 55 mph on the state highways, 30 mph within city limits and residential areas, and 55–65 mph on the interstates and on Florida's Turnpike. These limits may vary, so be sure to **watch road signs for any changes in the speed limit.**

To avoid price gouging, **buy gas away from the interstates,** especially Florida's Turnpike, but don't risk running out of gas for the sake of saving such small sums.

Note that most beachfront communities rely on meters to control parking, and meter maids are quick to write tickets. At least some counties, including Dade—metro Miami's—will track you down by computer if you have rented a car in the state and not paid a parking fine. If you're not staying at a beachfront hotel with its own parking (and in many communities, the beachfront hotels are priced well out of the budget range), you'll probably be driving to the beach and looking for a place to park; **bring change.**

Insurance

Baggage Airline liability for your baggage is limited to $1,250 per person on domestic flights. On international flights, the airlines' liability is $9.07 per pound or $20 per kilogram for checked baggage (roughly $640 per 70-pound bag) and $400 per passenger for unchecked baggage. Insurance for losses exceeding the terms of your airline ticket can be bought directly from the airline at check-in for about $10 per $1,000 of coverage; note that it excludes a rather extensive list of items, shown on your airline ticket.

Flight You should **think twice before buying flight insurance.** Often purchased as a last-minute impulse at the airport, it pays a lump sum when a plane crashes, either to a beneficiary if the insured dies or sometimes to a surviving passenger who loses eyesight or a limb. Supplementing the airlines' coverage described in the limits-of-liability paragraphs on your ticket, it's expensive and basically unnecessary. Charging an airline ticket to a major credit card often automatically entitles you to coverage and may also embrace travel by bus, train, and ship.

For U.K. Travelers According to the Association of British Insurers, a trade association representing 450 insurance companies, it's wise to **buy extra medical coverage when you visit the United States.** You can buy an annual travel-insurance policy valid for most vacations during the year in which it's purchased. If you go this route, make sure it covers you if you have a preexisting medical condition or are pregnant.

Trip Without insurance, you will lose all or most of your money if you must cancel your trip due to illness or for any other reason. Especially if your airline ticket, cruise, or package tour is nonrefundable and cannot be changed, it's essential that you **buy trip-cancellation-and-interruption insurance.** When considering how much coverage you need, look for a policy that will cover the cost of your trip plus the nondiscounted price of a one-way airline ticket should you need to return home early. Read the fine print carefully, especially sections defining "family member" and "preexisting medical conditions." Also **consider default or bankruptcy insurance,** which protects you against a supplier's failure to deliver. However, such policies often do not cover default by a travel agency, tour operator, airline, or cruise line if you bought your tour and the coverage directly from the firm in question.

Local Transportation

Many cities have free or low-cost downtown shuttles, trolleys, or park-and-ride schemes that encourage you to use rapid transit, such as Metrorail in Miami. It pays to **use these systems as much as you can,** even if you have a car with you—you'll save on parking, gas, and possible theft.

Lodging

Cutting Costs Even the most glittery resort towns in Florida have affordable lodgings, typically motel rooms that may cost as little as $20–$25 a night—not in the best part of town, mind you, but not in the worst, either, perhaps along busy highways where you'll need the roar of the air-conditioning to drown out the roar of the traffic. Beachfront properties are always more expensive than comparable properties off the beach, yet many beachfront properties are surprisingly affordable, too.

Because Florida has more hotel rooms than any other state in America, competition for attracting guests is intense. You can **play the competition to your advantage** and save some money.

Lodgings cost more than anything else on your trip, and the season makes the difference. During high season, there's more demand for rooms, so prices go up and there's less room for negotiating. Off-season, however, hotels are looking for people, and since an unoccupied bed is lost revenue forever, most managers would rather fill a bed than maintain published rates. Be sure to **ask in advance for all discounts.** Typically that means identifying yourself as a member of AARP, AAA, or some other group that entitles you to reductions, but also ask if there are other discounts, such as those for senior citizens (*see* Senior-Citizen Discounts, *below*) or corporate travelers, even if you're not traveling on company business. If the desk clerk or manager is under instructions to fill beds, he or she may just be looking for an excuse to offer you a break, which could run 10%–25%. You can also ask if there are any special deals for families. Often instead of a discount, families are offered an upgrade to a better (and larger) room when one is available. And if you're staying for an entire week, you can usually get a weekly rate—typically a free seventh night after a stay of six nights. But remember, even when you're getting a bargain, you can always **ask to see the room before you sign the register.** Generally that's a good idea—staying in an unpleasantly noisy or unclean room may not be worth the few dollars you'll save.

If you're willing to take a chance, you can **save money by showing up at the last minute.** Even in high season rooms are often available at the end of day, and if you show up in midafternoon you may get the room discounted. Show up in early evening, however, and a discount is less likely even if the room is available, because desk clerks assume you really need the room.

Also **visit the local chamber of commerce or convention and visitors bureau,** where local hotels and motels (as well as area attractions) often post discount coupons. In smaller towns, a staff person may be able to tell you which lodgings in the area customarily offer the various types of discounts discussed above.

Some of the most affordable places to stay along the east coast are in the Florida Keys (but only relative to Key West), Hollywood Beach, Riviera Beach (in Palm Beach County), Melbourne Beach, Daytona Beach, and Jacksonville Beach. On the west coast, try Fort Myers Beach, Anna Maria Island, beaches along the Pinellas Suncoast, Tarpon Springs, and along the Panhandle coast, from Port St. Joe to Panama City Beach; in Fort Walton Beach, Navarre Beach, and Pensacola Beach; and on Perdido Key. Bargain rooms are always available in Kissimmee–St. Cloud.

Apartment and Villa Rentals If you want a home base that's roomy enough for a family and comes with cooking facilities, **consider a furnished rental.** It's generally cost-wise, too, although not always—some rentals are luxury properties (economical only when your party is large). Home-exchange directories do list rentals—often second homes owned by prospective house swappers—and some services search for a house or apartment for you (even a castle if that's your fancy) and handle the paperwork. Some send an illustrated catalogue and others send photographs of specific properties, sometimes at a charge; up-front registration fees may apply.

Home Exchange If you would like to find a house, an apartment, or other vacation property to exchange for your own while on vacation, **become a member of a home-exchange organization,** which will send you its annual directories listing available exchanges and will include your own listing in at least one of them. Arrangements for the actual exchange are made by the two parties to it, not by the organization.

Money and Expenses

ATMs Chances are that you can **use your bank card at ATMs** to withdraw money from an account and get cash advances on a credit-card account if your card has been programmed with a personal identification number, or PIN. Before leaving home, **check on frequency limits** for withdrawals and cash advances.

On cash advances, you are charged interest from the day you receive the money from an ATM or teller. Transaction fees for ATM withdrawals outside your home turf may be higher than for withdrawals at home.

Taxes Everybody everywhere in Florida pays a 6% tax on almost everything. On top of that, half of Florida's 67 counties impose a tourist development tax that ranges, county to county, from 1% to 4%. In Orlando and Daytona Beach, for example, there's a 4% tax added on to your hotel room rate. In metropolitan Miami, depending on the part of town where you stay, you'll pay a 2% tax in most areas (3% in Bal Harbour) on room and food. In Miami Beach and elsewhere in Dade County, your hotel room rate will include an additional 3% convention-development tax, as well as another 1% professional-sports-franchise-facility tax. Everywhere in the metro area you pay a ½% local sales tax. Add it all up and in Surfside you pay 8½%, in Bal Harbour 9½%, in Miami Beach 11½%, and elsewhere in Dade (Miami, Coconut Grove, Coral Gables, for instance) 12½%.

Traveler's Checks Whether or not to buy traveler's checks depends on where you are headed; **take cash to rural areas and small towns, traveler's checks to cities.** The most widely recognized are American Express, Citicorp, Thomas Cook, and Visa, which are sold by major commercial banks for 1% to 3% of the checks' face value—it pays to **shop around.** Both American Express and Thomas Cook issue checks that can be countersigned and used by you or your traveling companion. Record the numbers of the checks, cross them off as you spend them, and keep this information separate from your checks.

Wiring Money You don't have to be a cardholder to send or receive funds through MoneyGram[SM] from American Express. Just go to a MoneyGram agent, located in retail and convenience stores and in American Express Travel Offices. Pay up to $1,000 with cash or a credit card, anything over that in cash. The money can be picked up within 10 minutes in cash or check at the nearest MoneyGram agent. There's no limit, and the recipient need only present photo identification. The cost, which includes a free long-distance phone call, runs from 3% to 10%, depending on the amount sent, the destination, and how you pay.

You can also send money using Western Union. Money sent from the United States or Canada will be available for pickup at agent locations in 100 countries within 15 minutes. Once the money is in the system, it can be picked up at any one of 25,000 locations. Fees range from 4% to 10%, depending on the amount you send.

Nightlife

When you go out at night, **look for ladies' nights and clubs without cover charges.** They're everywhere and often the best liked by locals.

Packages and Tours

A package or tour to Florida can make your vacation less expensive and more convenient. Firms that sell tours and packages purchase airline seats, hotel rooms, and rental cars in bulk and pass some of the savings on to you. In addition, the best operators have local representatives to help you out at your destination.

A Good Deal? The more your package or tour includes, the better you can predict the ultimate cost of your vacation. Make sure you know exactly what is included, and **beware of hidden costs.** Are taxes, tips, and service charges included? Transfers and baggage handling? Entertainment and excursions? These can add up.

Most packages and tours are rated deluxe, first-class superior, first class, tourist, and budget. The key difference is usually accommodations. If the package or tour you are considering is priced lower than in your wildest dreams, **be skeptical.** Also, **make sure your travel agent knows the hotels** and other services. Ask about location, room size, beds, and whether the facility has a pool, room service, or programs for children, if you care about these. Has your agent been there or sent others you can contact?

Buyer Beware Each year consumers are stranded or lose their money when operators go out of business—even very large ones with excellent reputations. If you can't afford a loss, take the time to **check out the operator**—find out how long the company has been in business, and ask several agents about its reputation. Next, **don't book unless the firm has a consumer-protection program.** Members of the United States Tour Operators Association and the National Tour Association are required to set aside funds exclusively to cover your payments and travel arrangements in case of default. Nonmember operators may instead carry insurance; look for the details in the operator's brochure—and the name of an underwriter with a solid reputation. Note: When it comes to tour operators, **don't trust escrow accounts.** Although there are laws governing those of charter-flight operators, no governmental body prevents tour operators from raiding the till.

Next, **contact your local Better Business Bureau and the attorney general's office** in both your own state and the operator's; have any complaints been filed? Last, **pay with a major credit card.** Then you can cancel payment, provided that you can document your complaint. Always **consider trip-cancellation insurance** (*see* Insurance, *above*).

Big vs. Small An operator that handles several hundred thousand travelers annually can use its purchasing power to give you a good price. Its high volume may also indicate financial stability. But some small companies provide more personalized service; because they tend to specialize, they may also be experts on an area.

Using an Agent Travel agents are an excellent resource. In fact, large operators accept bookings only through travel agents. But it's good to **collect brochures from several agencies,** because some agents' suggestions may be skewed by promotional relationships with tour and package firms that reward them for volume sales. If you have a special interest, **find an agent with expertise in that area;** the American Society of Travel Agents can give you leads in the United States. (Don't rely solely on your agent, though; agents may be unaware of small-niche operators, and some special-interest travel companies only sell direct.)

Single Travelers Prices are usually quoted per person, based on two sharing a room. If traveling solo, you may be required to pay the full double-occupancy rate. Some operators eliminate this surcharge if you agree to be matched up with a roommate of the same sex, even if one is not found by departure time.

Packing for Florida

Dress is casual throughout the state, with sundresses, jeans, or walking shorts appropriate during the day. A pair of comfortable walking shoes or sneakers is a must for the theme parks. A few of the better restaurants request that men wear jackets and ties, but most do not. It's always a good idea to **take a sweater,** since air-conditioning is often working in overdrive. You might even want a jacket in winter, when nighttime temperatures can dip to the 50s, even in the Keys, and there may be frost at night in the Panhandle area. In summer, bring an umbrella in case of sudden storms; plastic raincoats are uncomfortable when it's hot and humid.

You can swim in most of peninsular Florida year-round. Be sure to take a sun hat and a good sunscreen because the sun can be fierce, even in winter. Bring an extra pair of eyeglasses or contact lenses in your carry-on luggage, and if you have a health problem, **pack enough medication** to last the trip. **Don't put prescription drugs or valuables in luggage to be checked,** for it could go astray.

Luggage Free airline baggage allowances depend on the airline, the route, and the class of your ticket; ask in advance. In general, on domestic flights you are entitled to check two bags—neither exceeding 62 inches, or 158 centimeters (length + width + height), or weighing more than 70 pounds (32 kilograms). A third piece may be brought aboard; its total dimensions are generally limited to less than 45 inches (114 centimeters), so it will fit easily under the seat in front of you or in the overhead compartment. In the United States, the FAA gives airlines broad latitude to limit carry-on allowances and tailor them to different aircraft and operational conditions. Charges for excess, oversize, or overweight pieces vary.

Safeguarding Your Luggage Before leaving home, **itemize your bags' contents** and their worth, and label them with your name, address, and phone number. (If you use your home address, cover it so that potential thieves can't see it.) Inside your bag, **pack a copy of your itinerary.** At check-in, **make sure that your bag is correctly tagged** with the airport's three-letter destination code. If your bags arrive damaged or not at all, file a written report with the airline before leaving the airport.

Parks and Preserves

On holidays and weekends, crowds flock to Florida's most popular parks—some on islands that are accessible only by boat; **come early or risk being turned away.** In winter, northern migratory birds descend on the state. Many resident species breed in the warm summer months, but others (such as the wood stork) time their breeding cycle to the winter dry season. In summer, mosquitoes are voracious and daily afternoon thundershowers add to the state's humidity, but during the start of this season is when sea turtles come ashore to lay their eggs and when you're most likely to see frigate birds and other tropical species.

Passports and Visas

Canadians No passport is necessary to enter the United States.

U.K. Citizens British citizens need a valid passport. If you are staying fewer than 90 days and traveling on a vacation, with a return or onward ticket, you will probably not need a visa. However, you will need to fill out the Visa Waiver Form, 1-94W, supplied by the airline. While traveling, **keep one photocopy of the data page** of your passport separate from your wallet and leave another copy with someone at home. If you lose your passport, promptly call the nearest embassy or consulate, and the local police; having the data page can speed replacement.

Rail Travel

Amtrak's All-Aboard fares are an economical way to travel. They cost about half as much as airline fares, and they typically allow three stopovers—traveling between Washington and Winter Park, for example, you could stop in Savannah, Georgia, or on your way to Miami you could stop in Orlando. Knowing you'll need a car once you get to Florida, you might **consider taking Amtrak's AutoTrain,** which travels down the East Coast to Miami. You can ride in a regular train compartment, while your car is shipped along with you. Fares are seasonally adjusted, so if you're going north or south when most of the traffic is going the other way, you can expect to save. And once you get to Florida, you'll have your own car with you and won't need to pay for car rental.

Within Florida Along the lower east coast the cheapest way to travel is with Tri-Rail, which links Miami, Fort Lauderdale, and West Palm Beach, including all three of their airports and several towns in between. Service operates seven days a week and the fares are the same every day, regardless of how far you travel: $3 one-way, $5 round-trip. If you're over 65 or between the ages of five and 12, you pay half fare. Students with ID also pay half fare; youngsters below the age of five ride free.

Amtrak also offers cheap options for getting around within the state. Routes connect Miami and Tampa with Orlando, Orlando with Jacksonville, and Jacksonville with Pensacola in the far western Panhandle. Sample round-trip fares: between Tampa and Orlando, $26–$36; between Jacksonville and Pensacola, $80–$146. Lower fares are available for advance bookings. Senior citizens get 15% off regular fares traveling any day.

Renting a Car

Cuttings Costs Florida is a car renter's bazaar, with more discount companies offering more bargains—and more fine print—than any other state in the nation. Shop around for the best combination rate for car and airfare.

To get the best deal, **book through a travel agent and shop around.** When pricing cars, **ask where the rental lot is located.** Some off-airport locations offer lower rates—even though their lots are only minutes away from the terminal via complimentary shuttle. You may also want to **price local car-rental companies,** whose rates may be lower still, although service and maintenance standards may not be up to those of a national firm. Also **ask your travel agent about a company's customer-service record.** How has it responded to late plane arrivals and vehicle mishaps? Are there often lines at the rental counter, and, if you're traveling during a holiday period, does a confirmed reservation guarantee you a car?

Insurance When you drive a rented car, you are generally responsible for any damage or personal injury that you cause as well as damage to the vehicle. Before you rent, **see what coverage you already have** by means of your personal auto-insurance policy and credit cards. For about $14 a day, rental companies sell insurance, known as a collision damage waiver (CDW), that eliminates your liability for damage to the car; it's always optional and should never be automatically added to your bill.

For U.K. In the United States you must be 21 to rent a car; rates may be high-
Citizens er for those under 25. Extra costs cover child seats, compulsory for
children under five (about $3 per day), and additional drivers (about
$1.50 per day). To pick up your reserved car you will need the reser-
vation voucher, a passport, a U.K. driver's license, and a travel policy covering each driver.

Surcharges Before picking up the car in one city and leaving it in another, **ask
about drop-off charges or one-way service fees,** which can be substantial. Note, too, that some rental agencies charge extra if you return
the car before the time specified on your contract. To avoid a hefty
refueling fee, **fill the tank just before you turn in the car.**

Senior-Citizen Discounts

To qualify for these discounts, which are common throughout Florida, **mention your senior-citizen status up front** when booking hotel
reservations, not when checking out, and before you're seated in
restaurants, not when paying your bill. (Note that in Florida, a senior citizen may be anyone 50 or over.) Where there are set discounts,
there might be restrictions. You might be limited to certain menus,
days, or hours at restaurants, for example, or required to fill out a
card and register, as at the Eckerd Drug chain. In many instances
there is no standard, but it's still a good idea to **ask if there are discounts.** Even if a hotel or motel doesn't normally offer a reduction,
just by asking you'll prompt the desk clerk to extend one. When
renting a car, **ask about promotional car-rental discounts**—they can
net lower costs than your senior-citizen discount. Amtrak and Greyhound both offer discounted fares for senior citizens (*see* Bus Travel
and Rail Travel, *above*).

Shopping

Malls in Florida are full of nationally franchised shops, major de-
partment-store chains, and one-of-a-kind shops catering to a mass
clientele. For the best souvenirs and most affordable gift items,
however, **seek out small shops in out-of-the-way places.**

Art and You don't have to be a Sotheby's client to find art that satisfies. For
Antiques the best buys, **visit small-town museums.** Inspired local artists often
price their work for local buyers, and you can get lucky. Antiques
lovers should explore Havana, north of Tallahassee; Micanopy,
south of Gainesville off I–75; the Antiques Mall in St. Augustine's
Lightner Museum; U.S. 17/92 between Orlando and Winter Park;
U.S. 1 north of Dania Beach Boulevard in Dania; and Southwest 28th
Lane and Unity Boulevard in Miami (near the Coconut Grove
Metrorail station).

Citrus Fruit Fresh citrus is available most of the year, except in summer. Two
kinds of citrus grow in Florida: the sweeter and more costly Indian
River fruit from a thin ribbon of groves along the east coast, and the
less-costly fruit from the interior, south and west of Lake Okeechobee. For best prices, buy during the height of the season, which in
most parts of Florida is midwinter.

Citrus is sold in ¼, ½, ¾, and full bushels. Many shippers offer special gift packages with several varieties of fruit, jellies, and other
food items. Some prices include U.S. postage, others may not. Shipping may exceed the cost of the fruit. If you have a choice of citrus
packaged in boxes or bags, **choose boxes.** They are easier to label and
harder to squash than the bags.

Native Native American crafts are abundant, particularly in the southern
American part of the state, where you'll find billowing dresses and shirts,
Crafts hand-sewn in striking colors and designs. At the Miccosukee Indian
Village, 25 miles west of Miami on the Tamiami Trail (U.S. 41), as

well as at the Seminole and Miccosukee reservations in the Everglades, you can also find handcrafted dolls and beaded belts.

Seashells   The best shelling in Florida is on the beaches of Sanibel Island, off Fort Myers, and of course it's free. Kitschy shell shops abound throughout Florida, but know that the coral and other shells sold in shops in the Florida Keys have been imported for sale because of restrictions.

Sports and Outdoor Activities

One of the reasons Florida is such a popular destination for travelers on a budget is that visitors can spend most of their time here outdoors, enjoying the sun, water, and nature. If you're interested in active sports, however, there is usually some cost entailed, and you'll want to **shop carefully to find bargains.**

Biking   Bicycling continues to grow in popularity because the terrain is flat in the south and gently rolling along the central ridge and in much of the Panhandle. In most cities of any size, **check with bike-rental shops for information on local bike paths.**

Canoeing   The Everglades has areas suitable for flat-water wilderness canoeing that are comparable to spots in the Boundary Waters region of Minnesota. Other popular canoeing rivers include the Blackwater, Econlokahatchee, Juniper, Loxahatchee, Peace, Oklawaha, Suwannee, St. Marys, and Santa Fe. To stand the best chance of avoiding torrential downpours and voracious mosquitoes, **canoe in winter, the dry season.**

Fishing   Opportunities for saltwater fishing abound from the Keys all the way up the Atlantic Coast to Georgia and up the Gulf Coast to Alabama. Many seaside communities have fishing piers that charge admission to anglers (and usually a lower rate to watchers). These piers usually have a bait-and-tackle shop, where you can **check on local fishing seasons and regulations on the number and size of fish of various species that you may catch and retain.**

Inland, there are more than 7,000 freshwater lakes to choose from. The largest—448,000-acre Lake Okeechobee, the third-largest natural lake in the United States—is home to bass, bluegill, speckled perch, and succulent catfish (which the locals call "sharpies"). In addition to the state's many natural freshwater rivers, south Florida also has an extensive system of flood-control canals. In 1989 scientists found high mercury levels in largemouth bass and warmouth caught in parts of the Everglades in Palm Beach, Broward, and Dade counties and have extended warnings to parts of northern Florida, so **don't eat fish from those areas.**

If it's deep water you're after, **hire a boat-charter service.** Some of the best are found in the Panhandle, where Destin and Fort Walton Beach have huge fleets. The Keys, too, are dotted with charter services, and Key West has a big sportfishing fleet. Depending on your taste, budget, and needs, you can charter anything from an old wooden craft to a luxurious, waterborne palace with state-of-the-art amenities.

For both freshwater and saltwater fishing, **get a license.** The fees for a saltwater fishing license are $30 for nonresidents and $12 for residents. A nonresident seven-day saltwater license is $14. Nonresidents can purchase freshwater fishing licenses good for seven days ($15) or for one year ($30); residents pay $12 for an annual license. Combined annual freshwater fishing and hunting licenses are also available at $22 for residents. Typically, you'll pay a $1.50 surcharge at most any marina, bait and tackle shop, Kmart, Wal-Mart, or wherever you buy your license.

Golf Except in the heart of the Everglades, you'll never be far from one of Florida's more than 1,050 golf courses, but be sure to **reserve tee-off times in advance**, especially in winter. To save money, **consider an afternoon tee time**, since greens fees are usually lower.

Hiking While hiking is fairly popular, you're not likely to run into other humans on Florida trails. Instead, **look for wild turkey and deer.**

Hunting There's a wide variety of resident game animals and birds in Florida, including deer, wild hog, wild turkey, bobwhite quail, ducks, and coots, but first you must **purchase a license.** A resident hunting license costs $11; the same license for nonresidents is $150, except for nonresidents from Alabama who pay $100. Nonresidents can get a 10-day hunting license for $25, except for nonresidents from Georgia, who pay $121.

Jogging, Running, and Walking All over Florida, you'll find joggers, runners, and walkers on bike paths and city streets—primarily in the early morning and after working hours in the evening. The first time you run in Florida, **be prepared to go a shorter distance than normal** because of higher heat and humidity. Also, **ask at your hotel for information on measured trails in the vicinity.**

Scuba Diving and Snorkeling South Florida and the Keys attract most of the divers, but you can **scuba all along Florida's Atlantic and Gulf coasts** thanks to the more than 300 dive shops throughout the state that schedule drift-, reef-, and wreck-diving trips. For lower-tech pleasures, **try snorkeling along the Overseas Highway in the Keys and elsewhere where shallow reefs hug the shore.**

Inland in north and central Florida, **explore any of the more than 100 grottoes, rivers, sinkholes, and springs.** In some locations, you can **swim near endangered manatees** ("sea cows"), which migrate in from the sea to congregate around warm springs during the cool winter months.

Scuba divers take note: **Do not fly within 24 hours of scuba diving.**

Tennis If your hotel has a resident tennis pro, **ask about special tennis packages with lessons.** Many local park and recreation departments throughout Florida operate modern tennis centers like those at country clubs, so **check if the local center welcomes nonresidents for a fee.**

Students on the Road

To save money, **look into deals available through student-oriented travel agencies.** To qualify, you'll need to have a bona fide student I.D. card. Members of international student groups also are eligible. *See* Students *in* Important Contacts A to Z, *above.*

Telephones

Long-Distance The long-distance services of AT&T, MCI, and Sprint make calling home relatively convenient and let you avoid hotel surcharges; typically, you **dial an 800 number to reach your phone carrier.**

When to Go

Florida is a state for all seasons, although most visitors prefer October–April, particularly in southern Florida. If you're looking to save money, however, **go during the off-season**—winter in the Panhandle, or, for south Florida, the period between Easter and summer break and again between Labor Day and mid-December. Off-season, hotel prices drop by a third to half—sometimes more. Summers have become nearly as busy as winters in most of the state, but prices are only about three-quarters of what they are at winter's peak.

Summer in Florida, as smart budget-minded visitors have discovered, is often hot and very humid, but ocean breezes make the season bearable along the coast. In the Panhandle, summer is the peak season; Walt Disney World and other Orlando attractions also draw crowds in summer.

For senior citizens, fall is the time for discounts to many attractions and hotels in Orlando and along the Pinellas Suncoast in the Tampa Bay area.

Winter is the height of the tourist season, when southern Florida is crowded with "snowbirds" fleeing the cold weather in the North. Hotels, bars, discos, restaurants, shops, and attractions are all crowded. Hollywood and Broadway celebrities appear in sophisticated supper clubs, and other performing artists hold the stage at ballets, operas, concerts, and theaters. From mid-December through January 2, Walt Disney World's Magic Kingdom is lavishly decorated, and there are daily parades and other extravaganzas, as well as the year's largest crowds. In the Panhandle, however, winter is the low season, so it's an excellent bargain.

For the college crowd, spring vacation is still the time to congregate in Florida, especially in Panama City Beach and to a lesser extent the Daytona Beach area; Fort Lauderdale, which city officials are trying to refashion more as a family resort, no longer indulges young revelers, so it's much less popular with college students than it once was.

Climate What follows are average daily maximum and minimum temperatures for major cities in Florida.

Key West (The Keys)	Jan.	76F	24C	May	85F	29C	Sept.	90F	32C
		65	18		74	23		77	25
	Feb.	76F	24C	June	88F	31C	Oct.	83F	28C
		67	19		77	25		76	24
	Mar.	79F	26C	July	90F	32C	Nov.	79F	26C
		68	20		79	26		70	21
	Apr.	81F	27C	Aug.	90F	32C	Dec.	76F	24C
		72	22		79	26		67	19

Miami	Jan.	74F	23C	May	83F	28C	Sept.	86F	30C
		63	17		72	22		76	24
	Feb.	76F	24C	June	85F	29C	Oct.	83F	28C
		63	17		76	24		72	22
	Mar.	77F	25C	July	88F	31C	Nov.	79F	26C
		65	18		76	24		67	19
	Apr.	79F	26C	Aug.	88F	31C	Dec.	76F	26C
		68	20		77	25		63	17

Orlando	Jan.	70F	21C	May	88F	31C	Sept.	88F	31C
		49	9		67	19		74	23
	Feb.	72F	22C	June	90F	32C	Oct.	83F	28C
		54	12		72	22		67	19
	Mar.	76F	24C	July	90F	32C	Nov.	76F	24C
		56	13		74	23		58	14
	Apr.	81F	27C	Aug.	90F	32C	Dec.	70F	21C
		63	17		74	23		52	11

Festivals and Seasonal Events

For exact dates and details about the following festivals and other events, call the listed numbers or inquire from local chambers of commerce.

Winter

Dec.: Month-long Victorian Seaside Christmas takes place oceanside on Amelia Island (tel. 800/226–3542).

Mid-Dec.: Walt Disney World's Very Merry Christmas Parade in the Magic Kingdom celebrates the season at the Magic Kingdom (Walt Disney World, Box 10000, Lake Buena Vista 32830-1000, tel. 407/931–7639).

Mid-Dec.: Grand Illumination is a colorful display in St. Augustine (tel. 904/829–5681).

Mid-Dec.: Winterfest Boat Parade is on the Intracoastal Waterway, Fort Lauderdale (tel. 305/767–0686).

Late Dec.: Coconut Grove King Mango Strut is a parody of the Orange Bowl Parade (tel. 305/858–6253).

Early January: Polo season opens at the Palm Beach Polo and Country Club (tel. 407/793–1440).

January 6: Greek Epiphany includes religious celebrations, parades, music, dancing, and feasting at the St. Nicholas Greek Orthodox Cathedral in Tarpon Springs (tel. 813/937–6109).

Mid-Jan.: Taste of the Grove Food and Music Festival is a popular fund-raiser put on in Coconut Grove's Peacock Park by area restaurants (tel. 305/444–7270).

Mid-Jan.: Martin Luther King, Jr., Festivals are celebrated throughout the state, for example in Tampa (tel. 813/223–8518) and in Orlando (tel. 407/246–2221).

Late Jan.: Miami Rivers Blues Festival takes place on the south bank of the river next to Tobacco Road (tel. 305/374–1198).

Feb.: Gasparilla Festival celebrates the legendary pirate's invasion of Tampa with street parades, an art festival, and music (tel. 800/448–2672).

Feb.: Edison Festival of Lights, in various locations around Fort Myers, celebrates Thomas A. Edison's long winter residence in the city (tel. 941/334–2550).

Feb.: International Carillon Festival takes place at the Bok Tower Gardens, Lake Wales (tel. 941/676–1408).

Feb.: Florida Strawberry Festival in Plant City, in its 61st year, celebrates its winter harvest for two weeks, with country music stars, rides, exhibits, and strawberry delicacies (tel. 813/752–9194).

Feb.: Olustee Battle Festival in Lake City, the second-largest Civil War reenactment in the nation after Gettysburg, features a memorial service, crafts and food festival, 10K run, and parade (tel. 904/752–3610 or 904/758–1312).

Feb.: Speed Weeks is a three-week celebration of auto racing that culminates in the famous Daytona 500 at the Daytona International Speedway in Daytona Beach (tel. 904/254–2700 or 800/854–1234).

Feb.–Mar.: Winter Equestrian Festival includes more than 1,000 horses and three grand-prix equestrian events at the Palm Beach Polo and Country Club in West Palm Beach (tel. 407/798–7000).

Mid-Feb.: Florida State Fair includes carnival rides and 4-H competitions in Tampa (tel. 813/621–7821).

Mid-Feb.: Miami Film Festival is 10 days of international, domestic, and local films sponsored by the Film Society of America (tel. 305/377–3456).

Mid-Feb.: Florida Manatee Festival, in Crystal River, focuses on both the river and the endangered manatee (tel. 904/795–3149).

Mid-Feb.: Florida Citrus Festival and Polk County Fair, in Winter Haven, showcases the citrus harvest with displays and entertainment (tel. 941/967–3175).

Mid-Feb.: Coconut Grove Art Festival is the state's largest (tel. 305/447–0401).

Last full weekend in Feb.: Labelle Swamp Cabbage Festival is a salute to the state tree, the cabbage palm (tel. 941/675–0125).

Early Mar.: 59th Annual Sanibel Shell Fair, which runs for four days starting the first Thursday of the month, is the largest event of the year on Sanibel Island (tel. 941/472–2155).

Early Mar.: Azalea Festival is a beauty pageant, arts and crafts show, and parade held in downtown Palatka and Riverfront Park (tel. 904/328–1503).

Early Mar.: Carnaval Miami is a carnival celebration staged by the Little Havana Tourist Authority (tel. 305/644–8888).

Spring   **Mid-Mar. and early July: Arcadia All-Florida Championship Rodeo** is professional rodeo at its best (tel. 941/494–2014 or 800/749–7633).

Mid-Mar.–early May: Springtime Tallahassee is a major cultural, sporting, and culinary event in the capital (tel. 904/224–5012).

Apr.: Arts in April presents a series of visual- and performing-arts events produced by independent Orlando arts organizations (tel. 407/425–0277).

Early Apr.: Delray Affair is the biggest event in the area and features arts, crafts, and food (tel. 407/278–0424).

Early Apr.–late May: Addison Mizner Festival in Boca Raton celebrates the arts in Palm Beach County (tel. 407/241–7432 or 407/930–6400).

Palm Sunday: Blessing of the Fleet is held on the bayfront in St. Augustine (tel. 904/829–5681).

Mid-Apr.: Cedar Key Sidewalk Arts Festival is celebrated in one of the state's most historic towns (tel. 904/543–5600).

Late Apr.: River Cities Festival is a three-day event in Miami Springs and Hialeah that focuses attention on the Miami River and the need to keep it clean (tel. 305/887–1515).

Late Apr.–early May: Sun 'n' Fun Festival includes a bathtub regatta, golf tournament, and nighttime parade in Clearwater (tel. 813/462–6531).

Late Apr.–early May: Conch Republic Celebration, in Key West, honors the founding fathers of the Conch Republic, "the small island nation of Key West" (tel. 305/296–0123).

First weekend in May: Sunfest includes a wide variety of cultural and sporting events in West Palm Beach (tel. 407/659–5980 or 800/833–5733).

Mid-May: Arabian Nights Festival, in Opa-locka, is a mix of contemporary and fantasy-inspired entertainment (tel. 305/758–4166).

Mid-May: Tropicool Fest for two weeks draws thousands to Naples for more than 30 concerts as well as arts and sports events all around town (tel. 941/262–6141).

Memorial Day weekend: Florida Folk Festival takes place in White Springs at the Stephen Foster State Folk Culture Center (tel. 904/397–2192).

First weekend in June: Miami-Bahamas Goombay Festival, in Miami's Coconut Grove, celebrates the city's Bahamian heritage (tel. 305/443–7928 or 305/372–9966).

Early–mid-June: Billy Bowlegs Festival, in Fort Walton Beach, is a week of entertaining activities in memory of a pirate who ruled the area in the late 1700s (tel. 800/322–3319).

Mid-June: Fiesta of Five Flags, in Pensacola, celebrates de Luna's landing with dancing and reenactments of the event (tel. 904/433–6512).

Summer   **July 4: Firecracker Festival,** in Palm Bay, is one of the state's most colorful Independence Day celebrations (tel. 407/727–0457).

Mid-July: Hemingway Days Festival, in Key West, includes plays, short-story competitions, and a Hemingway look-alike contest (tel. 305/294–4440).

Early Aug.: Annual Wausau Possum Funday & Parade is held in Possum Palace, Wausau (tel. 904/638–1460).

Labor Day: Worm Fiddler's Day is the biggest day of the year in Caryville (tel. 904/548–5571).

Early Sept.: Anniversary of the Founding of St. Augustine is held on the grounds of the Mission of Nombre de Dios (tel. 904/829–8379).

Autumn   **Oct.: Jacksonville Jazz Festival** is a three-day event featuring jazz superstars, performances, arts and crafts, food, and the Great American Jazz Piano Competition (tel. 904/353–7770).

Oct.: Destin Seafood Festival is a two-day affair where you can sample smoked amberjack, fried mullet, or shark kabobs (tel. 800/322–3319).

Mid-Oct.: Fall RiverFest Arts Festival takes place downtown along the St. Johns River in beautiful and historic Palatka (tel. 904/328–8998).

Mid-Oct.: Boggy Bayou Mullet Festival is a three-day hoedown in celebration of the "Twin Cities," Valparaiso/Niceville, and the famed scavenger fish, the mullet (tel. 904/678–1615).

Mid-Oct.: Cedar Key Seafood Festival is held on Main Street, Cedar Key (tel. 904/543–5600).

Late Oct.: Fantasy Fest, in Key West, is an unrestrained Halloween costume party, parade, and town fair (tel. 305/296–1817).

Early Nov.: Light Up Orlando is a street celebration of bands, international foods, and the Queen Kumquat Sashay Parade (tel. 407/363–5800).

Early Nov.: Florida Seafood Festival is Apalachicola's celebration of its seafood staple with oyster-shucking-and-consumption contests and parades (tel. 904/653–9419).

Early Nov.–late Feb.: Orange Bowl and **Junior Orange Bowl Festival,** best known for the King Orange Jamboree Parade and the Federal Express/Orange Bowl Football Classic, also include more than 20 youth-oriented events in the Miami area (tel. 305/371–3351).

Mid-Nov.: Jensen Beach Pineapple Festival is at the Martin County Fairgrounds (tel. 407/334–3444).

Mid-Nov.: 12th Annual Miami Book Fair International, the largest book fair in the United States, is held on the Miami-Dade Community College Wolfson Campus (tel. 305/237–3258).

2 Miami and Miami Beach

By Herb Hiller

Editor of the Ecotourism Society Newsletter, *Herb Hiller is also a freelance writer whose pieces often focus on backroad travel and cycling.*

Miami is an affordable miracle. The best part of town for vacationing—Miami Beach's South Beach district—is the easiest place to visit on the cheap, with budget hotels, budget restaurants, and the best free people-watching in the United States.

South Beach is but the latest historic Miami area neighborhood to be transformed into a hot vacation spot. Two decades ago, crash pads and free kitchens, communes and rock and roll made Coconut Grove a hip and affordable getaway for the young. Today the young, the gay, and the artistic have made South Beach and its Deco District the most written-about and photographed place in America, Disney notwithstanding. Summer especially brings young people; two of every three are male, and three of every four are single. Celebrities such as Madonna, Gloria Estefan, record mogul Chris Blackwell, and designer Gianni Versace have bought up Ocean Drive properties, taking geriatric homes and turning them into posh and trendy abodes or $200-a-night digs. Meanwhile, old hotels that weren't on Ocean Drive started taking in the attendant crowd of hopefuls—kids with good looks trying to break into modeling and low-on-cash dreamers who came to be part of the scene. The apartments behind Ocean Drive have been colonized by young professionals who want South Beach as part of their residential lifestyle.

Less than a five-minute walk from the beach, hotels no older than the Deco headliners—with rooms no smaller and service that's less condescending—offer double rooms at $60 and $70 a night in the height of the winter season (about $40 and $45 off season). At the official AYH International Youth Hostel you can get a bed for $12, and some beachfront hotels have in-season suites for two couples traveling together for $100 per couple. If you look hard, you can find restaurants in the best part of SoBe with dinners at $10 and $12, and we've looked hard so we can tell you where they are.

We've also scoped out the affordable tennis courts, golf courses, shopping, and museums, and nowhere else in the country has rental cars as inexpensive as in Miami, so you can get to the best buys in places that may be a little out of the way. (Public transportation isn't Miami's strong suit.)

What Miami's strong suit is is its international flavor. Long before Spain's gold-laden treasure ships passed offshore in the Gulf Stream, the Calusa Indians who lived here had begun to trade with mainland neighbors to the north and island brethren to the south. Repeating this pattern, more than 150 U.S. and multinational companies now locate their Latin American headquarters in Greater Miami. The city has unparalleled airline connections to the Western Hemisphere, its cruise port ranks number one in the world, and it leads the nation in the number of Edge Act banks. Miami hosts 20 foreign trade offices, 29 binational chambers of commerce, and 49 foreign consulates. No city of the Western Hemisphere is so universally simpatico.

First-time visitors are always struck by the billboards in Spanish. Initially these seem an affectation, an attempt to promote Miami's exotic international image. Only after you hear Spanish spoken by hotel help all around you or after the elevator you're in announces the floor stops as *primer piso* and *segundo piso* do you realize that the city *Newsweek* called "America's Casablanca" is really the capital of Latin America. Metro Miami is more than half Latin. Cubans make up most of this Spanish-speaking population, but significant communities come from Colombia, El Salvador, Nicaragua, Panama, Puerto Rico, and Venezuela. The Spanish place names George Merrick affixed to the streets in Coral Gables 75 years ago—Alhambra, Alcazar, Salzedo—may have been romantic pretense, but today's renamed Avenida Gen. Maximo Gomez and Carlos Arboleya Way are earnest celebrations of a contemporary city's heroes. Frank Sinatra and Barbra Streisand have given way in the hearts of Miamians to Julio Iglesias and Gloria Estefan.

In addition to the dominant Spanish-speaking population, Miami is home to some 200,000 Haitians along with Brazilians, Chinese, Germans, Greeks, Iranians, Israelis, Italians, Jamaicans, Lebanese, Malaysians, Russians, and Swedes—all speaking a veritable Babel of tongues. Most either know or are trying to learn English; you can help them by speaking slowly and distinctly.

Established Miami has warmed up to its newcomers. That's a big step forward. Only a few years ago metropolitan government enacted an ordinance forbidding essential public information from appearing in Spanish. In 1993 that restrictive affront was rescinded, and resisters have adjusted or moved north. Yesterday's immigrants have become today's citizens, and the nation's most international city now offers a style expressed in its many languages, its world-beat music, and its wealth of restaurants enjoyed by Miamians and visitors alike.

Miami keeps changing fast. Not only has South Beach come back. Lincoln Road, once the 5th Avenue of the South and only recently an embarrassing derelict row, has been stunningly brought back to life. On weekends it rivals the pedestrian malls of Cambridge, Lyons, or Munich for crowds and sheer hoi polloi festivity. Next slated for revival is North Beach, as all of Miami Beach becomes a magic kingdom in the real world, proving it's possible and relatively inexpensive to build community by preserving distinctive architecture rather than by "imagineering" pseudo worlds. (Miamians—especially Miami's immigrant newcomers—do still adore Disney, however.)

More changes are in store in this city that seems fueled on caffeine. (Stop by the window serving station of any Cuban café for a *tinto*, the city's high-test fuel.) Not surprisingly, much of the change is taking place to the south, in areas hard hit by Hurricane Andrew in 1992. In the Redland district, the Redland Conservancy is introducing bicycle trails and bed-and-breakfasts as a way of preserving the south county's agricultural heritage. Coral-rock walls and avocado groves may prove as distinctive in their own way as art deco hotels. A network of 200 miles of trails should link Biscayne and Everglades national parks by the end of the decade. For those interested in a quicker pace, Homestead has become a state-of-the-art hub for America's love affair with car racing (*see* Chapter 3, the Everglades).

As a big city, Miami also earns its bad rap. It has the highest percentage of citizens living in poverty. Its traffic is the fourth most congested in the United States. It ranks first in violent and property crimes and does the worst job of any city in putting and keeping criminals behind bars. Yet the widely publicized crimes against tourists in 1993 led to stepped-up visitor-safety programs that by 1995 had turned visitor safety around. Police patrols have been upgraded in primary visitor areas. New red, sunburst-logo, highway direction signs have been installed at ¼-mile intervals on major roads. Indicia that made rental cars conspicuous to would-be criminals have been removed, and multilingual pamphlets with tips on how to avoid crime are widely distributed. Despite all the problems and hyped headlines, Miami is still incredibly appealing. It has the climate, the beaches, and the international sophistication that few places can match.

Four major-league sports franchises call Miami home, as do the Doral-Ryder Open Tournament, the Lipton Championships, the Miami City Ballet, and Florida Grand Opera. On the verge of its centennial year and barely two years after Hurricane Andrew roared through, Miami played host to the Summit of the Americas, the Super Bowl, and the National Conference of Mayors. Visitors find in Miami a multicultural metropolis that works and plays with vigor and that welcomes the world to celebrate its diversity.

Miami and Miami Beach Basics

Arriving and Departing

By Plane
Airports and Airlines
Miami International Airport (MIA), 6 miles west of downtown Miami, is Greater Miami's only commercial airport. With a daily average of 1,450 flights, it handled 30.2 million passengers in 1994, 43% of them international travelers. (It's also the nation's busiest airport for air cargo.) Altogether 149 airlines serve 188 cities around the world with nonstop or one-stop service. MIA has 118 aircraft gates and eight concourses; the newest, Concourse A, opened in late spring of 1995.

Anticipating continued growth, the airport has begun a more than $3 billion expansion program that will require much of the decade to complete. Passengers will mainly notice rebuilt and expanded gate and public areas, which should reduce congestion.

A greatly underused convenience for passengers who have to get from one concourse to another in this long, horseshoe-shape terminal is the cushioned Moving Walkway, on the skywalk level, with access points at every concourse. Also available on site is the 263-room **Miami International Airport Hotel** (Concourse E, upper level, tel. 305/871–4100), which has the Top of the Port restaurant on the seventh floor and Port Lounge on the eighth. MIA, the first airport to offer duty-free shops, now boasts 14, carrying liquors, perfumes, electronics, and various designer goods.

When you fly out of MIA, plan to check in 55 minutes before departure for a domestic flight and 90 minutes before departure for an international flight. Services for international travelers include 24-hour multilingual information and paging phones and foreign-currency conversion booths throughout the terminal. There is an information booth with a multilingual staff and 24-hour currency exchange at the entrance of Concourse E on the upper level. Other tourist information centers are available at the customs exit, Concourse E, lower level, 5 AM–11 PM; customs exit, Concourse B, lower level, 11–7; Concourse G, lower level, 11–7; Concourse D, lower level, 11–11; and Satellite Terminal, 11–7.

Airlines that fly into MIA include **ACES** (tel. 305/265–1272), **Aero Costa Rica** (tel. 800/237–6274), **Aeroflot** (tel. 800/995–5555), **Aerolineas Argentinas** (tel. 800/333–0276), **Aeromexico** (tel. 800/237–6639), **AeroPeru** (tel. 800/777–7717), **Air Aruba** (tel. 800/882–7822), **Air Canada** (tel. 800/776–3000), **Air France** (tel. 800/237–2747), **Air Guadeloupe** (tel. 800/522–3394), **Air Jamaica** (tel. 800/523–5585), **Air South** (tel. 800/247–7688), **Airways International** (tel. 305/887–2794), **Alitalia** (tel. 800/223–5730), **ALM** (tel. 800/327–7230), **American** and **American Eagle** (tel. 800/433–7300), **American TransAir** (tel. 800/225–2995), **APA** (tel. 305/599–1299), **Avensa** (tel. 800/428–3672), **Avianca** (tel. 800/284–2622), **Aviateca** (tel. 800/327–9832), **Bahamasair** (tel. 800/222–4262), **British Airways** (tel. 800/247–9297), **BWIA** (tel. 305/371–2942), **Caribbean Airlines** (tel. 305/594–3232), **Carnival** (tel. 800/437–2110), **Cayman Airways** (tel. 800/422–9626), **Comair** (tel. 800/354–9822), **Continental** (tel. 800/525–0280), **Copa** (tel. 800/359–2672), **Delta** (tel. 800/221–1212), **Dominicana** (tel. 800/327–7240), **El Al** (tel. 800/223–6700), **Faucett** (tel. 800/334–3356), **Finnair** (tel. 800/950–5000), **Gulfstream International** (tel. 800/871–1200), **Guyana Airways** (tel. 800/242–4210), **Haiti Trans Air** (tel. 800/394–5313), **HANAIR** (tel. 305/757–7247), **Iberia** (tel. 800/772–4642), **LAB** (tel. 800/327–7407), **Lacsa** (tel. 800/225–2272), **Ladeco** (tel. 305/670–3066), **Lan Chile** (tel. 800/735–5526), **LAP** (tel. 800/677–7677), **Lauda Air** (tel. 800/645–3880), **LTU** (tel. 800/888–0200), **Lufthansa** (tel. 800/645–3880), **Martinair Holland** (tel. 800/366–4655), **Mexicana** (tel. 800/531–7921), **Nica** (tel. 800/831–4396), **Northwest** (tel. 800/225–2525), **Paradise Island** (tel. 800/432–8807), **Saeta** (tel. 800/827–2382), **Sahsa** (tel. 800/327–1225 or 800/432–9818 in FL), **Servivensa** (tel. 800/428–3672), **South African Airways** (tel. 800/722–9675), **Surinam Airways** (tel. 800/432–1230), **Taca** (tel. 800/535–8780), **Tower Air** (tel. 800/348–6937), **Transbrasil** (tel. 800/872–3153), **TWA** (tel. 800/221–2000), **United** (tel. 800/241–6522), **USAir** and **USAir Express** (tel. 800/842–5374), **ValuJet** (tel. 800/825–8538), **Varig** (tel. 800/468–2744), **VASP** (tel. 800/732–8277), **Viasa** (tel. 800/468–4272), **Virgin Atlantic** (tel. 800/862–8621), and **Zuliana** (tel. 800/223–8780).

Budget Airport Transport

By Bus: The county's **Metrobus** (tel. 305/638–6700) still costs $1.25, though equipment has improved. From the airport you can take Bus 7 to downtown (weekdays every 40 minutes 5:30 AM–9 PM; weekends 6:30–7:30), Bus 37 south to Coral Gables and South Miami (every 30 minutes 6 AM–11:30 PM) or north to Hialeah (every 30 minutes 5:30 AM–11:30 PM), Bus J south to Coral Gables (every 30 minutes 6 AM–12:30 AM) or east to Miami Beach (every 30 minutes 4:30 AM–11:30 PM), and Bus 42 to Coconut Grove (hourly 5:40 AM–7 PM).

By Taxi: Except for the flat-fare trips described below, cabs cost $1.70 per mile plus a $1 toll for trips originating at MIA or the Port of Miami. Approximate fares from MIA include $10 to Coral Gables, $15–$20 to downtown Miami, and $25–$30 to Key Biscayne. Newly established flat fares to the beaches are $38 to Golden Beach and Sunny Isles, north of Haulover Beach Park; $32 from Surfside through Haulover Beach Park; $27 between 63rd and 87th streets; and $22 from 63rd Street south to the foot of Miami Beach. These fares are per trip, not per passenger, and include tolls and $1 airport surcharge but not tip. The flat fare between MIA and the Port of Miami, in either direction, is $15.75.

For taxi service to destinations in the immediate vicinity, ask a uniformed county taxi dispatcher to call an **ARTS (Airport Region Taxi Service)** cab for you. These special blue cabs offer a short-haul flat fare in two zones. An inner-zone ride is $5.60; the outer-zone fare is $9. The area of service is north to 36th Street, west to the Palmetto Expressway (77th Avenue), south to Northwest 7th Street, and east to Douglas Road (37th Avenue). Maps are posted in cab windows on both sides.

By Van: SuperShuttle (tel. 305/871–2000 from MIA, 305/764–1700 in Broward [Fort Lauderdale], or 800/874–8885 from elsewhere) vans transport passengers between MIA and local hotels, the Port of Miami, and even individual residences on a 24-hour basis. The company's service area extends from Palm Beach to Monroe County (including the Lower Keys). Drivers provide narration en route. Service from MIA is available around the clock, on demand, but for the return it's best to make reservations 24 hours in advance, although the firm will try to arrange pickups within Dade County on as little as four hours' notice. The cost from MIA to downtown hotels is about $8. Additional members of a party pay a lower rate for many destinations, and children 3 and under ride free with their parents. There's a pet transport fee of $5 for animals in cages.

By Rental Car: Six rental-car firms—**Avis** (tel. 800/831–2847), **Budget** (tel. 800/527–0700), **Dollar** (tel. 800/800–4000), **Hertz** (tel. 800/654–3131), **National** (tel. 800/227–7368), and **Value** (tel. 800/468–2583)—have booths near the baggage-claim area on MIA's lower level.

By Boat If you're entering the United States along Florida's Atlantic Coast south of Sebastian Inlet, you must call the **U.S. Customs Service** (tel. 800/432–1216). Customs clears by phone most boats of less than 5 tons, but you may be directed for further inspection to one or another marina.

By Bus **Greyhound** (tel. 800/231–2222) buses stop at five bus terminals in Greater Miami (700 Biscayne Blvd., Miami; 4111 N.W. 27th St., Miami; 16250 Biscayne Blvd., North Miami; 7101 Harding Ave., Miami Beach; and 5 N.E. 3rd Rd., Homestead). There are no reservations.

By Car The main highways into Greater Miami from the north are Florida's Turnpike (a toll road) and I–95. From the northwest take I–75 or U.S. 27 into town. From the Everglades to the west, use I–75 or the Tamiami Trail (U.S. 41), and from the south use U.S. 1 and the Homestead Extension of Florida's Turnpike. Continuous reconstruction of I–95 forever slows traffic in one place or another in south Florida. A $400 million, 46-mile widening project between Miami and West Palm Beach was completed in 1995, and the huge plate of spaghetti known as the Golden Glades interchange, north of downtown, which carries between 300,000 and 400,000 vehicles a day, has a new nine-story-high, $32 million car-pool overpass. On the flip side, a three- to four-year repaving project will keep I–95 from operating at peak capacity through most of the decade. The new Brickell Avenue Bridge, from the south into downtown, is scheduled to open during 1996; meanwhile, drivers must cross the Miami River on the Miami Avenue twin bridges, across I–95, or on the Southwest 3rd Avenue Bridge. On the other hand, driving across the newly widened MacArthur Causeway, which connects downtown with Miami Beach, has become easier, thanks to a new highrise span that eliminates frequent openings for boat traffic.

By Train **Amtrak** (tel. 800/872–7245) runs two trains daily between New York City and Miami (8303 N.W. 37th Ave., tel. 305/835–1221 for recorded arrival and departure information or 305/835–1222 for shipping); the *Silver Meteor* and *Silver Star* make different stops along the way. The thrice-weekly *Sunset Limited* operates between Miami and Los Angeles, stopping in Jacksonville and Pensacola and other Florida towns en route.

The seven-year-old **Tri-Rail** (1 River Plaza, 305 S. Andrews Ave., Suite 200, Fort Lauderdale, tel. 305/728–8445 or 800/874–7245) commuter train system connects Miami with Broward and Palm Beach daily.

Getting Around on the Cheap

Greater Miami resembles Los Angeles in its urban sprawl and traffic congestion. You'll need a car to visit many of the attractions and points of interest listed in this book, though some are accessible via the public transportation system, run by a department of the county government—the **Metro-Dade Transit Agency**. It consists of almost 600 **Metrobuses** on 71 routes, the 21-mile **Metrorail** elevated rapid-transit system, and the **Metromover,** an elevated light-rail system. Free maps, schedules, and a "First-Time Rider's Kit" are available. *Government Center Station, 111 N.W. 1st St., Miami 33128; Maps by Mail, tel. 305/654–6586; route information, tel. 305/638–6700 weekdays 6 AM–10 PM, weekends 9–5.*

By Bus **Metrobus** (tel. 305/638–6700) stops are marked by blue-and-green signs with a bus logo and route information. The frequency of service varies widely, so call in advance to obtain specific schedule information. The fare is $1.25 (exact change), transfers 25¢; 60¢ with 10¢ transfer for the disabled, senior citizens (65 and older), and students. Some express routes carry surcharges of $1.50. Reduced-fare tokens sold 10 for $10 are now available from Metropass outlets. Lift-equipped buses for people with disabilities are available on 16 routes, including one from the airport that links up with many routes in Miami Beach as well as Coconut Grove, Coral Gables, Hialeah, and Kendall. All but four of these routes connect with Metrorail. Those unable to use regular transit service should call **Special Transportation Services** (tel. 305/263–5400) for information on such services as curb-to-curb van pickup.

By Car In general, Miami traffic is the same as in any big city, with the same rush hours and the same likelihood that parking garages will be full at peak times. The large immigrant population creates additional problems, however, introducing a different cultural attitude toward traffic laws. Many drivers who don't know their way around turn and stop suddenly, and you may often find drivers dropping off passengers where they shouldn't. Some drivers are short-tempered and will assault those who cut them off or honk their horn.

Motorists need to be careful even when their driving behavior is beyond censure, however, especially in rental cars. Despite the removal of identifying marks, cars piled with luggage or otherwise showing signs that a tourist is at the wheel remain prime targets for thieves. Longtime residents know that reports of crime against tourists are blown way out of proportion by the media and that Miami is more or less as safe for a visitor as any American city its size. Still, before setting off on any drive, make sure you know where you're going and carry a map. Ask where you rent your car or at your hotel if there are any areas between your point of departure and your destination that you should especially avoid. A new system indicates the main tourist routes in a series of red sunbursts on special directional signs. You can't miss them. Keep your doors locked, and ask questions only at toll booths, gas stations, or other obviously safe locations. Don't stop if your car is bumped from behind or if you're asked for directions. One hesitates to foster rude behavior, but at least for now the roads are too risky to stop any place you're not familiar with (other than as traffic laws require).

By Taxi One cab "company" stands out immeasurably above the rest. It's actually a consortium of drivers who have banded together to provide good service, in marked contrast to some Miami cabbies, who are rude, unhelpful, unfamiliar with the city, or dishonest, taking advantage of visitors who don't know the area. To plug into this consortium—they don't have a name, simply a number—call the dispatch service (tel. 305/888–4444). If you have to use another company, try to be familiar with your route and destination.

Since 1974 fares have been $1.75 per mile, 25¢ a minute waiting time, and there's no additional charge for extra passengers, luggage, or tolls. Taxis can be hailed on the street, although you may not always find one when you need one—it's better to call for a dispatch taxi or have a hotel doorman hail one for you. Some companies with dispatch service are **Central Taxicab Service** (tel. 305/532–5555), **Diamond Cab Company** (tel. 305/545–5555), **Metro Taxicab Company** (tel. 305/888–8888), **Miami-Dade Yellow Cab** (tel. 305/633–0503), **Miami Springs Taxi** (tel. 305/888–1000), **Society Cab Company** (tel. 305/757–5523), **Speedy Cab** (tel. 305/861–9999), **Super Yellow Cab Company** (tel. 305/888–7777), **Tropical Taxicab Company** (tel. 305/945–1025), and **Yellow Cab Company** (tel. 305/444–4444). Many now accept credit cards; inquire when you call.

By Train Elevated **Metrorail** trains run from downtown Miami north to Hialeah and south along U.S. 1 to Dadeland, daily 5:30 AM–midnight. Trains runs every five minutes in peak hours, every 15 minutes at other times. The fare is $1.25. Transfers, which cost 25¢, must be bought at the first station entered. Parking at train stations costs $1.

Metromover has two loops that circle downtown Miami, linking major hotels, office buildings, and shopping areas (*see* Tour 2 *in* Exploring Miami, *below*). The system has been expanded from 1.9 miles to 4.4 miles, including the 1.4-mile Omni extension, with six stations to the north, and the 1.1-mile Brickell extension, with six stations to the south. Service runs daily every 90 seconds, 6 AM–midnight. The fare is 25¢. Transfers to Metrorail are $1.

By Water Taxi The service inaugurated in 1987 in Fort Lauderdale began Miami area operations in 1994 and expanded service between Miami Beach Marina and the Eden Rock Hotel in 1995. Canopied boats, 28 feet and longer, connect Miami Beach, Coconut Grove, and Key Biscayne from Bayside Marketplace. Routes cover downtown and Miami Beach hotels and restaurants and the Watson Island airboat station. Taxis operate daily 10 AM–2:30 AM. One-way fares around downtown Miami are $3, longer runs $7. For information, call 305/858–6292.

Important Addresses and Numbers

Emergencies Dial 911 for **police** or **ambulance**. You can dial free from pay phones.

Ambulance **Randle Eastern Ambulance Service Inc.** (35 S.W. 27th Ave., Miami 33135, tel. 305/642–6400) operates at all hours.

Hospitals The following hospitals have 24-hour emergency rooms:

In Miami Beach: **Miami Heart Institute** (4701 N. Meridian Ave., Miami Beach, tel. 305/672–1111; physician referral, tel. 305/674–3004), **Mt. Sinai Medical Center** (off Julia Tuttle Causeway, I–195 at 4300 Alton Rd., Miami Beach, tel. 305/674–2121; emergency, tel. 305/674–2200; physician referral, tel. 305/674–2273), and **South Shore Hospital & Medical Center** (630 Alton Rd., Miami Beach, tel. 305/672–2100).

In the north: **Golden Glades Regional Medical Center** (17300 N.W. 7th Ave., North Miami, tel. 305/652–4200; no physician referral).

In central Miami: **Coral Gables Hospital** (3100 Douglas Rd., Coral Gables, tel. 305/445–8461), **Jackson Memorial Medical Center** (1611 N.W. 12th Ave., near Dolphin Expressway, Miami, tel. 305/585–1111; emergency, tel. 305/585–6901; physician referral, tel. 305/547–5757), **Mercy Hospital** (3663 S. Miami Ave., Coconut Grove, tel. 305/854–4400; emergency, tel. 305/285–2171; physician referral, tel. 305/285–2929), and **Pan American Hospital** (5959 N.W. 7th St., Miami, tel. 305/264–1000; emergency, tel. 305/264–6125; physician referral, tel. 305/264–5118).

In the south: **Baptist Hospital of Miami** (8900 N. Kendall Dr., Miami, tel. 305/596–1960; emergency, tel. 305/596–6556; physician referral, tel. 305/596–6557) and **South Miami Hospital** (6200 S.W. 73rd St., South Miami, tel. 305/661–4611; emergency, tel. 305/662–8181; physician referral, tel. 305/633–2255).

Doctors **Dade County Medical Association** (1501 N.W. North River Dr., Miami, tel. 305/324–8717) is open weekdays 9–5 for medical referral.

Dentists **East Coast District Dental Society** (420 S. Dixie Hwy., Suite 2E, Coral Gables, tel. 305/667–3647) is open weekdays 9–4:30 for dental referral. Services include general dentistry, endodontics, periodontics, and oral surgery.

Late-Night Pharmacies **Eckerd Drug** (1825 Miami Gardens Dr. NE, at 185th St., North Miami Beach, tel. 305/932–5740; 9031 S.W. 107th Ave., Miami, tel. 305/274–6776). **Terminal Rexall Pharmacy** (Concourse F, Miami International Airport, Miami, tel. 305/876–0556). **Walgreen** (500–B W. 49th St., Palm Springs Mall, Hialeah, tel. 305/557–5468; 12295 Biscayne Blvd., North Miami, tel. 305/893–6860; 5731 Bird Rd., Miami, tel. 305/666–0757; 1845 Alton Rd., Miami Beach, tel. 305/531–8868; 791 N.E. 167th St., North Miami Beach, tel. 305/652–7332).

Services for People with Hearing Impairments **Fire, police, medical, rescue** (TTY tel. 305/595–4749). **Operator and directory assistance** (TTY tel. 800/855–1155). **Deaf Services of Miami** (9100 S. Dadeland Blvd., Suite 104, Miami 33156, voice tel. 305/670–9099) operates 24 hours year-round. **Florida Relay Service** (voice tel. 800/955–8770, TTY tel. 800/955–8771).

Visitor Information **Greater Miami Convention & Visitors Bureau** (701 Brickell Ave., Suite 2700, Miami 33131, tel. 305/539–3063 or 800/283–2707). Satellite tourist information centers are located at Bayside Marketplace (401 Biscayne Blvd., Miami 33132, tel. 305/539–2980), Miami Beach Chamber of Commerce (*see below*), and South Dade Visitor Information Center (160 U.S. 1, Florida City 33034, tel. 305/245–9180 or 800/388–9669, fax 305/247–4335).
Coconut Grove Chamber of Commerce (2820 McFarlane Rd., Coconut Grove 33133, tel. 305/444–7270, fax 305/444–2498).
Coral Gables Chamber of Commerce (50 Aragon Ave., Coral Gables 33134, tel. 305/446–1657, fax 305/446–9900).
Florida Gold Coast Chamber of Commerce (1100 Kane Concourse, Suite 210, Bay Harbor Islands 33154, tel. 305/866–6020) serves the beach communities of Bal Harbour, Bay Harbor Islands, Golden Beach, North Bay Village, Sunny Isles, and Surfside.
Greater Miami Chamber of Commerce (1601 Biscayne Blvd., Miami 33132, tel. 305/350–7700, fax 305/374–6902).
Greater South Dade/South Miami Chamber of Commerce (6410 S.W. 80th St., South Miami 33143-4602, tel. 305/661–1621, fax 305/666–0508).
Key Biscayne Chamber of Commerce (Key Biscayne Bank Bldg., 95 W. McIntyre St., Key Biscayne 33149, tel. 305/361–5207).
Miami Beach Chamber of Commerce (1920 Meridian Ave., Miami Beach 33139, tel. 305/672–1270, fax 305/538–4336).

North Miami Chamber of Commerce (13100 W. Dixie Hwy., North Miami 33181, tel. 305/891–7811, fax 305/893–8522).

Surfside Tourist Board (9301 Collins Ave., Surfside 33154, tel. 305/864–0722 or 800/327–4557, fax 305/861–1302).

Where to Stay on a Budget

Few urban areas can match Greater Miami's diversity of hotel accommodations. The area has hundreds of hotels and motels with lodgings in all price categories, from as low as $12 for a night in a dormitory-style hostel bed to $2,000 for a night in the luxurious presidential suite atop a posh downtown hotel. Most visitors will want to be in the South Beach area, with its hip fashion scene, loads of affordable restaurants, and proximity to the beach, and we've identified several outstanding buys there. But there are good affordable lodgings in all parts of the city and some splurges that are worth the money for a special getaway.

The hotels listed below are organized according to their rates during the winter high season, but off-season you can do even better, with rates often dipping to $40. You'll find the best values between Easter and Memorial Day (a delightful time in Miami, though it doesn't fit into most travelers' schedules) and in September and October—the height of hurricane season. Nowadays the general path of hurricanes is forecast a week or more in advance, so even when they're close, there's time to decide to get out or stick it out, depending on the storm's severity. Hoteliers are happy to have the hurricane season business. If this is when you plan to come, make sure that any deposit you put down is fully refundable in case *you* decide it's unsafe and cut your stay short. Regardless of season, Miami Beach hotels are the best place to try negotiating for lower rates because of the intense competition there.

Bay Harbor Islands
$$

Bay Harbor Inn. Here you'll find down-home hospitality in the most affluent zip code in the county. Retired Washington lawyer Sandy Lankler operates this 38-unit lodging in two sections, two moods. Townside is the oldest building in Bay Harbor Islands, vaguely Georgian in style but dating from 1940. Behind triple sets of French doors under fan windows, the lobby is full of oak desks, hand mills, grandfather clocks, historical maps, and potted plants. Rooms are antiques-filled, and no two are alike. Along Indian Creek the inn incorporates the former Albert Pick Hotella, a shipshape tropical-style set of rooms on two floors, off loggias surrounded by palms, with all rooms facing the water. The decor here is mid-century modern, with chintz. A complimentary Continental breakfast and the *Miami Herald* are provided. The popular Miami Palm restaurant is located town-side and B.C. Chong's Seafood Garden creek-side, with the London Bar serving the best ½-pound hamburger in the city. *9660 E. Bay Harbor Dr., 33154, tel. and fax 305/868–4141. 25 rooms, 12 suites, penthouse. Facilities: 2 restaurants, lounge, heated outdoor freshwater pool. AE, DC, MC, V.*

Coral Gables
Splurge

David William Hotel. Easily the most affordable of the top Gables hotels, the DW (as aficionados call it) was the first high-rise of Miami's modern era, standing 13 stories tall with a distinctive waffled facade. That dates it from the 1960s, but the DW has been kept in top shape. The hotel is solidly built, like a fort, so the rooms are very private and very quiet. Guest rooms are large, with marble baths; all those facing south (the sunnier exposure) have balconies. Many rooms have kitchens, and some are no-smoking. The decor features new furniture trimmed with braids of varicolored wood, upholstered in tan and blue. The excellent desk staff is more concerned with helping guests than with maintaining airs. Rooftop cabana guest rooms are the best bargains. Room rates in season run about $125 a night. *700 Biltmore Way, 33134, tel. 305/445–7821 or 800/327–*

Miami Area Lodging

N

OCEAN

MIAMI BEACH

Collins Ave.

Broad Causeway

JFK Causeway

Julia Tuttle Causeway

NORTH MIAMI BEACH

NORTH MIAMI

Miami Gdns. Dr.

Beach Blvd.

N. Miami

Biscayne Blvd.

N.E. 6th Ave.

N.E. 135th St.

N.E. 103rd St.

N.E. 95th St.

N.E. 2nd Ave.

N. Miami Ave.

Biscayne Blvd.

Florida's Turnpike

Palmetto Expwy

7th Ave.

Gratigny Rd.

N.W. 135th St.

N.W. 27th Ave.

N.W. 103rd St.

N.W. 95th St.

N.W. 79th St.

N.W. 62nd St.

N.W. 54th St.

Robert Frost Expwy

N.W. 36th St.

Hialeah Dr.

E. 25th St.

8th Ave.

E. 49th St.

Miami Gdns. Dr.

Red Rd.

W. 4th Ave.

W. 49th St.

Palmetto Expwy

Okeechobee Rd.

N.W. 72nd Ave.

N.W. 39th St.

airy Rd.

N.W. 58th St.

87th Ave.

856

826

A1A

195

95

441

800

826

817

932

944

27

27

909

915

75

ATLANTIC

Bill Baggs Cape Florida
State Recreation Area

5 miles

5 km

Virginia
Key

Crandon
Park

KEY
BISCAYNE

Biscayne
Bay

Rickenbacker Causeway

MacArthur Causeway

Bay

MIAMI

N.W. 7th St.

W. Flagler St.

S.W. 8th St.

S.W. 22nd St.

COCONUT
GROVE

Matheson
Hammock
Park

Tamiami Trail

W. Miracle Mile

CORAL
GABLES

S. Dixie Hwy.

Old Cutler Rd.

Red Rd.

S.W. 57th Ave.

Coral Way

Bird Rd.

S.W. 72nd St.

Dolphin Expwy.

W. Flagler St.

S.W. 8th St.

S.W. 24th St.

S.W. 40th St.

S.W. 87th Ave.

Sunset Dr.

N. Kendall Dr.

Bay Harbor Inn, **3**
Brigham Gardens, **9**
Budgetel Inn, **5**
Cadet Hotel, **12**
Clay Hotel, **10**
David William
Hotel, **20**

Days Inn North
Beach, **2**
Dorchester Hotel, **6**
Hotel Place St.
Michel, **19**
Kenmore Hotel, **16**
Mango's, **13**

Mermaid Guest
House, **14**
Miami Beach
International
Traveller's Hostel, **15**
Miami River Inn, **18**
Paraclete Motel, **4**
Park Washington
Hotel, **17**

Sagamore Hotel, **8**
Shelborne Beach
Hotel, **7**
Suez Oceanfront
Resort, **1**
Villa Paradiso, **11**

8770 outside FL, fax 305/445–5585. 70 rooms, 54 suites. Facilities: restaurant, bar, rooftop freshwater pool. AE, DC, MC, V.

Splurge
★

Hotel Place St. Michel. Art-nouveau chandeliers suspended from vaulted ceilings grace the public areas of this intimate jewel in the heart of downtown. The historic low-rise hotel, built in 1926 and restored from 1981 to 1986, is filled with the scent of fresh flowers, circulated by the paddle fans hanging from the ceilings. Each room has its own dimensions, personality, and imported antiques from England, Scotland, and France. A complimentary Continental breakfast is served. Many consider the ambience worth the $125-a-night (in season) price tag. *162 Alcazar Ave., 33134, tel. 305/444–1666 or 800/247–8526, fax 305/529–0074. 24 rooms, 3 suites. Facilities: restaurant, lounge, snack shop. AE, DC, MC, V.*

Downtown Miami
$$

Miami River Inn. Preservationist Sallye Jude has restored these five 1904 clapboard buildings, the oldest continuously operating inn south of St. Augustine and the only concentration of houses in Miami remaining from that period. The inn is an oasis of country hospitality in a working-class neighborhood—one of Miami's safest even if it doesn't look that way—at the edge of downtown. The heart of the city is only a 10-minute walk across the 1st Street Bridge, and José Martí Park, one of the city's prettiest but lately a haven for the homeless, is only a few hundred feet from the inn gates. There are 40 antiques-filled rooms (some with tub only), a room with breakfast area, small meeting space, outdoor pool and patio, and an oval lawn. Guests receive a complimentary Continental breakfast and have use of a refrigerator. The best rooms look over and down the river from the second and third stories. Avoid the tiny rooms in Building D with a view of the stark condo to the west. As part of the same property—officially designated the Riverside Historic District—four modified-deco mid-century masonry buildings house long-term renters. *118 S.W. South River Dr., 33130, tel. 305/325–0045 or 800/468–3589, fax 305/325–9227. 40 rooms (2 with shared bath). Facilities: outdoor pool, Jacuzzi. AE, D, DC, MC, V.*

Miami
¢

Paraclete Motel. Still the best budget buy in Miami, this small two-story property on Biscayne Boulevard is a cut above the others nearby. It hosts honest-to-goodness budget travelers rather than the distressed lodgers who otherwise tend to frequent the neighborhood. The motel is on the fringes of a red-light district, but just across Biscayne Boulevard to the east is one of Miami's best old neighborhoods. Showing no signs of shabbiness, the Paraclete is quite clean, from the modest lobby through the plain corridors to the plainly furnished rooms. The carpets may look a bit worn and untidy, but at least there *are* carpets. There are in-room phones, too, though a 50¢ surcharge is added for every call you make. *7350 Biscayne Blvd., 33138, tel. 305/751–1622, fax 305/759–1701. 20 rooms. Facilities: outdoor freshwater pool, guest laundry, off-street parking. MC, V.*

Miami Airport Area
$

Budgetel Inn. Close to the airport, this four-story chain motel is the best value in the vicinity. Double-glazed windows minimize the roar of the air traffic overhead. All rooms have microwave ovens and small fridges, but breakfast is included in the room rate. Though the general minimum is $64 in season, a few rooms are always available at $59. If you want one, be sure to ask, but you may have to book well in advance. *3501 LeJeune Rd., 33142, tel. 305/871–1777 or 800/428–3438, fax 305/871–8080. 152 rooms, 25 suites. Facilities: outdoor pool, guest laundry. AE, D, DC, MC, V.*

Miami Beach Deco District
$$

Brigham Gardens. Thanks to a mother (architect) and daughter (horticulturist) team, this place is exactly right for South Beach. While maintaining the two buildings' deco and Mediterranean looks, they converted what were apartments to comfortable but unpretentious units and added attractive tropical gardens. You feel as if you were staying for months with your own furniture, a mix of old and modern. Floors are variously Cuban tile, mosaic tile, wood, or carpet. Art ranges from Haitian to store-bought. Some units have interior arches, arresting alcoves, and French doors; 10 have two entrances; and the eight in the rear building have private porches. Twelve units have full kitchens, while the others have either fridge and microwave or fridge, microwave, and hot plate. *1411 Collins Ave., 33139, tel. 305/531–1331. 15 units. Facilities: garden, barbecue, coin laundry. AE, MC, V.*

$$ **Kenmore Hotel.** Just north of the Park Washington, this three-story, mid-'30s hotel has just as good a location but is a notch better in value. Nice features include an elevator, pool, large terrazzo lobby, in-room refrigerators, quiet air conditioners, and a free Continental breakfast. There's a touch of styling to the rooms courtesy of pastel quilted bedcovers and original Deco furniture, but there's no art on the walls. *1050 Washington Ave., 33139, tel. 305/674–1930, fax 305/ 534–6591. 60 units. Facilities: pool. AE, D, DC, MC, V.*

$$ **Mango's.** The advantage of this small two-story property, formerly a new-age geriatric home, is that it's in the heart of Ocean Drive action. You can stay out until all the bands quit and then crash for what's left of a night's sleep. Return any earlier and you'll want the air-conditioning on as loud as it gets to drown out the small adjoining nightspot of the same name. A waterfall in the palm garden to the rear helps, too, so light sleepers should ask for a back room. Though units have kitchens, no cooking is allowed, but fridges can be used. Furnishings are basic—a bed, a table, and two chairs, though some rooms may have a sofa or easy chair. *900 Ocean Dr., 33139, tel. 305/ 672–7223, fax 305/674–0311. 14 rooms. Facilities: restaurant/bar. AE, D, DC, MC, V.*

$$ **Mermaid Guest House.** Shazam! Lightning in the form of a long-haired former investment banker transformed a Collins Avenue fleabag into this delightful guest house that goes by the name Mermaid. Part Caribbean hideaway, part bohemian youth hostel, the place oozes the same kind of exuberance that early on sparked the birth of the Deco District. Everything is framed in color: a back-of-the-house patio set in a jungle waiting to burst loose and retake Miami Beach; dresser drawers, each painted a different, vivid color; and louvered shutters outlined in bold graphics that bring the outdoor garden in. Beds are shrouded in mosquito netting, though rooms have air-conditioning (but not phones or TV), and small deco baths have tub-showers. There's a shared kitchen outside and a pay phone in the garden. A Continental breakfast is included, and frequent BYOB guest cookouts add to the family-style climate. A youthful and young-at-heart clientele adores this place. *909 Collins Ave., 33139, tel. 305/538–5324. 10 units. Facilities: kitchen, garden. MC, V.*

$$ **Park Washington Hotel.** The location, on lower Washington Avenue, is convenient: two short blocks from the beach, directly across from the Wolfsonian Foundation, and right in the midst of a slew of affordable restaurants. The staff is of the no-attitude school, and guest rooms are small and clean, with original pine Deco furniture and in-room refrigerators, but otherwise basic. Don't expect art on the walls. The quietest rooms are on the north side. Rates have gone up slightly of late, but a pool has been added and a complimentary Continental breakfast is provided. In the same complex and run by the same owners, the Bel-Aire has weekly rates that can work out to an even better value (about $490 for efficiencies in season). *1020 Washington Ave., 33139, tel. 305/532–1930, fax 305/672–6706. 30 rooms. Facilities: pool. AE, MC, V.*

$$ **Villa Paradiso.** This guest house a block from the beach dates from 1935, so it has high ceilings and good detailing—wood floors, bathroom tiles, and fluted fireplace hearths. Recently converted from apartment use, it was done more for cash flow than for taste, however, so the informal spaces have unimaginative treatments, such as

the slapdash baffling in front of fireplaces no longer in use. Still, that's what makes this place affordable. The under-furnished rooms are ideal for a couple bringing bikes, musical instruments, or anything else that needs space, and old but comfortable furniture is easily moved around. Each unit has a full kitchen. Suites feature French doors and separate dining and kitchen areas. The gardens are attractive. *1415 Collins Ave., 33139, tel. 305/532–0616, fax 305/ 667–0074. 17 units. Facilities: garden, coin laundry. AE, MC, V.*

¢ **Clay Hotel.** The official AYH International Youth Hostel is set in a series of seven Mediterranean Revival–style buildings listed on the National Register of Historic Places. Completely renovated in the mid-'80s, the hostel has been repainted and recarpeted every two years since. It's one of the top choices with international hostelers in the United States, and there's a long waiting list for high season (December 15–April 15), so make reservations as early as possible. There are 200 beds in spartan dorms (four-bunk rooms), separate for men and women, and shared bathrooms in the halls. Another 50 rooms with bath and in-room TV rent for hotel guests. Maxwell's Café, on the ground floor, serves affordable meals, and the guest lounge has a TV and kitchen for guests' use. *1438 Washington Ave., 33139, tel. 305/534–2988 or 800/479–2529, fax 305/673–0346. 200 beds in dormitories, 50 rooms with bath. Facilities: café, lounge, coin laundry. MC, V.*

¢ **Miami Beach International Travellers Hostel.** Like the Clay Hotel, this hostel has rock-bottom rates, rooms with bunk beds for four, and some private rooms ($31 double in season, $28 off-season). However, since it's not affiliated with American Youth Hostels, it's more informal and more youth oriented. Still, the Clay remains the mecca for budget travelers, and guests have only to walk the five blocks up Washington Avenue to check out the popular bulletin board there, which has notices about excursions, drive-away cars, and the like. The hostel is open 24 hours and has a 24-hour staff. *236 9th St., 33139, tel. 305/534–0268, fax 305/534–5862. 60 hostel rooms, 12 private rooms. Facilities: kitchen and dining area, coin laundry. MC, V (for reservations only).*

Miami Beach Lincoln Road District
$$
★

Dorchester Hotel. It's wonderful that such good-value, untrendy places remain in the Deco District. Here you'll find an older Miami Beach, from the pre-Disney era when all you had to do was offer good lodgings and service, even if not directly on the beach, and the family trade was yours. This hotel maintains those standards at distinctly affordable rates any time of year. Moreover, it's set back from the avenue for peace and quiet. Also appealing are a big pool in a tropical garden, a large lobby, and a dining room for inexpensive breakfasts. Guest rooms are spacious, carpeted, outfitted with a fridge, and furnished with rattan and floral bedcovers—all the usuals of traditional hotel rooms, here done in pink and green. The best buys are rooms with a kitchenette, only $5 more per night. *1850 Collins Ave., 33139, tel. 305/534–6971, 305/531–5745, or 800/327– 4739, fax 305/673–1006. 94 rooms, 6 suites. Facilities: breakfast room, pool, billiards, table tennis, free off-street parking, barbecues. AE, DC, MC, V.*

$ Cadet Hotel. A minute's walk from the Theater of the Performing Arts and the Miami Beach Convention Center, and less than five minutes from the beach, this little two-story hotel costs barely more than half of what you'd pay on Ocean Drive for the same size room— and you don't have to worry about the chic scene keeping you awake at night. The other big difference is that the desk staff doesn't act like they're doing you a favor by letting you stay here. The Cadet has an old St. Petersburg–like feel—bright and unglitzy, with soft pastels and potted palms in the terrazzo lobby. A complimentary cooked breakfast is served in the lobby or on the terrace. Rooms are carpeted and are decorated in blues and creams, with a mix of ordinary furniture—not necessarily matching sets, but not crummy stuff either. Bathrooms are tiled and have tubs. *1701 James Ave., 33139, tel. 305/672–6688, fax 305/532–1676. 44 rooms. AE, D, DC, MC, V.*

$ **Sagamore Hotel.** At this five-story oceanfront hotel, they like to say
★ they're in the Deco District, hoping to seem trendy. But the truth is that the Sagamore is *better* than anything along Ocean Drive. Built in the 1940s, it was meant to outdo the hotels to the south, which by then were considered small and passé. Though the current decor is nondescript, rooms at the Sagamore are large and comfortably furnished; they have a big closet and at least a large fridge (many have kitchens). The lobby is huge, too, with plush leatherette sofas. On the premises you'll find a convenience store, a coffee shop, and a popular poolside tiki bar that serves $7.50 pitchers of draft beer (it's open to the public, so the crowd is a good mix). A complimentary welcome cocktail is included. Best of all, the rates start at two-thirds of what you pay for smaller rooms in the Ocean Drive hotels; if you're in a group of four, you can book a suite with a kitchen for $75 in season—one of the top buys on the Beach. *1671 Collins Ave., 33139, tel. 305/538–7211 or 800/648–6068, fax 305/674–0371. 130 rooms. Facilities: restaurant, coffee shop, tiki bar, freshwater and heated saltwater pools, oceanfront, shuffleboard, game room. AE, D, DC, MC, V.*

Miami Beach **Shelborne Beach Hotel.** This long-popular oceanfront property has
Mid-Collins been renovated and is now a condominium, but there are still many
Avenue rooms for rent. The big lobby—like a troop transport terminal—has
District plush upholstered furniture. Throughout the 16 floors of guest
$$ rooms, pastels predominate, in fresh curtains, bedspreads, and mauve carpets. The largest rooms are the corners (those with ocean views are the most expensive); units on the city side are affordable. For recreation, try the large pool or the waterfront, where catamarans are for rent. The Shelborne isn't as affordable as the Sagamore (*see above*), but it has a sharper image. *1801 Collins Ave., 33139, tel. 305/531–1271 or 800/327–8757, fax 305/531–2206. 280 rooms. Facilities: 2 restaurants, pool bar, showroom with projection TV, outdoor pool, water-sports rentals, billiards, parking. AE, DC, MC, V.*

Miami Beach **Days Inn North Beach.** Despite talk that it's the next Deco District,
North Beach North Beach still feels like an intact old neighborhood to which one-
District time vacationers have retired and where everybody knows every-
$ body. Dating from 1941, this seven-story hotel with modified deco styling used to be the Broadmoor. It was—and still is—the pick of the neighborhood. It's across the long shore road from a beautiful section of beach backed by grassy dunes. The beach isn't crowded because the neighborhood isn't trendy yet, nor is the hotel. Rooms are dark, undistinguished Days Inn style with basic furnishings and fridges, but the lobby is spacious. Restaurant and bar service are provided on the lovely terrace. This is a good choice if you plan to use your room mostly for sleeping. Even in season, some rooms are available for just under $60. *7450 Ocean Terr., 33141, tel. 305/866–1631 or 800/325–2525, fax 305/868–4617. 95 rooms, 5 suites. Facilities: restaurant, bar, dining terrace. AE, D, DC, MC, V.*

Sunny Isles **Suez Oceanfront Resort.** They call this Miami Beach, and though it is
$$ on the beach, it's several miles north of the municipality of Miami
★ Beach, in the section called Sunny Isles—more popularly referred to as Motel Row. This is affordable Miami Beach, chockablock with fancified motels but few of distinction. The carousel-stripe Suez, however, stands out; generous with public space, it has been run by the detail-minded Lucas family since 1963. Father and son walk the grounds all the time to stay in touch with guests, and staff members speak seven languages. Get past the tacky sphinx icons, walk upstairs in the main building, and you're in a quiet, gardenlike rattan-and-palm lounge. A landscaped palm courtyard leads to the beach, where you find a popular bar and beachside restaurant, two pools, a

tennis court, and playground. Rooms are done with matched chinois furniture and dazzling color that counteracts the generally small spaces. The least expensive rooms, in the north wing, are the smallest and have views of the parking lot. Modified American Plan dining, fridges in all the rooms and kitchens in some, and special kids' rates make this an especially good value. Free laundry service is a bonus. *18215 Collins Ave., 33160, tel. 305/932–0661, 800/327–5278, or 800/432–3661 in FL, fax 305/937–0058. 196 rooms. Facilities: restaurant, bar, freshwater and saltwater pools, children's pool, beach, lighted tennis court, shuffleboard and volleyball courts, playground, laundry service. AE, D, DC, MC, V.*

Exploring Miami

Disney captured Miami's family trade, *Miami Vice* smacked the city upside the head with notoriety, South Beach made it a global resort for the turn of the 21st century, and through all this, the city went from an enclave of retired northeasterners to the ultimate joyride with a Latin beat. Hardly any part of the city isn't caught up in change. Where once people came to lie on the beach, even that's dangerous nowadays, though people do it anyway. (Good sunblock helps.) Meanwhile sightseeing—which used to be pretty much limited to picking fruit off citrus trees and watching alligator wrestling—has become a fun way to glimpse the city at work and at play.

Downtown has become the live hub of the mainland city, now more accessible thanks to the Metromover extension. Other major attractions include Coconut Grove, Little Havana, and South Beach/the Art Deco District, but since these districts are spread out beyond the reach of public transportation, you'll have to drive.

Finding your way around Greater Miami is easy if you know how the numbering system works. Miami is laid out on a grid with four quadrants—northeast, northwest, southeast, and southwest—which meet at Miami Avenue and Flagler Street. Miami Avenue separates east from west, and Flagler Street separates north from south. Avenues and courts run north–south; streets, terraces, and ways run east–west. Roads run diagonally, northwest–southeast.

Many named streets also bear numbers. For example, Unity Boulevard is Northwest and Southwest 27th Avenue, and LeJeune Road is Northwest and Southwest 42nd Avenue. However, named streets that depart markedly from the grid, such as Biscayne Boulevard and Brickell Avenue, have no corresponding numerical designations. Dade County and most other municipalities follow the Miami numbering system.

In Miami Beach, avenues run north–south; streets, east–west. Numbers rise along the beach from south to north and from the Atlantic Ocean in the east to Biscayne Bay in the west.

In Coral Gables, all streets bear names. Coral Gables uses the Miami numbering system for north–south addresses but begins counting east–west addresses westward from Douglas Road (Southwest 37th Avenue).

Hialeah has its own grid. Palm Avenue separates east from west; Hialeah Drive separates north from south. Avenues run north–south and streets east–west. Numbered streets and avenues are designated west, east, southeast, southwest, northeast, or northwest.

Miami for Free—or Almost

Without question the best Miami area attraction after the beaches and sea is people-watching, and the best neighborhoods for that are South Beach and downtown Coconut Grove. Plunk yourself down on one of the public benches along Ocean Drive, or spring for a coffee or sangria in order to sit at one of the many sidewalk cafés in South Beach (in the Grove, cafés *have* to let anyone sit down, whether they buy something or not).

Miami is also one of the great American street festival cities, and something wonderful is happening any time of the year. Contact the **Cultural Affairs Council** (111 N.W. 1st St., Miami, tel. 305/375–4634) and ask for a copy of the free *Calendar of Events*, published in January and July, which lists literally hundreds of events.

If it's a rainy day or you've had too much sun, consider one of Miami's great almost-for-free activities, a ride on the **Metrorail** or **Metromover.** Unlike most cities' commuter rail systems, Miami's is all above ground, which makes it a natural for sightseeing, despite the many gripes that daily riders have about the system. Of course, the ride will probably be far more enjoyable if you're not on at rush hour and not trying to beat the clock. For $1.25 you can ride the 21-mile Metrorail system from Hialeah in the north to Dadeland (*see* Malls *in* Shopping for Bargains, *below*), the city's largest shopping mall, in the south. The ride from one end of the system to the other takes about 50 minutes, and you can transfer to the Metromover for free. (If you transfer from Metromover onto Metrorail, you'll be asked to pay $1, since the initial Metromover fare is only 25¢.) For details on the Metromover route, *see* Tour 2, *below.*

Art There is no charge for admission to the **South Florida Art Center** (*see* Tour 1, *below*) or the **Centre Gallery** and the **Frances Wolfson Art Gallery** (*see* Tour 2, *below*, for both). Admission to the following is also free:

The **African Heritage Cultural Arts Center** presents a mixed program of visual arts, dance, and theater. *6161 N.W. 22nd Ave., Miami, tel. 305/638–6771. Open daily 9–6.*

The **Bakehouse Art Complex,** a two-story masonry building built as the Flowers Bakery in the 1920s, was revived in 1987 as a gallery and studios for area artists. An open house with visits to studios takes place on the second Sunday of every month, from 1 to 5. Call for an appointment at other times. *561 N.W. 32nd St., Miami, tel. 305/576–2828. Office open Tues.–Fri. 10–4.*

Gables Gallery Night takes place the first Friday of every month (except July, when it may be the second Friday), between 7 and 10 PM. Four trolleys continuously shuttle visitors around 16 or 17 galleries, bookstores, antiques shops, and furniture stores, all located in Coral Gables. Most places serve free wine, and some serve snacks. A good place to start is outside Artspace/Virginia Miller Galleries (169 Madeira Ave., Coral Gables, tel. 305/444–4493).

As part of **Gallery Walk,** as many as 20 Lincoln Road Mall galleries stay open from 6 to 10 on the second Saturday of every month except August. Other mall merchants host their own special art exhibits. These are some of the most festive nights of the year on the mall and are not to be missed. For more information, contact the Lincoln Road Partnership (1045 Lincoln Rd., Miami Beach 33139, tel. 305/531–3442, fax 305/531–7331).

The **Joan Lehman Museum of Contemporary Art** will become a major Florida contemporary art museum when it opens its 23,000-square-foot addition in early 1996. Gallery space will grow from 1,500 to 10,000 square feet, and a permanent collection will be launched. An additional multipurpose space will become the venue for productions ranging from video to performance art. Rotating exhibits feature contemporary paintings, photographs, and other work by artists from around the world. Avant-garde films are also screened. *12340 N.E. 8th Ave., North Miami, tel. 305/893–6211. Open Mon.–Sat. 11–4, Sun. 1–4.*

You can pay whatever amount you wish for admission to the **Cuban Museum of Arts and Culture** (*see* Tour 3, *below*) and to other museums on particular days: Tuesday at the **Bass Museum of Art** (*see* Tour 1, *below*) and the **Center for the Fine Arts** (*see* Tour 2, *below*) and Monday at the **Historical Museum of Southern Florida** (*see* Tour 2, *below*).

Beaches The best free beaches are along Miami Beach and the neighboring communities of Surfside and Sunny Isles (*see* Beaches, *below*).

Concerts **Bayside Marketplace** (*see* Tour 2, *below*) has free concerts every day.

Brunch on the Beach presents live jazz performances at various Lincoln Road locations on alternating Sundays February–March from 11 to 2.

New World Symphony (*see* the Arts and Nightlife, *below*) typically introduces its fall season with a series of free concerts at its Lincoln Road theater; a monthly Musicians' Forum is performed by symphony members.

Performing Arts for Community and Education (PACE) (tel. 305/948–7223) supports free concerts in parks and cultural and religious institutions throughout Greater Miami.

University of Miami School of Music/Gusman Concert Hall (1314 Miller Dr., Coral Gables, tel. 305/284–6477) offers many free concerts on campus.

Farmers Markets Among the best free events in winter are the colorful and eclectic weekly **Farmers Market at Merrick Park,** on Saturdays outside Coral Gables City Hall, and the **Lincoln Road Farmers Market,** on Sundays (*see* Outdoor Markets *in* Shopping for Bargains, *below*, for both).

Tour 1: Miami Beach

Numbers in the margin correspond to points of interest on the Tour 1: Miami Beach map.

Most visitors to the Greater Miami area don't realize that Miami and Miami Beach are separate cities. Miami, on the mainland, is southern Florida's commercial hub. Miami Beach, on 17 islands in Biscayne Bay, is sometimes considered America's Riviera, luring refugees from winter to its warm sunshine, sandy beaches, and graceful palms.

In 1912 what would become Miami Beach was little more than a sand spit in the bay. Then Carl Graham Fisher, a millionaire promoter who built the Indianapolis Speedway, began to pour much of his fortune into developing the island city.

Ever since, Miami Beach has experienced successive waves of boom and bust—thriving in the early 1920s and the years just after World War II, but enduring the devastating 1926 and 1992 hurricanes, the Great Depression, and travel restrictions during World War II. During the 1960s, jets full of onetime Miami Beach winter vacationers began winging to the more reliably warm Caribbean, and the flow of summer family vacationers was dammed mid-state in 1971 by Walt Disney World.

Today Miami Beach—chiefly known for the South Beach area—revels in renewed world glory as a lure for models and millionaires, an affordable multilingual resort where anything goes, from fancy dress to gender-free dress to undress. The comeback of the Beach was marked in 1993 by a record $232 million in building permits, almost double the previous high of $135 only five years before. The hub of South Beach is the mile-square Art Deco District. About 650 significant buildings in the district are listed on the National Register of Historic Places. That is not to say that the City of Miami Beach yet respects the resource. The section immediately below the official Art Deco District, which also includes several outstanding properties, is slated for massive overbuilding in the near future after years of neglect. Bulky skyscrapers seem destined for lower Ocean Drive.

From the mainland, cross the **MacArthur Causeway** (U.S. 41), which spans Biscayne Bay, to reach Miami Beach. (To reach the causeway from downtown Miami, turn east off Biscayne Boulevard north of Northeast 11th Street. From I–95, turn east onto I–395. The eastbound Dolphin Expressway, Route 836, becomes I–395 east of the I–95 interchange.) As you approach the MacArthur Causeway bridge across the Intracoastal Waterway, you'll see the *Miami Herald* building, which occupies the Biscayne Bayfront on your left.

① Cross the bridge to **Watson Island,** created by dredging in 1931. To your right is the seaplane base of **Chalk's International Airlines,** the oldest scheduled international air carrier, founded in 1919. Today it operates seaplanes to Key West, Bimini, and Nassau.

②③ East of Watson Island the causeway leaves Miami and enters Miami **④** Beach. On the left you'll pass the bridge to **Palm** and **Hibiscus islands** and then the bridge to **Star Island.** Celebrities who have lived on these islands include Al Capone (93 Palm Ave., Palm Island), author Damon Runyon (271 Hibiscus Island), and actor Don Johnson (8 Star Island).

⑤ East of Star Island the causeway mounts a high bridge. Look left to see an island with an obelisk, the **Flagler Memorial Monument.** The memorial honors Henry M. Flagler, who built the Florida East Coast Railroad, which opened all of east coast Florida to tourism and commerce, reaching Miami in 1896 and Key West in 1912. Flagler's hotels set a new standard for opulent vacationing and ushered in a long train of imperial developers, the list crowned in our own time by Walt Disney.

Just beyond the bridge, turn right onto Alton Road past the **Miami Beach Marina** (300 Alton Rd., tel. 305/673–6000), where dive boats depart for artificial reefs offshore in the Atlantic Ocean. Continue to the foot of Alton Road, turn left on Biscayne Street, and then right **⑥** at Washington Avenue to enter **South Pointe Park** (1 Washington Ave.). From the 50-yard Sunshine Pier, which adjoins the mile-long jetty at the mouth of Government Cut, you can fish while watching huge ships pass. No bait or tackle is available in the park. Other facilities include two observation towers and volleyball courts.

Exit the park onto Biscayne Street, turn right, go to the end, and turn left onto Ocean Drive. Right away you'll start to see a line of pastel-hue Art Deco hotels on your left, and then at 5th Street, palm-fringed **Lummus Park** and the beach on your right. This is the **★ Art Deco District,** a 10-block stretch along Ocean Drive that has become the most talked-about beachfront in America. Less than 10 years ago, the vintage hotels were badly run down, catering to infirm retired people. But a group of visionaries saw this collection of buildings as an architectural treasure, a peerless grouping of Art Deco modern architecture from the 1920s and 1930s.

In the early 1980s, investors started fixing up the interiors of these hotels and repainting their exteriors with vibrant colors. International bistro operators then moved in, sensing the potential for a new café society. The media took note, and celebrities came, among them singer Gloria Estefan, designer Gianni Versace, and record executive Chris Blackwell, who bought pieces of the action.

Now the place hums 24 hours a day, as fashion photographers pose beautiful models for shoots that make backdrops of the throngs of visitors. Pop singer and actress Madonna photographed scenes in her controversial 1992 book, *Sex,* up and down the beach.

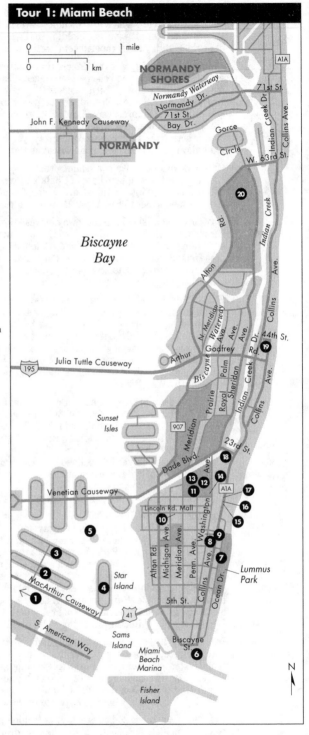

Tour 1: Miami Beach

As you progress up Ocean Drive, notice that the forms and decorative detail of buildings are drawn from nature (including birds, butterflies, and flowers); from ancient Aztec, Mayan, Babylonian, Chaldean, Egyptian, and Hebrew designs; and from the streamlined, aerodynamic shapes of modern transportation and industrial machinery. To get oriented, start at the **Art Deco District Welcome Center.** It is located on the beach side in the Oceanfront Auditorium (a 1950s building, not Deco). *1001 Ocean Dr., tel. 305/531–3484. Admission free. Open daily 11–6 (to later Thurs.–Mon. in season).*

You may want to get out of your car to stroll around the district, but from mid-morning on, parking is scarce along Ocean Drive. You'll do better on Collins and Washington avenues, the next two streets paralleling Ocean Drive to the west. Be warned: Tickets are handed out freely when meters expire, and towing charges are high. Additional parking garages are likely to materialize in 1996.

Turn left on 15th Street and left again at the next corner to cruise down **Collins Avenue.** Follow Collins south to 5th Street, and turn right. Turn right again at the next corner to go back north on **Washington Avenue,** a mix of chic restaurants, avant-garde shops, delicatessens, and produce markets.

Continue north on Washington Avenue to the new **Wolfsonian Foundation Gallery,** displaying the 50,000-item collection of modern design and so-called propaganda arts amassed by Miami native Mitchell Wolfson, Jr., a world traveler and connoisseur. The gallery and its adjoining study center open fully in 1995. *1001 Washington Ave., tel. 305/531–1001. Admission: $1 adults, 50¢ senior citizens and children. Open weekdays 1–5.*

Walk past 14th Street to **Espanola Way,** a narrow street of Mediterranean-revival buildings constructed in 1925 and frequented through the years by artists and writers. In the 1930s, Cuban bandleader Desi Arnaz performed in the Village Tavern, now part of the Clay Hotel (*see* Budget Lodging, *above*). For one block of Espanola Way, west of Washington Avenue to Drexel Avenue, the way for cars has been narrowed to a single lane, and Miami Beach's trademark pink sidewalks have been widened to accommodate new sidewalk cafés. As recently as 1990, this street was troubled by derelicts; now it has miraculously popped up clean, safe, and redeemed, chockablock with imaginative clothing, jewelry, and art shops.

Continue two blocks beyond Drexel to Meridian Avenue, and turn right. Three blocks north of Espanola Way is **Lincoln Road Mall.** Here you can expect throngs of new visitors who up until 1990 wouldn't have been caught dead on the mall, which had turned into a sideshow of freaks and panhandlers. During its heyday in the 1950s, Lincoln Road was known as the 5th Avenue of the South, but, like all of the Beach, by the '60s it had been bypassed. It was closed to traffic and turned into a pedestrian mall between Washington Avenue and Alton Road, but that couldn't halt the decline. When rents bottomed out, however, artists and arts groups moved in and rehabilitated their buildings. Cafés and restaurants followed, and then retailers. Today the mall is thriving, and even the Miami Beach City Commission, notoriously slow to recognize revival, is at least proving helpful here. A new, playful redesign, due for completion in 1996, includes a grove of 20 towering date palms with misters likely to spritz passersby, five linear pools divided by strips of jungle, and a simulated aquarium behind a curtainlike waterfall. The mall has become twinned with Ocean Drive as part of "must-see" South Beach, especially on Saturday nights, when art galleries schedule openings together. Don't miss it.

Park in the municipal lot half a block north of the mall, between Washington and Meridian avenues; then either walk along the mall or catch one of the trams that shuttle shoppers. At 541–545 Lincoln

Road you'll see a classical four-story Deco gem with its friezes repainted in wavy greens—this is where the **New World Symphony** (*see* the Arts and Nightlife, *below*) rehearses and performs. As you walk west, toward Biscayne Bay, the street is lined with chic food markets like **Lyon Freres** (600 Lincoln Rd., tel. 305/534–0600), with exotic businesses like the **Mideastern Dance Exchange** (622 Lincoln Rd., tel. 305/538–1608), with artistic cafés like the **Beehive Diner** (630–A Lincoln Rd., tel. 305/538–7484), and with brilliant boutiques like **Diamonds & Chicken Soup** (828 Lincoln Rd., tel. 305/532–7687). Go farther west, and you'll find the **South Florida Art Center** (924 Lincoln Rd., tel. 305/674–8278), one of the first arts groups to help resurrect the area. The building houses visual artists' studios and showrooms; they are open to the public, with no admission charge, weekdays 9–5. Farther on, a black-and-white Deco movie house with a Mediterranean barrel-tile roof has become the **Colony Theater** (*see* the Arts and Nightlife, *below*).

The first main street north of Lincoln Road Mall is 17th Street, named **Hank Meyer Boulevard** for the publicist who persuaded the late comedian Jackie Gleason to broadcast his TV show from Miami Beach in the 1950s. East on 17th Street, beside the entrance to **⑪ Miami Beach City Hall** (1700 Convention Center Dr., tel. 305/673–7030), stands *Red Sea Road*, a huge red sculpture by Barbara Neijna. Also to your left east across Convention Center Drive is the **⑫ Miami Beach Convention Center** (1901 Convention Center Dr., tel. 305/673–7311), a stucco 1960s-vintage building that gained its peach-tone, art deco look in a 1990 renovation and expansion. It's the Miami area's largest convention space, with 1.1 million square feet.

Behind the Convention Center, north along Convention Center Drive at the northwest end of the parking lot near Meridian Avenue, **⑬** is the **Holocaust Memorial** (1933–1945 Meridian Ave., tel. 305/538–1663 or 305/538–1673), a monumental sculpture and a graphic record in memory of the 6 million Jewish victims of the Holocaust. Admission is free, but a small donation is requested for literature on the memorial. A garden conservatory (2000 Convention Center Dr., tel. 305/673–7256) next door is worth a visit but has limited public hours.

Just south of the convention center, at 17th Street and Washington Avenue, you'll see another large sculpture, *Mermaid*, by Roy **⑭** Lichtenstein, in front of the **Jackie Gleason Theater of the Performing Arts** (1700 Washington Ave., tel. 305/673–7300), where Gleason's TV show originated. Now the 3,000-seat theater (*see* the Arts and Nightlife, *below*) hosts touring Broadway shows and classical-music concerts. Near the sculpture, performers who have appeared in the theater since 1984 have left their footprints and signatures in concrete. This **Walk of the Stars** includes the late George Abbott, Julie Andrews, Leslie Caron, Carol Channing, and Edward Villella.

Go one block east to Collins Avenue and turn right (south) toward three of the largest Art Deco hotels, all built in the 1940s. Their streamlined tower forms reflect the 20th century's transportation **⑮** revolution. The round dome atop the 11-story **Hotel National** (1677 Collins Ave., tel. 305/532–2311) resembles a balloon. The tower at **⑯** the 12-story **Delano Hotel** (1685 Collins Ave., tel. 305/538–7881) has fins suggesting the wings of an airplane or a Buck Rogers spaceship. (The hotel was acquired in 1994 by New York hotelier Ian Schrager, who has invested more than $20 million into the property and plans to turn it into a five-star urban resort in time for the 1995–96 winter **⑰** season.) The 11-story **Ritz Plaza** (1701 Collins Ave., tel. 305/534–3500) rises to a cylindrical tower resembling a periscope.

Go north on Collins Avenue. At 21st Street turn left beside the Miami Beach Public Library in Collins Park, go two blocks to Park Ave-

18 nue, and turn right. You're approaching the **Bass Museum of Art,** which houses a diverse collection of European art, including *The Holy Family*, a painting by Peter Paul Rubens; *The Tournament*, one of several 16th-century Flemish tapestries; and works by Albrecht Dürer and Henri de Toulouse-Lautrec. A current expansion project will double the museum's size to 40,000 square feet in time for the 1997–1998 winter season. Park in back and walk around to the entrance, past massive tropical baobab trees. *2121 Park Ave., tel. 305/673–7530. Admission: $5 adults, $4 students with ID and senior citizens, $3 youths 13–17, $2 children 6–12; donations Tues.; some exhibitions may be more expensive. Open Tues.–Sat. 10–5, 2nd and 4th Weds. of month 1–9; Sun. 1–5.*

Return on 21st or 22nd Street to Collins Avenue, and turn left. As you drive north, a triumphal archway looms ahead, framing a majestic white building set in lush vegetation beside a waterfall and tropical lagoon. This vista is an illusion—a 13,000-square-foot outdoor

19 mural on an exterior wall of the **Fontainebleau Hilton Resort and Towers.** Artist Richard Haas designed the mural to illustrate how the hotel and its rock-grotto swimming pool would look behind the wall. Locals call the 1,206-room hotel Big Blue. It's the giant of Miami Beach.

Turn left on 65th Street, left again at the next corner onto Indian Creek Drive, and right at 63rd Street, which leads into **Alton Road,** a winding, landscaped boulevard of gracious homes styled along art

20 deco lines. You'll pass **La Gorce Country Club** (5685 Alton Rd., tel. 305/866–4421), which developer Carl Fisher built and named for his friend Oliver La Gorce, then president of the National Geographic Society.

To return to the mainland on the MacArthur Causeway stay on Alton Road south to 5th Street, then turn right.

Tour 2: Downtown Miami

Numbers in the margin correspond to points of interest on the Tour 2: Downtown Miami map.

From a distance you see downtown Miami's future—a 21st-century skyline already stroking the clouds with sleek fingers of steel and glass. By day this icon of commerce and technology sparkles in the strong subtropical sun; at night it basks in the man-made glow of floodlights.

Here staid, suited lawyers and bankers share the sidewalks with Latino merchants wearing open-neck, intricately embroidered shirts called *guayaberas*. Fruit merchants sell their wares from pushcarts. European youths with backpacks stroll the streets. Foreign businesspeople haggle over prices in import-export shops. You hear Arabic, Chinese, Creole, French, German, Hebrew, Hindi, Japanese, Portuguese, Spanish, Swedish, Yiddish, and even a little English now and then.

The metropolis has become one of the great international cities of the Americas, yet Miami's downtown is sorely neglected. Although office workers crowd the area by day, the city, but for Bayside and the Miami Arena, is deserted at night, and patrons of the Arena rarely stay downtown when the basketball and hockey games or other events are over. Those who live close to downtown stay at its fringes, as on Claughton Island at the mouth of the Miami River, where a half dozen residential towers have risen to house thousands in the last decade. Visitors, too, spend as little time here as possible, since most tourist attractions are in other neighborhoods. Miami's oldest downtown buildings date from the 1920s and 1930s—not very old compared to the historic districts of St. Augustine and Pensacola. What's best in the heart of downtown Miami today is its Latinization and the sheer energy of Latin shoppers. The following walking tour doesn't include many must-see sights, but it can help you get to know this hub city.

Thanks to the Metromover, which has inner and outer loops through downtown plus north and south extensions, this is an excellent tour to take by rail. Attractions are conveniently located within about two blocks of the nearest station, so the tour approximately follows the outer loop. Parking downtown is no more inconvenient or expensive than in any city, but the best idea is to leave your car at an outlying Metrorail station and take the train downtown.

Get off the Metrorail train at **Government Center Station,** where the 21-mile elevated Metrorail commuter system connects with

❶ Metromover. As you leave the station, notice the **Dade County Courthouse** (73 W. Flagler St.). It's the building to the east with a pyramid at its peak, where turkey vultures roost in winter. Built in 1928, it was once the tallest building south of Washington, D.C.

❷ You'll enter **Metro-Dade Center** (111 N.W. 1st St.), the county government's sleek 30-story office building. Designed by architect Hugh Stubbins, it opened in 1985.

★ ❸ Across Northwest 1st Street stands the **Metro-Dade Cultural Center** (101 W. Flagler St.), one of the focal points of Miami's downtown. The city's main art museum, historical museum, and library are gathered here in a 3.3-acre complex. Opened in 1983, it is a Mediterranean expression of architect Philip Johnson's postmodern style. An elevated plaza provides a serene haven from the city's pulsations and an open-air setting for festivals and outdoor performances.

The **Center for the Fine Arts,** an art museum in the tradition of the European *kunsthalle* (exhibition gallery), has no permanent collection (though a push toward forming one has come with the arrival, in 1995, of a new director). Throughout the year CFA organizes and borrows temporary exhibitions on diverse themes. *Tel. 305/375–3000. Admission: $5 adults, $2 children 6–12; donations Tues. Open Tues.–Sat. 10–5, Thurs. 10–9, Sun. noon–5.*

The **Historical Museum of Southern Florida** is a regional museum that interprets the human experience in southern Florida from prehistory to the present. Artifacts on permanent display include Tequesta and Seminole Indian ceramics, clothing, and tools; a 1920 streetcar; and an original edition of Audubon's *Birds of America*. *Tel. 305/375–1492. Admission: $4 adults, $2 children 6–12; donations Mon. Open Mon.–Wed. and Fri.–Sat. 10–5, Thurs. 10–9, Sun. noon–5.*

The **Main Public Library** has nearly 4 million holdings and a computerized card catalog. Inside the entrance, look up at the rotunda mural, in which artist Edward Ruscha interpreted a quotation from Shakespeare: "Words without thought never to heaven go." You'll find art exhibits in the auditorium and second-floor lobby. *Tel. 305/375–2665. Open Mon.–Sat. 9–6, Thurs. 9–9, Sun. 1–5; closed Sun. May–mid-Oct.*

❹ Take the Metromover to the next stop, **Ft. Dallas Park Station,** and walk one block south to reach the **Miami Avenue Bridge,** one of 11 bridges on the Miami River that open to let ships pass. From the bridge approach, watch freighters, tugboats, research vessels, and luxury yachts ply this busy 5-mile waterway.

The next Metromover stop, **Knight Center Station,** nestles inside

❺ **NationsBank Tower** (100 S.E. 1st St.), a wedge-shape 47-story skyscraper designed by I. M. Pei and Partners. The building is brilliant-

❻ ly illuminated at night. Inside the tower follow signs to the **James L. Knight International Center** (400 S.E. 2nd Ave., tel. 305/372–0929),

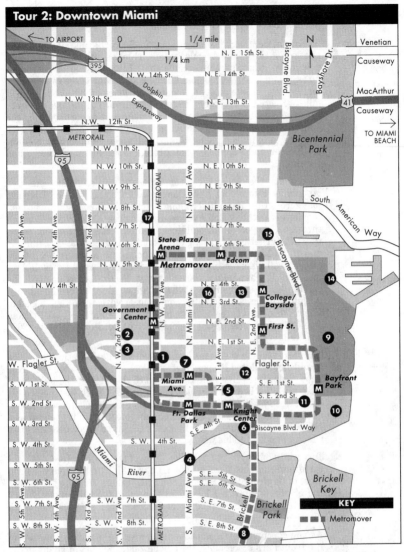

Tour 2: Downtown Miami

Bayside Marketplace, **14**

Brickell Avenue, **8**

Claude and Mildred Pepper Bayfront Park, **7**

Dade County Courthouse, **1**

Flagler Street, **7**

Freedom Tower, **15**

Gusman Center for the Performing Arts, **12**

Hotel Inter-Continental Miami, **10**

James L. Knight International Center, **6**

Metro-Dade Center, **2**

Metro-Dade Cultural Center, **3**

Miami Arena, **17**

Miami Ave. Bridge, **4**

Miami-Dade Community College, **13**

NationsBank Tower, **5**

Southeast Financial Center, **11**

U.S. Courthouse, **16**

a convention and concert hall in a bulbous concrete building appended to the Hyatt Regency Miami.

⑦ At Knight Center Station, you can transfer to the inner loop and ride one stop to the **Miami Avenue Station,** a block south of **Flagler Street,** downtown Miami's commercial spine. Like most such thoroughfares, Flagler Street has lost business in recent years to suburban malls—but, unlike most, it found a new lease on life. Today the ½ mile of Flagler Street from Biscayne Boulevard to the Dade County Courthouse is the most important retail import-export center in the United States. Its stores and arcades supply much of the world with bargain automotive parts, audio and video equipment, medical equipment and supplies, photographic equipment, clothing, and jewelry.

⑧ Also from the Knight Center Station, you can ride the new Metromover spur that links downtown with the Brickell District, just across the Miami River along **Brickell Avenue,** a southward extension of Southeast 2nd Avenue. Heading south on Brickell Avenue through a canyon of tall buildings, you pass the largest concentration of international banking offices in the United States. From the end of the Metromover line, you can look south to where several architecturally interesting condominiums rise between Brickell Avenue and Biscayne Bay. Israeli artist Yacov Agam painted the rainbow-hue exterior of **Villa Regina** (1581 Brickell Ave.). Arquitectonica, a nationally prominent architectural firm based in Miami, designed three of these buildings: the **Palace** (1541 Brickell Ave.), the **Imperial** (1627 Brickell Ave.), and the **Atlantis** (2025 Brickell Ave.).

⑨ The next stop on the outer loop is **Bayfront Park Station,** opposite **Claude and Mildred Pepper Bayfront Park,** which extends east from busy, palm-lined Biscayne Boulevard to the edge of the bay. Japanese sculptor Isamu Noguchi redesigned the park just before his death in 1989; it now includes a memorial to the *Challenger* astronauts, an amphitheater, and a fountain (most often turned off as a budget-tightening measure) honoring the late Florida congressman Claude Pepper and his wife.

⑩ Just south of Bayfront Park, the lobby of the **Hotel Inter-Continental Miami** contains *The Spindle*, a huge sculpture by Henry Moore. **⑪** West of Bayfront Park Station stands the tallest building in Florida, the 55-story **Southeast Financial Center** (200 S. Biscayne Blvd.); towering royal palms stand in the 1-acre Palm Court plaza beneath its steel-and-glass frame.

⑫ As you continue north on the Metromover, take in the fine view of Bayfront Park's greenery, the bay beyond, the Port of Miami in the bay, and Miami Beach across the water. The next Metromover stop, **First Street Station,** places you a block north of Flagler Street and the landmark **Gusman Center for the Performing Arts** (*see* the Arts and Nightlife, *below*), an ornate former movie palace restored as a concert hall. Resembling a Moorish courtyard with twinkling stars in the sky, it hosts performances by the Miami City Ballet and the New World Symphony.

⑬ The **College/Bayside Station** Metromover stop serves the downtown campus of **Miami-Dade Community College.** In Building 1, you can browse through two fine galleries: the **Centre Gallery** on the third floor, with various exhibitions, and the **Frances Wolfson Art Gallery** on the fifth floor, which houses traveling exhibits of contemporary art. *300 N.E. 2nd Ave., tel. 305/237–3278. Admission free. Both galleries open weekdays 10–6.*

★ ⑭ College/Bayside Station is also the most convenient stop for **Bayside Marketplace,** a waterside entertainment-and-shopping center built by the Rouse Company between Bayfront Park and the entrance to the Port of Miami. After completing an $11 million renovation in 1992 and adding the Hard Rock Cafe to its list of attractions, Bayside at last is attracting crowds of locals and visitors, including cruise passengers who come over from the port for a few hours' shopping before their ships head for the Caribbean. Bayside's 235,000 square feet of retail space houses 150 specialty shops, pushcarts in the center's Pier 5 area, outdoor cafés, and an international food court. Street performers entertain throughout the day and evening, and free concerts—typically calypso, jazz, Latin rhythms, reggae, and rock—take place every day of the year. *401 Biscayne Blvd., tel. 305/577–3344. Open Mon.–Thurs. 10–10, Fri.–Sat. 10–11, Sun. 11–8; extended hrs for restaurants and outdoor cafés; concerts (roughly): Mon.–Thurs. 7–11 PM, Fri.–Sat. 2–6 and 9 PM–1 AM, Sun. 1:30–5:30 and 7–11.*

Look just north of Bayside to see the twin-span bridge that leads to the Port of Miami. More than 1.5 million cruise passengers a year go through this port; its 12 terminals are home base for 20 cruise liners. The first series of passenger "pods" were built in 1964 in concrete shapes sculpted in the form of wind scoops. Though the pods are now enclosed and climate-controlled, in midweek when there are few ships docked here you can still see the graceful wavelike pod shapes inside.

As Metromover rounds the curve after College/Bayside Station, ⑮ look northeast to see **Freedom Tower** (600 Biscayne Blvd.), where the Cuban Refugee Center processed more than 500,000 Cubans who entered the United States to flee Fidel Castro's regime in the 1960s. Built in 1925 for the *Miami Daily News*, this imposing Spanish-baroque structure was inspired by the Giralda, an 800-year-old bell tower in Seville, Spain. After years in derelict condition, Freedom Tower was renovated in 1988 and opened for office use in 1990, although, oddly, it has remained untenanted. To see it up close, walk north from **Edcom Station** to Northeast 6th Street, then two blocks east to Biscayne Boulevard. (It's also at this point in the loop that the spur curves north to the Omni District.)

A two-block walk south from Edcom Station will bring you to the ⑯ **U.S. Courthouse,** a handsome building of coquina coral stone, erected in 1931 as Miami's main post office. In what was the second-floor central courtroom is *Law Guides Florida Progress*, a huge Depression-era mural by Denman Fink. Surrounding the central figure of a robed judge are several images that define the Florida of the 1930s: fish vendors, palm trees, beaches, and a Pan Am airplane winging off to Latin America. No cameras or tape recorders are allowed in the building. *300 N.E. 1st Ave. Building open weekdays 8:30–5; security guards open courtroom on request.*

As you round the northwest corner of the loop, at **State Plaza/Arena** ⑰ **Station,** look two blocks north to see the **Miami Arena** (701 Arena Blvd., tel. 305/530–4444), built in 1988 as a home for the Miami Heat, Miami's National Basketball Association team, and currently also home of the Florida Panthers of the National Hockey League. Round, squat, windowless, and pink, the arena hosts other sports and entertainment events when the teams aren't playing.

Tour 3: Little Havana

Numbers in the margin correspond to points of interest on the Tours 3–7: Miami, Coral Gables, and Key Biscayne map.

Some 35 years ago the tidal wave of Cubans fleeing the Castro regime flooded an older neighborhood just west of downtown Miami ★ with refugees. This area became known as **Little Havana.** Today, with a million Cubans and other Latins—more than half the metropolitan population—widely dispersed throughout Greater Miami,

Little Havana and neighboring East Little Havana remain magnets for Hispanics and Anglos alike. They come to experience the flavor of traditional Cuban culture. That culture, of course, functions in Spanish. Many Little Havana residents and shopkeepers speak little or no English.

From downtown go west on Flagler Street across the Miami River. Drive west on West Flagler Street to Teddy Roosevelt Avenue ❶ (Southwest 17th Avenue), and pause at **Plaza de la Cubanidad,** on the southwest corner. Redbrick sidewalks surround a fountain and monument with a quotation from José Martí, a leader in Cuba's struggle for independence from Spain: LAS PALMAS SON NOVIAS QUE ESPERAN (The palm trees are girlfriends who will wait), counseling hope and fortitude to the Cubans.

Turn left at Douglas Road (Southwest 37th Avenue), drive south to ❷ **Calle Ocho** (the Spanish name for Southwest 8th Street), and turn left again. You are now on the main commercial thoroughfare of Little Havana.

Drive east on Calle Ocho. After you cross Unity Boulevard (Southwest 27th Avenue), Calle Ocho becomes a one-way street eastbound through the heart of Little Havana, where every block deserves exploration. If your time is limited, try the three-block stretch from Southwest 14th Avenue to Southwest 11th Avenue. Parking is more plentiful west of Ronald Reagan Avenue (Southwest 12th Avenue).

At Avenida Luis Muñoz Marín (Southwest 15th Avenue) is ❸ **Dominoes Park** (technically Maximo Gomez Park), where elderly Cuban males, especially, pass the day with their black-and-white play tiles and their anti-Castro politics. Lately added here is a mural of the hemispheric Summit of the Americas held in Miami late in 1994; included are paintings of every leader who took part in the event. The park is open daily 9–6.

At Calle Ocho and Memorial Boulevard (Southwest 13th Avenue) ❹ stands the **Brigade 2506 Memorial,** commemorating the victims of the unsuccessful 1961 Bay of Pigs invasion of Cuba by an exile force. An eternal flame burns atop a simple stone monument with the inscription CUBA—A LOS MARTIRES DE LA BRIGADA DE ASALTO ABRIL 17 DE 1961. The monument also bears a shield with the Brigade 2506 emblem, a Cuban flag superimposed on a cross. Walk a block south on Memorial Boulevard to see other monuments relevant to Cuban history, including a statue of José Martí.

❺ Drive five blocks south on Ronald Reagan Avenue to the **Cuban Museum of Arts and Culture.** Created by Cuban exiles to preserve and interpret the cultural heritage of their homeland, the museum has expanded its focus to embrace the entire Hispanic arts community and work produced by young local artists in general. The museum includes among its collection the art of exiles and of artists who continue to work on the island. Other exhibits are drawn from the museum's small permanent collection. *1300 S.W. 12th Ave., tel. 305/858-8006. Donations welcome. Open Tues.–Fri. 11–3, Sat. noon–5.*

To return to downtown Miami take Ronald Reagan Avenue back north to Southwest 8th Street, turn right, drive east to Miami Avenue or Brickell Avenue, turn left, and continue north across the Miami River. To pick up the Coral Gables tour, which follows, drive south to the end of Ronald Reagan Avenue, where it intersects with Coral Way; turn right onto Coral Way and head west.

Tour 4: Coral Gables and South Miami

Coral Gables, a planned community of broad boulevards and Spanish Mediterranean architecture, justifiably calls itself "the City Beautiful." Developer George E. Merrick began selling Coral Gables lots in

1921 and incorporated the city in 1925. He named most of the streets for Spanish explorers, cities, and provinces. Street names are at ground level beside each intersection on whitewashed concrete cornerstones.

The 1926 hurricane and the Great Depression prevented Merrick from fulfilling many aspects of his plan. The city languished until after World War II but then grew rapidly. Today Coral Gables has a population of about 41,000. In its bustling downtown more than 140 multinational companies maintain headquarters or regional offices. The University of Miami campus, in the south part of Coral Gables, brings a youthful vibrance to its corner of the area.

From downtown Miami drive south on Southeast 2nd Avenue across the Miami River, where the street becomes Brickell Avenue. One-half mile south of the river turn right onto Coral Way, which at this point is Southwest 13th Street. Within ½ mile, Coral Way doglegs left under I–95 and becomes Southwest 3rd Avenue. It continues another mile to a complex intersection, Five Points, and doglegs right to become Southwest 22nd Street.

Along the Southwest 3rd Avenue and Southwest 22nd Street segments of Coral Way, banyan trees planted in the median strip in 1929 arch over the roadway. The banyans end at the Miami–Coral Gables boundary, where **Miracle Mile** begins. Actually only ½ mile long, this five-block retailing stretch of Coral Way, from Douglas Road (37th Avenue) to LeJeune Road (42nd Avenue), is the heart of downtown Coral Gables.

⑥ The **Colonnade Building** (133–169 Miracle Mile) once housed the sales office for Coral Gables's original developer, George Merrick. Its rotunda bears an ornamental frieze and a Spanish-tile roof 75 feet above street level. The Colonnade Building has been restored and connected to the 13-story Colonnade Hotel and an office building that echoes the rotunda's roofline.

Immediately west of LeJeune Road, bear softly to the left onto Biltmore Way. The ornate Spanish Renaissance structure facing **⑦** Miracle Mile is **Coral Gables City Hall,** opened in 1928. It has a three-tier tower topped with a clock and a 500-pound bell. A mural by Denman Fink inside the dome ceiling depicts the four seasons and can be seen from the second floor. *405 Biltmore Way, tel. 305/446–6800. Open weekdays 8–5.*

Continue west on Biltmore Way to the corner, turn right on Segovia, **⑧** left onto Coral Way, and right on Toledo Street to park behind **Coral Gables Merrick House and Gardens,** George Merrick's boyhood home. The city acquired the dwelling in 1976 and restored it to its 1920s appearance. It contains Merrick family furnishings and artifacts. *907 Coral Way, tel. 305/460–5361. Admission to house: $2 adults, $1 children; grounds free. House open Sun., Wed. 1–4; grounds open daily 8–sunset.*

As you leave the parking lot, turn left on Toledo Street and continue **⑨** to South Greenway Drive. You'll see the **Granada Golf Course** (2001 Granada Blvd., tel. 305/460–5367), a gorgeous green open space and one of two public courses in the midst of the largest historic district of Coral Gables.

Turn left on South Greenway Drive, follow it to Alhambra Circle, and turn right. One block ahead on your left, at the intersection of Alhambra Circle, Greenway Court, and Ferdinand Street, is the re-**⑩** stored **Alhambra Water Tower.** This city landmark dates from 1924, when it stored water and was clad in its decorative moresque, light-house-like exterior. After more than 50 years of disuse and neglect, the tower was completely restored in 1993 with a copper-ribbed dome and multicolor frescoes.

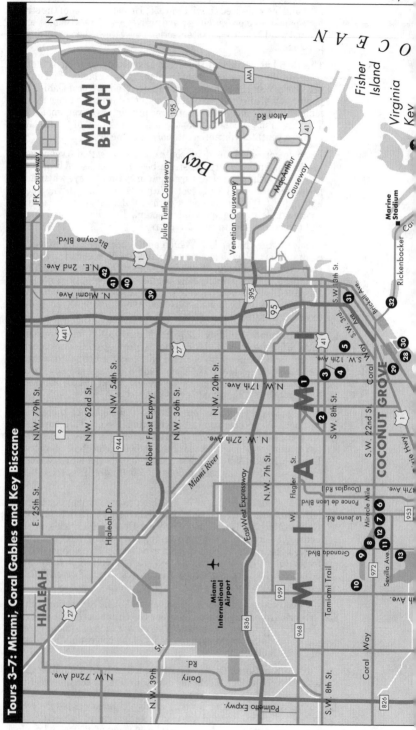

Tours 3–7: Miami, Coral Gables and Key Biscane

ATLANTIC

Bill Baggs Cape Florida State Recreation Area

KEY BISCAYNE

CORAL GABLES

SOUTH MIAMI

3 miles

3 km

0   3 km

0   3 miles

Alhambra Water Tower, **10**
Bakery Centre, **15**
Barnacle State Historic Site, **21**
Biltmore Hotel, **13**
Brigade 2506 Mem., **4**
Calle Ocho, **2**
Cape FL Lighthse., **38**

Caribbean Mktpl., **42**
Coconut Grove Convention Center, **24**
Coconut Grove Playhouse, **20**
CocoWalk, **22**
Colonnade Building, **6**
Coral Gables City Hall, **7**

Coral Gables Merrick House and Gardens, **8**
Crandon Park, **36**
Cuban Museum of Arts and Culture, **5**
De Soto Plaza and Fountain, **11**
Dinner Key Marina, **25**
Dominoes Park, **3**

Ermita de La Caridad, **28**
Eva Hewitt Munroe grave, **23**
Fairchild Tropical Garden, **17**
Former Cuban consulate, **41**
Granada Golf Course, **9**
Haitian Refugee Center, **40**

Kennedy Park, **27**
Matheson Hammock Park, **18**
Miami City Hall, **26**
Miami International Arts & Design District, **39**
Miami Museum of Science and Space Transit Planetarium, **29**

Miami Seaquarium, **33**
Old Rickenbacker Causeway Bridge, **32**
Parrot Jungle, **16**
Plaza de la Cubanidad, **1**
Plymouth Congregational Church, **19**
President Nixon's home, **37**

Simpson Park, **31**
University of Miami, **14**
Venetian Pool, **12**
Virginia Key Beach, **34**
Virginia Key Critical Wildlife Area, **35**
Vizcaya Museum and Gardens, **30**

Now drive south on Alhambra Circle four short blocks to Coral Way. Turn left, and after six blocks turn right onto Granada Boulevard.

⑪ You are now approaching **De Soto Plaza and Fountain,** a classical column on a pedestal with water flowing from the mouths of four sculpted faces. The closed eyes of the face looking west symbolize the day's end. Denman Fink designed the fountain in the early 1920s.

Follow the traffic circle almost completely around the fountain to northeast-bound De Soto Boulevard. On your right in the next block

⑫ is **Venetian Pool,** a unique municipal swimming pool transformed from a rock quarry. *2701 De Soto Blvd., tel. 305/460–5356. Admission (nonresident): $4 adults, $3.50 youths 13–17, $1.60 children 12 and under; free parking across De Soto Blvd. Open weekends 10–4:30 and June–Aug. weekdays 11–7:30; Sept.–Oct. and Apr.–May, Tues.–Fri. 11:30–5:30; Nov.–Mar., Tues.–Fri. 10–4:30.*

★ **⑬** Return to the De Soto Fountain, and follow De Soto Boulevard southwest to emerge in front of the **Biltmore Hotel** (1200 Anastasia Ave., tel. 305/445–1926). Like the Freedom Tower in downtown Miami, the Biltmore's 26-story tower is a replica of the Giralda Tower in Seville, Spain. After extensive renovations, the hotel reopened in 1992, looking better than ever. The Biltmore Golf Course, known for its scenic layout, has been restored to its original Donald Ross design.

Just to the west, in a separate building, is the **Biltmore Country Club.** Originally part of the hotel, the club then spent some years independent of it and was restored by the city in the late 1970s. In 1989 the richly ornamented Beaux Arts–style structure with a superb colonnade and courtyard was reincorporated into the hotel. On its ground floor are facilities for golfers. In the former club lounge, meeting rooms include one lofty space paneled with veneer from 60 species of trees.

From the hotel, turn right on Anastasia Avenue, go east to Granada Boulevard, and turn right. Continue south on Granada Boulevard over a bridge across the **Coral Gables Waterway,** which empties into Biscayne Bay. In the hotel's heyday, Venetian gondolas plied the waterway, bringing guests to a bay-side beach.

⑭ At Ponce de León Boulevard turn right. On your left is Metrorail's Stonehenge-like concrete structure, and on your right is the 260-acre main campus of the **University of Miami.** With almost 14,000 full-time, part-time, and noncredit students, UM is the largest private research university in the Southeast.

Turn right at the first stoplight (Stanford Drive) to enter the campus, and park in the lot on your right designated for visitors to UM's **Lowe Art Museum.** The Lowe's permanent collection of 8,000 works includes Renaissance and Baroque art, American paintings, Latin American art, and Navajo and Pueblo Indian textiles and baskets. The museum also hosts traveling exhibitions. *1301 Stanford Dr., tel. 305/284–3535 for recording or 305/284–3536 for museum office. Admission: $4 adults, $3 senior citizens, $2 students over 6. Open Tues.–Sat. 10–5, Sun. noon–5.*

Exit the UM campus on Stanford Drive, pass under Metrorail, and cross Dixie Highway. Just beyond the Burger King on your right, bear right onto Maynada Street. Turn right at the next stoplight onto **Sunset Drive.** Fine old homes and mature trees line this city-designated "historic and scenic road." Sunset Drive leads to and through **South Miami,** a pioneer farming community that grew into a suburb, but retains its small-town charm.

On the northwest corner of Sunset Drive and Red Road (57th Avenue), note the pink building with a mural in which an alligator seems ready to devour a horrified man. This trompe l'oeil fantasy, *South*

Florida Cascade, by illusionary artist Richard Haas, highlights the
⑮ main entrance to the **Bakery Centre** (5701 Sunset Dr., tel. 305/662–
4155). This oversize shopping mall, constructed on the former site of
the Holsum Bakery, has failed to attract the hoped-for hordes of
shoppers.

On the third level of the Bakery Centre, the **Miami Youth Museum**
features arts exhibits, hands-on displays, and activities to enhance
children's creativity and inspire interest in artistic careers. Late in
1996, the museum will move to quarters in neighboring Kendall that
more than double the current size. *5701 Sunset Dr., tel. 305/661–
3046. Admission: $3 adults and children over 1, $2 senior citizens.
Open Mon. and Fri. 10–5, Tues.–Thurs. 1–5, weekends 11–5;
closed holidays.*

Drive south on Red Road, and turn right just before Killian Drive
⑯ (Southwest 112th Street) into the 13-acre grounds of **Parrot Jungle,**
where more than 1,100 exotic birds are on display. Many of the par-
rots, macaws, and cockatoos fly free, and they'll come to you for
seeds, which you can purchase from old-fashioned gum-ball machines. Attend a trained-bird show, watch baby birds in training,
and pose for photos with colorful macaws perched on your arms. The
"jungle" is a natural hammock surrounding a sinkhole. Stroll among
orchids and other flowering plants nestled among ferns, bald cypress, and massive live oaks. Other highlights include a primate
show, small-wildlife shows, a children's playground, and a petting
zoo. Also see the cactus garden and Flamingo Lake, with a breeding
population of 75 Caribbean flamingos. Opened in 1936, Parrot Jungle is one of Greater Miami's oldest and most popular commercial
tourist attractions. *11000 S.W. 57th Ave., tel. 305/666–7834. Admission: $10.95 adults, $7.95 children 3–12. Open daily 9:30–6 (last admission at 5); café open daily 8–6.*

From Parrot Jungle follow Red Road ⅛ mile south, and turn left at
Old Cutler Road, which curves north along the uplands of southern
⑰ Florida's coastal ridge. Visit the 83-acre **Fairchild Tropical Garden,**
the largest tropical botanical garden in the continental United
States. Although the gardens lost most of their tropical foliage in
the 1992 hurricane, the cycads survived and the gardens are flour-
ishing again. Even so, visitors can get an idea of how tropical plants
regenerate themselves after severe storms by visiting a portion of
the gardens left untouched since Hurricane Andrew. In other devel-
opments, the rare-plant house is open again, concerts are a frequent
new feature, and the entry and parking lot have been relandscaped.
*10901 Old Cutler Rd., tel. 305/667–1651. Admission: $7 adults, un-
der 13 free with parents. Open daily 9:30–4:30; a free tram runs
hourly; Rain Forest Café open weekends 11–3. Closed Dec. 25.*

North of the garden, Old Cutler Road traverses Dade County's old-
⑱ est and most scenic park, **Matheson Hammock Park.** The Civilian
Conservation Corps developed the 100-acre tract of upland and mangrove swamp in the 1930s on land donated by a local pioneer, Commodore J.W. Matheson. The park's most popular feature is a
bathing beach, where the tide flushes a saltwater "atoll" pool
through four gates. A 90-slip marina is open, with an additional 162
slips to follow by 1997. *9610 Old Cutler Rd., tel. 305/667–3035. Parking fee for beach and marina: $3 per car, $5 per car with trailer, $6
per RV; limited free upland parking. Open daily 6–sunset. Pool lifeguards on duty winter (Eastern Standard Time), daily 8:30–5;
summer (Daylight Saving Time), daily 7:30–7.*

Continue north on Old Cutler Road to Cartagena Plaza, cross the
bridge over the waterway onto LeJeune Road, turn right on U.S. 1,
and return to downtown Miami.

Tour 5: Coconut Grove

Coconut Grove is southern Florida's oldest settlement, inhabited as early as 1834 and established by 1873, two decades before Miami. Its early settlers included Bahamian blacks, "Conchs" from Key West, and New England intellectuals. They built a community that attracted artists, writers, and scientists to establish winter homes. By the end of World War I more people listed in *Who's Who* gave addresses in Coconut Grove than anyplace else.

To this day Coconut Grove reflects its pioneers' eclectic origins. Posh estates mingle with rustic cottages, modest frame homes, and starkly modern dwellings—often on the same block. To keep Coconut Grove a village in a jungle, residents lavish affection on exotic plantings while battling to protect remaining native vegetation.

The historic center of the Village of Coconut Grove went through a hippie period in the 1960s, laid-back funkiness in the 1970s, and a teenybopper invasion in the early 1980s. Today the tone is upscale and urban, with a mix of galleries, boutiques, restaurants, bars, and sidewalk cafés. On weekends the Grove is jam-packed.

From downtown Miami follow U.S. 1 south to Southwest 27th Avenue (Grapeland Boulevard), turn left, and drive south to South Bayshore Drive. Turn right, and follow this road until it jogs right and becomes McFarlane Road. At the next intersection turn left onto Main Highway, which passes through the heart of the Village of Coconut Grove. Before you explore this trendy area, however, go on to **(19)** Devon Road, and turn right in front of **Plymouth Congregational Church.** Opened in 1917, this handsome coral-rock structure resembles a Mexican mission church. The front door, of hand-carved walnut and oak with original wrought-iron fittings, came from an early 17th-century monastery in the Pyrenees. Also on the 11-acre grounds are natural sunken gardens; the first schoolhouse in Dade County (one room), which was moved to this property; and the site of the original Coconut Grove waterworks and electric works. *3400 Devon Rd., tel. 305/444–6521. Call office 1 day in advance to see inside of church weekdays 9–4:30; Sun. service 10 AM.*

Return to Main Highway, and head northeast toward the historic **Village of Coconut Grove,** a trendy commercial district with redbrick sidewalks and more than 300 restaurants, stores, and art galleries. Parking can be a problem in the village—especially on weekend evenings, when police direct traffic and prohibit turns at some intersections to prevent gridlock. Be prepared to walk several blocks from the periphery into the heart of the Grove.

As you enter the village center, note the apricot-hue Spanish rococo **(20)** **Coconut Grove Playhouse** (*see* the Arts and Nightlife, *below*) to your left. Built in 1926 as a movie theater, it became a legitimate theater in 1956 and is now owned by the state of Florida.

Benches and a shelter opposite the playhouse mark the entrance to ★ **(21)** the **Barnacle State Historic Site,** a pioneer residence built by Commodore Ralph Munroe in 1891. Its broad, sloping roof and deeply recessed verandas channel sea breezes into the house. A central stairwell and rooftop vent allow hot air to escape. Many furnishings are original. *3485 Main Hwy., tel. 305/448–9445. Admission: $2. Reservations required for groups of 8 or more; others meet ranger on porch. Open Thurs.–Mon. 9–4; tours at 10, 11:30, 1, 2:30 (but best to double-check).*

At the north end of Commodore Plaza is Grand Avenue, a major ★ **(22)** shopping street. **CocoWalk** (3015 Grand Ave., tel. 305/444–0777), a multilevel open mall of Mediterranean-style brick courtyards and terraces overflowing with people, opened early in 1991 and has revitalized Coconut Grove's nightlife. The mix of shops, restaurants, and theaters has renewed the Grove by creating a new circuit for promenading between these attractions and the historic heart of the Grove along Commodore Plaza. Across Virginia Street, **Mayfair Shops at the Grove** (*see* Malls *in* Shopping for Bargains, *below*) gained new life in 1994, after several seasons of heavy vacancies, by the opening of the new club Planet Hollywood (3390 Mary St., tel. 305/445–7277). The area now teems with Manhattan-like crowds, especially on weekend evenings.

Leaving the village center, follow McFarlane Road east from its intersection with Grand Avenue and Main Highway. **Peacock Park,** site of the first hotel in southeast Florida, is on your right. In an iron enclosure to the side of the Coconut Grove Library (a branch of the main library system) is the **Eva Hewitt Munroe grave.** Ralph Munroe's first wife was reburied here at the site Munroe donated for the library.

If you turn north at the end of McFarlane Road onto South Bayshore Drive, you'll pass the 150,000-square-foot **Coconut Grove Convention Center** (2700 S. Bayshore Dr., tel. 305/579–3310), where antiques, boat, and home shows are held, and **Dinner Key Marina** (3400 Pan American Dr., tel. 305/579–6980), where seabirds soar and sailboats ride at anchor. Named for a small island on which early settlers held picnics, it's Greater Miami's largest marina, with 581 moorings at nine piers.

At the northeast corner of the same lot is **Miami City Hall,** built in 1934 as the terminal for the Pan American Airways seaplane base at Dinner Key. The building retains its nautical-style Art Deco trim. *3500 Pan American Dr., tel. 305/250–5357. Open weekdays 8–5.*

Continue north on South Bayshore Drive past Kirk Street to **Kennedy Park,** where you can park your car and walk toward the water. From a footbridge over the mouth of a small tidal creek, you'll enjoy an unobstructed view across Biscayne Bay to Key Biscayne. Film crews often use the park to make commercials and Italian westerns.

Drive north on South Bayshore Drive. At the entrance to Mercy Hospital, South Bayshore Drive becomes South Miami Avenue. At the next stoplight, turn right on a private road that passes St. Kieran's Church to **Ermita de La Caridad** (Our Lady of Charity Shrine), a conical building 90 feet high and 80 feet wide; it overlooks the bay so worshipers face toward Cuba. A mural above the shrine's altar depicts Cuba's history. *3609 S. Miami Ave., tel. 305/854–2404. Open daily 9–9.*

Another ⁹⁄₁₀ mile up South Miami Avenue, turn left to the **Miami Museum of Science and Space Transit Planetarium.** This is a participatory museum, chock-full of sound, gravity, and electricity displays for children and adults alike to manipulate and marvel at. A wildlife center houses native Florida snakes, turtles, tortoises, birds of prey, and large wading birds—175 live animals in all. Outstanding traveling exhibits appear throughout the year. *3280 S. Miami Ave., tel. 305/854–4247 or 305/854–2222 for 24-hr Cosmic Hotline for planetarium show times and prices. Admission: $6 adults, $4 senior citizens and children 3–12; planetarium show: $5 adults, $2.50 senior citizens and children; laser-light rock-and-roll concert shows: $6 adults, $3 senior citizens and children. Open daily 10–6.*

Across South Miami Avenue is the entrance to **Vizcaya Museum and Gardens,** an estate with an Italian Renaissance–style villa built in 1912–16 as the winter residence of Chicago industrialist James Deering. The house and gardens overlook Biscayne Bay on a 30-acre tract that includes a native hammock and more than 10 acres of formal gardens and fountains. The house contains 70 rooms, with 34 rooms of paintings, sculpture, antique furniture, and other decorative arts, open to the public. These objects date from the 15th through the 19th centuries and represent the Renaissance, Baroque, Rococo, and neoclassical styles. *3251 S. Miami Ave., tel. 305/250–9133. Admission: $8 adults, $4 children 6–12. Guided 45-min tours available, group tours by appointment. House and ticket booth open daily 9:30–4:30, garden daily 9:30–5:30. Closed Dec. 25.*

③ Continue north on South Miami Avenue to 17th Road, and turn left to **Simpson Park.** Enjoy a fragment of the dense tropical jungle—large gumbo-limbo trees, marlberry, banyans, and black calabash—that once covered the entire 5 miles from downtown Miami to Coconut Grove. You'll get a rare glimpse of how things were before the high-rises towered. Avoid the park during summer, when mosquitoes whine as incessantly today as they did 100 years ago. You may follow South Miami Avenue the rest of the way downtown or go back two stoplights and turn left to the entrance to the Rickenbacker Causeway and Key Biscayne. *55 S.W. 17th Rd., Miami, tel. 305/856–6801. Open sunrise–sunset, though park gate is unlocked by neighbors so opening sometimes delayed weekends and holidays.*

Tour 6: Virginia Key and Key Biscayne

Government Cut and the Port of Miami separate the dense urban fabric of Miami from two of the city's playground islands, Virginia Key and Key Biscayne—the latter no longer the laid-back village where Richard Nixon set up his presidential vacation compound. Parks occupy much of both keys, providing congenial upland with facilities for basking on the beach, golf, tennis, softball, and picnicking, plus uninviting but ecologically valuable stretches of dense mangrove swamp. Unfortunately, these islands were hit hard in 1992 by Hurricane Andrew, and, although all the hotels have reopened, the tourist attractions—many of which are outdoors and near the water—are still recovering their foliage.

To reach Virginia Key and Key Biscayne, take the **Rickenbacker Causeway** (toll: $1 per car) across Biscayne Bay from the mainland at Brickell Avenue and Southwest 26th Road, about 2 miles south of downtown Miami. The causeway links several islands in the bay.

The high-level **William M. Powell Bridge** rises 75 feet above the water to eliminate the need for a draw span. The panoramic view from the top encompasses the bay, keys, port, and downtown skyscrapers, with Miami Beach and the Atlantic Ocean in the distance.

㉜ Just south of the Powell Bridge, a stub of the **Old Rickenbacker Causeway Bridge,** built in 1947, is now a fishing pier. Park at its entrance, about a mile from the tollgate, and walk past anglers tending their lines to the gap where the center draw span across the Intracoastal Waterway was removed. Here you can watch boat traffic pass through the channel, pelicans and other seabirds soar and dive, and dolphins cavort in the bay.

Next along the causeway, on **Virginia Key,** stands the 6,536-seat **Miami Marine Stadium** (3601 Rickenbacker Causeway, tel. 305/361–3316), formerly the site of summer pop concerts, occasional shows by name entertainers, and a spectacular Fourth of July fireworks display. The stadium has been closed partly due to under-use and partly for needed repairs, and there's no date scheduled for reopening.

★ ㉝ Down the causeway from Marine Stadium is the **Miami Seaquarium,** a popular attraction with six daily shows featuring sea lions, dolphins, and Lolita, a killer whale who cavorts in a huge tank. Exhibits include a shark pool, a 235,000-gallon tropical-reef aquarium, and manatees. *4400 Rickenbacker Causeway, tel. 305/361–5705. Admis-*

*sion: $17.95 adults, $14.95 senior citizens, $12.95 children 3–12.
Open daily 9:30–6 (last admission at 4:30).*

(34) Opposite the causeway from the Seaquarium, a road leads north to **Virginia Key Beach,** a City of Miami park with a 2-mile stretch of oceanfront, shelters, barbecue grills, ball fields, nature trails, and a fishing area. Ask for directions at the entrance gate. Parking is $2 per car. Likely to be added later this decade are an RV park with various ball fields and an improved beach with windsurfing facilities.

(35) Plans are in progress to safeguard the 400-acre portion of this mangrove-edged island that has been dedicated as the **Virginia Key Critical Wildlife Area.** Birds to be seen here include reddish egrets, black-bellied plovers, black skimmers, and roseate spoonbills—but only May through July. The area is left undisturbed the other nine months, to be more amenable to migratory shorebirds. The entrance is at Virginia Key Beach.

(36) From Virginia Key the causeway crosses Bear Cut to the north end of **Key Biscayne,** where it becomes Crandon Boulevard. The boulevard bisects 1,211-acre **Crandon Park,** which has a popular 3½-mile Atlantic Ocean beach with a nature center. Turnouts on your left lead to four parking lots and adjacent picnic areas. *4000 Crandon Blvd., tel. 305/361–5421. Parking: $3 per vehicle. Open daily 8–sunset.*

On your right are entrances to the **Links at Key Biscayne** and the **Tennis Center at Crandon Park,** where in 1994 a $16.5 million, 7,500-seat tennis stadium was opened for use at the annual spring Lipton Championships (*see* Spectator Sports *in* Sports and the Outdoors, *below*).

(37) From the traffic circle at the south end of Crandon Park, Crandon Boulevard continues for 2 miles through the developed portion of Key Biscayne. You'll come back that way, but first detour to the site of **President Nixon's home** (485 W. Matheson Dr.). Turn right at the first stoplight onto Harbor Drive, go about a mile, and turn right at Matheson Drive. A later owner enlarged and totally changed the house.

Continue south on Harbor Drive to Mashta Drive; turn left and return to Crandon Boulevard. Turn right to reach the entrance to **Bill Baggs Cape Florida State Recreation Area,** named for a crusading newspaper editor whose efforts prompted the state to create this 406-acre park. After Hurricane Andrew turned 98 percent of the exotic Australian pine forest (600,000 trees) to kindling, park rangers engaged in a year of cleanup and two years of replanting. Gone are the high pines and other exotic plants. Except for a few coconut palms, they have been replaced with native species, including saw palmetto, cabbage palm, gumbo-limbo, pigeon plum, crabwood, and shoreline mangroves. The park is now reopened and largely transformed. Visitors find new boardwalks, 18 picnic shelters, and a bicycle and pedestrian path along the leeward shore as well as a nature trail, 1¼ miles of beach, and a seawall along Biscayne Bay where anglers catch bonefish, grouper, jack, snapper, and snook. Also in the **(38)** park is the oldest structure in south Florida, the brick **Cape Florida Lighthouse,** erected in 1845 to replace an earlier one destroyed in an 1836 Seminole attack, in which the keeper's helper was killed. Sometime during 1996, you should once again be able to climb the 95 feet to the top, and a replica of the keeper's house should open, too. *1200 S. Crandon Blvd., tel. 305/361–5811. Admission to park: $3.25 per vehicle with up to 8 people. Park open daily 8–sunset.*

When you leave Cape Florida, follow Crandon Boulevard back to Crandon Park through Key Biscayne's commercial center, a mixture of posh shops and more prosaic stores catering to the needs of the neighborhood. On your way back to the mainland, pause as you approach the Powell Bridge to admire the downtown Miami skyline. At night the brightly lighted NationsBank Tower looks from this angle like a clipper ship running under full sail before the breeze.

Tour 7: Little Haiti

Of some 200,000 Haitians who have settled in south Florida, almost half live in Little Haiti, an area on Miami's northeast side covering about 200 city blocks. More than 400 small Haitian businesses operate in Little Haiti. Yet the future of the district is uncertain: Immigration from Haiti has virtually ceased, while the majority already in Miami question their economic future in the ghetto. As their fortunes improve, many move out. Still, the neighborhood is one of the city's most distinctive. If you walk or drive along its side streets, you might see Haitian women carrying their burdens atop their heads, as they do on their home island.

For many Haitians, English is a third language. French is Haiti's official language, but much day-to-day conversation takes place in Creole, a French-based patois.

From downtown Miami, follow Biscayne Boulevard north to Northeast 38th Street; turn left, and drive about ⁴⁄₁₀ mile west as the street curves and becomes 39th Street. At North Miami Avenue, turn right, and at 40th Street, turn right again onto the main street of the
39 **Miami International Arts & Design District.** Here, close by Little Haiti, some 225 wholesale stores, showrooms, and galleries feature interior furnishings and decorative arts. Since 1993, the district has been undergoing a revival, and there are several new art studios and showrooms.

Immediately north is the gentrified neighborhood of Buena Vista, which merges with Little Haiti. The area contains some of Miami's oldest dwellings, dating from the dawn of the 20th century through the 1920s land-boom era. Drive the side streets to see elegant Mediterranean-style homes and bungalows with distinctive coral-rock trim.

Return to North Miami Avenue and drive north. A half block east on
40 54th Street is the tiny storefront office of the **Haitian Refugee Center** (119 N.E. 54th St., tel. 305/757–8538), a focal point of activity in the Haitian community. The building's facade is decorated by the painting of an uncomprehending Haitian standing in front of the Statue of Liberty, which denies him entry to America. Continue north on
41 North Miami Avenue past the **former Cuban consulate** (5811 N. Miami Ave.), a pretentious Caribbean-colonial mansion that is now the clinic of Haitian physician Lucien Albert.

North of 85th Street, cross the Little River Canal into **El Portal,** a tiny suburban village of modest homes, where more than a quarter of the property is now Haitian-owned. Turn right on Northeast 87th Street and right again on Northeast 2nd Avenue. You are now southbound on Little Haiti's tree-lined main commercial street. Along Northeast 2nd Avenue between 79th and 45th streets, rows of storefronts in faded pastels reflect a first effort by area merchants to dress up their neighborhood and attract outsiders.

Barely more successful, and showing the strains of uncertainty in
42 this immigrant community, is the **Caribbean Marketplace** (5927 N.E. 2nd Ave., no phone), which the Haitian Task Force (an economic-development organization) opened in 1990. The building beautifully evokes the Iron Market in Port-au-Prince. Its handful of merchants surrounding a medical clinic sell handmade baskets, Caribbean art and craft items, books, records, videos, and ice cream.

To return to downtown Miami follow Northeast 2nd Avenue south to Northeast 35th Street, turn left, drive east one block to Biscayne Boulevard, and turn right to go south.

Tour 8: South Dade

Numbers in the margin correspond to points of interest on the Tour 8: South Dade map.

This tour directs you to major attractions in the suburbs southwest of Dade County's urban core. Although the population was largely dislocated by Hurricane Andrew in the fall of 1992, little damage is evident today. All attractions have reopened.

From downtown Miami follow the Dolphin Expressway (Route 836) west to the Palmetto Expressway (Route 826) southbound. Bear left south of Bird Road (Southwest 40th Street) onto the Don Shula Expressway (Route 874). Exit westbound onto Killian Drive (Southwest 104th Street), and drive west to Lindgren Road (Southwest 137th Avenue). Turn left, and drive south to Southwest 128th Street, the entrance to the Tamiami Airport and **Weeks Air Museum.** Rebuilt since its destruction by hurricane, the museum now displays some 30–35 planes, including a B-17 Flying Fortress bomber and a P-51 Mustang from World War II. Most of the fragile WWI planes were destroyed by the storm. *14710 S.W. 128th St., tel. 305/233–5197. Admission: $5 adults, $4 senior citizens, $3 children 12 and under. Open daily 10–5; closed Thanksgiving, Dec. 25.*

Continue south on Lindgren Road to Coral Reef Drive (Southwest 152nd Street). Turn left, and drive east to **Metrozoo,** a cageless 290-acre zoo where animals roam free on islands surrounded by moats. Devastated by the hurricane, the zoo has reopened but without its monorail or "Wings of Asia," a 1.5-acre aviary where hundreds of exotic birds from Southeast Asia fly through a rain forest beneath a protective net. Although that is not scheduled to reopen before the end of 1996 at the earliest, most of the animals, including elephants, koalas, and flamingos, are back, after having been shipped to other zoos after the storm. "Paws," a petting zoo for children, features three shows daily. *12400 Coral Reef Dr. (S.W. 152nd St.), tel. 305/251–0401 or 305/251–0400 for recorded information. Admission during rebuilding: $5.33 adults, $2.66 children; 45-min. tram tour: $2. Open daily 9:30–5:30 (last admission at 4).*

Next to the zoo, the **Gold Coast Railroad Museum** displays a 1949 *Silver Crescent* dome car and the *Ferdinand Magellan,* the only Pullman car ever constructed specifically for U.S. presidents, used by Roosevelt, Truman, Eisenhower, and Reagan. The museum was damaged in the hurricane, but most trains were expected back at the site before the end of 1995, when the replacement of the great shed over the trains should be nearing completion. *12450 Coral Reef Dr. (S.W. 152nd St.), tel. 305/253–0063. Admission: $4 adults (train rides included). Open weekends 11–4 until repairs completed.*

Drive south on the Homestead Extension of Florida's Turnpike, exit at Hainlin Mill Drive (Southwest 216th Street), and turn right. Cross South Dixie Highway (U.S. 1), drive 3 miles west, and turn right into **Monkey Jungle,** home to more than 400 monkeys representing 35 species—including orangutans from Borneo and Sumatra, golden lion tamarins from Brazil, and brown lemurs from Madagascar. Its rain-forest trail, damaged in the hurricane, is expected to reopen fully in 1996. Performing-monkey shows begin at 10 and run continuously at 30-minute intervals. The walkways of this 30-acre attraction are caged; the monkeys roam free. *14805 Hainlin Mill Dr. (S.W. 216th St.), tel. 305/235–1611. Admission:*

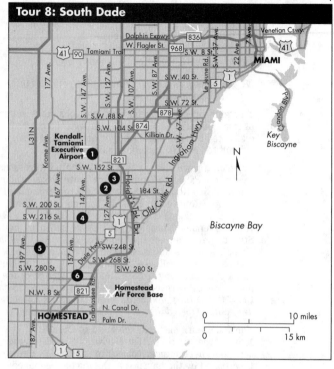

Tour 8: South Dade

$10.50 adults, $9.50 senior citizens, $5.35 children 4–12. Open daily 9:30–5 (last admission at 4).

Continue west on Hainlin Mill Drive, past Krome Avenue (Southwest 177th Avenue), to Redland Road (Southwest 187th Avenue), and turn left to Coconut Palm Drive (Southwest 248th Street). You are at the **Redland Fruit & Spice Park,** a Dade County treasure since 1944, when it was opened as a 20-acre showcase of tropical fruits and vegetables. It has since expanded to 30 acres, and there's the prospect of a 3-acre lake by 1996. Two of the park's three historic buildings were ruined by the hurricane, as well as about half of its trees and plants, but relandscaping has begun, and the park has reopened. Plants are now grouped by country of origin and include more than 500 varieties of exotic fruits, herbs, spices, nuts, and poisonous plants from around the world. A sampling reveals 50 varieties of bananas, 40 varieties of grapes, and 100 varieties of citrus. A gourmet-and-fruit shop offers many varieties of tropical-fruit products, jellies, seeds, aromatic teas, and reference books. *24801 Redland Rd. (S.W. 187th Ave.), tel. 305/247–5727. Admission: $1 adults, 50¢ children; guided tour: $1.50 adults, $1 children. Open daily 10–5; tours weekends at 1, 3.*

Drive east on Coconut Palm Drive (Southwest 248th Street) to Newton Road (Southwest 157th Avenue). Continue south on Newton Road to South Dixie Highway (U.S. 1), and turn left. Almost immediately you'll find **Coral Castle of Florida,** on your right. It was built by Edward Leedskalnin, a Latvian immigrant, between 1920 and 1940. The 3-acre castle has a 9-ton gate a child can open (though it was still not functioning in 1995), an accurate working sundial, and a telescope of coral rock aimed at the North Star. *28655 S. Dixie Hwy., tel. 305/248–6344. Admission: $7.75 adults, $6.50 senior citizens, $4.50 children 7–12. Open daily 9–6.*

To return to downtown Miami after leaving Coral Castle, take South Dixie Highway to Biscayne Drive (Southwest 288th Street) and go east to the turnpike. Follow the turnpike back to the Don Shula Expressway (Route 874), which leads to the Palmetto Expressway (Route 826), which leads to the Dolphin Expressway (Route 836).

Guided Tours

Miami is such an unsatisfactory city for public transportation that if you want to see the sights and you don't want to spend money on a rental car, you'll need to sign up for a guided tour. Most are near public transportation stops, so they're inexpensive to get to. Exploring downtown, however, is best and most cheaply done on the Metromover (*see* Tour 2, *above*).

Boat Tours *Island Queen, Island Lady,* and *Pink Lady* (401 Biscayne Blvd., tel. 305/379–5119) are 150-passenger double-decker tour boats docked at Bayside Marketplace. They go on daily 90-minute narrated tours of the Port of Miami and Millionaires' Row. The cost is $10 adults, $5 children 12 and under.

Heritage of Miami II (401 Biscayne Blvd., tel. 305/442–9697), a two-masted, 85-foot topsail schooner, sails from Bayside Marketplace. Tours loop through lower Biscayne Bay, offering views of Vizcaya, movie stars' homes, the Cape Florida Lighthouse, Port of Miami, and several residential islands. One hour costs $5 per person, two hours are $10, and children under 12 can ride for half price.

Ecotours **EcoTours Miami** (Box 22, Miami 33256–0022, tel. 305/232–5398), consisting of longtime environmentalist Ginni Hokanson and friends, conducts customized interpretive tours of the Everglades, Big Cypress Swamp, Fackahatchee Strand, Florida Bay, and wherever else in south Florida's native environment visitors want to explore. Tour guides—environmental educators and natural history specialists—are available who speak German, Italian, Portuguese, and Spanish. Price quotes are given on request.

Historic Tours **Art Deco District Tour** (1001 Ocean Dr., Miami Beach, tel. 305/672–2014), operated by the Miami Design Preservation League, is a 90-minute guided walking tour departing from the league's welcome center at the Ocean Front Auditorium at 10:30 AM Saturday. Private group tours can be arranged with advance notice. A two-hour bike tour at 10:30 Sunday leaves from Cycles on the Beach (713 5th St., Miami Beach, tel. 305/673–2055). The walking tour costs $6; the bike tour is $10 with a rental bike, $5 with your own bike.

Deco Tours Miami Beach (420 Lincoln Rd., Suite 412, Miami Beach, tel. 305/531–4465) also offers walking tours of the Art Deco District. These 90-minute tours, which cost $10, depart from various locations and take in Lincoln Road, Washington Avenue, Espanola Way, Ocean Drive, Lummus Park, and the Art Deco Welcome Center.

Professor Paul George (1345 S.W. 14th St., Miami, tel. 305/858–6021), a history professor at Miami-Dade Community College and past president of the Florida Historical Society, leads a variety of walking tours as well as boat tours and tours that make use of Metrorail and Metromover. Tours generally last about two hours and 20 minutes. Covering downtown and other historic neighborhoods, they start Saturday at 10 and Sunday at 11 at various locations, depending on the tour. Call for each weekend's schedule and for additional tours by appointment. The fee is $10 for adults.

Rickshaw Tours **Majestic Rickshaw** (75 N.E. 156 St., Biscayne Gardens, tel. 305/256–8833) offers two-person rickshaw rides along Main Highway in Coconut Grove's Village Center, nightly 8 PM–2 AM. It's $3 per person for a 10-minute ride through Coconut Grove or $6 per person for a 20-minute lovers' moonlight ride to Biscayne Bay.

Self-Guided
Tours The **Junior League of Miami** (2325 Salzedo, Coral Gables 33134, tel. 305/443–0160) publishes excellent self-guiding tours to architectural and historical landmarks in downtown Miami, the northeast, and south Dade. Each costs $3.

The **Miami Design Preservation League** (Bin L, Miami Beach 33139, tel. 305/672–2014) sells the *Art Deco District Guide*, a book of six detailed walking or driving tours of the Art Deco District, for $10.

Beaches

Key Biscayne Two of metro Miami's best beaches are on Key Biscayne. Nearest the causeway is the 3½-mile county beach in **Crandon Park,** popular with families and rated among the top 10 beaches in North America by many. The sand is soft, and parking is both inexpensive and plentiful. At the north end of the beach, the Marjory Stoneman Douglas Biscayne Nature Center interprets a variety of natural habitats through exhibits and year-round tours. *4000 Crandon Park Blvd., tel. 305/361–5421 or 305/642–9600 for nature center. Park admission: $3 per vehicle, nature center free. Open daily 8–sunset, nature center hrs vary.*

The other nice beach is in the **Bill Baggs Cape Florida State Recreation Area** (*see* Tour 6, *above*), which has a bounty of appealing features.

Miami Beach
Area A sandy, 300-foot-wide beach extends for 10 continuous miles from the foot of Miami Beach to Haulover Beach Park, with several distinct sections. Amazingly, it's all man-made. Seriously eroded during the mid-1970s, the beach was restored by the U.S. Army Corps of Engineers in a $51.5 million project between 1977 and 1981. Between 23rd and 44th streets, Miami Beach built boardwalks and protective walkways atop a sand dune landscaped with sea oats, sea grape, and other native plants whose roots keep the sand from blowing away.

The new beach lures residents and visitors alike to swim and stroll—without question, Miami's favorite activities. Here's a guide to where kindred spirits gather:

From **1st to 15th streets** senior citizens predominate early in the day. The section from 5th to 15th, known as **Lummus Park,** lies in the heart of the Deco District and attracts a mix of perfect-bod types and those of all ages who can only ogle. Volleyball, in-line skating along the paved upland path, and a lot of posing go on here, and children's playgrounds make this a popular area for families. Along these beaches, city officials don't enforce the law against female bathers going topless, as long as everyone on the beach behaves with decorum. Gays like the beach between 11th and 13th streets. Sidewalk cafés parallel the entire beach area, which makes it easy to come ashore for everything from burgers to quiche. At 23rd Street, the boardwalk begins, and no skates or bicycles are allowed.

French-Canadians frequent the **72nd Street beach** and the area from **Surfside to 96th Street,** which is colonized by winter visitors from Québec.

Families and anybody else who likes things quiet prefer **North Beach,** along Ocean Terrace between 73rd and 75th streets. Metered parking is ample right behind the dune and on Collins Avenue, a block behind, along a pleasant, old shopping street. The area, however, is slated for redevelopment with the intensity, if not the size, of South Beach.

North Shore State Recreation Area is still more quiet. The 40-acre park is, for a change, backed by lush tropical growth rather than hotels. *Collins Ave., between 79th and 87th Sts., Miami Beach; office: Oleta/North Shore GEOpark, 3400 N.E. 163rd St., North Miami*

*Beach, tel. 305/940–7439. Admission: $2 plus parking. Open daily
9–6.*

During the winter, wealthy condominium owners cluster on the
beach from **96th to 103rd streets** in Bal Harbour.

Older visitors especially complain about just how wide the beaches
have become—feet burn easily on long marches across hot sand before reaching the water. If you want the water closer to the upland,
try the beaches from **Haulover Beach Park** north through **Sunny
Isles.** The eroded sand was never replaced here, and the strand is
mercifully narrow. *Haulover Beach Park: 10800 Collins Ave., Miami, tel. 305/947–3525. Admission: $3 per vehicle. Open daily 8–
sunset.*

Shopping for Bargains

Visitors to Greater Miami are never more than 15 minutes from a
major shopping area. Downtown Miami long ago ceased to be the
community's central shopping hub, as most residents moved to the
suburbs. Today Dade County has more than a dozen major malls, an
international-free-trade zone, and hundreds of miles of commercial
streets lined with storefronts and small neighborhood shopping centers. Many of these local shopping areas have an ethnic flavor, catering primarily to one or another of Greater Miami's immigrant
cultures. In the Latin neighborhoods, for example, children's stores
sell *vestidos de fiesta* (party dresses) made of organza and lace.
Men's stores sell the guayabera, a pleated, embroidered shirt that
replaces the tie and jacket in much of the tropics. Traditional bridal
shops display formal dresses that Latin families buy or rent for a
daughter's *quince*, a lavish 15th-birthday celebration.

No standard store hours exist in Greater Miami, though most malls
observe the typical seven-day hours of malls everywhere. Call
ahead. When you shop, expect to pay Florida's 6% sales tax unless
you have the store ship your goods out of Florida.

**Shopping
Districts** The three most extensive bargain areas are the Miami Fashion District, the Miami Free Zone (MFZ), and the Wholesale District, all a
bit off the beaten path. At the **Miami Fashion District** (5th Ave. east
of I–95, between 25th and 29th Sts., Miami), you can buy the wares
of the 500 garment manufacturers in Miami and Hialeah. (Greater
Miami is the fashion marketplace for the southeastern United
States, the Caribbean, and Latin America.) Most of the more than
30 factory outlets and discount fashion stores are open Monday–Saturday 9–5. The **Miami Free Zone** (2305 N.W. 107th Ave., Miami) is
an international wholesale trade center open to the public, a vast operation occupying 850,000 square feet on three floors. You can buy
goods duty-free for export or pay duty on goods released for domestic use. More than 140 companies sell products from more than 100
countries, including aviation equipment, chemicals, clothing, computers, cosmetics, electronics, liquor, and perfumes. The 51-acre
MFZ is 15 minutes west of Miami International Airport off the Dolphin Expressway (Route 836) and about 40 minutes from the Port of
Miami. It's open weekdays 9–5. In the old section known as
Allapattah, the **Wholesale District** (20th St., between N.W. 17th and
27th Aves.) comprises hundreds of merchants lining either side of
the street. Merchandise includes apparel, shoes and handbags, luggage and accessories, jewelry, perfumes, and electronic and phar-
maceutical products, and many small, affordable restaurants are
tucked in as well. The district is about 10 minutes east of Miami International Airport off the East–West Expressway.

The **Miami International Arts & Design District** (*see* Tour 7, *above*),
also known as 40th Street, is full of showrooms and galleries specializing in interior furnishings and decorative arts. **Miracle Mile** (Cor-

al Way between 37th and 42nd Aves., Coral Gables) consists of some 160 shops along a wide, tree-lined boulevard. Shops range from posh boutiques to bargain-basement, from beauty salons to chain restaurants. As you go west, the quality increases.

Malls   Shops in the malls tend to be expensive. If you want to splurge or window-shop, consider **Aventura Mall** (19501 Biscayne Blvd., Aventura), anchored by Macy's, Lord & Taylor, JCPenney, and Sears, and the swank **Bal Harbour Shops** (9700 Collins Ave., Bal Harbour), featuring Gucci, Cartier, Nina Ricci, Fendi, Bruno Magli, Neiman Marcus, and Saks Fifth Avenue.

The two festival marketplaces are more affordable and also offer free entertainment and people-watching. **Bayside Marketplace** (401 Biscayne Blvd., Miami), the 16-acre showcase on Biscayne Bay, has 150 specialty shops, entertainment, tour-boat docks, and a food court. It's open late (10 during the week, 11 on Friday and Saturday). **Cocowalk** (3015 Grand Ave., Coconut Grove) has three floors of specialty shops that stay open almost as late as the popular restaurants and clubs.

A complex of clapboard, coral-rock, and stucco buildings, **Cauley Square** (22400 Old Dixie Hwy., Goulds) was erected in 1907–20 for railroad workers who built and maintained the line to Key West. Crafts, antiques, and clothing shops are here now. The only Sundays that stores are open are from Thanksgiving to Christmas Eve. The oldest retail mall in the county but always upgrading, **Dadeland** (7535 N. Kendall Dr., Miami) sits at the south side of town close to the Dadeland North and Dadeland South Metrorail stations. Retailers include Florida's largest Burdines, Saks Fifth Avenue, JCPenney, Lord & Taylor, and more than 175 specialty stores plus 17 restaurants. **The Falls** (S.W. 136th St. at U.S. 1, Miami), which derives its name from the several waterfalls inside, is the most upscale mall on the south side of the city. It contains Miami's only Bloomingdale's and Macy's, as well as another 60 specialty stores, restaurants, and theaters. **Mayfair Shops at the Grove** (2911 Grand Ave., Coconut Grove) is a higher-end version of people-friendly CocoWalk, just across the street. **Omni International Mall** (1601 Biscayne Blvd., Miami) rises vertically alongside the atrium of the Crowne Plaza Miami, where the eye-popping feature is an old-fashioned carousel. Among the 85 shops are a JCPenney, many restaurants, and 10 movie screens. The shortest and most elegant shopping arcade in the metropolis, the **Shops at 550** (550 Biltmore Way, Coral Gables) is in the marble halls of the Aztec-like 550 Building, three blocks west of Miracle Mile. Most shops are open weekdays 10–5, though some close later.

Outdoor   Several farmers markets have set up around Miami since the **Coco-**
Markets   **nut Grove Farmers Market** (Grand Ave., 1 block west of MacDonald Ave. [S.W. 32nd Ave.], Coconut Grove) began in 1977. It still takes place Saturdays 8 to 2 year-round. At the **Farmers Market at Merrick Park** (LeJeune Rd. [S.W. 42nd Ave.] and Biltmore Way, Coral Gables), some 25 produce and plant vendors set up in a little downtown park on Saturdays from 8 to 1, mid-January through March. Gardening workshops, cooking demonstrations, and children's activities are standard features. On Sundays November through March, the **Lincoln Road Farmers Market** (between Meridian and Euclid Avenues, Miami Beach) brings some 15 local produce vendors coupled with plant workshops and children's activities. Every weekend since 1984, more than 500 vendors have sold a variety of goods at the **Flagler Dog Track** (401 N.W. 38th Ct., Miami) from 9 to 4.

Specialty   Greater Miami's best English-language bookstore, **Books & Books,**
Shops   **Inc.** (296 Aragon Ave., Coral Gables, tel. 305/442–4408; Sterling
Books   Bldg., 933 Lincoln Rd., Miami Beach, tel. 305/532–3222) specializes in books on the arts, architecture, Floridiana, and contemporary

and classical literature. Collectors enjoy browsing through the rare-book room upstairs, which doubles as a photography gallery. Both locations always have tables of remaindered titles. There are frequent poetry readings and book signings.

Children's **A Kid's Book Shoppe** (1895 N.E. Miami Gardens Dr., North Miami
Books and Toys Beach, tel. 305/937–2665), an excellent children's-book resource, has been at this location since 1984. The friendly staff at **A Likely Story** (5740 Sunset Dr., South Miami, tel. 305/667–3730) has been helping Miamians choose books and educational toys appropriate to children's interests and stages of development since 1978.

Clothing **Allure** (550 Biltmore Way, Coral Gables, tel. 305/444–5252), in the luxurious Shops at 550 mall, sells fine women's wear—pricey but excellent value. **Ninth Street Bizaare** (900 Ocean Dr., Miami Beach, tel. 305/534–2254) is a trendy Miami Beach minimart with vendors selling clothing and accessories from around the world.

Decorative and **American Details** (3107 Grand Ave., Coconut Grove, tel. 305/448–
Gift Items 6163) sells colorful, trendy crafts items. **Art Deco Welcome Center** (1001 Ocean Dr., Miami Beach, tel. 305/531–3484) has a gift shop worth checking out for deco-phernalia, much of it very affordable. The **Indies Company** (101 W. Flagler St., Miami, tel. 305/375–1492), the Historical Museum of Southern Florida's gift shop, offers interesting artifacts reflecting Miami's history, including some inexpensive reproductions.

Jewelry **Stones of Venice** (550 Biltmore Way, Coral Gables, tel. 305/444–4474), operated by a three-time winner of the DeBeers Diamond Award for jewelry, sells affordable creations. Customers have included actor Elliott Gould, Pope John Paul II, and film director Barbet Schroeder, among others.

Sports and the Outdoors

Participant Sports

Miami's subtropical climate is ideal for active people. Here refugees from the frozen north can enjoy warm-weather outdoor sports, such as boating, swimming, and golf, all year long. During Miami's hot, humid summers, people avoid the sun's strongest rays by playing early or late in the day. Below are listed some of the most popular individual and group sports.

Biking Dade County has about 100 miles of off-road bicycle trails. A color-coded map outlining Dade's 4,000 miles of roads suitable for bike travel is available for $3.50 from area bike shops and from the **Dade County Bicycle Coordinator** (Metropolitan Planning Organization, 111 N.W. 1st St., Suite 910, Miami 33128, tel. 305/375–4507). For information on dozens of monthly group rides contact the **Everglades Bicycle Club** (Box 430282, South Miami 33243–0282, tel. 305/598–3998). Among the best shops for renting bicycles are **Dade Cycle** (3216 Grand Ave., Coconut Grove, tel. 305/444–5997 or 305/443–6075) and **Gary's Megacycle On the Beach** (1260 Washington Ave., Miami Beach, tel. 305/534–3306).

Boating Listed below are the major marinas in Greater Miami. The dock masters at these marinas can provide information on other marine services you may need. Also ask the dock masters for *Teall's Tides and Guides, Miami–Dade County,* and other local nautical publications.

Crandon Park Marina sells bait and tackle. *4000 Crandon Blvd., Key Biscayne, tel. 305/361–1281. Office open 7–6.*

Dinner Key Marina has dockage with space for transients and a boat ramp. *3400 Pan American Dr., Coconut Grove, tel. 305/579–6980. Open daily 7 AM–midnight.*

Haulover Marine Center offers a bait-and-tackle shop, marine gas station, and boat launch. *10800 Collins Ave., Miami Beach, tel. 305/ 945–3934. Open weekdays 9–5; bait shop and gas station open 24 hrs a day.*

Miamarina is closed until early 1996, when it is expected to reopen with about 100 slips. *Next to Bayside Marketplace, 401 Biscayne Blvd., Miami, temporary tel. 305/579–6955.*

Miami Beach Marina has become the "happening" marina. A multi-million-dollar expansion completed in 1995 has yielded restaurants, charters, boat and vehicle rentals, a complete marine hardware store, dive shop, large grocery store, fuel dock, concierge services, and 400 boat slips accommodating vessels up to 190 feet. New, too, is the Thursday evening Art al Fresco, a sunset celebration with original art, crafts, and music, plus free admission and parking. Facilities include air-conditioned rest rooms, washers and dryers, U.S. Customs clearing, and a heated swimming pool expected in 1996. This is the nearest marina to the South Beach Deco District, about a 15-minute walk away. *300 Alton Rd., Miami Beach, tel. 305/673– 6000. Open daily 8–6.*

Watson Island Marina will probably become a mega-yacht marina with a boutique hotel before the end of the decade, while maybe keeping a few charter and dive boats operating out of a facility that has become dilapidated from official neglect. Chalk's International Airlines will likely remain, and a new heliport could be added. A potential botanical garden may include a refurbished Japanese Garden. Currently 10 slips are available. *1050 MacArthur Causeway, Miami, tel. 305/579–6955. Call for hrs.*

Diving   Summer diving conditions in Greater Miami have been compared to those in the Caribbean. Winter diving can be adversely affected when cold fronts come through. Dive-boat schedules vary with the season and with local weather conditions.

Fowey, Triumph, Long, and Emerald reefs are all shallow 10- to 15-foot dives good for snorkelers and beginning divers. These reefs are on the edge of the continental shelf, ¼ mile from depths greater than 100 feet. You can also paddle around the tangled prop roots of the mangrove trees that line Florida's coastline, peering at the fish, crabs, and other onshore creatures that hide there.

In 1994, a greatly expanded artificial-reef program was begun off the shores of Miami. The first units of 100,000 tons of lime-rock boulders were placed on mostly sand and silt sea bottom where sea life had been destroyed by Hurricane Andrew. Early reports confirm that fish life was quickly attracted to the new sites.

Look for instructors affiliated with the Professional Association of Dive Instructors (PADI) or the National Association of Underwater Instructors (NAUI). Dive shops and charter services include:

Bubbles Dive Center is an all-purpose dive shop with PADI affiliation. Its boat, *Divers Dream,* is kept on Watson Island on MacArthur Causeway. *2671 S.W. 27th Ave., Miami, tel. 305/856– 0565. Open weekdays 10–7, Sat. 9–6.*

Divers Paradise of Key Biscayne has a complete dive shop and diving-charter service, including equipment rental and scuba instruction, with PADI affiliation. *4000 Crandon Blvd., Key Biscayne, tel. 305/ 361–3483. Open weekdays 10–6, weekends 7:30–6.*

The **Diving Locker** is a 24-year-old, PADI-affiliated dive shop that offers three-day and three-week Professional Diving Instructors Corporation certification courses, wreck and reef dives aboard the *Native Diver*, and full sales, service, and repairs. *223 Sunny Isles Blvd., North Miami Beach, tel. 305/947-6025. Open weekdays 9-9:30, Sat. 8-9:30, Sun. 8-6.*

Team Divers, a PADI five-star facility in the Miami Beach Marina, is the only dive shop in the South Beach area. Daily dives are arranged. *300 Alton Rd., tel. 305/673-0101 or 800/543-7887. Open Oct.-Mar., weekdays 10-7, weekends 9-6; Apr.-Sept., weekdays 10-7, weekends 7:30-6.*

Fishing   A few ocean fishing-charter operators sailing out of various parts of town are ***Abracadabra*** (4000 Crandon Blvd., Key Biscayne, tel. 305/361-5625), **Blue Waters Sportfishing Charters** (16375 Collins Ave., Sunny Isles, tel. 305/944-4531), ***Therapy IV*** (Haulover Marine Center, 10800 Collins Ave., Miami Beach, tel. 305/945-1578), and ***Reward II*** (Miami Beach Marina, 300 Alton Rd., MacArthur Causeway, Miami Beach, tel. 305/372-9470).

Golf   From the famed "Blue Monster" at the Doral Golf Resort and Spa to the scenic Links at Key Biscayne, overlooking Biscayne Bay, Greater Miami has more than 30 private and public courses. For information contact the appropriate parks-and-recreation department: City of Miami (tel. 305/575-5256), City of Miami Beach (tel. 305/673-7730), or Metro-Dade County (tel. 305/857-6868). Relatively affordable play is found at **Biltmore Golf Course** (1210 Anastasia Ave., Coral Gables, tel. 305/460-5364), **Links at Key Biscayne** (6700 Crandon Blvd., Key Biscayne, tel. 305/361-9129), **Normandy Shores Golf Course** (2401 Biarritz Dr., Miami Beach, tel. 305/868-6502), and **Presidential Country Club** (19650 N.E. 18th Ave., North Miami Beach, tel. 305/933-5266). **Don Shula's Hotel & Golf Club** (7601 Miami Lakes Dr., at the Palmetto Expressway, Miami Lakes, tel. 305/821-1150), **Doral Golf Resort and Spa** (4400 N.W. 87th Ave., Doral, tel. 305/592-2000 or 800/223-6725), and **Williams Island California Club** (20898 San Simeon Way, North Miami Beach, tel. 305/651-3590), open to the public after noon daily, become more affordable off-season or with a late tee time.

Jogging   Try these recommended jogging routes: in Coconut Grove, along the pedestrian/bicycle path on South Bayshore Drive, cutting over the causeway to Key Biscayne for a longer run; from the south shore of the Miami River, downtown, south along the sidewalks of Brickell Avenue to Bayshore Drive, where you can run alongside the bay; in Miami Beach, along Bay Road (parallel to Alton Road); and in Coral Gables, around the Riviera Country Club golf course, just south of the Biltmore Country Club. Two good sources of running information are the **Miami Runners Club** (7900 SW 40th St., Miami, tel. 305/227-1500) and **Foot Works** (5724 Sunset Dr., South Miami, tel. 305/667-9322), a running-shoe store.

Sailing   Dinner Key and the Coconut Grove waterfront remain the center of sailing in Greater Miami, although sailboat moorings and rentals are located along other parts of the bay and up the Miami River. **Easy Sailing** offers a fleet ranging from 19 to 127 feet for rent by the hour or the day. Services include sailboat lessons, scuba-diving lessons and certification, and on-board catering. *Dinner Key Marina, 3360 Pan American Dr., Coconut Grove, tel. 305/858-4001. Reservation and advance deposit required. Open daily 9-sunset.*

Tennis   Greater Miami has more than 60 tennis centers, of which more than a dozen are open to the public. All public tennis courts charge nonresidents an hourly fee. A sampling around the county includes:

Biltmore Tennis Center has 10 hard courts. *1150 Anastasia Ave., Coral Gables, tel. 305/460-5360. Nonresident day rate $4.30, night rate $5 per person per hr. Open weekdays 8 AM-9 PM, weekends 8-8.*

Flamingo Tennis Center has 19 clay courts. *1000 12th St., Miami Beach, tel. 305/673–7761. Day rate $2.67, night rate $3.20 per person per hr. Open weekdays 8 AM–9 PM, weekends 8–7.*

North Shore Tennis Center has 6 clay courts and 5 hard courts. *350 73rd St., Miami Beach, tel. 305/993–2022. Day rate $2.67, night rate $3.20 per person per hr. Open weekdays 8 AM–9 PM, weekends 8–7.*

Tennis Center at Crandon Park, a new $18 million facility and one of America's best, is the site of the annual Lipton Championships held each March (the only time when the courts are off-limits to the public). Included are 2 grass, 8 clay, and 17 hard courts. Reservations are necessary for night play. *7300 Crandon Blvd., Key Biscayne, tel. 305/365–2300. Laykold courts: day rate $2, night rate $3 per person per hr; clay courts: $4 per person per hr. Open daily 8 AM–10 PM.*

Windsurfing The safest and most popular windsurfing areas in city waters are south of town at Hobie Island and Virginia Key on Key Biscayne. The best windsurfing on Miami Beach is at 1st Street, just north of the Government Cut jetty, and at 21st Street. You can also windsurf at Lummus Park at 10th Street and in the vicinity of 3rd, 14th, and 21st streets. Lifeguards discourage windsurfing from 79th to 87th streets.

Sailboards Miami, on Hobie Island, just past the tollbooth for the Rickenbacker Causeway to Key Biscayne, rents windsurfing equipment. *Key Biscayne, tel. 305/361–7245. Cost: $17 per hr, $95 for 10 hrs; 2-hr lesson: $39. Open daily 10–5:30.*

Spectator Sports

Greater Miami boasts franchises in all major-league sports—baseball, basketball, football, and ice hockey—plus top-rated events in boat racing, jai alai, and tennis. In addition to contacting the addresses below directly, you can get tickets to major events from **Ticketmaster** (Dade County, tel. 305/358–5885; Broward County, tel. 305/523–3309; Palm Beach, tel. 407/839–3900) and charge them to your credit card. Generally you can find daily listings of local sports events in the sports section of the *Miami Herald.* Friday's Weekend section carries detailed schedules and coverage of spectator sports.

Activities of the annual **Orange Bowl** and **Junior Orange Bowl Festival** take place from early November to late February. Best known for its King Orange Jamboree Parade and the Federal Express/Orange Bowl Football Classic, the festival also includes two tennis tournaments: the Rolex–Orange Bowl International Tennis Tournament, for top amateur tennis players 18 and under, and an international tournament for players 14 and under. The Junior Orange Bowl Festival is the world's largest youth festival, with more than 20 events between November and January, including sports, cultural, and performing arts activities. The showcase event is the HealthSouth/Junior Orange Bowl Parade, held in downtown Coral Gables.

Auto Racing **Hialeah Speedway,** the Greater Miami area's only independent raceway, holds stock-car races on a ⅛-mile asphalt oval in a 5,000-seat stadium. Five divisions of stock cars run weekly. The Marion Edwards, Jr., Memorial Race for late-model stock cars is held in November. The speedway is on U.S. 27, ¼ mile east of the Palmetto Expressway (Route 826). *3300 W. Okeechobee Rd., Hialeah, tel. 305/821–6644. Admission: $10 ages 13 and over, special events $12. Open late Jan.–early Dec., Sat.; gates open at 5, racing 7–11.*

The **Toyota Grand Prix of Miami** is typically held in February or March on a 1.9-mile, E-shape track in downtown Miami, south of MacArthur Causeway and east of Biscayne Boulevard. Drivers race for three hours; the driver completing the most laps wins. Contact Miami Motor Sports, Inc. (1110 Brickell Ave., Suite 206, Miami 33131, tel. 305/379–5660 for information or 305/379–7223 for tickets).

Baseball The **Florida Marlins** (100 N.E. 3rd Ave., Fort Lauderdale 33301, tel. 305/626–7400) begin their fourth season in 1996 in the Eastern Division of the National League. Home games are played at Joe Robbie Stadium—also home to the Miami Dolphins (*see* Football, *below*)— which is 16 miles northwest of downtown Miami, accessible from I–95 and Florida's Turnpike. On game days the Metro-Dade Transit Agency (tel. 305/638–6700) runs buses to the stadium.

Basketball The **Miami Heat** (Miami Arena, 701 Arena Blvd., Miami 33136-4102, tel. 305/577–4328), Miami's National Basketball Association franchise, plays home games November–April at the Miami Arena, a block east of Overtown Metrorail Station.

Dog Racing The Biscayne and Flagler greyhound tracks in Greater Miami divide the annual racing calendar. Check with the individual tracks for dates.

At the **Biscayne Greyhound Track,** greyhounds chase a mechanical rabbit around illuminated fountains in the track's infield. *320 N.W. 115th St., near I–95, Miami Shores, tel. 305/754–3484. Admission: $1 table seats and grandstand, $2 sports room, $3 clubhouse; parking: 50¢–$2.*

Flagler Greyhound Track, in the middle of Little Havana, is five minutes east of Miami International Airport off the Dolphin Expressway (Route 836) and Douglas Road (N.W. 37th Ave. and 7th St.). *401 N.W. 38th Ct., Miami, tel. 305/649–3000. Admission: $1, $3 clubhouse; parking: 50¢–$2.*

Football The **Miami Dolphins** of the National Football League play at state-of-the-art Joe Robbie Stadium—JRS, as the fans call it—which has 73,000 seats and a grass playing-field surface with built-in drainage under the sod to carry off rainwater. It's on a 160-acre site 16 miles northwest of downtown Miami, 1 mile south of the Dade-Broward county line, accessible from I–95 and Florida's Turnpike. On game days the Metro-Dade Transit Agency (tel. 305/638–6700) runs buses to the stadium. *Joe Robbie Stadium, 2269 N.W. 199th St., Miami 33056, tel. 305/620–2578. Box office open weekdays 10–6, also Sat. during season.*

The **University of Miami Hurricanes** (1 Hurricane Dr., Coral Gables 33146, tel. 305/284–2655), perennial contenders for top collegiate ranking, play their home games at downtown Orange Bowl Stadium (1400 N.W. 4th St., Miami) September through November.

Horse Racing **Calder Race Course,** opened in 1971, is Florida's largest glass-enclosed, air-conditioned sports facility. Calder accordingly has an unusually extended season, from late May to early January—though it's a good idea to call the track for specific starting and wrap-up dates. Each year between November and early January, Calder holds the Tropical Park Derby for three-year-olds. The track is on the Dade-Broward county line near I–95 and the Hallandale Beach Boulevard exit, ¾ mile from Joe Robbie Stadium. *21001 N.W. 27th Ave., Miami, tel. 305/625–1311. Admission: $2, $4 clubhouse; parking: $1–$3. Gates open at 11, racing 1–5:30.*

A superb setting for thoroughbred racing, **Hialeah Park** has 228 acres of meticulously landscaped grounds surrounding paddocks and a clubhouse built in a classic French-Mediterranean style. Since it opened in 1925, Hialeah Park has survived hurricanes and now seems likely to survive even changing demographics, as the racetrack crowd has steadily moved north and east. Racing dates are usually March–May. The park is open year-round for free sightseeing, during which you can explore the gardens and admire the park's breeding flock of 800 Cuban flamingos. Metrorail's Hialeah Station is on the grounds. *2200 E. 4th Ave., Hialeah, tel. 305/885–8000. Admission: weekdays $1 grandstand, $2 clubhouse; weekends $2 grandstand, $4 clubhouse; parking: $1–$4. Gates open at 10:30, racing 1–5:30.*

Ice Hockey The **Florida Panthers** (Miami Arena, 701 Arena Blvd., Miami 33136-4102, tel. 305/577–4328) made the playoffs in their inaugural season in the National Hockey League. They play their third season in 1995–96 at the Miami Arena, one block east of Overtown Metrorail Station.

Jai Alai Built in 1926, the **Miami Jai-Alai Fronton,** a mile east of the airport, is the oldest fronton in America. Each evening it presents 13 games—14 on Friday and Saturday—some singles, some doubles. This game, invented in the Basque region of northern Spain, is the world's fastest. Jai-alai balls, called pelotas, have been clocked at speeds exceeding 170 miles per hour. The game is played in a 176-foot-long court called a fronton. Players climb the walls to catch the ball in a cesta—a woven basket—with an attached glove. You can bet on a team to win or on the order in which teams will finish. Dinner is available. *3500 N.W. 37th Ave., Miami, tel. 305/633–6400. Admission: $1, $3 reserved seats, $5 Courtview Club. Open Mon., Wed., Fri., Sat. noon–5 and 7–midnight; Tues., Thurs., Sun. 7–midnight.*

Tennis The **Lipton Championships** (7300 Crandon Blvd., Key Biscayne, tel. 305/442–3367), a 10-day spring tournament at the 64-acre Tennis Center at Crandon Park, is one of the largest in the world in terms of attendance and, with $4.1 million in prize money in 1995, was fifth-largest in purse. It's played in a new permanent stadium that seats 7,500 for big events.

Where to Eat on a Budget

The good news for budget-minded travelers is that the best—and most abundant—of Miami's affordable places to eat are, like the most affordable places to stay, on South Beach. From diners to sidewalk cafés to full-service restaurants, South Beach entrepreneurs have figured out how to feed the hip crowds, many of whom are low on cash, without going broke. And at these restaurants, the wait staff is often so friendly and non-condescending that you'll feel good about leaving a generous tip.

But you'll find inexpensive choices all over the Miami area. Miami is full of refugees from around the world, who have opened every imaginable kind of ethnic restaurant. Thus Miami offers not just Latin fare but dishes distinctive to Spain, Cuba, Nicaragua, and other Hispanic countries; not just Asian food but specialties of China, India, Thailand, Vietnam, and other Asian cultures. And don't neglect American fare just because it's not "foreign." In recent years the city has gained eminence for the distinctive cuisine introduced by chefs who have migrated north from the tropics and here combine fresh, natural foods—especially seafoods—with classically inspired dedication. Dining is definitely one of the signs of Miami's coming of age.

Coconut **Cafe Tu Tu Tango.** Local artists set up their easels in the rococo-
Grove modern arcades of this eclectic café-lounge on the second story of the
$$ highly popular CocoWalk. It's as if a bunch of imaginative kids were let loose on every surface. The end result: You'll be blown away, whether you sit indoors or out. Outside offers some of the best people-watching in the South. Inside, beneath ceiling fans in the oak-floored dining room, guests at the more than 250 seats graze on chips, dips, breads, and spreads. House specials include frittatas,

crab cakes, *picadillo empanadas* (spicy ground beef served with cilantro sour cream), and chicken and shrimp orzo paella, all to be enjoyed with some of the best sangria in the city. A few wines are also available, none of which costs too much. *3015 Grand Ave. (CocoWalk), tel. 305/529–2222. No reservations. Dress: casual but neat. AE, MC, V.*

$ Green Streets Cafe. In the village that started Miami's sidewalk café revival, this is *the* sidewalk café. It sits across Main Highway from the Barnacle and puts out eclectic international food. Breakfast is available daily to 3, and there are big choices among pastas, pizzas, and salads. Though seats inside are suitable for an infrequent cold winter morning, Groveites prefer to sit outside beneath the umbrellas. Everything is also available to go. *3110 Commodore Plaza, tel. 305/567–0662. No reservations. Dress: casual. AE, DC, MC, V.*

Coral Gables
$$ Coral Gables Executive Club. Atop the stunning Aztec-style 550
★ Building, with big windows overlooking tree-filled Coral Gables, is the most affordable prime luncheon place in metropolitan Miami. It's a club in name only; there's no membership. Elevators of burled-wood paneling lift you from the smartest-looking office-building lobby in town to an equally lovely setting of Asian silk murals, fresh flowers and palms, and outdoor terraces with terra-cotta pools. It looks like the kind of place where $10 tips would be flourished for window tables, but the prices are actually quite reasonable—the three-course daily specials run about $12.50. The à la carte menu features lots of luncheon salads (Asian steak with sesame-oil dressing, fresh Florida lobster, Mexican chicken), sandwiches, and such other entrées as honey basil chicken and salmon with saffron sauce and pasta. Unfortunately, it's only open until 3 PM. *550 Biltmore Way, tel. 305/447–9299. Reservations accepted. Dress: casual but neat. AE, DC, MC, V. Closed weekends, holidays. No dinner.*

$$ Darbar. Owner Bobby Puri's impeccably arranged Darbar (Punjabi
★ for "Royal Court") is the glory of Miami's Indian restaurants. Although small, it reigns with authenticity, down to the portraits of turbaned Puri ancestors, kings, and princes. Flavors rise as if in a dance from the *bangan bharta*, a dish of eggplant skinned and mashed with onions, tomatoes, herbs, and spices and baked in a tandoor. The limited menu's focus is on northern Indian or frontier cuisine, although there are also curries from different regions and *biryani* specialties prepared with basmati rice and garnished with boiled egg, tomato, nuts, and raisins. Among the northern Indian and Khyber Pass specialties, you'll find various kebabs, tandoori platters, and *tikkas*—pieces of chicken or lamb marinated in yogurt and spices and cooked tandoori style. Everything, including the unusual Indian breads, is cooked to order. *276 Alhambra Circle, tel. 305/448–9691. Reservations advised. Dress: casual but neat. AE, DC, MC, V. Closed lunch Sun.*

$$ Rodeo Grill. Skewers aloft, waiters at the imaginative Rodeo Grill race about (just hope they don't trip!), ready to carve off hunks and slices of 10 kinds of meats. The philosophy at this novel 180-seat restaurant in the heart of downtown Coral Gables seems to be "Eat 'til you drop." The idea comes from *rodizio*, a Portuguese word referring to a continuous feed—"rodeo" is an easy-to-pronounce corruption that makes you think "meat"—and in southern Brazil, where they're big meat eaters, that means beef ribs, chicken, lamb, London broil, pork, sausage, and turkey, with sides of rice, potatoes, fried yucca, and a big salad bar. If you have room for dessert you might want to split an order of *quindim*, a cake-and-custard combination made with coconuts and eggs. Restaurateur Tito Valiente, a native of São Paulo and former owner of the largest electronics store on Flagler Street, and his wife, Teresa, have made the Rodeo Grill a great favorite among the 40,000 Brazilians who live in Dade County, as well as with other locals and hordes of visiting Brazilians. The dining room is filled with mostly whimsical Brazilian art, much of it for sale through the adjacent gallery. *2121 Ponce de León Blvd., tel. 305/447–6336. Weekend reservations advised. Dress: casual but neat. AE, D, DC, MC, V. No lunch Sun.*

$ **Bugatti, The Art of Pasta.** Though it's short on looks, this storefront restaurant just below Miracle Mile, in the heart of the Gables, is long on value. Three-course pasta dinners—with sauces that range from classic pestos and marinaras to brandied leek and tomato sauce and smoked salmon cream—can be had for $11–$14. For $2–$3 more, pasta comes stuffed with a variety of meats, cheese, chicken curry, or lobster. Pizzas are imaginatively topped: One has shrimp; another has ricotta, sautéed onions, gorgonzola cheese, arugula, and walnuts. The menu also features wonderful gnocchi (potato dumplings), soups and salads, and such desserts as *zabaione freddo* (chilled wine and Italian dipping cookies). *2504 Ponce de León Blvd., tel. 305/441–2545. No reservations. Dress: casual but neat. AE, DC, MC, V. Closed Thanksgiving, Dec. 25, Jan. 1. No lunch Sun.*

$ **Jones Meats & Delicatessen.** At noontime everybody in downtown Gables who wants a quick lunch hits this landmark meat market on restaurant row. You line up at the meat counter to order fresh grilled chicken breasts; bagels filled with prosciutto, liverwurst, and pastrami; cold shrimp plates; and smoked salmon platters. Then sit in the little adjoining deli dining room amid a mix of secretaries and the international set. There's always a soup of the day, sandwiches are big, and coffee's only 55¢. Help yourself to drinks from the cooler. It's not fancy, but it's definitely affordable. *127 Giralda Ave., tel. 305/444–6183. No reservations. Dress: casual. No credit cards. Closed Sun., holidays. No dinner.*

$ **LB's Eatery.** Town and gown meet at this sprout-laden haven a half block from the University of Miami's baseball stadium. Kitschy food-related posters cover the walls of this relaxed restaurant with low prices. There are no waiters: You order at the counter and pick up your food when called. Vegetarians thrive on LB's salads and daily meatless entrées, such as lasagna and moussaka. The place is famous for Saturday-night lobster—if you plan to come after 8, call ahead to reserve one. Other specialties include barbecued baby-back ribs, lime chicken, croissant sandwiches, and carrot cake. *5813 Ponce de León Blvd., tel. 305/661–7091. No reservations. Dress: casual. D, MC, V. Closed Sun., holidays.*

¢ **Biscayne–Miracle Mile Cafeteria.** In the heart of downtown Coral Gables's Miracle Mile shopping district, this cafeteria has been dishing out lunch and dinner since 1946. A dozen or so entrées are offered daily, but no beer or wine is served. Service is buffet-style, although waiters will carry your tray for a tip. *147 Miracle Mile, tel. 305/449–9005. No reservations. Dress: casual. No credit cards. Closed Dec. 25.*

Splurge **Didier's.** After more than a year's hiatus when the building their res-
★ taurant occupied was sold from under them, the three brothers Colongette have reestablished their corner of Provence in Coral Gables. Didier (the business brother), Olivier (the host), and Thierry (the chef) have reassembled the elements that earned them their fame. The new restaurant is larger, dividing 120 seats among three rooms with a sunny French style that's distinct from Florida's own. Flower boxes with seasonal blooms show through the eyelet-curtained windows, tulips brighten tables in spring, and floral embellishment continues on menus. Chair seats are straw, floors terracotta tile, and walls white stucco. Service is informed and attentive. For starters, choose fresh basil soup or snails cooked in clay pots with garlic butter. Follow that up with a seafood entrée, such as bouillabaisse; a free-range chicken marinated in rosemary and served with wild mushrooms and glazed shallots; or roasted rack of lamb with fine herbs and fava beans with a fresh mint sauce. Desserts include crème brûlée, apple tart, and a strawberry with passion fruit sabayon. All is wonderful and affordable for the quality.

2530 Ponce de León Blvd., tel. 305/567–2444. Reservations accepted. Dress: casual but neat. AE, DC, MC, V. Closed Sun. No lunch Sat.

Downtown Miami
$$

East Coast Fisheries. This family-owned restaurant and retail fish market on the Miami River features fresh Florida seafood from its own 38-boat fleet in the Keys. From tables along the second-floor balcony, watch the cooks prepare your dinner in the open kitchen below. Specialties include a complimentary fish-pâté appetizer, blackened pompano with owner David Swartz's personal herb-and-spice recipe, lightly breaded fried grouper, and a homemade Key lime pie so rich it tastes like ice cream. *360 W. Flagler St., tel. 305/373–5515. Reservations accepted for parties of 6 or more. Dress: casual. AE, DC, MC, V. Beer and wine only.*

$$
Las Tapas. Overhung with dried meats and enormous show breads, this popular spot with terra-cotta floors and an open kitchen offers a lot of imaginative creations. Tapas ("little dishes") give you a variety of tastes during a single meal. Specialties include *la tostada* (smoked salmon on melba toast, topped with a dollop of sour cream, baby eels, black caviar, capers, and chopped onion) and *pincho de pollo a la plancha* (grilled chicken brochette marinated in brandy and onions). Also available are soups, salads, sandwiches, and standard-size dinners. *Bayside Marketplace, 401 Biscayne Blvd., tel. 305/ 372–2737. Reservations required for large parties. Dress: casual. AE, D, DC, MC, V.*

$$
Los Ranchos. Carlos Somoza, owner of this beautiful bay-side establishment, is a nephew of Nicaragua's late president Anastasio Somoza. Carlos, who came to south Florida in 1979, sustains a tradition begun more than 30 years ago in Managua, when the original Los Ranchos instilled in Nicaraguan palates a love of Argentine-style beef—lean, grass-fed tenderloin with *chimichurri,* a green sauce of chopped parsley, garlic, oil, vinegar, and other spices. Nicaragua's own sauces are a tomato-based marinara and the fiery *cebollitas encurtidas,* with slices of jalapeño pepper and onion pickled in vinegar. Specialties include chorizo, *cuajada con maduro* (skim cheese with fried bananas), and shrimp sautéed in butter and topped with creamy jalapeño sauce. Don't look for veggies or brewed decaf, but you do get live entertainment at lunch and dinner. *Bayside Marketplace, 401 Biscayne Blvd., tel. 305/375–8188 or 305/375–0666; 125 S.W. 107th Ave., Little Managua, tel. 305/221–9367; Kendall Town & Country, 8505 Mills Dr., Kendall, tel. 305/596–5353; the Falls, 8888 S.W. 136th St., Suite 303, South Miami, tel. 305/238–6867; 2728 Ponce de León Blvd., Coral Gables, tel. 305/446–0050. Reservations accepted. Dress: casual. AE, DC, MC, V. Closed Good Fri., Dec. 24, Jan. 1.*

$$
★
Tony Chan's Water Club. One of a pair of outstanding new Chinese restaurants on the mainland, this beautiful dining room just off the lobby of the high-rise Grand Prix Hotel looks onto a bay-side marina. The long room is filled with art and chrome modern rather than stock Chinese. From the care that servers take in dispensing food to the delicate flavorings and fresh broccoli, execution is noteworthy. Add to that a menu of more than 100 appetizers and entrées. Start with a minced quail tossed with bamboo shoots and mushrooms wrapped in lettuce leaves, or maybe abalone and scallops in chicken broth. Then you might try a seafood spectacular with shrimp, conch, scallops, fish cake, and crabmeat tossed with broccoli in a bird's nest, pork chops sprinkled with green pepper in a black bean–garlic sauce, or any of innumerable beef, vegetable, tofu, and rice and noodles dishes. *1717 N. Bayshore Dr., tel. 305/374–8888. Reservations accepted. Dress: casual but neat. AE, MC, V. No lunch weekends.*

¢
Jamaican Restaurant. This open-air Jamaican restaurant, open for breakfast and lunch, is so authentic, you'll think you're in Kingston. The jukebox pours reggae onto Miami Avenue while waitresses pour the native beer, Red Stripe, which goes well with the oxtail stew or curried goat. Choose counter or table seating. *245 N. Miami Ave.,*

tel. 305/375–0156. No reservations. Dress: casual. No credit cards. No dinner.

Five Points, Miami
$

Mykonos. A Miami fixture since 1973, this 74-seat restaurant brightens the intersection at Five Points in the Roads section of town with a beautiful mural of the Aegean. That sweet sense of faraway islands carries inside in a sparkling blue-and-white setting dressed up with Greek travel posters. Specialties include gyros, moussaka, marinated lamb and chicken, calamari and octopus sautéed in wine and onions, and sumptuous Greek salads thick with feta cheese and briny olives. Vegetarian moussaka, eggplant rolls, lasagna, and a Greek-style omelet are new to the menu. *1201 Coral Way, tel. 305/856–3140. Reservations accepted for dinner. Dress: casual. AE, DC, MC, V. Closed July 4, Thanksgiving, Dec. 24–25, Dec. 31, Jan. 1. No lunch Sun.*

Kendall (Southwest Suburb)
$

Shorty's Bar-B-Q. Shorty Allen opened his barbecue restaurant in 1951 in a log cabin, and this place has since become a tradition; a second location opened in 1989 in Davie, in southeast Broward County. Parents bring their teenage children here to show them where Mom and Dad ate on their honeymoon. Huge fans circulate fresh air through the single, screened dining room, where meals are served family-style at long picnic tables. On the walls hang an assortment of cowboy hats, horns, saddles, an ox yoke, and heads of boar and caribou. Specialties include barbecued pork ribs, chicken, and pork steak slow-cooked over hickory logs and drenched in Shorty's own warm, spicy sauce, and side orders of tangy baked beans with big chunks of pork, corn on the cob, and coleslaw. *9200 S. Dixie Hwy., tel. 305/670–7732; 5989 S. University Dr., Davie, tel. 305/680–9900 or 305/944–0348 from Miami. No reservations. Dress: casual. MC, V at Davie location. Closed Thanksgiving, Dec. 25.*

Key Biscayne
$$

Sundays on the Bay. This is a rarity among Miami-area restaurants—a free-standing waterfront bar and restaurant. You can tie up your boat and step onto the big outdoor deck under canvas or sit inside surrounded by aqua and pink at banquettes and free-standing tables. The best deal is the 60-item Sunday brunch, served 10:30 to 3:30, but the restaurant also serves lunch and dinner daily—seafood, salads, pasta—as well as drinks. *5420 Crandon Blvd., tel. 305/361–6777. Reservations accepted. Dress: casual but neat. AE, D, DC, MC, V.*

Little Haiti
$

Chez Moy. A fixture in its neighborhood, Chez Moy is utterly without pretense about being anywhere but in an outpost of Haiti. The music is Haitian, the TV in the corner plays Haitian programs, everyone speaks Creole, and the food is as authentic as on the rue Delmas in Port-au-Prince. Seating is outside on a shaded patio or in a pleasant room with oak tables and high-back chairs. Specialties include *grillot* (pork boiled then fried with spices), fried or boiled fish, stewed goat, and conch with garlic and hot pepper. Try a tropical fruit drink such as sweetsop (also called *anon* or *cachiman*) or soursop (also called *guanabana* or *corrosol*), blended with milk and sugar, and sweet-potato pie for dessert. *1 N.W. 54th St., tel. 305/757–5056. Reservations accepted. Dress: casual. No credit cards. No smoking.*

$
★

Hy-Vong Vietnamese Cuisine. Beer-savvy Kathy Manning has introduced a half-dozen top brews since taking over in 1989 (Double Grimbergen, Moretti, and Spaten, among them), and magic continues to pour forth from the tiny kitchen of this plain little restaurant with its 36 seats packed close together. Come before 7 to avoid a wait. Favorites include spring rolls (a Vietnamese version of an egg roll, with ground pork, cellophane noodles, and black mushrooms wrapped in homemade rice paper), whole fish panfried with *nuoc man* (a garlic-lime fish sauce), and thinly sliced pork, barbecued with sesame seeds and fish sauce, served with bean sprouts, rice noodles, and slivers of carrots, almonds, and peanuts. *3458 S.W. 8th*

St., tel. 305/446–3674. Reservations accepted for parties of 5 or more. Dress: casual. No credit cards. No smoking. Closed Mon., American and Vietnamese/Chinese New Years, 2 wks in Aug. No lunch.

Little Havana
$$
★

Casa Panza. Decorated with a tile-countered tapas bar, flamenco dolls, Spanish posters, and hanging hams, chorizos, and chilis, this little cavelike hideaway clicks with the authenticity of castanets, bringing a trace of Spain to the main drag of Little Havana. Tuesday and Thursday evenings, the tiny corner stage showcases a Spanish folkloric show, and the businesspeople over from Madrid or Barcelona relax as if at home. Food is made from scratch: tapas and soups to start, followed by big portions of shellfish, fish, the favored rice stews with clams or shrimp, paella for two, and meats. You can't do better than a big, bubbling bowl of codfish in green sauce. Special orders are accommodated, and there are very affordable selections of Spanish wines and sangria. Traditional desserts (lemon or vanilla cremes, puddings of the region) finish meals off nicely. Be warned that lunch service doesn't start until 1. *1620 S.W. 8th St., tel. 305/643–5343. Reservations required. Dress: casual but neat. MC, V. Closed Sun.*

$

Islas Canarias. Since 1976 this has been a gathering place for Cuban poets, pop-music stars, and media personalities. Wall murals depict a Canary Islands street scene (the grandfather of the current owner, Santiago Garcia, came from Tenerife). The menu includes such Canary Islands dishes as baked lamb, ham hocks with boiled potatoes, and tortilla *Española* (Spanish omelet with onions and chorizo), as well as Cuban standards including *palomilla* (a flat beefsteak) and fried kingfish. Don't miss the three superb varieties of homemade chips—potato, malanga, and plantain. Islas Canarias has another location in Westchester. *285 N.W. Unity Blvd. (N.W. 27th Ave.), tel. 305/649–0440; Coral Way and S.W. 137th Ave., Westchester, tel. 305/559–6666. No reservations. Dress: casual. No credit cards. Closes at 6 on Dec. 24 and Dec. 31.*

$

Versailles. WE ASK THAT GUESTS COMING JUST TO TALK PLEASE DO SO OUTSIDE reads a sign in Spanish, which should tell you something about this restaurant—*the* most popular place in all Miami since 1971. There's a roar of rapid-fire Spanish both inside and out—staccato at the counter and redoubled at the tables inside, where walls of etched mirrors bounce the sound around. For a total sensory experience, come for a full meal, though many come just to snack. Most of the servers don't speak English; you order by pointing to a number on either the English or Spanish menu. Specialties include palomilla; *ropa vieja* (literally, old clothes), a shredded-beef dish in tomato sauce; and arroz con pollo (chicken and yellow rice). *3555 S.W. 8th St., tel. 305/445–7614. Reservations accepted. Dress: casual but neat. AE, D, DC, MC, V.*

Miami Beach
$$

Da Leo. Tables from this little restaurant spill all over the mall, staying full thanks to consistently good food at prices only half what the trendy places charge. The volume keeps the mood festive and the standards high. Inside you won't find youthful in-line skaters, but you will be amazed by the art, which so completely covers the walls you might think the canvases provide structural support. The look is ancient Roman town house (though owner Leonardo Marchini hails from Lucca), with high ceiling fans, banquettes along one wall, and wainscoting along the other. Pastas, a few fish, a couple of veal, and a fowl choice make up most of the entrées. The house salad is shiny with olive oil lavished over fresh garden veggies served in a big bowl. *819 Lincoln Rd. Mall, tel. 305/674–0350. No reservations. Dress: casual but neat. AE, DC, MC, V. Closed some holidays. No lunch weekends.*

$$

Granny Feelgood's. "Granny" is a shrewd gentleman named Irving Field, who caters to health-conscious lawyers, office workers, and cruise-ship crews downtown and to locals and tourists on Lincoln

Road on the Beach. Specialties include chicken salad with raisins, apples, and cinnamon; spinach fettuccine with pine nuts; grilled tofu; apple crumb cake; and carrot cake. *647 Lincoln Rd. Mall, tel. 305/673–0408; 190 S.E. 1st Ave., Miami, tel. 305/358–6233; 111 N.W. 1st St., Miami, tel. 305/579–2104. No reservations. Dress: casual. AE, MC, V. No smoking. Closed Sun. downtown. No dinner.*

$$ **Mezzanotte.** Sometime between 6 and 10 each night, the big square room with the square bar in the middle transforms from an empty catering hall to a New Year's Eve party. Trendoids call for their *capellini* with fresh tomato and basil; calamari in clam juice, garlic, and red wine; or scaloppine with mushroom, pepper, and white wine—everything a gift from tomato heaven—and then top it off with their *dolci*: fresh napoleon, chocolate mousse, or tiramisù. Chic but not intimate, Mezzanotte has been known since 1988 for fine food at moderate prices, but watch out for the coffee at $2.25 a pop! *1200 Washington Ave., tel. 305/673–4343. Reservations accepted for parties of 5 or more. Dress: casual but neat. AE, DC, MC, V. Closed Thanksgiving. No lunch.*

$$ **Norma's on the Beach.** Put this wonderful reggae-style hole-in-the-
★ wall near the top of your list. The interior is small, but a wall of mirrors makes it look larger and tables outside on the mall add seating. Color bursts from seat cushions and cut-tin Haitian tap taps (jitneys) on the walls (all the art is for sale). Instead of bud vases on tables, there are entire palm trees in pots on the floor. Adding to the mood is Thursday evening's Brazilian music, Friday's anything-goes group, and Saturday's jazz duo. The cuisine melds French finesse with Caribbean seasonings. Dishes might include Red Stripe–beer baby-back ribs with Appleton rum glaze; Rasta chicken breast with *callaloo* (West Indian spinach), cream cheese, and roasted sweet peppers in a white-wine sauce; or pan-sautéed pompano with tropical rum banana sauce. Hey! This is fun. *646 Lincoln Rd. Mall, tel. 305/532–2809. Reservations accepted. Dress: casual. AE, D, DC, MC, V. Closed Mon., Thanksgiving, Dec. 25.*

$$ **Pineapples.** Art-filled, tropical pink-and-green café seating occupies half of this popular mid-Beach neighborhood emporium; on the other side of the wall is a retail health foods store. Daily seafood, chicken, and vegetarian specials add variety to longtime favorites: lasagna filled with tofu and mushrooms, spinach fettuccine with feta cheese, and a good variety of salads. Organic wine and beer are newly added. *530 Arthur Godfrey Rd., tel. 305/532–9731. No reservations. Dress: casual. AE, MC, V. No smoking.*

$$ **Thai Toni.** Since 1989, Thai silks, bronze Buddhas, dramatic ceiling drapes, private dining alcoves, and two raised platforms for those who want to dine seated on cushions have set this exceptional Thai restaurant apart from everything trendy in the neighborhood. The mellow Thai Singha beer sets you up for the spicy jumping squid appetizer prepared with chili paste and hot pepper or the hot hot pork. Choose from a large variety of inexpensive noodle, fried-rice, and vegetarian dishes or such traditional entrées as beef and broccoli, basil duck, or hot-and-spicy deep-fried whole snapper garnished with basil leaves and mixed vegetables. Desserts are routine, but the homemade lemonade is distinctly tart. *890 Washington Ave., tel. 305/538–8424. Reservations accepted. Dress: casual but neat. AE, MC, V. Closed Thanksgiving, Dec. 25. No lunch.*

$ **11th Street Diner.** A poor man's News Cafe (*see below*), this is anoth-
★ er place to see and be seen while chowing down affordably. There's a big line for Sunday breakfast, when half the tables seem to be filled by models working their cellular phones. Still it retains the folksiness of its origins as a 1948 stainless-steel diner, trucked down from Wilkes Barre, Pennsylvania, and set on the site of a former gas station. Sit at the counter, in one of the vintage leatherette booths, or on white wicker seats on the patio. At the full bar under a big '30s-style mural, you can order food and an Anchor Steam. Down-home cooking—hot turkey sandwiches drenched in thick gravy, meat

loaf, baby-back ribs, honey-baked ham—is joined by some new-age dishes, such as marinated dolphin, tofu, and veggies. From 11 to 4, you can get a cup of soup and either a half sandwich or house salad for $3.95. Breakfasts and nightly main course specials, served 5 to midnight, are also great buys. And there are lots of sugar shocks for dessert (pecan pie, a brownie hot-fudge sundae, cheesecake, cinnamon buns). The place is open 24 hours, and the divine smell of fresh-brewed hazelnut decaf coffee is always in the air. Note: 15% is added to bills. *11th St. and Washington Ave., tel. 305/534–6373. No reservations. Dress: casual. AE, D, DC, MC, V.*

$ **Gertrude's.** If a great cup of coffee is what you crave, this will be your high. What you get with it is a high-ceilinged coffeehouse atmosphere with arty walls and a guaranteed freshly ground bean bouquet. There are some 20 tables inside, 20 out on the mall. Before your coffee, try a soup, salad, or sandwich (turkey breast on sourdough, garden burger with trimmings, grilled chicken with tarragon mayo on herb rye). Desserts include outrageous chocolate cakes, berry tarts, and pies—many choices either fat-free or sugar-free—and there's a good selection of affordable wines by the bottle or glass. Coffees—Kona, mocha java, Hawaiian coconut, and macadamia nut to name but a few of the 20 or so choices, many also in decaf—are ground on the spot and individually brewed in your cup. Espresso, cappuccino, and tea are also offered. *826 Lincoln Rd. Mall, tel. 305/538–6929. No reservations. Dress: casual. AE, DC, MC, V. Closed Dec. 25.*

$ **Lulu's.** The logo features a fat beribboned pig eyeing a steaming platter, a hint of the pig paraphernalia and secondhand-store trash—old-time Coke signs and discarded license plates—that decorate this hip, colorful, sophomoric spot. Come here if you want to pig out on southern fried cooking: barbecued pork, BLTs, pork chops, and authentic lumpy mashed potatoes. For non-pig eaters, there are salads, all kinds of sandwiches (crab cake, fried catfish, smoked marlin salad, plus an Elvis fried peanut butter 'n' banana), and such main courses as boneless chicken breast, chicken-fried steak, and strip steak. You sit at cafeteria-style tables with red-and-white-check tablecloths downstairs and on the mezzanine; the upstairs room, favored by the T-shirt crowd, is overwhelmed with Elvis memorabilia. January 18 and August 16—the King's birth and death days—are big events at Lulu's, and everybody dresses up Elvis-style. Though the place is zany, the food's good. *1053 Washington Ave., tel. 305/532–6147. No reservations. Dress: casual. MC, V.*

$ **News Cafe.** This is the hippest joint on Ocean Drive. Owners Mark Soyka, who trained on the cosmopolitan beach scene in Tel Aviv, and Jeffrey Dispenzieri, from New York, are right on the money. Quick, friendly servers don't hurry guests who have come to schmooze or intellects deep in a Tolstoy novel picked out of the book rack. A raw bar has been added in back with 15 stools, but most visitors prefer sitting outside to feel the salt breeze and look at whom they're not with. Offering a little of this and a little of that—bagels, pâtés, chocolate fondue—the café attracts a big all-the-time crowd, with people coming in for a snack, a light meal, or an aperitif and, invariably, to indulge in the people parade. It's open 24 hours. *800 Ocean Dr., tel. 305/538–6397. No reservations. Dress: casual. AE, DC, MC, V.*

$ **Puerto Sagua Restaurant.** On the back wall, a 3-D mural shows the original Puerto Sagua, in old Havana on the Number 43 bus route. The owners jumped the chaos there in '62 and headed for South Beach, where they now serve the same delicious black beans and rice 365 days a year. If you're looking for atmosphere, the best place to sit is at the counter, where the gab's as quick as the service. Also on the menu are fried red snapper, pork fillet, and pickled kingfish, along with a *cafecito* (small coffee) for $1, sangria, and Spanish wines and cider. Don't miss it (or the convenience of the new artsy parking lot across the street). *700 Collins Ave., tel. 305/673–1115. No reservations. Dress: casual. AE, DC, MC, V.*

$ **13th Street Cafe.** This little Caribbean neighborhood café adds sparkle to a side street with colorful fruit sculptures, a colored-chalk blackboard, and ceiling drops with world-beat drawings. A few sidewalk stools and pass-throughs make it easy for locals to nosh without missing the action on the street. The menu has mostly sandwiches, pita pizzas, and pasta salads, though there's always a fixed-price dinner special—maybe a spinach fettuccine Alfredo or a baked turkey dish, plus salad and dessert—for $6.95. There are lots of juices, coolers, and revitalizers, and bagels, brownies, and monster cookies stare back at anybody seated at the counter. Breakfast is served all day. *227 13th St., tel. 305/532–8336. No reservations. Dress: casual. No credit cards.*

$ **Titi's Tacos.** Next door to the very affordable Mango's hotel (*see* Budget Lodging, *above*) is this convivial spot for quality fajitas, tacos, enchiladas, and *pollo mole* (chicken cooked in poblano sauce) with rice and beans. Or try the shrimp sautéed with peppers and onions and served with tons of melted cheese, sour cream, and rice, and finish the meal off with flan or *tres leches* (a puddinglike concoction of whipped cream and evaporated and condensed milk). The owner, who is from Vera Cruz, has put together a very Caribbean-Mexican look—terra-cotta tiles, ceramic-tile tabletops, and lots of Mexican wall murals. Though Titi's has no liquor license, waitresses come in from Mango's, the Cuban café next door, to take drink orders. Breakfast is also offered. *900 Ocean Dr., tel. 305/672–8484. No reservations. Dress: casual. AE, D, DC, MC, V.*

$ **Van Dyke Cafe.** Mark Soyka's second restaurant has quickly attracted the artsy crowd, just as his News Cafe (*see above*) draws the fashion crowd. Of course, tourists like it too. It features the same style menu, but instead of facing south, this place, in the restored, 1924 Van Dyke Hotel, faces north and is shadier. Save the News Cafe for winter, the Van Dyke for summer. Three meals are served, and a 15% gratuity is included. *846 Lincoln Rd., tel. 305/534–3600. No reservations. Dress: casual. AE, DC, MC, V.*

$ **World Cafe.** If there's another way to do something, South Beach will find it. Here on the Lincoln Road Mall, food gets combined with furniture and crafts from around the globe. Mostly the displays and menus are Third World, and live nightly world-beat music adds to the global village ideal. Guests sit surrounded by Indian wood vases, Nigerian drums, and Indonesian batiks and dine on cuisine that's mainly Thai but with a natural-foods touch. So there's beef basil, green-curry chicken, and Thai stir-fry with shrimp and chicken as well as vegetarian spring rolls, vegetable *panang* curry (with coconut milk and peanuts), and vegetable stir-fry with tofu. Brown rice, available at all meals, is $1 extra. Desserts range from tiramisù and a Middle Eastern walnut roll to fruit crisp and home-baked cookies. It's a wonderful change of pace. *719 Lincoln Rd. Mall, tel. 305/534–9095. No reservations. Dress: casual. MC, V. Closed Thanksgiving, Dec. 25, Jan. 1.*

$ **WPA Restaurant & Bar.** "We think it's time again for WPA" is this restaurant's motto, and it has already done plenty for the public good just by reviving food service in this choice Deco building. Once Friedman's Bakery, it was one of the first restorations in South Beach and helped to ignite the Deco District comeback. The decor is didactically 1930s—high open-beam ceilings, a big labor mural in the Mexican socialist style, and a signature display case of ketchup, mustard, and a dozen varieties of spicy sauces. The menu features lots of grazing food: Tex-Mex dishes, egg rolls, potato skins, a few stir-fries and grills, plus sandwiches, salads (Greek, fruit, tostada), burgers, ribs, wings, pizzas, and pastas. *685 Washington Ave., tel. 305/534–1684. Reservations accepted. Dress: casual but neat. AE, D, DC, MC, V. No lunch weekends.*

¢ **Beehive Diner.** Though seating extends onto Lincoln Road Mall, the
★ real pleasure here is to be found behind the ornamental iron gates
that lead to the fountain and ceramic pond in front of the Courtyard
630 Shops. Cross the big bee pavement mural, like crossing the Yellow Brick Road to reach the Emerald City. You'll find a place that's
as much an art gallery as a restaurant, filled with work by local artists as well as plants. Take your pick of inside or courtyard tables,
and enjoy some of the most affordable food around, including a big
variety of specialties (chicken breast six different ways, meat loaf,
catfish, pizzas, pastas) starting at $6 and most well under $10.
Wednesday evening features a gay show, magic, and fire eating. *630
Lincoln Rd. Mall, tel. 305/538–7484. No reservations. Dress: casual. AE, D, DC, MC, V. Closed Dec. 24, Dec. 31. No lunch Sun.*

¢ **Muff'n Man.** Although 8 or 10 kinds of tasty sandwiches and homemade soups are served here, most people come for the baked goods.
Multiberry, apple, and cinnamon-raisin muffins, among others (all
$1.50); brownies; and cookies are baked here daily. The interior is
filled with Deco District photos and silk pillows, and it's next door to
the laundromat with the out-of-town papers, the racing sheet, and
*Variety. 234 12th St., tel. 305/538–6833. No reservations. Dress: ca-
sual. No credit cards. No dinner.*

Splurge **Osteria del Teatro.** This 20-table dining room is the culinary equiva-
★ lent of Pavarotti. Thanks to word of mouth of knowledgeable diner-
outers, this northern Italian restaurant is consistently full, and despite a tiny kitchen, the preparations are just as consistent. Orchids
grace the tables in the intimate, low-ceilinged, gray, gray, and gray
room with a laced canvas ceiling, deco lamps, and the most refined
clink and clatter along this remarkable restaurant row. Everything
comes carefully detailed, starting with large, unevenly sliced hunks
of homemade bread lightly toasted. Specialties included an appetizer of grilled Portobello mushroom topped with fontina cheese and
served over a bed of arugula with a green peppercorn–brandy
sauce, and among entrées, linguine sautéed with chunks of jumbo
shrimp, roasted peppers, capers, black olives, fresh diced tomato,
and equally fresh herbs in a tangy garlic–olive oil sauce. Make room
for dessert and coffee so you don't feel guilty lingering in this tiny
but special room. *1443 Washington Ave., tel. 305/538–7850. Reservations required. Dress: casual but neat. AE, DC, MC, V. Closed
Tues., Dec. 25, Jan. 1. No lunch.*

North Miami **Salty's Seafood.** As at Sundays on the Bay (*see above*), the view is
Beach everything at this waterfront bar and restaurant in Baker's
$$ Haulover Park. The best seating is outdoors, looking out on upper
Biscayne Bay, and the best items include seafood, pastas, and a
wide selection of salads at lunchtime. *10880 Collins Ave., tel. 305/
945–6065. Reservations accepted. Dress: casual but neat. AE, D,
DC, MC, V.*

$$ **Unicorn Village Restaurant & Marketplace.** Longtime owner Terry
★ Dalton sold the marketplace early in 1995 but has kept the restau-
rant, which remains far and away the top choice in its field in the
north end of the city. This 300-seat restaurant, now in its 16th year,
caters to vegetarian and nonvegetarian diners. In an outdoor setting of free-form ponds and fountains by a bayfront dock, or in the
plant-filled interior under three-story-high wood-beam ceilings,
guests enjoy *seitan* medallions (wheat meat in a mushroom gravy
sauce) and a line of homemade organic pizzas. Other favorites include spinach lasagna; a Tuscan vegetable sauté with Italian seasonings; grilled honey-mustard chicken; wok-barbecued shrimp; spicy
seafood cakes; fresh fish, poultry, and Coleman natural beef; and the
Unicorn's spring roll of uncooked veggies wrapped in thin rice paper
with cellophane noodles. Very popular are the early dinner specials—typically eight entrées with soup or salad, basket of rolls,
veggies, and coffee—offered 4:30–5:30 for up to $10.95. The
nondairy, fat-free chocolate-mocha cake is tasty, and there are or-

ganic cappuccinos. The adjacent 16,000-square-foot food market is the largest natural-foods source in Florida and features desserts baked on the premises. *3565 N.E. 207th St., tel. 305/933–8829. No reservations. Dress: casual. AE, MC, V. No smoking.*

The Arts and Nightlife

For information on what's happening around town, Greater Miami's English-language daily newspaper, the *Miami Herald*, publishes reliable reviews and comprehensive listings in its Weekend section on Friday and in the Lively Arts section on Sunday. Call ahead to confirm details.

If you read Spanish, check *El Nuevo Herald* (a Spanish version of the *Miami Herald*) or *Diario Las Américas* (the area's largest independent Spanish-language paper) for information on the Spanish theater and a smattering of general performing-arts news.

Another good source of information on the performing arts and nightspots is the calendar in *Miami Today*, a free weekly newspaper available each Thursday in downtown Miami, Coconut Grove, and Coral Gables. The best, most complete source is the *New Times*, a free weekly distributed throughout Dade County each Wednesday. Various tabloids reporting on Deco District entertainment and society come and go on Miami Beach. *Wire* reports on the gay community; *Ocean Drive* out-glosses everything else.

The free *Greater Miami Calendar of Events* is published twice a year by the Dade County Cultural Affairs Council (111 N.W. 1st St., Suite 625, Miami 33128, tel. 305/375–4634).

Guide to the Arts/South Florida is a pocket-size publication produced 10 times a year ($2 per issue, $15 per year) that covers all the cultural arts in Dade, Broward, and Palm Beach counties and is available from Kage Publications (3800 S. Ocean Dr., Hollywood 33019, tel. 305/456–9599).

Real Talk/WTMI (93.1 FM) provides classical concert information on its **Cultural Arts Line** (tel. 305/358–8000, ext. 9398), as well as on-air reports three times daily at 7:30 AM and 12:50 and 6:30 PM. WLVE (93.9 FM) sponsors an **Entertainment Line** (tel. 305/654–9436) with information on touring groups of all kinds except classical. **Blues Hot Line** (tel. 305/666–6656) lists local blues clubs and bars. **Jazz Hot Line** (tel. 305/382–3938) lists local jazz programs.

The Arts

Performing-arts aficionados in Greater Miami will tell you they survive quite nicely, despite the area's historic inability to support a county-based professional symphony orchestra. In recent years this community has begun to write a new chapter in its performing-arts history.

The New World Symphony, a unique advanced-training orchestra, begins its ninth season in 1996. The Miami City Ballet has risen rapidly to international prominence in its 10-year existence. The Florida Grand Opera ranks among America's largest and best, and a venerable chamber-music series brings renowned ensembles here to perform. Several churches and synagogues run classical-music series with international performers. In theater, Miami offers English-speaking audiences an assortment of professional, collegiate, and amateur productions of musicals, comedy, and drama. Spanish theater also is active. In the cinema world, the Miami Film Festival attracts more than 45,000 people annually to screenings of new films from all over the world—including some made here.

To order tickets for performing-arts events by telephone, call **Ticketmaster** (Dade County, tel. 305/358–5885; Broward County, tel. 305/523–3309; Palm Beach, tel. 407/839–3900) and charge tickets to a major credit card.

Performing Arts Centers

Colony Theater (1040 Lincoln Rd., Miami Beach 33139, tel. 305/674–1026), once a movie theater, has become a 465-seat, city-owned performing-arts center featuring dance, drama, music, and experimental cinema.

Dade County Auditorium (2901 W. Flagler St., Miami 33135, tel. 305/545–3395) satisfies patrons with 2,498 comfortable seats, good sight lines, and acceptable acoustics. Opera, concerts, and touring musicals are usually on the schedule.

Gusman Center for the Performing Arts (174 E. Flagler St., Miami 33131, tel. 305/372–0925), in downtown Miami, has 1,739 seats seemingly made for sardines—and the best acoustics in town. Concerts, ballet, and touring stage productions are seen here. An ornate former movie palace, the hall resembles a Moorish courtyard. Lights twinkle, starlike, from the ceiling.

Jackie Gleason Theater of the Performing Arts (TOPA) (1700 Washington Ave., Miami Beach 33139, tel. 305/673–7300) has finally brought its acoustics and visibility up to par for all 2,750 seats. The Broadway Series each year presents five or six major productions (or other performances); contact the box office (505 17th St., Miami Beach 33139, tel. 305/673–8300).

Theater

Acapai (6161 N.W. 22nd Ave., Miami 33142, tel. 305/758–3534), whose name stands for African Caribbean American Performing Artists, Inc., mounts productions year-round at various area stages.

Acme Acting Company (955 Alton Rd., Miami Beach 33139, tel. 305/372–9077) presents thought-provoking, on-the-edge theater by new playwrights in its winter and summer seasons.

Actor's Playhouse (280 Miracle Mile, Coral Gables 33134, tel. 305/444–9293) is a nine-year-old professional Equity company. Late in 1995, it moved into the renovated Miracle Theater but still presents adults' and children's productions year-round.

Area Stage (645 Lincoln Rd., Miami Beach 33139, tel. 305/673–8002) performs provocative off-Broadway-style productions throughout the year.

Coconut Grove Playhouse (3500 Main Hwy., Coconut Grove 33133, tel. 305/442–4000 for box office or 305/442–2662 for administrative office) stages Broadway-bound plays and musical reviews and experimental productions in its 1,100-seat main theater and 100-seat cabaret-style Encore Room. Parking is $2 in the day, $4 evenings.

The **Florida Shakespeare Festival** (2304 Salzedo Ave., Coral Gables 33134, tel. 305/446–1116) performs classic and contemporary theater with one Shakespeare production a year at the 200-seat Carrusel Theater (235 Alcazar Ave., Coral Gables).

Gold Coast Mime Company (905 Lincoln Rd., Miami Beach 33139, tel. 305/538–5500) performs an October–June season in the studios of the Miami City Ballet.

New Theatre (65 Almeria St., Coral Gables 33134, tel. 305/443–5909) showcases contemporary and classical plays.

Ring Theater (1380 Miller Dr., Coral Gables 33146, tel. 305/284–3355) is the 311-seat hall of the University of Miami's Department of Theatre Arts, where eight plays a year are performed.

Spanish Theater

Spanish theater prospers, although many companies have short lives. About 20 Spanish companies perform light comedy, puppetry, vaudeville, and political satire. To locate them, read the Spanish newspapers. When you call, be prepared for a conversation in Spanish—few box-office personnel speak English.

Prometeo (Miami-Dade Community College, New World Center Campus, 300 N.E. 2nd Ave., Miami 33132, tel. 305/237–3263), in its

23rd year, produces two major plays and holds many workshop productions. Admission is free.

Teatro de Bellas Artes (2173 S.W. 8th St., Miami 33135, tel. 305/325–0515), a 255-seat theater on Calle Ocho, Little Havana's main commercial street, presents eight Spanish plays and musicals year-round.

Music **Concert Association of Florida** (555 Hank Meyer Blvd. [17th St.], Miami Beach 33139, tel. 305/532–3491), a not-for-profit organization directed by Judith Drucker, is the South's largest presenter of classical artists.

Friends of Chamber Music (44 W. Flagler St., Miami 33130, tel. 305/372–2975) presents an annual series of chamber concerts by internationally known guest ensembles, such as the Beaux Arts Trio, the Tokyo Quartet, and the Juilliard String Quartet.

Gusman Concert Hall (1314 Miller Dr., Coral Gables 33146, tel. 305/284–2438), a 600-seat concert hall on the University of Miami's Coral Gables campus, has good acoustics and plenty of room. Parking is a problem when school is in session.

New World Symphony (541 Lincoln Rd., Miami Beach 33139, tel. 305/673–3331 for box office or 305/673–3330 for main office), conducted by Michael Tilson Thomas, performs October–May. Greater Miami has no resident symphony orchestra, and this group helps fill the void. Musicians ages 22–30 who have finished their academic studies perform here before moving on to other orchestras.

Opera **Florida Grand Opera** (1200 Coral Way, Miami 33145, tel. 305/854–7890, box office open weekdays 10–4) is south Florida's leading opera company. It presents five operas each year in the Dade County Auditorium, featuring the Florida Philharmonic Orchestra (James Judd, artistic director). The annual series brings such luminaries as Placido Domingo and Luciano Pavarotti. (Pavarotti made his American debut with the company in 1965 in *Lucia di Lammermoor*.) All operas are sung in the original language, with surtitles in English projected onto a screen above the stage.

Dance The **Miami City Ballet** (905 Lincoln Rd., Miami Beach 33139, tel. 305/532–7713 or 305/532–4880) is Florida's first major, fully professional, resident ballet company. Edward Villella, the artistic director, was a principal dancer of the New York City Ballet under George Balanchine. Now the Miami City Ballet re-creates the Balanchine repertoire and introduces new works of its own during its September–March season. Performances are held at TOPA in Miami Beach; at the Broward Center for the Performing Arts; Bailey Concert Hall, also in Broward County; the Raymond F. Kravis Center for the Performing Arts; and at the Naples Philharmonic Center for the Arts. Demonstrations of works in progress take place at the 800-seat Lincoln Theater in Miami Beach. Villella narrates the children's and works-in-progress programs.

Film The **Alliance Film/Video Project** (Sterling Building, Suite 119, 927 Lincoln Rd. Mall, Miami Beach 33139, tel. 305/531–8504) presents cutting-edge cinema from around the world, with special midnight shows.

The **Miami Film Festival** (444 Brickell Ave., Suite 229, Miami 33131, tel. 305/377–3456) screens new films from all over the world for 10 days every February, in the Gusman Center for the Performing Arts.

Nightlife

Greater Miami has found a new concentration of nightspots in South Beach along Ocean Drive, Washington Avenue, and most recently along Lincoln Road Mall. Other nightlife centers on Little Havana, Coconut Grove, and on the fringes of downtown Miami.

Individual clubs offer jazz, reggae, salsa, various forms of rock, and Top-40 sounds on different nights of the week. Some clubs refuse entrance to anyone under 21; others set the age limit at 25. On South Beach, where the sounds of jazz and reggae spill into the streets, fashion models and photographers frequent the lobby bars of small Art Deco hotels. Throughout the Greater Miami area, bars and cocktail lounges in larger hotels operate discos nightly, with live entertainment on weekends. Many hotels extend their bars into open-air courtyards, where patrons dine and dance under the stars throughout the year. It's a good idea to inquire in advance about cover charges. Policies change frequently.

Bars and Lounges
Coconut Grove

Hungry Sailor (3064½ Grand Ave., tel. 305/444–9359), with two bars, serves up Jamaican-English food, British beer, and music Wednesday to Saturday. **Taurus Steak House** (3540 Main Hwy., tel. 305/448–0633) is an unchanging oasis in the trendy Grove. The bar, built in 1922 of native cypress, draws an over-30 singles crowd nightly that drifts outside to a patio. A band plays Wednesday through Saturday.

Coral Gables

In a building that dates from 1926, **Stuart's Bar-Lounge** (162 Alcazar Ave., tel. 305/444–1666) was named one of the best new bars of 1987 by *Esquire*; nine years later, locals still favor it. The style is fostered by beveled mirrors, mahogany paneling, French posters, pictures of old Coral Gables, and art-nouveau lighting. It's closed Sunday.

Key Biscayne

Sundays on the Bay (5420 Crandon Blvd., tel. 305/361–6777) is a classic Miami over-the-water scene on Key Biscayne with an upscale menu. The clientele includes lots of Latins who love Miami the way it was. There's a disco nightly and live entertainment Friday–Sunday ($5–$10 cover).

Miami

Tobacco Road (626 S. Miami Ave., tel. 305/374–1198), opened in 1912, holds Miami's oldest liquor license. Upstairs, in space occupied by a speakeasy during Prohibition, local and national blues bands perform nightly. There's excellent bar food and a dinner menu.

Miami Beach

Bash (655 Washington Ave., tel. 305/538–2274) has bars inside and out and dance floors with music—sometimes reggae, sometimes Latin, plenty of loud disco, and world-beat sounds in the garden, where there are artsy benches. Inside it's grottolike. Not quite SoBe, **Blue Steel** (2895 Collins Ave., tel. 305/672–1227) is a cool but unpretentious hangout with pool tables, darts, live music, comfy old sofas, and beer paraphernalia. Open-mike night is Fridays, and there's a jam on Mondays. **Mac's Club Deuce** (222 14th St., tel. 305/673–9537) is a South Beach gem where top international models pop in to have a drink and shoot some pool. All you get late at night are minipizzas, but the pizzazz lasts. Up in a nondescript motel row with nudie bars, baby stores, bait-and-tackle shops, and bikini warehouse stores, **Molly Malone's** (166 Sunny Isles Blvd., tel. 305/948–9143) is the only cool, down-to-earth spot that thrives in this neighborhood. The Irish pub, a big local fave, has live Irish music Fridays, acoustic sounds Saturdays, and poetry readings Thursdays. **Rose's Bar & Lounge** (754 Washington Ave., tel. 305/532–0228) features the best in local bands from Hendrix-style rock and rap/funk to jazz jams and Afro-Cuban/world beat, with the occasional national act. Though it doesn't take credit cards, there is an ATM. It's open seven nights, but it's packed Wednesday through Saturday. **Shabeen Cookshack and Bar** (Marlin Hotel, 1200 Collins Ave., tel. 305/673–8770), open Thursday–Sunday, is Jamaican all the way—brilliant island decor, upbeat Caribbean music, and a couple of pool tables. **Union Bar** (653 Washington Ave., tel. 305/672–9958), like Bash with bare concrete floors, features progressive/alternative music. It comes complete with a pool table, an informal dining area, strobe lighting, an unusual bubble fish tank in back-to-back rooms, and an immense dog sculpture.

Discos and **Baja Beach Club** (3015 Grand Ave., CocoWalk, tel. 305/445–0278),
Rock Clubs the number one party place in the Grove, has waiters and waitresses
Coconut Grove dressed in beach attire.

Key Biscayne **Stefano's of Key Biscayne** (24 Crandon Blvd., tel. 305/361–7007) is a
northern Italian restaurant–cum–disco; the music's live Tuesday–
Sunday.

Miami Beach **Amnesia** (136 Collins Ave., tel. 305/531–5535), open Thursday–Sunday, feels like a luxurious amphitheater in the tropics, complete
with rain forest, what used to be called go-go dancers, and frenzied
dancing in the rain when showers pass over the open-air ground-lev-
el club. The full-service Portobello restaurant, on an upper level, has
picture windows for taking in the scene without the decibels. **Bermuda Bar & Grille** (3509 N.E. 163rd St., tel. 305/945–0196) plays
LOUD MUSIC for disco dancing. Male bartenders wear knee-length
kilts whereas the female BTs dress in miniskirt kilts. The atmosphere and crowd, though, are stylish island casual, and there's a big
tropical forest scene, booths you can hide in, and six bars and pool
tables, too. One drawback is that there's no draft brew. It's closed
Monday. **Glam Slam** (1235 Washington Ave., tel. 305/672–4858) is
where Club Z, 1235, and Paragon all hit the heights of fashion before
falling out of favor. The artist formerly known as Prince has dressed
the place up with his motorcycle from *Purple Rain* in the foyer, and
there's a secret passage for his celeb pals. Theme nights include
Southern Fried Soul, Glamour Girls, Gay Night, and Saturday's
wild, packed Disco Party Time. It's open Wednesday through Sunday. **Ruby's** (300 Alton Rd., Miami Beach Marina, tel. 305/673–3444)
was dreamed up for the crowd that wants to be SoBe chic but without the "trash crowd" that helps give SoBe its character. This ritzy
disco is filled with overstuffed seating, wall-to-wall tropical-print
carpeting, and a fortune in A/V gear. It sits to the side of Nick's Miami Beach Restaurant and attracts the same stylish dressers.

Jazz Club **MoJazz Cafe** (928 71st St., tel. 305/865–2636) arrived on the scene in
Miami Beach 1993 with its easy neighborhood style, combining a local café with
real (nonfusion) jazz. It's in the Normandy Isle section—a long over-
looked neighborhood just right for hosting the occasional national
name, like Mose Allison, and the national attention–deserving local
talents of Ira Sullivan, Little Nicky, Joe Donato, and a stellar roster
of Miami's longtime jazz best. A nightly happy hour, food from the
country kitchen, and late-night breakfast are all on tap.

Nightclubs **Les Violins Supper Club** (1751 Biscayne Blvd., tel. 305/371–8668) is a
Miami reliable standby owned for 35 years by the Cachaidora-Currais family, who ran a club and restaurant in Havana. There's a live dance
band and a wood dance floor. Reservations are advised; the cover
charge is $15.

Miami Beach **Club Tropigala at La Ronde** (Fontainebleau Hilton, 4441 Collins
Ave., tel. 305/672–7469)—lately discovered by such stars as Sylves-
ter Stallone, Madonna, and Elton John—is a four-tier round room
decorated with orchids, banana leaves, philodendrons, cascading
waterfalls, and a dancing fountain, creating the effect of a tropical
jungle. The band plays standards as well as Latin music for dancing
on the wood floor. Reservations are advised.

3 The Everglades

By Herb
Hiller

Miami is the only metropolitan area in the United States with two
national parks—Everglades and Biscayne—in its backyard.
Everglades National Park, created in 1947, was meant to preserve
the slow-moving "River of Grass"—a freshwater river 50 miles wide
but only 6 inches deep, flowing from Lake Okeechobee through
marshy grassland into Florida Bay. Biscayne National Park, established as a national monument in 1968 and 12 years later expanded
and upgraded to park status, is the nation's largest marine park and
the largest national park in the continental United States with living
coral reefs. A small portion of the park's almost 274 square miles
consists of mainland coast and outlying islands, but 96% is under water, much of it in Biscayne Bay.

Unfortunately, Miami's "backyard" is being threatened by the suburban sprawl that has long characterized metro area development.
Added to the mix is the presence nearby, between the suburbs and
the parks, of one of the most productive, albeit shrinking, agricultural districts in the eastern United States. The result is competition between environmental, agricultural, and development
interests—for land, for government money, and for rules to govern
this one-of-a-kind region's future.

The biggest issue centers on control of water. Originally, the natural cycle of alternating floods and dry periods in the Everglades
maintained wildlife habitat and regulated the quality and quantity
of water that flowed into Florida Bay. The brackish seasonal flux
sustained a remarkably vigorous bay, including the most productive
shrimp beds in American waters and thriving mangrove fringes and
coral reefs at its Atlantic edge. The system nurtured both sea life
and recreationists, who flocked to the region for fishing and diving.
Starting in the 1930s, however, a giant flood-control system began
diverting water to canals that run to the Gulf and the Atlantic.
As you travel Florida's north–south routes, you cross this network of canals, symbolized by a smiling alligator that represents

the South Florida Water Management District, "Protector of the Everglades."

The unintended result of flood control has been devastation of the wilderness that lies within the boundaries of Everglades National Park, the Big Cypress National Preserve, and a series of water conservation areas to the northeast. Park visitors decry diminished bird counts (a 90% reduction over 50 years), the black bear has been eliminated, and the Florida panther nears extinction. Exotic plants once imported to drain the Everglades and feral pigs released for hunting are crowding out indigenous species. In 1995 the nonprofit group American Rivers ranked the Everglades among the most threatened rivers of North America. Meanwhile in Florida Bay, the loss of all that fresh water has made the bay more salty, creating dead zones where pea-green algae has replaced sea grasses and sponges, devastating sea-life breeding grounds.

Ultimately, priorities change, and new policies, still largely on paper, hold promise for an ecosystem that continues to diminish. Tourism and fishing industries, preservationists, and aggressive park management have pushed for improvement. The federal and state governments are now working together to advance environmental protection toward the top of water-management priorities. Congressional appropriations to study restoration of the Everglades have increased. The state has acquired the Frog Pond, some 1,800 acres of critical farmland to the east of the Everglades, in order to allow more natural flooding. Passage in 1994 of Florida's Everglades Forever Act mandates creation of 40,000 acres of filtration marshes to remove nutrients before they enter the protected wetlands. Within the next decade, farming must sharply reduce its phosphorus runoff, and the U.S. Army Corps of Engineers, which maintains Florida's flood-control system, proposes restoring a more natural flow of water into the Everglades and its related systems. Although the future of the natural system hangs uncertainly in this time of transition, these are promising signs.

Much like Florida Bay, Biscayne Bay functions as a lobster sanctuary and a nursery for fish, sponges, and crabs. Manatees and sea turtles frequent its warm, shallow waters, and the ocean east of the islands harbors the northernmost sections of Florida's tropical reef. At the park's boundary, the continental shelf runs to 60 feet deep; farther east, the shelf falls rapidly away to a depth of 400 feet at the edge of the Gulf Stream. Lamentably, this bay, too, comes under assault from similar forces at work in Florida Bay, and coral is additionally damaged by boat anchors and commercial ships that run off course onto the reefs.

The farm towns of Homestead and Florida City provide the closest visitor facilities to the two parks. They date from early in the century, when Henry Flagler extended his railroad to Key West and decided that farming in South Dade would do more for rail revenues than would passengers. Although both towns were devastated by Hurricane Andrew in 1992, both have fully recovered. Farms, including U-pick fields, extend west to the edge of Everglades National Park, and a vast network of almost 200 miles of bicycle and hiking trails is under development along the banks of flood-control canals. Routes are likely to connect the two national parks before the end of the decade.

Another way to see the Everglades is via a 15-mile probe that extends south from the Tamiami Trail (U.S. 41) between Miami and Naples. Miccosukee Indians in the area operate a range of cultural attractions and restaurants. The remaining entrance to the park is Everglades City, 35 miles southeast of Naples just off the Tamiami Trail. This community, originated in the late 19th century, offers lodgings, restaurants, and guided tours.

Everglades Basics

Budget Lodging

While this region provides a sufficient supply of reasonably priced accommodations, these mainly consist of standard chain motels in the Homestead–Florida City area and a couple of small Everglades City lodgings that are oriented toward adventure travelers—folks who will be exploring the watery western part of the Everglades. You may want to visit Biscayne National Park on a day trip from Miami and save yourself the hassle of checking out of your hotel there. The best bet at Everglades National Park is to overnight at Flamingo Lodge, inside the park.

If you do choose to spend several nights here and you really want to encounter the wilderness, you can stay at one of the primitive and backcountry campsites available in both parks, some accessible only by canoe. All have chemical toilets. Call ahead for information on accessibility for travelers with disabilities and updates. Carry all your food, water, and supplies in; carry out all trash.

Seasonal considerations affect lodging prices in this area; like most of south Florida, the parks are at their best and busiest—and most expensive—in winter.

Budget Dining

Although the two parks are wilderness areas, there are restaurants within a short drive of all park entrances: between Miami and Shark Valley along the Tamiami Trail (U.S. 41), in the Homestead–Florida City area, in Everglades City, and in the Keys along the Overseas Highway (U.S. 1). You can also find fast-food establishments that offer carryout in these places. The only food service actually *in* either park is at Flamingo Lodge in the Everglades.

If you don't plan to eat at a restaurant, you can buy fresh fruits, drinks, and novelties from roadside stands and other food from supermarkets in Homestead (near entrances to Everglades and Biscayne national parks) and in Naples (north along U.S. 41 from the Everglades City entrance of Everglades National Park). Many local fish houses sell freshly steamed shrimp or smoked fish, and many of the restaurants reviewed in this chapter will pack picnic fare that you can take to the parks.

In winter, when there are few mosquitoes, find a picnic place along the Barron River in Everglades City or on Chokoloskee Island (reached by a toll-free causeway). Between Royal Palm and Flamingo on the main road into Everglades National Park, picnic wherever it looks good to you; just be mindful to leave no trash, and don't feed the gators.

Bargain Shopping

Aside from gift shops at the parks (Convoy Point for Biscayne National Park, Flamingo Lodge Marina in Everglades National Park), there are few shopping opportunities around this area. Unusual crafts items made by the Miccosukee Indians are available near the Shark Valley entrance to the Everglades. In Florida City, there are several pick-your-own farm fields and roadside produce stands. Antiques stores are found in the heart of old Homestead, and shopping centers with major department stores are 10–20 miles north of Homestead along South Dixie Highway (U.S. 1).

Sports and the Outdoors

Most of the sports and recreational opportunities in Everglades National Park and Biscayne National Park are related in some way to water or nature study, or both. Boating, fishing, canoeing, diving, and swimming are great ways to explore the watery wilderness, and even on land, be prepared to get your feet wet on the region's marshy hiking trails. Ask the rangers for "Foot and Canoe Trails of the Flamingo Area," a leaflet that also lists bike trails.

In summer, save your outdoor activities for early or late in the day to avoid the sun's strongest rays, and use a sunscreen. Carry mosquito repellent at any time of year.

Boating   Bring aboard the proper *NOAA Nautical Charts* before you cast off to explore the waters of the parks. The charts cost $15–$15.95 each and are sold at many marine stores in south Florida, at the Convoy Point Visitor Center in Biscayne National Park, and in Flamingo Marina.

Waterway Guide (southern regional edition) is an annual publication that many boaters use as a guide to these waters. Bookstores all over south Florida sell it, or you can order it directly from the publisher (Argus Business, Book Department, 6151 Powers Ferry Rd., Atlanta, GA 30339, tel. 800/233–3359) for $33.95 plus $3 shipping and handling.

Florida Marine Patrol (tel. 305/325–3346), a division of the Florida Department of Natural Resources, maintains a 24-hour telephone service for reporting boating emergencies and natural resource violations. **Miami Beach Coast Guard Base** (100 MacArthur Causeway, Miami Beach, tel. 305/535–4300 or 305/535–4314, VHF-FM Channel 16) responds to local marine emergencies and reports of navigation hazards.

Guided Tours

Tours of Everglades and Biscayne national parks typically focus on native wildlife, plants, and park history. Concessionaires operate tram tours in the Everglades and boat cruises in both parks. In addition, the National Park Service organizes a variety of free programs at Everglades National Park. Ask a ranger for the daily schedule.

All Florida Adventure Tours (8263-B S.W. 107th Ave., Miami 33173-3729, tel. 305/270–0219) operates one-day to two-week custom tours and standard 10-day tours for groups, emphasizing nature, history, and ecology.

Tour 1: Everglades National Park

Winter is the best time to visit Everglades National Park. Temperatures and mosquito activity are moderate. Low water levels concentrate the resident wildlife around sloughs that retain water all year. Migratory birds swell the avian population. Winter is also the busiest time in the park. Make reservations and expect crowds at the most popular visitor service areas—Flamingo, the main visitor center, and Royal Palm.

In spring the weather turns increasingly hot and dry, and tours and facilities are less crowded. Migratory birds depart, and you must look harder to see wildlife. Be especially careful with campfires and matches; this is when the wildfire-prone saw-grass prairies and pinelands are most vulnerable.

The Everglades and Biscayne National Parks

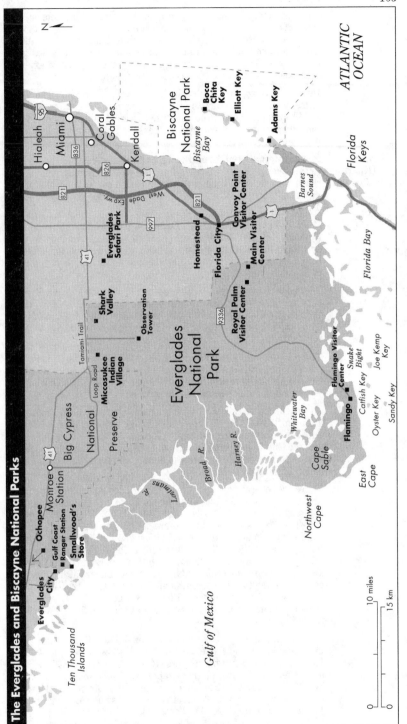

Summer brings intense sun and billowing clouds that unleash torrents of rain on the Everglades. Thunderstorms roll in almost every afternoon; water levels rise and wildlife disperses. Mosquitoes hatch, swarm, and descend on you in voracious clouds. It's a good time to stay away, although some brave souls do come to explore. Europeans constitute 80% of the summer visitors.

In mid-October, the first cold front sweeps through. The rains cease, water levels start to fall, and the ground begins to dry out. Wildlife moves toward the sloughs. Flocks of migratory birds and tourists swoop in, as the cycle of seasons builds once more to the winter peak activity.

Arriving and Departing By Plane **Miami International Airport** (MIA), the closest commercial airport to the Everglades, is 83 miles from the park's Flamingo resort. To reach the park you'll need to either rent a car or take one of the modes of transportation to Homestead or Florida City (*see* Tour 2, *below*).

By Boat If you're entering the United States by boat, you must phone **U.S. Customs** (tel. 800/432–1216) either from a marine phone or on first arriving ashore. At its option, customs will direct you to Dodge Island Seaport (Miami), will otherwise rendezvous with you, or will clear you by phone.

By Car The eastern gateway to Everglades National Park is via Florida City and Homestead (*see* Tour 2, *below*). To reach the Main Visitor Center and Flamingo, turn right (west) onto Route 9336 in Florida City, and follow signs to the park. From Homestead, the Main Visitor Center is 11 miles, and Flamingo is 49 miles.

To get to the park's south end in the Florida Keys, take U.S. 1 south from Homestead. It's 27 miles to the Key Largo Ranger Station (between mile markers 98 and 99, BS, Overseas Hwy.), which is not always staffed but has maps and information.

To reach the park's northern and western entrances, take the Tamiami Trail (U.S. 41). The Shark Valley visitor center is 70 miles east of Naples and 40 miles west of Miami. To reach Everglades City and the Gulf Coast Ranger Station, take the Tamiami Trail 35 miles east of Naples or 83 miles west of Miami, and turn south onto Route 29 for a few miles.

Guided Tours There are several ways to tour the Everglades, and many of the best are on the water. At **Flamingo Lodge Marina & Outpost Resort** (1 Flamingo Lodge Hwy., Flamingo 33034, tel. 305/253–2241 or 941/695–3101, fax 941/695–3921), a number of services are offered, including help in arranging for individualized tours given by charter fishing-boat captains. The cost is $265 a day for up to two people, $185 per half day, and $25 each additional person. **Back Country Tour** gives two-hour cruises aboard a 40-passenger catamaran. The cost (including tax) is $12 adults and $6 children 6–12. **Florida Bay Cruise** runs 90-minute tours of Florida Bay aboard *Bald Eagle*, a 90-passenger catamaran. It costs $8.50 adults and $4.50 children 6–12 (including tax).

In Everglades City, **Everglades National Park Boat Tours** (Gulf Coast Ranger Station, Rte. 29, tel. 941/695–2591 or 800/445–7724 in FL) carries 40 to 140 passengers (the two largest boats have food and drink concessions) on three separate 14-mile tours through the Ten Thousand Islands region along the Gulf of Mexico on the western margin of the park. The cost is $11 adults and $5.50 children 6–12. **Majestic Tours** (Box 241, 33929, tel. 941/695–2777) is led by exceptionally well-informed guides, Frank and Georgia Garrett. The 3½- to four-hour trips, on a 24-foot pontoon boat, depart from Glades Haven, just shy of a mile south of the circle in Everglades City; take in the Ten Thousand Islands; and visit the Watson Place, site of a turn-of-the-century wilderness plantation run by a fearsome outlaw. Tours are limited to six passengers and include brunch or afternoon snacks. The cost is $60 per person, $30 children under 12.

Airboats are another popular way to see the river of grass (*see below* for attractions with their own airboat rides). **Florida Boat Tours** (200 Rte. 29, Everglades City, tel. 941/695–4400 or 800/282–9194 in FL) runs 30- to 40-minute backcountry tours aboard custom-designed jet-airboats. The cost is $11.95 adults and $5.50 children 7–12; one-hour tours for a maximum of six people are $30 adults and $15 children 12 and under. **Swampland Airboat Tours** (Box 619, Everglades City 33929, tel. 941/695–2740 or 800/344–2740) offers personalized tours of the Everglades or the Big Cypress National Preserve. The cost is $60 per hour for up to six persons. Reservations are required. **Wooten's Everglades** (Wooten's Alligator Farm, Tamiami Trail, tel. 941/695–2781 or 800/282–2781) runs a variety of airboat and swamp-buggy tours. (Swamp buggies, giant tractor-like vehicles with over-size rubber wheels, can take up to 20 people at a time.) Tours of approximately 30 minutes cost $12 for ages 7 and over; younger children are free.

For those who'd like to see the area under their own power, **North American Canoe Tours** (Ivey House, 107 Camellia St., Box 5038, 33929, tel. 941/695–4666 or 941/695–3299; May–Sept. tel. 203/739–0791; fax 941/695–4155) leads one-day to six-night Everglades tours November–April for up to 10 participants. Highlights include bird and gator sightings, mangrove forests, no-man's-land beaches, relics of the hideouts of infamous and just plain reclusive characters, and spectacular sunsets. Included in the cost of extended tours ($450–$750) are canoes, all necessary equipment, a guide, meals, and lodging for the first and last nights at the Ivey House B&B in Everglades City. Day trips cost $40, and one-day bicycling and hiking tours are also offered.

If you'd prefer to stay on dry land, try one of the tram tours. **Wilderness Tram Tour** (Flamingo Lodge, Flamingo, tel. 305/253–2241 or 941/695–3101) visits Snake Bight, an indentation in the Florida Bay shoreline, aboard a 42-passenger screened tram. This two-hour tour passes through a mangrove forest and a coastal prairie to a 100-yard boardwalk over the mud flats at the edge of the bight. The cost (including tax) is $7.95 adults, $4 children 6–12. **Shark Valley Tram Tours** (Box 1729, Tamiami Station, Miami 33144, tel. 305/221–8455) starts at the Shark Valley visitor center and follows a 15-mile elevated loop road into the interior, stopping at a 50-foot observation tower built on the site of an oil well drilled in the 1940s. Reservations are recommended December–March. The cost is $8 adults, $7.20 senior citizens, $4 children 12 and under.

Everglades Air Tours (Homestead General Aviation Airport, 28790 S.W. 217th Ave., Homestead, tel. 305/248–7754) gives narrated, bird's-eye tours of the Everglades and Florida Bay that last 50 minutes and cost $55 per person.

The Main Park Road to Flamingo

Everglades National Park: Main Visitor Center (40001 Rte. 9336, Florida City 33034-6733, tel. 305/242-7700), Flamingo Ranger Station (1 Flamingo Lodge Hwy., Flamingo 33034-6798, tel. 941/695-2945).

★ The main **Everglades park road** (Route 9336) travels 38 miles from the Main Visitor Center to Flamingo, across a cross section of the park's eight distinct ecosystems: hardwood hammock, freshwater prairie, pineland, freshwater slough, cypress, coastal prairie, mangrove, and marine/estuarine. Highlights of the trip include a dwarf cypress forest, the ecotone (transition zone) between saw grass and mangrove forest, and a wealth of wading birds at Mrazek and Coot Bay ponds. Boardwalks and trails along the main road and several short spurs allow you to see the Everglades on dry land.

Enter the park at the **Main Visitor Center,** where a full range of interpretive materials is to be displayed in the new, more cracker-style park headquarters, expected by mid-1996. The new structure replaces a temporary facility with limited materials, which in turn replaced a structure destroyed by Hurricane Andrew. *40001 Rte. 9336, tel. 305/242–7700. Park admission: $5 per car; $3 per person on foot, bicycle, or motorcycle; free for U.S. citizens over 62 with Golden Age Passport ($10, good for life). Visitor center open daily 8–5.*

At the **Royal Palm Visitor Center** (4 mi west on Rte. 9336 and south on a side road), you can stroll along the Anhinga Trail boardwalk or follow the Gumbo Limbo Trail through a hardwood hammock (a tree island). The visitor center has an interpretive display, a bookstore, and vending machines and is open 8–noon and 1–4:30.

At the far end of the park road, **Flamingo** offers access to Florida Bay; tour boats and fishing guides leave from here. A visitor center, open daily 8–5, provides an interpretive display, and you can also make use of a lodge, restaurant, lounge, gift shop, marina, and campground.

Budget Lodging $–$$

Flamingo Lodge Marina & Outpost Resort. This plain low-rise motel offers the only lodging inside Everglades National Park. Accommodations are basic but well kept, and an amiable staff with a sense of humor helps you adjust to the alligators who sometimes bellow in the sewage-treatment pond down the road, the raccoons roaming the pool enclosure at night, and the flock of ibis grazing on the lawn. Rooms have carpeting, wood-paneled and plaster walls, contemporary furniture, floral bedspreads, and art prints of bird life. Bathrooms are tiny. All motel rooms face Florida Bay but don't necessarily overlook it. The cottages, in a wooded area on the margin of a coastal prairie, have kitchenettes and accommodate six people, except for the two disabled-accessible units, which accommodate four. Note that by park regulations, the concessionaire is obliged to offer two units to accommodate travelers on a budget. If you're interested, ask about their availability when you call for reservations, as well as about arranging for tours, skiffs, and canoes. *1 Flamingo Lodge Hwy., Flamingo 33034, tel. 305/253–2241 from Miami, 941/695–3101 from Gulf Coast, or 800/600–3813 for reservations, fax 305/695–3921. 101 motel rooms, 24 cottages. Facilities: restaurant, lounge, outdoor pool, marina, marina store with snack bar, gift shop, coin laundry. AE, D, DC, MC, V.*

Camping

The park includes three developed campsites with drinking water, a sewage dump station, and rest rooms. **Long Pine Key** offers 108 campsites. **Flamingo** offers 235 drive-in sites, 60 walk-in sites, and cold showers. **Chekika** has 20 sites plus a group site for up to 20, and additionally offers both hot and cold showers. Come early to get a good site, especially in winter. Bring plenty of insect repellent. *Admission: $8 per site in winter, free in summer except for walk-in sites at Flamingo, which are $4 year-round. Stay limited to 14 days Nov.–Apr. Checkout time 10 AM. Register at campground.*

There are 48 designated backcountry sites, two of which are accessible by land, the others only by water. Fifteen have chickees (raised wood platforms with thatch roofs), and all have chemical toilets, including the 18 beach sites and 15 inland sites. Four chickee sites and nine of the ground sites are within an easy day's canoeing of Flamingo. Carry all your food, water, and supplies in; carry out all trash. You'll need a free permit, issued for a specific site. Capacity and length of stay are limited, and sites are available on a first-come, first-served basis. For information on accessibility for those with disabilities, updates, and permits, contact the Flamingo Ranger Station (*see above*).

Budget Dining
$$

Flamingo Restaurant. The grand view, convivial lounge, and casual style mark the best of the mix introduced here by TW Recreational Services, the park concessionaire. Big picture windows on the visitor center's second floor overlook Florida Bay, revealing variously soaring eagles, gulls, pelicans, terns, and vultures. Dine at low tide, and you get to see the birds flock to the sandbar just offshore. Less satisfying is the food itself. All the seafood comes frozen—unless it's your own catch, which the kitchen will prepare after you've cleaned it at the marina. Otherwise look for pastas and a few grills. Service is limited to buffets in summer, though the snack bar at the marina store stays open all year to serve pizza, sandwiches, and salads, and you can always order a picnic basket. *Flamingo Lodge, 1 Flamingo Lodge Hwy., Flamingo, tel. 305/253–2241 from Miami or 941/695–3101 from Gulf Coast. Reservations advised for dinner. Dress: casual. AE, D, DC, MC, V.*

Participant
Sports
Boating

Flamingo Lodge Marina & Outpost Resort (1 Flamingo Lodge Hwy., Flamingo, tel. 305/253–2241 from Miami or 941/695–3101 from Gulf Coast) has a 50-slip marina that rents 10 power skiffs and five houseboats; several private boats are also available for charter. Of the two boat ramps, one is for Florida Bay, the other for Whitewater Bay and the backcountry. The hoist across the plug dam separating Florida Bay from the Buttonwood Canal can take boats up to 26 feet long. A small marina store sells food, camping supplies, bait and tackle, and automobile and boat fuel.

Canoeing

There are six well-marked canoe trails in the Flamingo area, including the southern end of the 99-mile Wilderness Trail from Flamingo to Everglades City. **Flamingo Lodge Marina & Outpost Resort** (*see above*) has 40 canoes for rent.

Along the Tamiami Trail

Another way to visit the Everglades is to follow the Tamiami Trail (U.S. 41) for the scenic 83 miles between Miami and Naples. The attractions below are listed starting near Miami and continuing west, but you can just as easily travel in the opposite direction. (Keep in mind that the sun will be in your eyes after noon while driving the tour east to west.)

Coopertown Airboat Ride operates a 30- to 35-minute airboat trip through the Everglades saw grass, visiting two hammocks (subtropical hardwood forests) and alligator holes. *5 mi west of Krome Ave. on Tamiami Trail, tel. 305/226–6048. Cost: $9 ages 7 and over, $22 minimum for the boat. Open winter (Eastern Standard Time), daily 8–6; summer (Daylight Saving Time), daily 8–7.*

Located 14 miles west of Florida's Turnpike, the **Everglades Safari Park** offers airboat rides, a jungle trail, observation platform, alligator wrestling, wildlife museum, gift shop, and restaurant. *Tamiami Trail, tel. 305/226–6923 or 305/223–3804, fax 305/554–5666. Admission: $14 adults, $6 children under 12. Open daily 8:30–5.*

Continue on U.S. 41 to **Shark Valley,** site of a park entrance and a visitor center, which has rotating exhibits and a bookstore. From here you can walk along a ¼-mile boardwalk, follow hiking trails, or take one of the **Shark Valley Tram Tours** (*see* Guided Tours, *above*), which visit a 50-foot observation tower from which you can view the vast river of grass sweeping south toward the Gulf of Mexico. Shark Valley Tram Tours also rents bikes, for $3.25 per hour, to ride along the Shark Valley Loop Road. *Visitor center: Tamiami Trail, tel. 305/ 221–8776. Park admission: $4 per car; $2 per person on foot, bicycle,* *or motorcycle; free for U.S. citizens over 62 with Golden Age Passport. Visitor center open daily 8:30–5.*

★ Near the Shark Valley entrance to Everglades National Park, the Miccosukee tribe operates the **Miccosukee Indian Village** as a tourist attraction. You can watch Indian families cooking and making the clothes, dolls, beadwork, and baskets that are sold at the village's shop; see an alligator-wrestling demonstration; or take **Buffalo Tiger's Florida Everglades Airboat Ride.** The 40- to 45-minute ride, led by a former chairman of the Miccosukee tribe, stops at an old Native American camp. The village also has a boardwalk and a museum. *12 mi west of Krome Ave. on Tamiami Trail, tel. 305/559–5250. Village admission: $5 adults, $3.50 children 5–12; airboat rides: $10 adults, $5 children under 10 (family rates available). Village open daily 9–5; airboat rides Mon.–Thurs. and Sat. 10–sunset, Sun. 11– sunset.*

Continuing west on the Tamiami Trail, you will drive through the **Big Cypress National Preserve,** with its variegated pattern of wet prairies, ponds, marshes, sloughs, and strands. Just west of the Miccosukee Indian Reservation turn left onto Route 94, the 29-mile

★ **Loop Road.** The way starts out paved, turns to dirt, and traverses deep, clear cypress swamps of rare beauty. Be sure to keep car windows rolled up when you stop, especially in summer, because mosquitoes can be a severe problem—lather on repellent if you leave the car to explore the road beside ponds. Walk silently and you may see gators, deer, rabbits, and other wildlife, as well as orchids and bromeliads. The road returns to the Tamiami Trail at Monroe Station, midway between the Miccosukee Indian Reservation and Everglades City.

Budget Lodging
$

Everglades Tower Inn. If you're overnighting in Shark Valley, odds are you just need a plain, serviceable, and affordable room, and that's just what you get here. This Miccosukee family-run lodging is 1 mile west of the Shark Valley entrance to Everglades National Park. Rooms have double doubles and baths but no phones. Next door are the Gator Hut Cafe, for affordable meals, and the Everglades Shark Valley Crafts Center. *Tamiami Trail, mile marker 70, SR Box E–4910, Ochopee 33943, tel. 305/559–7779 or 800/423– 6218 in FL. 20 rooms. MC, V.*

Budget Dining
$

Miccosukee Restaurant. Murals with Native American themes depict women cooking and men engaged in a powwow. Specialties include catfish and frogs' legs breaded and deep-fried in peanut oil, Indian fry bread (a flour-and-water dough deep-fried in peanut oil), pumpkin bread, Indian burger (ground beef browned, rolled in fry bread dough, and deep-fried), and Indian tacos (fry bread with chili, lettuce, tomato, and shredded cheddar cheese on top). *Tamiami Trail, near Shark Valley park entrance, tel. 305/223–8380, ext. 332. No reservations. Dress: casual. No credit cards.*

Everglades City

Everglades National Park: Gulf Coast Ranger Station (Rte. 29, Everglades City 33929, tel. 941/695–3311). Everglades City Chamber of Commerce (Rte. 29 and Tamiami Trail, Everglades City 33929, tel. 941/695–3941).

Just before Route 29 leaves the Tamiami Trail for Everglades City, you will pass through **Ochopee,** site of the smallest post office in North America. Buy a picture postcard of the little one-room building and mail it to a friend, thereby helping to keep this picturesque post office in business.

From here, turn south onto Route 29, and drive the 3 miles to **Everglades City** and the **Gulf Coast Ranger Station.** The visitor center here offers exhibits and a gift shop, and backcountry campers can pick up the required free permits. This station offers access to the Ten Thousand Islands region along the Gulf of Mexico, but there are no roads from here to other sections of the park. *Rte. 29, tel. 941/ 695–3311. Admission free. Open Nov.–Apr., daily 7–4:30; reduced hrs May–Oct.*

★ Stop at the **Rod and Gun Club** (*see* Budget Lodging, *below*), and take a time-warp trip back to the 1920s, when wealthy hunters, anglers, and yachting parties from all over the world came here for the winter season. Founded in 1889, the club is built on the foundations of the first house on the south bank of the Barron River. Sit on the screened porch, have a beer, and watch the yachts and the fishing boats go by.

Three miles from Everglades City across a free causeway is
★ **Smallwood's Store,** a perfectly restored old trading post that dates from 1906. Ted Smallwood pioneered this last American frontier deep in the Everglades and built a 3,000-square-foot pine store raised on pilings in Chokoloskee Bay. Smallwood's granddaughter Lynn McMillin reopened it in 1989, after it had been closed several years, and installed a small museum and gift shop. *360 Mamie St., Chokoloskee Island, tel. 941/695–2989. Admission: $2.50 ages over 12, $2 senior citizens. Open Dec. 1–May 1, daily 10–5; May 2–Nov. 30, Fri.–Tues. 10–4.*

Budget Lodging
$$

Rod and Gun Club. Hurricane Donna in 1960 did more damage than Andrew in 1992, but the pool and veranda were quickly restored at this landmark inn on the banks of the Barron River. With dark cypress and a nautical theme, the Rod and Gun is a vestige of backwoods glory days when imperial developer Barron Collier greeted U.S. presidents, Barrymores, and Gypsy Rose Lee here for days of leisurely fishing. Most of them flew in to the private landing strip; in the evenings they were fed by one of Collier's big catches, a chef who once worked for Kaiser Wilhelm. The old guest rooms, upstairs from the restaurant and bar, aren't open anymore, but you can stay in comfortable cottages (basic, with the standard amenities except room phone). The food's more than passable. Breakfast, lunch, and dinner are still served in the original dining room or on the wide veranda, and, as in days of yore, if you catch a "keeper" fish, the chef will prepare it for your dinner. *200 Riverside Dr., 33929, tel. 941/ 695–2101. 25 rooms. Facilities: restaurant, lounge, screened freshwater pool, tennis courts. No credit cards.*

¢

Ivey House. It's clean, homey, friendly, and a bargain, run by the very likable veteran innkeeper Catlin Maser for the folks who operate North American Canoe Tours. There are always adventure travelers around in the big living room, and lots of chatter over breakfast. The house is trailerlike, set upon blocks, and was a popular boardinghouse in the days when workers stayed here while building the Tamiami Trail. Earl and Agnes Ivey ran it from 1928 to 1974. There was nothing at all fancy about it then, or now. Men's and women's baths are down the hall, but the rooms are private. *107 Camellia St., 33929, tel. 941/695–3299. 10 rooms with shared baths. Facilities: recreation/breakfast room, TV lounge, library, bicycles. MC, V. Closed May–Oct.*

Camping

Of the 48 backcountry sites in the Everglades (*see* Camping *in* The Main Park Road to Flamingo, *above*), five ground sites are within an easy day's canoeing of Everglades City. You can get a free permit from the Gulf Coast Ranger Station.

Budget Dining
$$
★

Oyster House. An established local favorite, this rustic seafood house was built in 1984. The Florida fishing-village look is accented by mounted swampcats, gator heads, deer, crabs, nets, shells, and anchor chains. Lanterns from the A-frame ceiling burnish plank walls. You sit at booths and tables set without cloths. They'd serve on the porch, too, but the insects can get too pesty—though winters, when the bugs relent, guests sit outside with a drink from the bar to wait for a table. Fresh oysters are shucked daily, and main course favorites include the broiled or grilled pompano, black-tip shark, frog's legs, gator tail, and custom-cut steaks. Desserts include a homemade Key lime pie, carrot cake, and Black Forest cake. *Rte. 29 (Chokoloskee Causeway), tel. 941/695–2073. Reservations accepted. Dress: casual. MC, V. Closed Thanksgiving, Dec. 25.*

¢–$ **Susie's Station.** Susie Olson fell in love with Everglades City and made good here, opening this 85-seat restaurant in 1992 and running it until a car accident carried her away. Now her longtime sweetheart, Biss Williams, runs it exactly the way Susie did. You'd swear the place dates from Everglades City's heyday, with its white-balustered screened porch, the gas station memorabilia, the 1898 horse-drawn oil tanker, the old Ford pickup truck, and the Chevy coupe. Replica '20s lamps are strung over booths set with beige cloths. There are three dining areas, one with original area art by Camille Baumgartner, another fixed up like an old general store, and the third on the screened porch. Biss serves stone crabs in season, a cold seafood plate with lobster salad, seafood, steaks, and pizzas. The best buy is the nightly dinner special—maybe lasagna, baked chicken, or Salisbury steak. The homemade Key lime pie sells out daily (whole pies to go cost $14). *103 S.W. Copeland Ave., tel. 941/695–2002. Reservations accepted. Dress: casual. No credit cards. Beer and wine only. Closed Thanksgiving, Dec. 25.*

Canoeing The 99-mile **Wilderness Trail** is a canoe trail running from Flamingo to Everglades City. **Everglades National Park Boat Tours** (Gulf Coast Ranger Station, Rte. 29, tel. 941/695–2591 or 800/445–7724 in FL) rents canoes for $15 per half day, $20 per full day.

North American Canoe Tours (Ivey House, 107 Camellia St., Box 5038, 33929, tel. 941/695–4666) is an established source for canoes, sea kayaks, and guided Everglades trips (*see* Guided Tours, *above*). Canoes cost $20 the first day, $18 for every day after. Kayaks are $35–$45 per day. Car shuttles for canoeists paddling the Wilderness Trail are $135 with NACT canoe ($150 with your own) plus $5 park entrance fee. Reservations are required.

Tour 2: Homestead and Florida City

Homestead and Florida City sprang up early in this century as agricultural communities attached to the Florida East Coast Railroad built by Henry Flagler. Over the years, they developed a triple personality—part farming towns, part Miami suburbs, and part gateway to the parks. The area's better restaurants are in Homestead, whereas the best choices for overnighting are in Florida City.

Arriving and Departing
By Plane
Miami International Airport (MIA) is 34 miles from Homestead. From there, **SuperShuttle** (tel. 305/871–2000) operates 11-passenger air-conditioned vans to Homestead. Service is available around the clock, on demand; booths are located outside most luggage areas on the lower level. For the return to MIA, a 24-hour advance reservation is requested. The cost is $40 for the first person, $12 for each additional person at the same address.

Airporter (tel. 800/830–3413) runs shuttle buses three times daily off-season, four times daily in winter, that stop at the Hampton Inn in Florida City on their way between MIA and the Florida Keys. Shuttle service, which takes approximately an hour, runs 6:10 AM–5:20 PM from Florida City, 7:30 AM–6 PM from the airport, but reservations must be made in advance. Pick-ups can be arranged for all baggage claim areas. The cost is $20 one way.

Metrobus Route 1A runs from Homestead to MIA only during peak weekday hours: 6:30–9 AM and 4–6:30 PM.

Greyhound Lines operates three buses daily in each direction between the Homestead bus stop (5 N.E. 3rd Rd., tel. 305/247–2040) and Miami's Greyhound depot (4111 N.W. 27th St., tel. 305/871–1810), from which it's about a $5 cab ride to MIA. You can take a blue ARTS (Airport Region Taxi Service) car from MIA to the Greyhound depot for about $5.

By Car From Miami, the main highways to Homestead–Florida City are U.S. 1, the Homestead Extension of Florida's Turnpike, and Krome Avenue (Rte. 997/old U.S. 27).

Getting Florida City is immediately southwest of Homestead on Route 997.
Around If you don't have your own car, you'll want to rent one to get from
By Car Homestead–Florida City to the parks. Agencies in the area include **A&A Auto Rental** (30005 S. Dixie Hwy., Homestead 33030, tel. 305/246–0974), **Enterprise Rent-a-Car** (30428 S. Federal Hwy., Homestead 33030, tel. 305/246–2056), and **Thrifty Car Rental** (406 N. Krome Ave., Homestead 33030, tel. 305/245–8992).

By Taxi The local cab company is **New Taxi** (tel. 305/247–7466). Others servicing the area include **Action Express Taxi** (tel. 305/743–6800) and **South Dade Taxi** (tel. 305/256–4444).

Homestead

Homestead–Florida City Chamber of Commerce (43 N. Krome Ave., Homestead 33030, tel. 305/247–2332).

After being devastated by Hurricane Andrew, Homestead has been revived. Downtown Homestead has become a preservation-driven Main Street city, Homestead Air Force Base is becoming a civil air facility with commercial development, and the large Homestead Motorsports Complex will open by 1996.

You might want to stop off to view a portion of a historic photo collection at the restored 1917 **City Hall** (43 N. Krome Ave., tel. 305/247–2332), which also houses the chamber of commerce. More of the collection is displayed in a storefront across the street.

Homestead Bayfront Park has a marina as well as a saltwater atoll pool, adjacent to Biscayne Bay, which is flushed by tidal action. It's popular with local family groups and teenagers. Highlights include a "tot-lot" playground, ramps for people with disabilities (including a ramp that leads into the swimming area), and four barbecues in the picnic pavilion. *9698 S.W. 328th St., tel. 305/230–3033 for marina or 305/230–3034 for pool. Admission: $3 per car, $5 for boat ramp, $10 for hoist. Open daily 7–sunset.*

Budget Dining **Tiffany's.** This country-French cottage with shops and a restaurant
$ under a big banyan tree looks like a converted pioneer house with its high-pitched roof and lattice. That's because fourth-generation Miamian Rebecca DeLuria, who built it in 1984 with her husband, Robert, wanted a place that reminded her of the Miami she remembered. Teaberry-colored tables, satinlike floral place mats, marble-effect floor tiles, fresh flowers on each table, and lots of country items lend to the tearoom style found here. Featured entrées include hot crabmeat au gratin, asparagus supreme (rolled in ham with hollandaise sauce), and quiche of the day. Homemade desserts are to die for: old-fashioned (very tall) carrot cake, strawberry whipped-cream cake, and a harvest pie with double crust that layers apples, cranberries, walnuts, raisins, and a caramel topping. *22 N.E. 15th St., tel. 305/246–0022. Reservations accepted. Dress: casual but neat. MC, V. Closed Mon., Dec. 25, Jan. 1. No dinner.*

¢–$ **El Toro Taco.** The Hernandez family came to the United States from
★ San Luis Potosí, Mexico, to pick crops. In 1976 they opened this

Homestead-area institution, where they make their own salt-free tortillas and nacho chips with corn from Texas that they grind themselves. The cilantro-redolent salsa is mild, for American tastes; if you like more fire on your tongue, ask for a side dish of minced jalapeño peppers to mix in. Specialties include *chiles rellenos* (green peppers stuffed with meaty chunks of ground beef and topped with three kinds of cheese) and chicken fajitas (chunks of chicken marinated in Worcestershire sauce and spices, grilled in butter with onions and peppers, and served with tortillas and salsa). *1 S. Krome Ave., tel. 305/245–8182. No reservations. Dress: casual. MC, V. BYOB.*

¢–$ **Potlikker's.** This southern country-style restaurant takes its name from the broth—pot liquor—left over from the boiling of greens. Live plants dangle from the sides of open rafters in the lofty pine-lined dining room. Specialties include a lemon-pepper chicken breast with lemon sauce, fresh-carved roast turkey with homemade dressing, and at least 11 different vegetables to accompany lunch and dinner entrées. For dessert, try Key lime pie—4 inches tall and frozen; it tastes great if you dawdle over dessert while it thaws. *591 Washington Ave., tel. 305/248–0835. No reservations. Dress: casual. AE, MC, V. Closed Dec. 25.*

Shopping for Bargains In addition to Homestead Boulevard (U.S. 1) and Campbell Drive (S.W. 312th St. and N.E. 8th St.), **Krome Avenue** (Route 997) is a popular street for shopping. In the heart of old Homestead, it has a new brick sidewalk and many antiques stores.

Boating Aside from **Homestead Bayfront Park** (*see above*), whose marina has a dock and wet slips, dry slips, fuel, bait and tackle, ice, boat hoist, and ramp, there are a few other marinas in nearby Miami.

Five miles north, **Black Point Park** is a 155-acre Metro–Dade County park with a hurricane-safe harbor basin. Although badly mauled by Hurricane Andrew, it reopened in early 1993. **Black Point Marina**'s facilities include storage racks for 300 boats, 178 wet slips, 10 ramps, fuel, a bait-and-tackle shop, a canoe-launching ramp, powerboat rentals from Marine Management, and the Tugboat Annie Restaurant, serving lunch and dinner with a full bar. From Florida's Turnpike, exit at Southwest 112th Avenue, go two blocks north, turn east on Coconut Palm Drive (Southwest 248th Street), and drive to the end. *24777 S.W. 87th Ave., Miami, tel. 305/258–3500. Office open daily 8:30–5 (later in summer); park open daily 6–sunset.*

Pirate's Spa Marina (8701 Coconut Palm Dr. [S.W. 248th St.], Miami, tel. 305/257–5100), just west of the Black Point Park entrance, offers boat hoist, wet and dry storage, fuel, bait and tackle, and boat rental.

Florida City

South Dade Visitor Information Center (160 U.S. 1, Florida City 33034, tel. 305/245–9180 or 800/388–9669, fax 305/247–4335).

Most visitors use Florida City mainly for sleeping, but you might want to inquire whether the **Florida Pioneer Museum** (826 N. Krome Ave., tel. 305/246–9531) has reopened. In this former station agent's house, you could, until Hurricane Andrew, pore over a collection of articles from daily life that evoke the homestead period of the area, on the last frontier of mainland America. Items recall a time when Henry Flagler's railroad vaulted the development of the Florida Keys all the way to Key West, and Homestead and Florida City were briefly the take-charge supply outposts. Another part of the museum, the old East Coast Railway Station, was demolished by Hurricane Andrew, but its caboose, which was tumbled on its side, has since been righted.

For the sheer fun as well as the bargain, you can't beat a stint in any of the local fields that welcome visitors to pick their own produce. The season runs from November to April, and you can expect to find strawberries for maybe $2 a pound, corn at $1.25 a dozen ears, and tomatoes for 50¢ a pound. Drive and look for signs—in season they're everywhere among the fields—or call the South Dade Visitor Information Center (*see above*).

Southwest of Florida City near the entrance to Everglades National Park, **Everglades Alligator Farm** presents free hourly alligator shows and feedings and runs a 4-mile, 30-minute tour of the river of grass. No reservations are necessary. *40351 S.W. 192nd Ave., tel. 305/247–2628. Tour and show: $11 adults, $10 senior citizens, $6 children 4–12; show only: $5 adults and senior citizens, $3 children 4–12. Open daily 9–6; tours depart 20 mins after the hr.*

Budget Lodging
$$

Best Western Gateway to the Keys. New at the end of 1994, this two-story motel sits well back from the highway and contains such amenities as full closets, a heat lamp in the bathroom, and complimentary Continental breakfast. More expensive rooms come with wet bar, fridge, microwave, and coffeemaker. Otherwise it's a standard modern motel with floral prints and twin reading lamps. *1 Strano Blvd., 33034, tel. 305/246–5100, fax 305/242–0056. 114 units. Facilities: pool, spa, laundry. AE, D, DC, MC, V.*

$$

Hampton Inn. This two-story motel just off the highway has good clean rooms (including a post–Hurricane Andrew wing added in 1993) and public-friendly policies, including free Continental breakfast daily, free local calls, and a movie channel available at no extra charge. All rooms have at least two upholstered chairs, twin reading lamps, and a desk and chair. Units are color-coordinated and carpeted. Baths have tub-showers. *124 E. Palm Dr., 33034, tel. 305/ 247–8833 or 800/426–7866, fax 305/247–8833. 122 units. Facilities: outdoor pool. AE, D, DC, MC, V.*

$

Super 8 Motel. Standard rooms in a pair of one-story buildings would hardly rate notice anywhere else, but in Florida City your only other choices are to pay more or to opt for a non-chain motel. Avoid rooms 148–151 and 101–104, which are nearest the road. *1202 N. Krome Ave., 33034, tel. 305/245–0311, fax 305/247–9136. 52 units. Facilities: outdoor pool, coin laundry. AE, D, DC, MC, V.*

Budget Dining
$$

Mutineer Restaurant. Former Sheraton Hotels builder Allan Bennett built this upscale roadside restaurant with its indoor-outdoor fish and duck pond at a time (1980) when Florida City was barely on the map. Bilevel dining rooms are divided by sea scenes in etched glass, and there are striped velvet chairs, stained glass, and a few portholes, but no excess. The Wharf Lounge behind its solid oak doors is imaginatively decorated with a magnified aquarium and nautical antiques, including a crow's nest with a stuffed crow, gold parrot, and treasure chest. The big menu features 18 seafood entrées plus another half dozen daily seafood specials, as well as game, ribs, and steaks. Favorites include barbecued baby-back ribs, whole Dungeness crab, and snapper Oscar (topped with crabmeat and asparagus). Enjoy live music Thursday–Saturday evenings. *11 S.E. 1st Ave., tel. 305/245–3377. Reservations accepted. Dress: casual but neat. AE, D, DC, MC, V.*

$–$$
★

Richard Accursio's Capri Restaurant and **King Richard's Room.** One of the oldest family-run restaurants in Dade County—since 1958— this is where locals dine out: business groups at lunch, the Rotary Club each Wednesday at noon, and families at night. Specialties include pizza with light, crunchy crusts and ample toppings; mild, meaty conch chowder; mussels in garlic-cream or marinara sauce; Caesar salad with lots of cheese and anchovies; antipasto with a homemade, vinegary Italian dressing; pasta shells stuffed with rigatoni cheese in tomato sauce; yellowtail snapper française; and Key lime pie with plenty of real Key lime juice. *935 N. Krome Ave., tel.*

305/247–1544. Reservations advised. Dress: casual. AE, D, MC, V. Closed Dec. 25, Sun. except Mother's Day.

$ **Angie's Place.** Less than ½ mile south of the end of Florida's Turnpike, in a little shedlike building set with farmhouse country cupboards and gewgaws, sisters Angie and Tina Strano and Joyce Strano Sutton serve the kinds of breakfasts and lunches they grew up on locally. Food is fresh and cooked to order and includes nice specials. The fisherman's pleasure lunch to go earns a breakfast at half price, and the special of the month might consist of a pancake, an egg, a strip of bacon, sausage, and coffee for less than $4. Hot lunches include the likes of liver and onions, catfish, and marinated chicken breast. *404 S.E. 1st Ave., tel. 305/245–8939. No reservations. Dress: casual. No credit cards. Closed Easter; Thanksgiving; Dec. 24, 25, and 31; Jan. 1. No dinner.*

$ **Farmers' Market Restaurant.** On the grounds of the big state-operated farmers market, this large, modern dining room is up a ramp overlooking the produce vendor bays. The fare is fresh, cooked to order, and affordably priced. Breakfasts are hearty; lunches include baskets of fried and charbroiled seafood and chicken plus subs, sandwiches, burgers, and a few salads; and dinners feature home-style cooking: seafood pasta, catch of the day, fried seafood, country-fried steak, turkey, roast beef, pork chops, and spaghetti with meatballs or sausage. All entrées come with salad, potato or rice, veggie of the day, and rolls and butter. Coffee is only half a buck. *Florida City Farmers Market, Unit 17, 300 N. Krome Ave., tel. 305/ 242–0008. No reservations. Dress: casual. No credit cards. Closed holidays. No dinner Sun.*

Shopping for Bargains

Robert Is Here (19200 Palm Dr. [S.W. 344th St.], tel. 305/246–1592) is a remarkable fruit stand that sells vegetables and some 40 kinds of tropical fruits, including carambola, egg fruit, litchis, monstera, sapodilla, soursop, sugar apple, and tamarind, as well as fresh juices. It's open daily 8–7.

Florida Keys Factory Shops (250 E. Palm Dr.) offer discount shopping at some 50 stores plus a small food court.

Tour 3: Biscayne National Park

Biscayne National Park, the nation's largest marine park, includes 18 miles of mainland coast and 45 barrier islands 7 miles to the east across Biscayne Bay. The islands (called keys) are fossilized coral reefs that emerged from the sea when glaciers trapped much of the world's water supply during the Ice Age. Today a tropical hardwood forest grows in their rocky crevices. From December through April, when the mosquito population is relatively quiescent, you can comfortably explore several of the keys by boat, either your own or the park concessionaire's.

East of the keys another 3 miles lies the park's main attraction: living coral reefs, some the size of a student's desk, others as large as a football field. Once again, you must take a boat ride to see this underwater wonderland, and you really have to snorkel or scuba dive to appreciate it fully. A diverse population of colorful fish—angelfish, gobies, grunts, parrot fish, pork fish, wrasses, and many more—flits through the reefs. Fortunately, Hurricane Andrew did the reefs only minor damage and, scientists now believe, may actually have helped regenerate them.

Arriving and Departing By Plane

MIA (*see* Arriving and Departing by Plane *in* Tour 2, *above*) is the closest airport to Biscayne National Park. You'll have to drive from the airport to the park.

By Car To reach Biscayne National Park, take the Homestead Extension of Florida's Turnpike from Miami to the Tallahassee Road (Southwest 137th Avenue) exit, turn left, and go south. Turn left at North Canal Drive (Southwest 328th Street), go east, and follow signs to park headquarters at Convoy Point. The park is about 30 miles from downtown Miami.

To reach Biscayne National Park from Homestead, take U.S. 1 or Krome Avenue to Lucy Street (Southeast 8th Street), and turn east. Lucy Street becomes North Canal Drive (Southwest 328th Street). Follow signs for about 8 miles to the park headquarters.

Guided Tours Tours at Biscayne National Park are now run by people-friendly
★ **Biscayne National Underwater Park, Inc.** (Convoy Point, east end of North Canal Dr. [S.W. 328th St.], Box 1270, Homestead 33090, tel. 305/230–1100, fax 305/230–1120). Daily trips (10–1) explore the park's living coral reefs 10 miles offshore on *Reef Rover IV*, a 53-foot glass-bottom boat that carries up to 49 passengers. On days when the weather is unsuitable for reef viewing, an alternative two-hour, ranger-led, interpretive tour visits Elliott Key. Reservations are recommended, especially in summer. The cost is $16.50 adults, $15.50 senior citizens, and $8.50 children under 13.

Biscayne National Park

Biscayne National Park: Convoy Point Visitor Center (9700 S.W. 328th St., Box 1369, Homestead 33090-1369, tel. 305/230–7275).

Though a new park headquarters was opened in 1993, a replacement for the **Convoy Point Visitor Center,** which was badly damaged in Hurricane Andrew, will not open until the last half of 1996. A temporary visitor center offers books for sale, limited exhibits, an eight-minute slide orientation, and an 18-minute video on Hurricane Andrew's effects on the park. A short trail and boardwalk lead to a jetty, boat dock, and launch ramp. *9700 S.W. 328th St., Homestead, tel. 305/230–7275. Admission free. Park open daily 8–sunset; visitor center open weekdays 8:30–4:30 (to 5:30 June–Aug.), weekends 8:30–5. By 1996, park may resume its pre-hurricane closing hr of sunset.*

The visitor centers on the park's remote islands, which already attracted fewer visitors than they deserved, were the worst hit by the hurricane. None are now open. Happily, a new park concessionaire, **Biscayne National Underwater Park, Inc.** (*see* Guided Tours, *above*), is offering glass-bottom boat trips to the keys as well as reef tours.

Elliott Key has a 30-foot-wide sandy beach, about a mile north of the harbor on the west (bay) side; boaters like to anchor off it for a swim. Before Hurricane Andrew, rangers used to lead informal nature walks on the key. Check whether these have resumed, or walk the length of the 7-mile key on your own, along a rough path locally referred to as the "spite highway," which developers bulldozed before the park was created. The **Elliott Key Reception Center** had been converted to a ranger station before Hurricane Andrew. By 1996, the ground level is scheduled to be open for environmental education programs, interpretive displays, a slide show, and video. Additionally available are rest rooms, showers, and fresh water.

Just north at **Boca Chita Key,** which was once owned by Mark C. Honeywell, former president of Minneapolis's Honeywell Company, most of the historical structures have been repaired and stabilized. Revegetation, harbor repair, and rest room construction are expected to be complete by 1996, at which time the island will be reopened to the public. Overnight docking and camping is to be allowed. Access will be by private boat only.

On **Adams Key,** rest rooms and a picnic shelter are also scheduled for 1996, at which time the island will be reopened to the public for day use (camping to follow at a later date). A public dock and nature trail will be available. Here, too, access will be by private boat only.

Camping You can camp on designated keys 7 miles offshore at primitive sites or in the backcountry. Carry all your food, water, and supplies onto the keys, and carry all trash off when you leave. Bring plenty of insect repellent. Inquire at the park concessionaire office about boats to the keys, as there are no regular ferries or boats for rent. No reservations are made, but for backcountry camping, you need to get a free permit from rangers at Convoy Point, Elliott Key, or, when it reopens, Adams Key.

4 Fort Lauderdale

By Herb
Hiller

With its rejuvenated beachfront and downtown like balanced weights on the ends of a barbell, Fort Lauderdale has bench-pressed its way out of a reputation for rowdy spring breaks, and urban renewal has replaced scantily clad collegians as the most-talked-about attraction of vacationing here. You can ride the free midweek trolley, drive between beach and town along beautiful Las Olas Boulevard, or—the best bet for experiencing this canal-laced city—cruise aboard the city's water taxi. All these, plus the new expressway system that connects city and airport (including Florida's only vehicular tunnel), make getting around Fort Lauderdale, unlike elsewhere in congested Florida, remarkably hassle-free.

Also unlike elsewhere, where gaudy tourist zones stand aloof from workaday downtowns, Fort Lauderdale exhibits uncommon consistency at both ends of the 2-mile Las Olas corridor. The sparkling new look results from a decision to thoroughly improve both beachfront and downtown rather than focus design integrity in town and let the beachfront fall prey to design by T-shirt retailers. Fort Lauderdale also differs from other Florida coastal resorts in its long stretch of undeveloped beachfront. For 2 miles beginning just north of the new welcome center and the big Radisson Bahia Mar Beach Resort, strollers and café-goers along Atlantic Boulevard enjoy clear views, typically across rows of colorful beach umbrellas, to the sea and ships passing in and out of nearby Port Everglades. Those on the beach can look back to an exceptionally graceful promenade.

Pedestrians rank ahead of cars in Fort Lauderdale. Broad walkways line both sides of the shore road, and traffic has been trimmed to two gently curving northbound lanes, where in-line skaters dance alongside the slow-moving cars. On the beach side, a low masonry wall, which serves as an extended bench, edges the promenade with wavelike curls. Where side streets reach the shore road, the wave crests and then breaks for pedestrian access to the beach. At night, the wall is wrapped in ribbons of fiber-optic color. On the upland side of Atlantic Boulevard, the 17-story Beach Place residential, retail, and entertainment complex is under construction two blocks north of Las Olas. Otherwise there are mostly low-rise hotels plus a defining row of smart cafés, restaurants, bars, and shops.

North of the redesigned beachfront are another 2 miles of open and natural upland and seaside. Much of the way parallels the Hugh Taylor Birch State Recreation Area, which preserves a patch of primeval Florida.

As lovely as the renewed beach is, the downtown area along the New River, site of a new arts and entertainment district, is equally attractive. Where drug deals went down less than five years ago, pricey tickets now sell for *Miss Saigon* and other touring Broadway shows at the riverfront Broward Center for the Performing Arts. Clustered within a five-minute walk are the Museum of Discovery and Science with its Blockbuster Imax Theater, the expanding Fort Lauderdale Historical Society Museum, and the Museum of Art with its leading collection of 20th-century CoBrA works. Restaurants, sidewalk cafés, delis, and blues, folk, jazz, reggae, and rock clubs flourish. Brickell Station, along several blocks once owned by pioneers William and Mary Brickell, is expected to open its multistory entertainment stages, restaurants, and shops in 1996. A year later will bring the $40 million New World Aquarium, and in 1998, a living historical complex called Old Fort Lauderdale will open, with re-enactments and docents in pioneer dress centered on the Museum of History.

Tying this district together is the Riverwalk, which extends a mile along the river's north bank and a half mile along the south. Tropical gardens with benches and interpretive displays fringe the walk on one side, boat landings on the other. East along Riverwalk is Stranahan House, where in the late 19th century beloved Frank Stranahan ran a pioneer trading post. A block away, Las Olas attractions begin. Tropical landscaping sets off fine shops, restaurants, and popular nightspots. From here it's five minutes by car or 30 minutes by water taxi back to the beach.

Broward County is named for Napoleon Bonaparte Broward, Florida's governor from 1905 to 1909, whose drainage schemes around the turn of the century opened much of the marshy Everglades region for farming, ranching, and settlement (in retrospect an environmental disaster). Fort Lauderdale's first known white settler, Charles Lewis, established a plantation along the New River in 1793. Major William Lauderdale built a fort at the river's mouth in 1838 during the Seminole Indian wars—hence the name.

Incorporated in 1911, with just 175 residents, Fort Lauderdale grew rapidly during the Florida boom of the 1920s. Today the city has a population of 150,000, while its suburban areas keep growing and growing—1.3 million in the county. New homes, offices, and shopping centers have filled in the gaps between older communities along the coastal ridge. Now they're marching west along I–75, I–595, and the Sawgrass Expressway. Broward County is blessed with near-ideal weather, with some 3,000 hours of sunshine a year. The average temperature is about 77°F—66°F in winter, 84°F in summer. Once a home for retirees, the county today attracts younger, working-age families, too. It's always been known as a sane and pleasant place to live. Now it's also becoming one of Florida's most diverse and dynamic places to vacation.

Fort Lauderdale Basics

Arriving and Departing

By Plane **Fort Lauderdale–Hollywood International Airport (FLHIA)** (tel. 305/359–6100), 4 miles south of downtown Fort Lauderdale and just off U.S. 1, is Broward County's major airline terminal and is becoming one of Florida's busiest—more than 10 million arrivals and departures a year, a figure that's expected to triple within 20 years. FLHIA is especially favored by new low-cost carriers. Scheduled airlines include **Airways International** (tel. 305/887–2794), **American** (tel. 800/433–7300), **Bahamasair** (tel. 800/562–7661), **Carnival Air Lines** (tel. 305/359–7886), **Chalk's International** (tel. 800/424–2557), **Comair** (tel. 800/354–9822), **Continental** (tel. 800/525–0280), **Delta** (tel. 800/221–1212), **Eagle Air** (tel. 800/332–4533), **Icelandair** (tel. 305/359–2735), **Martinair** (tel. 800/366–4655), **Midwest Express** (tel. 800/452–2022), **Northwest** (tel. 800/225–2525), **Paradise Island** (tel. 800/432–8807), **TWA** (tel. 800/221–2000), **United** (tel. 800/241–6522), **USAir** (tel. 800/842–5374), and **Valujet** (tel. 800/825–8538).

Budget Airport Transport **Broward Transit** (tel. 305/357–8400) operates bus route No. 1 between the airport and its main terminal at Broward Boulevard and Northwest 1st Avenue in the center of Fort Lauderdale. Service from the airport begins daily at 5:40 AM; the last bus from the downtown terminal to the airport leaves at 9:30 PM. The fare is 85¢. **Gray Line** (tel. 305/561–8886) provides limousine service to all parts of Broward County. Fares to most Fort Lauderdale beach hotels are in the $6–$10 range.

Rental-car agencies located in the airport include **Avis** (tel. 305/359–3255), **Budget** (tel. 305/359–4700), **Dollar** (tel. 305/359–7800), **Hertz** (tel. 305/359–5281), and **National** (tel. 305/359–8303). In season you'll pay about $120–$130 by the week; the collision damage waiver adds about $11 per day.

By Bus **Greyhound Lines** (tel. 800/231–2222) buses stop in Fort Lauderdale (515 N.E. 3rd St., tel. 305/764–6551).

By Car Access to Broward County from the north or south is via Florida's Turnpike, I–95, U.S. 1, or U.S. 441. I–75 (Alligator Alley) connects Broward with Florida's west coast and runs parallel to Route 84 within the county.

By Train **Amtrak** (tel. 800/872–7245) provides daily service to the Fort Lauderdale station (200 S.W. 21st Terr., tel. 305/463–8251) as well as to the other Broward County stops, Hollywood and Deerfield Beach.

Tri-Rail (tel. 305/728–8445) operates train service daily, 5 AM–11 PM (more limited on weekends), through coastal Broward, Dade, and Palm Beach counties. There are six stations in Broward County, all of them west of I–95.

Getting Around on the Cheap

If you're staying near the beach, it isn't necessary to have a car to get around. Each of the beachfront communities has a good mix of lodgings and restaurants, and supermarkets, malls, and just about anywhere you'd want to go are close by or within easy and affordable range by bus.

By Bus and Trolley **Broward County Mass Transit** (tel. 305/357–8400) serves the entire county. The fare is 85¢ (40¢ senior citizens, people with disabilities, and students), plus 10¢ for a transfer. Service on all beach routes starts before 6 AM and continues past 10 PM except on Sundays. Call for route information. Special seven-day tourist passes, which cost $8, are good for unlimited use on all county buses. These are available at some hotels, at Broward County libraries, and at the main bus terminal (Broward Blvd. at N.W. 1st Ave.).

Supplementary bus and trolley services include the expanding free **Downtown Trolley,** which operates weekdays 7:30–5:30 on the Red Line (Courthouse Line) and 11:30–2:30 on the Green (Arts & Science to Las Olas) and Blue (Las Olas to Courthouse) lines. The wait is rarely more than 10 minutes. The lines connect major tourist sites in the Arts and Science District, offices, banks, and government and academic buildings to water-taxi stops along the Riverwalk and to the main bus terminal. Along the beach, the **Wave Line Trolley** (tel. 305/527–5600) costs $1 and operates daily every hour 10:15–8:15 except half hourly 4:45–6:15 PM. It runs along Route A1A from the Galleria Mall on Sunrise Boulevard in the north to close by the Hyatt Regency Pier Sixty-Six in the south.

By Car Should you opt for a car, however, Broward County is a fairly easy place to drive, except during rush hour. East–west I–595 runs from westernmost Broward County to link I–75 and U.S. 1, providing handy access to Fort Lauderdale–Hollywood International Airport. The scenic but slow Route A1A generally parallels the beach.

By Taxi It's difficult to hail a cab on the street. Sometimes you can pick one up at a major hotel. Otherwise, phone ahead. Fares are not cheap; meters run at a rate of $2.45 for the first mile and $1.75 for each additional mile; waiting time is 25¢ per minute. The major company serving the area is **Yellow Cab** (tel. 305/565–5400).

By Water Taxi **Water Taxi** (tel. 305/565–5507) provides service along the Intracoastal Waterway between Port Everglades and Commercial Boulevard 10 AM–1 AM and between Atlantic Boulevard and Hillsboro Boulevard in Pompano Beach noon–midnight. The boats stop at more than 30 restaurants, hotels, shops, and nightclubs; the fare is $6 one-way, $14 ($8 for children under 12) for an all-day pass, and $45 ($25 for kids) weekly.

Important Addresses and Numbers

Emergencies Dial 911 for **police** or **ambulance.**

Florida Poison Information Center (tel. 800/282–3171).

Hospitals The following hospitals have a 24-hour emergency room: **Broward General Medical Center** (1600 S. Andrews Ave., Fort Lauderdale, tel. 305/355–4400; physician referral, tel. 305/355–4888), **Coral Springs Medical Center** (3999 Coral Hills Dr., Coral Springs, tel. 350/344–3000; physician referral, tel. 305/355–4888), **Hollywood Medical Center** (3600 Washington St., Hollywood, tel. 305/985–6274; physician referral, tel. 800/237–8701), **Holy Cross Hospital** (4725 N. Federal Hwy., Fort Lauderdale, tel. 305/492–5753; physician referral, tel. 305/776–3223), **Imperial Point Medical Center** (6401 N. Federal Hwy., Fort Lauderdale, tel. 305/776–8500; physician referral, tel. 305/355–4888), **North Broward Medical Center** (201 E. Sample Rd., Pompano Beach, tel. 305/941–8300; physician referral, tel. 305/355–4888), **Plantation General Hospital** (401 N.W. 42nd Ave., Plantation, tel. 305/797–6470; physician referral, tel. 305/472–8879), and **Universal Medical Center in Plantation** (6701 W. Sunrise Blvd., Plantation, tel. 305/581–7800; physician referral, tel. 305/581–0448).

Late-Night Pharmacies **Eckerd Drug** (1385 S.E. 17th St., Fort Lauderdale, tel. 305/525–8173; 1701 E. Commercial Blvd., Fort Lauderdale, tel. 305/771–0660; 154 University Dr., Pembroke Pines, tel. 305/432–5510). **Medical Associates Plaza Pharmacy** (3700 Washington St., Hollywood, tel. 305/963–2008 or 800/793–2008). **Walgreen** (2855 Stirling Rd., Fort Lauderdale, tel. 305/981–1104; 5001 N. Dixie Hwy., Oakland Park, tel. 305/772–4206; 289 S. Federal Hwy., Deerfield Beach, tel. 305/481–2993).

Visitor
Information

Chamber of Commerce of Greater Fort Lauderdale (512 N.E. 3rd Ave., Fort Lauderdale 33301, tel. 305/462–6000). The walk-up, official **Visitors Information Center** (600 Seabreeze Blvd.), on the beach three blocks south of Las Olas Boulevard, is an excellent source of maps, transportation schedules, and event information; it's open Monday–Saturday 9–6, Sunday 11–6.

Dania Chamber of Commerce (100 W. Dania Beach Blvd., Dania 33004, tel. 305/927–3377).

Greater Deerfield Beach/North Broward Chamber of Commerce (1601 E. Hillsboro Blvd., Deerfield Beach 33441, tel. 305/427–1050).

Greater Fort Lauderdale Convention & Visitors Bureau (200 E. Las Olas Blvd., Suite 1500, Fort Lauderdale 33301, tel. 305/765–4466 or 800/227–8669 for brochures).

Hollywood Chamber of Commerce (2410 Hollywood Blvd., Hollywood, FL 33019, tel. 305/923–4000).

Latin Chamber of Commerce of Broward County (4000 Hollywood Blvd., Hollywood 33021, tel. 305/966–0767).

Lauderdale-by-the-Sea Chamber of Commerce (4201 N. Ocean Dr., Lauderdale-by-the-Sea 33308, tel. 305/776–1000).

Pompano Beach Chamber of Commerce (2200 E. Atlantic Blvd., Pompano Beach 33062, tel. 305/941–2940).

Where to Stay on a Budget

In Broward County, you'll want to stay near the beach, as inland communities have little to offer vacationers. In Fort Lauderdale, Pompano Beach, and the Hollywood–Hallandale area, dozens of hotels face the Atlantic Ocean. In much of Fort Lauderdale, however, lodgings are limited to the upland side of the beach roads, and, in much of Hollywood, they're limited to the upland side of the Broadwalk, leaving the beaches open to pedestrians and motorists. Luckily, if you stay at any of the beachfront places listed below, you'll be able to walk or ride the bus to almost everywhere you'll want to go. More affordable motels and hotels are available within a 5- to 10-minute walk of the beach. Those with cars might find these lodgings preferable, as overnight street parking is more accessible a block or two away from the ocean.

An innovative Superior Small Lodging program, set up by the Greater Fort Lauderdale Convention & Visitors Bureau and administered by the hospitality department of Broward County's Nova University, has led to substantial upgrading of many smaller properties. Some of the best are described below, but try to get a copy of the entire listing (it's free) because these are great buys, almost all within walking distance of the beach. Most of them offer seven nights for the price of six, even in high season. Many offer discounts to senior citizens, though the definition of "senior" may vary, there may be minimum-stay or double-occupancy requirements, and discounts may apply only to superior or deluxe rooms. Still, it's well worth asking.

Wherever you plan to stay in Broward County, reservations are a good idea throughout the year. Tourists from the northern United States and Canada fill up the hotels from Thanksgiving through Easter. In summer, southerners and Europeans create a second season that's almost as busy. The rate categories below are based on the all-year or peak-season price; off-peak rates may be lower.

Deerfield
Beach
$$

Carriage House Resort Motel. Run by a French-American couple (who speak German and some Spanish as well), this near-beachfront motel sits one block from the ocean. Very clean and tidy, the two-story, black-shuttered white Colonial-style lodging is actually two buildings connected by a second-story sundeck. Steady improvements have been made to the facility, including the addition of Bahama beds that feel and look like sofas. Kitchenettes are equipped with

Fort Lauderdale Area Lodging

Banyan Marina Apartments, **7**

Bermudian Waterfront Motel & Apartments, **6**

Blue Seas, **3**

Carriage House Resort Motel, **2**

Driftwood on the Ocean, **15**

International House, **4**

Maison Harrison, **13**

Manta Ray Inn, **14**

Martindale Apartments/Motel, **10**

Nina Lee Motel, **11**

Pelican Beach Resort, **5**

The Pillars, **8**

Royal Flamingo Villas, **1**

Sea Downs, **12**

Sol-Y-Mar International Youth Hostel, **9**

good-quality utensils. Rooms are self-contained and quiet and have walk-in closets and room safes. *250 S. Ocean Blvd., 33441, tel. 305/ 427–7670, fax 305/428–4790. 6 rooms, 14 efficiencies, 10 apts. Facilities: heated pool, sundeck, shuffleboard, coin laundry. AE, MC, V.*

Fort Lauderdale: Beach
$$

Martindale Apartments/Motel. On a short, quiet street a block from the beach, this three-story hotel is set around a landscaped but somewhat dark interior courtyard. There's a stylish blue canopy over the entry, and the rooms, efficiencies, and one-bedroom apartments are compact but fully furnished with table and chairs. The look is hodgepodgy rather than coordinated, but the spaces are clean and modestly comfortable. All units have in-room phone, cable TV, and refrigerator; a microwave or a storage safe costs $1 a day additional. Whereas most similar hotels have their pools right on the street, the Martindale's pool and garden are to the rear, for more privacy. If you book for a week, efficiencies can get downright inexpensive, as can one-bedroom apartments if shared by four people. *3006 Bayshore Dr., 33304, tel. 305/467–1841 or 800/666–1841, fax 305/653–8109. 19 units. Facilities: pool, 3 holes of miniature golf, gardens, coin laundry. AE, MC, V.*

$$

Nina Lee Motel. This is typical of the modest, affordable 1950s-style lodgings that can be found within a block or two of the ocean along the Fort Lauderdale shore. Be prepared for plain rooms—homey and clean, but not tiny, with at least a toaster, coffeemaker, and fridge; efficiencies have gas stoves, large closets, and tub-showers. The pool is set in a garden, and the entire property is removed just enough from the beach causeway so that it's quiet. *3048 Harbor Dr., 33316, tel. 305/524–1568. 14 units. Facilities: heated pool. MC, V.*

$$

Pelican Beach Resort. This ever-expanding, oceanfront, mom-and-pop operation consists of a row of seven different-looking two- and three-story motels dating from the 1950s. All the motels were refurbished between 1990 and 1992, and 25 rooms were added in 1995. Although the furnishings are bland and commercial, not homelike, the friendly management adds a personal touch. Affordable rooms don't overlook the ocean—you'll have to pay more for those views—but all rooms have access to the great facilities: pool, free parking, coin laundry, and a big beach you don't have to cross a street to get to. What's more, a Continental breakfast is included, and the innkeepers occasionally sponsor a barbecue for the guests. Given the large number of rooms, you're likely to do well negotiating here when rooms are available late in the day—maybe getting an upgrade into oceanfront space or a unit with kitchen facilities. *2000 N. Atlantic Blvd., 33305–3727, tel. 305/568–9431 or 800/525–6232, fax 305/565–2622. 56 rooms, 18 efficiencies, 12 suites. Facilities: heated oceanfront pool, beach, exercise room, coin laundry. AE, D, DC, MC, V.*

$$

The Pillars. Scott Anthony has spent seven years turning this 1936 estate house into a friendly waterfront compound. Pool, docks, and deck all overlook the Intracoastal Waterway, and Scott organizes barbecues here from time to time, especially when he has a lot of repeat guests, which he does often. The clean and comfortable Pillars attracts a quiet rather than partying clientele. Only three rooms qualify as being moderately priced and they face the street, but since they're 200 yards off the beach, nights are quiet. Rooms are small but adequate, with a cream-and-green color scheme, carpeting, and standard furniture—table, a couple of chairs, bed, and night table with reading lamp. Each does have a fridge, toaster, and coffeepot, so you can save money by fixing your own breakfast. The real reason to stay here, though, is what's outside: grass leading to the docks, lawn furniture around the pool, and a convivial atmosphere. If you stay for at least a week, you can get a 40% discount, which makes the room rate inexpensive. *111 N. Birch Rd., 33304, tel. 305/467–9639 or 800/800–7666, fax 305/763–2845. 12 rooms, 7 ef-*

ficiencies, 3 1-bedroom apts. Facilities: outdoor pool, dock with water taxi service, coin laundry. AE, D, DC, MC, V.

¢ **Bermudian Waterfront Motel & Apartments.** This is about as affordable as you can get in Fort Lauderdale. In season, a small single room goes for $30—and not a bad room at that, with French doors and a sash window overlooking the pool and the Intracoastal Waterway. More spacious rooms start at $56, efficiencies run $62–$80, one-bedroom apartments go for $82–$103, and two-bedroom apartments, $95–$150, sleep up to four. Children under 12 stay free. Only a block from the ocean, the place has good facilities. There are in-room phones, but a 40¢ surcharge is added for each call. *315 N. Birch Rd., 33304, tel. 305/467–0467, fax 305/467–0467, ext. 2. 4 rooms, 4 efficiencies, 16 apts. Facilities: pool, shuffleboard, barbecue, coin laundry. MC, V.*

¢ **International House.** This hostel, affiliated with the network of Hostelling International–American Youth Hostels, contains four- and eight-bunk dorms with a bathroom and TV in each room. It's a block from the beach and across the street from a 24-hour grocery store. Unlike many AYH facilities, International House sets no curfew. Free lockers are provided. *3811 N. Ocean Blvd., 33308, tel. 305/568–1615, fax 305/568–1595. 96 beds. Facilities: pool, scuba diving center, kitchen, picnic area, barbecue, coin laundry. MC, V.*

¢ **Sol-Y-Mar International Youth Hostel.** For just $12 a night (tax included), you can stay only a block from the beach. Of course, you'll have to share one of the seven multibunk rooms with either three or five other hostelers and you'll have to rent sheets (unless you bring your own), but each room has its own bath, TV, and fridge. Or you can opt for one of the four private rooms at $50 a night. There's a fully equipped communal kitchen and dayroom, and you can use the safe free. The hostel has operated since the mid-1980s and is very popular with international guests. It's a good idea to call ahead. *2839 Vistamar St., 33304, tel. 305/565–1419. 11 rooms. Facilities: kitchen, dayroom. Inquire about credit cards.*

Fort Lauderdale: Downtown
$$
★

Banyan Marina Apartments. French doors have been added to guest quarters, further fine-tuning these already outstanding waterfront apartments on a residential island just off Las Olas Boulevard. Imaginative landscaping includes a walkway through the upper branches of a banyan tree. Luxurious units with leather sofas, springy carpets, real potted plants, sheer curtains, custom drapes, high-quality art, and jalousies for sweeping the breeze in make these units as comfortable as any first-class hotel—but for a considerably lower price. Also included are a water view, beautiful gardens, dock space for eight yachts, and exemplary housekeeping. This is Florida the way you want it to be. *111 Isle of Venice, 33301, tel. 305/524–4430, fax 305/764–4870. 10 rooms, 1 efficiency, 4 1-bedroom apts., 2 2-bedroom apts. Facilities: pool, waterfront deck. MC, V.*

Hillsboro Beach
Splurge

Royal Flamingo Villas. This small community of houselike villas, built in the 1970s, reaches from the Intracoastal Waterway to the sea. The roomy and comfortable one- and two-bedroom villas are all condominiums, so they're fully furnished the way owners want them. All are so quiet that you hear only the soft click of ceiling fans and kitchen clocks. Some living rooms have tile floors, but there's carpet in the bedrooms. The development is wisely set back a bit from the beach, which is eroded anyway, though enjoyable at low tide. Lawns are so lushly landscaped you might trip. If you don't need lavish public facilities, this is your upscale value choice, and it's an especially good buy for two couples traveling together. *1225 Hillsboro Mile (Rte. A1A), 33062, tel. 305/427–0669, 305/427–0660, or 800/241–2477, fax 305/427–6110. 40 villas. Facilities: heated pool, beach, putting green, dock, boat rentals, shuffleboard, coin laundry. D, MC, V.*

Hollywood **Driftwood on the Ocean.** This attractive 36-year-old resort motel
$$ faces the beach at the secluded south end of Surf Road. The setting is
★ what draws guests, but attention to maintenance and frequent re-
furbishing are what adds value for the money. Most units have a
kitchen, one-bedroom apartments have a daybed, and standard
rooms have a queen-size Murphy bed. All have balconies. *2101 S.
Surf Rd., 33019, tel. 305/923–9528, fax 305/922–1062. 10 rooms, 39
efficiencies. Facilities: heated pool, beach, bicycles, shuffleboard,
barbecue, laundry. AE, MC, V.*

$$ **Maison Harrison.** This house feels very much like the '20s and '30s,
when developer Joseph Young planned and built Hollywood in what
seemed like overnight. As a result, it feels comfortable but a little
dated. Living room lighting is all by floor lamp—more suggestive
than illuminating. The sunporch, where breakfast is served, overlooks the street, which, as was customary for the time, is extraordi-
narily wide even though houses are cheek by jowl. The house
originally housed Young's salesmen, so bedrooms have private
baths. Today Millie Poole competently manages it in a style that's as
much commercial as engaging; it's good for those who want neither a
sterile motel nor that sense of obligation that sometimes comes with
doting hosts. Rooms are complete if a little fussy (various swags,
poufs, and an enormous canopy). Here and there a closet or bath-
room-cabinet door doesn't quite close, or unplugged screw holes remain where a towel rack once hung. Beds are firm, there's plenty of
hot water, and a couple of rooms have usable balconies. Furnishings
are mostly traditional, with much upholstery and Oriental-style
rugs. An expanded Continental breakfast is included. *1504 Harrison St., 33020, tel. 305/922–7319. 4 rooms. Facilities: living/dining
area. V.*

$$ **Manta Ray Inn.** Canadians Donna and Dwayne Boucher run this ex-
★ emplary two-story lodging on the beach, keeping the place immacu-
late and the rates affordable. Dating from the 1940s, the inn offers
the casual, comfortable beachfront vacationing Hollywood is famous
for. Nothing's fussy—white spaces with burgundy trim and rattan
furniture—and everything's included. Kitchens are equipped with
pots, pans, and mini-appliances that make housekeeping conve-
nient. All apartments have full closets, and except for second baths
with stall showers in two-bedroom units, baths have tub-showers.
*1715 S. Surf Rd., 33019, tel. 305/921–9666, fax 305/929–8220. 12
units. Facilities: beach, barbecue grills. No credit cards.*

$$ **Sea Downs.** This three-story lodging directly on the Broadwalk is a
good choice for efficiency living. Views vary from full on the beach to
rear-of-the-house prospects of neighborhood motels, and luck of the
draw determines what you get. All units are comfortably done in
chintz, however, with blinds, no drapes. Kitchens are fully
equipped, and most units have tub-showers and closets. Every room
has a ceiling fan, and of course everything is air-conditioned and has
TV and phone. Housekeeping is provided once a week. In between,
you receive fresh towels daily and sheets on request, but you make
your own bed. Bougainvillea on the Beach (2813 N. Surf Rd., tel.
305/925–1368), under the same ownership, also has efficiencies and
one-bedroom apartments. A block off the beach, it's similar to its
sister, but its decor is a slim notch lower. Guests here are welcome to
use the Sea Downs pool, and those at Sea Downs can enjoy
Bougainvillea's gardens. *2900 N. Surf Rd., 33019-3704, tel. 305/923–
4968, fax 305/923–8747. 5 efficiencies, 8 1-bedroom apts. (some can
be joined to make 2-bedroom apts.). Facilities: pool, beachfront. No
credit cards.*

Lauderdale- **Blue Seas.** Bubbly innkeeper Cristie Furth runs this one- and two-
by-the-Sea story motel with her husband, Marc, and small as it is, they keep in-
$ vesting their future in it. Newly added are lattice fencing and gar-
★ dens of cactus and impatiens in front, so there's more privacy around
the brick patio and garden-set pool. Guest quarters feature kitchenettes, terra-cotta tiles, bright Haitian and Peruvian art, and gener-

ally Tex-Mex and Danish furnishings, whose woody textures work well together. Handmade painted shutters and indoor plants add to the look. This remains an excellent buy in a quiet resort area just a block from the beach. *4525 El Mar Dr., 33308, tel. 305/772–3336. 13 units. Facilities: heated pool, coin laundry. MC, V.*

Exploring Fort Lauderdale

Fort Lauderdale for Free—or Almost

Low-cost activities are not limited to people-watching, though there's plenty of that to be had, either on the beaches or the downtown Riverwalk. Fort Lauderdale also has plenty of festivals; in April alone, these include the Fort Lauderdale Seafood Festival, the New River Jazz Festival, and the Downtown Festival of the Arts. Senior citizens can get discounts at many attractions. Dania Jai-Alai Palace (*see* Spectator Sports *in* Sports and the Outdoors, *below*), for example, offers visitors 55 and over free matinee admission before noon and reduced admission on Thursday before 8, and museum admission for those 65 and over at the International Swimming Hall of Fame (*see* Tour 2, *below*) is one-third the regular price.

Beaches The best things in Fort Lauderdale—the beaches—are free. From Hallandale and Hollywood in the south to Deerfield Beach in the north, all you have to do is walk onto the sand—no fee, no pass needed.

For the best beachside people-watching, ensconce yourself at a sidewalk café along the Broadwalk in Hollywood, near 876-foot-long Anglin's Pier in Lauderdale-by-the-Sea, and just about anywhere along the restored Fort Lauderdale beachfront between Las Olas and Sunrise boulevards.

Concerts Free jazz concerts are usually held the first Sunday of the month, August through December, along the Riverwalk in downtown Fort Lauderdale. A public band shell along the Broadwalk in Hollywood is also the site of occasional free concerts sponsored by the city.

Parks Broward County's fine parks system includes 14 regional parks that offer a wide range of activities including biking, jogging, swimming, canoeing, horseback riding, tennis, hiking on nature trails, and picnicking. Many parks offer special facilities. For example, **Brian Piccolo Park** (Sheridan St. and N.W. 101st Ave., Cooper City, tel. 305/437–2626) has a velodrome, where you can cycle or skate for two hours for $3. There's cable waterskiing at **Quiet Waters Park** (*see* Participant Sports *in* Sports and the Outdoors, *below*), and **C.B. Smith Park** (900 N. Flamingo Rd., Pembroke Pines, tel. 305/437–2650) has 700-foot water slides. It's open daily from when school's out in June to Labor Day, weekends only the rest of the year; admission is $5.75 adults, $4.25 children 4–12. The park system also schedules special events throughout the year. Call 305/563–7275 for a brief recorded description of that week's events.

Shopping for Bargains Every Saturday from 8 to 1, the **Homegrown Marketplace** (City Park Mall Garage, 115 S.E. 1st Ave.) sets up in downtown Fort Lauderdale. Special holiday events are sometimes offered at this farmer's market. At the **Seminole Native Village** (4150 N. Rte. 7, Hollywood, tel. 305/961–5140 for recording or 305/961–3220 for information), Seminoles sell native arts and crafts. (The village also features a bingo parlor and low-stakes poker tables, but these may or may not be "for free—or almost" depending on your luck.) Across the road is the **Anhinga Indian Museum and Art Gallery** (5791 S. Rte. 7, Fort Lauderdale, tel. 305/581–0416), where Joe Dan and Virginia Osceola display a collection of artifacts from the Seminoles and other tribes and sell contemporary Native American art and craft objects. Both the village and the museum and gallery are open daily 9–5.

Tour 1: Downtown Fort Lauderdale

Numbers in the margin correspond to points of interest on the Fort Lauderdale Area map.

1 This tour begins, appropriately enough, at **Stranahan House,** home of pioneer businessman Frank Stranahan and the oldest standing structure in Fort Lauderdale. Stranahan arrived in 1892 and with his wife, Ivy, befriended the Seminoles, traded with them, and taught them "new ways." In 1901 he built a store and later made it his home. Now it's a museum with many of his furnishings on display. *1 Stranahan Pl. (S.E. 6th Ave. at Las Olas Blvd.), tel. 305/524–4736. Admission: $5 adults, $2 children under 12. Open Wed.–Sat. 10–4, Sun. 1–4.*

Go north on Southeast 6th Avenue to **Las Olas Boulevard.** Between Southeast 6th and Southeast 11th avenues, Las Olas is an upscale shopping street with Spanish-colonial buildings housing high-fashion boutiques, jewelry shops, and art galleries. If you drive east on **2** Las Olas, you'll cross into **The Isles,** Fort Lauderdale's most expensive and prestigious neighborhood, where the homes line a series of canals with large yachts beside the seawalls.

Return west on Las Olas to Andrews Avenue, turn right, and park in one of the municipal garages while you walk around downtown Fort **★ 3** Lauderdale. First stop is the **Museum of Art,** which features a major collection of works from the CoBrA (Copenhagen, Brussels, and Amsterdam) movement, plus Native American, pre-Columbian, West African, and Oceanic ethnographic art. Edward Larabee Barnes designed the museum building, which opened in 1986. The museum has a notable collection of works by celebrated Ashcan School artist William Glackens and other early 20th-century American painters. *1 E. Las Olas Blvd., tel. 305/525–5500. Admission: $5 adults, $4 senior citizens, $3 students over 12. Open Tues. 11–9, Wed.–Sat. 10–5, Sun. noon–5.*

4 Walk one block north to the **Broward County Main Library,** in a distinctive building designed by Marcel Breuer. On display here are many works from Broward's Art in Public Places program, including a painting by Yaacov Agam; a wood construction by Marc Beauregard; an outdoor, aluminum-and-steel sculpture by Dale Eldred; and ceramic tile by Ivan Chermayeff. (Art in Public Places displays more than 200 works—painting, sculpture, photographs, weaving—by nationally renowned and Florida artists. Works are located at 13 major sites, including the main bus terminal and the airport [*see* Arriving and Departing *in* Fort Lauderdale Basics, *above*, for both]). Productions from theater to poetry readings are presented in a 300-seat auditorium. *100 S. Andrews Ave., tel. 305/357–7444 or 305/357–7457 for self-guided Art in Public Places walking tour brochure. Admission free. Open Mon.–Thurs. 9–9, Fri.–Sat. 9–5, Sun. noon–5:30; closed holidays.*

Go west on Southeast 2nd Street to Southwest 2nd Avenue, turn **★ 5** left, and head toward palm-lined **Riverwalk,** a lovely, paved promenade on the north bank of the New River. (SunBank sponsors a jazz brunch along Riverwalk the first Sunday of every month.) By the late 1990s, it will extend 2 miles on both sides of the beautiful urban stream, connecting a cluster of new facilities collectively known as **6** the **Arts and Science District.** The district includes the outdoor **Esplanade,** which features several exhibits, including a hands-on display of the science and history of navigation.

The major science attraction is the $30 million **Museum of Discovery and Science,** opened in 1992. It contains a 55-foot-by-71-foot screen

Fort Lauderdale Area

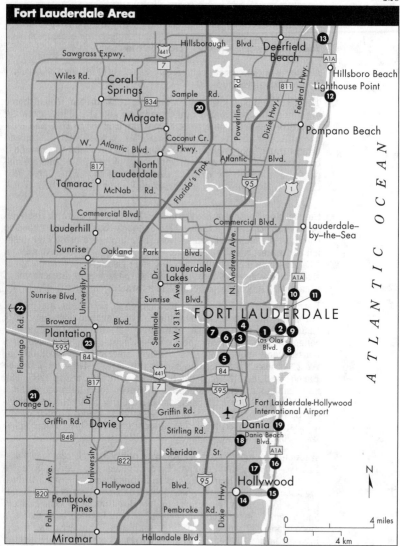

Art and Culture Center of Hollywood, **14**

Arts and Science District, **6**

Bonnet House, **11**

Broadwalk, **15**

Broward County Main Library, **4**

Butterfly World, **20**

Deerfield Island Park, **13**

Flamingo Gardens, **21**

Fort Lauderdale beachfront, **9**

Graves Museum of Archeology & Natural History, **18**

Hillsboro Light, **12**

Hollywood North Beach Park, **16**

Hugh Taylor Birch State Recreation Area, **10**

International Swimming Hall of Fame Museum and Aquatic Complex, **8**

The Isles, **2**

John U. Lloyd Beach State Recreation Area, **19**

Museum of Art, **3**

Riverwalk, **5**

Sawgrass Recreation Park, **22**

Sailboat Bend, **7**

Stranahan House, **1**

West Lake Park, **17**

Young at Art Children's Museum, **23**

in the Blockbuster IMAX Theater, which has six-channel sound, and interactive exhibits on ecology, health, and outer space. Many displays focus on the local environment, including a replica of an oak forest complete with mosses, lichens, and air plants, which grow without soil. Another unusual exhibit offers a cutaway of an Indian shell mound. *401 S.W. 2nd St., tel. 305/467–6637 for museum or 305/463–4629 for IMAX. Admission to museum: $6 adults, $5 senior citizens and children over 3; to IMAX: $5 adults, $4 senior citizens and children over 3; to both: $8 adults, $7 senior citizens and children over 3. Open weekdays 10–5, Sat. 10–8:30, Sun. noon–5.*

The adjacent **Broward Center for the Performing Arts** (201 S.W. 5th Ave., tel. 305/462–0222), a massive glass-and-concrete structure by the river, opened in 1991.

East of the Esplanade along the Riverwalk is the **Fort Lauderdale Historical Society Museum,** which by 1997 is expected to expand into several historic buildings, including the King-Cromartie House and the old New River Inn, adjacent to its longtime site. The museum surveys the city's history from the Seminole era to World War II. A model in the lobby depicts old Fort Lauderdale. The building also houses a research library and a bookstore. *219 S.W. 2nd Ave., tel. 305/463–4431. Admission: $2 adults, $1 students and children 6–12. Open Tues.–Sat. 10–4, Sun. 1–4.*

For a look at one of Fort Lauderdale's reviving, historic residential districts, go five blocks west along Las Olas Boulevard to Southwest **7** 7th Avenue and the entrance to **Sailboat Bend.** Between Las Olas and the river, as well as just across the river, lies a neighborhood with much the character of Old Town in Key West and historic Coconut Grove in Miami. No shops or services are located here. You can return to the start of the tour by traveling east along Las Olas Boulevard.

Tour 2: North on Scenic A1A

Go east on Southeast 17th Street across the **Brooks Memorial Causeway** over the Intracoastal Waterway, and bear left onto Seabreeze Boulevard (Route A1A). You will pass through a neighborhood of older homes set in lush vegetation before emerging at the south end of Fort Lauderdale's beachfront strip. On your left at the newly renovated **Radisson Bahia Mar Beach Resort** (801 Seabreeze Blvd., tel. 305/764–2233 or 800/327–8154) novelist John McDonald's fictional hero, Travis McGee, is honored with a plaque at marina slip F-18, where he docked his houseboat.

★ **8** Three blocks north, visit the **International Swimming Hall of Fame Museum and Aquatic Complex,** which celebrates its 31st anniversary in 1996. It contains two 10-lane, 50-meter pools and an exhibition building featuring photos, medals, and other souvenirs from major swimming events around the world, as well as a theater that shows films of onetime swimming stars Johnny Weismuller and Esther Williams. *1 Hall of Fame Dr., tel. 305/462–6536 for museum or 305/468–1580 for pool. Museum admission: $3 adults; $1 senior citizens, children 6–12, and military personnel; $5 family. Pool admission: $3 adults; $2 nonresident senior citizens and students; $1.50 resident senior citizens and students and military personnel. Museum and pro shop open daily 9–7; pool open weekdays 8–4 and 6–8, weekends 8–4. Pool closed mid-Dec.–mid-Jan.*

★ **9** As you approach Las Olas Boulevard, you will see the lyrical new styling that has given a distinctly European flavor to the **Fort Lauderdale beachfront.** A wave theme unifies the setting—from the low, white wave wall between the beach and widened beachfront promenade to the widened and bricked inner promenade in front of shops, restaurants, and hotels. Alone among Florida's major beachfront resorts, Fort Lauderdale Beach remains open and unbuilt-upon, and throughout the beach area, you'll see distinctive signs and street furniture. More than ever, the boulevard is worth promenading.

⑩ Turn left off Route A1A at Sunrise Boulevard, then right into **Hugh Taylor Birch State Recreation Area.** Amid the 180-acre park's tropical greenery, you can stroll along a nature trail, visit the Birch House Museum, picnic, play volleyball, pitch horseshoes, and paddle a canoe. *3109 E. Sunrise Blvd., tel. 305/564–4521. Admission: $3.25 per vehicle with up to 8 people. Open 8–sunset; ranger-guided nature walks Fri. at 10:30.*

★ ⑪ Cross Sunrise Boulevard and visit the **Bonnet House.** Closed in winter, when Evelyn Fortune Bartlett (now 107) is in residence, this charming mansion, built by Mrs. Bartlett's late husband, artist Frederic Clay Bartlett, stands on land he was given by his first father-in-law, Hugh Taylor Birch. The house and its subtropical 35-acre estate contain original works of art, whimsically carved animals, a swan pond, and, most of all, tranquility. *900 N. Birch Rd., tel. 305/563–5393. Admission (by reserved tour only): $8 adults; $6 senior citizens, students over 6, and military personnel. Tours May–Nov., Tues.–Thurs. at 10 and 1:30, Sun. at 1:30.*

North of Birch Park, Route A1A edges back from the beach through a section known as the **Galt Ocean Mile,** marked by beach-blocking high-rises. The pattern changes again in **Lauderdale-by-the-Sea,** a low-rise family resort town. Construction over three stories is banned, and dozens of good restaurants and shops are nearby, so vacationers don't bother to use their cars. One block east of Route A1A, you can drive along lawn-divided El Mar Drive, lined by garden-style motels.

North of Lauderdale-by-the-Sea, Route A1A enters **Pompano Beach,** where the high-rise procession begins again. Take Atlantic Boulevard east to the beach road, which is first called Pompano Beach Boulevard and then again A1A. Behind a low coral rock wall, a park extends north and south of **Fisherman's Wharf** along the road and beach. The road swings back from the beach, and then returns to it crossing **Hillsboro Inlet.** To your right across the inlet you can
⑫ see **Hillsboro Light,** the brightest light in the Southeast. The light is on private property and is inaccessible to the public.

Route A1A now enters onto the so-called **Hillsboro Mile** (actually more than 2 miles), which only a few years ago was one of Florida's outstanding residential corridors—a millionaire's row. Changes in zoning laws, however, have altered it; except for sections in the south and north, the island seems destined to sink under the weight of its massive condominiums. The road runs along a narrow strip of land between the Intracoastal Waterway and the ocean, with bougainvillea and oleander edging the way and yachts docked along both banks. In winter, the traffic often creeps at a snail's pace along here, as vacationers and retirees gawk at the views.

Turn left on Hillsboro Boulevard (Route 810). Make a sharp right just over the bridge onto Riverview Road, and park at the Riverview
⑬ Restaurant to take a free boat ride to **Deerfield Island Park.** This 8½-acre island, officially designated an urban wilderness area, resulted from the dredging of the Intracoastal Waterway and from construction of the Royal Palm Canal. Its mangrove swamp provides a critical habitat for gopher tortoises, gray foxes, raccoons, and armadillos. *1 Deerfield Island, Deerfield Beach, tel. 305/360–1320. Admission free. Open Wed., Sat. 8:15–sunset.*

At this point you're not far from the Palm Beach County line (*see* Chapter 5, Palm Beach and the Treasure Coast). You can return to Fort Lauderdale along Route A1A or turn west and head south along U.S. 1 or I–95.

Tour 3: Hollywood

Begin exploring at the junction of U.S. 1 and Hollywood Boulevard, called Young Circle after Joseph W. Young, a California real estate developer who in 1921 began developing the community of **Hollywood** from the woody flatlands. Just east of here, you can visit the
🚺 **Art and Culture Center of Hollywood.** A visual and performing arts center, it is set in a 1924 Mediterranean-style residence, typical of its era, and by 1996 will have expanded to 3,500 square feet. Facilities include an art reference library, outdoor sculpture garden, arts school, and a museum store. *1650 Harrison St., tel. 305/921–3274. Admission: $3 Wed.–Sat., $5 Sun. (including a classical or jazz concert); donations welcome Tues. Open Tues.–Sat. 10–4, Sun. 1–4.*

Drive east along wide Hollywood Boulevard, a reminder of the glory of the Young era. Cross the Intracoastal Waterway in front of the **Hollywood Beach Resort Hotel** (101 N. Ocean Dr., tel. 305/921–0990), opened by Young in 1922 and now filled with time-share condominiums and some available by the night. To the rear of the hotel is the separately operated retail and entertainment mall **Oceanwalk**—a good idea that only inconsistently achieves the right execution.

Take the ramp north onto Route A1A. The Intracoastal Waterway parallels it to the west, and the beach and ocean lie just on the other
🚺 side of the 2.2-mile-long, 27-foot-wide **Broadwalk.** A paved promenade since 1924, it's popular with pedestrians and cyclists. Expect to hear French spoken, especially during the winter; Hollywood Beach has been a favorite winter getaway for Québecois ever since Joseph Young hired French-Canadians to work here in the 1920s.

🚺 The Broadwalk ends at **Hollywood North Beach Park.** No high-rises overpower the scene, nothing hip or chic, just a laid-back old-fashioned place for enjoying sun, sand, and sea. *Rte. A1A and Sheridan St., tel. 305/926–2444. Admission free; parking: $5 until 2, $3 after. Open daily 8–6.*

Turn west onto Sheridan Street and proceed ½ mile. On your left,
🚺 enter 1,400-acre **West Lake Park.** By early 1996, Broward County's outstanding new resource-preserving nature facility and its wide range of recreational and interpretive attractions should be up and running. Canoes, kayaks, and boats with electric motors (no fossil fuels allowed in the park) will be available, and more than $1 million in nature exhibits will be on display at the Anne Kolb Nature Center, where a shop is expected to carry a large stock of books on the region's environment. Extensive boardwalks will traverse a mangrove community, and a 65-foot observation tower will yield views of the entire park and miles of contrasting development. *1200 Sheridan St., tel. 305/926–2410. Admission fees and hrs to be determined.*

Drive west to Federal Highway (U.S. 1), turn right (you have now entered **Dania**), and continue past one of Florida's largest antiques
🚺 districts (*see* Shopping for Bargains, *below*) to the **Graves Museum of Archaeology & Natural History.** After 15 years of using makeshift facilities in various locations, the museum has settled into a 50,000-square-foot permanent home. Exhibits include collections of pre-Columbian art and underwater artifacts from St. Thomas harbor as well as displays of Greco-Roman materials, a 3-ton quartz crystal, and dioramas of Tequesta Indian life and a jaguar habitat. A 9,000-square-foot dinosaur hall and additional wildlife dioramas are expected in late 1996. Monthly lectures, conferences, field trips, and a summer archaeological camp are offered, and the museum bookstore is one of the best in Florida. *481 S. Federal Hwy., tel. 305/925–7770, fax 305/925–7064. Admission: $5 adults, $4 senior citizens on Tues.*

only, $3 children 4–12. Open Tues.–Wed. and Fri.–Sat. 10–4, Thurs. 10–8, Sun. 1–4.

★ ⑲ Continue north to Dania Beach Boulevard (Route A1A), turn right, and drive to the beach. Just before turning left to enter the **John U. Lloyd Beach State Recreation Area,** you'll find the Dania Pier (*see* Fishing *in* Sports and the Outdoors, *below*) and the colorful SeaFair, a small collection of shops and diversions yet to hit their stride. The recreation area has a pleasant pine-shaded beach and a jetty pier where you can fish, and it offers good views, north almost to Palm Beach County and south to Miami Beach. From the road, look west across the waterway to Port Everglades, with its deep-water freighters and cruise ships. *6503 N. Ocean Dr., tel. 305/923–2833. Admission: $3.25 per vehicle with up to 8 people. Open 8–sunset.*

From here return via A1A and Hollywood Boulevard to where you began, or take Dania Beach Boulevard north into Fort Lauderdale.

Other Attractions

⑳ **Butterfly World** is a screened-in aviary in a tropical rain forest on 2.8 acres of land. Thousands of caterpillars, representing up to 150 species, pupate and emerge as butterflies. *3600 W. Sample Rd., Coconut Creek, tel. 305/977–4400. Admission: $8.95 adults, $7.95 senior citizens, $5 children 3–12. Open Mon.–Sat. 9–5, Sun. 1–5.*

㉑ **Flamingo Gardens** has gators, crocodiles, river otters, birds of prey, a 23,000-square-foot walk-through aviary, a plant house, and an Everglades Museum in the pioneer Wray Home. Admission includes a ½-hour guided tram ride through a citrus grove and wetlands area. *3750 Flamingo Rd., Davie, tel. 305/473–0010. Admission: $8 adults, $6.40 senior citizens, $4.50 children 4–12. Open daily 9–5.*

㉒ **Sawgrass Recreation Park** is on the site of a 16½-acre former fish camp at the edge of the Everglades. Here you can rent fishing boats, get bait and tackle, and enjoy a 90-minute series of three tours in one that includes an airboat ride, a tour of a Native American village replica, and an educational live reptile exhibit with alligators and caimans. A snack and gift shop is also available. *2 mi north of I–75 on U.S. 27, tel. 305/389–0202 or 800/457–0788. Tour package: $13.40 adults, $12.40 senior citizens, $6.50 children 4–12. Tours daily 9–5; shop open daily 6–6.*

㉓ **Young at Art Children's Museum** teaches kids to work in paint, graphics, sculpture, and crafts according to themes that change three times a year. Visitors can view work hung, mounted on pedestals, and even in motion. *801 S. University Dr. in the Fountains Shoppes, Plantation, tel. 305/424–0085. Admission: $3 ages over 2. Open Tues.–Sat. 11–5, Sun. noon–5.*

Guided Tours

Carrie B. (Riverwalk at S.E. 5th Ave., tel. 305/768–9920), a 300-passenger day-cruiser, gives 90-minute tours up the New River and Intracoastal Waterway for $7.95 adults, $3.95 children under 12.

Ecofloat (401 S.W. 2nd St., tel. 305/467–6637), offered by the Museum of Discovery and Science, is a 30-minute narrated tour on the New River covering flora, fauna, history, and legends of the New River. Tickets cost $3 adults, $2.50 senior citizens, and $2 children 12 and under.

Jungle Queen III and ***IV*** (Radisson Bahia Mar Beach Resort, 801 Seabreeze Blvd., tel. 305/462–5596) are 155-passenger and 578-passenger tour boats that take day and night cruises up the New River, through the heart of Fort Lauderdale. Three-hour narrated sightseeing cruises are $7.50 adults, $4.95 children under 12.

River and Walking Tours (219 S.W. 2nd Ave., tel. 305/463–4431), cosponsored by the Fort Lauderdale Historical Society, trace the New River by foot and by boat. River tours are $16 for two hours; walking tours are $10–$12.50 depending on what extra admission charges are involved.

South Florida Trolley Tours (Visitors Information Center, Rte. A1A, tel. 305/522–7701) are fully narrated, 90-minute trips on *Lolly the Trolley*. They start from the visitor center and make pickups along Las Olas Boulevard. Tickets are $10.

Beaches

Through much of the county, the beachfront is not built on, extending for miles without interruption and allowing for easy access. The character of the communities behind the beach does change, however. For example, in Hallandale at far south Broward County, the beach is backed by towering condominiums; in Hollywood, by motels and the hoi-polloi Broadwalk; and just north of there—blessedly—there's nothing at all.

The most crowded portion of beach is along **Ocean Boulevard,** between Las Olas Boulevard and Sunrise Boulevard in Fort Lauderdale. This is the onetime "strip" famed from *Where the Boys Are* and the era of spring-break madness, now but a memory. Parking is readily available, often at parking meters.

Dania, Lauderdale-by-the-Sea, Pompano Beach, and **Deerfield Beach** each have piers where you can fish in addition to beaches.

John U. Lloyd Beach State Recreation Area (*see* Tour 3, *above*), in Dania, is the locals' favorite beach area. It offers a beach for swimmers and sunners but also 251 acres of mangroves, picnic facilities, fishing, and canoeing.

Shopping for Bargains

Malls Even the more upscale malls are good places for window-shopping and for hunting up bargains at holiday and end-of-season sales. **Broward Mall** (8000 W. Broward Blvd., at University Dr., Plantation), the county's largest shopping center, features such stores as Burdines, JCPenney, and Sears. A three-level, 669,000-square-foot, landscaped, glass-enclosed facility, **Fashion Mall** (University Dr., just north of Broward Blvd., Plantation) counts Macy's and Lord & Taylor among its 150 shops, boutiques, and restaurants. **Galleria Mall** (2414 E. Sunrise Blvd., just west of the Intracoastal Waterway, Fort Lauderdale) occupies more than 1 million square feet and includes Neiman-Marcus, Lord & Taylor, Saks Fifth Avenue, and Brooks Brothers. **Pompano Square** (2001 N. Federal Hwy., Pompano Beach) has 110 shops with three department stores and food stalls. **Sawgrass Mills Mall** (Flamingo Rd. and Sunrise Blvd., Sunrise) is a 2 million-square-foot, candy-color, Disney-style discount mall containing restaurants and entertainment activities in addition to 250 stores that include Donna Karan, Saks, and Spiegel's outlets; Loehmann's; JCPenney; Ann Taylor; Alfred Angelo Bridal; Levi's; and TJ Maxx. On weekdays, two shuttle buses run: One calls at major beach hotels between 8:55 and 9:30 AM, arrives at the huge mall around 10, and returns at 2:30, while the other leaves between 11:30 and 12:15 and returns just past 5. To schedule a pickup, call 305/846–2350 or 800/356–4557. The charge is $4 each way and includes a coupon book for use at the mall.

Flea Markets Some 600 vendors set up at the **Festival Flea Market** (2900 W. Sample Rd., at Florida's Turnpike, Pompano Beach). The largest market of its type in the county, it's open Tuesday–Friday 9:30–5, weekends to 6. The **Swap Shop** (W. Sunrise Blvd., between I-95 and Florida's Turnpike, Fort Lauderdale) claims to be the second-largest flea market in the United States, with more than 2,000 vendors spread over an 80-acre complex. There's a free circus each day plus an air-conditioned entertainment and food court area. Outside is open daily 7:30-6, inside daily 7:30-7:30.

Specialty More than 75 dealers line Federal Highway (U.S. 1) in **Dania,** ½ mile
Stores south of the Fort Lauderdale airport and ½ mile north of Hollywood.
Antiques Take the Stirling Road or Griffin Road East exits off I-95.

Upscale If only for a stroll and some window-shopping, don't miss the **Shops**
Boutiques **of Las Olas** (a block off the New River just east of U.S. 1, Fort Lauderdale). The city's best one-of-a-kind boutiques plus top restaurants (many affordable) and art galleries line a beautifully landscaped street.

Sports and the Outdoors

Participant Sports

Biking Cycling is popular in Broward County, though the bad news is that metro Fort Lauderdale is one of the most dangerous places to bike in Florida. The good news is that you can ride the 330-meter **Brian Piccolo Park velodrome** (Sheridan St. and N.W. 101st Ave., Cooper City) in western Broward County. For a schedule of public hours and spectator events, as well as a copy of the new "Bicycling in Fort Lauderdale" brochure, contact the **County Bicycle Coordinator** (115 S. Andrews Ave., Fort Lauderdale 33301, tel. 305/357-6661). Another safe cycling option is along the 2½-mile **Broadwalk** on Hollywood Beach. Between April 16 and November 15, the cycling lane can be used at all hours. Other times of the year, use of the lane is restricted to between sunrise and 8 AM and between 4 PM and sunset. Otherwise, the most popular routes include Route A1A and Bayview Drive, especially early in the morning before traffic builds; the 7-mile bike path that parallels Route 84 and the New River and leads to Markham Park, which has mountain bike trails; a 4-mile loop that connects Pompano City Park, the Goodyear blimp hangar, and shopping in the vicinity of Copans Road and Federal Highway; and plenty of roads in the southwest and northwest sections of the county. Many shops along the beach rent bikes. A map for cycling Broward's streets is available in bike stores or from the county bicycle coordinator.

Diving Good diving can be enjoyed within 20 minutes of the shore along Broward County's coast. Among the most popular of the county's 80 dive sites is the 2-mile-wide, 23-mile-long **Fort Lauderdale Reef,** the product of Florida's most successful artificial reef-building program. The project began in 1984 with the sinking of a 435-foot freighter donated by an Oklahoma marine electronics manufacturer. Since then more than a dozen houseboats, ships, and oil platforms have been sunk in depths of 10 to 150 feet to provide a habitat for fish and other marine life, as well as to help stabilize beaches. The most famous sunken ship is the 200-foot German freighter *Mercedes*, which was blown onto Palm Beach socialite Mollie Wilmot's pool terrace in a violent Thanksgiving storm in 1984; the ship has now been sunk a mile off Fort Lauderdale beach. For more information, contact the Greater Fort Lauderdale Convention & Visitors Bureau (*see* Important Addresses and Numbers *in* Fort Lauderdale Basics, *above*).

Dive shops and charter boats include:

Force E (2700 E. Atlantic Blvd., Pompano Beach, tel. 305/943-3483; 2160 W. Oakland Park Blvd., Oakland Park, tel. 305/735-6227) stores rent scuba and snorkeling equipment, provide instruction at all skill levels, and run charters.

Lauderdale Diver (1334 S.E. 17th St. Causeway, Fort Lauderdale, tel. 305/467–2822 or 800/654–2073), which is PADI affiliated, arranges dive charters throughout the county. Dive trips typically last four hours. Nonpackage reef trips are also open to divers for $35, to snorkelers for $25; scuba and snorkel gear are extra.

Pro Dive (Radisson Bahia Mar Beach Resort, 801 Seabreeze Blvd., Fort Lauderdale, tel. 305/761–3413 or 800/772–3483), a PADI five-star facility, is the area's oldest diving operation and offers packages with Radisson Bahia Mar Beach Resort, from where its 60-foot boat departs. Snorkelers can go out for $25 on the four-hour dive trip or $20 on the two-hour snorkeling trip, which includes snorkel equipment but not scuba gear. Scuba divers pay $35 using their own gear.

Fishing Four main types of fishing are available in Broward County: bottom or drift-boat fishing from party boats, deep-sea fishing for large sport fish on charters, angling for freshwater game fish, and dropping a line off a pier.

For bottom fishing, party boats typically charge between $20 and $22 per person for up to four hours, including rod, reel, and bait. Three operators are **Captain Bill's** (south dock, Radisson Bahia Mar Beach Resort, Fort Lauderdale, tel. 305/467–3855), *Fish City Pride* (Fish City Marina, 2621 N. Riverside Dr., Pompano Beach, tel. 305/781–1211), and *Sea Leg's III* (5400 N. Ocean Dr., Hollywood, tel. 305/923–2109).

Two primary centers for saltwater charter boats are **Radisson Bahia Mar Beach Resort** (801 Seabreeze Blvd., Fort Lauderdale, tel. 305/764–2233) and the **Hillsboro Inlet Marina** (2629 N. Riverside Dr., Pompano Beach, tel. 305/943–8222). Be warned that charters can be quite expensive: A half day for up to six people runs up to $325 and a full day (8 hours) up to $595. Skipper and crew, plus bait and tackle, are included. Split parties can be arranged at a cost of about $85 per person for a full day.

Among marinas catering to freshwater fishing are **Sawgrass Recreation** (U.S. 27 north of I–595, tel. 305/426–2474) and **Everglades Holiday Park** (21940 Griffin Rd., tel. 305/434–8111). For $47.50 for five hours, you can rent a 14-foot, flat-bottom johnboat (with a 9.9-horsepower Yamaha outboard) that carries up to four people. A rod and reel rent for $9 a day, and bait is extra. For two people, a fishing guide for a half day (4 hours) is $110, for a full day (8 hours) $170; a third person adds $25 for a half day, $50 for a full day. You can also buy a freshwater fishing license (mandatory) here.

Fishing piers, the least-expensive option, draw anglers for pompano, amberjack, bluefish, snapper, blue runners, snook, mackerel, and Florida lobsters. Pompano Beach's **Fisherman's Wharf** (tel. 305/943–1488) extends 1,080 feet into the Atlantic. The cost is $2.65 for adults, $1.06 for children under 10; rod-and-reel rental is $10.07 (including admission and initial bait). **Anglin's Fishing Pier** (tel. 305/491–9403), in Lauderdale-by-the-Sea, reaches 876 feet and is open for fishing 24 hours a day. Fishing is $3 for adults and $2 for children up to 12, tackle rental is an additional $10 (plus $10 deposit), and bait averages $2. Newly reopened in 1995 after complete rebuilding following Hurricane Andrew, the 920-foot **Dania Pier** (tel. 305/927–0640), in Dania, is open around the clock. Fishing is $3 for adults (including parking), tackle rental is $6, bait's about $2, and spectators pay $1. A snack bar is to open by mid-1996.

Golf More than 50 courses, public and private, green the landscape in metro Fort Lauderdale, including famous championship links. The most affordable, with greens fees $10–$40 depending on time of year and time of day, are: in Fort Lauderdale, **Arrowhead Golf &**

Sports Club (8201 S.W. 24th St., tel. 305/475–8200) and **Sabal Palms Golf Course** (5101 W. Commercial Blvd., tel. 305/731–2600); in Hallandale, **Diplomat Resort & Country Club** (501 Diplomat Pkwy., tel. 305/457–2082); in Hollywood, **Hollywood Golf & Country Club** (1600 Johnson St., tel. 305/927–1751) and **Orange-Brook Golf Course** (400 Entrada Dr., tel. 305/921–4653); in Margate, **Oriole Golf and Tennis Club** (8000 W. Margate Blvd., tel. 305/972–8140); in Miramar, **Laurelton Park Golf & Country Club** (3700 S. Douglas Rd., tel. 305/431–3800); and in Pembroke Pines, **Flamingo Lakes** (701 Flamingo West Dr., tel. 305/435–6110) and **Pembroke Lakes Golf Club** (10500 Taft St., tel. 305/431–4144). The best way to play any of the more upscale courses is to book with **Next Day Golf** (tel. 305/772–2582 or 800/948–1239), which provides 10%–25% discounts to golfers willing to wait until after 5 PM to book tee times for next-day play. Among courses the service works with are several normally closed to the public.

Tennis   Some 20 sites offer public courts throughout the county. Best known to Broward Countians (and largest) is **Holiday Park** (701 N.E. 12th Ave., Fort Lauderdale, tel. 305/761–5378), which has 18 clay (14 lighted) and three hard-surface courts in the downtown area, 10 minutes from the beach. This is where former tennis pro Jimmy Evert taught his daughter Chris.

Waterskiing   A unique waterskiing cableway, which pulls water-skiers across the water, is found at **Quiet Waters Park,** just north of the Pompano Harness Track. **Ski Rixen** operates the waterskiing, which includes skis and life vests. *Power Line Rd., Pompano Beach, tel. 305/360–1315 for park or 305/429–0215 for Ski Rixen. Park admission: free weekdays, $1 per person weekends; waterskiing: $12 for 1 hr, $14 for 2 hrs. Park open daily 8–6:30, waterskiing daily 10–6.*

Spectator Sports

In addition to contacting the addresses below directly, you can get tickets to major events from **Ticketmaster** (tel. 305/523–3309).

Dog Racing   **Hollywood Greyhound Track** has plenty of dog-racing action during its season, from December 26 to April 26. There is a clubhouse dining room. *831 N. Federal Hwy., Hallandale, tel. 305/454–9400. Admission: 50¢–$1 box seats, $1 grandstand, $2 clubhouse, senior citizens free at matinees. Racing Tues., Thurs., Sat. at 12:30, 7:30; Sun.–Mon., Wed., Fri. at 7:30.*

Horse Racing   **Gulfstream Park Race Track** is the home of the Florida Derby, one of the Southeast's foremost horse-racing events. The park greatly improved its facilities during the past two years: Admission costs have been lowered, time between races shortened, and the paddock ring elevated for better viewing by fans. Racing is held January–mid-March. *901 S. Federal Hwy., Hallandale, tel. 305/454–7000. Admission: $3 general admission (including parking and program), $5 clubhouse plus $2 for reserved seat or $1.75 for grandstand. Racing daily at 1.*

Pompano Harness Track, Florida's only harness track, was sold in early 1995 to Casino America. However, since Florida doesn't allow casino gambling, this 327-acre facility continues to operate as a harness track 11 months of the year. The Top o' the Park restaurant overlooks the finish line. *1800 S.W. 3rd St., Pompano Beach, tel. 305/972–2000. Admission: $1 grandstand, $2 clubhouse. Racing Mon., Wed.–Sat. at 7:30.*

Jai Alai   **Dania Jai-Alai Palace** offers one of the fastest games on the planet. Games are held year-round. *301 E. Dania Beach Blvd., Dania, tel. 305/428–7766. Admission: $1 general admission, $1.50–$7 reserved seats, senior citizens free 11:30–noon. Games Tues., Thurs., Sat. at noon, 7:15; Wed., Fri. at 7:15. Closed Wed. in June.*

Rodeo **Davie Arena for Rodeo** holds rodeos throughout the year, but you have to call for the dates. For five-star rodeos, show up at 6:30, when gates open, and you can buy your way into the very popular country barbecue that precedes the events. *6591 S.W. 45th St. (Orange Dr.), Davie, tel. 305/797–1145. Admission: jackpot events: $5 adults, $2 children; 5-star rodeo: $9 adults, $5 children.*

Rugby The **Fort Lauderdale Knights** play September–April on the green at Croissant Park. *S.W. 17th St. at 2nd Ave., Fort Lauderdale, tel. 305/ 561–5263 for recording. Admission free. Games Sat. at 2.*

Soccer In their 12th season of play, the **Fort Lauderdale Strikers** will host 12 games, April to September, at 9,500-seat Lockhart Stadium (next door to the team's office). The Strikers play against U.S. and Canadian squads in the eight-team American Professional Soccer League. *5301 N.W. 12th Ave., Fort Lauderdale, tel. 305/771–5677. Admission: $8 adults, $4 children 16 and under. Most games at 7 or 7:30, occasional weekend day games.*

Where to Eat on a Budget

Deerfield **Brooks.** This is one of the area's best and most affordable restau-
Beach rants thanks to a French perfectionist, Bernard Perron, from Poi-
$$ tiers. Meals are served in a series of brilliantly set rooms, filled with
★ replicas of Old Masters, cut glass, antiques, and tapestry-like floral
wallpapers, though the shedlike dining room still feels very Florida.
For Perron the secret is fresh ingredients, which translate into a
distinctly Floridian cuisine. Main courses include red snapper in
papillote, broiled fillet of pompano with seasoned root vegetables,
and a sweet lemongrass linguine with bok choy and julienne of crisp
vegetables. Desserts include southern pecan pie with banana ice
cream, a phyllo purse filled with chocolate ganache and strawber-
ries, and rum-basted bananas with coconut ice cream and toasted
macadamia nuts. *500 S. Federal Hwy., tel. 305/427–9302. Reserva-
tions accepted. Dress: casual but neat. AE, D, MC, V. Closed Super
Bowl Sun., Dec. 25.*

Fort **Mistral.** This is the first and best of the gourmet cafés along the
Lauderdale: dreamily restyled beach drive. The open-air restaurant rates high
Beach for both taste and looks. About 75 can sit inside surrounded by tropi-
$$ cal art and pottery, with another 35 on the wave-theme sidewalk.
★ The kitchen staff is knowledgeable about pastas, turning out a
hearty *primavera* redolent with garlic and herbs and *tagliolini* (an
angel-hair pasta) with prosciutto, pine nuts, and tomato. Other favorites from the sun-drenched cuisine are grilled shrimp and black-
bean cakes as well as pan-seared dolphin. Pizzas, big salads, and a
strong selection of affordable wines, including by the glass, are also
served. *201 Rte. A1A, tel. 305/463–4900. Reservations accepted for
parties of 6 or more. Dress: casual. AE, D, DC, MC, V.*

$–$$ **Sea Watch.** It's back from the road and easy to miss—but not missed
by many. Waiting for a table, you're likely to hear announced, "Party of 47, your tables are ready!" After more than 20 years, this nauti-
cal-theme restaurant by the sea stays packed during lunch and
dinner. Waits can be as long as 30 minutes, but the time passes
quickly in the sumptuous upstairs lounge with its comfy sofas and
high-back rattan chairs. The menu has all the right appetizers: oysters Rockefeller, Florida Gulf shrimp, clams casino, and Bahamian
conch fritters. Typical daily specials might be sautéed yellowtail
snapper, oat-crusted with roasted red bell pepper sauce and basil,
or a charbroiled dolphin fillet marinated with soy sauce, garlic,
black pepper, and lemon juice. Desserts include a Granny Smith apple crisp cheesecake, cappuccino brownie, and strawberries Roma-
noff. Good early-bird specials are offered May–mid-December. *6002
N. Ocean Blvd., tel. 305/781–2200. No reservations. Dress: casual
but neat. AE, MC, V. Closed Dec. 25.*

Bimini Boatyard. With a sky-high sloped roof, loads of windows, and paddle fans, this is a rarity among architecturally distinctive restaurants: affordable menu, ambience, and a quality bar. Try a Bass ale with a loaf of Bimini bread or Buffalo chicken wings. Heartier fare? Go for the fettuccine *al salmone affumicato* (smoked salmon, capers, whole-grain mustard, white wine, cream, and leeks). The extensive menu includes salads, burgers, and dishes from the cookbooks of the Bahamas, Jamaica, and Indonesia (grilled chicken breast with peanut sauce). The restaurant is on the 15th Street canal, where outdoor seating lets you look at the year-round boat show. On weekends Bimini hosts live entertainment. Friday night's happy hour draws the biggest crowds. *1555 S.E. 17th St., tel. 305/ 525–7400. Reservations accepted for parties of 8 or more. Dress: casual. AE, MC, V. Closed Dec. 25.*

$$ **Good Planet Cafe.** A half block from the Florida East Coast Railroad track in a neighborhood that's turned from run-down to trendy, thanks to the Broward Center for the Performing Arts and all the nearby museums, this 50-seat eatery has primed the scene for food. Modeled after the Last Ditch Cafe in Silver City, New Mexico, run by sister Julie, the Good Planet is run by the Good family, especially brother Jonathan. Mom and pop handle the contracting and pick out the thrift-shop furniture, which, with the local art on the walls, creates a feel of hand-me-down chic. Most of the long list of entrées are served with *posole* (a corn chowder) or rice and beans. Try the bite-size chunks of lean pork marinated in red chili and fruit juices with a fresh mango-pineapple salsa, the Last Ditch pasta *pollo verde* (chicken chunks with diced green chili and fresh tomato tossed in a cream sauce with fettuccine), or the Szechuan scallop and shrimp angel hair. There are lots of vegetarian choices, and everything comes in big portions. *214 S.W. 2nd St., tel. 305/527–4663. Reservations accepted. Dress: casual. AE, MC, V. Closed Sun., Thanksgiving, Dec. 25. No lunch Sat.*

$$ **Rustic Inn Crabhouse.** Wayne McDonald started with a cozy one-room roadhouse saloon in 1955, when this was a remote service road just west of the little airport. Now, the plain, rustic place seats 700. Steamed crabs seasoned with garlic and herbs, spices, and oil are served with mallets on tables covered with newspapers; peel-and-eat shrimp are served either Key West–style (with garlic and butter) or spiced and steamed with Old Bay seasoning. The big menu includes other seafood items as well. Pies and cheesecakes are offered for dessert. *4331 Ravenswood Rd., tel. 305/584–1637. No reservations. Dress: casual. AE, D, DC, MC, V. Closed Thanksgiving.*

$$ **Shirttail Charlie's.** Overlooking the New River, you can watch the world go by from the outdoor deck or upstairs dining room of this restaurant, named for a yesteryear Seminole Indian who wore his shirts in the traditional way with the tails out. Diners may take a free 30- to 40-minute after-dinner cruise on *Shirttail Charlie's Express*, which chugs upriver past an alleged Al Capone speakeasy or across the river to and from the Broward Center for the Performing Arts. Charlie's itself is built to look old, with a 1920s tile floor that leans toward the water. Florida-style seafood offerings include an alligator-tail appetizer served with tortuga sauce (a béarnaise with turtle broth and sherry), conch served four ways, crab balls, blackened tuna with Dijon mustard sauce, crunchy coconut shrimp with a not-too-sweet piña colada sauce, three fresh catches nightly, and a superbly tart Key lime pie with graham-cracker crust. *400 S.W. 3rd Ave., tel. 305/463–3474. Reservations advised upstairs. Dress: casual but neat. AE, D, MC, V.*

$ **Bread of Life.** Big luncheon and dinner choices are offered at this 110-seat restaurant attached to a popular natural-foods store on the north side of town. The decor is typical of the genre—ceiling fans, hanging plants, deco posters—but the food is something special, all of it fresh. There are always at least two soups, one of them miso, and a dozen starters and salads (vegetable pâté, warm Brie, grilled shrimp, spinach and mushroom salad, field greens and French feta cheese). Typical entrées include chicken stir-fry, a macrobiotic plate (beans, brown rice, steamed veggies, and seaweed), fettuccine and fresh fish with dill cream sauce, tofu ravioli, and spanakopita (Greek spinach pie). House-baked desserts finish off the meal. If you want faster service, sit at one of the counter seats. There's live jazz Friday and Saturday nights and a Sunday jazz brunch. *2388 N. Federal Hwy., tel. 305/565-7423. Reservations accepted. Dress: casual. AE, D, DC, MC, V. No smoking.*

$ **Ernie's Bar-B-Q & Lounge.** Soup you can chew, thick barbecue between slabs of Bahama bread, and a wacky collection of memorabilia from a previous owner make Ernie's a must. The two-story eatery has an open-deck patio upstairs overlooking six-lane Federal Highway, while downstairs, murals tout zany slogans and are adorned with former owner Ernie Siebert's dodo birds. Since 1976, Jeff Kirtman (from Brooklyn) has managed the place and has supplied plenty of reasons for visiting, including his conch-rich thick chowder, the hot barbecued pork-and-beef sandwiches, and the ribs-and-chicken combo dinner with corn on the cob and baked beans. *1843 S. Federal Hwy., tel. 305/523-8636. No reservations. Dress: casual. MC, V.*

$ **Japanese Village.** In a row of little ethnic restaurants along tree-shaded Las Olas Boulevard, just east of the Riverside Hotel, this Japanese spot stands out. You can sit at a sidewalk table, at the sushi bar, or in the simply furnished black-and-white dining room, with mirrors, tiles, striking light fixtures, and big sprays of flowers on each table. For a small restaurant, the menu offers big variety—lots of tofu, tempura, stir-fries, and teriyaki dishes. A bowl of hearty ramen noodles and chicken broth, with added chicken strips, sprouts, shrimp, snow crab, and greens, is a meal in itself. *716 E. Las Olas Blvd., tel. 305/653-8163. Reservations accepted. Dress: casual but neat. AE, MC, V. Closed Dec. 23-25. No lunch weekends.*

$ **Las Olas Cafe.** Charming indoors and out, this café is tucked away in
★ an arcade between a couple of boutiques off Las Olas Boulevard. Outside you can dine beneath oak and schefflera trees hung with Christmas bulbs; inside are tables with candles and bud vases, floral art, chintz drapes, and a wall of mirrors that makes the room look larger than it is. Favorite appetizers include shrimp Berardi (with mozzarella and prosciutto) and scallops *en croute* (scallops with mushrooms and onions wrapped in flaky pastry, with an orange-saffron sauce). Among pastas, winners are pasta Andre (penne pasta with spinach and mushrooms in a creamy red sauce) and a shrimp-and-scallop sauté tossed with leeks, mushrooms, and fresh tomatoes and served over angel-hair pasta. The walnut-crusted dolphin, served on a bed of apples and sweet onions, is also popular. *922 E. Las Olas Blvd., tel. 305/524-4300. Weekend reservations advised. Dress: casual but neat. AE, DC, MC, V. Beer and wine only. Closed some holidays.*

$ **Sage.** This joyous, country-French café presents a country-American setting: exposed brick walls, captain's chairs, lace curtains, herbal art, and baskets of dried grains and flowers. The menu is a happy mix of very affordable quiches and pâtés, savory and dessert crepes, salads, and main course specialties. Entrées include coq au vin, beef bourguignonne, cassoulet *à l'Armagnac* (layers of duck and garlic sausage with white beans), and a platter of fresh vegetables that's a veritable garden of legumes. Early-bird dinners (weekdays 4:30-6) feature four courses for $12.50. There is a good selection of beers, including Anchor Steam and Sam Adams, and wines by the glass. *2378 N. Federal Hwy., tel. 305/565-2299. No reservations. Dress: casual but neat. AE, D, MC, V.*

$ **Studio One French Bistro.** As if one great bargain French restaurant
★ weren't enough, Fort Lauderdale offers a second. More like a gallery of art—intimate, black-and-white, mirrored—this restaurant

serves up bountiful portions at ridiculously low prices. The extraordinary profusion of food is thoughtfully presented, from high-gluten breads through a dozen or so appetizers, dinner-size salads, and entrées that include a grilled salmon in puff pastry with lobster sauce, Camembert-stuffed chicken breast with French cranberry sauce, and crispy roasted duckling with vanilla sauce. For dessert try the mildly sweet custard apple tart. Chef Bernd Asendorf now has charge of the kitchen, and his wife, Roberta, carries on the tradition of greeting by name the locals who return time and again, often bringing out-of-town guests. *2447 E. Sunrise Blvd., tel. 305/565-2052. Reservations accepted. Dress: casual but neat. AE, DC, MC, V. Closed Mon. mid-May–mid-Dec. No lunch.*

¢–$ **Juice Extractor.** Three guys from Pittsburgh, Philadelphia, and New York have made a splash in the arts district's Himmarshee Village with their inexpensive, deli-style organic foods and Champion Juicer blends. Frothy and light, juices are made from fresh apples, pears, strawberries, citrus, and veggies and can be enjoyed with bagels, whitefish salads, and homemade breads for breakfast. Lunch features dairy-free veggie burgers, pita sandwiches, and organic salads (at least three pasta versions). Free-range chicken prepared with mushrooms and veggies, marinated in lemon and honey with veggies, or served with organic pasta and red sauce; steamed salmon; bison steaks, whole or ground; and a vegetarian choice with brown rice and beans are just some of the dinner platters, which come with a choice of soup or salad. There are 28 seats inside (no-smoking) and 32 outside at this restaurant among five shops with imported art and crafts. *320 S.W. 2nd St., tel. 305/524-6935. Reservations accepted. Dress: casual. D, MC, V. Closed Thanksgiving, Dec. 25, Jan. 1.*

¢ **Cafe Europa.** The best advertisement for this popular sidewalk café in the heart of the Las Olas Boulevard shopping district is the aroma of pizza toppings that waft from within. In addition to a wide choice of pizzas, including vegetarian pizza (topped with zucchini, broccoli, spinach, and green peppers) and a pizza *pomodoro* (with fresh tomatoes, mozzarella, olive oil, and basil), you can get calzones, focaccia, spinach rolls, sandwiches, and salads. Eat under the sun-shielding canopy or inside among the posters and movie-star photos. Top the meal off with your choice of 36 coffees and cappuccinos (amaretto to vanilla). *726 E. Las Olas Blvd., tel. 305/763-6600. No reservations. Dress: casual. No credit cards. Closed holidays.*

Hollywood **Istanbul.** So there you are on the beach—hungry, without a picnic ¢–$ basket, but not yet ready to pack it in. Leave your significant other on the blanket and go grab a take-out order from this Turkish fast-food place. Actually fast food is a misnomer, since everything is prepared from scratch: hummus, tabbouleh, *adana* kebab (partially grilled, chopped lamb on skewers on a bed of yogurt-soaked pita squares, oven finished with hot butter sauce), pizza, salads, soups, and phyllo pie fingers filled with spinach, chicken, or meat. The creamy rice pudding, baklava, and pastries are equally transportable. To be sure, you can also sit and eat at one of the few tables, but how often do you get to lounge on the beach with a reasonably priced Turkish picnic? *707 N. Broadwalk, tel. 305/921-1263. No reservations. Dress: casual. No credit cards.*

¢ **Coral Rose Cafe.** You'll find this unpretentious little restaurant on Young Circle in downtown Hollywood, in a neighborhood that's lately been revived after years of neglect. The place has more than doubled in size to more than 40 seats—a sure sign that locals still love its folksy, friendly character. Hanging baskets and cane-back chairs, cypress-paneled walls, and colorful art prints provide the decor. Meals are strictly breakfast, lunch, and Sunday brunch. The breakfast menu is standard stuff; at lunch, soups, salads, sandwiches, quiche, omelets, and burgers are all made to order. The Sunday brunch menu—no buffet here—features various Benedicts, waffles, and *huevos rancheros*. Hot-cereal lovers are in heaven with a choice of oatmeal, Cream of Wheat, or Wheatena. *1840 Harrison St., tel. 305/925–4414. No reservations. Dress: casual. No credit cards. Closed Sun.–Mon., holidays. No dinner.*

Hollywood Beach
$
★

Le Tub. Since 1975, this quirky saloon has occupied a former Sunoco station ½ mile north of the Hollywood Beach Hotel on the Intracoastal Waterway. Hand-painted claw-foot bathtubs are everywhere, under ficus, sea grape, and palm trees. Le Tub is highly favored by locals for affordable waterside food (don't call it dining, thanks). Shrimp and barbecue are popular, as are steaks and Greek salad. *1100 N. Ocean Dr., tel. 305/921–9425. No reservations. Dress: casual. No credit cards.*

Lauderdale-by-the-Sea
$
★

Aruba Beach Cafe. Basically it's just a big beachside barn with lamps, but there's always a crowd here, summers as well as winters. Every night feels like a party. The bar crowd watches the three TVs, while everybody else stares at the sea—or at each other. The comfortable mood matches the general down-home atmosphere of Lauderdale-by-the-Sea. Portions are huge. Try the Caribbean conch chowder or Cuban black bean soup to start, and go on to fresh tropical salads, burgers, sandwiches, pastas, stir-fries, or seafood entrées (grouper, coconut-fried shrimp, grilled seafood brochette). Desserts are made on the premises: walnut fudge brownie sundae, Granny Smith apple pie, and peach cheesecake. *E. end of Commercial Blvd., tel. 305/776–0001. Reservations accepted. Dress: casual but neat. AE, D, DC, MC, V.*

Lighthouse Point
$$
★

Cafe Grazia. This happy green, red, and white recollection of an Italian garden is so close to the highway that its bar glasses jiggle to the passing of 18-wheelers. Not to worry—exuberance is what really shakes the scene. Chef Ace Gonzalez and his wife, Estelita, have created a happy case of the best for less: dinners on the low side of "moderate" and downright inexpensive if you come between 4:30 and 5:30 for the early-bird specials, a choice of three-course dinners priced at $6.95–$9.95 year-round. Pocketbook-pleasing, too, are the regular menu's 15 pasta selections, including penne pasta with hot chilies, vodka, tomatoes, and cream, and fresh pasta rosettes with fontina cheese, smoked ham, and spinach in a blush cream sauce. Other entrées include fowl, veal, and grills. *3850 N. Federal Hwy., tel. 305/942–7206. Reservations accepted. Dress: casual but neat. AE, MC, V. No weekend lunch.*

$$
★

Cap's Place. On an island that was once a bootlegger's haunt, this restaurant is reached by launch and has served such luminaries as Winston Churchill, Franklin D. Roosevelt, and John F. Kennedy. "Cap" was Captain Theodore Knight, born in 1871, who, with partner-in-crime Al Hasis, floated a derelict barge to the area in the 1920s. Today the rustic restaurant, built on the barge, is run by descendants of Hasis, who make freshness and excellence a priority. Baked wahoo steaks are lightly glazed and meaty, the long-cut french fries arouse gluttony, hot and flaky rolls are baked fresh several times a night, and tangy lime pie is the finishing touch. Turn east off Federal Highway onto Northeast 24th Street (two blocks north of Pompano Fashion Square); follow the double yellow line to the launch. *Cap's Dock, 2765 N.E. 28th Ct., tel. 305/941–0418. No reservations. Dress: casual. AE, MC, V. No lunch.*

Oakland Park
$$
★

Primavera. Night becomes brilliant Tuscan day in this creamy setting of etched glass dividers, statuary, figureheads, gorgeous planters, balusters, and pilasters. Taste redeems the lavish display of thematic decor—taste and larger than usual tables set with double covers, burgundy napkins, and fresh flowers, placed generously apart from each other atop thick, sound-muffling carpet. There's no piped-in music either, just the hum of content. Waiters do not merely recite the evening's specials but guide guests through the subtleties of the various pastas, risottos, and scaloppines. Among pasta

choices are a green-and-white pasta in a pink sauce with baby peas
and ham, and a linguine with clam sauce or seafood. A fresh catch is
prepared with sun-dried tomato sauce and topped with fried leeks.
Desserts are rich yet delicate. Consider sun-dried mangoes and banana in phyllo pastry, baked with a touch of passion fruit, coulis of
raspberry, and kiwifruit under whipped cream. *840 Plaza, Oakland
Park Blvd., tel. 305/564–6363. Reservations advised. Dress: casual
but neat. AE, D, DC, MC, V. Closed Mon. except after holidays,
Thanksgiving, Dec. 25, Jan. 1, 3 wks in Aug., Sept.*

Pompano **Cafe Maxx.** New-wave epicurean dining had its south Florida start
Beach here in the early '80s, and Cafe Maxx remains very popular among
Splurge regional gourmets. The setting, in a little strip of stores, is ordinary
★ to the extreme, but inside there's a holiday glow year-round. From
the open kitchen to booths that rim the boxy dining room, guests
and the culinary staff under chef Oliver Saucy engage in ritual devo-
tion to the preparation of fine cuisine and the pleasure of polishing it
off. A menu that changes nightly showcases foods from the tropics:
jumbo stone crab claws with honey-lime mustard sauce, Florida lobster with *salsa verde*, and black bean and banana pepper chili with
Florida avocado. Desserts, too, reflect a tropical theme, from pra-
line macadamia mousse over chocolate cake with butterscotch sauce
to candied ginger with Sekel pears poached in muscatel and sun-
dried cherry ice cream. More than 200 wines are offered by the bottle, another 20 by the glass. *2601 E. Atlantic Blvd., tel. 305/782–
0606. Reservations advised. Dress: casual but neat. AE, D, DC,
MC, V. Closed Super Bowl Sun., July 4. No lunch.*

Wilton **Old Florida Seafood House.** Owner Bob Wickline has run this tradi-
Manors tional seafood restaurant since 1978 with a West Virginian's eye to-
$$ ward giving value for money: It's plain on atmosphere and friendly
on price, with nothing frozen and nothing portion-controlled. He'll
bring out a whole swordfish to show that it's fresh. Try the veal
Gustav (sautéed veal topped with a lobster tail) or a snapper New
Orleans (sautéed with mushrooms and artichokes, laced with a light
brown sauce). There's usually a 30-minute wait on weekends. *1414
N.E. 26th St., tel. 305/566–1044; 4535 Pine Island Rd., Sunrise, tel.
305/572–0444; 9980 Pines Blvd., Pembroke Pines, tel. 305/436–
0200. No reservations. Dress: casual but neat. AE, MC, V. Closed
Thanksgiving, Dec. 25. No lunch weekends.*

The Arts and Nightlife

For the most complete weekly listing of events, read the
"Showtime!" entertainment insert and events calendar in the Fri-
day *Fort Lauderdale News/Sun Sentinel.* "Weekend" in the Friday
edition of the *Herald,* the Broward edition of the *Miami Herald,*
carries similar listings. The weekly *XS* is principally an entertain-
ment and dining paper with a relic "underground" look. A 24-hour
Arts & Entertainment Hotline (tel. 305/357–5700) provides updates
on art, attractions, children's events, dance, festivals, films, litera-
ture, museums, music, opera, and theater.

Tickets are sold at individual box offices and through **Ticketmaster**
(tel. 305/523–3309).

The Arts

Bailey Concert Hall (Central Campus of Broward Community Col-
lege, 3501 S.W. Davie Rd., Davie, tel. 305/475–6884) is a popular
place for classical music concerts, dance, drama, and other perform-
ing arts activities, especially October–April.
Broward Center for the Performing Arts (201 S.W. 5th Ave., Fort
Lauderdale, tel. 305/462–0222) is the waterfront centerpiece of Fort
Lauderdale's new cultural arts district. More than 500 events a year

are scheduled at the performing arts center, including Broadway musicals, plays, dance, symphony and opera, rock, film, lectures, comedy, and children's theater.

Sunrise Musical Theatre (5555 N.W. 95th Ave., Sunrise, tel. 305/741–8600) stages Broadway musicals, a few dramatic plays with name stars, and concerts by well-known singers throughout the year. The theater is 14 miles west of Fort Lauderdale Beach via Commercial Boulevard.

Theater   **Parker Playhouse** (707 N.E. 8th St., Holiday Park, Fort Lauderdale, tel. 305/763–2444) features Broadway plays, musicals, drama, and local productions.

Vinnette Carroll Repertory Company (503 S.E. 6th St., Fort Lauderdale, tel. 305/462–2424), a multi-ethnic theater company housed in a renovated church, has mounted productions of such Broadway hits as *Your Arms Too Short to Box with God* and *Don't Bother Me I Can't Cope.*

Music   The **Florida Philharmonic Orchestra** (3401 N.W. 9th Ave., Fort Lauderdale, tel. 305/561–2997), south Florida's only fully professional orchestra, is Broward-based but performs in six locations in Broward, Dade, and Palm Beach counties.

Opera   **Florida Grand Opera** (221 S.W. 3rd Ave., Fort Lauderdale, tel. 305/728–9700), formed in 1994 by the merger of the Opera Guild of Fort Lauderdale and the Greater Miami Opera, is now the 10th-largest opera company in the United States. It presents five productions a season at the Broward Center for the Performing Arts.

Nightlife

As an alternative to designated drivers, Fort Lauderdale's famous water taxi offers a Tuesday and Thursday evening "pub crawl" from 7 to midnight except holidays. The price is about $30 per person, including visits to three clubs with a drink at each. For pick-up and drop-off points, call 305/565–5507.

Bars and Lounges   **Baja Beach Club** (Coral Ridge Mall, 3200 N. Federal Hwy., Fort Lauderdale, tel. 305/561–2432) offers trendy entertainment: karaoke, lip sync, virtual reality, performing bartenders, temporary tattoos—plus a 40-foot free buffet. There are free drinks for women Wednesday night. **Bloody Mary's** (101 N. Beach Rd., Dania, tel. 305/922–5600), a canal-front bar just across from the John U. Lloyd Beach, is popular on winter weekends, when live acts perform. **Cheers** (941 E. Cypress Creek Rd., Fort Lauderdale, tel. 305/771–6337) is a woody nightspot with two bars and a dance floor. Every night has something special. Local favorite **Club M** (2037 Hollywood Blvd., Hollywood, tel. 305/925–8396) features live blues, dancing, and every kind of paraphernalia that starts with the letter M. **Confetti** (2660 E. Commercial Blvd., Fort Lauderdale, tel. 305/776–4080) is a high-energy "in" spot for adults up to 50. **Crocco's** (3339 N. Federal Hwy., Oakland Park, tel. 305/566–2406) is the action place for singles. Women drink free Wednesday and Sunday nights from 8 to 11. A long-running venue for the best of blues, jazz, rock-and-roll, and reggae performers, **Musicians Exchange** (729 W. Sunrise Blvd., Fort Lauderdale, tel. 305/764–1912) has a new Italian-American café. Events include national acts on weekends and a Monday blues jam. **O'Hara's Pub & Sidewalk Cafe** (722 E. Las Olas Blvd. Fort Lauderdale, tel. 305/524–2801) features live jazz and blues nightly. It's packed for TGIF, though usually by the end of each day the trendy crowd spills onto this prettiest of downtown streets. The **Parrot Lounge** (911 Sunrise La., Fort Lauderdale., tel. 305/563–1493) is a loony feast for the eyes, with a very casual, friendly, local crowd. Fifteen TVs and frequent sing-alongs add to the fun. A jukebox jams all night. **Squeeze** (401 S. Andrews Ave., Fort Lauderdale, tel. 305/522–2068) welcomes a wide-ranging clientele—hard-core new-wavers to yuppie types. Along with serving great Japanese food, **Sushi Blues** (1836 S. Young Circle, Hollywood, tel. 305/929–9560) hosts live music Thursday through Saturday evenings.

Comedy Clubs The **Comic Strip** (1432 N. Federal Hwy., Fort Lauderdale, tel. 305/565–8887) headlines stand-up comedians from New York and nationally touring comics, performing among framed old newspaper funnies. **Uncle Funny's Comedy Club** (9160 Rte. 84, Davie, tel. 305/474–5653) features national and local comics; two shows Friday and Saturday.

Country-and-Western Clubs **Desperado** (2520 S. Miami Rd., Fort Lauderdale, tel. 305/463–2855) features a mechanical bull and free line-dancing lessons.

5 Palm Beach and the Treasure Coast

By Herb
Hiller

After a century, the Flagler influence finally wanes. Henry Flagler, railroad and real-estate magnate, *created* Palm Beach. Before him, it was an island of fisherfolk and coconut planters, premodern pioneers who lived escapist lives and traveled by boat over sea and inland lagoon because there was no road. Then, suddenly, 100 years ago, the piney woods echoed with the whistle of Flagler's trains. He extended his railroad from Jacksonville and St. Augustine and connected south Florida to New York and the world. In the blink of history's eye, the area exchanged wilderness for luxury. It became the playground of Vanderbilts and Rockefellers, and the Gold Coast was born.

At the same time, West Palm Beach began as the scullery of Palm Beach. Flagler ousted the workers who were helping build his New World Riviera, relocating them across Lake Worth to his freight yards. Palm Beach was for society. West Palm was for servants. Nevertheless, West Palm would have its day. In the '20s the town roared. Then after World War II, suburbs spread in all directions (except east, where Palm Beach remained apart). As recently as a decade ago, West Palm had the most boarded-up downtown in Florida, and one-third of everything standing—77 acres' worth—was torn down and scraped bare.

But failure finally brought action. A strong administration and solid planning have brought new ideas about good downtown living. Residents are returning to live above storefronts; job-skills programs are being underwritten by a consortium of philanthropies; big projects, such as the $124 million County Judicial Center and Courthouse and the $60 million Kravis Center for the Performing Arts, have meant jobs; and a mix of cultural and entertainment organizations and facilities has taken root.

From Flagler's time through the '20s, everything came from the north, but today's prevailing influences come from the south. Fort

Lauderdale reinvented its downtown a few years ago. Miami Beach's Deco District set the standard for south Florida nightlife. Now it's West Palm's turn to get caught up in the action. Latin influence grows, too, as Palm Beach County absorbs rich and poor from South and Central America (now 10%–12% of a county population of nearly a million).

What all this means for visitors is a treasury of arts attractions; downtown preservation; and a beautifully landscaped Clematis Street with boutique shopping, good restaurants, and exuberant nightlife that mimics South Beach. There's a free downtown shuttle by day, free on-street parking at night and on weekends. West Palm Beach, born as an afterthought, has become the cultural, entertainment, and business center of the county and of the region to the north.

Elsewhere in Palm Beach County, the arts also flourish. From Boca Raton in the south to Jupiter in the north, there's a profusion of museums, galleries, and theaters and towns committed to historic preservation.

As for Palm Beach, socialites and celebrities still flock here. They attend charity galas at the Breakers. They browse in the stores along Worth Avenue, still one of the world's classiest shopping districts. They swim on secluded beaches that are nominally public but lack convenient parking and access points. They pedal the world's most beautiful bicycle path beside Lake Worth. And what they do, *you* can do—if you can afford it. But despite its prominence and affluence, the town of Palm Beach occupies far less than 1% of the land area of the remarkably diverse political jurisdiction that Palm Beach County has become.

Budget-minded vacationers can find excellent bargains in almost all parts of the county. To the south in Delray Beach, revival has been aimed largely at middle-class retirees. Their fixed-income lifestyles yield a good mix of affordable restaurants and good-quality lodgings. Between Delray and West Palm, Lake Worth is far and away the value leader of the Gold Coast, providing everything from gas and photocopies to food and lodging at bargain prices. In the north, an affordable district extends directly to the beach in Palm Beach Shores.

Also worth exploring is the region just north of Palm Beach County; called the Treasure Coast, it encompasses Martin, St. Lucie, and Indian River counties. Remote and sparsely populated as recently as the late 1970s, the Treasure Coast lost its relative seclusion in 1987, when I–95's missing link from Palm Beach Gardens to Fort Pierce was completed. Now malls crowd corridors between I–95 and the beaches from Palm Beach north to Vero Beach. Martin and Indian River counties are known for their high environmental standards (though not St. Lucie County in between). Stuart, the Martin County seat, has revived its downtown with restaurants and shops, while Vero Beach, the Indian River County seat, is a hub of Treasure Coast arts. It even has a few lodgings and restaurants along its beachfront that are excellent buys.

Inland, the Treasure Coast is largely devoted to citrus production, with cattle ranching in rangelands of pine-and-palmetto scrub. Along the coast, the broad tidal lagoon called the Indian River separates the barrier islands from the mainland. It's a sheltered route for boaters on the Intracoastal Waterway, a nursery for many saltwater game fish, and a natural radiator keeping frost away from the tender orange and grapefruit trees that grow near its banks. Sea turtles come ashore at night from April to August to lay their eggs on the beaches, and you can join organized turtle watches run by local conservation groups, chambers of commerce, and resorts.

Palm Beach and the Treasure Coast Basics

Budget Lodging

Palm Beach County deserves its nickname "the Gold Coast"—hotel prices hover at the high end of the scale, and it's tough to find a bargain. The best ways to save money are to stay in Delray Beach, Lake Worth, and Palm Beach Shores or to visit in the off-season, when rates are significantly lower.

If you plan to stay overnight along the Treasure Coast, reservations are a must. There's less to choose from because tourism came later to the Treasure Coast than to the Gold Coast, but prices are generally lower. Even beachfront lodgings can be affordable.

Budget Dining

The wealth and sophistication of Palm Beach County's seasonal residents ensure a good supply of top-end restaurants here; quick, casual, cheap restaurants are a bit harder to find. Along the Treasure Coast, however, restaurants woo business with dollar-saving early-bird menus.

Bargain Shopping

Palm Beach County is known for its exclusive shopping. Even if you don't feel like emptying your wallet on a shopping spree, however, you can still have a great time window-shopping, people-watching, and taking the pulse of these upscale towns.

Beaches

Beaches remain the main attraction in Palm Beach County and along the Treasure Coast to the north, and everywhere except Palm Beach (where access is made particularly difficult) beaches are freely accessible. Many of the beaches in Palm Beach County, especially those in Palm Beach itself, have begun to erode; the widest ones are in the Jupiter area, on Singer Island, and in Boca Raton. For those without a car, CoTran buses go to beaches in Boca Raton, Lake Worth, Lantana, and Singer Island.

Sports and the Outdoors

The spectator sport that's distinctive to the region is polo. Though played by the rich, polo is often quite affordable to watch, and attending a polo match provides a great opportunity to rub elbows (well, almost) with the elite. If you'd rather be active yourself, there's a wealth of sporting opportunities in the area.

Biking Parks with bicycling trails include Dreher (where the zoo is), John Prince, and Okeeheelee. In downtown Boynton Beach, Delray Beach, and Hypoluxo, marked bicycle lanes are going in along U.S. 1. For on-the-road rides, group rides, and schedules of longer rides and general cycling savvy, contact Wendell Phillips, the **Palm Beach County Bicycle Coordinator** (tel. 407/684–4170), who can put you in touch with the West Palm Beach Bicycle Club.

Diving You can drift dive or anchor dive along Palm Beach County's 47-mile Atlantic Coast. Drift divers take advantage of the Gulf Stream's strong currents and proximity to shore—sometimes less than a mile. A group of divers joined by nylon line may drift across coral reefs with the current; one member of the group carries a large, orange float that the charter-boat captain can follow. Drift diving works best from Boynton Beach north. South of Boynton Beach, where the Gulf Stream is farther from shore, diving from an anchored boat is more popular. Among the more intriguing artificial reefs in the area is a 1967 Rolls-Royce Silver Shadow in 80 feet of water off Palm Beach.

Scuba and snorkeling equipment can be rented throughout Palm Beach County from longtime, family-owned **Force E** (1399 N. Military Trail, West Palm Beach, tel. 407/471–2676; 155 E. Blue Heron Blvd., Riviera Beach, tel. 407/845–2333; 11911 U.S. 1, Suite 101–G, North Palm Beach, tel. 407/624–7136; 877 E. Palmetto Park Rd., Boca Raton, tel. 407/368–0555; 7166 Beracasa Way, Boca Raton, tel. 407/395–4407; 660 Linton Blvd., Delray Beach, tel. 407/276–0666). All stores have PADI affiliation and provide instruction at all skill levels; dive-boat charters are also available.

Fishing Palm Beach County and the Treasure Coast are fisherfolks' heaven, from deep-sea strikes of fighting sailfish and wahoo to the bass, speckled perch, and bluegill of Lake Okeechobee. In between there are numerous fishing piers, bridges, and waterways where pompano, sheepshead, snapper, and grouper are likely catches. To request a free Palm Beach County "Fish Finder Kit," with information on artificial reefs, boat ramps, charters, fish camps, marinas, tides, and tournament schedules, write to the **West Palm Beach Fishing Club** (c/o Fish Finder, Box 468, West Palm Beach 33402).

Golf There are 150 public, private, and semiprivate golf courses in the Palm Beach County area, and at last count 43 were open to the public, some with quite reasonable greens fees. Off-season fees are lower, and you can often pay less by playing later in the day.

Hiking Short hikes are available in most state parks and some county parks. The best long hikes in the area are in the **DuPuis Reserve State Forest,** in western Martin County. A mix of terrain includes wet prairie, broad-leaf marsh and saw grass, pasture, native flatwoods, and cypress and scrub cypress lands. Wildlife that might be seen include bobcat, feral hog, bald eagle, white-tailed deer, armadillo, wild turkey, and otter. The reserve also includes horse trails and primitive campsites. *6 mi west of Indiantown on Rte. 76, tel. 407/924–8021 or 941/763–2191. Admission: $1 per vehicle including driver, 50¢ each additional passenger.*

The Arts and Nightlife

Palm Beach County is booming as an affordable hub of the arts. Although its newest facility, the 2,200-seat Kravis Center for the Performing Arts in downtown West Palm Beach, is a high-priced venue, there are plenty of outlying centers meant to attract a wider population with lower admissions.

The *Palm Beach Post,* in its "TGIF" entertainment insert on Friday, lists all events for the weekend, including concerts. Admission to some cultural events is free or by donation. Call **Ticketmaster** (tel. 407/839–3900) for tickets for performing-arts events.

Guided Tours

Audubon Society of the Everglades (tel. 407/588–6908) leads field trips through Palm Beach County, the Treasure Coast, and the Space Coast (the region centered on the Kennedy Space Center), except during midsummer. Shorter nature walks take place Saturdays, January through March.

Tour 1: Palm Beach and West Palm Beach

Palm Beach is an island community 12 miles long and no more than ½ mile across at its widest point. Three bridges connect Palm Beach to West Palm Beach and the rest of the world. When Henry Flagler created this resort in 1894, it attracted the affluent for the Season: New Year's Day to Washington's Birthday. These rich people then departed for Europe, extolling Palm Beach's virtues and collecting great art to ship back to the mansions they were building on the island. Today, West Palm Beach is a year-round community, but Palm Beach still changes with the seasons—as do the hotel rates.

Arriving and Departing

By Plane

Palm Beach International Airport (PBIA) (Congress Ave. and Belvedere Rd., West Palm Beach, tel. 407/471–7400) is served by **Air Canada** (tel. 800/776–3000), **American/American Eagle** (tel. 800/433–7300), **American Trans-Air** (tel. 800/225–2995), **Canadian Holidays** (tel. 800/661–8881), **Carnival Airlines** (tel. 800/824–7386), **Comair** (tel. 800/354–9822), **Continental** (tel. 800/525–0280), **Delta** (tel. 800/221–1212), **KIWI Intl. Airlines** (tel. 800/538–5494), **Laker Airways Ltd.** (tel. 800/331–6471), **Northwest** (tel. 800/225–2525), **Paradise Island** (tel. 800/432–8807), **Republic Air Travel** (tel. 800/233–0225), **TWA** (tel. 800/221–2000), **United** (tel. 800/241–6522), and **USAir/USAir Express** (tel. 800/428–4322).

Route 10 of **Tri-Rail Commuter Bus Service** (tel. 800/874–7245) runs from the airport to Tri-Rail's nearby Palm Beach Airport station daily. **CoTran** (*see* Getting Around on the Cheap, *below*) Route 4–S operates from the airport to downtown West Palm Beach every two hours at 35 minutes after the hour from 7:35 AM until 5:35 PM. The fare is $1.

Palm Beach Transportation (tel. 407/689–4222) provides taxi and limousine service from PBIA. Reserve at least a day in advance for a limousine. The lowest fares are $1.50 per mile, with the meter starting at $1.25. Depending on your destination, a flat rate (from PBIA only) may save money. Wheelchair-accessible vehicles are available.

By Bus

Greyhound Lines (tel. 800/231–2222) buses arrive at the station in West Palm Beach (100 Banyan Blvd., tel. 407/833–8534).

By Car

I-95 runs north–south, linking West Palm Beach with Miami and Fort Lauderdale to the south and with Daytona, Jacksonville, and the rest of the Atlantic Coast to the north. To get to central Palm Beach, exit at Belvedere Road or Okeechobee Boulevard. Florida's Turnpike runs up from Miami through West Palm Beach before angling northwest to reach Orlando.

By Train

Amtrak (tel. 800/872–7245) connects West Palm Beach (201 S. Tamarind Ave., tel. 407/832–6169) with cities along Florida's east coast and the Northeast daily and via the *Sunset Limited* to New Orleans and Los Angeles three times weekly.

Getting Around

A new **Downtown Transfer Facility** (Banyan Blvd. and Clearlake Dr., West Palm Beach) is to open in 1996, off Australian Avenue at the western entrance to downtown. It links the Palmtran shuttle, Amtrak, Tri-Rail (the commuter line of Dade, Broward, and Palm Beach counties), CoTran (the county bus system), and taxis. Greyhound is also expected to tie in.

By Bus

CoTran (Palm Beach County Transportation Authority) buses require exact change. The cost is $1, 50¢ for students, senior citizens (plus $1 for ID), and people with disabilities; transfers are 20¢, 10¢ for students, senior citizens, and people with disabilities. Service operates between 5 AM and 8:30 PM, though pickups on most routes are 5:30 to 7. For details, call 407/233–1111.

The **Palmtran** shuttle system (tel. 407/833–8873) provides free transportation around downtown West Palm Beach from 6:30 AM to 7:30 PM weekdays.

By Car Downtown West Palm Beach, because of the still high vacancy rate in its office buildings, has plenty of parking on the street and in competitively priced garages—the rate is pretty much standard at 50¢ an hour. Moreover, after 4 o'clock weekdays and all weekends and holidays, all on-street parking is free. Still better, all cafés participating in downtown's Free and Easy program offer two hours of free parking.

In 1995 a new nonstop four-lane route, Okeechobee Boulevard, began carrying traffic from west of downtown West Palm Beach, near the Amtrak station in the airport district, directly to the Flagler Memorial Bridge and into Palm Beach. Flagler Drive will be turned over for pedestrian use before the end of the decade. Southern Boulevard (U.S. 98) runs east–west from West Palm Beach to Lake Okeechobee.

By Taxi **Palm Beach Transportation** (tel. 407/689–4222) has a single number serving several cab companies. Meters start at $1.25, and the charge is $1.25 per mile within West Palm Beach city limits; if the trip at any point leaves the city limits, the fare is $1.50 per mile. Some cabs may charge more. Waiting time is 25¢ per 75 seconds.

By Train **Tri-Rail** (tel. 305/728–8445 or 800/874–7245), the commuter rail system, has six stations in Palm Beach County (13 stops altogether between West Palm Beach and Miami). The round-trip fare is $5, $2.50 for students and senior citizens.

Guided Tours **Old Northwood Historic District Tours** (tel. 407/863–5633) offers two-hour group walking tours on Sundays year-round through the 1920s-era historic district of West Palm Beach, including historic home interiors. The district is listed on the National Register of Historic Places and hosts special events much of the year. A $5 donation is requested.

Star of Palm Beach (tel. 407/842–0882) runs year-round from Singer Island, each day offering one dinner-dance and three sightseeing cruises of the Intracoastal Waterway.

Palm Beach

Palm Beach Chamber of Commerce (45 Cocoanut Row, Palm Beach 33480, tel. 407/655–3282).

Numbers in the margin correspond to points of interest on the Palm Beach and West Palm Beach map.

❶ Begin at Royal Palm Way and County Road in the center of Palm Beach. Go north on County Road to Episcopal **Bethesda-by-the-Sea**, built in 1927 by the first Protestant congregation in southeast Florida. Spanish-Gothic design and ornamental gardens mark the site. *141 S. County Rd., tel. 407/655–4554. Gardens open daily 8–5; services Sept.–May, Sun. at 8, 9, and 11 AM; June–Aug., Sun. at 8 and 10; phone for weekday schedule.*

★ ❷ Continue north on County Road past the **Breakers** (*see* Budget Lodging, *below*), an ornate Italian renaissance hotel built in 1926 by Henry M. Flagler's widow to replace an earlier hotel, which had burned twice.

❸ Farther up County Road, at Royal Poinciana Way, go inside the **Palm Beach Post Office** to see the murals depicting Seminole Indians in the Everglades and royal and coconut palms. *95 N. County Rd., tel. 407/832–0633 or 407/832–1867. Lobby open 24 hrs.*

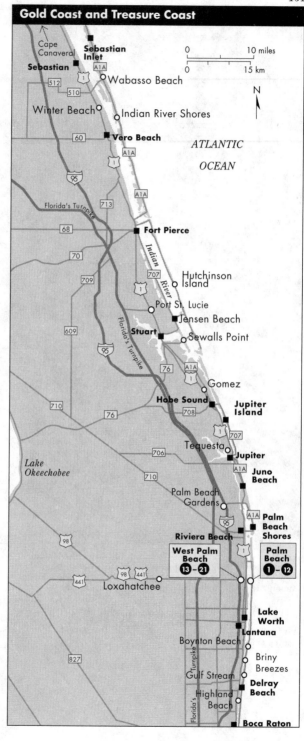

Gold Coast and Treasure Coast

Cape Canaveral

Sebastian Inlet

Sebastian

A1A

512

510

Wabasso Beach

Winter Beach

Indian River Shores

60

Vero Beach

A1A

1

ATLANTIC

OCEAN

95

Florida's Turnpike

713

A1A

68

Fort Pierce

70

707

Hutchinson Island

709

1

Port St. Lucie

Jensen Beach

609

95

76

Stuart

Sewalls Point

A1A

1

Gomez

710

76

Hobe Sound

708

Jupiter Island

706

Tequesta

1

707

Jupiter

Lake Okeechobee

710

A1A

Juno Beach

Palm Beach Gardens

95

A1A

Palm Beach Shores

98

Riviera Beach

1

West Palm Beach

13-21

Palm Beach

1-12

441

98 441

Loxahatchee

Lake Worth

Lantana

Boynton Beach

Briny Breezes

827

Gulf Stream

Delray Beach

Highland Beach

Florida's Turnpike

Boca Raton

0   10 miles

0   15 km

N

Indian River

Palm Beach and West Palm Beach

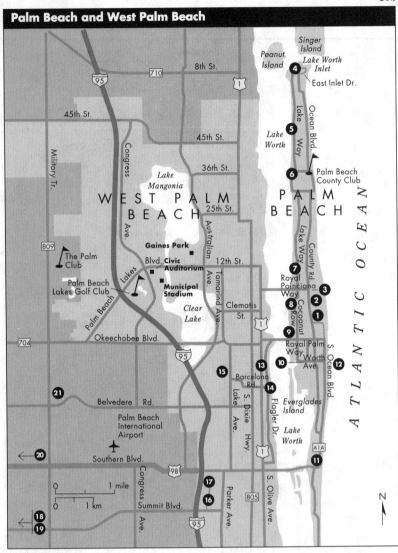

Continue 3.9 miles on North County Road/North Ocean Boulevard, past the very private Palm Beach Country Club and a neighborhood of expansive (and expensive) estates. Among these, at 1095 North Ocean Boulevard, is the former home of the Kennedy family, unoccupied, decaying, and lately for sale. You must turn around at **East Inlet Drive,** the northern tip of the island, where a dock offers a view of Lake Worth Inlet. Observe the no-parking signs; Palm Beach police will issue tickets.

Turn south and make the first right onto Indian Road, then the first left onto Lake Way. You'll return to the center of town through an area of newer mansions, past the posh, private Sailfish Club. Along the shoreline of Lake Worth, the **Palm Beach Bicycle Trail,** a palm-fringed path through the backyards of some of the world's priciest homes, parallels Lake Way.

Lake Way runs into Country Club Road, which takes you through the **Canyon of Palm Beach,** a road cut about 25 feet deep through a ridge of sandstone and oolite limestone.

As you emerge from the canyon, turn right onto Lake Way and continue south. Lake Way becomes Bradley Place. You'll pass the **Palm Beach Biltmore Hotel,** now a condominium. Another flamboyant landmark of the Florida boom, it cost $7 million to build and opened in 1927 with 543 rooms.

As you cross Royal Poinciana Way, Bradley Place becomes Cocoanut Row. Stop at **Whitehall,** the palatial 73-room mansion that Henry M. Flagler built in 1901 for his third wife, Mary Lily Kenan. In 1960 Flagler's granddaughter, Jean Flagler Matthews, bought the building. She turned it into a museum, with many of the original furnishings on display. In addition to an art collection, the house features a 1,200-pipe organ and exhibits on the history of the Florida East Coast Railroad. Flagler's personal railroad car, "The Rambler," is parked behind the building. A tour by well-informed guides takes about an hour. *Cocoanut Row at Whitehall Way, tel. 407/655–2833. Admission: $7 adults, $3 children 6–12. Open Tues.–Sat. 10–5, Sun. noon–5.*

Continue south on Cocoanut Row to Royal Palm Way. Turn right and then right again onto the grounds of the **Society of the Four Arts.** This 60-year-old cultural and educational institution is privately endowed and incorporates an exhibition hall for art, concerts, films, and lectures; a library open without charge; 13 distinct gardens; and the Philip Hulitar Sculpture Garden. *Four Arts Plaza, tel. 407/655–7226. Admission: $3 suggested donation. Concert and lecture tickets for nonmembers may be purchased 1 wk in advance; tickets for Fri. films available at time of showing. Exhibitions and programs: Dec.–mid-Apr., Mon.–Sat. 10–5, Sun. 2–5; library and children's library open weekdays 10–5, also Sat. 9–1 Nov.–Apr.; gardens open Mon.–Sat. 10–5, also Sun. 2:30–5 Jan.–Apr. 15.*

Return to Royal Palm Way and County Road, where we began this tour. Now go south on County Road, until you reach **Worth Avenue** (*see* Shopping for Bargains, *below*), one of the world's finest shopping streets.

County Road runs south along a mansion row fronted by thick stands of palm trees and high hedges, some hedge rows higher than 20 feet. You will see de rigueur barrel-tile roofs on the houses. After a mile, County Road joins Ocean Boulevard to become the shore road (now officially designated A1A). A low wall separates the road from the sea and hides the badly eroded beach. Here and there where the seaside strand deepens a bit, homes have been built directly on the beach.

Grandest of homes along this road is **Mar-A-Lago** (1100 S. Ocean Blvd.), its Italianate towers silhouetted against the sky. Mar-A-

Lago, the former estate of breakfast-food heiress **Marjorie Meriweather Post**, has lately been owned by real-estate magnate Donald Trump, who has turned it into a membership club. The property curves for ⅛ mile along the road.

Rather than cross the bridge to the mainland, turn back along Ocean Boulevard, heading north along one of Florida's most scenic drives. The road follows the dune top, with some of Palm Beach's most opulent mansions on your left. As you approach Worth Avenue, the **public beach** begins. Parking meters along Ocean Boulevard between Worth Avenue and Royal Palm Way signify the only stretch of beach in Palm Beach with convenient public access.

Budget Lodging *$$* **Sea Lord Hotel.** If you don't need glamour or brand names, and you're not the bed-and-breakfast type, this garden-style hideaway is for you. Choose from accommodations that overlook Lake Worth, the pool, or the ocean; all were given a face-lift in 1993–94—new paint, new furniture, and new bedspreads and drapes as needed. The reasonably priced 20-seat café, now with tablecloths and cloth napkins in the evening, adds to the at-home, comfy feeling and attracts repeat customers. Rooms are plain but not cheap and come with carpet, at least one comfortable chair, small or large fridge, and tropical print fabrics. *2315 S. Ocean Blvd., 33480, tel. and fax 407/582–1461. 19 rooms, 11 apts., 6 efficiencies. Facilities: restaurant, pool, beach. D, MC, V.*

Splurge ★ **The Breakers.** Only the Breakers can complete a five-year, $50 million renovation and immediately follow it up with a commitment for $40 million more. This palatial seven-story oceanfront resort hotel, built in Italian Renaissance style in 1926 and enlarged in 1969, sprawls over 140 acres of splendor in the heart of some of the most expensive real estate in the world. Cupids wrestle alligators in the Florentine fountain in front of the main entrance. Inside the lofty lobby, your eyes lift to majestic ceiling vaults and frescoes. The hotel still blends formality with tropical-resort ambience, even if, conceding to the times, men and boys are no longer *required* (only requested) to wear jackets and ties after 7 PM. Room decor follows two color schemes: cool greens and soft pinks in an orchid-pattern English cotton chintz fabric, and shades of blue with a floral and ribbon chintz. Both designs include white plantation shutters and wall coverings, Chinese porcelain table lamps, and original 1920s furniture restored to its period appearance. The original building has 15 different room sizes and shapes. If you prefer more space, ask to be placed in the newer addition. *1 S. County Rd., 33480, tel. 407/655–6611 or 800/833–3141, fax 407/659–8403. 567 rooms, 48 suites. Facilities: 4 restaurants, lounge, outdoor heated freshwater pool, ½ mi of beachfront, 2 golf courses, 20 tennis courts, lawn bowling, croquet, shuffleboard, health club with Keiser and Nautilus equipment, saunas, shopping arcade. AE, DC, MC, V.*

Budget Dining *$$* **Chuck & Harold's.** Ivana Trump, Larry Holmes, Brooke Shields, and Michael Bolton are among the celebrities who frequent this combination power-lunch bar, celebrity sidewalk café, and nocturnal big-band/jazz garden restaurant. Locals who want to be part of the scenery linger in the front-porch area, next to pots of red and white begonias mounted along the sidewalk rail. Specialties include a mildly spiced conch chowder with a rich flavor and a liberal supply of conch; an onion-crunchy gazpacho with croutons, a cucumber spear, and a dollop of sour cream; a frittata (an omelet of bacon, spinach, the hot salami-like pepperoncini, potatoes, smoked mozzarella, and fresh tomato salsa); and a tangy Key lime pie with a grahamcracker crust and a squeezable lime slice for even more tartness. A big blackboard lists daily specials and celebrity birthdays. There's a full bar. *207 Royal Poinciana Way, tel. 407/659–1440. Reservations advised. Dress: casual but neat. AE, DC, MC, V.*

$$ Dempsey's. A New York–style Irish pub under the palms: paisley table covers, plaid café curtains, brass rods, burgundy banquettes, paddle fans, horse prints, and antique coach lanterns. George Dempsey was a Florida cattle rancher until he entered the restaurant business 17 years ago. This place is packed, noisy, and as electric as a frenzied Friday at the stock exchange when major sports events are on the big TV. Along with much socializing, people put away fresh Maine lobster, fresh Florida seafood, plates of chicken hash Dempsey (with a dash of Scotch), shad roe, prime rib, and hot apple pie. There's live piano Thursday to Sunday evenings, Sunday brunch 10–2:30, and round-the-clock valet parking. *50 Cocoanut Row, tel. 407/835–0400. Reservations advised for parties of 6 or more. Dress: casual but neat. AE, MC, V. Closed Thanksgiving, Dec. 25.*

$$ Ta-boo. Real-estate investor Franklyn P. deMarco, Jr., has teamed up with Maryland restaurateur Nancy Sharigan to successfully re-create the legendary Worth Avenue bistro that debuted in 1941. Decorated in gorgeous pinks, greens, and florals, the space is divided into discrete salons: One resembles a courtyard; another, an elegant living room with a fireplace; a third, a gazebo under a skylight. The Tiki Tiki bar serves as an elegant saloon for the neighborhood crowd. Nightly dinners include chicken and arugula from the grill, prime ribs and steaks, gourmet pizzas, and main-course salads (a tangy warm steak salad, for instance, comes with grilled strips of marinated filet mignon tossed with greens, mushrooms, tomato, and red onion). A dish of portobello mushrooms, arugula, and asparagus with tomatoes and pine nuts has been added for lighter dining. *221 Worth Ave., tel. 407/835–3500. Reservations advised. Jacket preferred. AE, MC, V.*

$ TooJay's. New York deli food served in a California-style setting—what could be more Florida? Menu includes matzoh ball soup, corned beef on homemade rye, killer cake with five chocolates, and homemade whipped cream. A sandwich of Hebrew National kosher salami layered with onions, Muenster cheese, coleslaw, and Russian dressing on rye is a house favorite. There's also dill chicken; seafood with crabmeat, shrimp, and sour cream; and for the vegetarians, hummus, tabbouleh, and a wheatberry salad. On the High Holidays look for carrot *tzimmes* (a sweet compote), beef brisket with gravy, potato pancakes, and roast chicken. Wisecracking waitresses set the fast pace of this bright restaurant with a high, open packing-crate board ceiling and windows overlooking the gardens. In addition to this location, there are nine other TooJay's restaurants along the Gold and Gulf coasts and in mid-Florida. *313 Royal Poinciana Plaza, tel. 407/659–7232. No reservations. Dress: casual. AE, DC, MC, V. Beer and wine only. Closed Thanksgiving, Dec. 25.*

¢ Green's Pharmacy. Palm Beach's not-to-be-missed luncheonette has a higher ratio of *New York Times* copies per counter seat than anyplace outside New York City. Breakfasters peel off dollar tips from fat wads of bills. Cooks banter with waitresses while French toast, eggs, home fries, and grits sizzle and simmer. It's a good place to be on a cold day because the griddle's always hot. Breakfast foods are served until 6 (closing time Monday–Saturday), but the lunch counter also serves triple-decker sandwiches, soups, salads, and burgers, plus chili, crab cakes, fried shrimp or fish, and chicken breasts. *151 N. County Rd., tel. 407/832–9171. No reservations. Dress: casual. AE, MC, V. No dinner Sun.*

¢ ★ Murray's Palm Beach Diner. Simply one of the best in the budget range, Murray's has a great location at the foot of the beachfront ramp of the bridge from Lake Worth. It's on the site of a former HoJo's and still carries 22 flavors of its ice cream. Three separate seating areas comprise an outdoor deck under canvas, smartly tiled counter and booth sections with attractive potted greenery, and a room in the rear with walls of tropical art. Great deals include breakfast served all day; a pot of coffee for 95¢; two-course blue-plate luncheon specials for under $5; three-course specials for the smaller appetite, served noon–7; and 10% off dinners for senior citizens (55 and up) on Tuesday. Also available are a kids' menu, homemade cakes and pies, and a full bar. *2880 S. Ocean Blvd., tel. 305/ 582–9661. No reservations. Dress: casual. AE, D, DC, MC, V.*

Splurge **Cafe L'Europe.** Sumptuous oak paneling, shirred curtains over fan-
★ light windows, elaborate dried-flower bouquets, and vintage Sinatra in the background set the mood here. Even the bar habitués are elegantly coiffed, surrounded by details of brass, etched and leaded glass, and tapestry fabrics. Under chef Joseph Eisenbuchner the Mandarin cuisine has given way, and spa cuisine has been folded into the luncheon menu. Guests at dinner dine expensively on specialty pastas, such as spinach, shiitake mushroom, and mascarpone raviolis with pine-nut hazelnut butter; seafoods that may include a sautéed potato-crusted fresh Florida snapper, shaved baby fennel, and garlic-scallion beurre blanc; or the likes of roast Cornish hen, double lamb chops, and black Angus steak. Desserts include numerous fruit tarts and chocolate cakes prepared daily in the café bakery, as well as the signature apple pancake with lingonberries. *150 Worth Ave., in the Esplanade, tel. 407/655–4020. Reservations required in winter. Jacket required in main dining room. AE, DC, MC, V. No lunch Sun.*

Shopping for One of the world's showcases for high-quality shopping, **Worth Ave-**
Bargains nue runs ¼ mile east–west across Palm Beach, from the beach to Lake Worth. The street has more than 250 shops, and many upscale stores (Cartier, Gucci, Hermès, Pierre Deux, Saks Fifth Avenue, and Van Cleef & Arpels) are represented, their merchandise appealing to the discerning tastes of the Palm Beach clientele. Most merchants open at 9:30 or 10 and close at 5:30 or 6. Even if you don't care to pay their astronomical prices, window-shopping can be fun. Parking on and around Worth Avenue is quite limited. On-street parking has a strictly enforced one- or two-hour limit. An alternative is Apollo Valet Parking at Hibiscus and Peruvian avenues, a block off Worth Avenue. Merchants will stamp your parking ticket if you buy something (or if you look like a prospective customer); each stamp is good for an hour of free parking.

More affordable are shops along the six blocks of **South County Road,** north of Worth Avenue.

For specialty items (out-of-town newspapers and health foods in particular), try the shops along the north side of **Royal Poinciana Way.**

Participant Bike lanes are marked by stripes on Palm Beach streets. A good ride
Sports for less-experienced cyclists is the 10-mile path bordering Lake
Biking Worth, from the Flagler Bridge to the Lake Worth Inlet. Rentals, including mopeds and in-line skates, are available at **Palm Beach Bicycle Trail Shop** (223 Sunrise Ave., tel. 407/659–4583).

Golf You can pay a lot to play golf in Palm Beach. You can also pay $15.50 to walk (in high season), another $15.50 to rent a cart, at the oceanfront **Palm Beach Par 3 Golf Course** (2345 S. Ocean Blvd., tel. 407/ 582–4462).

Spectator **Palm Beach Kennel Club** opened in 1932 and has 4,300 seats. *1111 N.*
Sports *Congress Ave., 33409, tel. 407/683–2222. Admission: 50¢ general*
Dog Racing *admission, $1 terrace level; free parking. Racing Mon. at 12:30; Wed., Thurs., Sat. at 12:30, 7:30; Fri. at 7:30; Sun. at 1. Simulcasts Mon., Fri. at noon; Tues. at 12:30.*

The Arts and Not surprisingly, the arts flourish in Palm Beach, with equity thea-
Nightlife ter, the Society of the Four Arts, galleries galore, and a singular
The Arts commitment to historic preservation. **Royal Poinciana Playhouse** (70 Royal Poinciana Plaza, 33480, tel. 407/659–3310) presents seven productions each year between December and April.

Nightlife **Au Bar** (336 Royal Poinciana Way, tel. 407/832–4800), still popular even though the Kennedy-Smith scandal has faded, has a packed dance floor on weekends.

West Palm Beach

Palm Beach County Convention & Visitors Bureau (1555 Palm Beach Lakes Blvd., Suite 204, West Palm Beach 33401, tel. 407/471–3995). Chamber of Commerce of the Palm Beaches (401 N. Flagler Dr., West Palm Beach 33401, tel. 407/833–3711).

Royal Palm Way runs across the Royal Palm Bridge from Palm Beach into West Palm Beach. Okeechobee Boulevard leads west from here to downtown, but rather than drive there, turn left onto Flagler Drive. Running along the west shore of Lake Worth, the body of water that separates Palm Beach from the mainland, Flagler Drive has been spruced up with a $4.2 million waterfront restoration project.

★ ⑬ One-half mile south of the bridge, turn right onto Actaeon Street leading to the **Norton Gallery of Art.** Founded in 1941 by steel magnate Ralph H. Norton, the Norton Gallery boasts an extensive permanent collection of 19th- and 20th-century American and European paintings with emphasis on 19th-century French Impressionists, Chinese bronze and jade sculptures, a sublime outdoor patio with sculptures on display in a tropical garden, and a library housing more than 3,000 art books and periodicals. Visitors in 1996 will find a new wing under construction, expected to open in 1997. *1451 S. Olive Ave., tel. 407/832–5194. Admission: $5 suggested donation. Open Tues.–Sat. 10–5, Sun. 1–5.*

⑭ Return to Flagler Drive, go ½ mile south to Barcelona Road, and turn right again. You're at the entrance to the **Ann Norton Sculpture Gardens,** a monument to the late American sculptor Ann Weaver Norton, second wife of Norton Gallery founder Ralph H. Norton. In three distinct areas of the 3-acre grounds, the art park displays seven granite figures and six brick megaliths. Plantings were designed by Norton, an environmentalist, to attract native birdlife. *253 Barcelona Rd., tel. 407/832–5328. Admission: $3 ages over 12. Open Tues.–Sat. 10–4 (call ahead because schedule not always observed) or by appointment.*

⑮ Continue west on Barcelona Road to Lake Avenue, turn right, and go three blocks to Park Place and the former Palm Beach County National Guard Armory, now the **Armory Art Center.** Designed as a WPA project in 1939, the armory today serves as a complete visual-arts center with exhibitions, classes, workshops, and special events. *1703 S. Lake Ave., tel. 407/832–1776. Admission free. Open weekdays 9–5.*

⑯ Head back on Lake Avenue to Southern Boulevard (U.S. 98). Turn right and go west one block, turn left onto Parker Avenue, and go south about a mile. Turn right onto Summit Boulevard, and at the next stoplight you'll find the **Dreher Park Zoo.** The 22-acre zoo has more than 500 animals representing more than 100 species, including an endangered Florida panther. *1301 Summit Blvd., tel. 407/533–0887 or 407/547–9453 for a recording. Admission: $5.50 adults, $5 senior citizens over 60, $4.50 children 3–12; boat rides: $1. Open daily 9–5 (to 7 on spring and summer weekends); boat rides every 15 mins.*

⑰ About ¼ mile from the zoo is the **South Florida Science Museum.** Here you'll find hands-on exhibits, aquarium displays with touch-tank demonstrations, planetarium shows, and a chance to observe the heavens Friday nights through the most powerful telescope in south Florida (weather permitting). *4801 Dreher Trail N, tel. 407/832–1988. Admission: $5 adults, $4.50 senior citizens, $3 students*

13–21, $2 children 4–12; Aldrin Planetarium: $1.75 extra, laser show $2 extra. Open Sat.–Thurs. 10–5, Fri. 10–10.

Leaving the science museum, head west on Summit Boulevard to the **Pine Jog Environmental Education Center.** The 150-acre site is mostly undisturbed Florida pine flatwoods. There are now two self-guided ½-mile trails, and formal landscaping around the five one-story buildings features an array of native plants. Dioramas and displays show native ecosystems. *6301 Summit Blvd., tel. 407/686-6600. Admission free. Open weekdays 9–5, weekends 1–4; closed holidays.*

Continuing west on Summit, turn left (south) on Jog Road and right on Forest Hill Boulevard; a mile farther is another regional environmental resource, the **Okeeheelee Nature Center.** Here you can explore 5 miles of trails through 90 acres of native pine flatwoods and wetlands. A spacious visitor center and gift shop has hands-on exhibits. *7715 Forest Hill Blvd., tel. 407/233-1400. Admission free. Visitor center open Tues.–Fri. 1–4:45, Sat. 8:15–4:45; trails open daily.*

Continue west on Forest Hill Boulevard, turn right on U.S. 441 and take it for about 15 miles (as it bears west and joins Southern Boulevard) to **Lion Country Safari.** Here you drive (with car windows closed) on 8 miles of paved roads through a 500-acre cageless zoo where 1,000 wild animals roam free. Lions, elephants, white rhinoceroses, giraffes, zebras, antelopes, chimpanzees, and ostriches are among the species in residence. *Southern Blvd. W, tel. 407/793-1084. Admission: $11.95 adults, $8.55 senior citizens over 65, $9.95 children 3–16; car rental: $5 per hr. Open daily 9:30–5:30.*

Returning east on Southern Boulevard, turn left on Military Trail, which runs alongside the western perimeter of Palm Beach International Airport. On the right just north of Belvedere Road (less than 2 miles) is the 14-acre **Mounts Horticultural Learning Center,** where you can walk among displays of tropical and subtropical plants. Free guided tours are given. *531 N. Military Trail, tel. 407/233-1749. Admission free. Open Mon.–Sat. 8:30–5, Sun. 1–5; tours Sat. at 11, Sun. at 2:30.*

Okeechobee Boulevard, the next cross street north, will take you back to anywhere in the Palm Beaches, to Florida's Turnpike, or to I-95.

Budget Lodging
$$
★
Hibiscus House. Few B&B hosts in Florida work harder at hospitality and at looking after their neighborhood than Raleigh Hill and Colin Rayner. As proof, since the inn opened in the late 1980s, 11 sets of guests have bought houses in Old Northwood, which is listed on the National Register of Historic Places thanks to Hill and Rayner's efforts. Their Cape Cod–style bed-and-breakfast is full of the antiques Hill has collected during decades of in-demand interior designing: a 150-year-old four-square piano in the Florida room, a gorgeous green and cane planter chair beside an Asian fan and bamboo poles, and Louis XV pieces in the living room. Outstanding, too, is the landscaped, tropical pool-patio area behind a high privacy fence. Both Hill and Rayner are informed about the best—as well as the most affordable—dining in the area. This is an excellent value. *501 30th St., 33407, tel. 407/863-5633 or 800/203-4927. 8 rooms. Facilities: heated pool. AE, DC, MC, V.*

$$
Parkview Motor Lodge. This long-standing one-story motel just south of downtown is well kept up, homey, and with a bit of charm, such as bougainvillea planted here and there. The least expensive rooms are nearer the street, and you'll also save by taking a king- or queen-size bed, rather than two double beds. Rooms are carpeted and have a couple of chairs and a table. Though the motel has no restaurant, a Continental breakfast is included, and Howley's (*see* Budget Dining, *below*), next door, serves down-home meals that are

budget priced. *4710 S. Dixie Hwy., 33405, tel. 407/833–4644, fax 407/833–4644. 28 rooms. AE, D, MC, V.*

$$ **West Palm Beach Bed & Breakfast.** Like Hibiscus House, this cottage-style B&B is also in Old Northwood, but it's more informal and Key West–like, with a clump of rare paroutis palms out front. All rooms are vividly colored. (The aqua room is AQUA; the formerly pink room is now AMETHYST.) However, the splashy poolside carriage house and the new, brightly striped cottage with the fruity fabrics and Peter Max–style posters are where you want to be. The parlor has a delightful montage of work by Florida's favorite painter of hotel art, Eileen Seitz. Owners are Dennis Keimel and Ron Seitz (unrelated to the artist). *419 32nd St., 33407, tel. 407/848–4064 or 800/736–4064, fax 407/842–1688. 2 rooms, carriage house, cottage. Facilities: pool, reading room. AE, MC, V.*

Budget Dining **Basil's Neighborhood Cafe.** California tropical but distinctively Palm
$$ Beach, Basil's, in a West Palm shopping center, is the kind of place
★ that makes quick food an event. The service is friendly and efficient, and there's a full bar. The decor has lots of texture—tile, blackboards, stone, fabrics, decorative paints, greenery—but the standout feature is the big mural with caricatures of such Palm Beach personalities as Donald and Ivana Trump, Prince Charles and Princess Di (you can tell Basil's has been around a while), Burt Reynolds, socialite Molly Wilmot, and Zsa Zsa Gabor, plus gators, limos, pelicans, and yachts. Dine outside on the patio or inside at banquettes and free-standing tables. The menu has lots of pizzas and pastas, big dinner salads (pecan chicken, seafood in puff pastry, Greek, chili-blackened chicken), dolphin, steamed fish, meat loaf, burgers, chicken pot pie, and lamb chops. *771 Village Blvd. at Village Commons, tel. 407/687–3801. No reservations. Dress: casual. MC, V. Closed Mon., Thanksgiving, Dec. 25, 3 wks beginning mid-Aug. No lunch weekends.*

$$ **Comeau Bar & Grill.** Everybody still calls it Roxy's, its name from 1934 until it moved into an art deco downtown high-rise's lobby in 1989. Outside there are tables under the canopy; inside, behind the authentic old saloon, is a clubby, pecky cypress–paneled room that serves no-surprise, all-American food: steaks, shrimp, chicken, duck, some pastas, and Caesar and Greek salads. Try the Roxy Burger—a combination of veal and beef herbed and spiced. *319–323 Clematis St., tel. 407/833–2402 or 407/833–1003. Reservations accepted. Dress: casual but neat. AE, MC, V. Closed Dec. 25. No dinner Sun.*

$$ **Narcissus.** Get acquainted with the vitality of downtown West Palm Beach at this lively two-level jazz café across the park from the public library. The grazing menu features salads, pastas, crab cake, tuna pizza melt, burgers, and specialty sandwiches like falafel. Top-value twilight dinner specials are $8.95 for a selection of entrées, soup or salad, plus beverage and dessert. During the daily happy hour, 4:30–7, drinks and hors d'oeuvres are half price. There's a live jazz brunch Sunday noon–4 and jazz jamming 5–10. *200 Clematis St., tel. 407/659–1888. Reservations accepted. Dress: casual but neat. AE, MC, V.*

$ **Sagami.** Black lacquer walls, bamboo, and tatami mats strike a stylish Japanese note, while the acoustic-tile ceiling reminds you you're in a shopping center. Booths, tables, and counter seats (at the sushi bar) all get fast service. Tempura, stir-fries, and teriyaki dishes are among the favorites, as are the kettle dishes served with rice and salad. Try either the *yosenabe* (assorted seafood and vegetables) or the *sukiyaki* (thin sliced sirloin of beef and veggies), each cooked in a savory broth. Green tea and red-bean ice cream, as well as fresh fruits and banana tempura, are good after-dinner choices. *871 Village Blvd., Village Corner Shopping Center, tel. 407/683–4600. Reservations accepted. Dress: casual but neat. AE, V. Closed Thanksgiving. No lunch weekends.*

¢ **Howley's.** Since 1950, the neighborhood has been filling this multiroom diner just south of downtown for the best reason in the world: home cooking at prices you can hardly match cooking for yourself. You can get 65¢ coffee, a rare vegetarian breakfast (home fries, mushrooms, green peppers, and onions) for $2.95, an entire bowl of oatmeal for $1.65, a ¼-pound burger for $1.95 ($1 more with fries, pickle, lettuce, tomato, onion, and mayo), and a half-dozen lunches under $4 or $5 daily. Tuesday, Wednesday, and Friday lunch and every evening have all-you-can-eat items. Six nights a week you can get a half-dozen dinner entrées with two vegetables for around $6 or less. Sunday prices are a little higher, but the fare is a little fancier. All evenings you can add soup, salad, pudding, and coffee or tea for an extra $1.75. Waitresses greet the regulars by name. *4700 S. Dixie Hwy., tel. 407/833-5691. No reservations. Dress: casual. No credit cards. Closed Dec. 25.*

¢ **Wholly Harvest.** This natural-foods store and restaurant, the only one for miles around, is the anchor keeping its failing shopping center south of downtown from going under. The corner soda fountain–deli of the natural-foods crowd, it serves up prepared foods at 30 two-tops and a counter. Fare includes fresh soups, lots of grain and bean dishes, daily specials that might include a grilled seitan (wheat meat) sandwich, and usually crisps for dessert. *7735 S. Dixie Hwy., tel. 407/585-8800; 2200 Glades Rd., Boca Raton, tel. 407/392-5100. No reservations. Dress: casual. D, MC, V. Closed Thanksgiving, Dec. 25.*

Participant Sports

Biking Since it's almost completely free of cross streets, the 5-mile ride along Flagler Drive on the Intracoastal Waterway is good for beginning cyclists. Much of redone Okeechobee Boulevard through downtown now has marked bike lanes.

Tennis You can play for $4 day or night at the **South Olive Tennis Center** (345 Summa St., tel. 407/582-7218) and $5 day or night on the new clay courts at **Howard Park** (901 Lake Ave., tel. 407/582-7218).

Spectator Sports

Baseball The **Atlanta Braves** and the **Montreal Expos** both conduct spring training in Municipal Stadium (1610 Palm Beach Lakes Blvd., Box 3087, 33402, tel. 407/683-6012), which is also home to the **Palm Beach Expos,** a Class-A team in the Florida State League. For tickets, contact the Expos (Box 3566, 33402, tel. 407/684-6801) or the Braves (Box 2619, 33402, tel. 407/683-6100).

Polo **Palm Beach Polo and Country Club,** founded in 1979, has the longest season in Florida and the top players. It's the Wimbledon of polo in North America and site each spring of the $100,000 World Cup competition. *13420 South Shore Blvd., 33414, tel. 407/793-1440. Admission: $8 general admission, $15-$25 ($27-$35 for World Cup) box seats and chalet. Games Dec.-Apr., Sun. at 3.*

The Arts and Nightlife

The Arts The **Raymond F. Kravis Center for the Performing Arts** (701 Okeechobee Blvd., tel. 407/832-7469) is the three-year-old, $55 million, 2,200-seat, glass, copper, and marble showcase that occupies the highest ground in town. Its newest stage is the 250-seat Rinker Playhouse, which in late 1994 added a "black box" space for children's programming, family productions, and other special events. Some 300 performances of drama, dance, and music—everything from gospel and bluegrass to jazz and classical—are scheduled each year. Performing at the center are the **Palm Beach Opera** (415 S. Olive Ave., 33401, tel. 407/833-7888), which stages three productions each winter, and **Ballet Florida** (500 Fern St., 33401, tel. 407/659-2000 or 800/540-0172), one of Florida's chief artistic companies, which, in addition to having a winter season at the center, also goes on tour.

Quest Theatre (444 24th St., 33407, tel. 407/832-9328) enters its sixth season showcasing African-American productions in its own performance hall and on tour throughout the county. **Carefree Thea-**

tre (2000 S. Dixie Hwy., 33401, tel. 407/833–7305) is Palm Beach County's premier showcase of foreign and art films. **Narcissus** (*see* Budget Dining, *above*) gives free movie passes with dinner.

Nightlife   Thursday evening after work West Palm Beach closes Clematis Street to traffic. Local country, folk, and rock bands come out. Tables come out. People eat. People drink. People dance and carry on. Friday and Saturday nights after the three-piece-suiters drive home, the street unmasks. Clematis becomes the hub of West Palm's California-style indoor-outdoor nightclubs—lighter, less smoky and boozy, and more given to jazz brunches and reggae. Hip young professionals living in new downtown apartments supply the sense that something real is happening, and for the first time in 100 years West Palm is rivaling Palm Beach for night action.

The pick of the downtown nightspots is **Narcissus** (200 Clematis St., tel. 407/659–1888), which, in addition to food (*see* Budget Dining, *above*), features daily live jazz and a Sunday jazz brunch and jazz jam. Downstairs from Narcissus is the **Underground Coffeeworks** (105 Narcissus Ave., tel. 407/835–4792), a sort of '60s spot. **Respectable Street Cafe** (518 Clematis St., tel. 407/832–9999) explodes in high energy like an indoor Woodstock.

Palm Beach Shores

Even though this unpretentious middle-class community on the southern tip of Singer Island is separated only by an inlet from glitzy Palm Beach, to get between the two you must cross over to the mainland before returning to the beach. It's a distinctly affordable nook of Palm Beach County resortdom, and its main attraction is affordable beachfront lodging. By staying here, you get Palm Beach weather and a Palm Beach view without the pretense and for half the price of anything comparable in Palm Beach.

Budget   **The Sailfish Marina.** This long-established, one-story motel has a
Lodging   marina with 94 deep-water slips and 15 rooms and efficiencies that
$$ open to landscaped grounds. None is directly on the waterfront, but
★   units 9–11 have water views across the blacktop drive. Rooms have peaked ceilings, carpeting, king or twin beds, stall showers, the usual variety of dressers and cushioned chairs; many have ceiling fans. Much of the art is original, traded with artists who display in an informal show on the dock every Thursday night. Lately this has attracted some 35 artists and as many as 4,000 browsers and buyers each week. From the seawall, there's a good view of fish through the clear inlet water. The staff is informed and helpful, the proprietors as promotional as they are friendly. Inquire about May–September, Sunday–Thursday two-for-one packages (holidays and tournament days excluded) and other slow-season specials. There are neither no-smoking rooms nor in-room phones, but there are several pay phones on the property and messages are taken. *98 Lake Dr., 33404, tel. 407/844–1724 or 800/446–4577, fax 407/848–9684. 15 units. Facilities: restaurant, bar, pool, marina, water taxi cruises, barbecue grills, grocery store, gift shop. AE, MC, V.*

$–$$ **Capri Apartments.** You can swim right off the dock here in the crys-
★   tal waters of Lake Worth Inlet or walk five minutes to a big beach, not the eroded spit that the rich of Palm Beach have to make do with. And you'll feel safe walking at night in this quiet, residential neighborhood. The best accommodation is the spacious one-bedroom apartment upstairs, which overlooks the inlet, but even the least expensive units are efficiencies. Decor is more mixed than coordinated and rooms in the motel block tend to be darker, but all are clean and of good value. There's even a free fruit basket on arrival. Weekly rates offer even greater savings. *66 Lake Dr., 33404, tel. 407/844–5104 or 800/521–4433. 11 units. Facilities: dock, fishing pier, shuffleboard, laundry facilities, free airport transportation. MC, V.*

$-$$ **Ship Ahoy Apartments.** Four hundred feet from the ocean and looking like a small-town place from the 1950s, the Ship Ahoy is run by Elmer and Miriam Kovacic, who have been here for years and are devoted to their guests. The lodging is located in a safe, residential neighborhood, a two- to three-minute walk to the beach. Upstairs spaces are preferable for their better view, though all rooms are pleasant. They all have full kitchens with plenty of utensils, but there are no in-room phones. Furnishings are mostly Danish modern, nothing to write home about—what you will write home about is the value, especially if you get a weekly rate. *124 Bamboo Rd., 33404, tel. 407/842–9159. 10 units. Facilities: shuffleboard, barbecue. No credit cards.*

Tour 2: South to Boca Raton

This tour carries you along the coast of south Palm Beach County, nearly 40 miles along Route A1A through an almost uninterrupted realm of the rich and famous that has earned the sobriquet "the Gold Coast." Little commuter traffic occurs, but the route all the way is two-lane and slow-moving in winter. Watch for cyclists and joggers.

Arriving and Departing
Whether by plane, car, train, or bus, the ways to get to this part of the county are similar to those for the Palm Beaches (*see* Arriving and Departing *in* Tour 1, *above*).

Getting Around
If you're traveling by car, the most scenic road is Route A1A, along the coast. Paralleling it but inland are U.S. 1 and I–95. **CoTran** (tel. 407/930–5123) and **Tri-Rail** serve this part of Palm Beach County as well (*see* Getting Around on the Cheap *in* Tour 1, *above*).

Guided Tours
Boca Raton Historical Society (71 N. Federal Hwy., tel. 407/395–6766) offers afternoon tours of the Boca Raton Resort & Club on Tuesdays year-round, as well as group tours to other south Florida sites. (Call for departure points.)

Loxahatchee Everglades Tours (tel. 407/482–6107) operates year-round airboat tours from west of Boca Raton through the marshes between the built-up coast and Lake Okeechobee.

Ramblin' Rose Riverboat (tel. 407/243–0686) operates luncheon, dinner-dance, and Sunday-brunch cruises from Delray Beach along the Intracoastal Waterway.

Lake Worth

★ Heading south of Palm Beach on **Route A1A,** you come to the town of Lake Worth. Like Palm Beach Shores, its main interest for tourists lies in its stock of affordable lodgings and restaurants.

Turn right at the causeway leading over from Palm Beach into **Casino Park** (also known as Lake Worth Municipal Park). The park has an Olympic-size swimming pool, a free 1,300-foot fishing pier, picnic areas, shuffleboard, restaurants, and shops on the upland side of the street. Metered parking, however, is no longer one of the "affordables" here. In the past two years it has shot up four-fold to 25¢ per quarter hour. *Rte. A1A at end of Lake Worth Bridge, tel. 407/533–7367. Admission to beach: free; to pool: $2 adults, $1 senior citizens and children 15 and under. Open daily 9–4:45.*

Budget Lodging
$$
★
Holiday House. Ah, Lake Worth—the budget traveler's destination. Standing out amid a strip of wall-to-wall motels, a five-minute walk from the heart of town, is this uncommercial-looking, shipshape lodging of bright white plaster trimmed in blue, with bougainvillea twined around crosshatched balconies and rich tropical gardens. Units—motel rooms, efficiencies, and one-bedroom apartments—live up to expectations. Located in two adjacent two-story buildings dating from the late 1940s, but kept up nicely, each is warmly fur-

nished with carpet, upholstered chairs, table, desk, and miscellaneous art. Though the units are different, they are all clean and contain fridge, phone, and reverse-cycle air-conditioning. Those rooms that don't already have a microwave are getting one, and units possess either tub-showers or stalls. The owners are thoughtful enough to keep windows open when rooms are vacant. Maid service is provided daily for motel rooms, weekly for efficiencies and apartments. *320 N. Federal Hwy., 33460, tel. 407/582–3561, fax 407/582–3561, ext. 314. 30 units. Facilities: pool, coin laundry. MC, V.*

$ **New Sun Gate Motel.** Clean, comfortable lodgings don't get more affordable than this two-story motel near downtown Lake Worth, less than a 10-minute drive to the beach. Few places at any price pay more attention to what travelers want. Guests have use of a pool and sauna, parking close by their units, coffeemaker and microwave in most units, laundry facilities, and the Terrace Restaurant, which serves full breakfasts with coffee for under $5, dinners under $10. All these advantages are thanks to owner Roger Stjernvall, a former cruise-ship general manager and hotelier in Scandinavia, who knows how to keep costs down by setting prices that keep his units filled. Strictly a gimmick, all the units are named for celebrities—a poster makes the Elvis Suite, and an icon makes the Greta Garbo. High-season prices that top out at $55 a night for a small suite are no gimmick, though. *901 S. Federal Hwy., 33460, tel. 407/588–8110, fax 407/588–8041. 32 rooms. Facilities: restaurant, pool, sauna, barbecue grill, coin laundry. AE, D, DC, MC, V.*

Budget Dining **Farmer Girl Restaurant.** People eat free on Thanksgiving, thanks to
$ owner Peter Roubekous, an immigrant from Greece who has made it
★ here and wants to give something back to his adopted community. It's no surprise that people love the place, and it stays busy year-round. All meals allow you to sample from the 30-item salad bar and to slice away at loaves of fresh home-baked bread. The blue-and-white decor is dotted with lots of greenery, old farm equipment, and stained-glass lamps around the booths and tables. The food is strictly home cooking with an international range: chicken, pork, steaks, shish kebab, ham steak, veal parmigiana, Wiener schnitzel, moussaka, grilled liver and onions, catfish, scrod, and swordfish; there are pies, cakes, and puddings for dessert. It closes at 7 on Sunday. *1732 N. Dixie Hwy., tel. 407/582-0317. No reservations. Dress: casual but neat. MC, V. Closed Dec. 25.*

¢ **John G's.** About the only time the line lets up here is when the place
★ closes. Otherwise, there's little to complain about: certainly not the service, the prices, or the cheery hubbub. The menu is as big as the crowd: eggs every which way, including a UN of ethnic omelets; big fruit platters; sandwich board superstars; grilled burgers; and seafood. The Greek shrimp come on fresh linguine topped by feta cheese. Decor is not the focus in this big open room with tables and counter seats under nautical bric-a-brac. *On the beach, Lake Worth Casino, tel. 407/585-9860. No reservations. Dress: casual. No credit cards. Closed Dec. 25, Jan. 1. No dinner.*

Participant In high season, greens fees at the **Lake Worth Municipal Golf Course**
Sports (1 7th Ave. N, tel. 407/582-9713), are only $20 to walk ($11 after 2
Golf PM) and $60 for two with a cart ($42 after 2 PM).

Spectator **Gulf Stream Polo Club,** the oldest club in Palm Beach, began in the
Sports 1920s and plays medium-goal polo (for teams with handicaps of 8–16
Polo goals). It has six polo fields. *4550 Polo Rd., 33467, tel. 407/965-2057. Admission free. Games Dec.–Apr., Fri. at 3, Sun. at 1.*

Lantana

Continue on Route A1A, and cross Ocean Avenue (Route 812). On your left is **Lantana Public Beach** (100 N. Ocean Ave., tel. 407/586-0217). It has a decided advantage over Boynton Beach, farther south, because parking is only 25¢ for 20 minutes, as opposed to a flat rate of $5–$10 at Boynton, depending on the time of year.

Budget Dining **Dune Deck Cafe.** Fresh cheap food is in store in this million-dollar setting on the little boardwalk overlooking the beach and sea. Order $4 breakfasts or, for lunch, a burger with coffee for under $5 or a gyro on pita bread with fries and a milk shake that brings change from $10. There's always a fresh-fish choice with salad, pita, and coffee that's shy of $10, too. *100 N. Ocean Blvd., tel. 407/582–0472. No reservations. Dress: casual. No credit cards. No dinner.*

Fishing For deep-sea fishing, try **B-Love Fleet** (314 E. Ocean Ave., tel. 407/ 588–7612); a half day costs $20 per person ($16 for senior citizens on weekdays), including rod, reel, and bait.

Boynton Beach

Continuing south, you come to Boynton Beach. The main attraction here is actually inland. The **Arthur R. Marshall Loxahatchee National Wildlife Refuge** covers 221 square miles—the healthiest part of the Everglades system. From the visitor center, there are two walking trails—a boardwalk through a dense cypress swamp and a marsh trail to a 20-foot-high observation tower overlooking a pond—as well as a 5½-mile canoe trail. Wildlife viewing is good year-round. You can fish for bass and panfish or paddle your own canoe through this watery wilderness. *10119 Lee Rd., off U.S. 441 between Boynton Beach Blvd. (Rte. 804) and Atlantic Ave. (Rte. 806), west of Boynton Beach, tel. 407/734–8303. Admission: $4 per vehicle, $1 per pedestrian. Open 6–sunset.*

Golf **Boynton Beach Municipal Golf Course** (8020 Jog Rd., tel. 407/969–2200) is a good public course and has 27 holes.

Delray Beach

Just below the crossing of Route 804 (East Ocean Avenue), a niche road (Old Ocean Boulevard) cuts off directly along the beach to enter **Briny Breezes,** a wonderful old blue-collar town, 42 acres directly on the sea. It's an incongruous neighbor in these precincts of the high and mighty, but here it has been, incorporated since 1963.

Beyond this you'll pass another anomaly in this ritzy area—a row of mildly ramshackle houses, with overgrown yards full of rusting gear—and then come to the beautiful little community of **Gulf Stream.** You'll pass the very private St. Andrews Country Club and the bougainvillea-topped walls of the Gulfstream Club, part of the Addison Mizner legacy, where a private police officer may come onto the road to halt traffic for the moment it takes a golfer to cross in his or her cart.

Delray Beach, which began as an artists' retreat and a small settlement of Japanese farmers, recently won the title of All-American City. At the edge of town, across Northeast 8th Street (George Bush Boulevard), begins a lovely pedestrian way along the big broad swimming beach that extends north and south of Atlantic Avenue. This avenue, Delray's main street, has revived retailing thanks to historic preservation and pedestrian friendliness. The chief landmark along the 12 mostly store-lined blocks leading west from the ocean is the Mediterranean-revival **Colony Hotel** (525 E. Atlantic Ave., tel. 407/276–4123), still open only for the winter season as it has been for more than 60 years. Just off Atlantic Avenue, the **Old School Square Cultural Arts Center** (51 N. Swinton Ave., tel. 407/ 243–7922) houses several museums, notably the **Cornell Museum of Art & History,** and a performing-arts center in restored school buildings dating from 1913 and 1926. On the next street north is **Cason Cottage** (5 N.E. 1st St., tel. 407/243–0223), a home that dates from about 1915 and that now serves as offices of the Delray Beach Historical Society.

A block south of the Old School Square, the charmingly old-fashioned **Sundy House** (106 S. Swinton Ave., tel. 407/278–2163 or 407/272–3270) has a restaurant, which serves lunch and a traditional afternoon tea; antiques trove; and gift shop. Flagler foreman John Shaw Sundy, who became the first mayor of Delray, and his family lived here. The house has beautiful gardens and five gingerbread gables that complement Delray's finest wraparound porch.

★ Apart from downtown, the main tourist attraction in Delray Beach is the **Morikami Museum and Japanese Gardens,** a 200-acre cultural and recreational facility. Some programs and exhibits are in the lakeside museum building and theater; an earlier building, modeled after a Japanese imperial villa, houses a permanent exhibition detailing the history of the Yamato Colony, an agricultural community of Japanese, which dated from 1905. The grounds include a nature trail, picnic pavilions, library and audiovisual center on Japanese culture, museum shop, snack bar–café, and various gardens, including the only collection known to exist of bonsai Florida plants. *4000 Morikami Park Rd., tel. 407/495–0233. Admission: $4.25 adults, $3.75 senior citizens, $2 children 6–18, free Sun. 10–noon. Park open daily sunrise–sunset; museum open Tues.–Sun. 10–5, closed Jan. 1, Easter, July 4, Thanksgiving, Dec. 25.*

Budget **Sea Breeze of Delray Beach.** Though most of its units are a little more
Lodging than moderately expensive (book early for the cheaper ones), this
$$ lodging in very resorty but quiet Delray is an exceptional buy considering its top location. It's across from both the Gulfstream Bath & Tennis Club and the beach (though a three- to five-minute walk to access it). The look is garden-apartment white with aqua trim; the one- and two-story buildings are set around beautiful lawns. Each of the studios and one- or two-bedroom apartments has a full kitchen; the updated ones have microwaves. Some floors are being redone with cool resort tiles, while others still have carpets. Furnishings include lots of floral prints, brocaded pieces, and French provincial reproductions, which create a beachy yet homey look. Despite its 1950s vintage, the place remains beautifully maintained and clean, though guests may find kitchenware mismatched. There is twice-weekly maid service May to October. *820 N. Ocean Blvd., 33483, tel. 407/276–7496. 23 units. Facilities: heated pool, shuffleboard, gas barbecue, coin laundry. MC, V.*

$–$$ **Riviera Palms Motel.** This small 1950s-era motel has two chief virtues: It's clean and it's well located, across Route A1A from mid-rise apartment houses on the water, with beach access between them. Hans and Herter Grannemann have owned this two-story property, three wings surrounding a grassy front yard and heated pool, since 1978, and they have lots of repeat guests—you'll have to book early in winter. The decor comprises Danish modern furniture and colors of blue, brown, and tan. Rooms have at least a fridge but no phone. *3960 N. Ocean Blvd., 33483, tel. 407/276–3032. 17 rooms, efficiencies, and suites. Facilities: heated pool. No credit cards.*

Budget Dining **Jean Marees'.** They're a little old-fashioned at this popular, family-
¢ run breakfast and lunch restaurant along the main downtown shopping street. Home-baked muffins, salads, potatoes, dressings, and soups are all made from scratch. The eggs Benedict is locally acclaimed, and the coleslaw is made from grandmother's recipe. Choose from counter seats, inside tables, or four tables on Atlantic Avenue. For under $5, you can get a "he-man's breakfast" of two eggs, tomato, and ham (coffee's only 75¢) or any of several lunch specials—maybe an antipasto salad with a basket of bagel chips or stuffed tomato and crab. Deli sandwiches are stacked high but are still only $3 or $4. *450 E. Atlantic Ave., tel. 407/265–0120. No reser-*

vations. Dress: casual. No credit cards. Closed Thanksgiving, Dec. 25. No dinner.

Shopping for Bargains Unlike many cities along this resort coast, Delray Beach has a thriving old-fashioned downtown with hundreds of shops and restaurants, centered on a mile of east–west Atlantic Avenue that ends at the oceanfront. Delray also offers a year-round flea market, the **Delray Swap Shop** (2001 N. Federal Hwy.), open daily 6–3.

Tennis The **Delray Beach Tennis Center** (201 W. Atlantic Dr., tel. 407/243–7360) lets you play for $7.95 per person for the entire day, $3.18 additional per person for night play.

Boca Raton

South of Linton Boulevard the beachfront character changes, becoming more high-rise. You enter the town of **Highland Beach,** which has been completely developed from bare dune in the last 25 years. Today the shoreside is packed with condominiums, and across the Intracoastal Waterway, mansions. The road here is called South Ocean Boulevard.

Where the road rises along the dune, you enter into **Boca Raton.** This visionary city, developed by architect Addison Mizner in the 1920s, had barely made it off the drawing board when the Depression hit. For half a century after, Boca grew along the beach and along U.S. 1 without any town center. Off to the right ahead you will see the peachy-plum-color Boca Tower of the **Boca Raton Resort & Club** (*see* Budget Lodging, *below*); alongside it, lower to the ground, is the nucleus of the hotel, the original Cloister Inn built by Mizner. To the left is the Boca Beach Club, a newer part of the same property.

Cross the drawbridge over Boca Inlet and drive onto Camino Real, a six-lane boulevard with a double row of Malaysian dwarf palms down the center. Cross Federal Highway (U.S. 1), and just before Dixie Highway, turn left into the parking lot of **Addison's Flavor of Italy** (2 E. Camino Real, tel. 407/391–9800). Built in 1925 by the Mizner Development Corporation to house the city administration, this building shows Mizner's characteristic Spanish revival architectural style: pecky cypress, wrought-iron grills, a barrel tile roof, and handmade tiles around the courtyard.

Turn right onto South Dixie Highway. Immediately on your left is the restored **Boca Raton Florida East Coast Railroad Station,** now used for small community meetings.

As you continue north on Dixie Highway, on your right notice the distinctive Boca look: buildings in pink and burnt sienna, all with barrel-tile roofs, many with canopies and iron balconies. One block past Palmetto Park Road, turn right onto Boca Raton Road; on your right is the gold-domed **Old Town Hall,** built in 1927 to a Mizner design. A gift shop with unusual Boca items, especially good books and prints, is located in the original mayor's office. Historical exhibits rotate in the hall gallery. *71 N. Federal Hwy., tel. 407/395–6766. Admission free. Open weekdays 10–4.*

Turn left on North Federal Highway, and at Northeast 3rd Street you'll find **Mizner Park** (Federal Hwy. between Palmetto Park Rd. and Glades Rd., tel. 407/362-0606), the new heart of downtown Boca Raton, with its shopping promenade, apartments, and offices. This successful development has quickly given the community the focal point it sorely needed. A potential blockbuster, the **International Museum of Cartoon Art,** long championed by *Beetle Bailey* artist Mort Walker, is expected to open here before the end of 1996.

Exit Mizner Park across Northeast 2nd Street and continue west across the railroad tracks. The new **Boca Raton City Hall** is on your left, designed in the style of the original and set among enormous banyan trees.

Return to Palmetto Park Road and continue west to visit the **Boca Raton Museum of Art,** with its whimsical metal sculptures outdoors on the lawn. The museum's permanent collection includes works by Picasso, Degas, Matisse, Klee, and Modigliani as well as notable pre-Columbian art. *801 W. Palmetto Park Rd., tel. 407/392–2500. Admission free. Open weekdays 10–4, weekends noon–4.*

The residential area behind the museum is **Old Floresta,** developed by Addison Mizner starting in 1925 and landscaped with many varieties of palms and cycads. The houses are mainly Mediterranean-style, many with upper balconies supported in the Mizner style by exposed wood columns.

For kids, there are a handful of attractions worth seeing. **Children's Museum of Boca Raton at Singing Pines** is a learning center featuring hands-on exhibits, workshops, and special programs, such as introductions to Florida Philharmonic performances. There are five changing exhibits each year. *498 Crawford Blvd., tel. 407/368–6875. Admission: $1. Open Tues.–Sat. noon–4.*

Children's Science Explorium features some 40 hands-on exhibits and workshops on special themes that change quarterly, such as computers, electricity, oceans, and weather. *Royal Palm Plaza, Suite 15, 131 Mizner Blvd., tel. 407/395–8401. Admission: $2 ages over 3. Open Tues.–Sat. 10–5, Sun. noon–5.*

Gumbo Limbo Nature Center lets children view four 20-foot-diameter saltwater sea tanks, stroll a 1,628-foot boardwalk through a dense tropical forest, and climb a 50-foot tower to overlook the tree canopy. The center's staff leads guided turtle walks to the beach to see nesting females come ashore and lay their eggs. *1801 N. Ocean Blvd., tel. 407/338–1473. Donations welcome; turtle tour: $3, tickets must be obtained in advance. Open Mon.–Sat. 9–4, Sun. noon–4; turtle tours late May–mid-July, Mon.–Thurs. 9 PM–midnight.*

Budget Lodging *Splurge* ★   **Boca Raton Resort & Club.** Architect-socialite Addison Mizner designed and built the original Mediterranean-style Cloister Inn in 1926; the 27-story tower was added in 1961 and the ultramodern Boca Beach Club in 1980. In 1991 an eight-year, $55 million renovation was completed, upgrading the tower accommodations, adding a new fitness center, redesigning the Cloister lobby and adjacent golf course, and creating a new restaurant, Nick's Fishmarket, at the Beach Club. In 1992 the 27-story-high Top of the Tower Italian Restaurant opened. Room rates during the winter season are European Plan (no meals included), but a daily MAP supplement (breakfast and dinner) can be had for $50 per person. Rooms in the Cloister tend to be small and warmly traditional; those in the tower are in like style but larger, while rooms in the Beach Club are light, airy, and contemporary in color schemes and furnishings. In-room safes are available. An international concierge staff speaks at least 12 languages. *501 E. Camino Real, 33431-0825, tel. 407/395–3000 or 800/327–0101. 963 rooms, suites, studio rooms, and golf villas. Facilities: 7 restaurants, 3 lounges, 5 outdoor pools, ½-mi beach, 2 championship golf courses, 34 tennis courts (9 lighted), indoor basketball court, 23-slip marina, fishing and sailing charters, 3 fitness centers. AE, DC, MC, V.*

Budget Dining *$*   **Tom's Place.** "This place is a blessing from God," says the sign over the fireplace, to which, when you're finally in and seated (this place draws long lines) you'll add, "Amen!" That's in between mouthfuls of Tom Wright's soul food—sauce-slathered ribs, pork chop sandwiches, chicken cooked in a peppery mustard sauce over hickory and oak, sweet potato pie. You'll want to leave with a bottle or two of Tom's barbecue sauce: $2.25/pint—the same price for years—and to return, just as Lou Rawls, Ben Vereen, Sugar Ray Leonard, and a rush of NFL players do. You can bet the place is family run. *7251 N. Federal Hwy., tel. 407/997–0920. No reservations. Dress: casual but neat. MC, V. Closed Sun., Mon. May–mid-Nov., holidays, and sometimes a month around Sept.*

Beaches Three of the most popular beaches in town are **South Beach Park** (400 N. Rte. A1A), which has no picnic facilities, and **Red Reef Park** (1400 N. Rte. A1A) and **Spanish River Park** (3001 N. Rte. A1A), both with picnic tables, barbecue grills, and playgrounds. All are open 8–sunset.

Participant Sports For information on bike trails and group rides as well as general local bicycling tips, contact Jeff Borick, the **Boca Raton Bicycle Coordina-**
Biking **tor** (tel. 407/393–7797).

Tennis For $4.50 per person per hour ($5.75 October–March), you can play at **Patch Reef Park** (2001 N.W. 51st St., tel. 407/997–0881).

Spectator Sports **Royal Palm Polo,** founded in 1959 by Oklahoma oilman John T. Oxley, has seven polo fields with two stadiums. The complex is home
Polo to the $100,000 International Gold Cup Tournament. *6300 Old Clint Moore Rd., 33496, tel. 407/994–1876. Admission: $6 general admission, $10–$25 box seats. Games Jan.–Apr., Sun. at 1, 3.*

The Arts and Nightlife **Caldwell Theatre Company** (7873 N. Federal Hwy., 33487, tel. 407/ 241–7432 in Boca Raton, 407/832–2989 in Palm Beach, or 305/462–
The Arts 5433 in Broward County), a professional Equity regional theater, hosts the annual multimedia Mizner Festival each April–May and presents four productions each winter.

Jan McArt's Royal Palm Dinner Theatre (303 S.E. Mizner Blvd., Royal Palm Plaza, 33432, tel. 407/392–3755 or 800/841–6765), an Equity theater in its 18th year, presents five or six musicals on a year-round schedule.

Nightlife **Wildflower Waterway Cafe** (551 E. Palmetto Park Rd., tel. 407/391–0000) has nightly DJs spinning the top of the pop charts for a mostly young crowd.

Tour 3: The Treasure Coast

This tour takes you north from Palm Beach along the coast as far as Sebastian Inlet, but you can break away at any intermediate point and return to Palm Beach on I-95. Inland are citrus groves, but along the coast are some lovely nature refuges and unpretentious resort towns.

Arriving and Departing The same routes that access the Palm Beaches bring you here (*see Arriving and Departing in* Tour 1, *above*).

Getting Around As you move up the coast, Route A1A crosses back and forth from the barrier islands to the mainland, joining and rejoining U.S. 1. The interstate, I–95, runs parallel to U.S. 1 a bit farther inland.

Guided Tours **Capt. Doug's** (tel. 407/589–2329) offers three-hour lunch or dinner cruises from Sebastian along the Indian River on board the 35-foot sloop *Bobo*. Accommodating up to four couples, the sailboat tour costs $100 per couple, the same price as in 1984, including the meal, tips, beer, and wine.

Indian River County Historical Society (tel. 407/778–3435), which maintains an exhibit center at the old Florida East Coast Railroad Station (2336 14th Ave., Vero Beach), leads walking tours of downtown Vero on Wednesday at 11 and 1 (by reservation) and occasional driving tours of the historic 7-mile Jungle Trail along the Indian River.

Jonathan Dickinson's River Tours (tel. 407/746–1466) runs two-hour narrated river cruises from Jonathan Dickinson State Park in Hobe Sound daily at 9, 11, 1, and 3 and one night trip a month (at the full moon) at 7. The cost is $10 adults, $5 children under 12.

Louie's Lady (tel. 407/744–5550) gives steamboat-style sightseeing and luncheon tours of Jupiter Island and the Intracoastal Waterway. The boat leaves from docks behind Harpoon Louie's Restaurant on the Jupiter River.

Manatee Queen (tel. 407/744–2191), a 49-passenger catamaran, offers day and evening cruises on the Intracoastal Waterway and into the cypress swamps of Jonathan Dickinson State Park, November to May.

The Spirit of St. Joseph (tel. 407/467–2628) offers seven lunch and dinner cruises weekly along the Indian River, leaving from alongside the St. Lucie County Historical Museum, November through April.

Riviera Beach

To get started seeing the Treasure Coast, head north on U.S. 1 from downtown West Palm Beach. After about 5 miles, you'll reach Blue Heron Boulevard (Route A1A) in Riviera Beach.

Budget Dining
$
★

Crab Pot. A big local favorite since 1974, this restaurant directly over the Intracoastal Waterway offers fresh seafood at fair prices. If you want one of the waterside booths, come early or be prepared for a wait—you can sit outside at the deck bar and watch the pelicans. The reason for the big crowd is the early-bird special. Served from 4 to 6, it features eight fish and seafood dinners along with crab soup to start, a bottomless salad bowl, rice or potatoes, beverage, and dessert, all at a top price of $7.95. Even after 6, meals are still very favorably priced. Popular entrées are dolphin, grouper, swordfish, big broiled or fried platters, and specialties like shrimp steamed with beer and Old Bay spice, seafood Alfredo, flounder with crab stuffing, and Baltimore-style crab cakes. Desserts include Key lime pie, cheesecake, and sizzling apple pie topped with rich ice cream and brandy sauce. *386 E. Blue Heron Blvd. (north of bridge ramp), tel. 407/844–2722. No reservations. Dress: casual. AE, DC, MC, V. Closed Thanksgiving.*

Diving

Ocean Reef Park (3860 N. Ocean Dr., tel. 407/966–6655) is attractive for snorkeling because the reefs are close to shore in shallow water. You may see angelfish, sergeant majors, rays, robin fish, and occasionally a Florida lobster (actually a species of saltwater crayfish). Wear canvas sneakers and cloth gloves.

Juno Beach

Continue on Route A1A as it turns north onto Ocean Boulevard, past hotels and high-rise condominiums to **John D. MacArthur State Park,** which offers almost 2 miles of beach and interpretive walks to a mangrove estuary along the upper reaches of Lake Worth. *10900 Rte. A1A, North Palm Beach, tel. 407/624–6950 for office or 407/ 624–6952 for nature center. Admission: $3.25 per vehicle with up to 8 people. Open 8–sunset; nature center open Wed.–Mon. 9–5.*

North of MacArthur State Park, Route A1A rejoins U.S. 1, then veers east again 1½ miles north at **Juno Beach.** Take Route A1A north to Donald Ross Road, west to U.S. 1, and north immediately to enter **Loggerhead Park Marine Life Center of Juno Beach,** established by Eleanor N. Fletcher, "the turtle lady of Juno Beach." Museum displays interpret the sea turtles' natural history. Also on view are displays of coastal natural history, sharks, whales, and shells. *1200 U.S. 1 (entrance on west side of park), tel. 407/627–8280. Donations welcome. Open Tues.–Sat. 10–4, Sun. noon–3.*

Biking   For cycling information, contact Susan Kenney, the **Juno Beach Bicycle Coordinator** (tel. 407/626–1122).

Jupiter, Jupiter Island, and Hobe Sound

From Juno Beach north to **Jupiter,** Route A1A runs for almost 4 miles atop the beachfront dunes. At Jupiter Beach Road, turn right and immediately left onto Dubois Road. At its end in **Dubois Park** is the **Dubois Home,** a modest pioneer home that dates from 1898. The house, with design features that include Cape Cod as well as "cracker," sits atop an ancient Jeaga Indian mound 20 feet high, looking onto Jupiter Inlet. Even if you arrive when the house is closed, the park is worth the visit for its lovely beaches around swimming lagoons. *Dubois Rd., tel. 407/747–6639. Donations welcome. Open Sun. 1–4.*

Return to A1A, turn right to U.S. 1, and then turn left (south) for ⅓ mile. On the east side of the highway, in Burt Reynolds Park (actor Burt Reynolds grew up in Jupiter; his father was a Palm Beach County sheriff), is the **Florida History Center and Museum.** Permanent exhibits review Seminole Indian, steamboat era, and pioneer history on the Loxahatchee River, shipwrecks, railroads, and modern-day development. *805 N. U.S. 1, tel. 407/747–6639. Admission: $3 adults, $2 senior citizens, $1 children 6–18. Open Tues.–Sat. 10–4, Sun. 1–5.*

Take a side trip to the **Burt Reynolds Ranch and Mini Petting Farm,** a 160-acre working horse ranch owned by the famous actor. Visitors can take a 1½-hour tour by air-conditioned bus, with stops that include movie sets, a chapel, tree house, and wherever else filming may be in progress. You can pet both farm and exotic animals. *16133 Jupiter Farms Rd. (2 mi west of I-95 at Exit 59-B), tel. 407/747–5390. Admission free to petting farm; tour: $10 adults, $5 children. Open daily 10–4:30; closed holidays.*

Return north on U.S. 1 and cross the Loxahatchee River onto **Jupiter Island;** just across the Jupiter Inlet Bridge, pick up Route 707 (Beach Road). On your right is the **Jupiter Inlet Light Station,** a redbrick Coast Guard navigational beacon that has operated here since 1866. The 105-foot structure is open Sunday through Wednesday 10–4. Tours of the lighthouse and visit to a small museum cost $5, used for restoring the property.

Head north on Route 707 and stop at the Nature Conservancy's 73-acre **Blowing Rocks Preserve.** Within the preserve you'll find plant communities native to beachfront dune, strand (the landward side of the dunes), marsh, and hammock (tropical hardwood forest). Sea grape, cabbage palms, saw palmetto, and sea oats help to anchor the dunes. Also on the grounds are pelicans, seagulls, ospreys, red-bellied and pileated woodpeckers, and a profusion of warblers in spring and fall. The best time to visit is when high tides and strong offshore winds coincide, causing the sea to blow spectacularly through holes in the eroded outcropping. Park in the small lot; Jupiter Island police will ticket cars parked along the road shoulder. *Rte. 707, tel. 407/575–2297 for office or 407/747–3113 for preserve. $3 donation requested. Open daily 6–5.*

Continue north through the town of Jupiter Island, a carefully laid-out community with estates screened from the road by dense vegetation. At the north end of town, **Hobe Sound National Wildlife Refuge** has a 3½-mile beach where turtles nest and shells wash ashore. High tides and strong winds have severely eroded the beach; during winter high tides only a sliver of beach remains to walk along. *Beach*

Rd., off Rte. 707, tel. 407/546–6141. Admission: $4 per vehicle. Open sunrise–sunset generally.

To visit the refuge headquarters and the **Elizabeth W. Kirby Interpretive Center,** return to the mainland and U.S. 1, pass through the town of **Hobe Sound,** turn left on U.S. 1, and travel approximately 2½ miles. An adjacent ½-mile trail winds through a forest of sand pine and scrub oak—one of Florida's most unusual and endangered plant communities. *13640 S.E. Federal Hwy., tel. 407/546–6141. Admission free. Trail open sunrise–sunset; nature center open weekdays 9–11 and 1–3, call for Sat. hrs; group tours by appointment.*

From the interpretive center, go south 2½ miles to the entrance to **Jonathan Dickinson State Park.** Follow signs to Hobe Mountain, an ancient dune topped with a tower, from which you have a panoramic view across the park's 10,285 acres of varied terrain. The Loxahatchee River is part of the federal government's wild and scenic rivers program and is populated by manatees in winter and alligators all year. The park has bicycle and hiking trails, a campground, and a snack bar, and it's a great place to canoe (*see* Canoeing, *below*) or to take a narrated river cruise (*see* Guided Tours, *above*). *16450 S.E. Federal Hwy., tel. 407/546–2771. Admission: $3.25 per vehicle with up to 8 people. Open daily 8–sunset.*

Budget Dining
$$
★

Charley's Crab. The grand view across the Jupiter River complements the soaring ceiling and striking interior architecture of this 350-seat marina-side restaurant, much preferred by the affluent retirees of Jupiter. Between about November and Easter, weather accommodates outdoor seating. Otherwise, tiered seating and a second level of window seats on an indoor balcony provide good water views. Early diners save about 25%, but a better argument can be made for coming late and watching the searching beam of historic Jupiter Light (just downriver), a reminder of the region's long seafaring history. Ultimately the best reason to eat here is the expertly prepared seafood, including outstanding pasta choices: *pagliara* with scallops, fish, shrimp, mussels, spinach, garlic, and olive oil; fettuccine *verde* with lobster, sun-dried tomatoes, fresh basil, and goat cheese; and shrimp and tortellini boursin with cream sauce and tomatoes. Consider also such fresh fish as citrus-marinated halibut with black-bean basmati rice and pineapple relish or the tender, flaky swordfish. A big Sunday brunch features 75 items and a glass of champagne. Other Charley's are in Boca Raton, Deerfield, Fort Lauderdale, Palm Beach, and Stuart. *1000 N. U.S. 1, Jupiter, tel. 407/744–4710. Reservations advised. Dress: casual but neat. AE, D, DC, MC, V.*

$

Lighthouse Restaurant. Amsterdam-born brothers John and Bill Verehoeven bought this long-established place late in 1991 and have since toned the place up by bringing in the former chef of the Jupiter Island Club and Old Port Cove Yacht Club. Though the prices are still low, you can get items like chicken breast stuffed with sausage and fresh vegetables, burgundy beef stew, fresh fish, and king crab cakes. A full-time pastry chef's at work, too. In addition the restaurant still has the same people-pleasing formula of more than 60 years: round-the-clock service (except 10 PM Sunday–6 AM Monday) and daily menu changes that take advantage of the best market buys. Typical specials are veal parmigiana with spaghetti, hearty beef stew, and grilled center-cut pork chops with apple sauce. Also served nightly are affordable "lite dinners." You can get breakfast 24 hours a day and Sunday dinner at 1. *1510 U.S. 1, Jupiter, tel. 407/746–4811. No reservations. Dress: casual. D, DC, MC, V. Closed Dec. 24.*

$
★

Log Cabin Restaurant. "Too much!" exclaim first-timers, responding to the decor and whopping portions of American food at this rustic roadhouse (very easy to miss driving past). Everybody takes home a doggie bag, unless you've ordered the nightly all-you-can-eat special, for which the policy is suspended. Many also tote an antique home, because everything hung on the walls and from the rafters is for sale: old bikes, sleds, clocks, and quilts. The surprising menu variety starts with the big early-bird breakfast (7–8) for $1.99 and continues with old-fashioned pit barbecue, steaks, country dinners (e.g., roasted half chicken, liver and onions, pot roast, meat loaf), and fresh seafood—all with many side dishes—plus salad bar and hot sandwiches. Dine indoors or on the newly enclosed and air-conditioned front porch. There's a full bar and happy hour. *631 N. Rte. A1A, Jupiter, tel. 407/746–6877. No reservations. Dress: casual. AE, D, DC, MC, V.*

Beaches **Carlin Park** (400 Rte. A1A, Jupiter, tel. 407/964–4420) provides beachfront picnic pavilions, hiking trails, a baseball diamond, playground, six tennis courts, and fishing sites. The Park Galley, serving snacks and burgers, is usually open daily 9–5.

Canoeing **Canoe Outfitters of Florida** (4100 W. Indiantown Rd., Jupiter, tel. 407/746–7053) runs trips along the Loxahatchee River. **Jonathan Dickinson's River Tours** (16450 S.E. Federal Hwy., Hobe Sound, tel. 407/746–1466), a concessionaire, rents canoes at Jonathan Dickinson State Park.

The Arts The **Jupiter Dinner Theatre** (1001 E. Indiantown Rd., Jupiter, tel. 407/747–5566) was formerly the Burt Reynolds Jupiter Theater. More than 150 Broadway and Hollywood stars have performed here since the theater opened in 1979.

Stuart

Stuart/Martin County Chamber of Commerce (1650 S. Kanner Hwy., Stuart 34994, tel. 407/287–1088). Stuart Main Street Office (151 S.W. Flagler Ave., Stuart 34994, tel. 407/286–2848.

Return to U.S. 1 and proceed north. Quality of life is important in Stuart—the Martin County seat—a one-time fishing village that has become a magnet for sophisticates who want to live and work in a small-town atmosphere. Strict architectural and zoning standards ★ guide civic renewal projects in the **historic downtown,** which now claims eight antiques shops, nine restaurants, and more than 50 specialty shops within a two-block area. The old courthouse has become the **Court House Cultural Center** (80 E. Ocean Blvd., tel. 407/288–2542), which features art exhibits. The Old Stuart Feed Store has become the **Stuart Heritage Museum** (161 S.W. Flagler Ave., tel. 407/220–4600). The **Lyric Theatre** (59 S.W. Flagler Ave., tel. 407/220–1942) has been revived for performing and community events (and recently listed on the National Register of Historic Places), and a new gazebo features free music performances.

Continue north on Route A1A to Hutchinson Island. At Indian River Plantation, turn right onto MacArthur Boulevard, and go 1½ miles to the **House of Refuge Museum,** built in 1875. It's the only one remaining of nine such structures erected by the U.S. Life Saving Service (a predecessor of the Coast Guard) to aid stranded sailors. Exhibits include antique lifesaving equipment, maps, artifacts from nearby wrecks, and boat-making tools. *301 S.E. MacArthur Blvd., tel. 407/225–1875. Admission: $2 adults, 50¢ children 6–13. Open Tues.–Sun. 11–4; closed holidays.*

Return to Route A1A and go ³⁄₁₀ mile north to the pastel-pink **Elliott Museum,** built in 1961 in honor of Sterling Elliott, inventor of an early automated addressing machine and a four-wheel bicycle. In addition, the museum features antique automobiles, dolls and toys, and fixtures from an early general store, blacksmith shop, and apothecary shop. *825 N.E. Ocean Blvd., tel. 407/225–1961. Admission: $4 adults, 50¢ children 6–13. Open daily 11–4.*

Across the road is the **Coastal Science Center** (890 N.E. Ocean Blvd., tel. 407/225–0505) of the Florida Oceanographic Society. Its nearly 44-acre site combines a coastal hardwood hammock and mangrove forest. A 2,000-square-foot visitor center opened at the end of 1994, with aquariums, an auditorium, research laboratory, and permanent library to follow.

Budget **HarborFront.** On a quiet site that slopes to the St. Lucie River in a
Lodging historic enclave west of U.S. 1, this bed-and-breakfast combines an
$$ unusual mix of accommodations and imaginative extras—a Friday fresh-fish grill, picnic baskets, and conciergelike custom planning. Rooms and cottages are cozy and eclectic. Choose from a spacious chintz-covered suite or apartment or maybe the 33-foot moored sailboat (small rowing dinghy provided). Rooms include wicker and antiques, some airy and bright with private deck, others more tweedy and dark. From hammocks in the yard you can watch pelicans and herons. *310 Atlanta Ave., 34994, tel. 407/288–7289. 8 apts., cottages, suites, rooms, boat. Facilities: guest lounge, kayak. MC, V.*

$$ **The Homeplace.** The house was built in 1913 by pioneer Sam Matthews, who contracted much of the early town construction for railroad developer Henry Flagler. Jean Bell has restored the house to its early look, from hardwood floors to fluffy pillows. Fern-filled dining and sunrooms, full of chintz-covered cushioned wicker, overlook a pool and patio. Three guest rooms are Captain's Quarters, Opal's Room, and Prissy's Porch. A full breakfast is included. *501 Akron Ave., 34994, tel. 407/220–9148. 3 rooms. Facilities: pool, hot tub. MC, V.*

Budget Dining **Scalawags.** The look is plantation tropical—coach lanterns, ginger-
$$ bread, wicker, slow-motion paddle fans—but the top-notch buffets are aimed at today's resort guests. Standouts are the all-you-can-eat Wednesday evening seafood buffet, which features jumbo shrimp, Alaskan crab legs, clams on the half shell, marinated salmon, and fresh catch, and the Friday prime rib buffet with traditional Yorkshire pudding and baked potato station. Each features a 10-foot dessert table. A regular menu with a big selection of fish, shellfish, and grills, plus a big salad bar, is also offered. Seating is in the main dining room, overlooking the Indian River; in the private 20-seat wine room; or on the terrace, looking out on the marina. *555 N.E. Ocean Blvd., Hutchinson Island, tel. 407/225–3700. No reservations on buffet evenings. Dress: casual but neat. AE, DC, MC, V.*

$–$$ **The Ashley.** Since expanding in late 1993, this restaurant, the first of a number of immensely popular eateries in revived downtown Stuart, has more tables, more art, and more plants. Now with seating for 100 and a full bar, it still has elements of the old bank that was robbed here three times early in the century by the Ashley Gang (hence the name). The big outdoor mural in the French Impressionist style was paid for by good sports helping to revive the downtown, their names duly inscribed on wall plaques inside. The Continental menu appeals with the freshest foods and features lots of salads, fresh fish, and pastas. Breakfast is served on Sunday. *61 S.W. Osceola St., tel. 407/221–9476. No reservations. Dress: casual but neat. AE, MC, V. Closed Mon. in off-season. No lunch or dinner Sun.*

$–$$ **Jolly Sailor Pub.** This eatery in an old bank building is owned by a retired 27-year British Merchant Navy veteran, which may account for the endless ship paraphernalia. A veritable Cunard museum, it has a model of the *Brittania*, prints of 19th-century side-wheelers, and a big bar painting of the *QE2*. There's a wonderful brass-railed wood bar, a dart board, and such pub grub as fish-and-chips, cottage pie, and bangers (sausage) and mash, with Guinness and Double Diamond ales on tap. Dinner specials might be a blackened steak salad with romaine, charbroiled dolphin, or marinated tuna fillet. *1 S.W. Osceola St., tel. 407/221–1111. Reservations accepted. Dress: casual. AE, D, MC, V.*

$ **The Emporium.** Indian River Plantation's coffee shop is an old-fashioned soda fountain and grill that also serves hearty breakfasts. Specialties include eggs Benedict, omelets, deli sandwiches, and salads. *555 N.E. Ocean Blvd., Hutchinson Island, tel. 407/225–3700. No reservations. Dress: casual. AE, DC, MC, V.*

$ **The Porch.** This casual indoor-outdoor restaurant overlooks the tennis courts at Indian River Plantation. Come for the all-you-can-eat dinners and weekend breakfast buffet. *555 N.E. Ocean Blvd., Hutchinson Island, tel. 407/225–3700. No reservations. Dress: casual. AE, DC, MC, V.*

Shopping for Bargains More than 60 shops and restaurants featuring antiques, art, and fashions have opened along **Osceola Street** in the restored downtown, with hardly a vacancy. The 500-dealer **B & A Flea Market** (2885 S.E. Federal Hwy.), a block north of Indian Street, operates Saturday and Sunday 8–3.

Jensen Beach

The town of Jensen Beach has few attractions, but **Indian River Drive** (Route 707) is a scenic road full of curves and dips. Along its course were early 20th-century pineapple plantations.

Budget Lodging
$$ **Hutchinson Inn.** Sandwiched among the high-rises, this modest and affordable two-story motel from the mid-1970s has the feel of a bed-and-breakfast, thanks to its pretty canopies, bracketing, and the fresh produce stand across the street. You do in fact get an expanded Continental breakfast in the well-detailed, homey lobby, and you can also borrow a book or a stack of magazines to take to your room, where homemade cookies are served in the evenings. On Saturdays there's a barbecue at noon. Rooms range from small but comfy, with chintz bed covers, wicker chair, and contract dresser, to fully equipped efficiencies and seafront suites with private balconies. You have to book a year ahead to get a room in winter. *9750 S. Ocean Dr., 34957, tel. 407/229–2000, fax 407/229–8875. 21 units. Facilities: heated pool, beach, tennis court. MC, V.*

Budget Dining
$$ **Conchy Joe's.** This classic Florida stilt-house full of antique fish mounts, gator hides, and snakeskins dates from the late 1920s, but Conchy Joe's, like a hermit crab sidling into a new shell, only sidled up from West Palm Beach in '83 for the relaxed atmosphere of Jensen Beach. Under a huge Seminole-built chickee with a palm through the roof, you get the freshest Florida seafoods from a menu that changes daily—though some things never change: grouper marsala, the house specialty; broiled sea scallops; fried cracked conch. Try the rum drinks with names like Goombay Smash, Bahama Mama, and Jamaica Wind, while you listen to steel-band calypsos Thursday through Sunday nights. Happy hour is 3–6 daily and during all NFL games. *3945 N. Indian River Dr., tel. 407/334–1131. No reservations. Dress: casual. AE, D, MC, V. Closed Thanksgiving, Dec. 25, Super Bowl Sun. No dinner Dec. 24.*

$$ **11 Maple Street.** This 16-table cracker-quaint restaurant run by
★ Margee and Mike Perrin offers Continental gourmet specialties on a nightly changing menu. For food and setting, this is as good as the Treasure Coast gets. An old house alive with waxed floors, plank walls hung with local art and flower baskets, soft recorded jazz, and earnest, friendly staff satisfy as fully as the brilliant presentations served in ample portions. Appetizers might include walnut bread with melted fontina cheese; pan-fried conch with balsamic vinegar; or pear, Gorgonzola, and pine-nut salad with balsamic vinegar and grilled polenta. Among the entrées might be rosemary-spiced salmon with leeks, lobster and blue-crab cake, or dried porcini mushroom risotto. Desserts might include a cherry *clafouti* (like a bread pudding), a white-chocolate custard with blackberry sauce, or an old-fashioned chocolate cream pie with poached pear. *3224 Maple*

Ave., tel. 407/334–7714. Reservations required. Dress: casual but neat. MC, V. Closed Mon., Tues., Dec. 25. No lunch.

Fort Pierce

St. Lucie County Tourist Development Council (2300 Virginia Ave., Fort Pierce 34954, tel. 407/468–1535 or 800/344–8443).

At Midway Road (Route 712), 14 miles north of Jensen Beach, turn left and go ½ mile to the **Savannahs Recreation Area.** This 550-acre site was once a Fort Pierce reservoir but has been allowed to return to its natural state. Today it's semiwilderness with campsites, a petting zoo, botanical garden, boat ramps, and trails. *1400 E. Midway Rd., tel. 407/464–7855. Admission: $1 per vehicle. Open daily 8 AM–9 PM.*

Return to Route 707 and continue north to Savannah Road, turn left, go ⁸⁄₁₀ of a mile, and turn right immediately after Heathcote Road to **Heathcote Botanical Gardens.** A self-guided tour takes in a palm walk, Japanese garden, and subtropical foliage. *210 Savannah Rd., tel. 407/464–4672. Donations welcome. Open Tues.–Sat. 9–5, also Sun. 1–5 Nov.–Apr.*

A mile farther on Route 707, visit the **A. E. "Bean" Backus Gallery,** home of the Treasure Coast Art Association. Beanie Backus was Florida's foremost landscape artist until his death in 1990 at age 84. Many of his masterpieces are displayed here. The gallery also mounts changing exhibits and offers exceptional buys on locally produced art. *500 N. Indian River Dr., tel. 407/465–0630. Admission free. Open Tues.–Sun. 1–5.*

Turn right over the South Beach Causeway Bridge. On the east side, take the first road left onto the grounds of the **St. Lucie County Historical Museum.** Among its exhibits are historic photos, early 20th-century memorabilia, vintage farm tools, a restored 1919 American La France fire engine, replicas of a general store and the old Fort Pierce railroad station, and the restored 1905 Gardner House. *414 Seaway Dr., tel. 407/468–1795. Admission: $2 adults, $1 children 6–11. Open Tues.–Sat. 10–4, Sun. noon–4.*

From here, backtrack to the mainland, turn north (right) on U.S. 1, and then take your pick of two routes to Vero Beach. To proceed along the coast, head east across North Beach Causeway. Follow Route A1A north to Pepper Park and the **UDT-Seal Museum,** beside the beach where more than 3,000 Navy frogmen trained during World War II. In 1993 exhibit space was tripled (further expansions are planned through the decade). Numerous patrol boats and vehicles constitute an outdoor exhibit area. *3300 N. Rte. A1A, tel. 407/595–1570. Admission: $2 adults, $1 children 6–12. Open Tues.–Sat. 10–4, Sun. noon–4.*

About 1 mile north of Pepper Park, turn left to the parking lot for the 958-acre **Jack Island Wildlife Refuge,** accessible only by footbridge. The 1½-mile Marsh Rabbit Trail across the island traverses a mangrove swamp to a 30-foot observation tower overlooking the Indian River. Trails cover 4⅓ miles altogether. *Rte. A1A, tel. 407/468–3985. Admission free. Open 8–sunset.*

Back on Route A1A, go north to Vero Beach. If you'd rather take the mainland route from Fort Pierce, continue north from there along Route 707, which becomes Old Dixie Highway (Route 605). Just after the intersection of Immokalee Road (Route 608), turn right into **St. Lucie Village.** This is one of Florida's rare old settlements, largely left to change at its own pace. Old houses with screened porches behind broad lawns face the Indian River Lagoon across a narrow shore road. Some once served as lodgings for prominent northerners, including President William McKinley, who around the turn of the century enjoyed winter hunting and fishing here.

Continue north on Route 605 to the **Harbor Branch Oceanographic Institution,** a diversified research and teaching facility with a staff of some 200 and an international reputation. Its fleet of research vessels—particularly its two submersibles—operates around the world for NASA, NOAA, and NATO, among other contractors. Visitors can take a 90-minute tour of the 500-acre facility, which contains submersibles; aquariums of sea life indigenous to the Indian River Lagoon; exhibits of marine technology; learning facilities; lifelike and whimsical bronze sculptures created by founder J. Seward Johnson, Jr.; and a gift shop of imaginative items related to the sea. *5600 Old Dixie Hwy., tel. 407/465–2400. Admission: $5 adults, $3 students. Tours Mon.–Sat. at 10, noon, 2, except Thanksgiving, Dec. 25.*

Budget Lodging
$$
Harbor Light Inn. The pick of the pack of lodgings lining the Fort Pierce Inlet along Seaway Drive is this modern, nautical, blue-trimmed gray motel. Spacious units on two floors feature kitchen or wet bar, carpeting, tub-shower, and routine but well-cared-for furnishings. Most rooms have either a waterfront porch or balcony. Augmenting the motel units are a set of four apartments across the street (off the water), where, if you can get one, in-season weekly rates are $350. Book everything here early—at least a year in advance. *1156–1160 Seaway Dr., 34949, tel. 407/468–3555 or 800/433–0004. 25 units. Facilities: pool, fishing pier with 17 boat slips, coin laundry. AE, D, DC, MC, V.*

$$
Mellon Patch Inn. This new bed-and-breakfast has an excellent location—across the shore road from a beach park, at the end of a canal leading to the Indian River Lagoon. One side of the canal has a bank of attractive new homes; the other, the Jack Island Wildlife Refuge. Andrea and Arthur Mellon opened their two-story B&B in 1994. The delightful decor features half melons everywhere—in pillows, in crafts, in candies on night tables. The four guest rooms (two upstairs, two down) are named Seaside Serenity, Santa Fe Sunset, Patchwork Quilt, and Tropical Paradise. Each has imaginative accessories, art, and upholstery appropriate to its theme. The cathedral-ceiling living room features a wood-burning fireplace and "Howie," a Native American in effigy who will surprise you every time you enter. Full breakfast is included. *3601 N. Rte. A1A, North Hutchinson Island 34949, tel. 407/461–5231. 4 rooms. MC, V.*

Budget Dining
$$
Mangrove Mattie's. Since its opening eight years ago, this upscale rustic spot on Fort Pierce Inlet has provided dazzling views and imaginative decor with seafood to match. Try the coconut-fried shrimp or the chicken and scampi, or come by for the happy hour with free buffet (Monday through Friday 5–8). The dinner-at-dusk early-bird special (4:30–6 except Sunday) offers a choice of a half-dozen entrées with a glass of wine for under $10. *1640 Seaway Dr., tel. 407/466–1044. Reservations advised. Dress: casual but neat. AE, D, DC, MC, V. Closed Dec. 25.*

$$
P. V. Martin's. This atmospheric seaside restaurant dates from the days when you were allowed to build on the dunes. With a weather vane atop its weathered-wood exterior, it's situated on an ever-blowy site along an eroded beach with its own boardwalk. Behind the jaunty red-and-white-stripe front awning, a large dark bar area gives way to a dining room with an open-beam, sloping roof. Rattan and bentwood chairs, blue-tile and wood-plank tabletops, ship models under glass, and old navigating lamps create an appropriately well-seasoned nautical look, put together over the years. Favorite Florida seafoods are featured: grouper baked with bananas and almonds; shrimp fried in a Parmesan, garlic, and spice batter; and crabmeat pasta with shrimp and mushrooms. Chicken, veal, rib, and steak entrées are also on the menu. Smaller-appetite entrées are all

priced under $10, and there's a children's menu, too. For dessert, try the Heath Bar crunch pie served with champagne sherbet, or strawberries over vanilla ice cream sprinkled with brandy and whipped cream. *5150 N. A1A, tel. 407/465–7300 or 407/569–0700. Reservations accepted. Dress: casual but neat. MC, V.*

$ **Theo Thudpucker's Raw Bar.** Businesspeople dressed for work mingle here with people who come in off the beach wearing shorts. On squally days everyone piles in off the jetty. Specialties include oyster stew, smoked fish spread, conch salad and fritters, fresh catfish, and alligator tail. New early-bird menus (Monday through Friday 3–5:30) feature $6–$7 entrées with potatoes. *2025 Seaway Dr. (South Jetty), tel. 407/465–1078. No reservations. Dress: casual. No credit cards. Closed Thanksgiving, Dec. 25.*

Shopping for Bargains One of Florida's best discount malls, the **Manufacturer's Outlet Center** (Rte. 70, off I–95 at Exit 65) contains 41 stores offering such brand names as American Tourister, Jonathan Logan, Aileen, Polly Flinders, Van Heusen, London Fog, Levi Strauss, and Geoffrey Beene.

Baseball The **New York Mets** hold spring training in the 7,300-seat St. Lucie County Sport Complex (525 N.W. Peacock Blvd., 34986, tel. 407/ 871–2115), home stadium for the Florida League's **St. Lucie Mets.** Take Exit 63C off I–95 and follow St. Lucie West Boulevard east to Peacock Boulevard.

Vero Beach

Indian River County Tourist Council (1216 21st St., Box 2947, Vero Beach 32961, tel. 407/567–3491).

Vero is an affluent city of about 30,000 (retirees make up half the winter population), with a strong commitment to the environment and the arts. At 17th Street, head east across the 17th Street Bridge to the beach, where you can turn north onto A1A. In the exclusive Riomar Bay section, north of the 17th Street Bridge, "canopy roads" are shaded by massive live oaks.

At Beachland Boulevard, turn left (west), and after less than a mile, just east of the new high-rise Merrill Barber Bridge, is Riverside Park. Here you'll find the **Civic Arts Center,** a cluster of cultural facilities that includes theaters (*see* the Arts, *below*) and the **Center for the Arts** (3001 Riverside Park Dr., tel. 407/231–0707). In its ninth season, the center presents a full schedule of exhibitions, art movies, lectures, workshops, and other events, with a focus on Florida artists.

Return to Route A1A and continue north past the John's Island development. Turn left onto Old Winter Beach Road: The pavement turns to hard-packed dirt as the road curves north, indicating the
★ old **Jungle Trail.** For nearly 9 miles the trail meanders through largely undeveloped forestland across from Pelican Island, which harbors the first national wildlife refuge established in the United States, dating from 1903. State agencies are creating a buffer for the trail to shield it from sight of further development and are stabilizing its surface for improved recreational use.

Budget Lodging
$$ **Aquarius Resort Motel.** Like its sister property (*see below*), this North Beach motel provides good value and a quiet beachfront (rare in southeast Florida) that's great for vacationing in the high season. All units are efficiencies or one- and two-bedroom apartments. Owner Paul Kelley has been known to drop the printed rates when demand is slow—which sometimes happens even in winter. *3544 Ocean Dr., 32963, tel. 407/231–1133. 27 units. Facilities: heated pool, beachfront, shuffleboard. D, DC, MC, V.*

$$ **Islander Resort.** The aqua-and-white-trim Islander has a snoozy Key West style that contrasts stylishly with the smart shops across from

the beach along Ocean Drive. Jigsaw-cut brackets and balusters and beach umbrellas dress up the pool. All rooms feature white wicker, pickled paneled walls, Caribbean art, colorful carpets, floral bed covers, paddle fans hung from vaulted ceilings, and fresh flowers. It's just right for beachside Vero. *3101 Ocean Dr., 32963, tel. 407/ 231–4431 or 800/952–5886. 16 rooms, 1 efficiency. Facilities: pool, barbecue grill. AE, DC, MC, V.*

$–$$ **Aquarius Oceanfront Resort.** Along South Beach, this two-story lodging is priced lower than its sister (*see above*) but is still on a quiet stretch of beach. Book far enough in advance, and you can get one of the two double-bedded motel rooms available at $60 per night. They lack a view, to be sure, and they're small, but they're not dingy. Furnishings include a table and two chairs, carpet, chintz bed covers, standard tropical art, and a shower stall in the bathroom. All other units are efficiencies and are a bit more expensive. *1526 S. Ocean Dr., 32963, tel. 407/231–5218. 27 units. Facilities: heated pool, beachfront, shuffleboard, barbecues. D, DC, MC, V.*

Budget Dining **Black Pearl.** This intimate restaurant (19 tables) with pink and
$$ green art deco furnishings offers entrées that combine fresh local
★ ingredients with the best of the Continental tradition. Specialties include chilled leek-and-watercress soup, local fish in parchment paper, feta cheese and spinach fritters, mesquite-grilled swordfish, and pan-fried veal with local shrimp and vermouth. Pearl's Bistro (54 Royal Palm Blvd., tel. 407/778–2950), a more casual and less expensive sister restaurant, serves Caribbean-style food for lunch and dinner. *1409 Rte. A1A, tel. 407/234–4426. Reservations advised. Dress: casual but neat. AE, MC, V. Closed Super Bowl Sun., holidays. No lunch.*

$$ **Ocean Grill.** Opened by Waldo Sexton as a hamburger shack in 1938, the Ocean Grill is nowadays furnished with Tiffany lamps, wrought-iron chandeliers, and Beanie Backus paintings of pirates and Seminole Indians. The menu includes black-bean soup, crisp onion rings, jumbo lump crabmeat salad, at least three kinds of fish every day, prime rib, and a tart Key lime pie. The bar looks out on the remains of the *Breconshire*, an 1894 near-shore wreck, from which 34 British sailors escaped. The event is commemorated by the Leaping Limey, a curious blend of vodka, blue curaçao, and lemon. *1050 Sexton Plaza (Beachland Blvd. east of Ocean Dr.), tel. 407/231–5409. Reservations accepted for parties of 5 or more. Dress: casual but neat. AE, D, DC, MC, V. Closed Super Bowl Sun., 2 wks following Labor Day, Thanksgiving. No lunch weekends.*

$$ **The Patio.** What immediately catches your eye is the tile bar from Spain, the Druze-tribe wood panels from Lebanon, and rafter ceilings and lighting fixtures from the Dodge, Mizner, Rockefeller, and Stotesbury estates. Everyone from young professionals to retirees packs the place from 4 to 6, when hot hors d'oeuvres—ample as a meal—are served in the happy-hour bar. Twilight dinners from 4 to 5:30 (check! this may change) are great buys—$7.95 for four courses with wine. Early-bird specials, served until 8, are only $11.95 and are followed by nightly live entertainment. On Sunday, there's an all-you-can-eat champagne brunch (60-plus items with endless bubbly and mimosas) at $11.95. Otherwise it's all-American fare: steaks, prime rib, chicken, and seafood. *1103 Miracle Mile (U.S. 1), tel. 407/567–7215. Reservations accepted. Dress: casual but neat. AE, MC, V.*

Beaches All through town there are beach-access parks (admission free; open daily 7 AM–10 PM) with boardwalks and steps bridging the foredune. **Humiston Park** (Ocean Dr., just below Beachland Blvd.) has a large children's play area and picnic tables and is across the street from shops.

Participant Snorkelers and divers can swim out to explore reefs 100–300 feet off
    Sports the beach. Summer offers the best diving conditions. At low tide you
    Diving can see the boiler and other remains of an iron-screw steamer,
Breconshire, which foundered on a reef just south of Beachland
Boulevard in 1894.

    Fishing For marsh fishing, two sites west of town are tops for bluegills, cat-
fish, largemouth bass, shellcrackers, and speckled perch. Cypress-
lined 3-by-7-mile Blue Cypress Lake is 5 miles north of Route 60 on
Blue Cypress Lake Road. Stick Marsh, farther up Blue Cypress
Lake Road, produces even greater catches, but it's strictly catch-
and-release. The best contact for either site is **Middleton Fish Camp**
(Blue Cypress Lake, tel. 407/778-0150).

Spectator The **Los Angeles Dodgers** train each March in the 6,500-seat Holman
    Sports Stadium at Dodgertown (4101 26th St., Box 2887, 32961, tel. 407/
    Baseball 569-4900).

    Polo **Windsor** is the home of the annual Prince of Wales Cup in late Febru-
ary or early March. (Prince Charles helped inaugurate Windsor polo
in February 1989 with a special charity game.) The cup benefits the
international Friends of Conservation, of which the prince is a pa-
tron. *3125 Windsor Blvd., 32963, tel. 407/589-9800. Admission: $10
general admission, $50 fieldside; Prince of Wales Cup $20, $125.
High-goal season games Jan.–Mar., Sun. at 2.*

The Arts **Riverside Theatre** (3250 Riverside Park Dr., 32963, tel. 407/231-
6990) stages six productions each season in its 633-seat performance
hall. Children's productions are mounted in the compound at the **Agnes Wahlstrom Youth Playhouse** (tel. 407/234-8052).

Sebastian Area

Just north of where the Jungle Trail rejoins Route A1A, the
McLarty Museum, a National Historical Landmark site, has displays dedicated to the 1715 hurricane that sank a fleet of Spanish
treasure ships. *13180 N. Rte. A1A, Sebastian, tel. 407/589-2147.
Admission: $1 ages over 6. Open daily 10–4:30.*

At the northern end of Orchid Island is **Sebastian Inlet,** where a high
bridge offers spectacular views. Along the sea is a dune area that's
part of the **Archie Carr National Wildlife Refuge,** a haven for sea turtles and other protected Florida wildlife. The 587-acre **Sebastian Inlet State Recreation Area,** on both sides of the bridge, is the best-
attended park in the Florida state system because of the inlet's
highly productive fishing waters. *9700 S. Rte. A1A, Melbourne
Beach, tel. 407/984-4852 or 407/589-9659 for camping. Bait and
tackle shop open daily 7:30–6, concession stand 8–5.*

Backtrack along Route A1A to Wabasso Beach Road and turn right.
On the south side of the road you'll see the finished first phase of the
Disney Vacation Club at Vero Beach, the first Disney resort separate
from a theme park. Completed so far are a 115-room inn and 60 of the
320 vacation villas.

Cross the bridge to the mainland, and immediately turn left and follow the signs to the **Environmental Learning Center.** This outstanding 51-acre facility has a new wet lab with aquariums filled with
Indian River Lagoon life in addition to its preexisting 600-foot
boardwalk through mangrove shore and 1-mile canoe trail. *255 Live
Oak Dr., Vero Beach, tel. 407/589-5050. Admission free. Open
weekdays 9–5, weekends 1–4.*

Take Wabasso Beach Road west and U.S. 1 north for 4½ miles, just
past Route 512, to the little fishing village of **Sebastian.** At **Mel Fisher's Treasure Museum,** you can view some of the recovery from the
treasure ship *Atocha* and its sister ships of the 1715 fleet. *1322 U.S.*

1, tel. 407/589–9874. Admission: $5 adults, $4 senior citizens, $1.50 children 6–12. Open Mon.–Sat. 10–5, Sun. noon–5.

Budget Lodging
$–$$

Captain's Quarters. Four Key West–style units—three overlooking the Indian River Lagoon and the marina at Capt. Hiram's and one two-room suite—are all cute. They are painted in bright colors with matching fabrics and contain pine and white wicker furniture, pine plank floors with grass rugs, a ceiling fan, a little fridge, air-conditioning and heat, and nautical and miscellaneous art. The adequate bathrooms have large stall showers. Glass doors open to a plank porch with two molded chairs, but the porches are all within sight of each other. *1606 Indian River Dr., Sebastian 32958, tel. 407/589–4345. 3 rooms, 1 suite. Facilities: restaurant, marina. AE, D, MC, V.*

$–$$

Davis House Inn. Vero native Steve Wild modeled his two-story inn after the clubhouse at Augusta National. Wide overhung roofs shade wraparound porches. In a companion house that Steve calls the Gathering Room, he serves a complimentary expanded Continental breakfast. Though the inn only opened in 1992, it looks established, fitting right in with the fishing-town look of Sebastian, on the Indian River Lagoon. Rooms are huge—virtual suites, with a large sofa sitting area—though somewhat underfurnished. Each has a hand-painted, pine, king-size bed and microwave kitchenette. It's a terrific value. *607 Davis St., Sebastian 32958, tel. 407/589–4114. 12 efficiencies. Facilities: bicycles. MC, V.*

Budget Dining
$$

Hurricane Harbor. A year-round crowd of retirees and locals frequent this down-home, open-beam, Old Florida–style waterfront restaurant (though note, it's all indoors), built in 1927 as a garage and during Prohibition used as a smuggler' den. Guests love the window seats on stormy nights, when sizeable waves break outside in the Indian River Lagoon. The menu features seafood, steaks, and grills, along with sandwiches, soups, and salads. Friday and Saturday nights they open the Antique Dining Room, with its linen, stained glass, and a huge antique breakfront. There's live music nightly—jazz, pop, Dixieland, German, country and western, or oldies. *1540 Indian River Dr., Sebastian, tel. 407/589–1773. Reservations accepted. Dress: casual. AE, D, MC, V. Closed Mon., Dec. 25.*

Participant Sports
Canoeing

Bill Rogers Outdoor Adventures (1541 DeWitt La., Sebastian, tel. 407/388–2331) outfits canoe trips down the Sebastian River, along Indian River Lagoon, through Pelican Island Wildlife Refuge, and for more distant locations.

Fishing

The best inlet fishing in the region is at **Sebastian Inlet State Recreation Area** (*see above*), where the catch includes bluefish, flounder, jack, redfish, sea trout, snapper, snook, and Spanish mackerel.

6 The Florida Keys

By Herb
Hiller

Though they're connected by a thread of concrete—U.S. 1, known down here as the Overseas Highway—these islands strung together off the tip of Florida are still islands, and everything that doesn't grow or swim here has to be trucked in from the mainland. As a result, the Keys can be an expensive place to visit, especially its liveliest and most vital town, Key West. Yet the laid-back, casual nature of the Keys favors the budget traveler. Even the expensive resorts resist formality, while the mom-and-pop motels and roadside restaurants don't fuss at all.

The Florida Keys are a wilderness of flowering jungles and shimmering seas, a jade necklace of mangrove-fringed islands dangling toward the tropics. The Florida Keys are also a 110-mile traffic jam lined with garish billboards, hamburger stands, shopping centers, motels, and trailer courts. Unfortunately, in the Keys you can't have one without the other. A river of tourist traffic gushes along the Overseas Highway. Residents of Monroe County live by diverting that river's green dollar flow to their own pockets. In the process, however, the fragile beauty of the Keys—or at least the 45 that are inhabited, linked to the mainland by 43 bridges—has paid the price.

Despite a state-mandated county development slowdown, the Keys' natural resources are still imperiled. Since 1992, new building has been severely restricted, with an eye to protecting the environment as well as to improving hurricane evacuation procedures. Nevertheless, increased salinity in Florida Bay has caused large areas of sea grass to die off, drift in mats out of the bay onto the coral reefs, and prevent sunlight from reaching the corals, thereby stifling their growth and threatening the Keys' significant recreational diving economy and tourism in general. In 1996 the National Oceanic and Atmospheric Administration (NOAA) begins implementing a controversial management plan for the 200-mile-long Florida Keys National Marine Sanctuary (the largest in the nation). The sanctuary plan is intended to help protect the coral reefs and restore badly depleted fish reserves, but it has been challenged by short-sighted interests, even while many of these same interests agree on the need to renourish Florida Bay. The management plan calls for a new maritime zoning concept that restricts commercial and recreational activities in designated areas. Dive shops and places where visitors stay are to alert people to these restrictions.

For now, however, take pleasure as you drive down U.S. 1 along the islands. Most days show only the silvery blue and green Atlantic and its still-living reef on your left; Florida Bay, the Gulf of Mexico, and the backcountry on your right. (The Keys extend east–west from the mainland.) At some points, the ocean and the Gulf are 10 miles apart; on the narrowest landfill islands, they are separated only by the road.

The Overseas Highway varies from a frustrating traffic-clogged trap to a mystical pathway skimming the sea. More islands than you can remember appear. Pay attention to the green mile markers by the side of the road, and even if you lose track of the names of the islands, you won't get lost.

Things to do and see are everywhere, but first you have to remind yourself to get off the highway. Once you do, you can rent a boat and find a secluded anchorage at which to fish, swim, and marvel at the sun, sea, and sky. In the Atlantic, you can dive to spectacular coral reefs or pursue dolphin, blue marlin, and other deep-water game fish. Along the Florida Bay coastline you can seek out the bonefish, snapper, snook, and tarpon that lurk in the grass flats and in the shallow, winding channels of the backcountry.

Along the reefs and among the islands are more than 600 kinds of fish. Diminutive deer and pale raccoons, related to but distinct from their mainland cousins, inhabit the Lower Keys. And throughout the islands you'll find such exotic West Indian plants as Jamaica dogwood, pigeon plum, poisonwood, satinwood, and silver and thatch palms, as well as tropical birds, including the great white heron, mangrove cuckoo, roseate spoonbill, and white-crowned pigeon.

Another Keys attraction is the weather: In the winter it's typically 10° warmer than on the mainland; in the summer it's usually 10° cooler. The Keys also get substantially less rain, around 30 inches annually compared to 55–60 inches in Miami and the Everglades. Most of the rain falls in quick downpours on summer afternoons. In winter, continental cold fronts occasionally stall over the Keys, dragging overnight temperatures down to the 40s.

The Keys were only sparsely populated until the early 20th century. In 1905, however, railroad magnate Henry Flagler began building the extension of his Florida railroad south from Homestead to Key West. His goal was to establish a rail link to the steamships that sailed between Key West and Havana, just 90 miles away across the Straits of Florida. The railroad arrived at Key West in 1912 and remained a lifeline of commerce until the Labor Day hurricane of 1935 washed out much of its roadbed. For three years thereafter, the only way in and out of Key West was by boat. The Overseas Highway, built over the railroad's old roadbeds and bridges, was completed in 1938, and many sections and bridges have recently been widened or replaced.

Although most mainlanders tend to see the Keys as much alike, they are actually quite different from each other. Key Largo, the largest and closest to the mainland, has become a bedroom community for Homestead, South Dade, and even the southern reaches of Miami. Most of the residents of the Upper Keys moved to Florida from the Northeast and Midwest; many are retirees. In the Middle Keys, fishing dominates the economy, and many residents descend from people who moved here from elsewhere in the South. The Lower

Keys reflect a diverse population: native "Conchs" (white Key Westers, many of whom trace their ancestry to the Bahamas), freshwater Conchs (longtime residents who migrated from somewhere else years ago), gays (who now make up at least 20% of Key West's citizenry), Bahamians, Hispanics (primarily Cubans), recent refugees from the urban sprawl of Miami and Fort Lauderdale, transient Navy and Air Force personnel, students waiting tables, and a miscellaneous assortment of vagabonds, drifters, and dropouts in search of refuge at the end of the road.

Florida Keys Basics

Budget Lodging

Accommodations in the Keys are more expensive than elsewhere in south Florida. In part this is due to the Keys' popularity and ability to command top dollar, but primarily it's because everything used to build and operate a hotel costs more in the Keys.

Key West is a particularly high-cost destination, though it also offers the greatest variety of lodgings, from large resorts to bed-and-breakfast rooms in private homes. Our choices are limited to a handful of affordable motels and a few guest houses with affordable rooms. Obviously, you must book these well in advance, and you probably won't be able to bargain on the price. The only time of year when there might be last-minute vacancies is midweek between Easter and Memorial Day, and during hurricane season, between Labor Day and Halloween.

You can do much better in the Keys north of Key West, where older lodgings have been fixed up by dreamers with an ambition to somehow make a living in the sun. They keep their prices affordable not only because of the competition, but also to build repeat business. Our choices of lodgings are typically mom-and-pop places.

A couple of negotiating strategies will help you get the best deals. If you book in advance, you'll pay the full rate, but show up off the road on an evening when rooms are available and you can bargain. Don't just complain that the price is too high— tactfully ask if the place offers a discount to families (if you're traveling with a family), AAA members, or AARP members, whichever would apply to you. If you'd like to spend more than one night there, ask if they discount multiple-night stays. Finally, you can just offer a lower rate than what you're quoted. Mention the names of some motels up or down the road in the direction you're heading, say that you were in fact heading to one of those places but you saw this one, you were attracted, and the kids said, or the wife said, or the husband said, or the mother-in-law said . . .

Off-season in the Keys is between Easter and mid-December (except for holiday weekends and other special events), when rates are often only half of what they are in winter. Lodging operators are even more willing to deal off season. It's not a bad idea, either, to go by the chambers of commerce and ask which motels offer the lowest rates—often motel owners will have instructed the chamber to offer added discounts to people who ask. Keep in mind that the best rooms in the Keys are those on the water—and the least desirable are those along the highway. No matter how the desk clerk assures you that the traffic noise abates at night, assume that there will always be cars without mufflers and heavy-duty trucks cranking up the highway. So if you're bargaining, consider asking for an upgrade in location. The motel would rather fill a bed than not, and if the more expensive room is going empty, you might as well sleep there as in a noisy room.

Some hotels in the Keys are historic structures with a charming patina of age; others are just plain old. Salty winds and soil play havoc with anything man-made in the Keys. Constant maintenance is a must, and some hotels and motels don't get it. Inspect your accommodations before checking in.

Budget Dining

Denizens of the Florida Keys may be relaxed and wear tropical-casual clothes, but these folks take food seriously. A number of young, talented chefs have settled here in the last few years to enjoy the climate and contribute to the Keys' growing image as a fine-dining center. The restaurant menus, the rum-based fruit beverages, and even the music reflect the Keys' tropical climate and their proximity to Cuba and other Caribbean islands. Freshly caught local fish have been on every Keys menu in the past, but that is starting to change, as many venerable commercial fish houses have abandoned the business in the past decade. There's a good chance the fish you order in a Keys restaurant may have been caught somewhere else—even queen conch, which is considered an endangered species in the United States. Florida lobster and stone crab should be local and fresh from August through March. Key lime pie—a yellow lime custard in a graham-cracker crust with a meringue top—is a famous local specialty, though it's getting hard to find an authentic one.

Note that small restaurants down here don't hold too strictly to their stated hours of business; sometimes they close for a day or a week, or cancel lunch for a month or two, just by posting a note on the door.

Bargain Shopping

You needn't worry that you just passed the last T-shirt shop in the Keys. There will always be another, just as there are plenty of stores that sell souvenirs. Luckily, there are also places with more out-of-the-ordinary wares: art, crafts, interesting foods, and books. Like everything in the Keys, however, prices tend to be a little higher than on the mainland.

Beaches

Keys shorelines are either mangrove-fringed marshes or rock outcrops that fall away to mucky grass flats. Most pleasure beaches in the Keys are man-made, with sand imported from the U.S. mainland or the Bahamas. There are public beaches in **John Pennekamp Coral Reef State Park** (MM 102.5), **Long Key State Recreation Area** (MM 67.5), **Sombrero Beach** (MM 50) in Marathon, **Bahia Honda State Park** (MM 37), and at many roadside turnouts along the Overseas Highway. Many hotels and motels also have their own small, shallow-water beach areas.

When you swim in the Keys, wear an old pair of tennis shoes to protect your feet from rocks, sea-urchin spines, and other potential hazards.

Sports and the Outdoors

In the Keys, you're always close to the water, so water sports are prime activities everywhere: diving, sailing, canoeing, fishing, swimming, and windsurfing. Motor yachts, sailboats, Hobie Cats, Windsurfers, canoes, and other water-sports equipment are all available for rent by the day or on a long-term basis. Some hotels have their own rental services; others will refer you to a separate vendor. There aren't many golf courses, however—the islands that make up the Keys just aren't big enough to devote a lot of acreage to golf links.

Biking   Touring opportunities steadily improve in the Keys, although riding along certain stretches of the Overseas Highways can still be dangerous. Key West is a cycling town, and getting around on a fat-tired "Conch cruiser" is a tradition.

Boating   Boaters can travel to Key West either along the Intracoastal Waterway through Florida Bay or along the Atlantic Coast. The Keys are full of marinas that welcome transient visitors, but they don't have enough slips for everyone who wants to visit the area. Make reservations in advance, and ask about channel and dockage depth—many Key marinas are quite shallow.

Florida Marine Patrol (MM 48, BS, 2796 Overseas Hwy., Suite 100, State Regional Service Center, Marathon 33050, tel. 305/289–2320), a division of the Florida Department of Natural Resources, maintains a 24-hour telephone service for reporting boating emergencies and natural-resource violations.

Coast Guard Group Key West (Key West 33040, tel. 305/292–8727) provides 24-hour monitoring of VHF-FM Channel 16. Safety and weather information is broadcast at 7 AM and 5 PM Eastern Standard Time on VHF-FM Channel 16 and 22A. There are three stations in the Keys: Islamorada (tel. 305/664–4404), Marathon (tel. 305/743–6778), and Key West (tel. 305/292–8856).

Diving and   Although diving is an expensive sport, for many visitors diving is the
Snorkeling   only reason for vacationing here. Reefs and wrecks elsewhere along the east coast of Florida simply don't match up to the warm-water attraction of the Keys, the state's most extensive diving and snorkeling grounds. Divers come for the quantity and quality of living coral reefs within 6 or 7 miles of shore, the kaleidoscopic beauty of 650 species of tropical fish, and the adventure of probing wrecked ships that foundered in these seemingly tranquil seas during almost four centuries of exploration and commerce.

Yet even if expensive, diving the reefs of the Keys is certainly cheaper than flying to the Cayman Islands, Bonaire, or elsewhere in the Caribbean and beyond. Divers willing to share rooms among four or more even in the winter can find rates no higher than $25 per person per night, as many of our lodging choices indicate.

For Keys visitors who don't scuba dive, many of the reefs can also be enjoyably snorkeled. Most dive shops that operate boats take snorkelers at substantially reduced rates and rent snorkels, masks, and fins. From shore or from a boat, snorkelers can easily explore grass flats, mangrove roots, and rocks in shallow water almost anywhere in the Keys. You may see occasional small clusters of coral and fish, mollusks, and other sea creatures. Ask dive shops for snorkeling information and directions.

Diving and snorkeling are prohibited around bridges and near certain keys. Be aware that certain weather conditions—say 2- or 3-foot seas—may be okay for dives but not good for surface snorkeling.

Dive shops all over the state organize Keys dives and offer diving instruction. South Florida residents fill dive boats on weekends, so plan to dive Monday through Thursday, when the boats and reefs are less crowded.

Fishing   You have a choice of deep-sea fishing on the ocean or the Gulf or flatwater fishing in the mangrove-fringed shallows of the backcountry. Each of the areas protected by the state or federal government has its own set of rigorously enforced regulations. Check with your hotel or a local chamber of commerce to find out what the rules are in the area where you're staying. The same sources can refer you to a reliable charter-boat or party-boat captain who will take you where the right kind of fish are biting.

The Arts and Nightlife

The Keys are more than warm weather and luminous scenery—a vigorous and sophisticated artistic community flourishes here. Key West alone currently claims among its residents 55 full-time writers and 500 painters and craftspeople. Arts organizations in the Keys sponsor many special events, some lasting only a weekend, others spanning an entire season. But street theater is the only cheap theater in Key West—for sit-down theater, expect tickets in the $12–$25 range (generally about $15, with the upper end for opera and headliners). Senior citizens typically get 10%–20% discounts, but not always.

The monthly *Island Navigator* (Box 430870, Big Pine Key 33034, tel. 305/664–2266 or 800/926–8412), Monroe County's only countywide, general-interest newspaper, is free at banks, campgrounds, and stores. Its monthly community calendar lists cultural and sports events. Other publications covering arts, music, and literature are available at hotels and other high-traffic areas: the daily *Miami Herald* (218 Whitehead St., Key West 33040, tel. 305/294–4683 or 800/437–2537), the daily (except Saturday) *Key West Citizen* (3420 Northside Dr., Key West 33040, tel. 305/294–6641), the weekly *Free Press* (Box 469, Islamorada 33036, tel. 305/664–2266 or 800/926–8412), and the monthly *Solares Hill* (Key West Publications, Inc., 330-B Julia St., Key West 33040, tel. 305/294–3602).

A night out at a tourist trap or the neighborhood bar is the best buy for nightlife in the Keys. Keys people like to party, and partying is about all that many can afford. Bars are plentiful, and they're usually informal—otherwise locals won't bother. We've identified some of the more popular hangouts; you can find more by asking at your hotel.

Festivals

In mid-January, the **Organized Florida Fishermen Seafood Festival** (tel. 305/664–5596) features a weekend of arts and crafts and lots of spiny lobster eating. In late April, the **Conch Republic Celebration** (tel. 305/294–2587 or 800/527–8539) in Key West honors the founding fathers of the Conch Republic, "the small island nation of Key West." Key West also hosts the **Hemingway Days Festival** (tel. 305/294–4440) in July, which includes plays, short-story competitions, and an Ernest Hemingway look-alike contest, and **Fantasy Fest** (tel. 305/296–1817) at Halloween, with a riotous costume party, parade, and town fair.

Tour 1: The Upper Keys

Arriving and Departing
By Plane

A popular option is to fly into Miami International Airport (MIA) and take a van or taxi to the Keys. The **Airporter** (tel. 305/852–3413 or 800/830–3413) operates scheduled van and bus service from MIA's baggage areas to wherever you want to go in Key Largo and Islamorada. Drivers post Airporter signs with the names of clients they are to meet. The cost is $30 per person to Key Largo and $33 per person to Islamorada; children under 12 ride for half fare. Reservations are required. **Keys Super Shuttle** (tel. 305/871–2000) charges $77 to Key Largo for the first person, $15 each additional person; the prices to Islamorada are $88 and $22. Super Shuttle requests 24-hour advance notice.

Island Taxi (tel. 305/664–8181, 305/743–0077, or 305/872–0128) meets arriving flights at MIA. Reservations are required 24 hours in advance for arrivals, one hour for departures. Fares for one or two persons are $80 to Key Largo, $100 to Islamorada; each additional person is $5. Accompanied children under 12 ride free.

By Bus   **Greyhound Lines** (tel. 305/374–7222 or 800/231–2222) has increased service to the Keys. Buses run from downtown Miami, MIA, and Homestead to Key Largo (Wings, MM 99.5, BS, tel. 305/296–9072 for all Keys stops) and Islamorada (Burger King, MM 83.5, BS).

By Car   U.S. 1 is the main highway from Florida's mainland to the Keys. From Florida City to Key Largo, it's only two lanes wide and choked with traffic, so you may want to take the Card Sound Road (Route 905A) instead. Although this is a toll road ($1.25), it's still the fastest way to go. Where the road ends on North Key Largo, turn right onto Route 905. You will rejoin U.S. 1 in Key Largo. Plans for four-laning U.S. 1 between Florida City and Key Largo are on hold because of environmental concerns. No improvements will occur until near the end of the decade at the earliest.

Getting   Finding your way around the Keys isn't hard once you understand
Around   the unique address system. The only address many people have is a mile marker (MM) number. The markers themselves are small green rectangular signs along the side of the Overseas Highway (U.S. 1). They begin with MM 126 a mile south of Florida City and end with MM 0 on the corner of Fleming and Whitehead streets in Key West. Keys residents use the abbreviation BS for the bay side of U.S. 1 and OS for the ocean side.

Guided Tours   ***Key Largo Princess*** (MM 100, OS, Key Largo, tel. 305/451–4655) offers glass-bottom boat trips and sunset cruises on a luxury 70-foot motor yacht with a 280-square-foot glass viewing area, departing from the Holiday Inn docks.

Sailors Choice (MM 100, OS, Key Largo, tel. 305/451–1802 or 305/451–0041) operates daily charters, including a nighttime trip, on a 50-foot, 49-passenger boat, departing from the Holiday Inn docks.

Key Largo

Key Largo Chamber of Commerce (MM 106, BS, 105950 Overseas Hwy., Key Largo 33037, tel. 305/451–4747 or 800/822–1088).

This tour begins on Key Largo, the northeasternmost of the Florida Keys accessible by road. The tour assumes that you have come south from Florida City on Card Sound Road (Route 905A). If you take the Overseas Highway (U.S. 1) south from Florida City, you can begin the tour with Key Largo Undersea Park.

Cross the Card Sound Bridge onto **North Key Largo,** where a new fence along Card Sound Road forms the eastern boundary of **Crocodile Lakes National Wildlife Refuge.** In the refuge dwell some 300 to 500 crocodiles, the largest single concentration of these shy, elusive reptiles in North America. There's no visitor center here—just 6,800 acres of mangrove swamp and adjoining upland jungle. For your best chance to see a crocodile, park on the shoulder of Card Sound Road and scan the ponds along the road with binoculars. In winter, crocodiles often haul themselves out to sun on the banks farthest from the road. Don't leave the road shoulder; you could disturb tern nests on the nearby spoil banks or irritate the rattlesnakes.

Take Card Sound Road to Route 905, turn right, and drive for 10 miles through **Key Largo Hammock,** the largest remaining stand of the vast West Indian tropical hardwood forest that once covered most of the upland areas in the Florida Keys. The state and federal governments are busy acquiring as much of the hammock as they can to protect it from further development, and they hope to establish

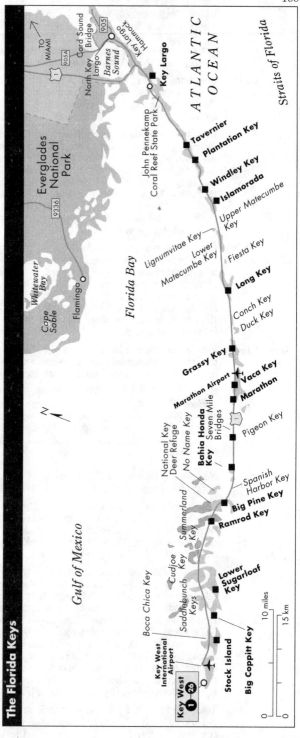

The Florida Keys

TO MIAMI

Card Sound Bridge
905
Card Sound
North Key Largo
1
905A
Barnes Sound
Key Largo Hammock
Key Largo

Key Largo

Everglades National Park

9336

Tavernier

John Pennekamp Coral Reef State Park

Plantation Key

Windley Key

Islamorada

Upper Matecumbe Key

Whitewater Bay

Cape Sable

Flamingo

Lignumvitae Key

Lower Matecumbe Key

Fiesta Key

Florida Bay

Long Key

Conch Key

Duck Key

N

Grassy Key

Vaca Key

Marathon Airport

Marathon

Gulf of Mexico

National Key Deer Refuge

No Name Key

Bahia Honda Key

Seven Mile Bridges

Pigeon Key

1

Spanish Harbor Key

Summerland Key

Big Pine Key

Ramrod Key

Cudjoe Key

Boca Chica Key

Saddlebunch Keys

Lower Sugarloaf Key

10 miles

15 km

Key West International Airport

Stock Island

Big Coppitt Key

Key West
1 — 26

ATLANTIC OCEAN

Straits of Florida

visitor centers and nature trails. For now, it's best to admire this wilderness from the road. According to law-enforcement officials, this may be the most dangerous place in the United States, a haven for modern-day pirates and witches. The "pirates" are drug smugglers who land their cargo along the ocean shore or drop it into the forest from low-flying planes. The "witches" are practitioners of voodoo, Santeria, and other occult rituals. What's more, this jungle is full of poisonous plants. The most dangerous, the manchineel or "devil tree," has a toxin so potent that rainwater falling on its leaves and then onto a person's skin can cause sores that resist healing. Florida's first tourist, explorer Juan Ponce de León, died in 1521 from a superficial wound inflicted by an Indian arrowhead dipped in manchineel sap.

Just after joining U.S. 1, you'll see the **St. Justin Martyr Catholic Church** (MM 105.5, BS, tel. 305/451–1316), notable for its architecture, which evokes the colors and materials of the Keys. Among its art are a beautiful fresco of the Last Supper and an altar table formed of a 5,000-pound mass of Carrara marble quarried in Tuscany.

Continue on U.S. 1 toward **Key Largo.** At Transylvania Avenue (MM 103.2), turn left to visit the **Key Largo Undersea Park.** Family attractions include an underwater archaeology exhibit that you have to snorkel or dive to reach, underwater music, and an air-conditioned grotto theater with a 13-minute multimedia slide show devoted to the history of people and the sea. Also at the site are a small submarine, which gives three-hour tours for up to six people, and Jules' Undersea Lodge. *51 Shoreland Dr., tel. 305/451–2353. Aquarium theater admission free; scuba fee, including tanks and gear: $20–$30; snorkel fee, including gear: $10, $35 for family of 4; submarine tour: $199. Open daily 9–3.*

Less than 1 mile south on the Overseas Highway is the **Maritime Museum of the Florida Keys.** This small but earnest museum offers exhibits depicting the history of shipwrecks and salvage efforts along the Keys: retrieved treasures, reconstructed wreck sites, and artifacts in various stages of preservation. Artifacts newly added in 1994 and 1995 have come from a fleet of treasure ships wrecked in 1715 by a hurricane 250 miles farther north along the Gulf Stream. *MM 102.5, BS, tel. 305/451–6444. Admission: $5 adults, $3 children 6–12. Open Fri.–Wed. 10–5.*

★ Across the road is the entrance to **John Pennekamp Coral Reef State Park.** The primary attraction here is diving on the offshore coral reefs, but even a landlubber can appreciate the superb interpretive aquarium in the park's visitor center. A concessionaire rents canoes and sailboats and offers boat trips to the reef. The park also includes a nature trail through a mangrove forest, a swimming beach, picnic shelters, a snack bar, a gift shop, and a campground. *MM 102.5, OS, tel. 305/451–1202. Admission: $3.25 per vehicle with up to 8 people, plus 50¢-per-person county surcharge. Open daily 8–sunset.*

Return to U.S. 1 and turn left. At MM 100, turn left again into the parking lot of the Holiday Inn Key Largo Resort. In the adjoining Key Largo Harbor Marina you'll find the *African Queen,* the steam-powered work boat on which Katharine Hepburn and Humphrey Bogart rode in their movie of the same name. Also displayed at the resort is the *Thayer IV,* a 22-foot mahogany Chris Craft built in 1951 and used by Ms. Hepburn and Henry Fonda in Fonda's last film, *On Golden Pond.*

Budget **Largo Lodge.** No two rooms are the same in this 1950s-vintage re-
Lodging sort, but all are cozy, with rattan furniture and screened porches
$$ with Cuban tile floors. The prettiest palm alley you've ever seen sets
★ the mood. Tropical gardens with more palms, sea grapes, and orchids surround the guest cottages. There's 200 feet of bay frontage,

and late in the day, wild ducks, pelicans, herons, and other birds come looking for a handout from longtime owner Harriet "Hat" Stokes. If you want a top-value tropical hideaway without going far into the Keys, this is it. *MM 101.5, BS, 101740 Overseas Hwy., 33037, tel. 305/451–0424 or 800/468–4378. 6 apts. with kitchen, 1 efficiency. Facilities: boat ramp, 3 slips. MC, V.*

$–$$ **Bay Harbor Lodge.** Owner Laszlo Simoga speaks German, Hungarian, and Russian and caters to an international clientele. Situated on two heavily landscaped acres, his little resort offers a rustic wood lodge, tiki huts, and concrete block cottages; every room has either a small fridge or full kitchen. Unit 14, a large efficiency apartment with a deck, has a wood ceiling, original oil paintings, and a dining table made from the hatch cover of a World War II Liberty Ship. Laszlo and his wife, Sandra, are the kind of caring hosts who make mom-and-pop lodges such as this worth your patronage. The rates and the waterfront setting make this place especially good. A pool is to be added by 1996. *MM 97.7, BS, 97702 Overseas Hwy., 33037, tel. 305/852–5695. 16 rooms. Facilities: weight equipment, 2 docks, paddleboats, rowboats, canoe, kayak, Jacuzzi, barbecue grills, boat-trailer parking. D, MC, V.*

¢ **Sunset Cove Motel.** Statues of lions, tigers, and dinosaurs seem to be attracting water birds, which fly in each morning and afternoon, while an orphaned manatee swims by for a daily visit. The dormitory house, which sleeps four and has a kitchen, falls into the budget range; otherwise, you'll pay moderate prices for 10 guest units, which all have kitchens and original hand-painted murals. A glass bar beneath a tiki hut in a garden with a waterfall is new, while the always appealing waterfront has tiki huts, big hanging woven chairs the size of beds to bliss out in, a sandy beach (even if coarse), and free use of sailboats (for experienced sailors), glass-bottom and regular paddleboats, canoes, rowboats, and Windsurfers. Special discounts are offered to senior citizens and members of conservation groups. *MM 99.5, BS, Box 99, 33037, tel. 305/451–0705. 10 units, dormitory. Facilities: water-sports equipment, 115-ft fishing pier, boat ramp. MC, V.*

Camping The State of Florida operates recreational-vehicle and tent campgrounds in **John Pennekamp Coral Reef State Park** (MM 102.5, OS, Box 1560, 33037, tel. 305/451–1202).

Budget Dining **Crack'd Conch.** The new floor and ceiling make no difference. Behind the white clapboard and lattice exterior and the green and violet trim, foreign money and patrons' business cards still festoon the main dining room, where vertical bamboo stakes support the bar. There's also a screened porch and an outdoor garden. This was originally a fish camp from the 1930s. Specialties include conch (cracked and in chowder, fritters, and salad), an award-winning lobster taco, fried alligator, smoked chicken, and 115 kinds of beer. Portions are big; they use lots of take-out containers. *MM 105, OS, 105045 Overseas Hwy., tel. 305/451–0732. No reservations. Dress: casual. AE, D, MC, V. Closed Wed. and holidays.*

$ **Harriette's Restaurant.** Typical of roadside places where the Coke signs outrank the restaurants', this eatery is thick with down-home personality. Owner Harriette Mattson makes it her business to know many of her guests by name and even takes the trouble to remember what they eat. Wise-cracking waitresses, perfectly styled for this joint, will tell you that the three-egg omelet is usually a six-egg omelet because Harriette has a heavy hand. Harriette's is famous for its breakfasts: steak and eggs with hash browns or grits and toast and jelly for $5.95, or old-fashioned hot cakes with whipped butter and syrup and sausage or bacon for $3.25. A new Keys mural, a little paneling, some carpet, and acoustic ceiling tiles touch things up, but you can still count on a homey style punctuated with local crafts and photos on consignment. *MM 95.7, BS, 95710*

Overseas Hwy., tel. 305/852–8689. No reservations. Dress: casual. No credit cards. Closed Thanksgiving, Dec. 25. No dinner.

$ **Mrs. Mac's Kitchen.** Hundreds of beer cans, beer bottles, and expired auto license plates from all over the world decorate the walls of this wood-paneled, open-air restaurant. At breakfast and lunch, the counter and booths fill up early with locals. Regular nightly specials are worth the stop: meat loaf on Monday, chef's choice on Tuesday, Italian on Wednesday, and seafood Thursday through Saturday. The chili is always good, and the beer of the month is $1.50 a bottle or can. *MM 99.4, BS, tel. 305/451–3722. Reservations accepted. Dress: casual. No credit cards. Closed Sun., holidays.*

¢ **Hideout Restaurant.** Located behind a grassy seafront yard in the Key Largo Undersea Park, where students learn marine science, this little place combines campus atmosphere with down-home Keys friendliness. Locals drive down for very affordable breakfasts and lunches and the $8.95 Friday-night all-you-can-eat fish fry, the only night dinner is served. You can get breakfast until 2 from a menu that includes oatmeal, omelets, Eggbeaters, fish and grits, lox, bagels and cream cheese, raisin toast, cinnamon toast, and hotcakes. Lunch fare comprises soups, sandwiches, burgers, and salads, plus specials like a fish sandwich, fried fish or clams, conch fritters, and shrimp baskets. Eat inside, in the windowed porch, or on the screened porch. *MM 103.5, OS, tel. 305/451–0128. No reservations. Dress: casual. No credit cards. No dinner Sat.–Thurs.*

Participant Sports

Biking

Riding along the 17 miles of the Card Sound Road from the mainland to the easier-to-navigate section on North Key Largo will remain difficult until the year 2000, when paved shoulders are expected to lessen the risks at least from the toll bridge to the south turn. By 1996, cyclists will be able to ride all but 2 of the next 20 miles south from MM 106 on Key Largo on a combination of bike paths and old roads separate from the Overseas Highway. **Key Largo Bikes** (MM 99, BS, 105 Laguna Ave. tel. 305/451–1910), just east of the Overseas Highway behind Blockbuster Video, stocks adult, children's, and tandem bikes—single-speed bicycles with coaster brakes and multispeed mountain bikes—for sale or rent.

Diving and Snorkeling

Captain Slate's Atlantis Dive Center (MM 106.5, OS, 51 Garden Cove Dr., tel. 305/451–3020 or 800/331–3483) is a full-service dive shop (NAUI, PADI, and YMCA certified) that also offers underwater weddings.

American Diving Headquarters (MM 105.5, BS, tel. 305/451–0037 or 800/634–8464) is the oldest dive shop in the Keys (since 1962) and operates a complete photographic department.

Quiescence Diving Service, Inc. (MM 103.5, BS, 103680 Overseas Hwy., tel. 305/451–2440) takes groups of up to six people per boat.

Capt. Corky's Diver's World of Key Largo (MM 92.5, OS, Box 1663, 33037, tel. 305/451–3200 or 305/852–5176) offers reef and wreck-diving packages, exploring the *Benwood*, Coast Guard cutters *Bibb* and *Duane*, and French and Molasses reefs.

Water Sports

Florida Bay Outfitters (MM 104, BS, tel. 305/451–3018) arranges camping, canoeing, kayaking, and sailing adventures in the Upper Keys and beyond, from 1 to 14 days. It also rents equipment, such as one- and two-person sea kayaks, by the hour, half day, or day.

Coral Reef Park Co. (John Pennekamp Coral Reef State Park, MM 102.5, OS, tel. 305/451–1621) runs scuba, snorkeling, and sailing trips on a 38-foot catamaran as well as glass-bottom boat tours. It also rents boats and equipment for sailing, canoeing, and windsurfing.

Nightlife

Breezers Tiki Bar (MM 103.8, BS, tel. 305/453–0000), in Marriott's Key Largo Bay Beach Resort, is popular with the smartly coiffed, brochure-look crowd. **Caribbean Club** (MM 104, BS, tel. 305/451–

9970) draws a hairy-faced, down-home crowd (and those drawn to them) to shoot the breeze while shooting pool. It's friendlier than you might imagine. **Coconuts** (MM 100, OS, tel. 305/451–4107), in the Marina Del Mar Resort, features year-round nightly entertainment. **Groucho's** (MM 100, OS, tel. 305/465–4329), in the Holiday Inn Key Largo, hosts comics Friday and Saturday nights. **Holiday Casino Cruises** (MM 100, OS, tel. 305/451–0000 or 800/971–1777) operates four-hour night (and day) sails aboard the 92-foot custom yacht *Pair-A-Dice* out beyond the 3-mile limit.

Tavernier and Plantation Key

Continuing south on U.S. 1 you'll cross Plantation Key (MM 93–86), named for the plantings of limes, pineapples, and tomatoes cultivated here at the turn of the century. In 1991, woodcarver and teacher Laura Quinn moved her **Florida Keys Wild Bird Rehabilitation Center** here. Enter at the sign that says, "Tern Here." Nowhere else in the Keys can you see bird life so close up. Many are kept for life because of injuries that can't be healed. Others are brought for rehabilitation and then set free. At any time the resident population can include ospreys, hawks, pelicans, cormorants, terns, and herons of various types. A short nature trail has been built into the mangrove forest (bring mosquito repellent), and a new office with a few items for sale has been added. A helpful notice explains that wild animals *do* feel pain when injured but don't scream because screaming would attract predators. *MM 93.6, BS, 93600 Overseas Hwy., Tavernier, tel. 305/852–4486. Donations welcome. Open daily sunrise–sunset.*

Budget Lodging **Tavernier Hotel.** This the oldest hotel in the Keys was built not long
$$ after the train came through in the first decade of this century. For years it verged on the flophouse side of fish camp, but Margaret Thompson, from Yorkshire, and her kids have fixed it up. Now the outside is all butter yellow with white trim and pretty gardens, and a hot tub, patio, and barbecues have been added. In the last year, improvements have been made inside; the windows have been double glazed to improve sleep, and the decor has been smartened up, though rooms are small as ever. Basic furnishings include either twin beds or a double bed with new chintz bed covers and Kmart art. There are no in-room phones, but each room has a fridge. Though the hotel isn't on the water, it's within easy walking distance of everything. Guests receive a 10% discount on meals at the Copper Kettle next door. Rates drop to inexpensive midweek. *91861 Overseas Hwy., Tavernier 33070, tel. 305/852–4131 or 800/515–4131, fax 305/852–4037. 17 rooms. Facilities: hot tub, barbecues, picnic tables, coin laundry. D, MC, V.*

Budget Dining **Craig's.** Like a scene from the 1950s, this is the sort of place where
$ locals fill the booths, tables, and counter stools; where waitresses
★ complain about their boyfriends; and where the male customers—fishermen, etc.—commiserate. The prices aren't quite 1950s-level, but they are affordable. Nightly $8.95 specials include Sunday's prime rib; Saturday's all-you-can-eat fish fry costs only $12.95. Specials sell out in two hours, so get there close to 7, when they start serving. The lunchtime specialty is a super fish sandwich made with grouper cheeks and served with American cheese (you can ask to have it left off), tomatoes, and tartar sauce. *MM 90.5, Plantation Key, tel. 305/852–9424. No reservations. Dress: casual. MC, V.*

Diving and Snorkeling **Florida Keys Dive Center** (MM 90.5, OS, 90500 Overseas Hwy., Box 391, Tavernier 33070, tel. 305/852–4599 or 800/433–8946) organizes dives from John Pennekamp Coral Reef State Park to Alligator Light. This center has two Coast Guard–approved dive boats and offers training from introductory scuba through instructor course.

Islamorada and Indian Key

Islamorada Chamber of Commerce (MM 82.5, BS, Box 915, Islamorada 33036, tel. 305/664–4503 or 800/322–5397).

Next down the Overseas Highway, on Windley Key, is **Islamorada,** notable for **Theater of the Sea,** where 12 dolphins, two sea lions, and an extensive collection of tropical fish swim in the pits of a 1907 railroad quarry. Allow at least two hours to attend the dolphin and sealion shows and visit all the exhibits, which include an injured birds of prey display, a "bottomless" boat ride, touch tank, a pool where sharks are fed by a trainer, and a 300-gallon "living reef" aquarium with invertebrates and small reef fishes. For an additional fee, you can even swim with dolphins for 30 minutes, after a 30-minute orientation. *MM 84.5, OS, Box 407, 33036, tel. 305/664–2431. Admission: $13.25 adults, $7.75 children 3–12. Swim with dolphins: $75, reservations required with 50% deposit; video or still photos: $70 (inquire at concession). Open daily 9:30–4.*

Watch for the **Hurricane Memorial** (MM 82) beside the highway. It marks the mass grave of 423 victims of the 1935 Labor Day hurricane. Many of those who perished were veterans who had been working on the Overseas Highway; they died when a tidal surge overturned a train sent to evacuate them. The art deco–style monument depicts wind-driven waves and palms bowing before the storm's fury.

Near here are three unusual state parks accessible only by water—and not easily at that; you'll need your own boat or a rental for each. The nearest boat source is **Robbie's Boat Rentals & Charters** (*see* Participant Sports, *below*). The **San Pedro Underwater Archaeological Preserve,** about 1 mile off the western tip of Indian Key, features an underwater, wrecked, 18th-century Spanish treasure fleet. You have to dive to see the remains.

Small as it is—only 11½ acres—**Indian Key State Historic Site** (OS) was a county seat town and base for wreckers (early 19th-century shipwreck salvagers) until an Indian attack wiped out the settlement in 1840. Dr. Henry Perrine, a noted botanist, was killed in the raid. Today you can see his plants overgrowing the town's ruins. Though no guide is available, trails are marked and sites labeled.

A virgin hardwood forest still cloaks **Lignumvitae Key State Botanical Site** (BS), punctuated only by the home and gardens that chemical magnate William Matheson built as a private retreat in 1919. Even with your own boat, you need to reserve a guided ranger tour, given Thursday–Monday at 10:30, 1, and 2:30 and costing $1 for ages over 6. Request a list of native and well-naturalized plants from the ranger. Contact **Long Key State Recreation Area** (*see* Long Key, *below*).

Budget Lodging
$$

Ragged Edge Resort. Most downstairs units now have screened porches at this unusually spacious, grassy little oceanside resort, quietly situated ¼ mile off the Overseas Highway. The two-story buildings are covered with rustic planks outside; inside, rooms are decorated with pine paneling, tile, carpet, chintz-covered furniture, and matching drapes. Each unit has a large tiled bath suite. The one motel room has a fridge, while all others have full kitchens with island counters, chopping blocks, lots of cabinets, and irons and ironing boards. Upper units have more windows and light and openbeam ceilings. The resort feels expensive, though it's surprisingly affordable because there's no staff to speak of and there aren't a lot of resort extras (like in-room phones). Amenities take the form of a two-story thatch-roof observation tower, picnic areas with barbecue pits, and free coaster-brake bikes. Though there's not much of a beach, you can swim off the large dock—a virtual rookery when boating activity isn't disturbing the pelicans, herons, anhingas, and terns. Look north and south, and only mangroves cluster the near distance. *MM 86.5, OS, 243 Treasure Harbor Rd., Islamorada 33036, tel. 305/852–5389. 10 units. Facilities: freshwater pool, bicycles, shuffleboard, barbecue grills. MC, V.*

$–$$ **Islamorada Inn Motel.** This 1950s-era one-story motel sits just far enough back from the highway that you can sleep. It is run in a real mom-and-pop style by Jay and Colleen Myers, who came from the Jersey shore in 1988. Rates vary based on demand, so you may save money if you show up at the last minute and negotiate. Rooms are clean and basic, with chintz bedspreads and bamboo wall decorations. There are no in-room phones and the TV isn't cable-connected, but there are efficiencies with kitchens. You can easily walk from here to Plantation Yacht Harbor, where the bay-side beach is open to the public, or to restaurants and shopping in town. *87760 Overseas Hwy., Islamorada 33036, tel. 305/852–9376. 7 rooms, 6 efficiencies. Facilities: pool. AE, D, DC, MC, V.*

$ **Bed & Breakfast of Islamorada.** Dottie Saunders, who has welcomed guests to the Keys since 1984, knows everything there is to do—and how to save. Guests feel at home in her modest house on quiet Old Highway and can pick from the guava, hog plum, and star fruit trees in the garden. Lots of nautical art, stained glass, and iron lamps are about, but the main mood setters at this relaxed place are cushiony furniture, an open kitchen (from which a full breakfast gets served daily), and good chatter. Both guest rooms are plainly furnished, each with its own tiled bath (one with shower-tub, the other with shower only). Bicycles and snorkeling gear are free for guests. In high season you pay between $45 and $55 for a double ($60 on holidays), and that includes breakfast for two. Book by the week and save even more. *81174 Old Highway, Islamorada 33036-9761, tel. 305/664–9321. 2 rooms. Facilities: bicycles, snorkeling gear. No credit cards.*

Budget Dining **Green Turtle Inn.** Once upon a time, around 1947, this was Sid & **$$** Roxie's Green Turtle Inn, and women in Betty Grable hairdos and guys in crew cuts would drive from miles around to socialize over dinner and dancing. Third owner Henry Rosenthal is still devoted to the era. Photographs of locals and famous visitors line the walls, and stuffed turtle dolls dangle from the ceiling over the bar. The background music is "Speak Low" and "In the Mood" in wood-paneled rooms kept on the dark side. Specialties remain from the old days, including a turtle chowder; conch fritters, nicely browned outside, light and fluffy inside; conch salad with vinegar, lime juice, pimiento, and pepper; alligator steak (tail meat) sautéed in an egg batter; and Key lime pie. Whole pies are available for carryout. *MM 81.5, OS, Islamorada, tel. 305/664–9031. No reservations. Dress: casual. AE, D, DC, MC, V. Closed Mon., Thanksgiving.*

$$ **Marker 88.** The best seats in chef-owner Andre Mueller's main din-★ ing room catch the last glimmers of sunset. Hostesses recite a lengthy list of daily specials and offer you a wine list with more than 200 entries. You can get a good steak or veal chop here, but 75% of the food served is seafood. Specialties include a robust conch chowder, banana-blueberry bisque, salad Trevisana (radicchio, leaf lettuce, Belgian endive, watercress, and sweet-and-sour dill dressing—President Bush's favorite), sautéed conch or alligator steak meunière, grouper Rangoon (served with chunks of papaya, banana, and pineapple in a cinnamon and currant jelly sauce), and Key lime pie. *MM 88, BS, Plantation Key, tel. 305/852–9315. Reservations advised. Dress: casual. AE, D, DC, MC, V. Closed Mon., Thanksgiving, Dec. 25. No lunch.*

$$ **Papa Joe's Landmark Restaurant.** Never mind the heavily chlorinated water and the pasty white bread when you can savor succulent dolphin and fresh green beans and carrots al dente. Here, they will still clean and cook your own catch: $8.95 up to one pound per person fried, broiled, or sautéed; $10.95 any other style, which includes meunière, blackened, coconut-dipped, Cajun, almandine, or Oscar (sautéed, topped with béarnaise sauce, crabmeat, and asparagus). Joe's—which dates from 1937—includes an upper-level, over-the-water tiki bar with 25 seats. "Early American dump" is how owner Frank Curtis describes the look: captain's chairs, mounted fish, hanging baskets, fish buoys, and driftwood strung year-round with Christmas lights. The decor never gets ahead of the food, which is first rate. An early-bird menu from 4 to 6 is priced at $7.95–$9.95. For dessert dive into the Key lime cake, peanut-butter pie, Grand Marnier cheesecake, mud pie, or rum chocolate cake. *MM 79.7, BS, 78786 Overseas Hwy., Islamorada, tel. 305/664–8756. Reservations accepted. Dress: casual. AE, MC, V. Closed Tues., Thanksgiving, Dec. 25.*

$$ **Squid Row.** It may look like just another cutely named, affordable
★ food stop on the way to Key West, but this attitude-free roadside eatery is devoted to serving the freshest fish you haven't caught yourself. Seafood wholesalers own it, and they supply the kitchen with fresh daily specials. Grouper grilled in a little vegetable oil, sprinkled with paprika, and drenched in fresh lemon comes divinely flaky. Alternately, enjoy it rolled in bread crumbs and sautéed, served with black pepper and citrus butter. Whatever's fresh and seasonal is best here: yellowtail, various snapper and shrimp dishes, and, of course, squid. Service is friendly and prompt, and the wait staff can talk about the specials without theatrics. They'll brew a fresh pot of coffee for guests and volunteer to wrap what's left of the flavorful, airy banana bread that comes at the start of the meal but is best kept for dessert. There's also a full bar with happy hour 5–7. *MM 81.9, OS, Islamorada, tel. 305/664–9865. Reservations accepted. Dress: casual. AE, D, DC, MC, V. Closed Wed.*

$$ **Whale Harbor Inn.** This coral-rock building has oyster shells cemented onto the walls, an old Florida Keys bottle collection, and a water mark at 7 feet as a reminder of Hurricane Donna's fury in 1960. Several restaurant employees rode out the storm in the building's lighthouse tower. The main attraction is the 50-foot-long, all-you-can-eat buffet, which includes a stir-fry area and a plentiful supply of shrimp, mussels, crayfish, and snow crab legs. The adjoining Dockside Restaurant and Lounge are open for breakfast, while the upstairs wood-trimmed raw bar and grill and the open-air bar, at eye level with the flying bridges of the marina charter fleet, are open to midnight. *MM 83.5, OS, Upper Matecumbe Key, tel. 305/ 664–4959. No reservations. Dress: casual. AE, D, DC, MC, V.*

Shopping for Good crafts buys can be found in two Islamorada shopping com-
Bargains pounds. **The Rain Barrel** (MM 86.7, BS, 86700 Overseas Hwy.), a 3-acre crafts village attended by free-running cats, represents 450 local and national artists and has eight resident artists. During the third weekend of March each year the largest arts show of the Keys takes place here, when some 20,000 visitors view the work of 100 artists. A tearoom and bakery are to be added by 1996.

Where salvage master Art McKee ran McKee's Treasure Museum in the 1950s and an enormous fabricated crustacean now stands, a dozen craft and specialty shops plus the excellent little Made to Order eat-in and carryout restaurant operate as **Treasure Village** (MM 86.7, OS).

Participant A new 4-mile section for bikes, south of Islamorada along Old High-
Sports way, extends most of the length of Lower Matecumbe Key. An addi-
Biking tional 1.8 miles along Indian Key Fill will be complete before the end of 1996.

Boating and **Treasure Harbor Marine** (MM 86.5, OS, 200 Treasure Harbor Dr.,
Fishing Islamorada, tel. 305/852–2458 or 800/352–2628, fax 305/852–5743) rents bareboat and crewed sailboats, from a 19-foot Cape Dory to a 41-foot custom-built ketch, plus a 43-foot Carver luxury cruising yacht. Reservations and advance deposit are required; there's a

$100-per-day captain fee. Also on site are a library of Keys videos for free use, a ship's store, and barbecue area.

Caloosa (MM 83.5, OS, Whale Harbor Marina, tel. 305/852–3200) is a 65-foot party fishing boat captained by Ray Jensen and his son David.

Gulf Lady (MM 79.8, OS, Islamorada, tel. 305/664–2628 or 305/664–2451) is a 65-foot deluxe party boat operating full day and night fishing trips from Bud 'n' Mary's Marina.

Robbie's Boat Rentals & Charters (MM 77.5, Islamorada 33036, tel. 305/664–9814) rents a 14-foot skiff with a 25-horsepower outboard (the smallest you can charter) for $25 an hour, $60 for four hours, and $80 for the day. Boats up to 27 feet are also available. At a second location (MM 84.5, OS, Holiday Isle, tel. 305/664–8070), Robbie's operates deep-sea- and reef-fishing boats.

Diving and Snorkeling **Lady Cyana Divers** (MM 85.9, BS, Box 1157, Islamorada 33036, tel. 305/664–8717 or 800/221–8717), a PADI five-star-rated training center, operates 40-, 45-, and 50-foot dive boats.

Nightlife Three of the most popular bars in the Keys are within a few miles of each other in Islamorada. The **Harbor Bar** (MM 83.5, OS, tel. 305/664–9888), next door to the Whale Harbor Inn (*see* Budget Dining, *above*) at Whale Harbor, is a rustic-looking wood-paneled upstairs bar with an immense shark strung from the rafters. It features live music nightly except Monday and has great views of the water. The liveliest bar in the Keys is the **Tiki in the Sky Bar** (MM 84.5, OS, tel. 305/664–2321 or 800/327–7070), actually built around a palm tree beneath a cane-and-shingle roof over the water at Holiday Isle. Every day from 4 to 8:30, live rock music plays at the over-the-water bar and grill at **Lorelei** (MM 82, BS, tel. 305/664–4656), behind the big mermaid across the road from the posh Cheeca Lodge resort. It's a big party scene for swells and swills alike.

Long Key

Continue on the Overseas Highway down to Long Key (MM 72–67), where you'll pass a tract of undisturbed forest on the right (BS) just below MM 67. Watch for a historical marker partially obscured by foliage. Pull off the road here and explore **Layton Trail,** named after Del Layton, who incorporated the city of Layton in 1963 and served as its mayor until his death in 1987. The marker relates the history of the Long Key Viaduct, the first major bridge on the rail line, and the Long Key Fishing Club, which Henry Flagler established nearby in 1906. Zane Grey, the noted western novelist, was president of the club. It consisted of a lodge, guest cottages, and storehouses—all obliterated by the 1935 hurricane. The clearly marked trail, which should take 20–30 minutes to walk, leads through tropical hardwood forest to a rocky Florida Bay shoreline overlooking shallow grass flats offshore.

Less than 1 mile below Layton Trail, turn left into **Long Key State Recreation Area,** then left again to the parking area for the **Golden Orb Trail.** This trail leads onto a boardwalk through a mangrove swamp alongside a lagoon where many herons and other water birds congregate in winter. The park also has a campground, a picnic area, a canoe trail through a tidal lagoon, and a not-very-sandy beach fronting on a broad expanse of shallow grass flats. Bring a mask and snorkel to observe the marine life in this rich nursery area. *MM 67.5, OS, Box 776, 33001, tel. 305/664–4815. Admission: $3.25 per vehicle with up to 8 people, plus 50¢ per person county surcharge. Bike or canoe rental: $10 deposit and $2.14 per hr (includes tax). Open daily 8–sunset.*

Below Long Key, the Overseas Highway crosses Long Key Channel on a new highway bridge beside the railroad's **Long Key Viaduct.** The second-longest bridge on the former rail line, this 2-mile-long structure has 222 reinforced-concrete arches. It ends at **Conch Key** (MM 63), a tiny fishing and retirement community.

Budget Lodging $$ **Lime Tree Bay Resort Motel.** Consider this the little resort that could—and did. New owners of this long-popular 2½-acre hideaway in the Middle Keys have spent two years at work on a makeover. Gone are the vestiges of a fish camp, replaced by attractive wicker- and rattan-furnished guest rooms, tropical art, and new kitchens in cottages. New, too, are a boat-rental hut, little sandy beach, landscaping, beautiful pool deck, hammocks, a gazebo, and covered walkway. The best units are the cottages out back (no bay views, unfortunately) and the four deluxe rooms upstairs, which have high cathedral ceilings and skylights. The upstairs Tree House is the best bet for two couples traveling together; it has a palm tree growing through its private deck and a divine canvas sling chair with a separately strung footrest. You can swim and snorkel in the shallow grass flats just offshore. *MM 68.5, BS, Box 839, Layton 33001, tel. 305/664–4740. 29 rooms. Facilities: restaurant, outdoor pool, beach, tennis court, shuffleboard, horseshoe pit, power and sailboat rentals, dive boats, charter boats, Jacuzzi, barbecue, picnic tables. AE, D, DC, MC, V.*

Camping RV and tent camping is available at **Long Key State Recreation Area** (MM 67.5, OS, Box 776, 33001, tel. 305/664–4815).

Fishing and Water Sports **Captain Kevin** (MM 68.5, BS, tel. 305/664–0750) arranges for backcountry fishing guides and operates recreational watercraft from Lime Tree Bay Resort.

Tour 2: The Middle Keys

Though fishing is king in the Middle Keys, in 1995 the town of Marathon, which is the main commercial hub, declared its intention to base its economy on what it calls ecotourism.

Arriving and Departing **By Plane** Direct service between Miami and newly expanded **Marathon Airport** (MM 52, BS, 9000 Overseas Hwy., tel. 305/743–2155) is provided by **American Eagle** (tel. 800/443–7300) and **Gulfstream International** (tel. 800/992–8532). **USAir Express** (tel. 800/428–4322) connects Marathon with Tampa.

Car-rental agencies at the airport are **Avis** (tel. 305/743–5428 or 800/331–1212) and **Budget** (tel. 305/743–3998 or 800/527–0700).

You can also fly into MIA and take a van or taxi to the Keys. To go to Marathon on **Keys Super Shuttle,** however, you must book an entire van (up to 11 passengers) at a cost of $250. For **Island Taxi** (*see* Arriving and Departing *in* Tour 1, *above,* for both), fares for one or two people are $175 to Marathon, and each additional person is $5. Reservations are required 24 hours in advance for arrivals, one hour for departures. Accompanied children under 12 ride free.

By Bus **Greyhound Lines** (tel. 305/374–7222 or 800/231–2222) stops in Marathon (Kingsail Resort, MM 50, BS).

Grassy Key

Past the Long Key Viaduct, you'll cross Conch Key, upscale Duck Key, and then come to Grassy Key (MM 60–57). Watch on the right for the **Dolphin Research Center** and the 35-foot-long concrete sculpture of the dolphin Theresa and her offspring Nat outside the former home of Milton Santini, creator of the original *Flipper* movie. The 14 dolphins here today are free to leave and return to the fenced area that protects them from boaters and predators. A half-day program called Dolph*Insight* teaches about dolphin biology and human-dolphin communications and allows you to touch the dolphins out of the water. A 2½-hour instruction-education program aptly called Swim with Dolphins enables you to do just that for 20 minutes. *MM 59, BS, Box 522875, Marathon Shores 33052, tel. 305/289–1121. Admission: $9.50 adults, $7.50 senior citizens, $6 children 4–12; Dolph*Insight*: $75; Swim with Dolphins: $90. Children 5–12 must swim with an accompanying, paying adult. Reserve for dolphin swim after 1st day of month for next month (e.g., Mar. 1 for Apr.). Open Wed.– Sun. 9–4; Dolph*Insight* Wed., Sat., Sun. at 9:15; walking tours Wed.–Sun. at 10, 11, 12:30, 2, 3:30. Closed Thanksgiving, Dec. 25, Jan. 1.*

Budget Lodging
$
★
Golden Grouper Motel. Jim and Linda Tyborchek run a wonderfully laid-back two-story place under the palms, with just enough of the ramshackle to be charming, but nothing shabby. It's back off the highway enough that traffic's no bother. Jim, a former social worker from Palm Beach County who opted for a low-stress lifestyle, turned to lobstering and bought this lodging. He named it the Golden Grouper, ostensibly because he bought it from people named Golden (anybody else in the Keys will tell you that "golden grouper" is a good-ole-boys' reference to an illicit substance). Linda's green thumb keeps the yard full of orchids, banana trees, and bougainvillea, where it's not covered with lobster traps, foam floats, hammocks, and cats. Aside from in-room phones, units have the basics—a laminate table and two chairs, small fridge, maybe an armchair with throw cushions, a quilted cover on the bed, a little dresser—but also some extras, like an eccentric sculpture or crown stenciling or maybe zappy aqua doors. The only caveat: Room 2 upstairs and the efficiency next to it share a partition that sound easily passes between. Otherwise it's affordable traveler heaven. *MM 57.5, OS, Marathon 33050, tel. 305/743–5285. 7 units. Facilities: fishing docks, rowboat, canoe, outdoor grill. MC, V.*

¢–$
★
Bonefish Resort. A caring, competent pair of nurses, Jackie and Paula, know how to make guests at their little oceanfront motel resort comfortable, to the point of driving them around if need be. They provide the hospitality of a B&B yet leave you a little more on your own. All the rooms and efficiencies are different—some have futons, some tub-showers, some tropical covers on director's chairs, some daybeds, some fishnets strung on walls, and others original art sent by former guests—but all are clean and well maintained, and all have newly painted palms on the doors. If you sleep lightly, ask for one of the rooms set back from the highway. The small waterfront has freely available canoes, a Windsurfer, pedal boat with ocean bucket for viewing beneath the surface, rowboat, shore pavilion, loaner fishing poles, and a Jacuzzi under a thatch hut. It's a wonderfully tropical atmosphere, utterly informal and perfect for slowing down. *MM 58, OS, 33050, tel. 305/743–7107. 12 units. Facilities: waterfront, boating facilities, Jacuzzi, gas grills, chickee with hammocks. MC, V.*

Budget Dining
$
Grassy Key Dairy Bar. New tables, new counters, and even white shirts in the kitchen are now found at this ever-improving little landmark that dates from 1959 and is marked by the Dairy Queen–style concrete ice-cream cones near the road. Locals and construction workers stop here for quick lunches. Owners-chefs George and Johnny Eigner are proud of their fresh-daily homemade bread, soups and chowders, and—a surprise to those who expect a vegetarian place—fresh seafood and fresh-cut beef. *MM 58.5, OS, tel. 305/743–3816. Reservations accepted. Dress: casual. No credit cards. Closed Sun., Mon. No lunch Sat.*

Marathon

Greater Marathon Chamber of Commerce (MM 48.7, BS, 3330 Overseas Hwy., Marathon 33050, tel. 305/743–5417 or 800/842–9580).

Continuing down U.S. 1, you will pass the road to **Key Colony Beach** (MM 54, OS), an incorporated city developed in the 1950s as a retirement community. It has a golf course and boating facilities. Soon after, you'll cross a bridge onto **Vaca Key** and enter **Marathon** (MM 53–47), the commercial hub of the Middle Keys.

★ On your right, across from the Kmart, are the **Museums of Crane Point Hammock.** This group of museums, part of a 63-acre tract that includes the last known undisturbed thatch-palm hammock, is owned by the Florida Keys Land Trust, a private, nonprofit conservation group. In the **Museum of Natural History of the Florida Keys,** behind a stunning bronze-and-copper door crafted by Roy Butler of Plantation, Florida, are dioramas and displays on the Keys' geology, wildlife, and cultural history. Also here is the **Florida Keys Children's Museum.** Outside, on the 1-mile indigenous loop trail, you can visit the remnants of a **Bahamian village,** site of the restored **George Adderly House,** the oldest surviving example of Conch-style architecture outside Key West. From November to Easter, weekly docent-led hammock tours may be available; bring good walking shoes and bug repellent. During **Pirates in Paradise,** an annual four-day festival held the first weekend in May, the museums sponsor a celebration of the region's history throughout the Middle Keys. *MM 50, BS, 5550 Overseas Hwy., Box 536, 33050, tel. 305/743–9100. Admission (including tour): $5 adults, $4 senior citizens, $2 students 13 and over. Open Mon.–Sat. 9–5, Sun. noon–5.*

Look to your left as you approach the new **Seven Mile Bridge**; there on **Knight's Key** (MM 47), the Pigeon Key Visitor's Center and gift shop have been set up in an old Florida East Coast Railway car. The key was an assembly site during construction of the bridge and today serves as the depot for shuttle access to **Pigeon Key** (MM 45). If you don't want to take the shuttle, you can walk across a 2-mile stretch of the **Old Seven Mile Bridge** (the entrance is across the highway from the shuttle depot); no private cars are allowed. Listed on the National Register of Historic Places, the old bridge is maintained by the Florida Department of Transportation to provide access to the key. An engineering marvel in its day, the bridge rested on 546 concrete piers spanning the broad expanse of water that separates the Middle and Lower keys. Pigeon Key itself was once a railroad work camp and later site of a bar and restaurant, a park, and government administration building. Should you decide to tour the key, where portions of the Arnold Schwarzenegger movie *True Lies* were filmed, you can watch a 1930 "home movie" of a trip on the Florida East Coast Railway from Key West to Miami. In 1993 the nonprofit Pigeon Key Foundation leased the site, a National Historic District, from Monroe County and started developing it as a center focusing on the encompassing culture of the Florida Keys. Its first project is the restoration of the old railroad work-camp buildings, the earliest of which date from 1908, and a museum recalling the history of the railroad and the Keys is taking shape, too. Among its first exhibits are two old Cuban fishing boats. The site is also being used for research on the Florida Bay system and for cancer studies involving sharks, conducted by Mote Marine Laboratories of Sarasota. For information, contact the Pigeon Key Foundation. *Box 500130, Pigeon Key 33050, tel. 305/289–0025, fax 305/289–1065. Shuttle: $1 each way; key admission and tour: $2. Shuttle: Tues.–Sun. 9–5.*

Return to U.S. 1 and proceed across the new Seven Mile Bridge (actually 6.79 miles long). Built between 1980 and 1982 at a cost of $45 million, it is believed to be the world's longest segmental bridge, with 39 expansion joints separating its cement sections. Each April runners gather in Marathon for the annual Seven Mile Bridge Run.

Budget Lodging
$$

Kingsail Resort Motel. For those who want a more professional, less mom-and-pop kind of place, this medium-size resort combines affordability with more facilities than you typically get for the price. The best units are the efficiencies, which come with private screened front porches and fully equipped kitchens. They have double beds with green bed covers, a wrought-iron glass-top table with four chairs, and an overall look of brick, rattan, and tile. Motel rooms are equally smart looking, with bentwood rattan pieces, pastel bed covers, and straw fans on the walls. The well-run property is large enough to make you feel part of a vacation community. *7050 Overseas Hwy., 33050, tel. 305/743–5246 or 800/423–7474, fax 305/743–8896. 13 rooms, 31 efficiencies. Facilities: pool, dock, boat ramp, tropical garden, outdoor grill, convenience store, laundry, trailer parking. AE, MC, V.*

$–$$

Valhalla Beach Resort Motel. Guests come back year after year to this unpretentious motel with the waterfront location of a posh resort. There are no fewer than three little beaches here, whereas many other Keys resorts have none. Bruce Schofield is the second-generation proprietor of this 1950s-era plain-Jane place. Clean and straightforward, with rattan and laminate furniture and refrigerators in the rooms, it's excellent for families because of the safe, shallow beaches. It's also far off the highway, so don't miss the sign. *MM 56.5, OS, Crawl Key, Rte. 2, Box 115, 33050, tel. 305/289–0616. 4 rooms, 8 efficiencies. Facilities: beaches, dock, boat ramp. No credit cards.*

$

Lagoon Resort & Marina. You don't expect a place this good to be this affordable in the Keys. Set ¼ mile back from the highway and with lots of land surrounding it, this '50s-era lodging comprises two rows of one-story units painted white with pink and soft-blue trim. A pebbly drive runs between the two rows—motel rooms and efficiencies backing onto the waterway on one side, two-bedroom cottages on the other. Sleeping rooms are small and have carpeting and flared bamboo headboards on the beds; some have a fridge. The tile bathrooms are fairly tiny. Efficiencies, too, are small, and the kitchenette amounts to a two-burner hot plate, but if four people share a two-room efficiency, the price becomes downright cheap. In a raised deck, the large swimming pool was retiled and painted in 1994. The property extends to a point of land along the bay, where, though there's no beach, chairs and chaises are set out on the pebbled, sandy shore. Pets are $5 per day. *MM 51, BS, 7200 Aviation Blvd., 33050, tel. 305/743–5463. 24 units. Facilities: pool, volleyball, dock, shuffleboard. AE, D, MC, V.*

¢

Sea Cove Motel. "So un–Sea Cove" is how one of the owners of this cheapest-of-the-cheap, yet not uncharming, motel described the considerable improvements lately made here. Next to the motel rooms and efficiencies, which poke down a gravel lane, are three houseboats at a plain but private dockside. One has multiple rooms on upper and lower decks; the other two are self-contained units. Rooms on the larger houseboat now have bathrooms with makeup lights, tile, and pretty floral papers. Low lighting over the beds gives the tiny rooms an intimate feel. Air-conditioning is now in all but one unit. Otherwise the motel has zero amenities. Don't expect housekeeping. Expect savings. Pets are allowed for an extra $5 a day. *MM 54, OS, 12685 Overseas Hwy., 33050, tel. 305/289–0800. 22 rooms (13 with shared baths), 4 efficiencies. Facilities: fishing pier, 3 barbecues, picnic tables. AE, D, MC, V.*

Budget Dining
$$
★

Gallagher's. You don't have to be dressed up to eat at this little, white, two-story roadhouse with an enclosed shack porch, but the hearty food is as gourmet as it gets along this highway. The portions here are so large they might register on the scales of the truck weighing station up the road. Humongous slabs of beef, huge portions of fish, and immense plates of chicken are served, accompanied by a relish tray, potatoes, salad, hot biscuits, and honey. Pies, cakes, sundaes, and sherbets round out the meal. For ambience, there's music from the 1930s and 1940s and a cozy, rustic decor composed of frame dividers, a big mural of palm trees and a sunset, and hanging ship lights. *MM 57.5, OS, tel. 305/289–0454. Reservations advised. Dress: casual. MC, V. Closed Tues.–Wed. May–Dec., Thanksgiving, Dec. 25, Super Bowl Sun. No lunch.*

$$ **Kelsey's.** The walls in this restaurant at the Faro Blanco Marine Resort are hung with boat paddles inscribed by the regulars and such celebrities as Joe Namath and Ted Turner. All entrées are accompanied by fresh-made yeast rolls brushed with drawn butter and Florida orange honey. You can bring your own cleaned and filleted catch for the chef to prepare. Dessert offerings change nightly and may include Mrs. Kelsey's original macadamia pie (even though she's sold out and gone to the old Riverview Hotel in New Smyrna Beach) and Key lime cheesecake. *MM 48, BS, 1996 Overseas Hwy., tel. 305/743–9018. Reservations required. Dress: casual. AE, MC, V. Closed Mon. No lunch.*

$$ **WatersEdge.** The name of this popular restaurant at the Hawk's Cay Resort has changed, but you can still dine indoors or under the dockside canopy. A collection of historic photos on the walls depicts the railroad era, the development of Duck Key (which later became Hawk's Cay), and many of the notables who have visited here. Dinners include soup and a 40-item salad bar. Specialties range from homemade garlic bread, Swiss onion soup, Florida stone crab claws (in season), and steaks to mud pie and coffee-ice-cream pie with a whipped-cream topping. *MM 61, OS, tel. 305/743–7000, ext. 3627. Reservations accepted. Dress: casual. AE, D, DC, MC, V. No lunch off-season (generally Easter–mid-Dec.).*

$ **Herbie's.** A local favorite for lunch and dinner since the 1940s and winner of many local awards, Herbie's has three small rooms with two counters. Indoor diners sit at wood picnic tables or the bar; those in the screened outdoor room use vinyl-covered concrete tables. Specialties include spicy conch chowder with chunks of tomato and crisp conch fritters with homemade horseradish sauce. *MM 50.5, BS, 6350 Overseas Hwy., tel. 305/743–6373. No reservations. Dress: casual. No credit cards. Closed Sun. and 1 month in fall (usually Oct.).*

$ **7 Mile Grill.** This open-air diner built in 1954 at the Marathon end of ★ Seven Mile Bridge has walls liberally lined with beer cans, mounted fish, sponges, and signs describing individual menu items. It's open breakfast, lunch, and dinner, and favorites include fresh-squeezed OJ, a cauliflower and broccoli omelet, conch chowder, the fresh fish sandwich of the day, and a foot-long chili dog on a toasted sesame roll. The daily special could be a Caesar salad with marinated chicken, popcorn shrimp, chicken almandine, grouper, or snapper. Even if you're not a dessert eater, don't pass up the authentic Key lime pie or, for a change, the peanut-butter pie, served near frozen, in a chocolate-flavor shell. Made with cream cheese, it's a cross between pudding and ice cream. *MM 47, BS, 1240 Overseas Hwy., tel. 305/743–4481. No reservations. Dress: casual. No credit cards. Closed Wed.–Thurs., Dec. 24–1st Fri. after New Year's, and at owner's discretion Aug.–Sept.*

$ **Village Cafe.** Set in the local shopping center, this place is wonderfully small-town America. The customers include high-schoolers, moms pushing infants in carriages, and guys from the hardware store, and the same crowd shows up mornings for breakfast, afternoons for coffee, and evenings for dinner. Many more show up for lunch, when a line often forms. The decor is clean and cool, gray and white, with floor tiles and acoustical ceiling tile. On the menu are pizzas, hot sandwiches, salads, pastas, and other Italian dishes—calamari, fettuccine Alfredo, gnocchi with red sauce, and various specialties cooked with oregano, sausage, meatballs, and Parmesan

cheese. Breakfasts are more American, and Sunday features breakfast and dinner buffets. *MM 50.5, BS, Gulfside Village Shopping Center, tel. 305/743–9090. No reservations. Dress: casual. D, MC, V. Closed some holidays.*

Shopping for Bargains **Food for Thought** (MM 51, BS, 5800 Overseas Hwy., tel. 305/743–3297), in the Gulfside Village, is a bookstore and a natural-foods store with a good selection of Florida titles—including *The Monroe County Environmental Story*, "must" reading for anyone who wants the big picture on the Keys ($35—not cheap but worth it).

T.L.C. Nursery & Botanical Garden (7455 Overseas Hwy., tel. 305/743–6428) lets you browse through a fairyland of brilliant plantings, indoors and out, all for sale. The displays make up one of the Keys' better attractions.

Participant Sports *Biking* The Marathon area is popular with cyclists. Some of the best paths include those along Aviation Boulevard on the bay side of Marathon Airport, the four-lane section of the Overseas Highway through Marathon, Sadowski Causeway to Key Colony Beach, Sombrero Beach Road from the Overseas Highway to the Marathon public beach, and the roads on Boot Key (across a bridge from Vaca Key on 20th St., OS). There's also easy cycling at the south end of Marathon, where a 1-mile off-road path connects to the 2 remaining miles of the Old Seven Mile Bridge to Pigeon Key, where locals like to ride to watch the sunset. **Equipment Locker Sport & Cycle** (MM 53, BS, 11518 Overseas Hwy., tel. 305/289–1670) rents mountain bikes, multispeed road bikes, and single-speed adult and children's bikes.

Boating and Fishing **Marathon Lady** and **Marathon Lady III** (MM 53, OS, tel. 305/743–5580) are a pair of 65-footers that offer half-day and full-day fishing charters from the Vaca Cut Bridge just north of Marathon.

Captain Pip's (MM 47.5, BS, ¼ mi east of Seven Mile Bridge, tel. 305/743–4403) lets you rent your own 20-foot or larger motor-equipped boat.

Diving and Snorkeling **Hall's Diving Center and Career Institute** (MM 48.5, BS, 1994 Overseas Hwy., tel. 305/743–5929 or 800/331–4255) offers trips to Looe Key, Sombrero Reef, Delta Shoal, Content Key, Coffins Patch, and the 110-foot wreck *Thunderbolt*.

Tour 3: The Lower Keys

Arriving and Departing **Greyhound Lines** (tel. 305/374–7222 or 800/231–2222) stops on Looe Key (Ramrod Resort, MM 27.5, OS).

Guided Tours **Reflections Kayak Nature Tours** (MM 30, OS/BS, Box 430861, Big Pine Key 33043, tel. 305/872–2896) operates daily trips into the Great White Heron Wildlife Refuge and Everglades National Park from the Upper and Lower keys. The Lower Keys are considered home, however, and "away" trips depend on the number who sign up. Tours last about three hours, and $45 per person covers granola bars, fresh fruit, raisins, spring water, as well as a tour guide familiar with bird life, a printed bird guide, and waterproof binoculars. Snorkeling gear (if you want it) is extra.

Strike Zone Charters (MM 29.5, BS, Big Pine Key, tel. 305/872–9863 or 800/654–9560), run by Lower Keys native Capt. Larry Threlkeld, offers fishing and island sightseeing into the backcountry; Looe Key and offshore snorkeling, diving, and deep-sea-fishing outings; and three- and five-day trips into the Dry Tortugas.

Bahia Honda Key

★ Here you'll find **Bahia Honda State Park** and its sandy (most of the time) beach. Lateral drift builds up the beach in summer; storms whisk away much of the sand in winter. The park's Silver Palm Trail leads through a dense tropical forest where you can see rare West Indian plants, including the Geiger tree, sea lavender, Key spider lily, bay cedar, thatch and silver palms, and several species found nowhere else in the Florida Keys: the West Indies yellow satinwood, Catesbaea, Jamaica morning glory, and wild dilly. The park also includes a campground, cabins, gift shop, snack bar, marina, and dive shop offering offshore-reef snorkel trips, scuba trips, and boat rentals. *MM 37, OS, Box 782, Big Pine Key 33043, tel. 305/872-2353. Admission: $3.25 per vehicle with up to 8 people, plus 50¢ per person county surcharge. Open daily 8–sunset; concession open 8–5 (food to 6:30).*

Camping   The State of Florida operates RV and tent campgrounds as well as rental cabins in **Bahia Honda State Park** (*see above*). The best bet to reserve one is to call at 8 AM 60 calendar days before your planned visit.

Big Pine Key

Lower Keys Chamber of Commerce (MM 31, OS, Box 511, Big Pine Key 33043, tel. 305/872-2411 or 800/872-3722).

Cross the Bahia Honda Bridge and continue past Spanish Harbor Key and Spanish Harbor Channel onto Big Pine Key (MM 32–30), where signs alert drivers to be on the lookout for Key deer. Every year cars kill 50 to 60 of the delicate creatures. A subspecies of the Virginia white-tailed deer, Key deer once ranged throughout the Lower and Middle keys, but hunting and habitat destruction reduced the population to fewer than 50 in 1947. In 1954 the **National Key Deer Refuge** was established to protect them, and the deer herd grew to about 750 by the early 1970s. But the government owns only about a third of Big Pine Key, and as the human population on the remaining land grew during the 1980s, the deer herd declined again until today only 250 to 300 remain. To visit refuge headquarters, turn right at the stoplight, bear left at the fork onto Key Deer Boulevard (Route 940), and follow the signs. A new, more accessible refuge office has opened in the Big Pine Shopping Plaza (off Wilder Rd., tel. 305/872-2239).

The best place in the refuge to see Key deer is on **No Name Key,** a sparsely populated island just east of Big Pine Key. To get there from the Refuge Headquarters, return east on Watson Boulevard to Wilder Road, and turn left. Go 3½ miles from Key Deer Boulevard across the Bogie Channel Bridge and onto No Name Key. At the end of the road you can get out of your car to walk around, but close all doors and windows to keep raccoons from wandering in. Deer may turn up along this road at any time of day—especially in early morning and late afternoon. Admire their beauty, but don't try to feed them—it's against the law.

Budget   **The Barnacle.** Three bed-and-breakfasts, all Keys-y, all up on stilts,
Lodging   all serving full breakfast, and all within a mile of each other, make
$$ Big Pine Key the B&B hub of the Keys shy of Key West. The Barna-
★   cle is run by Wood and Joan Cornell, who for years operated the well-known Reluctant Panther in Manchester, Vermont. There are two rooms in the main house, both on the second floor, and two in the Cottage, one upstairs and one down but each with its own kitchen. Guest rooms are large, and those in the main house open to an atrium, where a hot tub sits in a beautiful garden screened to the sea and sky. Throughout both houses, furnishings are colorful and whimsical, and many were collected from around the world. Wood Cornell's stained-glass windows are very impressive, and floors are mostly paver tiles. *Long Beach Dr., east off Overseas Hwy. just south of MM 33, Rte. 1, Box 780 A, 33043, tel. 305/872-3298. 4 rooms. Facili-*

ties: beach, bicycles, rafts, rubber boat, kayak, dock, boat ramp, hot
tub, tiki hut and barbecue. No credit cards.

$$ **Casa Grande.** This B&B, right next to the Barnacle, is run by Jon
★ and Kathleen Threlkeld, longtime friends and former business asso-
ciates of the Cornells in upstate New York. Though operated sepa-
rately, the inns share many facilities and are connected on the land
side by a pond and drive and on the sea side by the beach. (It's impor-
tant to note, however, that although all three B&Bs are on the
beach, the sea deepens very gradually and the shore is often covered
with seaweed. The B&Bs provide saltwater sneakers, or you may
take a boat to deeper water for swimming.) Casa Grande is marked-
ly Mediterranean, with a massive Spanish door and mucho Mexican
furnishings. The spacious guest rooms have carpeting, high open-
beam ceilings, and a small fridge. Here, too, there is a screened, sec-
ond-story atrium facing the sea. *Long Beach Dr., east off Overseas
Hwy. just south of MM 33, Box 378, 33043, tel. 305/872–2878. 3
rooms. Facilities: beach, bicycles, rafts, rubber boat, kayak, dock,
boat ramp, hot tub, tiki hut and barbecue. No credit cards.*

$$ **Deer Run.** Just down the road is the most casual of the three B&Bs,
populated by lots of animals: cats, caged birds, and a herd of deer,
which forages along the beach and lush seafront gardens. The inn is
run by burned-out real-estate operator and 35-year Big Pine resident Sue Abbott, who, like her fellow innkeepers, is caring and in-
formed, well settled and generously hospitable. Two downstairs
units occupy part of a onetime garage area. Though a wall blocks any
sea view from one of them, the other two units, including one upstairs, have wonderful sea views, variously through the trees and
mulched pathways. Guests have use of a living room and screened
porch. Like its neighbors, this offers some of the best value for the
money in the Keys. *Long Beach Dr., east off Overseas Hwy. just
south of MM 33, Box 431, 33043, tel. 305/872–2015. 3 rooms. Facilities: beach, gardens. No credit cards.*

Budget Dining **Island Reef Restaurant.** This Keys-perfect cottage restaurant by the
¢–$ road dates from the Flagler era. It has six counter seats, 15 tables
covered with bright beneath-the-sea-blue prints, and outdoor tables—not to mention outdoor rest rooms. Nightly changing dinner
specials that start at $9 are all served with soup or salad; choice of
potato; vegetable; rolls and scones; homemade pie, pudding, or ice
cream; and tea or coffee. Entrées include seafood, steaks, veal,
frogs' legs, and vegetarian stir-fry. *MM 31.25, BS, tel. 305/872–
2170. No reservations. Dress: casual. MC, V. Closed Dec. 25. No
breakfast or lunch Sun.*

Participant Opportunities in the Lower Keys are mostly for off-road bikes. On
Sports this key, a good 10 miles of paved and unpaved roads run from MM
Biking 30.3, BS, along Wilder Road across the bridge to No Name Key and
along Key Deer Boulevard into the National Key Deer Refuge. You
might even see some small Key deer. Stay off the trails that obviously lead into wetlands, where fat tires can do damage.

Diving and National Key Deer Refuge contains reefs where the Keys' northern
Snorkeling margin drops off into the Gulf of Mexico. It attracts fewer divers
than the better-known Atlantic Ocean reefs. Another favorite Gulf
spot for local divers is the Content Key (MM 30), 5 miles off Big Pine
Key.

The Torch Keys and Ramrod Key

Return to U.S. 1 and continue on across **Big Torch, Middle Torch,**
and **Little Torch** keys (named for the torchwood tree, which settlers
used for kindling because it burns easily even when green). Next
comes **Ramrod Key** (MM 27.5), a base for divers headed for **Looe Key
National Marine Sanctuary** (216 Ann St., Key West 33040, tel. 305/
292–0311), which contains a reef 5 miles offshore, perhaps the most

beautiful and diverse coral community in the entire region. It has large stands of elkhorn coral on its eastern margin, large purple sea fans, and abundant populations of sponges and sea urchins. On its seaward side, it has an almost-vertical drop-off to a depth of 50–90 feet. The reef is named for H.M.S. *Looe*, a British warship wrecked there in 1744.

Diving and Fishing **Looe Key Dive Center** (MM 27.5, OS, Box 509, Ramrod Key 33042, tel. 305/872–2215 or 800/942–5397), the dive shop closest to Looe Key National Marine Sanctuary, offers overnight dive packages.

Scandia-Tomi (MM 25, BS, Summerland Chevron Station, Summerland Key, tel. 305/745–8633 or 800/257–0978), under Capt. Bill Hjorth, takes up to six passengers on reef-, deep-drop-, and off-shore-fishing trips; he also takes divers and snorkelers to Looe Key.

Lower Sugarloaf Key

A performing dolphin named Sugar lives in a lagoon behind the very visible **Sugar Loaf Lodge** (*see* Budget Lodging, *below*). From the motel, follow the paved road northwest for ⁹⁄₁₀ mile, past an airstrip, and bear right down a newly paved road. One-tenth of a mile later, in bleak, gravel-strewn surroundings, you'll find a reconstruction of R. C. Perky's **bat tower.** Perky, an early real-estate promoter, built the tower in 1929 to attract mosquito-eating bats, but no bats ever roosted in it.

Budget Lodging $$ **Sugar Loaf Lodge & Marina.** This well-landscaped older motel overlooking mangrove islands and Upper Sugarloaf Sound has one building canal-side, with soft beds and an eclectic assortment of furniture, and another bayside, with high ceilings, wall murals, and balconies on the second floor. The friendly dolphin Sugar inhabits a lagoon just outside the restaurant; diners can watch her perform through a picture window. Several additional dolphins were at least temporarily cared for here in 1995 as part of a train-for-release program. *MM 17, BS, Box 148, 33044, tel. 305/745–3211, fax 305/745–3389. 44 rooms, 11 efficiencies. Facilities: restaurant, deli, lounge, pool, tennis court, miniature golf course, convenience store, coin laundry, 3,000-ft private airstrip. AE, D, DC, MC, V.*

Budget Dining $$ ★ **Mangrove Mama's.** This lattice-front conch house is a remnant from a time when trains outnumbered cars in the Keys, around 1919. Fresh fish, seafood, some decent beers, and rave-worthy Key lime pie are served. Capt. Eddie's Hideaway, a bar, has been relocated into an old house in back of the dining area. Its Tennessee oak, concrete floors, Keys art on the walls, and lights twinkling at night in the banana trees all contribute to the romantic ambience here. Free Sunday-night reggae and $9 barbecue make Mangrove Mama's a must. *MM 20, BS, tel. 305/745–3030. Reservations accepted. Dress: casual. MC, V. Closed Dec. 25.*

Biking Another 10 miles of roads with little car traffic, Routes 939 and 939-A leave the Overseas Highway on the ocean side at MM 20 (Mangrove Mama's) and loop back at MM 17 (Sugar Loaf Lodge).

Big Coppitt Key, Boca Chica Key, and Stock Island

Continue on through the Saddlebunch Keys and Big Coppitt Key to **Boca Chica Key** (MM 10), site of the **Key West Naval Air Station.** You may hear the roar of jet fighter planes in this vicinity.

At last you reach **Stock Island** (MM 5), the gateway to Key West. Pass the 18-hole **Key West Resort Golf Course,** then turn right onto Junior College Road and pause at the **Key West Botanical Garden,** where the Key West Garden Club has labeled an extensive assortment of native and exotic tropical trees.

Budget Dining
$

Rusty Anchor. They clang a big bell when orders are ready in this big barn of a place across the street from the old dog track on Stock Island. This restaurant has been here forever, part of a fishery that never had a proper street address and still hasn't. Customers—fisherfolk, businesspeople from Key West, Navy pilots from Boca Chica—come here looking for the freshest seafood. There's great service, too, motivated by a boss who sees that help gets major holidays off, including Fantasy Fest. Captains' chairs are set at hatch-cover tables, lots of local art and photos hang on walls, and a wood-trimmed bar sits at one end. Specialties include jumbo fried shrimp, steamed shrimp, broiled or fried sea scallops, fresh local yellowtail or grouper, conch steak, Florida lobster tail, stone crab claws in season, oysters and clams on the half shell, and what they call their gorilla burger (with bacon, cheese, and coleslaw). Try Key lime pie or mud pie for dessert. You'll groan when you stand up but not when you see the tab. *5th Ave., Stock Island, tel. 305/294–5369. No reservations. Dress: casual. AE, D, DC, MC, V. Closed Sun., holidays, including Fantasy Fest.*

Biking

A mile of Big Coppitt Key will get a separated path along the highway before the end of 1996.

Tour 4: Key West

In April 1982, the U.S. Border Patrol threw a roadblock across the Overseas Highway just south of Florida City to catch drug runners and illegal aliens. Traffic backed up for miles as Border Patrol agents searched vehicles and demanded that the occupants prove U.S. citizenship. City officials in Key West, outraged at being treated like foreigners by the federal government, staged a mock secession and formed their own "nation," the so-called Conch Republic. They hoisted a flag and distributed mock border passes, visas, and Conch currency. The embarrassed Border Patrol dismantled its roadblock, and now an annual festival recalls the secessionists' victory.

The episode exemplifies Key West's odd station in Florida affairs. Situated 150 miles from Miami and just 90 miles from Havana, this tropical island city has always maintained its strong sense of detachment, even after it was connected to the rest of the United States—by the railroad in 1912 and by the Overseas Highway in 1938.

The U.S. government acquired Key West from Spain in 1821 along with the rest of Florida. The Spanish had named the island Cayo Hueso (Bone Key) after the Native American skeletons they found on its shores. In 1822, Uncle Sam sent Commodore David S. Porter to the Keys to chase pirates away.

For three decades, the primary industry in Key West was "wrecking"—rescuing people and salvaging cargo from ships that foundered on the nearby reefs. According to some reports, when pickings were lean, the wreckers hung out lights to lure ships aground. Their business declined after 1852, when the federal government began building lighthouses along the reefs.

In 1845 the Army started construction of Ft. Taylor, which held Key West for the Union during the Civil War. After the war, an influx of Cuban dissidents unhappy with Spain's rule brought the cigar industry to Key West. Fishing, shrimping, and sponge-gathering became important industries, and a pineapple-canning factory opened. Major military installations were established during the Spanish-American War and World War I. Through much of the 19th century and into the second decade of the 20th, Key West was Florida's wealthiest city in per-capita terms.

In the 1920s the local economy began to unravel. Modern ships no longer needed to provision in Key West, cigar making moved to Tampa, Hawaii dominated the pineapple industry, and the sponges succumbed to a blight. Then the Depression hit, and even the military moved out. By 1934 half the population was on relief. The city defaulted on its bond payments, and the Federal Emergency Relief Administration took over the city and county governments.

Federal officials began promoting Key West as a tourist destination. They attracted 40,000 visitors during the 1934–35 winter season. Then the 1935 Labor Day hurricane struck the Middle Keys, sparing Key West but wiping out the railroad and the tourist trade. For three years, until the Overseas Highway opened, the only way in and out of town was by boat.

Ever since, Key West's fortunes have waxed and waned with the vagaries of world affairs. An important naval center during World War II and the Korean conflict, the island remains a strategic listening post on the doorstep of Fidel Castro's Cuba.

As a tourist destination, Key West has a lot to sell—superb frost-free weather with an average temperature of 79°F, quaint 19th-century architecture, and a laid-back lifestyle. Promoters have fostered fine restaurants, galleries and shops, and new museums to interpret the city's intriguing past. There's also a growing calendar of artistic and cultural events and a lengthening list of annual festivals (*see* Festivals *in* Florida Keys Basics, *above*). No other city of its size—a mere 2 miles by 4 miles—offers the joie de vivre of this one.

Yet as elsewhere that preservation has successfully revived once tired towns, next have come those unmindful of style, eager for a buck. Duval Street is becoming show biz—an open-air mall of T-shirt shops and tour shills. Mass marketers directing the town's tourism have attracted cruise ships, which dwarf the town's skyline and flood Duval Street with day-trippers who gawk at the earringed hippies with dogs in their bike baskets and the otherwise oddball lot of locals. You can still find fun, but the best advice is to come sooner rather than later.

Arriving and Continuous improvements in service now link airports in Miami,
Departing Fort Lauderdale/Hollywood, Naples, Orlando, and Tampa directly
By Plane with **Key West International Airport** (S. Roosevelt Blvd., tel. 305/296–5439 for information, 305/296–7223 for administration). Service is provided by **Airways International Airlines** (tel. 305/292–7777), **American Eagle, Cape Air** (tel. 800/352–0714), **Comair** (tel. 800/354–9822), **Gulfstream International,** and **USAir/USAir Express** (tel. 800/428–4322).

The airport has booths for **Avis** (tel. 305/296–8744 or 800/831–2847), **Budget** (tel. 305/294–8868), **Dollar** (tel. 305/296–9921 or 800/800–4000), **Hertz** (tel. 305/294–1039 or 800/654–3131), and **Value** (tel. 305/296–7733 or 800/468–2583). Companies in other Key West locations include **Thrifty** (3841 N. Roosevelt Blvd., tel. 305/296–6514 or 800/367–2277) and **Tropical Rent-A-Car** (1300 Duval St., tel. 305/294–8136). **Enterprise Rent-A-Car** (3031 N. Roosevelt Blvd., tel. 305/292–0220 or 800/325–8007) has several Keys locations, including participating hotels. Don't fly into Key West and drive out; there are substantial drop-off charges for leaving a Key West car in Miami.

For those flying to MIA, **Keys Super Shuttle** charges $300 for an entire van to Key West, while **Island Taxi** costs $200 for one or two people, $10 each additional person (*see* Arriving and Departing *in* Tour 1, *above*, for both).

By Bus **Greyhound Lines** (tel. 305/374–7222 or 800/231–2222) stops in Key West (615½ Duval St., tel. 305/296–9072).

By Car Allow five hours on U.S. 1 from Florida City to Key West on a good day. Without traffic tie-ups the drive may take only four. After midnight, you can make the trip in three—but then you miss the scenery.

Getting Around By Bus The **City of Key West Port and Transit Authority** (tel. 305/292–8165) operates two bus routes: Mallory Square (counterclockwise around the island) and Old Town (clockwise around the island). The fare is 75¢ (exact change) adults, 35¢ senior citizens, students, children under five, and people with disabilities.

By Taxi Four cab companies in Key West originate from the same dispatch area (1816 Flagler Ave.): **Island Transportation Services** (tel. 305/296–1800), **Maxi-Taxi Sun Cab System** (tel. 305/294–2222 or 305/296–7777), **Pink Cabs** (tel. 305/296–6666), and **Yellow Cabs of Key West** (tel. 305/294–2227). All operate around the clock. The fare from the airport for two or more to New Town is $5 per person with a cap of $15; to Old Town it's $6 and $20. Otherwise meters register $1.40 to start, 35¢ for each ⅕ mile, and 35¢ for every 50 seconds of waiting time.

Guided Tours The **Conch Tour Train** (tel. 305/294–5161) is a 90-minute, narrated tour of Key West, traveling 14 miles through Old Town and around the island, daily 9–4:30. Board at Mallory Square Depot every half hour, or at Roosevelt Boulevard Depot (just north of the Quality Inn) every hour on the half hour. The cost is $14 adults, $6 children 4–12.

Old Town Trolley (1910 N. Roosevelt Blvd., tel. 305/296–6688) operates 12 trackless trolley-style buses, departing every 30 minutes daily 9–4:30, for 90-minute, narrated tours of Key West. The trolleys are smaller than the Conch Tour Train and go places the train won't fit. You may disembark at any of 14 stops and reboard a later trolley. The cost is $14 adults, $6 children 4–12.

The **Key West Nature Bike Tour** departs from Moped Hospital (Truman Ave. and Simonton St., tel. 305/294–2882) on Sunday at 10:30 and Tuesday–Saturday at 9 and 3. The cost is $12 per person with your own bike, or you can rent a clunker for $3.

There are lots of boat tours around town. **Adventure Charters** (6810 Front St., 33040, tel. 305/296–0362) operates tours on the 42-foot catamaran *Island Fantasea* for a maximum of six passengers. Trips range from a half day into the backcountry to daylong and overnight sojourns. **M/V *Discovery*** (Land's End Marina, 251 Margaret St., 33040, tel. 305/293–0099) and the 65-foot **M/V *Fireball*** (Ocean Key House, 2 Duval St., 33040, tel. 305/296–6293 or 305/294–8704) are two glass-bottom boats. **M/V *Miss Key West*** (Ocean Key House, 2 Duval St., 33040, tel. 305/296–8865) offers a one-hour, narrated cruise that explores Key West's harbor up to ½ mile from shore. The sundown cruise includes live music. **Vicki Impallomeni** (23 Key Haven Terr., 33040, tel. 305/294–9731), an authority on the ecology of Florida Bay, features half-day and full-day charters in her 22-foot Aquasport open fisherman, *The Imp II*. Families especially like exploring with Captain Vicki because of her ability to teach youngsters. Tours depart from Murray's Marina (MM 5, Stock Island), and reservations are recommended, at least a month ahead in winter. *Wolf* (Schooner Wharf, Key West Seaport [end of Greene St.], 33040, tel. 305/296–9653) is Key West's tall ship and the flagship of the Conch Republic. The 74-foot, 44-passenger topsail schooner operates day cruises as well as sunset and starlight cruises with live music.

Mosquito Coast Island Outfitters & Kayak Guides (1107 Duval St., 33040, tel. 305/294–7178) runs full-day, guided sea kayak tours around the lush backcountry marsh just east of Key West. Reservations are required. The $45-a-day charge covers transportation and supplies, including snorkeling gear, water, and granola.

The Historic Florida Keys Preservation Board (*see* Exploring Key West, *below*) distributes a free detailed pamphlet and map of the self-guiding **Cuban Heritage Trail,** which comprises 36 sites embodying Key West's close connection to the historical affairs of Cuba.

"Pelican Path" is a free walking guide to Key West published by the Old Island Restoration Foundation. The tour discusses the history and architecture of 43 structures along 25 blocks of 12 Old Town streets. Pick up a copy at the Greater Key West Chamber of Commerce (*see* Exploring Key West, *below*).

"Solares Hill's Walking and Biking Guide to Old Key West," by historian Sharon Wells, contains eight walking tours, covering the city as well as the Key West cemetery. Free copies are available from the Greater Key West Chamber of Commerce and many hotels and stores.

Writers' Walk is a one-hour guided tour past the residences of prominent authors who have lived in Key West (Elizabeth Bishop, Robert Frost, Ernest Hemingway, Wallace Stevens, Tennessee Williams, among others). Guides share richly from the anecdotal trove. Tours depart at 10:30 Saturdays from the Heritage House Museum (410 Caroline St.) and on Sundays from in front of Hemingway House (907 Whitehead St.). Tickets, which are $10, can be purchased from Key West Island Bookstore (513 Fleming St.), Blue Heron Books (538 Truman Ave.), or Caroline Street Books (800 Caroline St.) or at time of departure if the tour isn't full.

Key West for Free—or Almost The best scheduled show in town is sunset at Mallory Square, Key West's signature ritual. An hour before sunset everybody begins to drift over. The Conch Salad Man's setting up, as are the sellers of Key lime tarts. So are the escape artist, the kilted bagpipers, the jugglers with their Indian clubs, the cats preparing to jump through hoops of fire. By a half hour before sunset, the dock is packed with the darnedest cocktail-party crush you ever saw—the salute to sunset's only an excuse. Just as the sun's about to drop behind Tank Island, usually somebody in a sailboat has figured the moment just right and sails silhouetted right across the flaming ball. The sun plops, everybody claps, the pipers play "Auld Lang Syne," and everybody drifts away for drinks and supper. It may be the best hour or two you'll spend in this town, and it's all free.

Otherwise try people-watching along Duval Street, or enjoy one of the well-detailed walking tours (*see* Guided Tours, *above*) for the price of their descriptive publications. Videos about the reef of the Florida Keys are free for the viewing at the offices of the **Reef Relief Environmental Center** (*see* Exploring Key West, *below*).

At the Land's End Marina, many colorful vendors operate from stalls. Stop for a drink at the open-air **Schooner Wharf Bar** (*see* the Arts and Nightlife, *below*); then drop in at the **Waterfront Market** (*see* Shopping for Bargains, *below*), where you can get a big deli sandwich for takeout.

Among the attractions described below, a few are free: the **San Carlos Institute,** for a good introduction to the Cuban connection with Key West and south Florida; **Old City Hall,** with its photo collection of old Key West; and the **City Cemetery.**

Exploring Key West

Florida Keys & Key West Visitors Bureau (Box 1147, Key West 33041, tel. 800/352–5397). Greater Key West Chamber of Commerce (402 Wall St., Key West 33040, tel. 305/294–2587 or 800/527–8539, fax 305/294–7806).

Numbers in the margin correspond to points of interest on the Key West map.

★ ❶ Start your tour at **Mallory Square,** named for Stephen Mallory, secretary of the Confederate Navy, who later owned the Mallory Steamship Line. On the nearby **Mallory Dock,** a nightly sunset celebration draws street performers, food vendors, and thousands of onlookers. (Parking is $1.50 an hour.)

❷ Facing Mallory Square is the **Key West Aquarium,** which features hundreds of brightly colored tropical fish and other fascinating sea creatures from the waters around Key West. A touch tank enables you to handle starfish, sea cucumbers, horseshoe and hermit crabs, even horse and queen conchs—living totems of the Conch Republic. Built in 1934 by the Works Progress Administration as the world's first open-air aquarium, the building has been enclosed for all-weather viewing, though an outdoor area with a small Atlantic shores exhibit, including red mangroves, remains. *1 Whitehead St., tel. 305/296–2051. Admission: $6.50 adults, $5.50 senior citizens, $3.50 children 8–15. Open daily 10–6; guided tours (with shark feeding) at 11, 1, 3, 4:30.*

For $4 you can get six (a dozen for $7.50) of what may be the Keys' most authentic conch fritters at the strictly stand-up **Original Conch Fritters** (1 Whitehead St., tel. 305/294–4849), previously a Cuban snack stand from the '30s. Current owners flaunt their buttermilk and peanut oil recipe. Aficionados say it's the conch that counts.

Turn east on Front Street and turn right to **Clinton Place,** where a Civil War memorial to Union soldiers stands in a triangle formed by the intersection of Front, Greene, and Whitehead streets. On your right is the **U.S. Post Office and Customs House,** a Romanesque revival structure designed by prominent local architect William Kerr and completed in 1891. Tour guides claim that federal bureaucrats required the roof to have a steep pitch so it wouldn't collect snow.

❸ On your left is the **Mel Fisher Maritime Heritage Society Museum,** which displays gold and silver bars, coins, jewelry, and other artifacts recovered in 1985 from the Spanish treasure ships *Nuestra Señora de Atocha* and *Santa Margarita.* The two galleons foundered in a hurricane in 1622 near the Marquesas Keys, 40 miles west of Key West. In the museum you can lift a gold bar weighing 6.3 Troy pounds and see a 77.76-carat natural emerald crystal worth almost $250,000. *200 Greene St., tel. 305/294–2633. Admission: $6 adults; $5 AAA and AARP members, military personnel; $2.50 children 6–12. Open daily 9:30–5 (last video showing 4:30).*

Mel Fisher's museum occupies a former Navy storehouse that he bought from Pritam Singh, a Key West hippie turned millionaire. Singh has been the developer (lately along with banks) behind ❹ **Truman Annex,** a 103-acre former military parade grounds and barracks. During World War II, Truman Annex housed some 18,000 military and civilian employees. Singh is successfully transforming it into a suburban community of pastel, picket, and lattice charm, a mix of affordable condominiums and grassy-yard family homes surrounded by colorful bougainvillea and allamanda vines. Recent additions have included three-story town houses in the old brick machine shop. The whole community, set behind high black wrought-iron gates, is designed in the Victorian style that knits Old Town together. Pedestrians and cyclists are welcome on the grounds daily between 8 AM and sunset. Also on the grounds is the **Harry S. Truman Little White House Museum,** the president's former vacation home, with Truman family memorabilia on display. *111 Front St., tel. 305/294–9911. Admission: $6 adults, $3 children 12 and under. Open daily 9–5.*

Key West

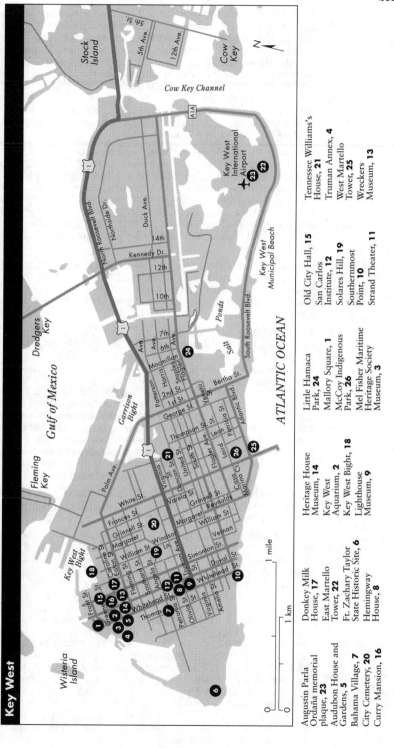

Augustin Parla
Ordaña memorial
plaque, **23**
Audubon House and
Gardens, **5**
Bahama Village, **7**
City Cemetery, **20**
Curry Mansion, **16**

Donkey Milk
House, **17**
East Martello
Tower, **22**
Ft. Zachary Taylor
State Historic Site, **6**
Hemingway
House, **8**

Heritage House
Museum, **14**
Key West
Aquarium, **2**
Key West Bight, **18**
Lighthouse
Museum, **9**

Little Hamaca
Park, **24**
Mallory Square, **1**
McCoy Indigenous
Park, **26**
Mel Fisher Maritime
Heritage Society
Museum, **3**

Old City Hall, **15**
San Carlos
Institute, **12**
Solares Hill, **19**
Southernmost
Point, **10**
Strand Theater, **11**

Tennessee Williams's
House, **21**
Truman Annex, **4**
West Martello
Tower, **25**
Wreckers
Museum, **13**

From Mel Fisher's museum, cross Whitehead Street to visit the
⑤ Audubon House and Gardens. A museum in this three-story dwelling
built in the mid-1840s commemorates ornithologist John James
Audubon's 1832 visit to Key West. On display are several rooms of
period antiques, a children's room, and a large collection of Audubon
engravings. A docent guides you through the first floor; then proceed on your own through the upper stories. A self-guided walking
tour of the tropical gardens is keyed to an updated 12-page brochure. *205 Whitehead St., tel. 305/294–2116. Admission: $6 adults;
$5 senior citizens, AAA members, military personnel; $4 children
6–12; $2 children under 6. Open daily 9:30–5.*

Continue on to 301 **Whitehead Street,** which was the original headquarters of Pan American Airways, one of the first U.S. airlines to
operate scheduled international air service. Its inaugural flight took
off from Key West International Airport on October 28, 1927, and
passengers paid $9.95 for the 90-mile, 80-minute flight from Key
West to Havana aboard *The General Machado,* a Fokker F–7
trimotor. The building is now occupied by **Kelly's,** a popular local
bar, grill, and the continental United State's southernmost brewery.

Pause for a libation at the open-air **Green Parrot Bar** (601 Whitehead
St., corner of Southard St., tel. 305/294–6133). Built in 1890, the bar
is said to be Key West's oldest, a sometimes-rowdy saloon where locals outnumber the tourists, especially on weekends when bands
play.

⑥ Turn right onto Southard Street and follow the signs to the **Ft.
Zachary Taylor State Historic Site.** Built between 1845 and 1866, the
fort served as a base for the Union blockade of Confederate shipping
during the Civil War. More than 1,500 Confederate vessels captured
while trying to run the blockade were brought to Key West's harbor
and detained under the fort's guns. What you will see at Ft. Taylor
today is a fort within a fort; a new moat suggests how the fort originally looked when it was surrounded by water. Because of an artificial reef, snorkeling is excellent here, except when the wind blows
south–southwest and muddies the water. *Tel. 305/292–6713. Admission: $3.25 per vehicle with up to 8 people, $1 per pedestrian or
bicyclist, plus 50¢ per person county surcharge. Park open daily 8–
sunset; fort open 9–5; free 50-min tour daily at noon and 2.*

Return to Thomas Street, and go right two blocks to the corner of
⑦ Petronia Street and the heart of **Bahama Village,** where Bahamians
settled Key West a century and a half ago.

Take Petronia Street east back to Whitehead Street, turn right, and
★ ⑧ go one block to the **Hemingway House,** now a museum dedicated to
the novelist's life and work. Built in 1851, this two-story Spanish colonial dwelling was the first house in Key West to have running water and a fireplace. Hemingway bought the house in 1931 and wrote
about 70% of his life's work here, including *For Whom the Bell Tolls*
and *The Old Man and the Sea.* Three months after Hemingway died
in 1961, local jeweler Bernice Dickson bought the house and its contents from Hemingway's estate and two years later opened it as a
museum. Of special interest are the huge bed with a headboard
made from a 17th-century Spanish monastery gate, a ceramic cat by
Pablo Picasso (a gift to Hemingway from the artist), the hand-blown
Venetian glass chandelier in the dining room, and the swimming
pool. The museum staff gives guided tours rich with anecdotes
about Hemingway and his family and feeds the more than 50 feline
habitants, descendants of Hemingway's own 50 cats. Tours begin every 10 minutes and take 25–30 minutes; then you're free to explore
on your own. *907 Whitehead St., tel. 305/294–1575. Admission:
$6.50 adults, $2.50 children 6–12. Open daily 9–5.*

Down the block and across the street from Hemingway House (behind a spic-and-span white picket fence) is the **Lighthouse Museum,** a 92-foot lighthouse built in 1847 and an adjacent 1887 clapboard house, where the keeper lived. You can climb 98 steps to the top of the lighthouse for a spectacular view of the island town, as well as of the first order (biggest) Fresnel lens, installed at a cost of $1 million in the 1860s. On display in the keeper's quarters are vintage photographs, ship models, nautical charts, and lighthouse artifacts from all along the Keys' reefs. *938 Whitehead St., tel. 305/294–0012. Admission: $5 adults, $1 children 7–12. Open daily 9:30–5 (last admission 4:30).*

Continue to the foot of Whitehead Street, where a huge concrete marker wrongly proclaims this spot to be the **Southernmost Point** in the United States. Most tourists snapping pictures of each other in front of the marker are oblivious to Key West's real southernmost point, on a nearby Navy base off limits to civilians but visible through the fence to your right. Bahamian vendors of shells and straw hats line the sidewalk and blow a conch horn at passing Conch Tour Trains and Old Town Trolleys.

Turn left on South Street. To your right are two dwellings both claimed to be the **Southernmost House:** the cream-brick Queen Anne mansion at 1400 Duval Street and the Spanish-style home at 400 South Street, built in the 1940s by Thelma Strabel, author of *Reap the Wild Wind,* a novel about the wreckers who salvaged ships aground on the reef in Key West's early days. Neither is open to the public. Turn right onto Duval Street, which ends at the Atlantic Ocean and the **Southernmost Beach** (*see* Beaches, *below*).

Now go north on Duval Street toward downtown Key West. Pause at the **Cuban Club** (1108 Duval St.). The original building—a social club for the Cuban community—burned in 1983 and has been replaced by shops and luxury condominiums; some of the original facade was retained. Continuing on, you'll pass several art galleries between the 1100 and 800 blocks.

Pause to admire the colorful marquee and ornamental facade of the **Strand Theater,** built in 1918 by Cuban craftsmen. After a period as a movie theater and a music hall, the Strand is now the **Odditorium,** one of a chain of **Ripley's Believe It or Not** museums, displaying weird and eccentric artifacts. *527 Duval St., tel. 305/293–9686. Admission: $8.95 adults, $5.95 children 4–11. Open Sun.–Thurs. 10–11, Fri.–Sat. 10–midnight.*

★ ⑫ Continue on to the **San Carlos Institute,** a Cuban-American heritage center, which houses a museum and research library focusing on the history of Key West and of 19th- and 20th-century Cuban exiles. The San Carlos Institute was founded in 1871 by Cuban immigrants who wanted to preserve their language, customs, and heritage while organizing the struggle for Cuba's independence from Spain. Cuban patriot Jose Martí delivered many famous speeches from the balcony of the auditorium. Opera star Enrico Caruso sang in the 400-seat hall of the Opera House, which reportedly has the best acoustics of any concert hall in the South. The original building (built in 1871) burned in the Key West fire of 1886, in which two-thirds of the city was destroyed, and a second version succumbed to the hurricane of 1919. The current building was completed in 1924, but after Cuba and the United States broke off diplomatic relations in 1961, it deteriorated. It was saved from demolition when Miami attorney Rafael A. Peñalver, Jr., secured a $3 million state grant for its restoration. The building reopened January 3, 1992, exactly 100 years after Martí founded the Cuban Revolutionary Party here. A self-guided tour takes close to an hour; on weekends you can top it off by watching the almost hour-long documentary *Nostalgia Cubano,* about Cuba in the 1930s to 1950s. *516 Duval St., tel. 305/294–3887.*

Admission: $3 adults, $1 children. Open Tues.–Fri. 11–5, Sat. 11–9, Sun. 11–6.

⓭ Continue north on Duval Street to the **Wreckers Museum,** alleged to be the oldest house in Key West. It was built in 1829 as the home of Francis Watlington, a sea captain and wrecker. He was also a Florida state senator but resigned to serve in the Confederate Navy during the Civil War. Six of the home's eight rooms are now a museum furnished with 18th- and 19th-century antiques. In an upstairs bedroom is an eight-room dollhouse of Conch design, outfitted with tiny Victorian furniture. *322 Duval St., tel. 305/294–9502. Admission: $3 adults, 50¢ children 3–12. Open daily 10–4.*

At Caroline Street, turn left and go half a block to the house known
⓮ as **Heritage House Museum.** This was until recently the home of Jessie Porter Newton, grand dame of Old Town restoration. The Caribbean-colonial house dates from the 1830s, when it was home to ship's captain George Carey, and it includes among its original furnishings antiques and seafaring artifacts from 19th-century China. Out back in beautiful gardens is a cottage that was often occupied by the late poet Robert Frost and where recordings of his poetry can be heard. *410 Caroline St., tel. 305/296–3573. Admission: $6 ages over 12, $5 senior citizens. Open Mon.–Sat. 10–5, Sun. 1–5.*

Return to Duval Street, turn left, continue to Greene Street, and
⓯ turn right to see the restored **Old City Hall** (510 Greene St.), where the City Commission has its meetings. Designed by William Kerr, the architect responsible for the Customs House, the hall opened in 1891. It has a rectangular tower with four clock faces and a fire bell. The ground floor was used as a city market for many years. Inside Old City Hall is a permanent exhibition of old Key West photographs, including an 1845 Daguerreotype, the oldest known photographic image of Key West. Behind an adjoining door on the second-story landing are the offices of the **Historic Florida Keys Preservation Board** (tel. 305/292–6718), the principal information source about preservation throughout the Keys.

Stop in at the **Cuban Coffee Queen Cafe** (512 Greene St., tel. 305/296–2711), run by a mother-daughter team from Central Chaparra, in Cuba's Oriente Province. Locals love the hot bollos (baked buns with butter), conch fritters, pigs' feet, ham and eggs, sangria, and Cuban coffee.

At Simonton Street, turn right, go one block to Caroline Street, and
⓰ turn right again. The 22-room Victorian **Curry Mansion,** built in 1899 for Milton Curry, the son of Florida's first millionaire, is an adaptation of a Parisian town house. It has Key West's only widow's walk open to the public. Owners Edith and Al Amsterdam have restored and redecorated most of the house and turned it into a winning bed-and-breakfast (*see* Budget Lodging, *below*). Take an unhurried self-guided tour with a comprehensive brochure, which includes floor plans and is full of detailed information about the history and contents of the house. *511 Caroline St., tel. 305/294–5349. Admission: $5 adults, $1 children under 12. Open daily 10–5.*

Return to Simonton Street; turn right and then left on Eaton Street
⓱ to get to the **Donkey Milk House.** This Key West classical revival house was built around 1866 by prominent businessman and U.S. marshal Peter "Dynamite" Williams, a hero of the great fire of 1886. Antiques and artifacts fill its two balconied floors. The house won a 1992 restoration award. *613 Eaton St., tel. 305/296–1866. Admission: $5. Open daily 10–5.*

Return to Simonton Street, turn right and then right again on Greene Street. A three-block walk with a jog at Elizabeth Street
⓲ onto Lazy Way brings you to the **Key West Bight** (also known as Harbor Walk). Formerly site of the Singleton Shrimp Fleet and Ice &

Fish House, this is the last funky area of Old Key West. The nearby Turtle Kraals is a historic site, and a restaurant adjoins. Also in the area are numerous charter boats, classic old yachts, and the **Reef Relief Environmental Center** (201 William St., tel. 305/394–3100), a public facility with videos, displays, and free information about the coral reef, open 9–5 weekdays and most weekends in season. Next door is the **Waterfront Market** (*see* Shopping for Bargains, *below*), the only natural-foods market and juice bar in town.

Go south on Margaret Street to Angela Street. To the west rises **(19) Solares Hill,** the "steepest" natural grade in Key West. Its summit, the island's loftiest elevation, is 18 feet above sea level.

★ **(20)** Go down Windsor Lane to Passover Lane, turn left, and go to Margaret Street and the entrance of the **City Cemetery.** Clustered near a flagpole resembling a ship's mast are the graves of 22 sailors killed in the sinking of the battleship U.S.S. *Maine.* Historian Sharon Wells leads six guided tours a week from the sexton's office at Margaret and Angela streets. No reservations are necessary. *Tel. 305/296–3913 for tour information. Admission free; tour donation: $5. Open sunrise–sunset; tours Tues., Wed. at 9, 10, 11.*

Walk east to White Street, turn right and go south to Duncan Street, and then go four blocks east to Leon Street. Here you find **(21) Tennessee Williams's House** (1431 Duncan St.), a modest two-story, red-shuttered Bahamian-style cottage behind a white picket fence, where the playwright lived from 1949 until his death in 1983. After years of neglect, the house was purchased in 1992 and fixed up by a couple named Paradise. The house is not open to the public, nor is there any historical marker.

The last few Key West sights are better visited on wheels, either car or bicycle. Take Truman Avenue (U.S. 1) east from downtown, past **Garrison Bight Yacht Basin,** where many charter fishing boats dock. Continue east, as U.S. 1 becomes North Roosevelt Boulevard. Past the turnoff to Stock Island at the east end of Key West, North Roosevelt Boulevard (now Route A1A) swings south and then, at the bottom of the island, turns west, becoming South Roosevelt Boulevard. On your left is a small community of houseboats. On your right, just ★ **(22)** past the entrance to Key West International Airport, stands **East Martello Tower,** one of two Civil War forts of similar design overlooking the Atlantic Ocean. Housed in a portion of this tower (restored in 1993) are military uniforms and relics of the battleship U.S.S. *Maine,* which was blown up in Havana Harbor in 1898. The Key West Art and Historical Society operates a museum in East Martello's vaulted casemates. The collection includes Stanley Papio's "junk art" sculptures, Cuban primitive artist Mario Sanchez's chiseled and painted wood carvings of historic Key West street scenes, memorabilia from movies shot on location in the Keys, and a display of books by many of the 60-some famous writers (including seven Pulitzer Prize winners) who have lived in Key West. Historical exhibits present a chronological history of the Florida Keys. A circular 48-step staircase in the central tower leads to a platform overlooking the airport and surrounding waters. *3501 S. Roosevelt Blvd., tel. 305/296–6206 or 305/296–3913. Admission: $5 adults, $1 children. Open daily 9:30–5.*

(23) Walk east to the terminal of Key West International Airport. In the front of the parking lot, facing the terminal, is the **Augustin Parla Ordaña memorial plaque.** Born in Key West in 1887 to Cuban exile parents, Ordaña was the first to fly the 119 miles from Key West to El Mariel, Cuba, in 1913.

Continue west on South Roosevelt Boulevard past **Smathers Beach** (*see* Beaches, *below*) on your left. To your right are the **salt ponds** where early residents evaporated seawater to collect salt. This area, a vestige of the old Key West and for years a wildlife sanctuary, was

㉔ saved from condo development in 1991 and turned into **Little Hamaca Park.** To enter, take Bertha Street to Flagler Avenue (Route 5-A), turning right and right again onto Government Road. The entrance is just ahead, and a boardwalk leads into the natural area. (Although the sign says that the park is open 7 to dusk, the gates are not necessarily open. Cyclists lift their bikes over.)

Return to Flagler Avenue, turn left on First Street, and turn right onto Atlantic Boulevard. Near White Street, where Atlantic Boulevard ends, are **Higgs Memorial Beach** (*see* Beaches, *below*) and **West Martello Tower,** a fort built in 1861 and used as a lookout post during the Spanish-American War. Within its walls the Key West Garden Club maintains an art gallery and tropical garden. *Atlantic Blvd. and White St., tel. 305/294–3210. Donations welcome. Open Wed.– Sun. 9:30–3:30; closed holidays.*

㉖ Turn right onto White Street; on your right is the city-operated **McCoy Indigenous Park.** The park contains more than 100 species of trees and shrubs; the largest collection of native tropical plants in the Florida Keys, including many fruit-bearing trees; migrating songbirds spring and fall; and many species of colorful butterflies. *Atlantic Blvd. and White St., tel. 305/292–8155. Admission free. Open weekdays 7–4.*

Budget Lodging Three services can help arrange for accommodations. **Key West Reservation Service** (628 Fleming St., Drawer 1689, 33040, tel. 305/294– 8850 or 800/327–4831, fax 305/296–6291) makes hotel reservations and helps locate rental properties (hotels, motels, bed-and-breakfasts, oceanfront condominiums, and luxury vacation homes). Generally more expensive properties, which still may be good buys for two or three couples traveling together for an extended time, are represented by the following: **Key West Vacation Rentals** (525 Simonton St., 33040, tel. 305/292–7997 or 800/621–9405, fax 305/ 294–7501) lists historic cottages and condominiums for rent. **Property Management of Key West, Inc.** (1213 Truman Ave., 33040, tel. 305/ 296–7744) offers lease and rental service for condominiums, town houses, and private homes, including renovated Conch homes.

$$ **Caribbean House.** Norman Moody had a great idea in 1989, when he took over this abandoned nightclub in Bahama Village. He painted it in brilliant tropical colors and installed guests in 11 very affordable rooms. Since then, demand has kicked in so heavily from independent European travelers that Norman has let his rates drift upward a bit. The rooms are tiny yet complete, with bathroom (shower, no tub), chair and table, French provincial–style dresser, Caribbean art, and a ceiling fan. The one drawback is that the place doesn't take reservations—you have to stop by early in the morning or risk not getting a room, though Norman has arranged with friends in the neighborhood to take in guests when he's full. Luck of the draw might get you a second-story kitchen "penthouse," a room with upper and lower beds, or the standard. It's very informal—guests have been known to throw in with each other in the little lobby and share a room. It's a good choice for the footloose and the young at heart. Continental breakfast is included. *226 Petronia St., 33040, tel. 305/ 296–1600 or 800/543–4518. 11 rooms. Facilities: coin laundry. MC, V.*

$$ **Eden House.** Some years ago this hotel with a Mediterranean revival facade and stucco arches was the low-end choice in Key West. Originally a general store and residence in 1924, it was later a working-class hotel; Mike Eden and his brother Stan bought it in 1974 in their late-hippie phase, charging $7 a night and often tapping a beer keg in the afternoon for new guests. Those days, as they say, are gone forever (though there is still a happy hour daily). The rates are more than 10 times that high now just for the so-called "European rooms," small but not without charm—a piece of Key West art, floral bed covers, a chair, and a drape of fabric. The rooms are air-conditioned,

though bathrooms are down the hall, a separate shower is across the hallway, and there's no TV (not that the expensive rooms have TV either). Eight of the 15 European rooms now have phones, and there's a pay phone, too. Out back, there are plank decks and a colorful canopy where reasonably priced Martin's Cafe serves German-American food. *1015 Fleming St., 33040, tel. 305/296–6868. 42 rooms share baths. Facilities: pool, bike rentals, Jacuzzi, gazebo, gift shop, parking. MC, V.*

$$ **Frances Street Bottle Inn.** With a rash of new guest houses in Key West and established ones going more and more for the luxury trade, this wonderful six-bedroom house, opened in 1994, offers a refreshing change. Owners Bob and Katy Elkins look after guests as if they were all favorite cousins coming down to get married. The two-story Conch house dates from the 1890s, and the clean and tidy rooms are all pale, with carpet and plain furniture, paddle fans, and ductless air-conditioning that's virtually silent. Dedicated to conservation, the Elkins have installed low-flow toilets and shower heads, and they compost and recycle. Two bedrooms are downstairs and open to a porch-patio (where a Jacuzzi may be coming), two upstairs open to a porch, and the two least-expensive rooms (the only ones that actually qualify as moderately priced) nonetheless have two exposures and four windows. The house's name comes from the antique bottles that Bob, a commercial spearfisherman, has collected over the years. Continental breakfast is included in the rate. *535 Frances St., 33040, tel. 305/294–8530 or 800/294–8530. 6 rooms. Facilities: patio. MC, V.*

$$ **Harborside Motel & Marina.** The motel is in a safe, pleasant section tucked between a quiet street and Garrison Bight (the charter boat harbor), between Old Town and New Town. Units (all efficiencies) are boxy, clean, basic, and carpeted and have little patios, phones, and basic color cable TV. *903 Eisenhower Dr., 33040, tel. 305/294–2780, fax 305/292–1473. 12 efficiencies. Facilities: freshwater pool, tiki hut, coin laundry. AE, D, DC, MC, V.*

$$ **Lord's Motel.** A tropical patio adds charm to this otherwise plain peach-color motel with white shutters, lattice accents, and carpeted floors. Close to Old Town in the motel district, Lord's is a couple of blocks from the beach. Rates here can be up or down depending on demand, even in winter. *625 South St., 33040, tel. 305/296–2829. 6 rooms, 9 efficiencies. AE, D, MC, V.*

$$ **Popular House/Key West Bed & Breakfast.** Unlike so many prissy ho-
★ tels that wall the world out, Jody Carlson brings Key West in. Doors stay open all day. Local art—large splashy canvases, a wall mural in the style of Gauguin—hangs on the walls, and tropical gardens and music punctuate the mood. Jody converted this onetime fat farm into a B&B in the late 1980s, offering low-cost shared-bath rooms and luxury rooms in the same house, reasoning that budget travelers deserve the same good local style as the rich. Low-end rooms burst by day with the bright yellows and reds of their furnishings. At night they glow by candlelight. Hand-painted dressers will make you laugh out loud. Spacious third-floor rooms, though, are best (and most expensive), decorated with a paler palette and brilliantly original furniture: a bench made of newel posts from the old Key West City Hall, another piece crafted of attic I-beams. Terra-cotta tiles, rockers with cane insets, and arched windows overlooking Key West rooftops provide added pleasures. The Continental breakfast is lavish. *415 William St., 33040, tel. 305/294–3630 or 305/296–7274. 10 rooms (5 with shared baths). Facilities: Jacuzzi, gardens. AE, D, DC, MC, V.*

$$ **Sea Shell Motel.** Connected to the Key West International Hostel (*see below*), this motel offers tiny guest rooms and efficiencies. The warrenlike rooms are dark, with terrazzo floors and tiny bathrooms, but they do have TVs. The standard of amenities is very low, but at least it's cheap (for Key West)—though at Christmas and spring break rates will jump up to $85 for a double room. At places like this,

try for a low confirmed rate in advance. *718 South St., 33040, tel. 305/296–5719, fax 305/296–0672. 10 rooms, 4 efficiencies. MC, V.*

¢ **Key West International Hostel.** The cheapest of the cheap, it's not recommended otherwise. A bed costs $13 a night if you belong to American Youth Hostels or just about any other hostel organization, $16 otherwise. A few years back, when the hostel was run by other folks, AYH disaffiliated the place for various reasons—they assigned hostelers to sleep on the floor when they ran out of bunks, and they mixed males and females. The current operators continue the same practices, arguing that the floor is better than turning people away when they show up late at night without reservations. Stacked bunks feel opium-den tight, and each room has six bunks and only one tiny bathroom. Incredibly cheap meals are served here—$1 dinners (burgers, hot dogs, chili, chicken à la king) and $2 Continental breakfasts with cereal included. The scene is beyond laid-back, bordering on flophouse. *718 South St., 33040, tel. 305/296–5719, fax 305/296–0672. 80 beds. Facilities: kitchen with microwave, bicycle rentals, barbecue, picnic patio, laundry. MC, V.*

Splurge **Artist House.** Dressed in French Empire and Victorian style, with lavender shutters on white clapboard, latticework, wrought-iron spear fencing, and a grand tin-shingled turret, this guest home is a real showstopper. All rooms are antiques-filled and have Dade County pine floors. Among the rooms you'll find a mix of brocade sofas, Japanese screens, pull-latch doors, claw-foot tubs, four-poster beds, and elaborate moldings. A small upstairs room configured into the upstairs rear of the house has a hot plate and full fridge, but it lacks the elegance of the others. The little garden out back has a Jacuzzi with a stone lion's head, surrounded by a brick deck, and there's a pond. A Continental buffet breakfast is included. *534 Eaton St., 33040, tel. 305/296–3977 or 800/582–7882, fax 305/296–3210. 7 units. Facilities: Jacuzzi, garden. AE, D, DC, MC, V.*

Splurge **Curry Mansion Inn.** Careful dedication to detail by Key West archi-
★ tect Thomas Pope and care for modern travelers by owners Al and Edith Amsterdam have made the annex rooms (most of those at the inn) exceptionally comfortable, even if not as precisely detailed as the now rarely used rooms in the main house, the first of the island's millionaire mansions (from 1899). Each room has a different color scheme using tropical pastels; all have carpeted floors, wicker headboards and furnishings, and quilts from the Cotton Gin Store in Tavernier. Rooms 1 and 8, honeymoon suites, feature canopy beds and balconies. In 1993 the Amsterdams added eight full-size suites at the restored James House across the street; 306 and 308 face south and have beautiful morning light. Guests are welcome to a complimentary expanded Continental breakfast and happy hour with an open bar and live piano music; they also receive privileges at Pier House Beach Club, Casa Marina, and the Reach. A wheelchair lift and wheelchair-accessible rooms are available. *511, 512 Caroline St., 33040, tel. 305/294–5349 or 800/253–3466, fax 305/294–4093. 15 rooms, 8 suites. Facilities: pool. AE, D, DC, MC, V.*

Budget Dining **Antonia's.** Northern Italian cooking reaches new heights in a smart
$$ setting that was once site of the Blue Boar Bar and the hippie coffee-
★ house Crazy Ophelia's. A woody bar opens to a darkly paneled and candlelit dining room with at most 30 tables. Chefs Antonia Berto and Phillip Smith turn out fluent renditions of Keys seafood and pasta, including a nightly grilled fish, a fresh catch prepared with a variety of sauces, *malfatti di ricotta e spinaci* (small dumplings of spinach and homemade ricotta in a light tomato sauce), and *capellini alla puttanesca* (angel hair pasta with fresh tuna, tomato sauce, capers, anchovies, olives, red pepper, and garlic). There's also veal, of course, and tenderloin filets, rack of lamb, chicken, and various salads. All pastas and focaccia are made in-house. Guests can order half-portions of pastas, and many Italian wines are offered by the

glass. *615 Duval St., tel. 305/294–6565. Reservations advised. Dress: casual but neat. AE, DC, MC, V. Closed Thanksgiving. No lunch.*

$$ ★ **Cafe Marquesa.** This intimate restaurant with attentive service and superb food is a felicitous counterpart of the excellent small hotel of which it's a part. Accommodating maybe 20 tables, the café has a mellow atmosphere with bluesy ballads played in the background and an open kitchen viewed through a trompe l'oeil pantry mural. Ten or so entrées are featured nightly and typically make good use of regional foods—mango relish with the grilled boneless quail, and veal and pork *boudin* sausage, coconut milk in the Caribbean shrimp chowder with sweet potatoes, and citrus marinade for the grilled chicken with roasted garlic light sauce. Many low-fat choices are featured, such as a grilled black grouper served in a tomato-ginger broth with white-bean succotash and baby bok choy. Desserts are quite the contrary: a Marquesa brûlée with almond chocolate macaroon, coconut cake with chocolate lattice and crème Anglaise, and a Key lime cheesecake with raspberry coulis. There's also a fine choice of microbrewery beers and fresh coffee. *600 Fleming St., tel. 305/292–1244. Reservations accepted. Dress: casual but neat. AE, DC, MC, V. Closed summer Tues. No lunch.*

$$ **Pepe's Cafe and Steak House.** Judges, police officers, carpenters, and fisherpeople rub elbows every morning in their habitual breakfast seats, at tables or high-back, dark pine booths under a huge paddle fan. Face the street or dine outdoors under a huge rubber tree if you're put off by the naked-lady art on the back wall. Pepe's was established downtown in 1909 (which makes it the oldest eating house in the Keys) and moved to the current site in 1962. The specials change nightly: barbecued chicken, pork tenderloin, ribs, steak, at least one fresh fish item, potato salad, red or black beans, and corn bread on Sunday; meat loaf on Monday; seafood Tuesday and Wednesday; a full traditional Thanksgiving dinner every Thursday; filet mignon on Friday; and prime rib on Saturday. *806 Caroline St., tel. 305/294–7192. No reservations. Dress: casual. D, MC, V.*

$–$$ ★ **Blue Heaven.** For the moment, anyway, this area has been spared the T-shirt hustle and general overdose of Mallory Square. The inspired remake of an old blue-on-blue clapboard, peach-and-yellow-trim Greek revival Bahamian house was, not too long ago, a bordello where Ernest Hemingway refereed boxing matches and customers watched cockfights. There's still a rooster graveyard out back, as well as a water tower hauled here from Little Torch Key in the 1920s. Upstairs is an art gallery of whimsical Key West work (check out the zebra-stripe bikes), and downstairs are affordable fresh eats, either in the old house or the big leafy yard. There are five nightly specials, and a good mix of offerings covers natural foods (carrot and curry soup, vegetarian black bean soup, grilled vegetable roulade, Caribbean tofu stir-fry) and more typical West Indian favorites (pork tenderloin pan-seared with sweet potato, veggies, plantains, chutney, and curry butter; Jamaican jerk chicken; Caribbean barbecued shrimp). Top it off with Banana Heaven (banana bread, flamed bananas with spiced rum, and homemade vanilla-bean ice cream). Three meals are served six days a week; on Sunday, there's a to-die-for Sunday brunch that includes humongous pancake or waffle platters, granola and fruit bowls, and the freshest coffee, all accompanied by an electric hammered dulcimer while kids swing on ropes and chase roosters through the richly decaying humus of the yard. Expect a line. Everybody knows how good this is. *729 Thomas St., tel. 305/296–8666. No reservations. Dress: casual. D, MC, V. Schedule may change in summer.*

$–$$ **Half Shell Raw Bar.** "Eat It Raw" is the motto, and even off-season the oyster bar keeps shucking. You eat at shellacked picnic tables and benches in a shed, with ship models, life buoys, a mounted dolphin, and old license plates hanging overhead. Classic signs offer homage to Keys' passions. Reads one: "Fishing is not a matter of life and death. It's more important than that." Once a fish market, the Half Shell looks out onto the deep-sea fishing fleet. Specials, chalked on the blackboard, may include broiled dolphin sandwich or linguine seafood marinara. Whatever it is, it's fresh. *Land's End Marina, tel. 305/294–7496. No reservations. Dress: casual. D, MC, V.*

$–$$ **Mangia Mangia.** Fresh homemade pasta comes served Alfredo, ma-
★ rinara, meaty, or pesto style, either in the twinkly brick garden with its specimen palms or in the classic old-house dining room with the splashy Save the Rain Forests mural, where another 12 much-needed seats and an equally needed coffee bar were added. One of the best—and best-value—restaurants in Key West, Mangia Mangia is run by Elliot and Naomi Baron, ex-Chicago restaurateurs who found Key West's warmth and laid-back style irresistible. Everything served from the open kitchen is outstanding, especially the pasta, made with 100% semolina and fresh eggs. Made-on-the-premises Key lime pie and Mississippi mud pie are winners for dessert, after which you can now get a decaf as well as espresso and cappuccino. The wine list, the largest in Monroe County, contains excellently priced "reserve" wines (a good selection always under $20), or try talking Elliot into letting you sample his flower-light home-brewed lager. *900 Southard St., tel. 305/294–2469. No reservations. Dress: casual but neat. MC, V. Closed Thanksgiving, Dec. 24–25. No lunch.*

$–$$ **Market Bistro.** Seat yourself at the Pier House's deli and fine-dining snack shop. The espresso bar supplies a cup of the perfect complement to the hotel's classic Key lime pie or the chocolate decadence: a triple chocolate flourless torte with raspberry sauce and rose petals. A cooler holds tropical fruit juices, beer, and mineral water. Other specialties include sandwiches, salads, gourmet cheeses, pâtés, and homemade pastries. *1 Duval St., in Pier House, tel. 305/ 296–4600. No reservations. Dress: casual. AE, DC, MC, V.*

$–$$ **South Beach Seafood & Raw Bar.** They don't call it the southernmost eatery (which it is), but even apart from that tacit distinction, it's worth stopping here for breakfast, lunch, or dinner. It's alongside the Southernmost Beach, and though the beach hardly boasts the award-winning sand of Florida's Panhandle, the breeze always seems to be blowing in the windows, creating a Keys-tropical mood. Fare is mostly seafood—a raw bar; several catches of the day; pastas made with clams, shrimp, and fish; plus various platters and a choice of lobster and shrimp dishes. *1405 Duval St., tel. 305/294–2727. No reservations. Dress: casual. MC, V.*

$ **El Siboney.** This sprawling, three-room, family-style restaurant serves traditional Cuban food, including a well-seasoned black bean soup that's a blessing for vegetarians. Specials include beef stew Monday, pepper steak Tuesday, chicken fricassee Wednesday, a weekly surprise Thursday, chicken and rice Friday, and oxtail stew with rice and beans on Saturday. Always available are roast pork with *morros* (black beans and white rice) and cassava, paella, and *palomilla* steak. *900 Catherine St., tel. 305/296–4184. No reservations. Dress: casual. No credit cards. Closed 2 wks in June, Thanksgiving, Dec. 25, Jan. 1.*

$ **Gato Gordo.** Replacing the popular El Loro Verde, Gato Gordo comes across lighter in look, more stylized, but whatever the name, you know it's Mexican. It's all a piece of eye candy—with gorgeous tiles and walls of tropical art—but it's no less comfy for that. Inside and out on the patio, where there's a roll-down tarp in case of rough weather, seating accommodates 150 plus whoever's standing at the bar. The plantings, including lots of hybrid hibiscus, are as beautiful as the art. Salsa and chips come free the first time around, followed by the usual tacos, tostadas, enchiladas, burritos, and fajitas. Also on the menu is a vegetarian special of fresh veggies steamed in a to-mato-cilantro sauce over Spanish rice with pinto beans and two flour tortillas, as well as chicken by the quarter or half served with the same sides. Homemade pumpkin, apple, or walnut pie (of course Key lime, too); flan; sopapillas (light, fried bread dough with sugar or honey); and ice cream are the desserts. *404 Southard St., tel. 305/ 294–0888. No reservations. Dress: casual. AE, D, MC, V. Closed holidays.*

$ **PT's Late Night Bar & Grill.** The name says it: Food is served to 3 AM, drinks to 4. Despite the pool tables, there's no hustle scene—just a regular guys' and gals' saloon-cum-foodery across from Land's End Marina. On Sunday the five TVs are all going with different ball games and movies. The food is equally eclectic. Pick your favorite among items like meat loaf, Yankee pot roast, barbecued baby-back ribs, fajitas, chicken-fried steak, and daily blue-plate specials. Dark wood decor is brightened with Haitian art and beer company neon. This is a Key West favorite. *920 Caroline St., tel. 305/296–4245. No reservations. Dress: casual. MC, V. Closed Dec. 25.*

$ **Sunset Pier Bar.** When the crowds get too thick on the Mallory Dock at sunset, you can thin your way out 200 feet offshore behind the Ocean Key House. A limited menu offers crispy conch fritters, potato salad, shrimp, and jumbo Hebrew National hot dogs. Live island music is featured nightly. *0 Duval St., tel. 305/296–7701. No reservations. Dress: casual. AE, D, DC, MC, V.*

¢–$ **Compass Rose.** It's kind of tacky, but the customers love it—when they can find it, tucked away at the side of the old Sandcastle Restaurant. You can eat indoors or out, even at the bar. The atmosphere is homey, courtesy of touches like fresh and dried flowers and the lunch menu scrawled on a blackboard. The food is homey, too: real mashed potatoes and gravy, pot roast, meat loaf, roast garlic chicken, country-fried steak, and what locals declare are the best ribs in town. Somewhat more refined offerings include grilled dolphin with olives or fruit sauce and a daily pasta special. There are three standard desserts—Snickers frozen pie, Key lime pie, and a white-chocolate swirl raspberry cheesecake. *532 Margaret St., tel. 305/294– 4394. No reservations. Dress: casual. No credit cards.*

¢–$ **Five Star Restaurant.** Here's a place where people from the neighborhood meet over a meal, keeping the neighborhood together. Whether you eat outdoors or stay inside under the ceiling fans, this homey little Cuban restaurant is a winner. Regulars are greeted by name by proprietor Anna Aguiar, who took over the place from her dad (he first opened it in the early 1970s). Traditional Cuban cooking includes roast pork, pork chops, palomilla steak, paella, grouper, dolphin, whole yellowtail, and *picadillo* (spicy minced beef), plus hot onions on the house ("good for the sex life," Anna assures customers). In 1993, Anna prepared the longest Cuban sandwich on record—112 feet long—for the annual Hemingway Festival. *1100 Packer St., tel. 305/296–0650. Reservations advised in winter. Dress: casual. MC, V. Closed Tues. in summer. Inquire about holidays the evening before.*

¢ **Bleeker Street Bagelry & Gourmet Delicatessen.** They claim to make authentic water bagels, though you can't taste the potato water or feel the gluten flour snarl back at every bite. But it is an affordable choice in New Town, and who expects the real thing anyway? You'll find big meaty, cheesy sandwiches; salad sandwiches; deli treats like knishes (either meat or vegetarian); and smoked fish, as well as assorted muffins, sour-cream coffee cake, rugelach, and brownies. It's in a plain storefront in the Overseas Market shopping center. There isn't quite enough space to park your car, so watch out for fender benders. *2796 N. Roosevelt Blvd., tel. 305/293–0665; 534 Fleming St., next to Fausto's, tel. 305/193–6956. No reservations. Dress: casual. No credit cards. Closed weekends.*

¢ **Chit-Chat Restaurant.** This place is purely for breakfast—though this being Key West, breakfast is served until 1 PM. If you come before 8, you get two eggs, toast, and grits or home fries for 99¢ ($1.99 after 8). Otherwise there are omelets, pancakes, crepes, and English muffins—not fancy, just breakfast. You sit on a terrace at a mishmash of plastic tables alongside locals reading their morning *Citizens*. The service is the best in town—maybe because everybody recognizes that early morning in Key West is the twilight zone and we have to be helpful to each other. *821 Duval St., tel. 305/294–6954. No reservations. Dress: casual. No credit cards.*

¢ **Duds & Suds.** The first gas station in Key West was the original occupant of this site. It has since been converted into a quirky Laundromat-café, where you can toss your clothes in the washing machine and then catch a casual meal at the adjoining eatery (where the service station's office used to be). Magazines and newspapers lay scattered around, along with fliers for local bands and parties. Jazz and blues music plays, and local art hangs on the walls, along with chalkboards where the menu is written. Every day, a homemade soup is featured (try the 15-bean soup); there are also fruit breads, spinach salad, cheese melt and vegetables, black beans and rice, and lots of subs made in the sandwich pit. *829 Fleming St., tel. 305/294–7837. No reservations. Dress: casual. No credit cards.*

Splurge **Cafe des Artistes.** By choosing the least expensive items on the ★ menu, you can have an affordable meal at this intimate, 75-seat restaurant. Otherwise consider this a splurge. The classic Key West dining here is so good that many guests, even clad in T-shirts and shorts, don't blanch at a $100 dinner check for two. The restaurant was once part of a hotel building constructed in 1935 by C.E. Alfeld, Al Capone's bookkeeper. For Key West, the look is studiously unhip: rough stucco walls, old-fashioned lights, and a knotty-pine ceiling. Haitian paintings and Keys scenes by local artists dress the walls. Guests dine in two indoor rooms or on a rooftop deck beneath a sapodilla tree. Chef Andrew Berman presents a French interpretation of tropical cuisine, using fresh local seafood and produce and light, flour-free sauces. Specialties variously include the restaurant's award-winning Lobster Tango Mango (lobster with cognac, served with shrimp in a mango-saffron beurre blanc), a half roast duckling with raspberry sauce, and the yellowtail Atocha (sautéed with shrimps and scallops in lemon butter with basil). Special orders can be accommodated, and the wine list is strong on both French and California labels. *1007 Simonton St., tel. 305/294–7100. Reservations advised. Dress: casual but neat. AE, MC, V. No lunch.*

Shopping for Key West shopping is pricey, with some of the most unpleasant T-**Bargains** shirt rip-offs in Florida. The legit operators still haven't figured out how to put the quietus on the scam artists, who keep showing up with new names and locations.

Following are some of the best shops in Key West:

Like a parody of Duval Street T-shirt shops, the hole-in-the-wall **Art Attack** (606 Duval St., tel. 305/294–7131) throws in every icon and trinket anyone nostalgic for the days of peace and love might fancy: beads, necklaces, medallions, yin-yang banners, harmony bells, and of course Dead and psychedelic T's.

Take time, even if you're not buying, to enjoy the smells at **Bailey's Place Espresso Bar** (1111 Duval St., tel. 305/292–3739), the "southernmost coffee roasters." Dozens of varieties of beans plus fresh-baked pastries are for sale.

Fast Buck Freddie's (500 Duval St., tel. 305/294–2007) sells imaginative items you'd never dream of, including battery-operated alligators that eat Muenster cheese, banana leaf–shape furniture, fish-shape flatware, and every flamingo item anyone's ever come up with.

Fausto's Food Palace (522 Fleming St., tel. 305/296–5663; 1105 White St., tel. 305/294–5221) may be under a roof, but it's a market in the traditional town-square style. Since 1926, Fausto's has been where everyone meets to catch up on the week's gossip, and it's also where you chill out in summer, because it's got the heaviest air-conditioning in town.

The oldest gallery in Key West, **Gingerbread Square Gallery** (1207 Duval St., tel. 305/296–8900) mainly represents Keys artists who have attained national prominence.

Haitian Art Co. (600 Frances St., tel. 305/296–8932) sells the works of 200 or more Haitian artists.

H.T. Chittum & Co. (725 Duval St., tel. 305/292–9002) sells the kind of informal clothing beloved by Key Westers (and Key West visitors)—aviator hats and fish-cleaning knives as well as smart ready-to-wear. There's also a branch in Islamorada (MM 82.7, OS, tel. 305/664–4421).

Inter Arts (506 Southard St., tel. 305/296–4081) features textiles to wear, display, walk on, and keep you warm in bed.

Key West Aloe (524 Front St., tel. 305/294–5592 or 800/445–2563) was founded in a garage in 1971; today it produces some 300 perfume, sunscreen, and skin-care products for men and women. You can also visit the factory store (Greene and Simonton Sts.), open seven days a week, where you can watch the staff measure and blend ingredients, then fill and seal the containers.

Key West Hand Print Fabrics (201 Simonton St., tel. 305/294–9535) was made famous in the 1960s by Lilly Pulitzer's designs. Weekday shoppers can watch workers making hand-printed fabric on five 50-yard-long tables in the Curry Warehouse, a brick building erected in 1878 to store tobacco. The shop is open seven days.

Key West Island Bookstore (513 Fleming St., tel. 305/294–2904) is the literary bookstore of the large Key West writers' community.

In this town with a gazillion T-shirt shops, **Last Flight Out** (710 Duval St., tel. 305/294–8008) offers classic namesake T's that recall the pre–World War II heyday of tourist flights between Key West and Havana.

Lazy Way Shops (Elizabeth and Greene Sts., tel. 305/294–3003) sells a constantly changing sampling of local arts and crafts in an old shrimpers' net shop.

Lucky Street Gallery (919 Duval St., tel. 305/294–3973) shows the best tropical work for hanging and mounting.

L. Valladares & Son (1200 Duval St., tel. 305/296–5032) is a fourth-generation newsstand selling more than 2,000 periodicals and 3,000 paperback books along with Florida, national, and international newspapers.

Pelican Poop (314 Simonton St., tel. 305/296–3887) sells Haitian and Ecuadorean art. It's worth buying something just to gain admittance to the lush, tropical courtyard garden with its gorgeous aqua pool—the kind of place you could imagine Tennessee Williams coming for inspiration. (Hemingway actually once lived here, in the apartments out back called Casa Antigua.)

A welcome survivor of Key West's seafaring days, **Perkins & Son Chandlery** (901 Fleming St., tel. 305/294–7635) offers the largest selection of used marine gear in the Keys among a pine tar– and kerosene-redolent trove of nautical antiques, books, outdoor clothing, and collectibles.

Plantation Pottery (521 Fleming St., tel. 305/294–3143) is not to be missed for local and brought-in-from-elsewhere pottery that's original, not commercial.

Tikal Trading Co. (129 Duval St., tel. 305/296–4463) sells its own well-known line of double-stitched women's clothing of hand-woven Guatemalan cotton and tropical prints.

Waterfront Market (201 William St., tel. 305/294–8418 or 305/296–0778) sells health and gourmet foods, deli items, fresh produce, salads, an outstanding selection of cold beer, and wine. If you're there, be sure to check out the baaadest bulletin board in Key West. Absorbed into the same building are Waterfront Fish Market, Inc. (tel. 305/294–0778) for fresh seafood and Waterfront Baits & Tackle (tel. 305/292–1961) for bait and fishing gear.

Potters Charles Pearson and Timothy Roeder are **Whitehead St. Pottery** (1011 Whitehead St., tel. 305/294–5067), which has displayed their raku-fired pieces since 1986.

Beaches **Atlantic Shores Motel** (510 South St.) has a beach where female visitors can go topless.

Dog Beach (Vernon and Waddell Sts.) is the only beach in Key West where dogs are allowed.

Ft. Zachary Taylor State Historic Site (*see* Exploring Key West, *above*) has several hundred yards of beach near the western end of Key West and an adjoining picnic area with barbecue grills in a stand of Australian pines. Snorkeling is good except when winds blow from the south–southwest. This beach is relatively uncrowded and attracts more locals than tourists; nude bathing is not allowed.

Higgs Memorial Beach (near the end of White St.) is a popular sunbathing spot. A nearby grove of Australian pines provides shade, and the West Martello Tower provides shelter should a storm suddenly sweep in.

Simonton Street Beach (north end of Simonton St.), facing the Gulf of Mexico, is a great place to watch boat traffic in the harbor, but parking here is difficult.

Smathers Beach features almost 2 miles of sand beside South Roosevelt Boulevard. Trucks along the road will rent you rafts, Windsurfers, and other beach "toys."

Southernmost Beach, on the Atlantic Ocean at the foot of Duval Street, is popular with tourists at nearby motels. It has limited parking and a nearby buffet-type restaurant.

Participant Key West is a cycling town, but many tourists aren't accustomed to
Sports driving with so many bikes around, so ride carefully. Paved road
Biking surfaces are poor, so it's best to ride a "Conch cruiser" (fat-tired bike). Some hotels rent bikes to guests; others will refer you to a nearby shop and reserve a bike for you. **Keys Moped & Scooter** (523 Truman Ave., tel. 305/294–0399) rents beach cruisers with large baskets as well as mopeds and scooters. **Moped Hospital** (601 Truman Ave., tel. 305/296–3344) supplies balloon-tire bikes with yellow safety baskets, as well as mopeds.

Diving and **Captain's Corner** (511-A Greene St., tel. 305/296–8865), a PADI five
Fishing star–rated shop, provides dive classes in English, French, German, Italian, Swedish, and Japanese. All captains are licensed dive masters. Reservations are accepted for regular reef and wreck diving, spear and lobster fishing, and archaeological and treasure hunting. The shop also runs fishing charters and a 60-foot dive boat—*Sea Eagle*—which departs twice daily.

Linda D III & IV (Dock 19, Amberjack Pier, City Marina, Garrison Bight, tel. 305/296–9798), captained by third-generation Key Wester Bill Wickers, Jr., offers half-day, full-day, and night sportfishing.

The Arts and   **Red Barn Theater** (319 Duval St. [rear], tel. 305/296–9911), a profes-
Nightlife   sional, 94-seat theater in its 15th year, performs dramas, comedies,
The Arts   and musicals, including plays by new playwrights.

Tennessee Williams Fine Arts Center (Florida Keys Community College, 5901 W. Junior College Rd., tel. 305/296–1520) presents chamber music, dance, jazz concerts, and plays (dramatic and musical)
with national and international stars, as well as other performing-
arts events, November–April.

Waterfront Playhouse (Mallory Sq., tel. 305/294–5015) is a mid-
1850s wrecker's warehouse that was converted into a 185-seat, non-
Equity community theater presenting comedy and drama November–May.

Nightlife   **Capt. Tony's Saloon** (428 Greene St., tel. 305/294–1838) is a landmark bar, owned until 1988 by a legend in his own right, Capt. Tony
Tarracino—a former bootlegger, smuggler, mercenary, gunrun-
ner, gambler, raconteur—and lately Key West mayor. The building
dates from 1851, when it was first used as a morgue and ice house;
later it was Key West's first telegraph station. The bar was the original Sloppy Joe's from 1933 to 1937. Hemingway was a regular, and
Jimmy Buffet got his start here. Live country and rhythm-and-blues
make the scene nowadays, and the house drink, the Pirates' Punch,
contains a secret rum-based formula.

Havana Docks Lounge (1 Duval St., tel. 305/296–4600, ext. 571, 572)
is a high-energy disco popular with young locals and visitors. The
deck is a good place to watch the sun set when Mallory Square gets
too crowded.

Margaritaville Cafe (500 Duval St., tel. 305/292–1435) is owned by
Key West resident and recording star Jimmy Buffett, who has been
known to perform here but more often just has lunch. The house special drink is, of course, a margarita. There's live music nightly. (The
Margaritaville Store is at the same address.)

Schooner Wharf Waterfront Bar (202 William St., tel. 305/292–9520)
amounts to a laid-back tiki hut. Called "the last little piece of Old
Key West," it's where the town's waiters and waitresses hang out.
You can hear live music weekends (and sometimes at other times) in
the warehouse space next door.

Sloppy Joe's (201 Duval St., tel. 305/294–5717) is the successor to a
famous speakeasy named for its founder, Capt. Joe Russell. Ernest
Hemingway liked to gamble in a partitioned club room in back. Decorated with Hemingway memorabilia and marine flags, the bar is
popular with tourists and is full and noisy all the time. Live entertainment plays daily, noon to 2 AM.

The Top Lounge (430 Duval St., tel. 305/296–2991) is on the seventh
floor of the La Concha Holiday Inn, Key West's tallest building, and
is one of the best places to view the sunset. (Celebrities, on the
ground floor, presents weekend entertainment and serves food.)

7 Walt Disney World® and the Orlando Area

Long before the strains of "It's a Small World" echoed through the palmetto scrub, other theme parks tempted visitors away from the beaches into the scruffy interior of central Florida. I–4 hadn't even been built when Dick and Julie Pope created Cypress Gardens, which now holds the record as the region's oldest continuously running attraction. Gatorland sprang up in 1949. But when the Magic Kingdom opened on October 1, 1971, and was immediately successful, the central Florida theme park scene became big business. Sea World filled its tanks two years afterward. Epcot Center debuted in 1982. Disney-MGM Studios Theme Park threw down the movie gauntlet in 1989; Universal Studios answered the challenge one year later. By the end of the decade, Disney will add a fourth major theme park, tentatively titled Wild Animal Kingdom, and Universal will counter with Islands of Adventure.

All this grew up around a clean, sleepy farming town founded as a military outpost, Fort Gatlin, in 1838. Though not on any major waterway, Orlando was surrounded by small, clear, spring-fed lakes, and transplanted northerners planted sprawling oak trees, which vary the original landscape of palmetto scrub and citrus groves. Though this graceful, quiet city often seems to visitors to be lost in the shadow of the theme parks, most of the tourist development is in southwest Orlando, along the I–4 corridor south of Florida's Turnpike. Orlando itself has become a growing center of national and international business activity, and north of downtown are several handsome, prosperous suburbs, most notably Winter Park, where the pace of life is still leisurely and refined.

The sheer volume of unmissable attractions in the Orlando area (each of them worth a visit and each of them fairly pricey) causes vacation costs to mount. However, there are several ways to keep the total down without missing the fun. The first option is to plan your trip for the off-season: any time the majority of American children are in school. Hotel rates and airfares during these times are often discounted, and crowds are smaller. Your second option is to stay in a hotel that isn't on Disney property; rates get lower the farther you get from the parks. Families can take advantage of the great rental-car deals in the area, since the cost of shuttling several people back and forth to attractions can add up. It's also essential to plan your budget in advance—and stick to it. The number of souvenir shops here is staggering, and buying a stuffed Mickey here and a Shamu baseball cap there can soon end up being expensive.

Walt Disney World and Orlando Area Basics

Arriving and Departing

By Plane More than 20 scheduled airlines and more than 30 charter firms operate in and out of **Orlando International Airport,** providing direct service to more than 100 cities in the United States and overseas. At last count, **Delta Airlines,** the official airline of Walt Disney World, had more than 60 flights daily to and from Orlando International. The airport is also a major hub for **United Airlines.** Other airlines serving the airport include **America West, American, Bahamasair, British Airways, Continental, Icelandair, KLM, Mexicana, Northwest, TransBrasil, TWA,** and **USAir.**

Budget Airport Find out in advance whether your hotel offers free airport shuttles;
Transit if not, ask for a recommendation.

Public buses operate between the airport and the main terminal of the **Tri-County Transit Authority** (1200 W. South St., Orlando, tel. 407/841–8240). Though the cost is only 75¢, other options are preferable since downtown is far from most of the hotels used by theme park vacationers.

Mears Transportation Group (tel. 407/423–5566) has meet-and-greet service—they'll meet you at the gate, help you with your luggage, and whisk you away, either in an 11-passenger van, a town car, or a limo. Vans run to Walt Disney World and along U.S. 192 every 30 minutes; prices range from $12.50 one-way for adults ($8.50 for children 4–11) to $22 round-trip adults ($16 children 4–11). Limo rates run around $50–$60 for a town car that will accommodate three or four and $90 for a stretch limo that will seat six. **Town & Country Limo** (tel. 407/828–3035) charges $30–$40 one-way for up to seven, depending on the hotel, while **First Class Transportation** (tel. 407/578–0022) charges $45 one-way for up to four people.

Taxis take only a half hour to get from the airport to most hotels used by WDW visitors and charge about $25 plus tip to the International Drive area, about $10 more to the U.S. 192 area.

By Bus **Greyhound** (tel. 800/231–2222) buses stop in Orlando (555 N. Magruder Ave., tel. 407/843–7720).

By Car From I–95, which runs down Florida's east coast, you can turn off onto I–4 just below Daytona; it's about 50 miles from there to Orlando. If you're taking I–75 down through the middle of the state, get off at Wildwood for Florida's Turnpike, which gets you to Orlando in about 50 miles. The Beeline Expressway is a scenic toll road linking Orlando and Cocoa Beach; it takes about an hour to drive.

By Train **Amtrak** (tel. 800/872–7245) operates the *Silver Star* and the *Silver Meteor* to Florida. Both stop in Winter Park (150 Morse Blvd.), in Orlando (1400 Sligh Blvd.), and then, 20 minutes later, in Kissimmee (416 Pleasant St.).

If you want to have your car in Florida without driving it there, board the **Autotrain** in Lorton, Virginia, near Washington, DC. Its southern terminus is Sanford, Florida, some 23 miles from Orlando.

Getting Around on the Cheap

Though public transportation in Orlando is practically nonexistent and taxis are expensive because of the distances involved, it is by no means absolutely necessary to rent a car when you are in Orlando. If you are staying at a Disney hotel, or if you purchase a four- or five-day passport instead of buying daily admission tickets to the Disney parks, your transportation within Walt Disney World is free (*see* Walt Disney World *in* Exploring the Orlando Area, *below*). Outside Walt Disney World, just about every hotel (and even many motels) is linked to one of several private transportation systems that shuttle travelers back and forth to most of the area attractions for only a few dollars. However, should you want to visit the major theme parks outside Walt Disney World, venture off the beaten track, or eat where most tourists don't, then a rental car is essential. Rental cars are also a money-saving option for families, since the cost of hotel shuttles can add up when several people are involved. Fortunately, Orlando offers some of the lowest rental car rates in the United States. Rates are lower from companies with offices in Orlando or near but not actually in the airport. These budget firms usually offer free pickup service at the hotels and the airport.

By Bus If you are staying along International Drive, in Kissimmee, or in Orlando proper, you can ride public buses to get around the immediate area. To find out which bus to take, ask your hotel clerk or call the **Tri-County Transit Authority Information Office** (tel. 407/841–8240) during business hours. Fares are 75¢ (10¢ extra for transfers), and exact change is required.

By Car The most important artery in the Orlando area is **I-4**. This interstate highway, which links the Atlantic Coast to Florida's Gulf of Mexico, ties everything together, and you'll invariably receive directions in reference to it. The problem is that I-4, though considered an east–west expressway in our national road system (where even numbers signify an east–west orientation and odd numbers a north–south orientation), actually runs north and south in the Orlando area. So when the signs say east, you are usually going north, and when the signs say west, you are usually going south.

Another main drag is **International Drive**, a.k.a. I-Drive, which has many major hotels, restaurants, and shopping centers. You can get onto International Drive from I-4 Exits 28, 29, and 30B.

The other main road, **U.S. 192**, cuts across I-4 at Exits 25A and 25B. This highway goes through the Kissimmee area and crosses Walt Disney World property, taking you to the Magic Kingdom's main entrance. U.S. 192 is sometimes called by its former names, Spacecoast Parkway and Irlo Bronson Memorial Highway.

By Shuttle Scheduled service and charters linking just about every hotel and major attraction in the area are relatively affordable options (if you don't want to rent a car) and are available from **Mears Transportation Group** (tel. 407/423–5566), **Gray Line of Orlando** (tel. 407/422–0744), **Rabbit Bus Lines** (tel. 407/291–2424), and **Phoenix Tours** (tel. 407/859–4211). In addition, many hotels run their own shuttles especially for guests; to arrange a ride, ask your hotel's concierge, inquire at the front desk, or phone the operator directly.

One-way fares are usually $6–$7 per adult, a couple of dollars less for children 4–11, between major hotel areas and the Disney parks. Excursion fares to Cypress Gardens are $27 per person, including admission as well as round-trip fare.

By Taxi Taxis are convenient, but certainly not cheap. Fares start at $2.45 and cost $1.40 for each mile thereafter. Call **Yellow Cab Co.** (tel. 407/699-9999) or **Town and Country Cab** (tel. 407/828-3035). Sample fares are: to WDW's Magic Kingdom, about $20 from International Drive, $11-$15 from U.S. 192; to Universal Studios, $6-$11 from International Drive, $25-$30 from U.S. 192; to downtown Orlando's Church Street Station, $20-$25 from International Drive, $30-$40 from U.S. 192.

Important Addresses and Numbers

Emergencies Dial 911 for **police** or **ambulance.** All the area's major theme parks have first-aid centers.

Hospitals Hospital emergency rooms are open 24 hours a day. The most accessible hospital, located in the International Drive area, is the **Orlando Regional Medical Center/Sand Lake Hospital** (9400 Turkey Lake Rd., tel. 407/351-8500).

Dentists **Emergency dental referral** (tel. 407/847-7474).

Late-Night Pharmacies **Eckerd Drugs** (908 Lee Rd., just off I-4 at the Lee Road exit, Orlando, tel. 407/644-6908) and **Walgreen** (6201 International Dr., opposite Wet 'n' Wild, Orlando, tel. 407/345-8311 or 407/345-8402; 4578 S. Kirkman Rd., just north of Universal Studios, tel. 407/293-8458).

Visitor Information For general information about Walt Disney World, contact **Walt Disney World** (Guest Letters, Box 10040, Lake Buena Vista 32830, tel. 407/824-4321, TTY 407/827-5141). Request the free *Walt Disney World Vacation Guide.* For reservations or accommodations and entertainment, phone the Central Reservations Office (CRO, tel. 407/934-7639; TTY, 407/345-5984). To be a member of the audience at a show being taped at Disney-MGM Studios, call Production Information (tel. 407/560-4651).

Other area visitors bureaus include:

Kissimmee/St. Cloud Convention and Visitors' Bureau (1925 E. Irlo Bronson Hwy., Kissimmee 34744, tel. 407/847-5000, 407/363-5800, or 800/327-9159).

Orlando/Orange County Convention and Visitors Bureau (8445 International Dr., Orlando 32819, tel. 407/363-5871).

Winter Park Chamber of Commerce (Box 280, Winter Park 32790, tel. 407/644-8281).

Where to Stay on a Budget

With nearly 80,000 hotel rooms, Orlando has a lodging to fit your budget—no matter what it is. Your basic options come down to properties that are (1) owned and operated by Disney on WDW grounds, (2) not owned or operated by Disney but located on Disney property, and (3) not located on WDW property. On-site hotels, whether Disney-owned or not, are generally expensive, though there are now some moderately priced establishments on Disney property. The best way to save money on lodging, as a rule, is to come off-season, that is, any time that most American children are in school. The next best way is to base yourself off Disney property; rates get lower the farther away you go.

For the best bargains but basic accommodations, head for the U.S. 192 strip in Kissimmee—a.k.a the Irlo Bronson Memorial Highway—crammed with mom-and-pop motels and bargain-basement hotels, cheap restaurants, fast-food spots, nickel-and-dime attractions, gas stations, and minimarts. Room rates start at $20 a night at the right time of year, if you can cut the right deal.

Disney's on-site hotels do offer a lot for their higher prices. Built with families in mind, rooms are usually large enough to accommodate up to five; all accommodations offer baby-sitting and cable TV with the Disney Channel. As an on-site guest, you can call in advance to make reservations at any of the restaurants in Epcot Center and Disney-MGM Studios. For Disney dinner show reservations, on-site guests can book as far in advance as they want (outsiders can only reserve seats 30 to 45 days in advance, depending on the show). In addition, on-site guests can gain admission to the Magic Kingdom one hour before regular park opening. Even when the theme parks or water parks have reached capacity (as River Country, Typhoon Lagoon, and Disney-MGM Studios sometimes do), on-site guests are guaranteed entry. Additionally, on-site hotels offer many of their own special events. Best of all, Walt Disney World buses and monorails are free to guests at on-site resorts (as well as to those who have purchased multiday passes), making it easy to shuttle from one Disney park to another. Because of the additional convenience of on-site accommodations, you can see more Disney in less time—and save money by shaving a day from your Disney vacation.

There are two ways of staying on-site for less: Choose one of the several new moderately priced Disney-owned properties, or lodge in one of the "official" Disney hotels. Although not owned or operated by the Disney organization, the latter offer their guests many of the same courtesies available to guests at Disney-owned properties— for instance, guests can make telephone reservations for restaurants and dinner shows in Walt Disney World in advance of the general public. At the moderately priced Disney hotels, you'll enjoy all the benefits of being a Disney guest; room decor is attractive and upscale, and there are fabulous, inventive swimming pools at each complex. The disadvantage is that rooms are somewhat smaller than at the high-priced resorts and can accommodate only four.

Hotels near Walt Disney World are clustered in several principal areas. In addition to Kissimmee, described above, there's International Drive, a few minutes south of downtown Orlando, and the Disney Maingate area around WDW's northernmost entrance, just off I–4. Nearly all hotels in all these areas provide frequent transportation to and from Walt Disney World.

In all but the smallest motels there is little or no charge for children under 18 who share a room with an adult.

All on-site accommodations, Disney-owned or not, may be booked through the **Walt Disney World Central Reservations Office** (Box 10100, Suite 300, Lake Buena Vista 32830, tel. 407/934–7639). You must give a deposit for your first night's stay within three weeks of making your reservation. Reservations should be made several months in advance—as much as a year in advance for the best rooms during high season (historically, Christmas vacation, summer, and from mid-February through the week after Easter). Many hotels and attractions offer discounts up to 40% from September to mid-December.

Packages, including cruises, car rentals, and hotels both on and off Disney property, can be arranged through your travel agent or **Walt Disney Travel Co.** (1675 Buena Vista Dr., Lake Buena Vista 32830, tel. 800/828–0228).

Inside Walt Disney World
$$

All-Star Sports and All-Star Music Resorts. This large complex, at the northwest quadrant of the World Drive/U.S. 192 interchange, southwest of the Disney-MGM Studios and Epcot Center, is the first phase of a project that is rumored to include a fourth major theme park. Meanwhile, guests can enjoy the zany design of these two new resorts, which opened in the spring and summer of 1994. Every aspect of the resorts' architecture, landscaping, and lighting displays an over-the-top devotion to their themes: The five three-story build-

231

Orlando Area Lodging

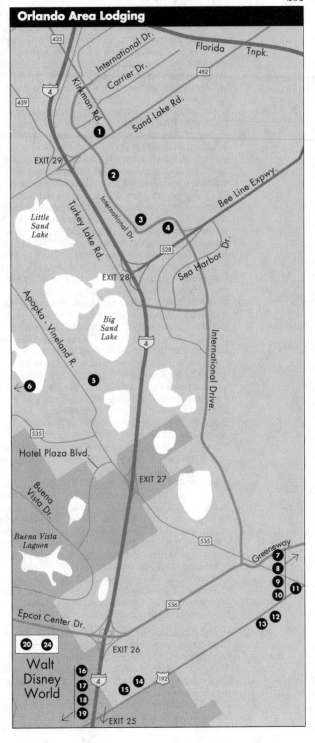

ings at each represent a different sport (baseball, football, tennis, surfing, and basketball) or type of music (Broadway, country and western, calypso, jazz, and rock and roll). Included are such eye-catching features as stairwells in the shape of soda cups, a courtyard that looks like a football field, a three-story silhouette of a sax player, and a pool shaped like a guitar. The rooms, which have two double beds, are intended to accommodate four. *Tel. 407/934–7639. 1,920 rooms at each. Facilities: 2 food courts, 2 poolside bars, 4 pools, game room, baby-sitting, guest laundry. AE, MC, V.*

$$ ★ **Caribbean Beach Resort.** This immensely popular 200-acre property surrounding a 42-acre lake, just east of Epcot Center and Disney-MGM Studios theme parks, comprises five palm-studded island "villages," awash with the bright colors of the Caribbean, each with its own pool and white-sand beach. Bridges over the lake connect the mainland with 1-acre Parrot Cay, where there's a play area for children. A mile-long promenade circles the lake and is favored by '80s joggers, '90s bikers, and old-fashioned romantic strollers. Attractive, pastel-hued guest rooms are equipped with minibars and coffeemakers. The only drawbacks compared to other on-site properties are somewhat smaller rooms, limited dining options, and no supervised children's program. *Tel. 407/934–7639. 2,106 rooms. Facilities: food court, lounge, 7 outdoor pools, children's pool, beach, bike rentals, marina, boat rentals, jogging track, whirlpool, game room, playground, baby-sitting. AE, MC, V.*

$ **Fort Wilderness Resort and Campground.** If you're seeking a calm spot amid the theme-park storm, you need go no farther than these 700 acres of scrubby pine, tiny streams, and peaceful canals on the shore of subtropical Bay Lake, about a mile from the Wilderness Lodge Resort. With a bunch of kids playing softball in one corner and a couple of families getting together for a cookout in another, you could easily forget the Magic Kingdom is only a Mouse's skip away. Sports facilities abound; the large number of waterways are great for fishing, canoeing, and sailing; and River Country and the Meadow Recreation Complex are nearby. And bringing a tent or RV is one of the cheapest ways to actually stay on WDW property, especially considering that sites accommodate up to 10. Tent sites, with water and electricity, are the best bargains, but RV sites, which cost more, come equipped with electric, water, and sewage hookups as well as outdoor charcoal grills and picnic tables. You can even get maid service for your trailer. Three hundred "preferred sites," those closest to the lake (numbering from 100 to 500, in the 700s, and in the 1400s), have higher prices but also have cable TV hookups. Each group of sites has rest rooms, showers, telephones, an ice machine, and a laundry room. You can also rent one of the fully equipped, air-conditioned Disney trailers (known as Wilderness Homes) parked on the property, but they're considerably more expensive. *Tel. 407/934–7639 or 407/824–2900 for same-day reservations and fax. 390 tent sites, 387 trailer sites. Facilities: cafeteria, snack bar, 3 outdoor heated pools, lakeside beach, bike paths, bike and canoe rental, horseback riding, volleyball, fitness trail, petting farm, game room, grocery store, guest laundry. AE, MC, V.*

Splurge **Grand Floridian.** Set on the shores of the Seven Seas Lagoon, this looks like a turn-of-the-century summer resort, with its gabled red roof, brick chimneys, rambling verandas, and delicate gingerbread. Although equipped with every modern convenience, the softly colored rooms have real vintage charm, especially the attic nooks, up under the eaves. Even the resort's monorail station carries the elegant Victorian theme. Deluxe suites are available in the smaller lodge. *Tel. 407/824–3000. 834 rooms, 71 suites. Facilities: 5 restaurants, 4 lounges, outdoor pool, beach, 2 lighted tennis courts, marina, boat rentals, health club, whirlpool, children's program, playground. AE, MC, V.*

Splurge **Walt Disney World Wilderness Lodge.** This mammoth, rustic lodge is
★ modeled after the early 20th-century structures in national parks of
the Pacific Northwest, but guests won't exactly rough it. The
pricey, six-story establishment opened in summer 1994 on the
southwest shore of Bay Lake, in the Magic Kingdom resort area. Its
massive lobby features a huge, three-sided stone fireplace constructed of rocks from the Grand Canyon, enormous iron chandeliers with Indian and buffalo motifs, and two authentic 50-foot totem
poles. Rooms all have western decor: hard-backed leather chairs,
patchwork quilts, and cowboy art. The large swimming pool area
begins as a hot spring in the main lobby, flows under a window wall
to an upper courtyard, and widens into a rushing waterfall. *Tel. 407/
934–7639. 697 rooms, 29 suites. Facilities: 3 restaurants, lounge,
heated outdoor pool, children's pool, golf, game room, children's
program. AE, MC, V.*

International **Fairfield Inn by Marriott.** This understated, few-frills, three-story
Drive hotel—the Marriott Corporation's answer to the Motel 6 and
$$ Econolodge chains—is a natural for single travelers or small fami-
lies on a tight budget. It's squeezed between International Drive
and the highway and doesn't have the amenities of top-of-the-line
Marriott properties, but nice perks such as complimentary coffee
and tea, free local phone calls, work desks, and cable TV give a sense
of being at a much fancier property. *8342 Jamaican Ct., Orlando
32819, tel. 407/363–1944 or 800/228–2800, fax 407/363–1944. 135
rooms. Facilities: heated outdoor pool, game room. AE, D, DC, MC,
V.*

$$ **Orlando Heritage Inn.** Smaller hotels do have more charm. The exte-
★ rior of this two-story structure—pale pink clapboard and white rail-
ings—was inspired by *Gone with the Wind*, but the interior is
modeled on Victorian-era Florida. It's full of reproduction turn-of-
the-century furnishings, French windows, patterned tin ceilings,
and brass lamps, interspersed with 19th-century antiques. In the
guest rooms, folk art hangs on the walls, lace curtains on the double
French doors, and quilted spreads cover the beds. Dinner shows are
presented in the rotunda several nights weekly. In-room safes are
provided. *9861 International Dr., Orlando 32819, tel. 407/352–0008
or 800/447–1890. 150 rooms. Facilities: restaurant, lounge, dinner
theater, outdoor pool, baby-sitting, guest laundry. AE, D, DC, MC,
V.*

$$ **Wynfield Inn–Westwood.** This three-story motel is a find. Its cheer-
ful, contemporary rooms are smartly appointed with colorful, floral-
print bedspreads and understated wall hangings. Complimentary
fruit, coffee, and tea are served in the lobby daily. The staff is
friendly and helpful. Children 17 and under stay free in their par-
ents' room (with a maximum of four guests per room). In-room mov-
ies are available. *6263 Westwood Blvd., Orlando 32821, tel. 407/345–
8000 or 800/346–1551. 300 rooms. Facilities: pool bar, 2 outdoor
pools, game room, guest laundry. AE, D, MC, V.*

Maingate **Perri House.** Exactly 1 mile from the Magic Kingdom as the crow
$$ flies and situated at the top of a sheltered side road, this modern,
★ bed-and-breakfast-style country inn, set amid 20 acres of serenity,
is a truly unique lodging in "build it bigger and they will come" Orlando. Nick and Angi Perretti and their three grown children
planned and built the clever circular house so that each neatly furnished room has an outside entrance. What really sets Perri House
apart, however, is that it is in the process of becoming an Audubon
Society–recognized bird sanctuary—including walking paths, ga-
zebos, a pond, feeding station, and so on. A Continental breakfast is
included. *10417 Rte. 535, Lake Buena Vista 32830, tel. 407/876–4830
or 800/780–4830. 6 rooms. Facilities: outdoor pool, bird sanctuary.
AE, D, MC, V.*

$$ **Wyndham Garden Hotel.** Formerly the Doubletree Club Hotel, this
★ six-story complex looks like an office building from the outside, but

don't be discouraged. Inside it's full of homey touches, such as a 5,000-square-foot club area with loads of big comfy couches and a giant-screen TV. The new owners have remodeled all public areas and redecorated rooms in Florida blues and greens. *8688 Palm Pkwy., Lake Buena Vista 32830, tel. 407/239–8500 or 800/996–3426. 167 rooms. Facilities: restaurant, lounge, outdoor pool, health club, whirlpool. AE, D, DC, MC, V.*

U.S. 192 Area
$$

Holiday Inn Maingate East. Everything seems to be the biggest something in Orlando, and Maingate East is the world's largest two-story Holiday Inn. The service is good, despite the size, but that's not the only reason to stay here. The whole interior recently got a multimillion-dollar makeover; all rooms now have a TV and VCR, and kitchenettes are fully equipped. You can rent videotapes and buy snacks and groceries in the lobby, and some of the restaurants serve buffet-style—an added convenience. There's also a supervised program for kids 3–12 from 8 AM to midnight. *5678 W. Irlo Bronson Memorial Hwy., Kissimmee 34746, tel. 407/396–4488, 800/366–5437, or 800/465–4329; fax 407/396–1296. 670 rooms. Facilities: 6 restaurants, café, 2 lounges, 2 Olympic-size pools (1 heated), wading pool, 2 lighted tennis courts, 2 game rooms, 2 whirlpools, children's program, 2 playgrounds, small convenience store, guest laundry. AE, D, DC, MC, V.*

$$

Hyatt Orlando Hotel. This is not a place for those who are prone to getting lost. Instead of a single tower, this very large hotel consists of 10 two-story buildings in four clusters. Each cluster is a community with its own heated pool, whirlpool, park, and playground at its center. The rooms are spacious, but otherwise unmemorable. The lobby is vast and mall-like, with numerous shops and restaurants: The Foi-Foi is upscale Italian, and there is also a very good deli. If you'll be spending most of your time attacking Orlando attractions, the reasonable rates and convenience (it's the closest independent property to WDW) will more than make up for the unremarkable nature of the place. *6375 W. Irlo Bronson Memorial Hwy., Kissimmee 34746, tel. 407/396–1234 or 800/228–3336, fax 407/396–5090. 888 rooms, 34 suites. Facilities: 4 restaurants, deli, lounge, 4 heated outdoor pools, 3 lighted tennis courts, jogging trail, game room, health club, 4 whirlpools, 4 playgrounds, baby-sitting, guest laundry. AE, D, DC, MC, V.*

$$
★

Radisson Inn Maingate. This sleek, twin-towered, seven-story modern hotel, just a few minutes from WDW's front door, has cheerful guest rooms, large bathrooms, and plenty of extras for the price. It's not fancy, but it is perfectly adequate. The best rooms are those with a view of the pool. Two floors in each tower are reserved for nonsmokers. *7501 W. Irlo Bronson Memorial Hwy., Kissimmee 34746, tel. 407/396–1400 or 800/333–3333, fax 407/396–0660. 575 rooms, 5 suites. Facilities: restaurant, deli, lounge, poolside bar, heated outdoor pool, 2 lighted tennis courts, jogging trail, exercise room, whirlpool, baby-sitting, guest laundry. AE, D, DC, MC, V.*

$$

Sheraton Lakeside Inn. This complex of 15 two-story buildings with balconies is spread over 27 acres with a small man-made lake. Comfortable though undistinguished, the resort offers quite a few recreational facilities for the money. The nondescript beige rooms have either two double beds or one king-size bed as well as a refrigerator and safe. *7769 W. Irlo Bronson Memorial Hwy., Kissimmee 34746, tel. 407/239–2650 or 800/848–0801. 651 rooms. Facilities: 2 restaurants, deli, lounge, 3 outdoor pools, children's pool, miniature golf, 4 lighted tennis courts, paddleboat and fishing-equipment rentals, children's program. AE, D, DC, MC, V.*

$

Best Western Kissimmee. Overlooking a nine-hole, par-3 executive golf course, this independently owned and operated three-story hotel is a hit with golf-loving seniors as well as with families. The two swimming pools in the garden courtyard are amply shaded. The spacious rooms are done in soft pastels, with light wood furniture and attractive wall hangings. Units with king-size beds and kitchenettes are available. *2261 E. Irlo Bronson Memorial Hwy., Kissimmee 34744, tel. 407/846–2221 or 800/944–0662. 282 rooms. Facilities: restaurant, lounge, 2 outdoor pools, playground, picnic area. AE, D, MC, V.*

$ **Comfort Inn Maingate.** This hotel is close to Walt Disney World—just a mile away—so you can save a bundle without unduly inconveniencing yourself. Standard rooms are light and airy with a mauve-and-soft-blue color scheme; deluxe rooms, overlooking a landscaped garden, have refrigerators, coffeemakers, and hair dryers. Children 17 and under stay free, and those under 12 eat free. *7571 W. Irlo Bronson Memorial Hwy., Kissimmee 34746, tel. 407/396–7500 or 800/228–5150, fax 407/396–7497. 281 rooms. Facilities: restaurant, lounge, outdoor pool, game room, gift shop, guest laundry. AE, D, DC, MC, V.*

$ **Quality Inn Lake Cecile.** Rooms at this plain-Jane inn are adequate, not fancy—but those close to the lake are prettier as well as quieter. *4944 W. Irlo Bronson Memorial Hwy., Kissimmee 34746, tel. 407/396–4455 or 800/846–4855, fax 407/396–4182. 222 rooms. Facilities: outdoor pool, lakeside beach, guest laundry. AE, D, DC, MC, V.*

$ **Red Roof Inn.** If you want a clean, quiet room but don't want to gamble on an independent, this three-story chain motel delivers consistently. The small, comfortable rooms are decorated in blues and grays. A big plus are the many fast-food and budget-priced eateries within walking distance. The complimentary daily newspaper and coffee each morning are pleasant surprises. *4970 Kyng's Heath Rd., Kissimmee 34746, tel. 407/396–0065 or 800/843–7663, fax 407/396–0245. 102 rooms. Facilities: outdoor pool, heated whirlpool, guest laundry. AE, D, DC, MC, V.*

¢ **Casa Rosa Inn.** For simple motel living—no screaming kids or loud music, please—this pink, Spanish-motif spot run by a Chinese immigrant family is the place you want. It's simple and doesn't have much in the way of facilities aside from its pool, complimentary morning coffee, and free in-room movies. Still, it's only 5 miles from the Magic Kingdom; it's a good, serviceable option; and the price is right. *4600 W. Irlo Bronson Memorial Hwy., Kissimmee 34746, tel. 407/396–2020 or 800/432–0665. 56 rooms. Facilities: outdoor pool, guest laundry. AE, D, DC, MC, V.*

¢ **Knights Inn–Maingate.** Part of a national chain, this one-story motel, with a prefab Old World facade, is not exactly an English charmer, but it does offer spacious, clean rooms at budget prices; some have kitchenettes and sofas. Don't expect fine antiques; serviceable veneer is the predominant design statement. *7475 W. Irlo Bronson Memorial Hwy., Kissimmee 34746, tel. 407/396–4200 or 800/843–5644, fax 407/396–8838. 120 rooms. Facilities: heated outdoor pool, game room, guest laundry. AE, D, MC, V.*

¢ **Park Inn International.** The Mediterranean-style architecture is not likely to charm you off your feet, but the staff is friendly and the property has all the facilities you're likely to want—and it's on Cedar Lake. Ask for a room as close to the water as possible. There is a restaurant, but for an extra $10 you can get a room with a kitchenette. *4960 W. Irlo Bronson Memorial Hwy., Kissimmee 34741, tel. 407/396–1376 or 800/327–0072. 197 rooms. Facilities: restaurant, outdoor pool, game room, whirlpool. AE, D, DC, MC, V.*

¢ **Record Motel.** This simple property is the kind of few-frills, rock-bottom-rates mom-and-pop operation that made U.S. 192 famous. Clean rooms with free HBO, complimentary morning coffee, and a solar-heated pool are the major amenities. What the place lacks in luxuries and ambience it more than makes up for with its friendly staff. *4651 W. Irlo Bronson Memorial Hwy., Kissimmee 34746, tel. 407/396–8400. 57 rooms. Facilities: outdoor pool, baby-sitting. AE, D, MC, V.*

¢ **Sevilla Inn.** This classy, family-operated motel is one of the best
★ buys in the Orlando area. Stucco and wood on the outside, the three-

story building has up-to-date rooms inside, with colorful bed-spreads, tasteful wall hangings, a fresh mauve or green paint job, and cable TV. The pool area, encircled by palm trees and tropical flowers, feels like something you'd find in a much fancier resort. *4640 W. Irlo Bronson Memorial Hwy., Kissimmee 34746, tel. 407/ 396–4135 or 800/367–1363. 46 rooms. Facilities: outdoor pool. AE, D, MC, V.*

Exploring the Orlando Area

Orlando for Free—or Almost

The Arts A number of free or very inexpensive offerings are clustered in or near Winter Park. **Rollins College** (*see* The Arts and Nightlife, *below*) presents a choral concert series during the school year. Local museums display everything from European and American art to Orlando memorabilia. Of special note are the **Cornell Fine Arts Museum, Charles Hosmer Morse Museum of American Art, Orange County Historical Museum,** and the **Orlando Museum of Art** (*see* Winter Park Area, *below*, for all).

Window-Shopping Though its trendy boutiques and restaurants are priced above a budget-watcher's budget, Winter Park's **Park Avenue** is a great place to people-watch and take in local color. It's divided by Central Park, where benches under the ancient trees offer a respite from the hustle and bustle. Another spot that's better for window-shopping than bargain-hunting is **Church Street Exchange** (*see* Shopping for Bargains, *below*), a complex of specialty shops. **Flea World** (*see* Shopping for Bargains, *below*) is a far cry from the chichi shops of Winter Park and Church Street. The people-watching alone (Tammy Faye Bakker used to be a regular) is worth the trip.

Parks **Mead Gardens** (*see* Winter Park Area, *below*), a natural preserve, provides a welcome change from the ultra-landscaped worlds of the theme parks. **Leu Botanical Gardens** (*see* Winter Park Area, *below*) and **Central Florida Zoological Park** (*see* Other Sites of Interest, *below*) display nice collections of flora and fauna, respectively.

Walt Disney World

Numbers in the margin correspond to points of interest on the Orlando Area map.

① **Walt Disney World** (WDW) has its own everything: its own resorts, its own complete transportation system, and its own lingo. Everything's fairly simple to understand once you get in the Disney swing.

WDW Essentials
Transportation The elevated **monorail** serves many important destinations. It has two loops: one linking the Magic Kingdom, an area known as the Transportation and Ticket Center (TTC), and a handful of resorts, including the Contemporary, Grand Floridian, and Polynesian Village; and the other looping from the TTC directly to Epcot Center.

Motor **launches** connect WDW destinations located on waterways. Specifically, they operate between the Epcot Center resorts (except the Caribbean Beach) and Disney-MGM Studios and between Discovery Island (in Bay Lake) and the Magic Kingdom, Wilderness Lodge, Grand Floridian, and the Fort Wilderness Campground, Polynesian, and Contemporary resorts (Discovery Island admission ticket, WDW resort ID, or multiday admission ticket required).

In addition, **buses** provide direct service from every on-site resort to both major and minor theme parks, and express buses go directly between the major theme parks. To Typhoon Lagoon, you can go directly from (or make connections at) the Disney Village Market-

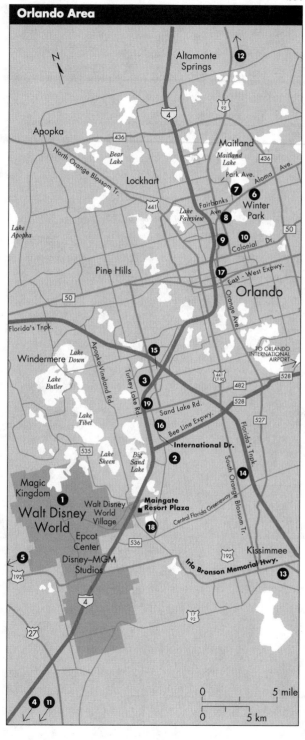

Orlando Area

Walt Disney World

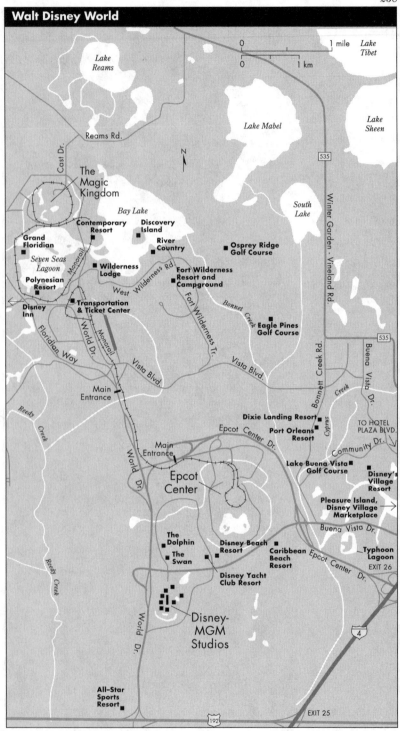

Lake Tibet

Lake Reams

Lake Sheen

Lake Mabel

Reams Rd.

Cast Dr.

535

South Lake

Winter Garden - Vineland Rd.

The Magic Kingdom

Bay Lake

Contemporary Resort

Discovery Island

River Country

Osprey Ridge Golf Course

Grand Floridian

Seven Seas Lagoon

Wilderness Lodge

Polynesian Resort

Fort Wilderness Resort and Campground

Wilderness Rd.

535

Disney Inn

Transportation & Ticket Center

West

Monorail

Fort Wilderness Tr.

Bonnet Creek

Eagle Pines Golf Course

Buena Vista Dr.

Floridian Way

World Dr.

Monorail

Vista Blvd.

Vista Blvd.

Bonnett Creek Rd.

Creek

Reedy Creek

Main Entrance

Dixie Landing Resort

Cypress

TO HOTEL PLAZA BLVD.

World Dr.

Main Entrance

Epcot Center Dr.

Port Orleans Resort

Community Dr.

Lake Buena Vista Golf Course

Disney's Village Resort

Epcot Center

Pleasure Island, Disney Village Marketplace

Buena Vista Dr.

Reedy Creek

The Dolphin

The Swan

Disney Beach Resort

Caribbean Beach Resort

Epcot Center Dr.

Typhoon Lagoon

EXIT 26

Disney Yacht Club Resort

World Dr.

Disney-MGM Studios

4

All-Star Sports Resort

192

EXIT 25

0 ___ 1 mile

0 ___ 1 km

N

place, Epcot Center, and the Epcot Center resorts (the Beach and Yacht clubs, the Caribbean Beach Resort, the Swan, and the Dolphin).

From the Epcot Center resort area, **trams** operate to the International Gateway of the park's World Showcase section.

Monorail, launches, buses, and trams all operate during the hours that you'll want them—usually from early in the morning until at least midnight. (Hours are shorter during early closing periods.) Check on the operating hours of the service you need if you plan to be out later than that.

All of this transportation is free if you are staying at an on-site resort, or if you hold a three-park ticket. If not, you can buy unlimited transportation within Walt Disney World for $2.50 a day.

Every theme park has a parking lot—and all are huge. Always write down exactly where you park your car and take the number with you. Trams make frequent trips between the parking area and the parks' turnstile areas. The cost is $5 for each lot (free to Walt Disney World resort guests with ID), except for Typhoon Lagoon, where parking is free.

Admission Fees and Tickets   Visiting Walt Disney World is not cheap, especially if you have a child or two along. Everyone 10 and older pays adult prices; reductions are available for children 3–9. Children under three get in free. No discounted family tickets are available.

In Disneyspeak, "ticket" refers to a single day's admission to the Magic Kingdom, Epcot Center, or the Disney-MGM Studios. A ticket is good in the park for which you buy it only on the day you buy it; if you buy a one-day ticket and later decide to extend your visit, you can apply the cost of it toward the purchase of any passport (but only before you leave the park). Exchanges can be made at City Hall in the Magic Kingdom, at Earth Station in Epcot Center, or at Guest Relations at Disney-MGM.

There are a number of options for those staying longer than three days. The **Four-Day Value Pass** allows you to visit each of the three parks on any three days and then one of the parks again on one more day. You cannot visit more than one park on any day. To avoid this restriction, you can get the **Four-Day Park Hopper,** a personalized photo-ID pass that allows unlimited admission to the three parks on any four days. The **Five-Day World Hopper** is also a photo ID; it includes unlimited visits to the three theme parks over five days, plus seven days' admission to WDW's minor parks—Pleasure Island, Typhoon Lagoon, River Country, Blizzard Beach, and Discovery Island. Disney says it introduced the new park-hopping passes as photo IDs to prevent counterfeiting and the illegal resale of passports. (First, however, there was quite a controversy over an earlier decision to allow park hopping only to guests registered at hotels on Disney property.)

These three passes can save you money. In fact, if you plan to visit the minor parks or go to Typhoon Lagoon more than once, it may pay to buy a Five-Day World Hopper Pass even if you're staying only four days. Each time you use a passport, the entry date is stamped on it; remaining days may be used years in the future. A variety of annual passes are also available, at a cost only slightly more than a World Hopper Pass; if you plan to visit twice in a year, these are a good deal.

Guests at Disney resorts can also purchase **Length of Stay Passes,** which are good from the time of arrival until midnight of the departure day. Passes may be purchased at the front desks of all resorts as well as in Guest Services at the three theme parks. Prices (not including tax) are based upon the number of room nights and range from $80 for a 1-night, 2-day adult pass to $262 for 9 nights, 10 days. The pass is good for all three theme parks, as well as the three water parks, Pleasure Island, and Discovery Island.

Disney changes its prices at least once a year and without any notice. At press time, WDW admission prices (including 6% tax) were as follows, but call as close as possible to the time of your trip for the most current information.

	Adults	Children
One-day ticket	$38.10	$30.60
Four-Day Value Pass	$130.95	$102.45
Four-Day Park Hopper	$141.55	$113.05
Five-Day World Hopper	$189.15	$151.10
River Country	$15.64	$12.19
Discovery Island	$10.60	$5.83
Combined River Country/ Discovery Island	$19.61	$14.05
Typhoon Lagoon	$23.85	$18.02
Blizzard Beach	$23.85	$18.02
Pleasure Island	$16.91	$16.91

Tickets and passports to Walt Disney World, Epcot Center, and Disney-MGM Studios Theme Park can be purchased at admission booths at the TTC, in all on-site resorts (if you're a registered guest), and at the Walt Disney World kiosk at Orlando International Airport (2nd floor, main terminal). American Express, Visa, and MasterCard are accepted, as are cash, personal checks (with ID), and traveler's checks. Many offices of the American Automobile Association (AAA) also sell discounted tickets; check with your local office for availability.

Opening and Closing Hours Operating hours for the Magic Kingdom, Epcot Center, and Disney-MGM Studios Theme Park vary widely throughout the year and change for school and legal holidays. In general, the longest days are during the prime summer months and over the year-end holidays, when the Magic Kingdom is open to midnight (later on New Year's Eve); Epcot Center is open to 11 PM; and Disney-MGM is open to 9 PM.

At other times, Epcot Center and Disney-MGM are open until 8 and the Magic Kingdom until 6 (Main Street until 7)—but there are variations, so call ahead.

Note that though the Magic Kingdom, Epcot Center's Future World, and Disney-MGM officially open at 9 AM, visitors may enter at 8:30, and sometimes at 8. The parking lots open at least an hour before the parks. Arriving at the Magic Kingdom turnstiles before "rope drop," the official opening time, you can breakfast in a restaurant on Main Street, which opens before the rest of the park, and be ready to dash to one of the popular attractions in other lands at rope drop. Arriving in Epcot Center or Disney-MGM studios, you can make dinner reservations before the crowds arrive and take in some of the attractions and pavilions well before the major crowds descend, which is usually at about 10.

Ratings Every visitor leaves the Magic Kingdom, Epcot Center, and Disney-MGM Studios with a different opinion about what was "the best."

Some attractions get raves from all visitors, while others are enjoyed mostly by young children or older travelers. To take this into account, our descriptions rate each attraction with ★ , ★ ★ , or ★ ★ ★, depending on the strength of its appeal to the visitor group noted by the italics.

Magic Kingdom For most people, the Magic Kingdom *is* Walt Disney World. Certainly it is both the heart and soul of the Disney empire. The Magic Kingdom is comparable to California's Disneyland; it was the first Disney outpost in Florida when it opened in 1971, and it is the park that traveled, with modifications, to France and Japan. For a park that wields such worldwide influence, the Magic Kingdom is surprisingly small: At barely 98 acres, it is the tiniest of Walt Disney World's Big Three. However, packed into six different "lands" are nearly 50 major crowd-pleasers, and that's not counting all the ancillary attractions: shops, eateries, live entertainment, cartoon characters, fireworks, and parades.

The park is laid out on a north–south axis, with Cinderella Castle at the epicenter and the various lands surrounding it in a broad circle. Upon passing through the entrance gates, you immediately discover yourself in **Town Square,** a central area containing **City Hall,** the principal information center. Here you can pick up the *Magic Kingdom Guide Book* and a schedule of daily events; search for misplaced belongings or companions; and ask questions of the omniscient staffers behind the desk.

Town Square directly segues into **Main Street,** a boulevard filled with Victorian-style stores and dining spots. Main Street runs due north and ends at the **Hub,** a large tree-lined circle in front of Cinderella Castle. Moving clockwise from the Hub, the Magic Kingdom's different lands are **Adventureland, Frontierland, Liberty Square, Fantasyland** (located directly behind Cinderella Castle), **Mickey's Starland,** and **Tomorrowland.**

Main Street Step right up to the elevated platform above the Magic Kingdom's entrance for a ride on the **Walt Disney World Railroad.** The 1½-mile track runs along the perimeter of the Magic Kingdom, through the woods and past Tom Sawyer Island and other attractions; stops are in Frontierland and Mickey's Starland. It's a great introduction to the layout of the park and a much-welcomed relief for tired feet. The four trains run at five- to seven-minute intervals; a complete circuit takes 21 minutes. *Audience: All ages. Rating:* ★

Although attractions with a capital "A" are minimal on Main Street, there are plenty of inducements to spend more than the 40 minutes most visitors usually take. The stores that most of the structures house range from the **House of Magic,** complete with trick-showing proprietors, to the **Harmony Barber Shop,** where you can have yourself shorn, to a milliner's emporium stocking Cat-in-the-Hat fantasies, to all sorts of snack and souvenir shops. The **Penny Arcade** lets you try vintage coin-operated games and kinescopes. The best time to shop is mid-afternoon, when the lines at the rides are long and slow.

Six screens run continuous vintage Disney cartoons in the cool, air-conditioned quiet of the **Main Street Cinema,** halfway up Main Street on the right. It's a great opportunity to see the genius of Walt Disney and to see *Steamboat Willie*, Mickey Mouse's debut cartoon. *Audience: All ages. Rating:* ★ ★

Adventureland From the scrubbed brick, manicured lawns, and meticulously pruned trees of the Central Plaza, an artfully dilapidated wooden bridge leads to Adventureland, Disney's version of jungle fever. The landscape artists went wild here: South African Cape honeysuckle droops, Brazilian bougainvillea drapes, Mexican flame vines cling, spider plants clone, and three different varieties of palm trees sway, all creating a seemingly spontaneous mess. **Swiss Family Treehouse** is the first attraction on your left (the camouflaged entrance is *way* over to the left). Based on the classic novel by Johann Wyss about the adventures of a family shipwrecked on the way to America, the treehouse shows what you can do with a big banyan and a lot of imagination: The kitchen sink is made of a giant clamshell, the boys' room, strewn with clothing, has two hammocks instead of beds, and an ingenious system of rain barrels and bamboo pipes provides running water in every room (German visitors seem especially fascinated by this). *Audience: All ages; toddlers unsteady on their feet may have trouble with the stairs. Rating:* ★ ★

During the **Jungle Cruise,** you glide through three continents along four rivers: the Congo, the Nile, the Mekong, and the Amazon. The canopied launches pack in visitors tighter than sardines, the safari-suited guide makes a point of checking his pistol, and the *Irrawady Irma* or *Mongala Millie* is off for another "perilous" journey. The guide's spiel is surprisingly funny, with just the right blend of cornball humor and the gently snide. *Audience: All ages. Rating:* ★ ★

"Avast, ye scurvy scum!" is the sort of greeting your kids will proclaim for the next week—which gives you an idea of the impact of the stellar **Pirates of the Caribbean.** This 10-minute boat ride is Disney at its best: memorable vignettes, incredible detail, a gripping story, and catchy music. Emerging from a pitch-black tunnel of time, you're literally in the middle of a furious battle as a pirate ship, cannons blazing, attacks a stone fortress. Audio-Animatronic pirates hoist the Jolly Roger while brave soldiers scurry to defend the fort. The wild antics of the pirates result in a conflagration, the town goes up in flames, and everyone goes to his or her just reward. *Audience: All ages. Rating:* ★ ★ ★

Inside the blessedly air-conditioned Polynesian longhouse that houses the **Enchanted Tiki Birds,** the "Tropical Serenade" is sung and whistled by hundreds of Audio-Animatronic figures: exotic birds, swaying flowers, and Tiki god statues with blinking red eyes. This was Disney's first Audio-Animatronics attraction; the animatronics still hold up fine but the audio could use an update. *Audience: All ages. Rating:* ★

Frontierland Located in the northwest quadrant of the Magic Kingdom, Frontierland invokes the spirit of the American frontier, with Disney staffers dressed in checked shirts, leather vests, cowboy hats, and brightly colored neckerchiefs. Banjo and fiddle music twangs from tree to tree.

At rope drop, the hordes hoof it to **Splash Mountain.** Based on the animated sequences in Disney's 1946 film, *Song of the South*, it features Audio-Animatronic creations of Brer Rabbit, Brer Bear, Brer Fox, and a menagerie of brer beasts. An eight-person hollowed-out log carries you through a lily pond and up the mountain. You get one heart-stopping pause at the top—just long enough to grab the safety bar—and then the boat plummets down the world's longest and sharpest flume drop right into a gigantic briar patch. *Audience: All but young children. No pregnant women or guests wearing back, neck, or leg braces; minimum height 44 inches. Rating:* ★ ★ ★

Scoot across the footbridge to another classic Disney ride, **Big Thunder Mountain Railroad.** As any true roller-coaster lover can tell you, this three-minute ride is a tame one, but the thrills are there, thanks to the intricate details and stunning scenery. Set in gold-rush days, the runaway train rushes and rattles past 20 Audio-Animatronic figures—including donkeys, chickens, a goat, and a grizzled old miner surprised in his bathtub—a derelict mining town, hot springs, and a flash flood. *Audience: All but young children. No pregnant women or guests wearing back, neck, or leg braces; minimum height 40 inches. Rating:* ★ ★ ★

No matter where you go, travel is easier when you know the code.[SM]

dial 1 800 CALL ATT®

Dial 1 800 CALL ATT and you'll always get through from any phone with any card* and you'll always get AT&T's best deal.** It's the one number to remember when calling away from home.

*Other long distance company calling cards excluded.
**Additional discounts available.

AT&T
Your True Choice

Head back across the footbridge past Splash Mountain and continue to your left along Frontierland's main drag to the landing stage for the rafts to **Tom Sawyer Island**—actually, two islands connected by an old-fashioned swing bridge. Most of the attractions are located on the main island: the mystery cave, a pitch-black (almost) labyrinth where the wind wails in a truly spooky fashion; Injun Joe's cave, all pointy stalactites and stalagmites; Harper's Mill, an old-fashioned grist mill (nothing scary here); and, in a clearing at the top of the hill, a rustic playground for younger children. On the other island is Fort Sam Clemens, a log fortress from which you can fire air guns (with great booms and cracks) at the soporific passengers on the Liberty Square Riverboat. *Audience: All ages. Rating:* ★★

Back on the main street, a row of barns, false-fronted buildings, and other structures straight out of Dodge City house shops, eateries, and two theaters. The first one on your right contains the **Country Bear Jamboree**, a stage show in which wise-cracking, corn-pone Audio-Animatronics bears joke, sing, and play country music and 1950s rock and roll. *Audience: All ages. Rating:* ★★★

The rip-roaring, raucous, corny, high-kicking **Diamond Horseshoe Jamboree** features a sextet of dance-hall girls and high-spirited cowboys, a lovelorn saloon keeper, and Lily, a shimmying, feather-boa-toting reincarnation of Mae West. Seating begins half an hour before curtain time, and snacks and light refreshments may be purchased at your table. *Show times: 10:45, 12:15, 1:45, 3:30, and 4:45; reservations essential. Audience: All but young children. Rating:* ★★

Liberty Square Weathered siding gives way to neat clapboard and solid brick, mesquite and cactus are replaced by stately oaks and masses of azaleas, and the rough-and-tumble western frontier gently slides into Colonial America. The shops in this area tend to sell more arts than kitsch, and the **Liberty Tree Tavern**, a gracious, table-service restaurant that could have been airlifted from Colonial Williamsburg, is one of the best at the Magic Kingdom; reservations are essential.

The **Hall of Presidents**, a 30-minute multimedia tribute to the Constitution, is another marvel of Audio-Animatronics. The two-part show starts with a film discussing the importance of the Constitution; the second half is a roll call of all 42 American presidents, including William Jefferson Clinton. The detail is lifelike right down to the brace on Franklin Delano Roosevelt's leg, and the robots can't resist nodding, fidgeting, and even whispering to each other while waiting for their names to come up. *Audience: Older children and adults. Rating:* ★★

The **Liberty Square Riverboat** is a real old-fashioned steamboat, the *Richard F. Irvine* (named for a key Disney designer), authentic from the big rear paddle wheel to the gingerbread trim on its three decks and its calliope whistle. The 15-minute trip is slow and certainly not thrilling, but it's a relaxing break for all concerned. *Audience: All but young children. Rating:* ★

The **Mike Fink Keel Boats** ply the same waters as the Liberty Square Riverboat, but these craft are short and dumpy and you have to listen to a heavy-handed, noisy spiel about those roistering, roustabout days along the Missouri. *Audience: All ages. Rating:* ★

Part walk-through, part ride on a "doom buggy," the eight-minute **Haunted Mansion** ride is scary but not terrifying, and the special effects are phenomenal. Catch the glowing bats' eyes on the wallpaper; the strategically placed gusts of damp, cold air; the wacky inscriptions on the tombstones; and the spectral xylophone player. *Audience: All but young children. Rating:* ★★★

Fantasyland You can enter Fantasyland from Frontierland or by skyway from Tomorrowland, but the classic introduction is a stroll through the glistening white towers of the **Cinderella Castle**. Although often confused with Disneyland's Sleeping Beauty Castle, at 180 feet this castle is more than 100 feet taller and, with its elongated towers and lacy fretwork, immeasurably more graceful.

The whirling, musical heart of Fantasyland—and maybe even of the entire Magic Kingdom—the antique **Cinderella's Golden Carrousel** has 90 prancing horses, each one completely different. The rich notes of the band organ—no calliope here—play favorite tunes from Disney movies. *Audience: All but young children. Rating:* ★ ★ ★

The first attraction on the left as you enter Fantasyland is **Legend of the Lion King.** Unlike many of the stage shows in the Magic Kingdom, this one showcases "humanimals," Disneyspeak for bigger-than-life-size figures that are manipulated by human "animateers" hidden from audience view. The preshow consists of the opening "Circle of Life" overture from the film. *Audience: All ages. Rating:* ★ ★

Moving clockwise through Fantasyland brings you to **Peter Pan's Flight,** a truly fantastic indoor ride. You board two-person (or one-adult, two-children) magic sailing ships, whose brightly striped sails catch the wind and soar into the skies above London en route to Never-Never-Land. Adults will especially enjoy the dreamy views of London by moonlight. *Audience: All ages. Rating:* ★ ★

Visiting Walt Disney World and *not* stopping for **It's a Small World**— why, the idea is practically un-American. Disney raided the remains of the 1964–65 New York World's Fair for this exhibit. Moving somewhat slower than a snail, barges inch through several barnlike rooms, each crammed with musical moppets dressed in various national costumes and madly singing the theme song, "It's a Small World After All." But somehow by the time you reach the end of the 11-minute ride, you're grinning and humming, too. *Audience: All ages. Rating:* ★ ★

Dumbo, the Flying Elephant is one of Fantasyland's most popular rides. Jolly Dumbos fly around a central column, each pachyderm packing a couple of kids and a parent. A joystick controls each Dumbo's vertical motion, so that it appears to swoop and soar. Alas, the ears do not flap. *Audience: Young children. Rating:* ★

In the **Mad Tea Party,** based on the 1951 Disney film of *Alice in Wonderland*, you hop into oversize, pastel-color teacups and whirl for two minutes around a giant platter. If the centrifugal force hasn't shaken you up too much, check out the soused mouse that pops out of the teapot centerpiece. *Audience: All ages. Rating:* ★

Mr. Toad's Wild Ride, based on the 1949 Disney release *The Adventures of Ichabod and Mr. Toad* (itself derived from Kenneth Grahame's classic children's novel, *The Wind in the Willows*), puts you in the jump seat of the speed-loving amphibian's flivver for a jolting, jarring three-minute jaunt through the English countryside. Marginally less scary than Snow White's Adventure, this ride may still startle young children. *Audience: All ages. Rating:* ★ ★

What was previously an unremittingly scary three-minute indoor spook-house ride reopened in December 1994 as a kinder, gentler **Snow White's Adventures.** Where once the dwarves might as well have been named Anxious and Fearful, the new ride—now with six-passenger cars and a mini-version of the movie—has been tempered. There's still the evil queen, her nose wart, and her cackle, but joining the cast at long last are the prince and Snow White herself. The trip is still packed with plenty of scary moments, but an honest-to-goodness kiss followed by a happily-ever-after ending might even get you heigh-ho-ing on your way. *Audience: All ages; toddlers may be scared. Rating:* ★ ★

The **Skyway to Tomorrowland** takes off on its one-way aerial trip to Tomorrowland from an enchanted attic perched above the trees in the far left corner of Fantasyland. *Audience: All ages. Rating:* ★

Mickey's Starland, built in 1988 to celebrate Mickey Mouse's 60th birthday, is a rarely crowded 3-acre niche set off to the side of Fantasyland. The attractions are located in the imaginary town of Duckburg (yes, Donald and Huey, Dewey, and Louie are all here, along with a cast of other Disney characters), whose pastel-color houses are positively Lilliputian, with miniature driveways and toy-size picket fences and signs scribbled with finger paint. **Mickey's Starland Show and Hollywood Theater,** held under a yellow-and-white-stripe big top, presents the television stars of "The Disney Afternoon" in a cheerful sing-along musical comedy that kids adore. Afterward, all the kids dash around backstage to **Mickey's Dressing Room,** where the star graciously signs autographs and poses for pictures with his adoring public. There's also a petting zoo with live animals at **Grandma Duck's Farm. Mickey's Treehouse** and **Minnie's Doll House** offer opportunities for climbing and exploring, and the **Mousekamaze** offers a place to get lost. *Audience: Young children, mainly. Rating:* ★ ★

Tomorrowland A brand-new Tomorrowland has made its long-awaited debut. To revitalize what had become the least appealing area of the Magic Kingdom, Disney artists and architects created new facades, restaurants, and shops for an energized Future City, which is more similar in mood to the themed villages of other lands. This time around the creators showed that they had learned their lesson: Rather than predict a tomorrow destined for obsolescence, they focused on "the future that never was"—the future envisioned by sci-fi writers and moviemakers in the '20s and '30s, when space flight, laser beams, and home computers belonged in the world of fiction, not fact.

Disney Imagineers have pulled out the stops on the **Transportarium in the Metropolis Science Centre.** Combining CircleVision 360 filmmaking with Audio-Animatronic figures, this attraction takes you on a time-traveling adventure to the past and on into the future. Hosted by Time Keeper, a C-3PO clone whose frenetic personality is provided by Robin Williams, and Nine-Eye, a slightly frazzled droid, the trip introduces you to famous inventors and visionaries of the machine age. *Audience: All ages. Rating:* ★ ★

There's almost never a wait at **Delta Dreamflight,** which should put your suspicions on red alert. Sponsored by Delta Airlines, this ride takes a look at the adventure and romance of flying. The idea is cute, but the execution—surprising given Disney's experience with special effects—falls far short of thrilling. *Audience: All ages. Rating:* ★

Despite a disappointing lack of truly special effects, **Alien Encounter** is still certain to become one of the Magic Kingdom's most popular new attractions. You enter the Future City's convention center to watch a test of a new teleportation system, but an attempt to transport the CEO of the device's manufacturer, an alien corporation called XS-Tech, fails. The catastrophic result is a close encounter with a frightening alien creature. *Audience: All but young children. Rating:* ★ ★

At the center of Future City is the **AstroOrbiter,** whose gleaming superstructure of revolving planets will most likely come to symbolize the new Tomorrowland as much as Dumbo represents Fantasyland. The ride itself, however, hasn't changed much from its previous life as StarJets. Ride vehicles—now looking more like Buck Rogers toys than space shuttles—sail past the whirling planets during a swing through space; you control the altitude if not the velocity. *Audience: All ages. Rating:* ★ ★

Just past AstroOrbiter, you'll find the **Tomorrowland Transit Authority** (TTA). The TTA takes a nice, leisurely ride around the perimeter of Tomorrowland, circling the AstroOrbiter and eventually gliding through the middle of Space Mountain. Disney's version of future mass transit is smooth and noiseless, thanks to an electromagnetic linear induction motor that has no moving parts, uses little power, and emits no pollutants. *Audience: All ages. Rating:* ★

First seen at the 1964–65 World's Fair, the **Carousel of Progress** has gotten a major face-lift. The 20-minute show, in a revolving theater, traces the impact of technological progress on the daily lives of Americans from the turn of this century into the near future. In each decade, an Audio-Animatronic family sings the praises of the new gadgets that technology has wrought. *Audience: All ages. Rating:* ★

Set off to the extreme left corner of Tomorrowland opposite the land's main block of shops and restaurants, **Grand Prix Raceway** incites instant addiction among kids: brightly colored Mark VII model gasoline-powered cars swerve around the four 2,260-foot tracks with much vroom-vroom-vrooming. But there's a lot of waiting: waiting to get on the raceway (it can take up to an hour), waiting for a car to pull up, then waiting to deliver it back after your five-minute lap. *Audience: Older children; minimum height 52 inches to drive. Rating:* ★

The needlelike spires and gleaming white concrete cone of **Space Mountain** are as much a Magic Kingdom landmark as Cinderella Castle. Inside this 180-foot-high structure is arguably the world's most imaginative roller coaster. The ride only lasts two minutes and 38 seconds and attains a top speed of 28 miles per hour, but the devious twists and invisible drops, and the fact that you can't see where you're going, make it seem twice as long and four times as thrilling. *Audience: All but young children; minimum height 44 inches. Rating:* ★ ★ ★

The brightly colored cable cars of the one-way **Skyway to Fantasyland** can be picked up at the station right outside of Space Mountain for the commute to the far western end of Fantasyland. *Audience: All ages. Rating:* ★

Entertainment A 30-minute-long **daily parade** proceeds down Main Street through Frontierland beginning at 3; it boasts floats, balloons, cartoon characters, dancers, singers (usually lip-synching to music played over the PA system), and much waving and cheering. **SpectroMagic** is a 30-minute nighttime extravaganza of battery-lighted floats, sequined costumes, sparkling decorations, and twinkling trees. **Fantasy in the Sky** is the Magic Kingdom fireworks display. Heralded by a dimming of all the lights along Main Street, a single spotlight illuminates the top turret of the Cinderella Castle and—poof!—Tinkerbell emerges in a shower of pixie dust to fly over the treetops and the crowds. Her disappearance signals the start of the fireworks.

Epcot Center Walt Disney World was created because of Walt Disney's dream of EPCOT, an "Experimental Prototype Community of Tomorrow." He envisioned a future in which nations coexisted in peace and harmony, reaping the miraculous harvest of technological achievement. He suggested the idea as early as October 1966. But with Disneyland hemmed in by development, Disney had to search for new land. He found it in central Florida. The permanent community that he envisioned has not yet come to be, but instead we have Epcot Center (which opened in 1982, years after Disney's death), a showcase, ostensibly, for the concepts that would be incorporated into the EPCOTs of the future. Then, as now, it was composed of two parts: **Future World,** whose 10 pavilions are sponsored by major American corporations, and **World Showcase,** whose 11 exhibition areas each represent a different country.

Epcot is that rare paradox—an educational theme park—and a very successful one, too. Although rides have been added over the years to try to amuse the young 'uns, the thrills are mostly in the mind. Consequently, Epcot is best suited for older children and adults. A dedicated visitor really needs two days to explore it all; to cram it into one day, get to the park early, don't waste time at sit-down meals, see the shows when the park is empty, and slow down and enjoy the shops and the live entertainment when the crowds thicken.

Air-conditioned 65-foot water taxis depart every 12 minutes from World Showcase Plaza at the border of Future World. There are two docks: Water taxis from the one on the left zip to the Germany pavilion, from the right to Morocco. In World Showcase, slow-moving double-decker buses depart every five–eight minutes and stop in front of every other pavilion.

Future World   Future World is made up of two concentric circles of pavilions. The inner core is composed of the Spaceship Earth geosphere and, just beyond it, the new Innoventions exhibit and Innoventions Plaza. The large Fountain of Nations serves as a dividing point between the inner core and the pavilions beyond.

Balanced like a giant golf ball waiting for some celestial being to tee off, the multifaceted silver geosphere of **Spaceship Earth** is to Epcot Center what the Cinderella Castle is to the Magic Kingdom. It weighs 1 million pounds, measures 164 feet in diameter and 180 feet in height, and encompasses more than 2 million cubic feet of space. The anodized aluminum sheath is composed of 954 triangular panels, not all of equal size or shape. Because it is not a geodesic dome (which is only a half sphere), the name "geosphere" was invented for it.

Earth Station, underneath Spaceship Earth, is the principal information center, the place to pick up schedules of live entertainment, park brochures, and the like. The computerized WorldKey Information System kiosks, located in Earth Station and in World Showcase near Germany, let you obtain detailed information about every pavilion, leave messages for companions, and most important of all, make reservations for Epcot restaurants.

Besides the Earth Station information center, Spaceship Earth contains the **Spaceship Earth ride** (★ ★ ★), hands down the most popular ride at Epcot Center. Scripted by science-fiction writer Ray Bradbury and now narrated by Jeremy Irons, the 15-minute journey begins in the darkest tunnels of time, proceeds through history as we know it, and ends poised on the edge of the future, including a dramatic look at a "virtual reality" classroom. Audio-Animatronic figures present history in astonishing detail.

Disney's latest addition to Future World is **Innoventions,** a two-building, 100,000-square-foot attraction situated at the center of the complex. Live stage demonstrations, interactive hands-on displays, and exhibits highlight new technology that affects daily living.

Universe of Energy (★ ★ ★), the first of the pavilions on the left (east) side of Future World, occupies a large, lopsided pyramid, sheathed in thousands of mirrors, which serve as solar collectors to power the ride and films within. One of the most technologically complex shows at Epcot Center, the Exxon-sponsored exhibit combines one half-hour ride, two films, the largest Audio-Animatronic animals ever built, 250 prehistoric trees, and enough cold, damp fog to make you think you've been transported to the inside of a defrosting icebox.

A towering statue of a DNA double helix stands outside the gold-crowned dome of Metropolitan Life's popular **Wonders of Life** pavilion, which takes an amusing but serious and educational look at health, fitness, and modern lifestyles. One improvisational theater revue, two films, and dozens of interactive gadgets that whiz, bleep, and blink make up the Fitness Fairground. Walt Disney World's first flight simulator, **Body Wars** (★ ★ ★), takes visitors on a five-minute bumpy platelet-to-platelet ride through the human circulatory system. And the 20-minute multimedia presentation, **Cranium Command** (★ ★ ★), reveals the workings of the mind of a typical 12-year-old boy during the course of an ordinary day.

At **Horizons** (★ ★), General Electric sponsors a relentlessly optimistic look at the once and future future. After being enjoined to "live your dreams," you ride a tram for 15 minutes past visions of the future, where great minds imagine what the world might have been like in a hundred years or so. The tram then moves past a series of tableaus of life in a future space colony. The Omega Centuri tableau, portraying a free-floating space colony, prefigures virtual reality with its games of zero-gravity basketball and simulated outdoor sports.

Shaped like a wheel, General Motors' **World of Motion** features the **TransCenter,** a 33,000-square-foot exhibit and auto showroom displaying new and experimental car models, and the 15-minute **World of Motion Ride** (★ ★) essentially a dippy, feel-good frolic through scenarios depicting the history of human attempts to get somewhere else faster.

United Technologies' **Living Seas** (★ ★ ★) is a favorite among children. An imaginative fountain flings surf in a never-ending wave against a rock garden beneath the stylized marquee. Inside is a 5.7 million-gallon central aquarium. The three-minute **Caribbean Coral Reef Ride** encircles the acrylic tank. Sometimes you'll catch sight of a diver, testing out the latest scuba equipment, surrounded by a cloud of parrot fish as he scatters food for the tank's denizens. After the ride, you may want to circumnavigate the tank at your own speed on an upper level, pointing out barracudas, stingrays, parrot fish, sea turtles, and even sharks, before exploring the two levels of **Sea Base Alpha,** a prototype undersea research facility. There are six interactive modules, each dedicated to a specific subject, such as the history of robotics, ocean exploration, ocean ecosystems, dolphins, porpoises, and sea lions.

Shaped like an intergalactic greenhouse, the enormous skylighted **The Land** pavilion dedicates 6 acres and a host of different attractions to everyone's favorite topic: food. You can easily spend two hours exploring here. The main event is a 14-minute ride called **Listen to the Land** (★ ★ ★), where you cruise through three biomes (rain forest, desert, and prairie ecological communities) and into an experimental greenhouse that demonstrates how food sources may be grown in the future, not only on Earth but also in outer space. **Food Rocks** (★) is a rowdy concert in which rock musicians taking the shape of favorite foods (the Peach Boys, Chubby Cheddar, and Neil Moussaka, among others) sing about the joys of nutrition. The **Harvest Theater** is home to a 20-minute, National Geographic–like film called *Symbiosis* (★ ★), an intelligent look at how we can profit from the earth's natural resources while ensuring that the earth benefits, too.

The last of the big three pavilions on the west side, **Journey into Imagination,** presented by Eastman Kodak, sets your mind spinning. The **Journey into Imagination Ride** (★ ★ ★) is a dreamy exploration of how creativity works. Laser beams zing back and forth, lightning crackles, letters leap out of a giant typewriter, an iridescent painting unfolds across a wall. The **Image Works** (★ ★ ★) is an electronic fun house crammed with interactive games and wizardry. The 3-D film *Honey, I Shrunk the Audience* (★ ★ ★) is one of the most popular attractions in Epcot. Like the two hit films on which it's based, the adventure stars Rick Moranis as Dr. Wayne Szalinski. While he's demonstrating his latest shrinking machine, things go really, really wrong. It's just too much fun to give anything else away, but be prepared to laugh and scream your head off, courtesy of the special in-theater effects, moving seats, and 3-D film technology developed by Walt Disney Studios.

World Showcase   The 40-acre World Showcase Lagoon is 1⅛ miles around, but in that space, you circumnavigate the globe.

A striking rocky chasm and tumbling waterfall make just one of the high points of **Canada.** Like that of the Rocky Mountains and the Great Canadian North, the scale of the structures seems immense; unlike the real thing, it's managed with a trick called forced perspective, which exaggerates the smallness of the distant parts to make the entire thing look humongous. The top attraction is the 17-minute CircleVision film *O Canada!* (★ ★ ★).

A pastiche of there-will-always-be-an-England architecture, the **United Kingdom** rambles between the elegant mansions lining a London square to the bustling, half-timbered shops of a village High Street to the thatched-roof cottages from the countryside (their thatch made of plastic broom bristles). The pavilion has no single major attraction. Instead, you can wander through shops selling tea and tea accessories, Welsh handicrafts, Royal Doulton figurines, and woolens and tartans from Pringle of Scotland, while outside, the strolling Old Globe Players coax audience members into participating in their definitely lowbrow versions of Shakespeare.

You don't need the scaled-down model of the Eiffel Tower to tell you that you've arrived in **France,** specifically Paris. There's the poignant accordion music wafting out of concealed speakers, solid mansard-roof mansions crowned with iron filigree, and delicious aromas surrounding the Boulangerie Pâtisserie bakeshop. The intimate Palais du Cinema, inspired by the royal theater at Fontainebleau, screens the 18-minute film *Impressions de France* (★ ★ ★), a five-screen homage to the glories of the country.

Walk through the pointed arches of the Bab Boujouloud gate, ornamented with beautiful wood carvings and encrusted with intricate mosaics, into **Morocco.** You can take a guided tour of the pavilion (inquire of any cast member), check out the ever-changing exhibit in the Gallery of Arts and History, and entertain yourself examining the wares at such shops as Casablanca Carpets, Jewels of the Sahara, the Brass Bazaar, and Berber Oasis. The belly-dancing in restaurant Marrakesh (reservations required) is tame, but youngsters like it.

A brilliant vermillion *torii* gate epitomizes the striking yet serene mood that pervades **Japan.** Disney horticulturists deserve a hand here for their achievement in constructing a very Japanese landscape, complete with rocks, pebbled streams, pools, and hills out of all-American plants and boulders. The heart of the pavilion is a brilliant blue winged pagoda, based on the 8th-century Horyuji Temple in Nara. Entertainment is provided by Japanese musicians and demonstrations of traditional Japanese crafts.

The **American Adventure,** housed in a scrupulous reproduction of Philadelphia's Liberty Hall, presents a 100-yard dash through history called the **American Adventure** (★ ★ ★), which uses evocative sets, the world's largest rear-projection screen (72 feet wide), enormous movable stages, and 35 Audio-Animatronic players. Beginning with the arrival of the Pilgrims at Plymouth Rock, Ben Franklin and a wry, pipe-smoking Mark Twain narrate 30 minutes of episodes—both praiseworthy and shameful—that have shaped the American spirit. Outside, a convoy of pushcarts offers heritage handicrafts, and directly opposite the pavilion on the edge of the Lagoon, the open-air **American Gardens Theatre** presents the **Magical World of Barbie,** a high-spirited, song-and-dance review about the world's most famous doll and her adventures around the world.

Saunter around the corner into the replica of Venice's Piazza San Marco and you've moved to **Italy.** The star is the architecture: a reproduction of Venice's Palace of the Doges that's true right down to the gold leaf on the angel perched 100 feet atop the Campanile, gondolas tethered to a seawall stained with age, and Romanesque columns, Byzantine mosaics, Gothic arches, and stone walls carefully "antiqued" to look historic. Inside, shops sell Venetian beads and glasswork, leather purses and belts, and Perugina chocolate "kisses."

Germany is a jovial make-believe village that distills the best folk architecture from all over that country. You'll hear hourly chimes from the specially designed glockenspiel on the clock tower, musical toots and tweets from multitudinous cuckoo clocks, folk tunes from the spinning dolls and lambs sold at Der Teddybär, and the satisfied grunts of hungry visitors chowing down on hearty German cooking. Other than the four-times-a-day oompah band show in the Biergarten restaurant (*see* Budget Dining, *below*; reservations required), Germany's pavilion doesn't offer any specific entertainment, but it does boast the most shops of any pavilion.

At **China,** a shimmering red-and-gold, three-tier replica of Beijing's Temple of Heaven towers over a serene Chinese garden, an art gallery displaying treasures from the People's Republic, a spacious emporium devoted to Chinese goods, and two restaurants. The garden, planted with rosebushes native to China, a 100-year-old mulberry tree, and water oaks (whose twisted branches look Asian but are actually Florida homegrown), is one of the most peaceful spots in Epcot Center. The 19-minute film *Wonders of China* (★ ★ ★) is dramatically portrayed on a 360° CircleVision screen.

In **Norway,** there are rough-hewn timbers and sharply pitched roofs (so the snow will slip right off), bloom-stuffed window boxes, figured shutters, and lots of smiling, blond and blue-eyed young Norwegians. The pavilion complex contains a 14th-century stone fortress that mimics Oslo's Akershus, cobbled streets, rocky waterfalls, and a wood stave church with wood dragons glaring from the eaves. The church houses an exhibit called "To the Ends of the Earth," which tells the story of two early 20th-century polar expeditions with vintage artifacts. Norway also has a dandy boat ride, **Maelstrom** (★ ★), in which dragon-headed longboats take a 10-minute voyage through time.

Housed in a spectacular Mayan pyramid surrounded with a tangle of tropical vegetation, **Mexico** contains an exhibit of pre-Columbian art, a restaurant, a shopping plaza, and the **El Rio del Tiempo ride** (★). This nine-minute journey from the jungles of the Yucatán to modern-day Mexico City is enlivened by video images of feathered Toltec dancers, by Spanish-colonial Audio-Animatronic dancing puppets, and by film clips of the cliff divers in Acapulco, the speedboats in Manzanillo, and snorkeling around Isla Mujeres.

Entertainment   Walt Disney World uses the lagoon for the spectacular **IllumiNations** sound-and-light show every night a half hour before closing. Best viewing spots are on the bridge between France and the United Kingdom, the promenade in front of Canada and Norway, and the bridge between China and Germany.

Disney-MGM Studios Theme Park

When Walt Disney Company chairman Michael Eisner opened Disney-MGM Studios in May 1989, he welcomed visitors to "the Hollywood that never was and always will be." Modeled after southern California's highly successful Universal Studios tour (an even more successful version of which is just down I–4), Disney-MGM combined Disney detail with MGM's motion-picture expertise in an amalgamation that blends theme park with fully functioning movie and television production center, breathtaking rides with instructional tours, nostalgia with high-tech wonders.

Although there are attractions that will interest young children, Disney-MGM is really best for teenagers old enough to watch old movies on television and catch the cinematic references.

When the lines are minimal, the park can be easily covered in a day with time for repeat rides. The **Crossroads of the World kiosk** in the Entrance Plaza dispenses park maps, entertainment schedules, brochures, and the like. The **Production Information Window** (tel. 407/560–4651), also in the Entrance Plaza, is the place to find out what's being taped when and how get a seat in the audience for any of these shows.

Hollywood Boulevard

With its palm trees, pastel buildings and flashy neon, Hollywood Boulevard paints a rosy picture of Tinseltown in the 1930s. The sense of having walked right onto a movie set is enhanced by vintage automobiles that putt-putt back and forth, strolling brass bands, and roving actors dressed in costume and playing everything from would-be starlets to nefarious agents. Hollywood Boulevard is crammed with souvenir shops and memorabilia collections, such as **Oscar's Classic Car Souvenirs & Super Service Station,** easily identified by the grape-color 1947 Buick parked in front; **Sid Cahuenga's One-of-a-Kind** antiques and curios, where you might find (and acquire) Brenda Vaccaro's shawl, Liberace's table napkins, or autographed stars' photos; and **Cover Story**, where you can have your picture put on the cover of a major magazine.

At the head of Hollywood Boulevard is the fire-engine-red, pagoda'd replica of Grauman's Chinese Theatre, which houses the **Great Movie Ride.** Disney-MGM pulls out all the stops on this 22-minute tour of great moments in film. Movie memorabilia fills the lobby. The preshow area screens film clips. Then you ride open trams—past Audio-Animatronic characters, scrim, smoke, and Disney magic—for a tour of cinematic climaxes. *Audience: All but young children (for whom it may be too intense). Rating:* ★ ★ ★

Sunset Boulevard

This newest of Disney-MGM's theme avenues pays tribute to famous Hollywood monuments. The **Theater of the Stars,** reminiscent of the famed Hollywood Bowl, is home to a musical production called **Beauty and the Beast—Live on Stage.** As guests turn onto Sunset Boulevard from Hollywood Boulevard, the first stop for hungry hordes is **Hollywood Junction Station,** where reservations can be made for restaurants throughout the park. Star-struck shoppers should find something to feed their fandom at **Legends of Hollywood,** which brims with books, videos, and posters of classic films, while the young at heart should stop by **Once Upon a Time,** which showcases vintage character toys.

Ominously overlooking Sunset Boulevard is the **Twilight Zone Tower of Terror.** You take an eerie stroll through the dimly lit lobby and decaying library to the boiler room before boarding the hotel's giant "elevator." As you head upward past seemingly deserted hallways, ghostly former residents appear around you, until suddenly—faster than you can say "Where's Rod Serling?"—the creaking vehicle abruptly plunges downward in a terrifying, 130-foot free-fall drop! *Audience: Older children and adults. No pregnant women or guests with back, neck, or heart problems; minimum height 42 inches. Rating:* ★ ★ ★

Studio
Courtyard

As you exit the Chinese Theatre, veer left through the high arched gateway to the Studio Courtyard. You're now at one end of Mickey Avenue. A boxy building on the left invites you to join Ariel, Sebastian, and the underwater gang in the **Voyage of the Little Mermaid** stage show, which condenses the movie into a 15-minute presentation of the greatest hits. *Audience: All ages. Rating:* ★ ★

The **Magic of Disney Animation,** a 30-minute self-guided tour through the Disney animation process, is one of the funniest and most engaging attractions at the park. You'll watch a hilarious eight-minute film in which Walter Cronkite and Robin Williams explain the basics of animation. You then follow walkways with windows overlooking the working animation studios, where you see actual salaried Disney artists at their drafting tables doing everything you just learned about. This is better than magic—this is real. *Audience: All but toddlers. Rating:* ★ ★ ★

Inside the Walt Disney Theater, *The Making of* **The Lion King** was originally produced for the Disney Channel and now runs for the masses at half-hour intervals. Narrated by Robert Guillaume (the voice of Rafiki, the film's psychic baboon), the film traces the making of the animated classic from concept to final scenes. *Audience: All ages. Rating:* ★ ★ ★

The **Backstage Studio Tour,** a combination tram ride and walking tour, takes you on a 25-minute tour of the back-lot building blocks of movies: set design, costumes, props, lighting, and special effects. You literally ride through working offices, peering through windows as Foley artists mix sound, as lighting crews sort cables, as costumers stitch seams, and so on. At Catastrophe Canyon, the tram bounces up and down in a simulated earthquake, an oil tanker explodes in gobs of smoke and flame, and a water tower crashes to the ground, touching off a flash flood. *Audience: All but young children. Rating:* ★ ★ ★

Hop off the tram and walk through the **Studio Showcase,** an exhibit of film and television memorabilia. Then follow Roger Rabbit's pink footsteps to the **Loony Bin,** where kids can have their picture taken in front of the directional signs indicating Thisaway and Thataway. The **Inside the Magic Special Effects and Production Tour,** a one-hour walking tour, explains how clever camera operators make illusion seem like reality through camera angles, miniaturization, matte backgrounds, and a host of other magic tricks. You visit the soundstages used for filming the *Mickey Mouse Club, Ed McMahon's Star Search,* and assorted movies. In the Post-Production area, Star Wars director George Lucas, aided by the robots R2D2 and C-3PO, explains how film editors use computers for editing, and Mel Gibson and Pee-Wee Herman switch voices in a lecture on sound tracks. *Audience: Older children and adults. Rating:* ★ ★ ★

The Backlot

In this rather amorphous area, you can tour the New York street sets on foot as long as crews aren't filming—and it's worth it, for the wealth of detail to be seen in the store windows. Take a left at the corner of Mickey Avenue and New York Street and let the kids run free in the *Honey, I Shrunk the Kids* **Movie Set Adventure,** a state-of-the-art playground based on the movie about lilliputian children in a larger-than-life world. *Audience: Children. Rating:* ★ ★ ★

Jim Henson's Muppet*Vision **3-D** is a combination of 3-D movie and musical revue. The theater was constructed especially for this spectacular 30-minute show, with special effects literally built into the walls. All the Muppet characters make an appearance. *Audience: All ages. Rating:* ★ ★ ★

Backlot Annex

This niche contains two of the park's most high-powered attractions. The **Indiana Jones Epic Stunt Spectacular** features the stunt choreography of veteran coordinator Glenn Randall (*Raiders of the Lost Ark, Indiana Jones and the Temple of Doom, E.T.*, and *Jewel of the Nile* are among his credits). Presented in a 2,200-seat amphitheater, this 30-minute show teaches the audience how breathtaking movie stunts are pulled off, with the help of 10 audience participants. *Audience: All but young children. Rating:* ★ ★ ★

The annex's other attraction, **Star Tours,** is a real showstopper: a flight simulator inspired by the *Star Wars* films. Piloted by Star Wars characters R2D2 and C-3PO, a 40-passenger StarSpeeder takes a seven-minute flight that soon goes awry: You shoot into deep space, dodge giant ice crystals and comet debris, innocently bumble into an intergalactic battle, and whiz through the canyons of some planetary city before coming to a heart-stopping halt. The lines are incredibly long, but don't go first thing in the morning—it'll spoil you for the rest of the park. *Audience: Older children and adults. Rating:* ★ ★ ★

Lakeside Circle Set off to the left, or west, side of Hollywood Boulevard, Lakeside Circle is an idealized California, with two major attractions.

At **SuperStar Television,** 28 volunteers are chosen from the 1,000-person audience to "play" the starring roles on everything from *I Love Lucy* to *Gilligan's Island*. While the volunteers are led off to makeup and costume, the audience files into a 1,000-seat theater reminiscent of the days of live television broadcasting. You watch on 6-foot-wide monitors, as electronic dubbing merges the onstage action with clips from classic shows. *Audience: All but young children. Rating:* ★ ★

Despite its name, the **Monster Sound Show** is anything but scary. Rather, it's a delightful, multifaceted demonstration of the use of movie sound effects. Volunteer sound-effects specialists dash around trying to coordinate their sound effects with the short movie being shown simultaneously, where a hilariously klutzy Chevy Chase plays an insurance man on a visit to a haunted house. *Audience: All ages. Rating:* ★ ★ ★

Discovery Island Originally conceived as a re-creation of the setting of Robert Louis Stevenson's *Treasure Island*, complete with wrecked ship and Jolly Roger, Discovery Island evolved gradually into its contemporary status as an animal preserve where visitors can see and learn about some 100 different species of exotic birds and animals amid 11½ lushly landscaped acres. Although it's possible to "do" Discovery Island in less than an hour, anything quicker than a stop-and-start saunter would do it an injustice. You can wander along the boardwalks at your own pace, stopping to inspect the bougainvillea or visit with a rhinoceros hornbill. You can picnic on the beach or on one of the benches in the shade and watch trumpeter swans glide by. The only thing you may not do is go swimming—the water sprites and motor launches come just too close for safety.

Just past the first right-hand bend in the boardwalk is the **Discovery Island Bird Show,** presented in an open amphitheater equipped with benches and numerous perches. There's usually a show every hour from 11 to 4; most last about 15 minutes.

Typhoon Lagoon Four times the size of River Country (*see below*), Typhoon Lagoon offers a full day's worth of activities: bobbing in 4-foot waves in a surf lagoon the size of two football fields; speeding down arrow-straight water slides and around twisty storm slides; bumping through white-water rapids; and snorkeling in **Shark Reef,** a 360,000-gallon snorkeling tank (closed November–April) containing an artificial coral reef and 4,000 real tropical fish. More mellow folks can float in inner tubes along the 2,100-foot **Castaway Creek,** which circles around the entire park (it takes about 30 minutes to do the whole circuit; you can stop as you please along the way). A children's area, **Ketchakiddie Creek,** replicates adult rides on a smaller scale (all children *must* be accompanied by an adult). It's Disney's version of a day at the beach—complete with lifeguards in spiffy red-and-white stripe, fisherman's T-shirts.

Typhoon Lagoon is popular—in the summer and on weekends, the park often reaches capacity (7,200 people) by mid-morning. If you must go during the summer, go for a few hours during the dreamy late afternoons or when the weather clears up after a thundershower. (Typically, rainstorms drive away the crowds, and lots of people simply don't come back.) If you plan to make a whole day of it, avoid weekends—Typhoon Lagoon is big among locals as well as tourists.

River Country In the backwoods setting of the Fort Wilderness Resort and Campground, kids can slide, splash, and swim about in an aquatic playground, complete with white-water inner-tubing channels and corkscrew water slides that splash down into a 300,000-gallon pond. The pool is heated during the winter, so kids can take a dip here year-round. During the summer, River Country can get very congested, so it's best to come late in the afternoon.

Blizzard Beach Blizzard Beach promises the seemingly impossible—a seaside playground with an Alpine theme. The park centers on **Mt. Gushmore,** a 90-foot "snow-capped" mountain. Here "skiers" slide down the face of the mountain, tackling moguls, slalom courses, and toboggan and sled runs. At the base of the mountain, there's a sandy beach featuring the de rigueur wave pool, a lazy river, and play areas for both young children and preteens.

Mt. Gushmore's big gun is **Summit Plummet,** which Disney bills as "the world's tallest, fastest free-fall speed slide." From Summit Plummet's "ski jump" tower, it's a wild 55-mph plunge straight down to a splash landing at the base of the mountain. **Teamboat Springs** is a "white-water raft ride" in which six-passenger rafts zip along a twisting 1,200-foot series of rushing waterfalls. No water park would be complete without a flume ride. Enter **Snow Stormers**—actually three flumes that descend from the top of Mt. Gushmore. Riders follow a switchback course through ski-type slalom gates. There are also rides for the slightly less adventurous.

Sea World, Universal Studios, and Beyond

Sea World Aptly named, 135-acre **Sea World** is the world's largest zoological **❷** park and is devoted entirely to the mammals, birds, fish, and reptiles that live in the ocean and its tributaries. Every attraction is designed to teach visitors about the beauty of the marine world and how it is threatened by human thoughtlessness. Yet the presentations are rarely dogmatic, never pedantic, and almost always memorable as well as enjoyable. The park rivals Disney properties for sparkly cleanliness, smiley staff, and attention to detail.

Sea World is organized around the nucleus of a 17-acre central lake. As you enter, the lake is to your right. You can orient yourself by the Sky Tower, whose revolving viewing platform is generally visible even above the trees; it's directly opposite Shamu Stadium.

Walk straight through the park to the **Sea World Theatre** to see the 20-minute *Window to the Sea* (★ ★), both to orient yourself and to get a sense of the larger vision of the park. Then whip into **Penguin Encounter** (★ ★) early, to visit one of the most spectacular attractions at its least crowded time. This refrigerated re-creation of Antarctica is home to 17 species of penguins; a Plexiglas wall on the viewers' side of the tank lets you see that the penguins are as graceful in the water as they are awkward on land. Proceed to **Terrors of the Deep** (★ ★ ★), where videos and walk-through Plexiglas tunnels let you get acquainted with the world's largest and most unique collection of such dangerous sea creatures as eels, barracuda, venomous and poisonous fish, and sharks. Then stop in to visit the hulking Clydesdale horses, the Anheuser-Busch trademark, at **Clydesdale Hamlet (★)**.

Follow the crowds across the bridge to **Shamu Stadium**; while they're watching Sea World's orca mascot perform, you can sneak into **Wild Arctic (★ ★ ★)**. The park's newest and most ambitious attraction, it provides a chilly encounter with polar bears. Stop by the nearby concession for shopping or food, or get a lakeside table at Mango Joe's to catch the show at the **Atlantis Water Ski Stadium (★ ★ ★)**.

While on this side of the lagoon, visit the **Pinniped Habitat (★ ★ ★)**, the 2½-acre home of fun-loving California sea lions and harbor and fur seals; **Manatees: The Last Generation? (★ ★ ★)**, where you can view a film and then watch manatees splash about in their 300,000-gallon tank (there's also a 30,000-gallon nursing lagoon for manatee moms and their babies); and **Shamu: Close Up (★ ★ ★)**. That should put you right in place for the afternoon **Shamu show (★ ★ ★)**. Go as much as 45 minutes early to get a seat—even the wait is fun, as you watch the whales swim around their tank.

Wander back across the bridge and treat yourself to some interactive exhibits: the **Dolphin Community Pool, Harbor Seal Community, Stingray Lagoon,** and **Tide Pool (★ ★ ★)**—some of the most rewarding experiences in the park for all ages. The snack-happy animals are obligingly hungry all day, but get there before the herring concessions close at dusk. Also keep an eye on the time: You'll want to intersperse these with the delightful shows at the **Whale & Dolphin Stadium** (20 minutes long, **★ ★ ★**) and the **Sea Lion & Otter Stadium** (40 minutes long, **★ ★ ★**). By now, you'll be feeling a little frayed. If you've got kids, this may be the time to let them unwind at **Shamu's Happy Harbor (★ ★)**, a 3-acre outdoor play area. Otherwise, head for the soothing **Tropical Reef (★ ★ ★)**, an indoor attraction built around a cylindrical mega-aquarium where more than 1,000 tropical fish swim around a 160,000-gallon man-made coral reef. The **Water Fantasy (★)**, back in the Sea World Theater, is another good option: After 5, the theater is turned into a giant wading pool with 36 revolving nozzles spraying water into fountains, waving plumes, and helices, all set to music and colored lights. Restored and in good humor for a few last shows, trek across the lake for **Shamu's Night Magic (★ ★ ★)** and watch an orca bop to Madonna. End the day with the lasers, fountains, and pyrotechnics of **Mermaids, Myths, & Monsters (★ ★ ★)**.

7007 Sea World Dr. (near intersection of I–4 and Bee Line Expressway), Orlando 32821, tel. 407/351–3600, 800/327–2424 outside FL, or 800/432–1178 in FL. Admission: 1-day: $35.95 adults, $30.95 children 3–9; 2-day: 40.95 adults, 35.95 children 3–9; parking: $5 per car, $7 per RV or camper. Open Sept.–June, daily 9–7; July–Aug. and Thanksgiving and Christmas holidays, daily 9–9.

Universal Studios Florida ③   Far from being a "me-too" version of Disney-MGM Studios, **Universal Studios Florida,** which opened in 1990, is a theme park with plenty of personality of its own. It's saucy, sassy, and hip—and doesn't hesitate to invite comparisons to the competition. When a stuntman in the Wild, Wild, Wild West Stunt Show falls into a well, he emerges spitting water and shouting, "Look, Ma, I'm Shamu!" Disney-MGM's strolling actors are pablum compared to the Blues Brothers peeling rubber in the Bluesmobile. And let's face it, even the Muppets are matched by the E.T., Tickli Moot Moot, and other inventions of Steven Spielberg, Universal's genius on call.

The lofty adult ticket price raises expectations very high indeed. They are met most of the time but can easily be dashed by long lines and the park's unabashed attempt to soak you extra at every step at ubiquitous concession stands and overpriced snackeries. With Disney-MGM just down the road, is Universal worth the visit? The answer is an unqualified yes. Actually, Universal Studios and Disney-MGM dovetail rather than replicate each other. Universal's attractions are geared more to older children than to the stroller set.

The 444 acres of Universal Studios are a bewildering conglomeration of stage sets, shops, reproductions of New York and San Francisco, and anonymous soundstages housing theme attractions as well as genuine movie-making paraphernalia. On the map, these sets are neatly divided into six neighborhoods, surrounding a huge blue lagoon, the setting for the **Dynamite Nights Stunt Spectacular (★ ★)**, a shoot-em-up stunt show (performed on water skis, no less!) presented nightly at 7. As you walk around the park, however, expect to get lost, and if you do, just ask directions of the nearest staffer.

The Front Lot is essentially a scene-setter, and the place to find many services. The main drag, the Plaza of the Stars, stretches from the marble-arched entrance gateway straight down to the other end of the lot.

Angling off to the right of Plaza of the Stars, Rodeo Drive forms the backbone of **Hollywood.** Among its attractions, **Lucy: A Tribute (★)** is basically just a walk-through collection of Lucille Ball's costumes, accessories, and other memorabilia, best for real fans of the ditzy redhead. The **Gory, Gruesome & Grotesque Horror Make-Up Show (★ ★)** is especially appreciated by kids and teens (young children may be frightened), showing as it does what goes into and oozes out of the most mangled monsters in movie history. You can play high-tech computer games at **AT&T at the Movies (★ ★)** and explore **Jurassic Park: Behind the Scenes (★ ★).**

Production Central comprises six huge warehouses containing working soundstages, as well as several attractions. Follow Nickelodeon Way left from the Plaza of the Stars to the embarkation point for the **Production Tram Tour (★)**, a 20-minute nonstop narrated ride around the park that neither orients you nor takes you inside any of the soundstages. It lets you off right back where you started, where the Green Slime Geyser entices visitors into **Nickelodeon Studios**, a 40-minute tour **(★ ★)** showing how a television show is produced. With its yellow stairwells and bright orange zigzags, black squiggles, and blue blobs, this is a postmodern fun house, appropriate for the home of the world's only television network designed for kids. About 90% of the Nickelodeon shows are made on Nick's pair of soundstages, so visitors can always expect to see some action. Lines are often long, so you may want to skip it if no shows are taping. The **Funtastic World of Hanna-Barbera (★ ★ ★)**, a combination ride-video-interactive display at the corner of Nickelodeon Way and Plaza of the Stars, is one of the most popular attractions at Universal Studios and is always crowded. Using Hanna-Barbera animated characters (Yogi Bear, the Jetsons, the Flintstones), you're shown how cartoons are made and given eight minutes of thrills in the process. (It may be too much for toddlers.) **Alfred Hitchcock's 3-D Theatre (★ ★ ★)**, across the Plaza of the Stars from Hanna-Barbera, is a dandy 40-minute multimedia tribute to the master of suspense. (Young children may be frightened.) *Murder, She Wrote* **Mystery Theatre (★ ★ ★)**, based on the popular TV series starring Angela Lansbury as senior-citizen sleuth Jessica Fletcher, is presented in a large sit-down theater, where the audience is placed in the role of executive producer, racing the clock to put together an episode of the show. The **Adventures of Rocky & Bullwinkle (★ ★)** is a musical revue starring Bullwinkle the Moose, his faithful friend Rocky the Flying Squirrel, and those two Russian no-goodniks, Boris Badenov and his slinky sidekick, Natasha, staged hourly on an animated set at the edge of Universal's New York back lot.

The **New York** back lot has been rendered with surprising verisimilitude, right down to the cracked concrete and slightly stained cobblestones. The **Blues Brothers Bluesmobile** regularly cruises the neighborhood, and musicians hop out to give impromptu performances at 70 Delancey. New York is also home to **Ghostbusters** (★ ★ ★), a 15-minute show that's part special-effects demonstration, part high-tech haunted house. **Kongfrontation** (★ ★ ★) is a very popular five-minute ride just down the street from Ghostbusters.

San Francisco/Amity combines two sets: one the wharves and warehouses of San Francisco's Embarcadero and Fisherman's Wharf district, with cable-car tracks and the distinctive redbrick Ghiradelli chocolate factory; the other the New England fishing village terrorized by the shark in *Jaws*. Attractions here include **Beetlejuice's Graveyard Revue** (★ ★ ★), a live 15-minute sound-and-light spectacle starring the ghoul of the same name, from the 1991 movie starring Michael Keaton. Its theme is rock and roll and monsters, and it's carried off with lots of noise, smoke, and wit. Just next door, **Earthquake—The Big One** (★ ★ ★) starts off with a preshow that reproduces choice scenes from the movie *Earthquake*, then takes you on San Francisco Bay Area Rapid Transit subway cars to ride out an 8.3 Richter scale tremor and its consequences: fire, flood, blackouts. Unlike Disney-MGM's Disaster Canyon, there are no "safe" seats on this ride; it's not for younger children. It lasts 20 minutes and the lines are always long. Stagger out of San Francisco into Amity to stand in line for the revamped **Jaws** ride, a terror-filled boat ride (★ ★ ★) with concomitant explosions, noise, shaking, and gnashing of sharp shark teeth. The **Wild, Wild, Wild West Stunt Show** (★ ★ ★), presented in a covered amphitheater at the very end of Amity Avenue, involves trapdoors, fistfights, bullwhips, water gags, explosions, shoot-outs, horseback riding, and jokes that skewer every other theme park in central Florida.

Expo Center, which takes up the southeastern corner of the park, contains another treasure trove of attractions. *Back to the Future. . . The Ride* (★ ★ ★) is the flight simulator to beat all others, even (probably) those yet to be built. A seven-story, one-of-a-kind Omnimax screen surrounds your Delorean-shape simulator so that you lose all sense of perspective as you rush backward and forward in the space-time continuum—and there are no seat belts. You may have to wait up to two hours for this five-minute ride. The same is true of the somewhat gentler **E.T. Adventure** (★ ★ ★), where you board bicycles mounted on a movable platform and pedal through fantastic forests and across the moon in an attempt to help the endearing extraterrestrial find his way back to his home planet. For younger children, **Fievel's Playland** (★ ★), just around the corner, is a true gift. Based on the adventures of Steven Spielberg's mighty, if miniature, mouse, this gigantic playground incorporates a four-story net climb, tunnel slides, water play areas, ball crawls, a 200-foot water slide, and a harmonica slide that plays music when you slide along the openings. **A Day in the Park with Barney** (★ ★), right next door, features America's most famous purple dinosaur and a host of activities for children.

1000 Universal Studios Plaza (entrance is ½ mi north of I–4 Exit 30B), Orlando 32819–7610, tel. 407/363–8000, TTY 407/363–8265. Tickets also available by mail through Ticketmaster (tel. 800/745–5000); discounted tickets available at Orlando/Orange County Convention and Visitors Bureau ticket office (8445 International Dr.). Admission: 1-day: $37 adults, $30 children 3–9; 2-day: $55 adults, $44 children 3–9; parking: $5 cars, $7 campers. Open daily 9–7 (extended as late as 10 in summer and holiday periods).

Cypress Gardens
❹

A botanical garden, amusement park, and waterskiing circus rolled into one, **Cypress Gardens** is a uniquely Floridian combination of natural beauty and utter kitsch. A 45-minute drive from Walt Disney World, the park encompasses 233 acres and contains more than 8,000 varieties of plants gathered from 75 countries. More than half the grounds are devoted to flora, ranging from natural landscaping to cutesy-poo topiary to chrysanthemum cascades. Even at a sedate pace, you can see just about everything in six hours.

The souvenir-shop-ridden main entrance funnels visitors straight to the **Water Ski Stadiums** (★ ★ ★) for a stunt-filled half-hour waterskiing revue presented every two hours. To the right are the Botanical Gardens, where you can board a boat for the **Botanical Gardens Cruise,** which floats through the cypress-hung canals of the Botanical Gardens, passing hoopskirted southern belles, flowering shrubs, 27 different species of palm, and the occasional baby alligator.

The path leading from the ski stadiums to the amusement park area meanders through the **Exhibition Gardens,** where the landscaping philosophy is heroic in intent and hilariously vulgar in execution.

The **Crossroads Arena** (★ ★ ★), at the far southern end of the park, presents a rotating collection of circus-theme acts, from acrobats to trained birds. Many of the park's attractions are clustered around Southern Crossroads, including the bird show at the **Cypress Theatre;** a huge walk-through butterfly conservatory; a museum of antique radios; **Cypress Junction,** the nation's most elaborate model railroad exhibit; and **Cypress Roots,** a clapboard shack chock-full of fascinating memorabilia about the gardens' founders, Dick and Julie Pope. **Kodak's Island in the Sky,** a 153-foot-high revolving platform, provides aerial views of the park, and **Carousel Cove** is the kids' playground, with lots of ball rooms and bouncing pads plus a lovely old carousel.

Box 1, Cypress Gardens 33884 (take I–4 to U.S. 27S and follow signs), tel. 941/324–2111, 800/237–4826 outside FL, or 800/282–2123 in FL. Admission: $24.95 adults, $21.20 senior citizens, $16.45 children 3–9; parking free. Open daily 9:30–5:30 (extended hrs in summer).

Splendid China
❺

Splendid China is more a superlative open-air museum than a theme park in the Mickey Mouse tradition. Here you can stroll among painstakingly re-created versions of China's greatest landmarks and watch artisans demonstrate traditional Chinese woodworking, weaving, and other crafts, while tinkling, meditative music plays in the background. It took $100 million and 120 Chinese craftspeople working for two years and using, whenever possible, historically accurate building materials and techniques to create the 60-plus replicas. Both man-made structures and natural phenomena are represented—some life size, others greatly reduced in scale. (The bricks in the Great Wall, for example, are only 2 inches long.) To appeal to theme-park-savvy western visitors, live entertainment and a playground are also offered.

The park is at its most magical at night, which is kicked off at 6:30 with a parade, so try to arrive after noon. As you come through the turnstile, you enter Splendid China's version of Main Street: **Suzhou Gardens,** a re-creation of a 14th-century Chinese village. Inside are most of the park's shops and restaurants, both of which are a cut above those at typical theme parks. Check with Guest Services (tel. 407/397–8825), inside the main entrance and to the right, for show times and any special events.

Before touring the park, stop at **Harmony Hall,** where the 15-minute film *This Is Splendid China* (★ ★) explains the park's history and construction. Then, when you're ready to see the monuments, head clockwise (rather than counter-clockwise, as the exhibits are numbered), in order to save the best for last.

Along the way you'll pass replicated **stone grottoes,** the originals of which are used as temples, and a maze of odd obelisks, the **Stone Forest,** replicas of limestone pillars whittled by aeons of erosion. In the far back corner of the park is the controversial reproduction of the **Potala Palace,** the traditional home of the Dalai Lama, Tibet's spiritual and political leader. The dusty rose-and-white structure seems even taller than it is, since the walls lean inward, creating a false perspective.

Splendid China's live-action venue is the **Temple of Light Amphitheater.** A **costume show** (★) and a **demonstration of folk dances and music** (★ ★) are presented on alternating hours. Both are slow-moving affairs (though the latter is considerably more interesting) and not improved by the mumbling Chinese announcer. A better choice is the **acrobatic show** (★ ★ ★), held in a nearby tent.

After having your fill of Chinese entertainment, be sure to see the **1,000 Eyes and 1,000 Hands Guanyin Buddha Statue,** whose many hands are said to ease the troubles of the world, and the nearby **Terra Cotta Warriors,** modeled after 7,000 life-size clay figurines unearthed in 1974.

Now take a walk along the **Great Wall.** Although it can't compare to the original—the 1,500-mile-long behemoth that is the only man-made structure visible from space—it's nonetheless impressive, especially when you realize that the 6.5 million tiny bricks used to make the wall were mortared by hand. As in China, on the other side of the wall lies Mongolia, and a **Mongolian Yurt** has scheduled Mongolian wrestling demonstrations.

The **Imperial Palace,** the centerpiece of Beijing's Forbidden City, is one of Splendid China's most impressive sights. The compound in Beijing, built in the early 1400s as the home of the royal family, was constructed with materials from all over China and decorated with centuries' worth of loot. It housed so many people that as many as 6,000 cooks were needed to feed them. Even the scale model gives a feeling of the immense size and artistry.

3000 Splendid China Blvd., Kissimmee 34747, tel. 407/397–8800 or 800/244–6226. Admission: $23.55 adults, $13.90 children 5–12; 10% discount AAA members and senior citizens. Open daily 9:30–8 (extended hrs in peak seasons); Suzhou Gardens shops and restaurants open to 9:30.

Winter Park Area

Once the winter refuge of some wealthy northerners, the community of Winter Park, though part of Orlando's metro area, maintains a proud, independent, and tony identity. **Park Avenue** in downtown Winter Park is lined with trendy boutiques and restaurants; long and narrow Central Park stretches through the heart of the shopping district.

6 Historic **Rollins College,** a private liberal arts school, is at the south end of Park Avenue. Take time to look at the Spanish-style architecture, especially Knowles Memorial Chapel, home to the Bach Festival Society. Also on campus is the **Cornell Fine Arts Museum,** which has the largest collection of American and European art in central Florida. *1000 Holt Ave., Winter Park, tel. 407/646–2526. Admission free. Open Tues.–Fri. 10–5, weekends 1–5; closed holidays.*

7 The elegant **Charles Hosmer Morse Museum of American Art** features an outstanding collection of stained-glass windows, blown glass, and lamps by Louis Tiffany (son of Charles Tiffany of New York jewelry fame). There's also a collection of paintings by 19th-

and 20th-century American artists, as well as jewelry and pottery. *133 E. Welbourne Ave., Winter Park, tel. 407/645–5311. Admission: $2.50 adults, $1 students and children. Open Tues.–Sat. 9:30–4, Sun. 1–4; closed holidays.*

Heading west out of town on Fairbanks Avenue, take a left fork onto Orange Avenue and, after ½ mile, turn left onto Denning Avenue for **8** a visit to 55-acre **Mead Gardens,** which has intentionally been left to grow as a natural preserve. The recently constructed boardwalk provides a good view of the delicate wetlands. *S. Denning Ave., Winter Park, tel. 407/623–3334. Admission free. Open daily 8–sunset.*

With entrances on both Rollins and Princeton streets (1 mile east off **9** I–4's Exit 43), **Loch Haven Park** is a grassy field with three of the city's museums. The **Orlando Science Center** is full of hands-on and interactive exhibits, including a special preschoolers' water play area and a planetarium. *810 E. Rollins St., Orlando, tel. 407/896–7151. Admission: $6.50 adults, $5.50 children 3–11; Cosmic Concerts: $6.50. Open Mon.–Thurs. and Sat. 9–5, Fri. 9–9, Sun. noon–5; Cosmic Concerts: Fri. and Sat. at 9 PM, 10, 11, midnight.*

The **Orange County Historical Museum** is a storehouse of Orlando memorabilia, photographs, and antiques. Permanent exhibits explore Native American and cracker (native Floridian) culture and show off a country store, a Victorian parlor, a print shop, and an actual 1926 brick firehouse. *812 E. Rollins St., Orlando, tel. 407/897–6350. Admission: $2 adults, $1.50 senior citizens, $1 children 6–11. Open Mon.–Sat. 9–5, Sun. noon–5.*

The **Orlando Museum of Art** displays 19th- and 20th-century American art and a permanent exhibit of pre-Columbian artifacts from a Mayan excavation. Young children will enjoy the first-class Art Encounter, created with the help of Walt Disney World. *2416 N. Mills Ave., Orlando, tel. 407/896–4231. Suggested donation: $4 adults, $2 children 4–11. Open Tues.–Sat. 9–5, Sun. noon–5; tours Sept.–May, Wed. and Sun. at 2; Art Encounter Tues.–Fri. and Sun. noon–5, Sat. 10–5.*

10 A short distance from Loch Haven Park is **Leu Botanical Gardens,** Orlando's 56-acre horticultural extravaganza. Formerly the estate of the late industrialist and citrus industry entrepreneur Harry P. Leu, it has a collection of historic blooms, many varieties having been established before 1900. You'll see ancient oaks, a 50-foot floral clock, an orchid conservatory, and one of the largest camellia collections in eastern North America (in bloom October through March). Mary Jane's Rose Garden is the largest rose conservatory south of Atlanta. The simple 19th-century Leu House Museum, once the Leu family home, preserves the furnishings and appointments of a well-to-do, turn-of-the-century Florida family. *1730 N. Forest Ave., Orlando, tel. 407/246–2620. Admission: $4 adults, $1 children 6–16. Open daily 9–5; museum Tues.–Sat. 10–3:30, Sun.–Mon. 1–3:30; closed Dec. 25.*

Other Sites of Interest

11 A one-hour drive south of Orlando, **Bok Tower Gardens** is a sanctuary of plants, flowers, trees, and wildlife native to subtropical Florida. Shady paths meander through pine forests in this peaceful world of silvery moats, mockingbirds and swans, blooming thickets, and hidden sundials. There is a quirky appeal to the majestic 200-foot Bok Tower, constructed of coquina (from seashells) and pink, white, and gray marble. The tower is carved with wildlife designs, each very symbolic, and bronze doors are decorated with reliefs that tell the complete story of Genesis. The tower houses a carillon with 57 bronze bells that ring every half hour after 10 AM. Also on the grounds is the 230-room, Mediterranean revival–style Pinewood House, built in 1930. Take I–4 to U.S. 27 south. About 5 miles past the Cypress Gardens turnoff, turn right on Route 17A to Alternate U.S. 27. Past the orange groves, turn left on Burns Avenue and follow about 1½ miles to the gardens. *Burns Ave. and Tower Blvd., Lake Wales, tel. 941/676–1408. Admission: $4 adults, $1 children 5–12; Pinewood House tour (suggested donation): $5 adults, $4 children under 12. Open daily 8–5; house tour Sept. 15–May 15, Tues. and Thurs. at 12:30 and 2, Sun. at 2.*

⑫ A visit to **Central Florida Zoological Park** will disappoint you if you're expecting a grand metro zoo. However, this is a respectable display of 230 animals on 110 acres, tucked under pine trees in a natural setting, and, like the city of Orlando, it continues to grow. A boardwalk extends through a wetland tour. The elephant exhibit is popular, as are the tortoises. The zoo is becoming specialized in small- and medium-size exotic cats, including servals, caracals, and jaguarundis. There is a petting area and daily pony rides are offered. *3755 N. U.S. 17–92, Sanford, tel. 407/323–4450. Admission: $5 adults, $3 senior citizens ($1.50 on Tues.), $2 children 3–12. Open daily 9–5; closed Thanksgiving and Dec. 25.*

⑬ The **Flying Tigers Warbird Air Museum** is a working aircraft restoration facility and a museum displaying about 30 vintage planes in its hangar, with a few big ones out on the tarmac. Tour guides are full of facts and personality and have an infectious passion for the planes. *231 Hoagland Blvd., Kissimmee, tel. 407/933–1942. Admission: $6 adults, $5 senior citizens and children 5–12. Open Mon.–Sat. 9–5:30, Sun. 9–5 (extended hrs in peak seasons).*

⑭ Long before Walt Disney World, there was **Gatorland,** a kitschy attraction south of Orlando on U.S. 441 that has endured since 1949. Through the monstrous aqua gator-jaw doorway lie thrills and chills in the form of thousands of alligators and crocodiles, swimming and basking in the Florida sun. In addition to the gators and crocs, a zoo houses many other reptiles, animals, and birds. A free train ride provides an overview of the park, and a three-story observation tower overlooks the gator breeding marsh. Don't miss the Gator Jumparoo show, the Gator Wrestling show, and the educational Snakes Alive show, with 30–40 rattlesnakes in the pit around the speaker. *14501 S. Orange Blossom Trail, between Orlando and Kissimmee, tel. 407/855–5496 or 800/393–5297. Admission: $10.95 adults, $7.95 children 3–11. Open daily 8–sunset.*

⑮ **Mystery Fun House** is an 18-chamber Mystery Maze, which comes with the warning that it is "90% dark" and full of gory and distorted images. Outside there's an 18-hole Mystery Mini-Golf, a video arcade, and the high-tech Starbase Omega laser game, in which you are suited up, given a reflector gun and badge, and transported to an arena for a group game of laser tag. *5767 Major Blvd., Orlando, tel. 407/351–3355. Admission: maze $7.95, minigolf $4.95, laser game $6.95, all 3 games $13.85. Open daily 10 AM–11 PM (to midnight in peak seasons).*

⑯ The **Ripley's Believe It or Not!** museum, in the heart of tourist territory, is part of a national chain displaying all sort of weird and amazing artifacts. Children love it, but the displays are strictly for looking—no touching. *8201 International Dr., Orlando, tel. 407/363–4418. Admission: $8.95 adults, $5.95 children 4–11. Open daily 10 AM–11 PM (extended hrs in peak seasons).*

⑰ Visit a haunted house all year round at **Terror on Church Street.** There's also a gift shop with all kinds of creepy things. *Church St. and Orange Ave., Orlando, tel. 407/649–3327. Admission: nonresidents: $12 adults, $10 students 17 and under; residents: $10 adults, $8 students 17 and under. Open Sun.–Thurs. 7 PM–midnight; Fri., Sat. 7 PM–1 AM.*

⑱ Water Mania has all the requisite rides and slides without the aesthetics you'll find at Walt Disney World. However, it's the only water park around to have Wipe Out, a surfing simulator, where you grab a body board and ride a continuous wave form. The giant Pirate Ship in the Rain Forest, one of two children's play areas, is equipped with water slides and water cannons. The Abyss, similar to Wet 'n' Wild's Black Hole (*see below*), is an enclosed tube slide through which you twist and turn on a one- or two-person raft for 300 feet of deep-blue darkness. The park also offers miniature golf, a sandy beach, snack bars, gift shops, and periodic concerts. *6073 W. Irlo Bronson Memorial Hwy., Kissimmee, tel. 407/239–8448, 407/396–2626, or 800/ 527–3092. Admission: $20.95 adults, $17.95 children 3–12. Open daily 10–5 (until about 8 in summer) except on very cold days.*

⑲ Wet 'n' Wild is best known for its outrageous water slides, especially the Black Hole—a 30-second, 500-foot, twisting, turning ride on a two-person raft through total darkness propelled by a 1,000 gallon-a-minute blast of water. There's also an elaborate kids' park, for those 4 feet tall and under, full of miniature versions of the bigger rides. The latest addition is the Bubba Tub, a six-story, triple-dip slide with a tube big enough for the entire family to ride in together. The park has snack stands, but visitors are allowed to bring their own food and picnic around the pool or on the lakeside beach. *6200 International Dr., Orlando, tel, 407/351–3200. Admission: $20.95 adults, $17.95 children 3–9. Open daily 10–5 (until about 9 in summer) except for really cold days.*

Guided Tours

Theme Park Tours
Walt Disney World's **Magic Kingdom** operates 3½- to 4-hour guided orientation tours ($5 per adult, $3.50 per child, plus park admission). Tours include visits to some of the rides, but don't expect to go to the head of the line—you still have to wait your turn. For schedules, ask at City Hall.

Reserve up to three weeks in advance for the two four-hour behind-the-scenes tours of **Epcot Center**, open to guests 16 and up ($20 plus park admission, tel. 407/345–5860): Hidden Treasures of the World Showcase (Sun., Wed., and Fri. at varying times) and Gardens of the World (Mon., Tues., and Thurs. at varying times).

Among many other educational programs, **Sea World** offers the guided, 90-minute **Animal Lover's Adventures** ($5.95 adults, $4.95 children 3–9). It provides a close-up look at the park's breeding, research, and training facilities and is as interesting to children as to adults, as is the 45-minute **Let's Talk Training** presentation ($5.95 adults, $4.95 children 3–9), which introduces guests to Sea World's animal behavior and training techniques.

Boat Tour
Scenic Boat Tour (312 E. Morse Blvd., Winter Park, tel. 407/644–4056) is a relaxing, hour-long cruise past 12 miles of fine old homes and through the grounds of Rollins College, on one of Winter Park's three main lakes, which are connected by 100-year-old canals.

Shopping for Bargains

Outlet Stores
The International Drive area is filled with factory outlet stores, including **Belz Factory Outlet World and Annexes** (5401 W. Oakridge Rd., Orlando), with nearly 170 stores. **Quality Outlet Center** and **Quality Center East** (5409 and 5529 International Dr., Orlando), two interconnected strip shopping centers, contain 20 brand-name factory outlet stores. **Kissimmee Manufacturers' Outlet Mall** (1 mi east of Rte. 535 on U.S. 192, Kissimmee) has approximately 20 stores.

Flea Market
Flea World (3 mi east of I–4 Exit 50 on Lake Mary Blvd., then 1 mi south on U.S. 17–92, Sanford) claims to be America's largest flea

market under one roof. More than 1,600 booths sell only new merchandise—everything from car tires, ginsu knives, and pet tarantulas to gourmet coffee, leather lingerie, and beaded evening gowns. Kids love Fun World next door, which offers miniature golf, arcade games, go-carts, bumper cars, bumper boats, kiddie rides, and batting cages.

Malls **Altamonte Mall** (451 Altamonte Ave., ½ mi east of I–4 on Rte. 436, Altamonte Springs) is an airy, spacious two-level mall containing Sears, Gayfers, Burdines, and JCPenney department stores and 165 specialty shops.

Church Street Exchange (Church St. Station, 129 W. Church St., Orlando) is a decorative, brassy, Victorian-theme "festival marketplace" filled with more than 50 specialty shops. Perhaps the best demonstration is at Augusta Janssen, where free samples are distributed during a lighthearted look at the process of making fudge. Across the street from the complex is Bumby Emporium, a Church Street souvenir shop, and across the railroad tracks is yet another collection of unusual shops and pushcarts, known as the Historic Railroad Depot. The prices here can be steep, but the window-shopping and people-watching make a visit worthwhile.

Crossroads of Lake Buena Vista (Rte. 535 and I–4, Lake Buena Vista), across the street from the entrance to the hotels at Lake Buena Vista, contains restaurants and nearly 20 shops that are convenient for tourists. The necessities, such as a 24-hour grocery and pharmacy, post office, bank, and cleaners, are all here, and while you shop, your offspring can entertain themselves at Pirate's Cove Adventure Golf.

Nestled along the shores of Buena Vista Lagoon, **Disney Village Marketplace** (Lake Buena Vista) is a complex of shops packed with art, fashions, crafts, and more. If you are looking for one-stop shopping for Disney collectibles and souvenirs, this is the place, although prices aren't any better than in the theme park. Stores are open until 10.

Florida Mall (8001 S. Orange Blossom Trail, 4½ mi east of I–4 and International Dr., Orlando), the largest in central Florida, includes Sears, JCPenney, Belk Lindsey, Gayfers, Dillard's, 200 specialty shops, seven theaters, and one of the better food courts around.

The Spanish-style **Mercado Mediterranean Village** (8445 International Dr., Orlando) houses more than 60 specialty shops. A walkway circles the courtyard, where live entertainment can be enjoyed throughout the day. The clean, quick, and large food court offers a selection of food from around the world.

Old Town (5770 W. Irlo Bronson Memorial Hwy., Kissimmee) is a shopping-entertainment complex featuring a 1928 Ferris wheel, a 1909 carousel, and more than 70 specialty shops in a re-creation of a turn-of-the-century Florida village.

Orlando Fashion Square (3201 E. Colonial Dr., 3 mi east of I–4 Exit 41, Orlando) has 130 shops including Burdines, JCPenney, Sears, Camelot Music, the Disney Store, the Gap, Lerner, and Lechters.

Sports and the Outdoors

Participant Sports

Fishing Central Florida is covered with freshwater lakes and rivers teeming with all kinds of fish: especially largemouth black bass, but also perch, catfish, sunfish, and pike.

At WDW, there's fishing off the dock at the **Ol' Man Island Fishing Hole** (Dixie Landings, tel. 407/934–5409). Catch and release is encouraged, but you can have your fish packed in ice to take home. You'll have to clean them yourself, though.

Lake Tohopekaliga is a popular camping and fishing destination (don't bother trying to pronounce it—it's Lake Toho to the locals) with a number of excellent fishing camps. Camp offices will generally help you hire fishing guides and sell you Florida state fishing licenses, which are necessary to fish in the lake. On East Lake Tohopekaliga, **East Lake Fish Camp** (3705 Big Bass Rd., Kissimmee, tel. 407/348–2040) has 283 RV sites, 40 tent sites, and 24 cabins; on West Lake Tohopekaliga, **Red's Fish Camp** (4715 Kissimmee Park Rd., St. Cloud, tel. 407/892–8795) has RV sites and **Richardson's Fish Camp** (1550 Scotty's Rd., Kissimmee, tel. 407/846–6540) has cabins with kitchenettes as well as RV and tent sites.

Golf Golfpac (Box 162366, Altamonte Springs 32701, tel. 407/260–2288 or 800/327–0878) packages golf vacations and prearranges tee times at more than 40 courses around Orlando. Rates vary based on hotel and course, and 60–90 days' advance notice is recommended to set up a vacation.

Golf is an extremely popular activity in Orlando. Be sure to reserve tee times well in advance. Greens fees usually vary by season—the highest and lowest figures are listed, all including mandatory cart rental.

At WDW Walt Disney World's five championship courses—all on the PGA Tour route—are among the busiest and most expensive in the region. The three older Disney courses have the same fees and discount policies: Guests at WDW resorts pay $85; all others pay $95 regardless of season. Prices at Eagle Pines and Osprey Ridge go up to $100 and $115 January–April. The twilight discount rate is $45 for everyone; it goes into effect at 2 PM during the winter and peak seasons, 3 PM during the summer and off seasons. For tee times and private lessons on any of the five, phone 407/824–2270. The five 18-hole courses are: **Eagle Pines** (Bonnet Creek Golf Club, 6,722 yds), **Lake Buena Vista** (Lake Buena Vista, 6,829 yds), **Magnolia** (Shades of Green, 7,190 yds), **Osprey Ridge** (Bonnet Creek Golf Club, 7,101 yds), and **The Palm** (Shades of Green, 6,957 yds). **Oak Trail,** a nine-hole layout, is for novice and preteen golfers.

Elsewhere **Cypress Creek Country Club** (5353 Vineland Rd., Orlando, tel. 407/351–2187) is a demanding 6,955-yard, 18-hole course with 16 water holes and lots of trees; greens fees run $25–$38.

Grenelefe Golf & Tennis Resort (3200 Rte. 546, Haines City, tel. 941/422–7511 or 800/237–9549), about 45 minutes from Orlando, has three excellent 18-hole courses, of which the toughest is the 7,325-yard West Course. Greens fees run $39–$110.

Hunter's Creek Golf Course (14401 Sports Club Way, Orlando, tel. 407/240–4653), designed by Lloyd Clifton, has large greens and 14 water holes. Greens fees are $35–$55.

Poinciana Golf & Racquet Resort (500 E. Cypress Pkwy., Poinciana, tel. 407/933–5300 or 800/331–7743), about 18 miles southeast of Disney World, is an 18-hole course. Greens fees are $30–$40.

Timacuan Golf & Country Club (550 Timacuan Blvd., Lake Mary, tel. 407/321–0010) has a two-part course designed by Ron Garl—the front nine is open with lots of sand, the back nine is heavily wooded. Greens fees are $40–$85.

Horseback Riding **Fort Wilderness Resort and Campground** (tel. 407/824–2832) offers tame trail rides through backwoods. Children must be over nine, and adults must be under 250 pounds. Trail rides cost $17 for 45 minutes. Rides are daily at 9, 10:30, noon, and 2.

Poinciana Riding Stables (3705 Poinciana Blvd., Kissimmee, tel. 407/847–4343) offers basic ($29.95) and advanced ($39.95) nature trail tours along old logging trails near Kissimmee. Reservations a day in advance are recommended for the popular advanced trail rides. Private lessons and pony rides are also available.

Jogging Walt Disney World has several scenic jogging trails. Pick up jogging maps at any Disney resort. **Fort Wilderness Resort and Campground** (tel. 407/824–2900) has a 2.3-mile jogging course with plenty of fresh air and woods as well as numerous exercise stations along the way.

In Winter Park, around **Rollins College,** you can jog along the shady streets and around the lakes. The **Orlando Runners Club** meets in the area every Sunday morning at 7AM for 3-, 6-, and 12-mile jaunts; for details, call the Track Shack (1322 N. Mills Ave., Orlando, tel. 407/ 898–1313).

Tennis You can play tennis at any number of Disney hotels. All have lights
At WDW and are open 7 AM–10 PM, and most have lockers and rental rackets ($4–$5 an hour). There seems to be a long-term plan to move from hard courts to clay, and the Contemporary has already converted. All courts are open to all players, but staff can opt to turn away nonguests when things get busy. (That doesn't often happen.)

The **Contemporary Resort** (tel. 407/824–3578, court reservations up to 24 hrs in advance) is the center of Disney's tennis program, with its sprawl of six clay courts. The cost is $12 per hour or $40 for length of stay.

The **Disney Beach and Yacht Clubs** (tel. 407/934–3256, court reservations up to 24 hrs in advance) have two blacktop courts, for which there is no charge. **Fort Wilderness Resort and Campground** (tel. 407/824–2900, no court reservations) has two courts out in the middle of a field, and there's no charge to play. As a result, they're popular with youngsters. If you hate players who are too free about letting their balls stray across their neighbors' court, this is not the place for you.

Elsewhere **Lake Cane Tennis Center** (5108 Turkey Lake Rd., Orlando, tel. 407/ 352–4913) has 13 lighted hard courts for $2 per hour weekdays, $4 per hour weekends.

Orange Lake Country Club (8505 W. Irlo Bronson Memorial Hwy., Kissimmee, tel. 407/239–0000) has 15 all-weather hard courts, nine of them lighted. It is five minutes from Walt Disney World's main entrance. Nonguests pay $4 per hour.

Orlando Tennis Center (649 W. Livingston St., Orlando, tel. 407/ 246–2162) offers 16 lighted tennis courts and two racquetball courts. For 1½ hours, courts are $5.80 for Har-Tru and $3.68 for asphalt.

Spectator Sports

Basketball The NBA **Orlando Magic** (Box 76, 600 W. Amelia St., 2 blocks west of I–4 Amelia St. exit, tel. 407/839–3900) plays in the 15,077-seat Orlando Arena.

Dog Racing **Sanford Orlando Kennel Club** (301 Dog Track Rd., Longwood, tel. 407/831–1600) has dog racing as well as south Florida horse-racing simulcasts, November–May.

Seminole Greyhound Park (2000 Seminole Blvd., Casselberry, tel. 407/699–4510), open May–October, is a newer track.

Jai Alai **Orlando-Seminole Jai-Alai** (6405 S. U.S. 17–92, Fern Park, tel. 407/ 331–9191), about 20 minutes north of Orlando off I–4, offers south Florida horse-racing simulcasts and betting in addition to jai alai at the fronton (closed May).

Where to Eat on a Budget

Drive down International Drive or U.S. 192 near Walt Disney World and you'll probably be convinced that some obscure federal law mandates that any franchise restaurant company doing business in the United States has to have at least one outlet in Orlando. If they batter it, fry it, microwave it, torture it under a heat lamp until it's ready to sign a confession, and serve it with a side of fries, you can find it in central Florida. Not all the franchises are burger barns, however, and even those that are try to put their best foot forward in Orlando, where food is consumed by millions of international visitors. The McDonald's on International Drive, for example, is the largest in the nation; the new Planet Hollywood at Pleasure Island is the biggest and most elaborate in the chain. Hotels tend, too, to have bigger and fancier restaurants than they would in another city of the same size. Restaurateurs build monuments here and usually try to offer superb food, so you'll ask "Hey, why don't they have one of these places in our town?" This fiercely competitive dining market even brings out the best from the hometown eateries that predate Disney. The result is that dining choices in Orlando are like entertainment choices. There's simply more than you can sample on any one trip. An added bonus is that bargains abound.

Grouper—fried, blackened, or broiled—is the closest thing central Florida has to a local dish. Most locals don't eat much alligator tail, but almost every fish restaurant offers it for the tourists, and it's fun to try. Also worthy are some of the treats imported from the Florida Keys and billed as local fare: stone crabs, in season October–March; the small, tasty Keys lobsters; and conch chowder. Fresh hearts of palm, served in the more upscale restaurants, are also good. One tip on Key lime pie: If it's green, especially fluorescent green, you've been had. Authentic Key lime pie is yellow, just like the fruit used to make it.

Because tourism is king here, casual dress is the rule, and almost no restaurants require fancier attire. At most places, you'll be safe wearing anything that wouldn't get you thrown out of a Burger King, and if your child is the only one wearing a hat with Goofy ears, you probably made a wrong turn and ended up in Georgia.

Reservations are always a good idea in a city where the phrase "Bus drivers eat free" is emblazoned on the coat of arms. If you don't have reservations, the entire Ecuadoran soccer team or the senior class from Platt City High School may arrive moments before you and keep you waiting a long, long time. Save that experience for the attractions. Orlando is not a big town, but getting to places is frequently complicated, so always call for directions. Some of the smaller, hungrier restaurant operators may offer to come get you. Disney has simplified its telephone reservation system. Whether you are staying in a Disney hotel or not, the number to call for WDW restaurants outside Epcot is 407/939–3463. For restaurants in Epcot, however, you must make reservations in person on the day you dine if you are not a Disney hotel guest. Kiosks for Epcot's electronic dining reservation system are located all around the park, with the biggest bank of electronic reservation machines near Earth Center.

Picnicking is not encouraged at WDW, and you can't bring in a cooler. You won't be run through a salami detector at the gate, though, so if you want to bring sandwiches, chips, and plastic bottles of water in a knapsack or diaper bag, you're free to do so. In general, you can find the most competitive prices on WDW property at the Disney Village Marketplace, largely because it's only a couple of blocks from the Crossings shopping center (on Route 535), which has a good supply of fast-food restaurants that charge virtually the same prices they charge anywhere else in the United States.

In and Around Walt Disney World

$$

★

Artist Point. This excellent restaurant offers those not booked at the Wilderness Lodge a good excuse to see the huge, hunting-lodge-style hotel. The northwestern salmon sampler is a good start, but you might also try the smoked duck breast, the maple-glazed steak, or the sautéed elk sausage. Most meats are hardwood grilled. The house specialty is Trail Dust Shortcake, a buttermilk biscuit with strawberries, vanilla bean ice cream, and whipped cream. Just to make sure you get that Pacific Northwest feeling, the sommelier can suggest one of the Washington State or Oregon wines. *Wilderness Lodge, Magic Kingdom resort area, tel. 407/939–3463. Reservations accepted. Dress: casual. AE, MC, V.*

$$ **Austin's.** Stephen F. Austin, founder of the Republic of Texas, was the inspiration for this Floridian fantasy of what a Texas beef palace should be. But it's a good fantasy. The barbecued ribs and chicken are quite tasty, and the Galveston Bay, which features ½ pound of ribs and a skewer of hickory-grilled shrimp, should satisfy those buckaroos who can't decide between surf and turf. The hickory-grilled fish is quite good, especially when Norwegian salmon is available. If you've already been to Disney World, the $6 price tag for the burgers won't phase you. *8633 International Dr., Orlando, tel. 407/363–9575. Dress: casual. AE, D, DC, MC, V.*

$$ **Biergarten.** Oktoberfest runs 365 days a year in this popular spot. The cheerful—some would say raucous—atmosphere is what you would expect in a place with an oompah band. Waitresses in typical Bavarian garb serve hot pretzels, hearty German fare such as sauerbraten and bratwurst, and stout pitchers of beer and wine, which patrons pound on their long communal tables—even when the yodelers, singers, and dancers aren't egging them on. *Germany, Epcot Center. Reservations required. Dress: casual. AE, D, DC, MC, V.*

$$

★

Cafe Tu Tu Tango. This très-chic bistro doesn't have a dance floor, but there's plenty of choreographing going on here. Multiple kitchens bombard you with different courses, which seem to arrive in waves if you follow the house custom and order a series of appetizers. (This you're bound to do anyway, since the entrées are appetizer size.) The menu gives the address (on International Drive) a new meaning. Try the Cajun chicken egg rolls, for instance, with blackened chicken, Greek goat cheese, Creole mustard, and tomato salsa, if you want to sample the world's major cuisines in one bite. Trendy dishes like sun-dried tomato pizza and smoked chicken quesadillas give this place a certain hip spin. For added atmosphere, artists work at easels while diners watch, sipping drinks like the Matisse margarita and the Renoir rum runner. The café is part of the empire of Orlando-based restaurant magnate Robert Earl, creator of Planet Hollywood, who strives to entertain customers as well as feed them. There's a limited selection of nonfancy food, like burgers and pizza, on the children's menu. Even though nothing is more than $8, it's easy to spend $50 on lunch for two, especially if you follow the server's suggestion and order sangria early and often. *8625 International Dr., Orlando, tel. 407/248–2222. No reservations. Dress: casual. AE, D, MC, V.*

$$ **Ciao Italia.** The location, almost in the shadow of Sea World, is a bit odd for a quiet, charming little Italian eatery, but even though it's in the tourism fast lane, nothing is hurried here. Every item on the menu is made to order, so you might want to bring along that copy of *War and Peace* you never finished. Your patience will be rewarded, however: The Italian-speaking proprietors have managed to re-create a piece of Italy in central Florida. The proof is in the sweet New Zealand mussels, served with either white garlic or marinara sauce, and the light, colorful *pollo alla Tonino* (chicken breast with red and yellow peppers). For dessert, try the *tartufo* (chocolate-coated ice cream). *6149 Westwood Blvd., Orlando, tel. 407/354–0770. Reserva-*

tions accepted. Dress: casual. AE, D, DC, MC, V. Beer and wine only. No lunch.

$$ Ming Court. The building is as important as the cooking here, and both the architect and the chef get high marks. A wall that looks like a dragon's back provides serenity in an enclosed courtyard, even on International Drive. Diners look out through glass walls over a beautiful series of floating gardens. Inside, touches like rosewood chopsticks and linen tablecloths add to the classy feel. If you eat Chinese a lot, you probably won't see any dishes you haven't heard of, but the versions here are expertly prepared. The jumbo shrimp in lobster sauce, flavored with crushed black beans, may cost more than you're used to ($15), but it's quite worthwhile. Another popular dish is the Hunan *kung pao* chicken, sautéed with red and green peppers and served with cashews and walnuts. The restaurant is within walking distance of the Orange County Convention Center. *9188 International Dr., Orlando, tel. 407/351–9988. Reservations advised. Dress: casual but neat. AE, DC, MC, V.*

$$ Mitsukoshi. This complex of dining areas overlooking tranquil gar-
★ dens is actually three restaurants: the Yakitori; the Tempura Kiku, where you can sit around a central counter and watch chefs prepare sushi, sashimi, and tempura; and a series of five Teppanyaki Rooms, where chefs skillfully chop vegetables, meat, and fish at lightning speed and then stir-fry them at grills set into communal dining tables. The Matsunoma Lounge to the right of this area pours Japanese sake, plum wine, and saketinis (martinis made with sake rather than vermouth). Food is authentic and tasty, as evidenced by the number of Japanese diners. If you just want sushi, go to the lounge to avoid a wait. *Japan, Epcot Center. Reservations required. Dress: casual. AE, D, DC, MC, V.*

$$ Pebbles. In the past few years, this has become one of the most popular local dining spots, perennially voted best in the city by the readers of the *Orlando Sentinel*. It offers the right blend of elegance and informality for a "casual gourmet" clientele. On tap is California cuisine, dude, with a Florida cracker touch that adds grouper and other regional favorites. Good entrée choices include angel hair pasta, smothered with smoked duck, scallops, and Asian spices, and the Mediterranean salad, where sun-dried tomatoes put in their obligatory appearance. The Caesar salad, tossed table-side, is memorable, which is difficult for such a common dish to accomplish. Desserts are worth the calories, and the wine list is intelligent without being a wallet breaker. *Crossroads of Lake Buena Vista, Orlando, tel. 407/ 827–1111; 17 W. Church St., Orlando, tel. 407/839–0892; 2516 Aloma Ave., Winter Park, tel. 407/678–7001; 2100 Rte. 434, Longwood, tel. 407/774–7111. No reservations. Dress: casual. AE, D, DC, MC, V.*

$$ Portobello Yacht Club. Operated by Chicago's venerable Levy brothers, this eatery has a much better pedigree than the one the Disney brain trust made up for the building. Supposedly, it was the home of Merriweather Adam Pleasure, the man for whom Pleasure Island was named. Of course, Pleasure never existed, but you'll still find great pleasure dining here. Start with something simple—the chewy, tasty sourdough bread, served with roast garlic. Then move on to bigger and better things like the spaghettini *alla Portobello*, a stick-to-your-ribs dish with scallops, clams, shrimp, mussels, tomatoes, garlic and herbs, and, of course, copious amounts of pasta. There's always a fresh catch of the day, and servers are attentive and knowledgeable. Since Pleasure Island is in Disney's own nightclub district, where party animals are a protected species, the people-watching can be quite interesting, especially after a little sangria. This is a good spot for a late meal since it's open until midnight. *Pleasure Island, Walt Disney World Village, tel. 407/934– 8888. Reservations accepted. Dress: casual. AE, DC, MC, V.*

$$ Restaurant Akershus. Norway's tradition of seafood and cold-meat dishes is highlighted at the *koldtboard* (Norwegian buffet) in this restaurant—four dining rooms that occupy a copy of Oslo's Akershus Castle. Hosts and hostesses explain the dishes and suggest which ones go together, then send you off to the buffet table. There is no need to shovel everything you see onto your plate at one time; it's traditional to make several trips. Start with appetizers (usually herring, which comes several ways here); then cold seafood, such as gravlax; next, cold salads and meats; and hot lamb, veal, or venison on your last foray. Desserts, offered à la carte, include cloudberries (in season only)—delicate seasonal fruits that grow on the tundra. *Norway, Epcot Center. Reservations required. Dress: casual. AE, D, DC, MC, V.*

$$ **Rosario's.** Housed in a New England–style clapboard house that looks refreshingly out of place in the unsightly jumble of motels known as Kissimmee, this understated and cheerful little place serves Italian food that's way above average. The spaghetti *aglio olio* is sauced with fresh garlic, basil, and diced tomatoes sautéed in olive oil. The hearty *pasta e fagioli* soup is filled with Italian white beans, prosciutto, escarole, pasta, and flavored with brandy and a touch of marinara sauce. All entrées come with a choice of soup or salad and plenty of crusty Italian bread. *4838 W. Irlo Bronson Memorial Hwy., Kissimmee, tel. 407/239–0118. Dress: casual. AE, D, DC, MC, V. Beer and wine only. No lunch.*

$$ **Rose and Crown.** If you love British street culture and a good thick beer, this friendly pub on World Showcase Lagoon is the place to soak up both. "Wenches" serve up simple pub fare, such as steak-and-kidney pie and fish-and-chips. Dark wood floors, sturdy pub chairs, and brass lamps create a warm, homey atmosphere. At 4, a traditional tea is served, and at day's end, visitors mingle with Disney employees over pints of Bass Ale and Guinness Stout with Stilton cheese. The food is relatively inexpensive, especially at lunch, and the terrace has a splendid view of IllumiNations. All things considered, it's one of the best bets in Epcot. *United Kingdom, Epcot Center. Reservations required. Dress: casual. AE, D, DC, MC, V.*

$$ **San Angel Inn.** The lush, tropical surroundings—cool, dark, and almost surreal—make this restaurant in the Mexican pavilion courtyard perhaps the most exotic in Walt Disney World. It's popular among Disney execs and tourists who treasure a respite, especially when the humid weather outside makes central Florida feel like Africa in August. The restaurant is open to the "sky" and filled with the music of folk singers, guitars, and marimbas. Above looms an Aztec pyramid, whose soft, fiery light evokes a sense of the distant past. The best seats are along the outer edge, away from the entrance and directly alongside the "river," where boatloads of sightseers stream by. On the roster of authentic dishes, one specialty is *mole poblano* (chicken simmered in a rich sauce of different chilies, green tomatoes, ground tortillas, cumin, and 11 other spices mixed with cocoa). Fresh tortillas are made each day and served with beef, chicken, and cheese fillings as well as fresh salsa *verde* (spicy green sauce). You probably won't see a Disney employee, even off duty, ordering one of the margaritas, incidentally; they're so bad as to be legendary. *Mexico, Epcot Center. Reservations required. Dress: casual. AE, D, DC, MC, V.*

$$ **White Horse Saloon.** Improbable as it sounds, this western-theme saloon is located in the Hyatt Regency Grand Cypress. You can get a barbecued half chicken for $20 or pay $1 more for prime rib. All entrées come with sourdough bread, baked or mashed potatoes, and your choice of creamed spinach or corn on the cob. A hearty hot apple pie with cinnamon-raisin sauce awaits those desperadoes who can still handle dessert. You also get music with your vittles. The Hand-Picked Trio, which has been here for years, plays evenings. *Hyatt Regency Grand Cypress, 1 Grand Cypress Blvd., Orlando, tel. 407/239–1234. Reservations advised. Dress: casual. AE, DC, MC, V.*

$ Enzo's at the Marketplace. This pizzeria and deli combines the real Italian flavor of its sister in Longwood with a more casual atmosphere and a location that's more convenient for tourists. Owner Enzo Perlini, a food purist, imported the pizza ovens from Italy to ensure that his pizza *napoli* would have the proper thin, crispy crust. It does. The toppings are Italian style—fresh tomatoes and mozzarella, seafood, or grilled vegetables. If you don't feel like pizza, order the chicken cacciatore (a half bird served in a tangy marinara sauce) or one of the many pasta dishes (chicken ravioli is a good bet). The deli has takeout. *7600 Dr. Phillips Blvd., Orlando, tel. 407/351–1187. Reservations in dining room only. Dress: casual. AE, D, DC, MC, V.*

$ Hard Rock Café Orlando. The motto at this place is "Save the Planet," but that was before founder Robert Earl jumped ship and moved on to found Planet Hollywood. Both chains purvey a similar fantasy: a few hours of being cool just for standing in line and getting inside. The Hard Rock, a huge, guitar-shaped building that is loaded down with memorabilia, is adjacent to Universal Studios Florida. There's usually a long line of Universal visitors. It's also a hangout for members of the NBA Orlando Magic, and, oh yes, it even serves food. Both menu and prices could be a lot worse, considering that the Rock's location guarantees its popularity, no matter what it served. The best bets are the pig sandwich, made of pork shoulder hickory smoked for 14 hours, and the old reliable, ⅓-pound charbroiled cheeseburger with all the trimmings. There's also an extensive collection of beers. Don't go if you can't tolerate noise that would drown out a 747 on takeoff; this place is a rock shrine and proud of it. *Universal Studios Florida, 5800 Kirkman Rd., Orlando, tel. 407/351–7625. No reservations. Dress: casual. AE, MC, V.*

$ Phoenician. This is the latest addition to the rich culinary clique at the Marketplace. Hummus flavored with tahini, *babaganoush* (roasted eggplant purée), and *lebneh* (soft, seasoned, yogurt-based cheese) top the menu. The best bet is to order a tableful of *mezes* and then sample as many as possible. *7600 Dr. Phillips Blvd., Orlando, tel. 407/345–1001. No reservations. Dress: casual. AE, MC, V.*

$ Planet Hollywood. On weekend nights, when nearby clubs are jumping, the line approaching this place is about as long as the one in front of Lenin's Tomb during the Soviet era. The rationale for standing here is similar: You queue up to see a piece of history. In this case, it's movie history, as assembled by club owners Demi Moore, Bruce Willis, Arnold Schwarzenegger, Sylvester Stallone, and the biggest showman among the partners, restaurateur Robert Earl. Memorabilia, like the bus that was used in the movie *Speed* and the leather jacket worn by Schwarzenegger in *The Terminator*, rotate between the Orlando Planet and its 17 sister restaurants around the country. At the souvenir shop, just outside, you can buy a few T-shirts while you ponder which day you'll get inside. In actuality, the wait is about two hours most evenings. If you want to minimize it, go in mid-afternoon. The menu doesn't change—fresh, healthful dishes like turkey burgers, smoked and grilled meats, unusual pastas and salads, and a wide range of desserts. But then the food is secondary to the 110-foot-tall, 20,000-square-foot building, complete with indoor waterfall. It cost $15 million, about as much as a new theme park attraction. If someone else is driving, try a Comet, the gargantuan souvenir-glass drink with vodka, rum, tequila, and orange and pineapple juices, all for $13. *Pleasure Island, Walt Disney World Village, tel. 407/363–7827. No reservations. Dress: casual. AE, DC, MC, V.*

$ Ran-Getsu. The surroundings are definitely a Disney version of the Orient—but the food is fresh and carefully prepared. Sit at the curved, dragon's tail–shape sushi bar and order the matsu platter— an assortment of *nigiri-* and *maki*-style sushis. Or, unless you're alone, have your meal Japanese-style at the low tables overlooking a carp-filled pond and decorative gardens. Specialties include sukiyaki and *shabu-shabu* (thinly sliced beef prepared table-side in a boiling seasoned broth and served with vegetables). If you feel more adventurous, try the deep-fried alligator tail. It helps to know a bit about Japanese cuisine, as servers are not great at educating customers. *8400 International Dr., Orlando, tel. 407/345–0044. Reservations advised. Dress: casual. AE, DC, MC, V. No lunch.*

¢ **McDonald's.** The nation's largest McDonald's is no plain-Jane burger joint. Although the menu is standard, the frills are pure Orlando: a 7,500-square-foot playground full of slides, tunnels, and seesaws; a theater where musicians and magicians perform; and even a gift shop, called Mickey D's, full of T-shirts. You can chow down in the tiki bar–style Sunset Terrace area; the Maui Room, with a 600-gallon saltwater aquarium; or the Rock and Roll Room, featuring '50s memorabilia and a jukebox. *6875 Sand Lake Rd. and International Dr., Orlando, tel. 407/351–2185. No reservations. Dress: casual. AE, MC, V.*

¢ **Siam Orchid.** One of Orlando's several elegant Asian restaurants, Siam Orchid occupies a gorgeous structure a bit off I-Drive. Waitresses, who wear costumes from their homeland, serve such authentic fare as Siam wings (a chicken wing stuffed to look like a drumstick) and *pla lad prig* (a whole, deep-fried fish covered with a sauce flavored with red chili, bell peppers, and garlic). If you like your food spicy, say "Thai hot" and grab a fire extinguisher. Otherwise, a request to make a dish spicy will be answered with a smile, and your food will come merely mild. *7575 Republic Dr., Orlando, tel. 407/351–0821. Reservations advised. Dress: casual. AE, DC, MC, V.*

Elsewhere Around Orlando **Enzo's on the Lake.** Enzo's is one of Orlando's most popular restaurants, even though it's on a tacky stretch of highway filled with used-car lots. The Roman charmer who owns the place, Enzo Perlini, has turned a rather ordinary lakefront house in suburban Longwood, about 30 minutes by car from I-Drive, into a delightful Italian villa. A wall in front shields it from its shabby surroundings and makes the grounds look rather bucolic. It's worth the trip to sample the antipasto (a huge array of fresh grilled vegetables), homemade frittatas and pâtés, bean salad, and marinated seafood salad, made up of tiny whole squid, tender calamari, and shrimp. The electricity in the air is such that even people with reservations don't mind waiting at the bar (as is often necessary); they simply get into the party. Once you've adjusted to the clamor, your only problem will be deciding what to eat, because all the choices are irresistible. *1130 S. U.S. 17–92, Longwood, tel. 407/834–9872. Reservations required. Dress: casual. AE, DC, MC, V. Closed Sun.*

$$ **Gargi's Italian Restaurant.** You can feel the building vibrate when Amtraks roll by only feet way, but that just adds to the charm of this delightful ma-and-pa pasta place. If you crave old-fashioned spaghetti and meatballs, lasagna, or manicotti made with sauces that you know have been simmering all day, this storefront hole-in-the-wall in Orlando's antiques district, just a little north of downtown, is the place. Well-heeled Orlandoans eat here before Orlando Magic games; it's also a favorite of water-skiers from Lake Ivanhoe across the street. Only a few hundred yards from I–4, it's worlds away from touristy I-Drive. *1421 N. Orange Ave., Orlando, tel. 407/894–7907. Reservations accepted. Dress: casual. MC, V. Beer and wine only. Closed Sun.*

$$ **Le Coq au Vin.** Louis Perrotte could run a stuffed-shirt kind of place, because his traditional French cuisine is as expertly prepared as any you'll find in the area. Instead, he chooses to run a modest little kitchen in a small but charming house in south Orlando. Perrotte and his wife, Magdalena, who acts as hostess, make the place feel warm and homey, and it's usually filled with friendly Orlando residents. The menu changes quarterly, reflecting the cooking of various regions of Perrotte's native France, but the fare is

always first class. Try homemade chicken liver pâté, fresh rainbow trout with champagne sauce, or Long Island duck with green peppercorns. For dessert, sample the crème brûlée, and pat yourself on the back for discovering a place that few tourists know about. Ask to be seated in the main dining room—it's the center of action. *4800 S. Orange Ave., Orlando, tel. 407/851–6980. Reservations advised. Dress: casual. AE, DC, MC, V.*

$$ ★ **Moorefield's.** Erudite but not snobby, this downtown restaurant attracts an after-theater crowd. The trendy menu and fresh, sophisticated, homemade dishes make you think Martha Stewart might be in the kitchen somewhere, but it's really owner-chef Elizabeth Moorefield. Though the menu changes constantly, you can always find some variation of grilled salmon, roast pork, and the very popular angel hair pasta with artichoke hearts, hearts of palm, chèvre, sun-dried tomatoes, and Parmesan. A favorite appetizer is a minipizza topped with mushrooms and roasted garlic. About 20 carefully selected wines are served by the glass. *123 S. Orange Ave., Orlando, tel. 407/872–6960. Reservations accepted. Dress: casual but neat. AE, MC, V.*

$$ **Positano.** One side of this cheerful restaurant is a bustling family-style pizza parlor; the other is a more formal dining room. Although you can't order pizza in the dining room, you can get anything on the entire menu in the pizzeria, which serves some of the best New York–style pies in central Florida. Try the unusual and piquant ziti *aum, aum* (with mozzarella, Parmesan, eggplant, and basil in a tomato sauce). The delicious homemade soups—included in the full dinner—can be a meal in themselves. Desserts are all old reliables: spumoni, tortoni, and cannoli. If this place were on Disney property, it would be much pricier—and you'd still be getting a good deal. *8995 West Colonial Dr., Good Homes Plaza, Orlando, tel. 407/291–0602. Reservations in dining room only. Dress: casual. AE, D, DC, MC, V.*

$ ★ **Dexter's.** With a facade so nondescript it almost blends into the Laundromat next door, this popular, trendy eatery and winery is sophisticated enough to offer its own wine label and publish a monthly newsletter for oenophiles. Much of the clientele comes from Rollins College, a liberal arts school a block away, and the SoHo-like menu reflects that. If you're over 40, however, you won't feel out of place, since this is also a hangout for those who live in the lakefront mansions nearby. Not surprisingly, wine and cheese are popular, with more than two dozen wines by the glass and an equal number of cheese boards on the appetizer menu. One of the best entrées is chicken tortilla pie, a stack of cheese-laden tortillas that looks more spaceship than a pie; it's topped with sour cream and stuffed with jalapeños, tomato salsa, and other tasty fillings. A similar ratt pie is filled with provolone and ratatouille, and thick deli sandwiches come with everything from pastrami to pesto. Jazz is frequently featured at night. This place may be too hip to represent the locals' Orlando, but it's definitely off the beaten tourism path. *200 W. Fairbanks Ave., Winter Park, tel. 407/629–1150. No reservations. Dress: casual. AE, MC, V.*

$ **Straub's Seafood.** Generally, the farther you drive from Disney, the less you pay, and Straub's is no exception. Escargots cost $6—less than you'd pay for a burger on U.S. 192 in Kissimmee. This is one of those minimalist restaurants that emphasizes food, not atmosphere (tablecloths are covered with Plexiglas). But owner Robert Straub, a fishmonger of many years, knows how to prepare a mighty mean mesquite-grilled Atlantic salmon with a little béarnaise on the side. He fillets his own fish and won't serve anything that's not fresh. Blackened dolphin Cajun style (the fish, not the Sea World inhabitant) is quite good. The menu lists the calorie count and fat content of every fish item, but for the coconut-banana cream pie, made on premises, you just don't want to know. *5101 E. Colonial Dr., Orlando, tel. 407/273–9330; 512 E. Altamonte Dr., Altamonte Springs,* tel. *407/831–2250. Reservations accepted. Dress: casual. AE, D, DC, MC, V.*

¢ **Amigo's.** Orlando is not exactly a hotbed of Mexican restaurants, but the best is this one, run by a family of transplanted Texans. The cuisine is built on good basics, like refried beans that would play well in San Antonio. Go for the Santa Fe dinner, so big it almost takes a burro to bring it to your table; you'll be able to sample tamales, enchiladas, chiles rellenos, and those heavenly frijoles and wash it down with a Mexican beer. *120 Westmoreland, Altamonte Springs, tel. 407/774–4334; 494 N. Semoran, Winter Park, tel. 407/657–8111. No reservations. Dress: casual. AE, MC, V.*

¢ **Forbidden City.** You're in for a treat if you can get past this former gas station's decor, or lack thereof, to the terrific Hunan-style food. Start with the diced chicken with pine seeds in a package (icy lettuce cups wrapped around spicy chicken), offering a delightful mix of cold and hot. The sesame chicken goes perfectly with bright-green broccoli in a subtle garlic sauce, and the traditional 10-ingredient lo mein is full of fresh shrimp, chicken, beef, and pork. *948 N. Mills Ave., Orlando, tel. 407/894–5005. Reservations accepted. Dress: casual. MC, V. Closed Sun. No lunch Sat.*

¢ **4-5-6.** Mirrored walls and emerald-green carpet create a setting as unadulterated as the food, made without MSG or preservatives. There's an extensive choice of vegetarian and steamed entrées, and brown rice is provided as an alternative to white. The best appetizer is steamed dumplings, served in the small aluminum dishes in which they're cooked; one person can easily consume an order. Dumplings sautéed in hot peanut butter sauce is a must for peanut butter fans. Specialties include chicken three ways (including General Tso's chicken, lemon chicken, and sliced chicken breast with snow peas), as well as Five Fresh Herbs Steamed Fresh Fish, made with sea bass. The friendly staff tries hard to accommodate, so be sure to speak up if you want your food spicy or served in a special casserole to keep it warm. *657 N. Primrose Dr., Orlando, tel. 407/898–1899. Reservations accepted. Dress: casual. AE, MC, V. Beer and wine only.*

¢ **Little Saigon.** As Orlando flourishes, so do its ethnic restaurants, in-
★ cluding some Vietnamese eateries about 1½ miles east of I–4's U.S. 50 exit. The folks here are friendly and love to introduce novices to their healthy and delicious national cuisine. Sample the spring rolls or the summer rolls (spring roll filling in a soft wrapper). Then move on to the grilled pork and egg, served atop rice and noodles, or the traditional soup, filled with noodles, rice, vegetables, and either chicken or seafood; ask to have extra meat in the soup if you're hungry, and be sure they bring you the mint and bean sprouts to sprinkle in. Request an English-speaking waiter if you're unfamiliar with the cuisine. *1106 E. Colonial Dr., Orlando, tel. 407/423–8539. Reservations advised. Dress: casual. MC, V. Beer and wine only.*

¢ **Numero Uno.** To the followers of this long-popular Latin restaurant,
★ the name is quite appropriate. The place calls itself "the home of paella," and that's probably the best dish. If you have time and a good appetite, try the paella Valenciana, made to order an hour and 15 minutes in advance, with yellow rice, sausage, chicken, fish, Spanish spices, and a side order of plantains. If you don't have that long, go for traditional Cuban fare like shredded flank steak or arroz con pollo. Good homemade lemonade, worthwhile flan, and a selection of sodas from south of the border are available. *2499 S. Orange Ave., Orlando, tel. 407/841–3840. Reservations accepted for parties of 4 or more. Dress: casual. AE, D, MC, V.*

¢ **Ronnie's.** A former Orlando dining critic used to call this place Ronnie's "totalitessen" because of the silly and strictly enforced rules about such things as how many condiments you could have on the table at one time. The owner's penchant for being a control freak can be forgiven because of the excellent, New York deli–style food. Go for the corned-beef sandwich and Dr. Brown's soda, on the menu so long it has become an institution. At lunchtime, city bigwigs fill up the back tables, and hours after other restaurants have closed for the night, Ronnie's is still serving coffee and Danish. You can get takeout and baked goods next door. *Colonial Plaza, 2702 E. Colonial Dr., Orlando, tel. 407/894–4951. Dress: casual. No credit cards.*

¢ **Spicy Pot.** One taste of the West Indian food in this luncheonette in a rather dingy shopping center will take you straight to Trinidad. The roti sandwich is wrapped around a delicately spiced and curried filling—vegetable, potato, beef, or chicken. Be sure to drink sorrel or *mauby*, nonalcoholic beverages made from the bark of trees and the perfect accompaniment to the hot food. The traditional entrée is Jamaican jerk chicken (very spicy chunks of poultry served with vegetables and rice). On weekends there's music and dancing in a back room. The neighborhood is not appealing, but it's safe. *6203 Silver Star Rd., Orlando, tel. 407/297–8255. No reservations. Dress: casual. No credit cards. Beer and wine only. Closed Sun., Mon.*

The Arts and Nightlife

The Arts

Check out the local fine arts scene in *The Weekly*, a local entertainment magazine, or "Calendar," which is printed every Friday in the *Orlando Sentinel*. They are available at most newsstands. Ticket prices for performing arts events in the Orlando area rarely exceed $12 and are often half that.

The **Carr Performing Arts Centre** (401 Livingston St., Orlando, tel. 407/849–2020) presents a different play each month, with evening performances Wednesday through Saturday and Sunday matinees. The Broadway series features new productions on the way to Broadway and current road shows.

Civic Theater of Central Florida (1001 E. Princeton St., Orlando, tel. 407/896–7365), in Loch Haven Park, stages productions throughout the year. The MainStage Series offers traditional Broadway musicals and dramas; the SecondStage Series has off-Broadway-style, cutting-edge works; and family classics are performed in the Theatre for Young People.

The **Orange County Convention and Civic Center** (south end of International Dr., Orlando, tel. 407/345–9800) and the **Orlando Arena** (W. Amelia St., Orlando, tel. 407/849–2020) play host to many big-name performing artists.

During the school year, Winter Park's **Rollins College** (tel. 407/646–2233) has a choral concert series that is open to the public and usually free. The first week of March there is a Bach Music Festival (tel. 407/646–2182) that has been a Winter Park tradition for more than 55 years. Also at the college, the Annie Russell Theater (tel. 407/646–2145) has a regular series of productions.

Nightlife

Disneyesque street signs with bright colors and engaging graphics are not the only new things in downtown Orlando. Nightspots have sprung up and are thriving in an area that used to be deserted after office workers went home. Orlando's club owners have figured out that there's big money to be made by luring tourists into the city center. The result is a diverse collection of nighttime activities offering everything from cutting-edge palaces and quiet coffeehouses to jousting tournaments and murder-mystery buffets. Even locals who haven't ventured out in a few years are surprised.

Nightclubs in Orlando proper have significantly more character than those in the areas around Walt Disney World, but clubs on Disney property are allowed to stay open later—you can get a drink there as late as 2:45 AM. The cover charges at clubs can be pretty steep, particularly at Pleasure Island and Church Street Station. Unfortunately, if you want to enjoy the nightlife scene, you'll have to resign yourself to spending some money.

Walt Disney World
Inside Walt Disney World, every hotel has its quota of bars and lounges. Jazz trios and bluegrass bands, DJs and rockers tune up and turn on their amps after dinner's done. In addition, there are two long-running dinner shows that give you and your family an evening of song, dance, and a meal for a single price—a pretty steep price, somewhere in the range of $30–$45 for adults, $15–$25 for children. The **Hoop-Dee-Doo Revue,** staged at Fort Wilderness Resort and Campground's rustic Pioneer Hall (tel. 407/934–7639 in advance, 407/824–2748 day of show), may be corny, but it is also the liveliest show in Walt Disney World. A troupe of jokers called the Pioneer Hall Players stomp their feet, wisecrack, and otherwise make merry while the audience chows down on barbecued ribs, fried chicken, corn on the cob, strawberry shortcake, and all the fixin's. There are three shows nightly; the prime times sell out months in advance in busy seasons. The **Polynesian Luau** (tel. 407/934–7639) is an outdoor barbecue with entertainment appropriate to its colorful, South Pacific setting at the Polynesian Resort. There are two shows nightly, plus an earlier wingding for children called Mickey's Tropical Revue, wherein Disney characters do a few numbers decked out in South Seas garb.

Pleasure Island (tel. 407/934–7781) is a 6-acre after-dark entertainment complex, an island with a cluster of vintage buildings, connected to Disney Village Marketplace and the mainland by three footbridges. In addition to seven clubs, there's also a 10-screen AMC movie theater (tel. 407/827–1309) that starts showing films at 1:30 PM. A pay-one-price admission ($16.91) gets you into all the clubs and shows except the movie house. The **Adventurers Club** whimsically recreates a private club of the 1930s; the **Comedy Warehouse** has an improvisational setup, with five shows nightly; **Mannequins Dance Palace** is a high-tech Top-40 dance club with a revolving dance floor and special effects; live country-and-western music is the focus of the **Neon Armadillo Music Saloon;** and the **Rock & Roll Beach Club** throbs with live rock music of the 1950s and 1960s. At the new **Planet Hollywood** (*see* Budget Dining, *above*), you may not see movie stars, but you can see plenty of movie memorabilia, much of which has a central Florida connection. (Check out the motorcycle from Wesley Snipes's *Passenger 57*, which was filmed north of Orlando in Sanford.)

Church Street Station
Church Street Station (129 W. Church St., Orlando, tel. 407/422–2434) is a complete entertainment complex, with old-fashioned saloons, dance halls, dining rooms, and shopping arcades that are almost Disneyesque in their attention to detail. Unlike much of what you see in Walt Disney World, this place doesn't just look authentic—it is. The train on the tracks is an actual 19th-century steam engine; the whistling calliope was especially rebuilt to blow its original tunes. Just about everything down to the cobblestones that clatter under the horse-drawn carriages is the real McCoy. For a hefty $15.95 admission price ($9.95 for children 4–12) you can wander freely and stay as long as you wish. Food and drink cost extra and are not cheap. Parts of the complex are open during the day, but the place is usually quiet then; the pace picks up at night, especially on weekends, with crowds thickest from 10 to 11.

Rosie O'Grady's Good Time Emporium, the original bar on Church Street, is a turn-of-the-century saloon with dark wood, brass trim, a full Dixieland band, can-can and tap dancers, and vaudeville singers. Quiet **Apple Annie's Courtyard** offers easy-listening music from Jimmy Buffett to James Taylor. **Lili Marlene's Aviator's Pub and Restaurant** has the relaxed wood-paneled atmosphere of an English pub and the finest dining on Church Street—hearty, upscale, very American food, mostly steaks, ribs, and seafood. **Phineas Phogg's Balloon Works,** a disco that plays contemporary dance tunes on a sound system that will blow your socks off, draws a good-looking yuppie tourist crowd and a few local young singles; the place is jammed by midnight. In the **Orchid Garden Ballroom,** iron latticework, arched ceilings, and stained-glass windows create a striking Victorian setting where visitors sit, drink, and listen to a first-rate band pounding out popular tunes from the 1950s to present. **Cracker's Oyster Bar,** behind the Orchid Garden, is a good place to get a quick gumbo or chowder fix; it also has one of the largest wine cellars in Florida. The immensely popular **Cheyenne Saloon and Opera House** occupies a tri-level former opera house, now full of moose racks, steer horns, buffalo heads, and Remington rifles; the seven-piece country-and-western band that plays there darn near brings the house down. The upstairs restaurant serves chicken-and-ribs fare.

Elsewhere Around Orlando Bars and Lounges

The two-story inland answer to a beach party, **Baja Beach Club** (8510 Palm Pkwy., Lake Buena Vista, tel. 407/239–9629) plays hits from the '60s to the '90s. It has a sand volleyball court and an open deck that serves sandwiches and just-grilled burgers. **Bennigan's** (6324 International Dr., Orlando, tel. 407/351–4436), a young singles spot, draws crowds in the early evening and during happy hours: 2–7 PM and 11 PM–midnight. With two big-screen TVs and a couple of satellite dishes, **Bloopers** (5715 Major Blvd., Orlando, tel. 407/351–3340) is your basic high-testosterone sporting establishment. They might even change the channel to find your favorite team, but don't even think of asking when the University of Florida or Florida State is playing. **Coaches Locker Room** (269 W. Rte. 436, Altamonte Springs, tel. 407/869–4446), a two-level sports palace, boasts six big-screen TVs and 12 smaller monitors. Coaches shows every pro football game, plus every other kind of sport imaginable. The food is not the major attraction, but the Buffalo wings are worth trying. It's in the strip mall behind the T.G.I.Friday's at the intersection of I–4 and Route 436. **Dad's Road Kill Cafe** (106 Lake Ave., Maitland, tel. 407/647–5288), in a strip mall on the corner of Lake and Orlando avenues, is a tiny bar-and-restaurant with an eclectic menu. The bar area is littered with things to keep you busy as you drink your beer and wine: games, puzzles, a computer, plus the obligatory pool table and dartboards. On Friday and Saturday nights, there's low-key live entertainment. A spacious, wood-hued rock-and-roll club, **Jani Lane's Sunset Strip** (26 S. Orange Ave., Orlando, tel. 407/649–4803) attracts acts in the Mötley Crüe vein. For a breather, stand out on the balcony and watch downtown Orlando's nightlife pass below. **Mulvaney's Irish Pub** (27 W. Church St., Orlando, tel. 407/872–3296) has seven imported beers on tap, including Guinness, and traditional Irish music Wednesday through Saturday. It's packed on weekends and on Orlando Magic game nights. The kitchen serves mostly sandwiches but also has such British staples as shepherd's pie, fish-and-chips, and bangers and mash. A jazz club with a gourmet menu, **Pinkie Lee's** (380 W. Amelia Ave., Orlando, tel. 407/872–7393) is among Orlando's most grown-up nightspots. The entertainment is usually top-notch, reflected in the $7.50 minimum and $11–$17 cover charge on weekends. **Yab Yum** (25 Wall St. Plaza, Orlando, tel. 407/422–3322) is a bohemian refuge from downtown's hustle and bustle. The crowd is heavy with aspiring poet types hunched over espresso while giving form to their latest angst, but you don't have to be tormented to enjoy a sandwich, specialty coffee, or a hunk of fresh carrot cake along with the music of local bands.

Country-and-Western Club	**Sullivan's Entertainment Complex** (1108 S. Orange Blossom Trail [U.S. 441], Orlando, tel. 407/843–2934) is a country-and-western dance hall where people of all ages come to strut their stuff. Big-name performers entertain on occasion; a house band plays Tuesday–Saturday. The cover charge runs $2 and up.
Dinner Shows	Dinner shows are an immensely popular form of nighttime entertainment around Orlando. A fixed price usually buys a theatrical production and a multiple-course dinner; unlimited beer, wine, and soda usually are included, but mixed drinks will cost extra. When you factor together what you'd spend on dinner and entertainment separately elsewhere, these aren't bad deals, though the food is usually forgettable and the entertainment decidedly lowbrow. What the shows lack in substance and depth they make up for in color and enthusiasm; children often love them. Most shows have seatings at 7 and 9:30, and at most you sit with strangers at long tables. Always call and make reservations in advance, especially for weekends.

Arabian Nights looks like an elaborate palace outside; inside it's more like an arena, with seating for more than 1,200. The show features some 25 acts with more than 80 performing horses, music, special effects, and a chariot race; keep your eyes open for a unicorn. The four-course dinners are of prime rib or vegetarian lasagna. *6225 W. Irlo Bronson Memorial Hwy., Kissimmee, tel. 407/396–7400, 407/239–9223, 800/553–6116, or 800/533–3615 in Canada. Admission: $34.95 adults, $19.95 children 3–11. AE, D, DC, MC, V.*

Capone's Dinner and Show returns to the gangland Chicago of 1931, complete with mobsters and their dames. The evening begins in an old-fashioned ice cream parlor, but say the secret password and you'll be ushered inside Al Capone's private Underworld Cabaret and Speakeasy. Dinner is an unlimited Italian buffet that's heavy on pasta. Beer and sangria are included. *4740 W. Irlo Bronson Memorial Hwy., Kissimmee, tel. 407/397–2378. Admission: $36.99 adults, $18 children under 12. AE, D, MC, V.*

King Henry's Feast, set in a Tudor-style building, features jesters, jugglers, dancers, magicians, and singers, ostensibly feting Henry VIII as he celebrates his birthday. Saucy wenches serve forth potato-leek soup, salad, and chicken and ribs. *8984 International Dr., Orlando, tel. 407/351–5151 or 800/883–8181. Admission: $31.95 adults, $19.95 children 3–11. AE, D, DC, MC, V.*

Mark Two stages complete Broadway musicals—such as *Oklahoma, My Fair Lady, West Side Story,* and *South Pacific*—throughout the year and musical revues chockablock with Broadway tunes during the Christmas holidays. For about two hours before curtain, you can order from the bar and help yourself at buffet tables laden with institutional seafood Newburg, baked whitefish, meats, and salad; dessert arrives during intermission. Unlike other dinner theaters, the Mark Two offers only tables for two and four. *Edgewater Center, 3376 Edgewater Dr., Orlando (from I–4 take Exit 44 and go west), tel. 407/843–6275. Tickets: $29–$33 adults, $24–$28 children under 12. AE, D, MC, V.*

Medieval Times, in a huge, medieval-style manor house, portrays a two-hour tournament of sword fights, jousting matches, and other games, featuring no fewer than 30 charging horses and a cast of 75 knights, nobles, and maidens. The bill of fare is heavy on the meat and potatoes. *4510 W. Irlo Bronson Memorial Hwy., Kissimmee, tel. 407/239–0214, 407/396–1518, or 800/239–8300. Tickets: $32 adults, $21.95 children 3–12. AE, D, MC, V.*

Wild Bill's Wild West Dinner Show, at Fort Liberty, is a mixed bag of real Indian dances, foot-stompin' sing-alongs, and acrobatics. The chow, served by a rowdy chorus of cavalry recruits, is beef soup, fried chicken, corn-on-the-cob, and pork and beans. *5260 W. Irlo Bronson Memorial Hwy., Kissimmee, tel. 407/351–5151. Admission: $31.95 adults, $19.95 children 3–11. AE, DC, MC, V. No smoking in showroom.*

8 The Tampa Bay Area

Updated by Pamela Acheson

Pamela Acheson splits her time between Florida and the Caribbean and writes extensively about both. She is a regular contributor to Travel & Leisure, Caribbean Travel and Life, *and* Florida Travel and Life *and is author of* The Best of the British Virgin Islands.

While Miami's international glitz and Orlando's Mickey Mouse and Donald Duck grab most of the Florida tourism headlines, the rapidly growing Tampa Bay area has quietly become a favorite spot for pleasure-seeking U.S. and international visitors. Over the last 25 years the region has become fully developed, but at a much slower pace and with a less commercial atmosphere than the east coast. As a result, this is a community with a varied economic base, not entirely dependent upon tourism.

It's a good destination for travelers on a budget, thanks to a host of year-round, no-cost attractions: a semitropical climate, plentiful sunshine, waterfront landscapes, picturesque settings, a lively international community, and astoundingly diverse terrain—from the rolling, pine-dotted northern reaches to the coast's excellent white-sand beaches and barrier islands, from mangroves to palm trees. Plenty of lodgings, some on the beach, are quite moderately priced all year long, and from Easter until Christmas, resorts, hotels, and motels in all price ranges can drop their rates as much as 50%. Many superior hotels and resorts cater to families, offering reasonably priced two-bedroom, two-bath suites with full kitchens and laundry facilities, in addition to supervised children's programs. Taking advantage of the facilities, mom and dad can pursue their own activities, which may include 18 holes of golf or a couple of tennis matches. They might also try their hand at boating or deep-sea fishing, both of which rank among the favorite pastimes here.

Tampa itself does not have a Gulf beach, and Tampa Bay, though lovely to look at, is not suitable for swimming. For that, visitors should head to neighboring St. Petersburg, which sits on a peninsula bordered on three sides by bays and the Gulf of Mexico, filled with pleasure and commercial craft.

What the Tampa Bay area does have is a wealth of nationalities, not surprising for a thriving international port. The Cuban community centers on the east Tampa suburb of Ybor City; north of St. Petersburg, in Dunedin, the heritage is Scottish; and the area north of Dunedin, in Tarpon Springs, has supported a large Greek population for decades.

Native Americans were the sole inhabitants of the region for many years (Tampa is an Indian phrase meaning "sticks of fire"). The Spanish explorers Juan Ponce de León, Pánfilo de Narváez, and Hernando de Soto passed through in the mid-1500s, and the U.S. Army and civilian settlers arrived in 1824. A military presence remains in Tampa in the form of MacDill Air Force Base, where the U.S. Operations Command is located.

Inland, to the east of Tampa, is a typical American residential area: suburban sprawl, freeways, shopping malls, and—the main draw—Busch Gardens.

The coastal area north of Tampa, from Weeki Wachee to Crystal River, can aptly be called the Manatee Coast. Extensive nature preserves and parks, designed to protect these water creatures and other wildlife indigenous to the area, are among the best spots to view manatees, also called sea cows. Only about 1,200 of these curious mammals, related to elephants, are alive today. It's believed that ancient mariners' tales of mermaids were based on sightings of manatees.

The southern end of Tampa Bay is anchored by the two cities of Bradenton and Sarasota, which also have their string of barrier islands with fine beaches. Sarasota is very much a resort town—Sarasota County has no less than 35 miles of Gulf beaches, as well as two state parks, 22 municipal parks, and 46 golf courses, many of them open to the public. But Sarasota also has a thriving cultural scene, thanks mostly to John Ringling, founder of the Ringling Brothers Barnum & Bailey Circus, who chose this area for the winter home of his circus and his family. Bradenton maintains a lower profile than Sarasota, though it also has its share of sugar-sand beaches, golf courses, and historic sites dating back to the mid-1800s. Many of Sarasota County's beaches are located around Venice, a few miles south on the Gulf Coast, which was the actual winter home of the circus; today Venice contains the world's only clown college.

Tampa Bay Area Basics

Budget Lodging

From January through April, room rates are generally double what they are the rest of the year, and weekend prices differ from those on weeknights. It pays to make a few phone calls to compare current rates and inquire about specials for senior citizens and families with children. Be specific about what you want, and be sure you understand exactly what you're getting, as terms can mislead. A room described as "waterfront," for example, might have a view of a pond, lake, or canal, not the Gulf as you expect. Even "Gulf view" doesn't necessarily mean the room is on the beach; it could be across the street.

Budget Dining

Bargain meals are easy to find in the area. The area's ethnic diversity means that visitors can enjoy Spanish paellas, Italian pastas, and Greek dishes, as well as fine fresh seafood, ample buffets, and the convenience of fast-food establishments. Good eateries are often tucked in between the shops of the malls and shopping areas, and even the best restaurants sometimes have inexpensive early-bird dinner specials, many year-round. Many visitors eat their major meal at noon, and then settle for a pizza or burger for dinner. Or, they prepare a couple of light meals at their motel and splurge at dinner.

Bargain Shopping

Like any sophisticated metropolitan area, the towns around Tampa Bay have their share of large malls with the usual chain stores, plus some smaller, more exclusive collections of shops in the resort areas. The most distinctive products of this area are the Cuban-style cigars hand-rolled in Tampa's Ybor City neighborhood, and the locally harvested natural sponges for sale along Dodecanese Boulevard in Tarpon Springs, along the Gulf Coast north of Clearwater.

Beaches

Boaters, marinas, and industry have polluted Tampa Bay to the point that it is no longer suitable for swimming. On the peninsula that holds St. Petersburg and Clearwater, however, there are a number of beaches lining the Gulf of Mexico. Clearwater Beach is southwest Florida's version of Daytona Beach, a popular, accessible beach area that attracts lots of teenagers and college students on break. There are plenty of causeways linking the barrier islands to the mainland, and most of the Gulf-front beaches on this peninsula have rest rooms, showers, and snack bars, or at least picnic areas.

Bradenton also has a number of public beaches, and Sarasota County has no fewer than 10 beaches on the Gulf.

Sports and the Outdoors

Biking There aren't many reserved bike paths around these cities and towns, but there are plenty of stores that rent bikes, should you want to pedal along the streets.

Boating People around here take to the water in everything from kayaks to tall ships. Canoe liveries abound—with half-day, one-day, and weekly rentals available. Some state parks have canoes for rent, as well as airboats. Sarasota has boat ramps at several locations around the city.

Fishing Anglers flock to the region for its good fishing. In the 1950s Sarasota began an artificial-reef program, and since then everything from railroad boxcars to boat molds piled high to resemble an apartment house has been sunk to serve as bases for reefs, fostering excellent fishing grounds. Tarpon, kingfish, speckled trout, snapper, grouper, sea trout, snook, sheepshead, and shark are among the species caught in coastal waters. Fishing excursions are especially plentiful from Clearwater and St. Petersburg marinas, and boat captains are sometimes willing to negotiate the price—especially off-season.

Golf As elsewhere in the state, golf is about the number one participant sport around here, and a regulation or shorter executive course is the centerpiece of many a housing and condominium development. Public courses, including some excellent ones, abound, and from May through December many private courses offer bargains—call the pro shop and see if you can strike a deal. Be prepared with hats and sunscreen, and watch for alligators, which have been known to sun themselves on fairways throughout Florida.

Tennis Most hotels and some motels have courts available for their guests, and municipal courts are plentiful. Inquire at chambers of commerce and tourist offices.

The Arts and Nightlife

The Tampa Bay region hums with cultural activity, so plan to purchase tickets before you arrive, especially during the winter tourist season. Most halls and theaters accept credit-card charges by phone. Area chambers of commerce (*see* specific tours) can supply schedules of upcoming events. Many discounts are available for senior citizens, particularly in summer—ask at the convention bureaus for coupon books.

Festivals

Gasparilla Festival, in early February, celebrates the legendary 18th-century pirate, Jose Gaspar. Festivities begin midmorning in Tampa, when the world's only fully rigged pirate ship sets sail from Ballast Point Pier and docks downtown, triggering a big party that includes parades, races, concerts, and fireworks. Call 813/223–4141 for more information. About a week later, Ybor City, the so-called "SoHo of the South," celebrates its ethnic heritage on **Fiesta Day** with sideshows, art fairs, crafts, and food booths. All this is topped off when the Knights of Sant'Yago (St. James) fill the streets with dozens of illuminated floats. For further information call 813/248–3712.

In Sarasota, one of the most spectacular events is the **Medieval Fair,** held in early March. The Ringling Museum is transformed into a medieval village, complete with jesters, jugglers, mimes, knights in shining armor, human chess players, artists, artisans, and musicians. For more information call 941/355–5101.

Perhaps one of the most unusual events is the **Sharks' Tooth Festival,** which is held in Venice every August. In addition to seeing prehistoric sharks' teeth, you can enter a sand-sculpting or kite-flying competition, wander through the arts-and-crafts display, or sample seafood from local vendors. Call 941/488–2236 for more information.

Tour 1: Tampa Bay and North

The city of Tampa dominates the Tampa Bay area commercially, and its top-end hotels and restaurants are oriented toward business travelers and conventioneers. The accent is more on leisure travelers on the St. Petersburg peninsula to the west, with its string of beaches on barrier islands fronting the Gulf of Mexico. But there are exceptions to this—families will want to stop off in Tampa to visit Busch Gardens, the huge safari-theme park just off I–275, and budget-minded travelers may want to save money by staying at certain Tampa motels that give price breaks to compensate for being far from the Gulf beaches. The springs, rivers, and creeks of the Manatee Coast to the north are among the best spots to see manatees, and the area's many scenic natural areas are wonderful spots to picnic.

Arriving and Departing **Tampa International** (6 mi west of downtown, tel. 813/870–8700) is served by **Air Canada** (tel. 800/776–3000), **Air Jamaica** (tel. 800/523–
By Plane 5585), **American** (tel. 800/433–7300), **Bahamasair** (tel. 800/222–4262), **British Airways** (tel. 800/247–9297), **Canadian Holidays** (tel. 800/282–4751), **Cayman Airlines** (tel. 800/422–9626), **Continental** (tel. 800/525–0280), **Delta** (tel. 800/221–1212), **Mexicana** (tel. 800/531–7921), **Northwest** (tel. 800/225–2525), **TWA** (tel. 800/221–2000), **United** (tel. 800/241–6522), **USAir** (tel. 800/428–4322), and **Virgin Atlantic** (tel. 800/862–8621).

St. Petersburg–Clearwater International Airport (Roosevelt Blvd. and Rte. 686, tel. 813/535–7600), just north of the city, is served by

Air South (tel. 800/225–2995), **American Trans Air** (tel. 800/225–2995), **Canada 3000** (tel. 800/993–4378), **Canadian Airlines** (tel. 800/661–8881), and **Sun Jet** (tel. 800/478–6538).

The cheapest way to get from the Tampa airport into town or to various other points is to take the **Hillsborough Area Regional Transit** (HART) (tel. 813/254–4278). Buses run every half hour, and the fare is $1, $1.50 for express buses. **The Limo** (tel. 813/572–1111 or 800/282–6817) van service handles both the Tampa and St. Petersburg-Clearwater airports for $12–$15 one-way to downtown Tampa or St. Pete. Expect taxi fares to be about $11–$21 from the Tampa airport for most of Hillsborough County, just north of Tampa, and about twice that for Pinellas County, around St. Petersburg.

By Bus **Greyhound Lines** (tel. 800/231–2222) has stops in Tampa (610 Polk St., tel. 813/229–2112) and St. Petersburg (180 Martin Luther King St., tel. 813/898–1496).

By Car I–75 spans the region from north to south. Once you cross the border into Florida from Georgia, it should take about three hours to reach Tampa. If you're coming from Orlando, you'll likely drive west into Tampa on I–4.

By Train **Amtrak** (tel. 800/872–7245) connects the Northeast, Midwest, and much of the South to Tampa (601 N. Nebraska Ave., tel. 813/221–7600), while Amtrak's Autotrain runs from Lorton, Virginia (near Washington, DC), to Sanford, Florida (near Orlando). Depending on the time of year and availability, round-trip fares from New York City to Tampa begin at $138; from Chicago, they range from $178 to $350.

Getting Around Around Tampa, the **Hillsborough Area Regional Transit** (HART) (tel. 813/254–4278) bus system serves most of the county. The fare is *By Bus* $1, 50¢ senior citizens, and $1.50 for express buses (no discounts). Buses now have bike racks, so combining bus transportation with biking can be a very cheap way to explore. The **Pinellas–Sun Coast Transit Authority** (tel. 813/530–9911) covers the St. Petersburg-Clearwater area. The fare is $1 adults, 50¢ senior citizens.

By Car To get from Tampa to St. Petersburg, take I–275 on the Howard Frankland Bridge or U.S. 92 on the Gandy Bridge. I–275 then swings south to cross the bay again on the Sunshine Skyway. Clearwater, at the neck of the peninsula, can be reached from Tampa by the Courtney Campbell Causeway. On U.S. 19, the major north-south artery through St. Petersburg, traffic can be heavy, and there are many lights, so allow extra time. Once you've left the congestion of St. Petersburg, however, traffic flows freely along U.S. 19, the prime route through manatee country. U.S. 41 (the Tamiami Trail) links the business districts of many communities, so you should avoid it and all bridges during rush hours, 7 AM–9 AM and 4 PM–6 PM.

In Tampa, you can park at meters 8–5 weekdays for 50¢ per half hour. The **Fort Brooke Municipal Parking Garage**, at the corner of Whiting and Franklin streets, close to the Convention Center and Harbour Island, costs $6 per day or 75¢ per hour.

By Trolley The **Tampa-Ybor Trolley** (tel. 813/254–4278) runs 7:30–5:30 in downtown Tampa. The adult fare is 50¢ (exact change).

Guided Tours **Around the Town** (tel. 813/932–7803) conducts tours for groups of 25 or more in the Tampa Bay area, plus Tarpon Springs and Sarasota, the dog tracks, and area theaters. Try to make reservations several weeks in advance.

Gulf Coast Gray Line (tel. 813/535–0208) makes daily trips at 8:25 AM from Tampa's Holiday Inn (4500 W. Cypress St.) to Walt Disney World, Sea World, Busch Gardens, and other attractions. Costs, including entry fees to the attractions, range from $42 (Busch Gardens) to $69 (Disney World). Reservations must be made at least a day in advance.

Among the many boats offering sightseeing cruises in the area are the *Lady Anderson* (St. Petersburg Causeway, 3400 Pasadena Ave., St. Petersburg Beach, tel. 813/367–7804), the *Admiral* (Clearwater Beach Marina, tel. 813/462–2628 or 800/444–4814), and the *Starlite Princess* (Hamlin's Landing, Indian Rocks Beach, tel. 813/595–1212). The last two have dinner as well as daytime cruises. During the day expect to pay $7 to $10 per person. For dinner cruises, which usually last three hours, expect to pay $9 to $12.50 for the cruise plus the cost of your dinner, which runs $8.95 to $16.95.

Tampa

The Greater Tampa Chamber of Commerce (Box 420, Tampa 33601, tel. 813/228–7777); for information on current area events, call the Visitors Information Department (tel. 813/223–1111). Tampa/ Hillsborough Convention and Visitors Association (111 Madison St., Suite 1010, Tampa 33601-0519, tel. 800/826–8358; information and hotel reservations, tel. 800/448–2672; vacation packages, tel. 800/284–0404).

Numbers in the margin correspond to points of interest on the Tampa/St. Petersburg and the Manatee Coast map.

Tampa is the business and commercial hub of this part of the state, with numerous high-rise buildings and heavy traffic. The city by the bay pays homage to its coastal setting with the **Florida Aquarium,** an $84 million complex that opened in the spring of 1995 at the intersection of Garrison and Ybor channels near downtown. The 83-foot-high glass dome is already a landmark. Included are more than 4,300 specimens of fish, other animals, and plants representing 550 species native to Florida. Visitors follow the path of a drop of water from the freshwater springs and limestone caves of the aquifer, through rivers and wetlands, to the beaches and open seas. Four major exhibit areas are covered: springs and wetlands, bay and barrier beach, a coral reef, and the Gulf Stream and open ocean. Perhaps the most spectacular is a 500,000-gallon tank, the aquarium's largest, with a full-scale replica of a Florida coral reef. Ringed with viewing windows, including an awesome 43-foot-wide panoramic opening, the tank features an acrylic tunnel where you can look up into an underwater thicket of elk horn coral teeming with tropical fish and into a dark cave, which reveals fish and animals you could otherwise only see on a night dive. *300 S. 13th St., tel. 813/229–8861. Admission: $13.95 adults, $12.55 senior citizens and ages 13–18, $6.95 children 3–12. Open Fri.–Wed. 9–6, Thurs. 9–8.*

★ ❷ **Ybor City,** with its cobblestone streets and wrought-iron balconies, is Tampa's Cuban community. To get there, take I–4 to Exit 1 (22nd St.) and go south five blocks to 7th Avenue. The Cubans brought their cigar-making industry to Ybor (pronounced EEbor) City in 1866, and this east Tampa area is still primarily Cuban. Although the number of cigar makers is dwindling, in the heart of Ybor City the smell of cigars—hand rolled by Cuban refugees—still drifts around the old-world architecture. Take a stroll past the ornately tiled Columbia restaurant (*see* Budget Dining, *below*) and the stores lining 7th Avenue, or step back to the past at **Ybor Square** (1901 13th St.), a restored cigar factory that is listed in the National Register of Historic Places and now houses boutiques, offices, and several restaurants. (Free guided walking tours are given at 1:30 PM Tuesday, Thursday, and Saturday.) You can watch as artisans continue the local practice of hand-rolling cigars.

For something a little more modern, head for the new skyscrapers downtown. From 7th Avenue, go west to Nebraska Avenue and turn

Tampa/St. Petersburg and the Manatee Coast

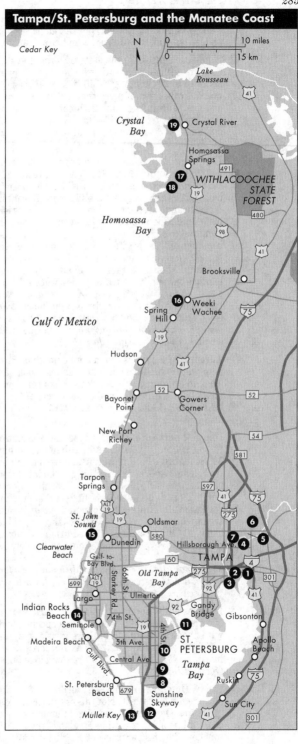

left. At Kennedy Boulevard, turn right and drive a few blocks to the vicinity of Franklin Street, one of Tampa's booming growth areas. A pedestrian mall runs down the center of Franklin Street.

❸ A few more blocks to the east you'll find the **Tampa Museum of Art,** near the Hillsborough River. The 35,000-square-foot museum presents 15 to 20 changing exhibitions yearly as well as a growing permanent collection of more than 7,000 works of art. It specializes in classical antiquities and 20th-century American art. *601 Doyle Carlton Dr., tel. 813/223–8130. Admission: $3.50 adults, $3 senior citizens, $2.50 students, $1.50 children 6–16. Open Tues.–Sat. 10–5, Wed. 10–9, Sun. 1–5.*

★ ❹ Eighteen miles northeast of downtown Tampa and 2 miles east of I–275, you'll find **Busch Gardens,** a sprawling, immaculately manicured complex combining a zoolike setting with a theme park. A main draw in the region, it is slightly different in style and approach from Orlando area attractions. The emphasis is on rides and live animals, and kids and adults find the mix appealing. In addition to a monorail ride that simulates an African safari—taking in free-roaming zebras, giraffes, rhinos, lions, and other exotic animals—the 300-acre park features thrill rides, live entertainment, animal exhibits, shops, restaurants, and games. Eight themed sections capture the spirit of turn-of-the-century Africa. In addition, there's a tasting room where guests of drinking age can sample complimentary beer. Allow at least six to eight hours. *3000 Busch Blvd. (Rte. 580), tel. 813/987–5082. Admission: $29.95 adults, (15% discount to senior citizens and military personnel), $23.95 children 3–9, plus $3 parking charge. Open daily 9:30–6.*

❺ **Adventure Island,** less than a mile north of Busch Gardens, is a 36-acre water wonderland. Water slides, pools, and man-made waves are the highlights; the park also has convenient changing rooms, snack bars, a gift shop, and a video arcade. *4545 Bougainvillea Ave., tel. 813/987–5660. Admission: $16.95 ages over 2. Open Mar.–Nov., daily 10–5.*

❻ One mile north of Busch Gardens, the **Museum of Science and Industry** could occupy you for another half day. A hands-on museum, the MOSI features both traveling and permanent exhibits. The Butterfly Encounter is an interactive garden inhabited by free-flying butterflies; the GTE Challenger Learning Center offers simulated "flights"; and the 100-seat Saunders Planetarium, Tampa Bay's only planetarium, offers afternoon and evening shows daily, including a trek through the universe and a chance to get blown away in a hurricane. A 110,000-square-foot addition, featuring an Omni Theatre with a 360° revolving dome, opened in early 1995. *4801 E. Fowler Ave., tel. 813/987–6300. Admission: $4.50 adult Florida residents, $5 other adults, $2 children; additional $1.50 for planetarium show; optional admission fee Mon. Open daily 9–4:30; hrs extended in peak season.*

❼ Families will also enjoy the **Lowry Park Zoo,** which has more than 600 species, including endangered species, and a manatee enclave with about a half dozen of these gentle, playful giants. Take I–275 exit 31 to Sligh Avenue. *7530 N. Boulevard, tel. 813/935–8552. Admission: $6.50 adults, $5.50 senior citizens, $4.50 children 3–11. Open daily 9–5.*

Budget Lodging
$$
★
Crown Hotel. Charming is a word too often applied to hotels that don't really deserve it. Not this one in Inverness, a small town north of Tampa. Owners Jill and Nigel Sumner have given Florida's west coast a bit of Merrie Olde England, their native land, via special touches like the portraits of English royalty that hang below the curving lobby staircase and the display case filled with replicas of the Crown Jewels. Guest rooms, on the second and third floors, have flowered wallpaper and huge, old-fashioned washbasins with bright

brass fixtures. Each room has a TV and either two twin, one double, or one queen-size bed. There's a small but beautiful pool out back, with a vine-covered wall for privacy. Churchill's is well worth trying for its Continental food, as well as its wine list; the cozy, dark-paneled Fox and Hounds is a good bet for less expensive meals. Though it has a full menu, it's also great for snacks, sandwiches, and British beer. *109 N. Seminole Ave., Inverness 32650, tel. 904/344–5555. 34 rooms. Facilities: restaurant, pub, pool. AE, MC, V.*

$$ **Holiday Inn Busch Gardens.** This well-maintained, family-oriented motor inn just 1 mile west of Busch Gardens is across the street from the University Square Mall, Tampa's largest mall. *2701 E. Fowler Ave., 33612, tel. 813/971–4710, fax 813/977–0155. 392 rooms, 7 suites. Facilities: restaurant, lounge, pool, exercise room. AE, DC, MC, V.*

$ **Days Inn Busch Gardens East.** Providing decent digs in a central location and all the necessities of life, this link in the national chain is low-budget even in winter. *2520 N. 50th St., 33619, tel. 813/247–3300 or 800/523–7513. 200 rooms. Facilities: restaurant, lounge, pool. AE, D, DC, MC, V.*

$ **Sailport Resort Inn.** This resort could be just the ticket for budget-minded travelers, especially families with small children. Rates are by the unit, not the number of people, and a suite in season is $97 but can cost as little as $60 in summer. All but 20 of the units are actually suites with a queen bed in the bedroom and a pull-out sofa in the living room. The hallway has two small bunks that can each accommodate a small child under 50 pounds. The living room has a full kitchen. You can save by preparing a meal or two each day (and by having the complimentary coffee and doughnuts), and the waterfront balconies are great for watching sunsets. *2506 Rocky Point Dr., 33607, tel. 813/281–9599 or 800/255–9599, fax 813/281–9510. 237 rooms. Facilities: pool. AE, DC, MC, V.*

¢ **Econo Lodge Busch Gardens.** This two- and three-story motel is just a mile from Busch Gardens, within 5 miles of golf and tennis, and close to museums and shopping. Rooms are well maintained, and the rates are a bargain, even in season. *1701 E. Busch Blvd., 33612, tel. 813/933–7681 or 800/783–7681, fax 813/251–8825. 238 rooms. Facilities: restaurant, pool. AE, DC, MC, V.*

¢ **Tahitian Inn.** This family-run motel offers comfortable rooms at budget prices. It's five minutes from Tampa Stadium, 20 minutes from Busch Gardens. *601 S. Dale Mabry Hwy., 33609, tel. 813/877–6721, fax 813/877–6218. 79 rooms. Facilities: restaurant, pool. AE, DC, MC, V.*

Splurge **Wyndham Harbour Island Hotel.** This first-class getaway is great for a day or two and not too expensive if you can make it for a weekend off-season. Thanks to its attentive service, central downtown location, nice views, excellent tennis facilities, and elegant ambience, enhanced by lots of dark wood paneling and substantial furniture, this hotel is worth the price (summer weekends $119–$129, weekdays $129–$179; 30%–50% more in winter). *725 S. Harbour Island Blvd., 33602, tel. 813/229–5000, fax 813/229–5322. 300 rooms. Facilities: restaurant, lounge, pool, tennis, health club, dock, boating. AE, DC, MC, V.*

Budget Dining **Colonnade.** The wharf-side location of this popular family restaurant is reflected in its nautical decor. Seafood—particularly grouper, red snapper, and lobster—is a specialty, but steak and chicken are also served. *3401 Bayshore Blvd., tel. 813/839–7558. No reservations. Dress: casual. AE, DC, MC, V.*

$$ **★** **Columbia.** A Spanish fixture in Ybor City since 1905, this magnificent structure with ceramic murals, high archways, and ornate railings occupies an entire city block. There are several airy and spacious dining rooms and a sunny atrium with tile decor. Specialties include the Columbia 1905 salad (lettuce, ham, olives, cheese, and garlic), paella (saffron rice with chicken, fish, and mussels), and black bean soup. There's also flamenco dancing. *2117 E. 7th Ave., tel. 813/248–4961. Reservations accepted. Dress: casual weekdays, jacket suggested weekends. AE, DC, MC, V.*

$$ **Selena's.** New Orleans Creole food, along with some Sicilian dishes, is served in antiques-filled dining rooms. Shrimp scampi and other fresh seafood are featured. *1623 Snow Ave., tel. 813/251–2116. Reservations advised. Dress: casual. AE, DC, MC, V.*

$ **Bella's Italian Cafe.** Brightly lit and slightly noisy, Bella's is filled
★ with the smells of such fare as angel-hair pasta, chicken cannelloni in Alfredo sauce, and *Bella! Bella!* (a truffle torte of bittersweet, semisweet, and white chocolate). Crayons and paper tablecloths and a late-night menu with half-price pizza and happy-hour drinks are further draws. *1413 S. Howard Ave., tel. 813/254–3355. No reservations. Dress: casual. AE, MC, V. No lunch Sat.*

$ **Cactus Club.** Southwestern cuisine, such as fajitas, is what you'll get at this casual but fashionable restaurant. Also available is a pretty good pizza. *1601 Snow Ave., Old Hyde Park Mall, tel. 813/251–4089. Reservations not needed. Dress: casual. AE, DC, MC, V.*

Splurge **Bern's Steak House.** Known well beyond the state line as perhaps the
★ best steak house in all of Florida, Bern's creates specialties from finely aged prime beef. In fact, owner-chef Bern Lexer ages his own beef, grows his own organic vegetables, roasts his own coffee, and even maintains his own saltwater fish tanks. Choose from an extensive wine list—some 7,000 choices, with selections ranging in price from $10 to $10,000 a bottle. Upstairs are the dessert rooms: small, glass-enclosed rooms where sumptuous desserts are served. Each room is equipped with a control panel for TV, radio, or listening in to the live entertainment in the lounge. *1208 S. Howard Ave., tel. 813/ 251–2421. Reservations advised. Dress: casual but neat. AE, DC, MC, V. No lunch.*

Shopping for **Old Hyde Park Village** (Swan Ave. near Bayshore Blvd.) is an ele-
Bargains gant outdoor shopping center that stretches more than seven blocks. **The Pier** (800 2nd Ave. NE), near the Museum of Fine Arts, is a five-story bay-front building that looks like an inverted pyramid. Inside are numerous shops and eating spots. If it's cigars you crave, **Ybor City** is your goal—they're still hand rolled in the historic district. **Ybor Square,** the famous restored cigar factory, is now a place for shopping and dining. **Big Top** (9250 Fowler Ave.) flea market, open weekends 8–5, has more than 600 booths featuring new and used items.

Participant Inland, there are several rivers that make for good canoeing. Just
Sports south of Tampa, **Canoe Outpost** (18001 U.S. 301 S, Wimauma, tel.
Canoeing 813/634–2228) offers half-day, full-day, and overnight canoe-camping trips from a number of southwest Florida locations, including the Little Manatee River.

Golf Golfers can play at **Apollo Beach Club** (tel. 813/645–6212), **Babe Zaharias Golf Course** (tel. 813/932–8932), **Bloomingdale Golfers Club** (Valrico, tel. 813/685–4105), **The Eagles** (Odessa, tel. 813/920–6681), **Rocky Point Golf Course** (tel. 813/884–5141), and **Saddlebrook Golf and Tennis Resort** (Wesley Chapel, tel. 813/973–1111).

Tennis Try the **City of Tampa Courts** (59 Columbia Dr., Davis Islands, tel. 813/253–3997), with 8 courts, or **City of Tampa Tennis Complex,** containing 32 courts and racquetball facilities, at Hillsborough Community College (3901 Tampa Bay Blvd., tel. 813/870–2383). Prices run $4.50 per person per hour.

Spectator A new Major League Baseball expansion franchise has been
Sports awarded to the area, and the **New York Yankees** will conduct spring
Baseball training in a new facility across from Tampa Stadium, scheduled for completion in 1996.

Football   NFL football comes in the form of the **Tampa Bay Buccaneers,** who play at Tampa Stadium (4201 N. Dale Mabry Hwy., tel. 813/461–2700 or 800/282–0683).

Horse Racing   **Tampa Bay Downs** (Race Track Rd., off Rte. 580, Oldsmar, tel. 813/855–4401) holds Thoroughbred races from mid-December to early May.

Ice Hockey   The NHL **Tampa Bay Lightning** (401 Channelside Dr., 33602, tel. 813/229–2658) will play in a new downtown waterfront stadium.

Jai Alai   **Tampa Jai-Alai Fronton** (S. Dale Mabry Hwy. and Gandy Blvd., tel. 813/837–2441) offers jai alai year-round.

The Arts and Nightlife
The Arts   Be sure to ask at visitor centers about free events and attractions as well as for discount coupon books, which are particularly plentiful in summer.

The **Tampa Bay Performing Arts Center** (1010 W.C. MacInnes Pl., Box 2877, tel. 813/221–1045 or 800/955–1045) occupies 9 acres along the Hillsborough River and is one of the largest such complexes south of the Kennedy Center in Washington, DC. The 290,000-square-foot complex, which includes a 2,400-seat festival hall, 900-seat playhouse, and small, 300-seat theater, can accommodate opera, ballet, drama, and concerts. The Tampa Ballet (tel. 813/229–7827) calls the center home.

The **Tampa Theater** (711 N. Franklin St., tel. 813/223–8981) presents shows, musical performances, and films.

The **Tampa Bay Convention Center** (333 S. Franklin St., tel. 813/223–8511) hosts concerts throughout the year.

Nightlife   **The Barn** (13815 Hillsborough Ave., tel. 813/855–9818) plays '50s and '60s hits. Weekends bring great jazz to the **Blue Ships Cafe** (1910 E. 7th Ave., Ybor City, tel. 813/248–6097). Head to **Comedy Works** (3447 W. Kennedy Blvd., tel. 813/875–9129) seven nights a week for live comedy with top-name performers. Crowds descend on noisy, boisterous **Dallas Bull** (8222 N. U.S. 301, tel. 813/985–6877) to stomp to country music. **Harbour Island Hotel** (Harbour Island, tel. 813/229–5000) has a bar with a great view of the bay, large-screen TV, and thickly padded, comfortable chairs. **MacDintons** (405 S. Howard Ave., tel. 813/254–1661) presents live rock music nightly, starting at 10. There's a full Continental menu for when the munchies strike. **Skippers Smokehouse** (910 Skipper Rd., tel. 813/971–0666) is a full-service restaurant and oyster bar featuring live reggae and blues. **Yucatan Liquor Stand** (4811 W. Cypress Ave., tel. 813/289–8454) is a trendy spot with live music, dancing, a performing disc jockey, and a nosh menu that includes seafood, burgers, and Mexican delights.

St. Petersburg–Clearwater

St. Petersburg Chamber of Commerce (100 2nd Ave. N, St. Petersburg 33701, tel. 813/821–4069). Greater Clearwater Chamber of Commerce (128 N. Osceola Ave., Clearwater 34615, tel. 813/461–0011). St. Petersburg–Clearwater Area Convention & Visitors Bureau (Thunderdome, 1 Stadium Dr., Suite A, St. Petersburg 33705–1706, tel. 813/582–7892).

Though their respective chambers of commerce may disagree, St. Petersburg and Clearwater are such close neighbors that it's difficult to distinguish when you have left one and entered the other. They share barrier islands and Tampa Bay and are the two most prominent of the eight resort communities that make up the Pinellas (Spanish for Point of Pines) County peninsula, enclosing Tampa Bay. Whereas Clearwater—an apt name—is the front door to some of the cleanest white-sand beaches in the United States, St. Petersburg is known more as a cultural center. However, in addition to its downtown, centered on the bay, it, too, has a beach area on a string of barrier islands facing onto the Gulf. Several causeways, many of which charge tolls, link these beach communities to the mainland. Both towns have myriad hotels, motels, cottages, and eateries and make great bases from which to take day trips up the coast as far as Crystal River.

In 1885, in one of many schemes planned to attract the idle rich and famous to the area, a Dr. van Bidder proposed that a "health city" be founded where St. Petersburg now stands. Early Florida entrepreneur Henry Plant built the Belleville Biltmore Hotel (now the Belleville Mido) on Bellair Beach, near Clearwater, and in 1928 the vast pink Don Cesar Hotel rose on St. Petersburg Beach. As can be expected during the January–April season, prices are posh, and patience is paramount—traffic is heavy and you must dodge oblivious beachgoers with their paraphernalia, marching like lemmings to the sea.

8 In **St. Petersburg,** just off Exit 9 of I–275, is **Great Explorations!,** a museum where you will never be told, "Don't touch!" Everything is designed for a hands-on experience. The museum is divided into theme rooms, such as the Body Shop, which explores health; the Think Tank, which features mind-stretching puzzles and games; the Touch Tunnel, a 90-foot-long, pitch-black maze you crawl through; and Phenomenal Arts, which displays such items as a Moog music synthesizer (which you can play) and neon-filled tubes that glow in vivid colors when touched. *1120 4th St. S, tel. 813/821–8885. Admission: $5 adults, $4.50 senior citizens, $4 children 4–17. Open Mon.– Sat. 10–5, Sun. noon–5.*

9 A few blocks north and one block east, at the **Salvador Dali Museum,** you will find the world's most extensive collection of art by the famous Spanish surrealist. The collection, valued at more than $125 million, includes 93 oil paintings, 200 watercolors and drawings, and 1,000 graphics, sculptures, and objets d'art. *1000 3rd St. S, tel. 813/ 823–3767. Admission: $5 adults, $4 senior citizens, $3.50 students. Open Tues.–Sat. 9:30–5:30, Sun.–Mon. noon–5.*

10 Eight blocks north and two blocks east, the **Museum of Fine Arts** has outstanding examples of European, American, pre-Columbian, and Far Eastern art, as well as photographic exhibits. *255 Beach Dr. NE, tel. 813/896–2667. Suggested donation: $4. Open Tues.–Sat. 10–5, Sun. 1–5.*

11 A little farther north on 4th Street lies one of Florida's most colorful spots, **Sunken Gardens.** Walk through an aviary with tropical birds, stroll among more than 50,000 exotic flowers and other plants, and stop to smell the rare, fragrant orchids. *1825 4th St. N, tel. 813/896– 3186. Admission: $11 adults, $6 children 3–11. Open daily 9–5:30.*

★ **12** There is a $1 toll for the trip over the **Sunshine Skyway,** heading south on I–275, but it's worth it for the view of the islands and Tampa Bay. You can also see what's left of the original twin span that collapsed and killed more than 30 people when a ship hit it in 1980. Turn around and come back north for a view of several small islands that dot the bay, as well as St. Petersburg Beach.

13 At the north end of the causeway, turn left on 54th Avenue South (Route 682), and cross the water on the Pinellas Bayway. Turn left on Route 679 and you'll cross the islands you saw from the Sunshine Skyway. Eventually you'll end up at **Fort De Soto Park,** at the mouth of Tampa Bay. This 900-acre park is spread over six small islands, called keys. The fort for which it's named was built on the southern end of Mullet Key to protect sea lanes in the Gulf during the Spanish-American War. Roam the fort (admission free) or wander the beaches of any of the islands that make up the park.

The Pinellas Bayway continues over to more barrier islands, beginning with Pass-A-Grille Beach and St. Petersburg Beach. Gulf Boulevard (Route 699) runs the length of these islands all the way to Clearwater Beach in the north. When pelicans become entangled in fishing lines, locals sometimes carry them to the **Suncoast Seabird Sanctuary,** a nonprofit rehabilitation center dedicated to the rescue, repair, recuperation, and release of sick and injured birds. At times, there are 500 to 600 land and seabirds residing at the sanctuary. Pelicans, egrets, herons, gulls, terns, cranes, ducks, owls, and cormorants are among the birds treated on-site. *18328 Gulf Blvd., Indian Shores, tel. 813/391–6211. Donations welcome. Open daily 9–5:30; guided tours Wed., Sun. at 2.*

U.S. 19 leads north from St. Petersburg through **Dunedin,** so named by two Scots in the 1880s. If the sound of bagpipes played by men in kilts appeals to you, head to Dunedin in March or April, when the Highland games and the Dunedin Heather and Thistle holidays pay tribute to the Celtic heritage.

Caladesi Island State Park lies 3 miles off Dunedin's coast, across Hurricane Pass. One of the state's few remaining undeveloped barrier islands, this 600-acre park is accessible only by boat. There's a beach on the Gulf side, mangroves on the bay side, and a self-guided nature trail winding through the island's interior. Park rangers are available to answer questions. This is a good spot for swimming, fishing, shelling, boating, and nature study. Facilities include boardwalks, picnic shelters, bathhouses, and a concession stand. Take the Dunedin Causeway to Honeymoon Island, to the north, and get on the ferry. *Ferry tel. 813/734–5263. Admission to park: $3.25 per car; ferry: $4 adults, $2.50 children 3–12. Open 8–sunset; ferry runs hourly 10–5 (good weather only).*

Return to U.S. 19 and continue on to **Tarpon Springs,** home of the region's Greek community. Sponge divers from the Dodecanese Islands of Greece moved here at the turn of the century, and it became the world's largest sponge center by the 1930s. Although a bacterial blight wiped out the sponge beds in the 1940s, the Greeks held on, and the sponge industry has returned, though in lesser force than during its heyday. Today, the Greek influence remains evident in the churches, the restaurants, and, often, the language spoken on the streets.

Budget Lodging
$$

Bayboro House. From the wide veranda complete with rocking chairs and a comfortable swing to the gabled roof and clapboard siding, this inn recalls a more peaceful time. Each room has different wallpaper and a different mix of furniture collected by the owners over the years. There are marble-top tables, mahogany four-poster beds, lace curtains, needlepoint pillows, paintings, photographs, old portraits, and antique clocks. Complimentary wine is available in the parlor each evening, and a light breakfast, included in the room rate, is served in the formal dining room. *1719 Beach Dr. SE, St. Petersburg 33701, tel. and fax 813/823–4955. 9 units. Facilities: dining room. AE, D, MC, V.*

$$ **Colonial Gateway Inn.** This well-maintained Gulf-front hotel is family oriented. Half of its rooms are equipped with kitchenettes, and all are nicely decorated with light-green floral prints. Water sports are available. *6300 Gulf Blvd., St. Petersburg Beach 33706, tel. 813/367–2711 or 800/237–8918, fax 813/367–7068. 200 rooms. Facilities: 2 restaurants, bar, lounge, pool. AE, DC, MC, V.*

$$ **New Comfort Inn.** This is a comfortable, unpretentious motor inn near the airport and Tampa Bay. *3580 Ulmerton Rd. (Rte. 688), Clearwater 34622, tel. 813/573–1171, fax 813/572–8736. 119 rooms. Facilities: restaurant, pool, fitness center. AE, DC, MC, V.*

Splurge **Tradewinds on St. Petersburg Beach.** Old Florida ambience is offered here, with white gazebos, gondolas gliding along canals, and hammocks swaying on 13 acres of beachfront property. *5500 Gulf Blvd., St. Petersburg Beach 33706, tel. 813/367–6461. 381 rooms. Facilities: restaurant, lounge, kitchens, pools, wading pool, sauna, tennis, exercise room, racquetball, beach, dock, scuba instruction, windsurfing, boating, waterskiing, fishing, bicycles, playground. AE, DC, MC, V.*

Camping If you are traveling by RV or with intentions to camp, contact the chambers of commerce listed above for current campground availability and costs. For information on state parks, call the **Florida Park Service** (tel. 904/488–9872). One option, north of Dunedin, is **Caladesi Island State Park** (Rte. 586, tel. 813/469–5918), where you can camp for as little as $5 per night, plus tax and additional amenities charges.

Budget Dining **Apropos.** Sit indoors or out at this little harbor-front café that is open
$$ all day. Some of the dinner entrées are moderately priced, but many items are downright inexpensive. You can certainly have lunch for less than $12. For breakfast, try the delicious blueberry pancakes. For lunch, choose either a light salad or one of the appealing sandwiches—filet mignon, tarragon chicken club, or ginger-marinated pork loin. Dinner entrées include salads, grilled meats, and a pasta special. *2nd Ave. at beginning of the Pier, St. Petersburg, tel. 813/823–8934. Reservations advised for dinner. Dress: casual. MC, V.*

$$ **Nick's on the Water.** Sitting at the end of the St. Petersburg Pier is
★ this peaceful place with tablecloths and pretty water views. Pizzas baked in a wood-burning stove are a specialty and come with different toppings: traditional cheese, barbecued chicken, and even Philly cheese steak! Rigatoni à la vodka, the signature dish, accompanies salads and classic Italian pasta dishes on the menu. Lunches here are a bargain. *800 2nd Ave. NE, St. Petersburg, tel. 813/898–5800. Reservations advised for dinner. Dress: casual. AE, MC, V.*

$ **Hurricane Seafood Restaurant.** Located right on historic Pass-A-Grille Beach (at the southern end of St. Pete Beach), this seafood joint is popular for its grilled, broiled, or blackened grouper; steamed shrimp; and homemade crab cakes. One of the few places in St. Petersburg with live jazz (Wednesday–Sunday), it also has an adjacent disco called Stormy's at the Hurricane, so it's well frequented even after mealtime. A sundeck on the third floor attracts crowds who come to see those gorgeous sunsets. *807 Gulf Way, St. Petersburg Beach, tel. 813/360–9558. Reservations advised. Dress: casual. MC, V.*

¢ **Ted Peters Famous Smoked Fish.** The menu is limited to mackerel, mullet, and salmon, but all are smoked and seasoned to perfection and served with heaping helpings of German potato salad. All meals are served outdoors. *1350 Pasadena Ave. S, Pasadena, tel. 813/381–7931. No reservations. Dress: casual. No credit cards. Closed Tues. No dinner.*

Shopping for **Hamlin's Landing** (401 2nd St. E, Indian Rocks Beach) has several
Bargains shops and restaurants along the Intracoastal Waterway, in a Victorian-style setting. **John's Pass Village and Boardwalk** (12901 Gulf Blvd., Madeira Beach) features a collection of shops and restaurants in an old-style fishing village near St. Petersburg. Pass the time watching the pelicans cavorting and dive-bombing for food. **Wagonwheel** (7801 Park Blvd., Pinellas Park), open weekends 8–4, is 100-plus acres containing some 2,000 vendors and a variety of food concessions. There is a tram from the parking lot to the vendor area.

Beaches **Bay Beach** (North Shore Dr. and 13th Ave. NE, St. Petersburg), on Tampa Bay, has showers and shelters.

Clearwater Beach is a popular hangout for teenagers and college students. On a narrow island between Clearwater Harbor and the Gulf, it is connected to downtown Clearwater by Memorial Causeway. Facilities include a marina, concessions, showers, rest rooms, and life-guards.

On five islands totaling some 900 acres, **Fort De Soto Park** (*see above*) has St. Petersburg's southernmost beaches. Facilities are two fish-ing piers, picnic sites overlooking lagoons, a waterskiing and boat-ing area, and miles of beaches for swimming. It's open daily until dark. To get there, take the Pinellas Bayway through three toll gates (cost: 85¢).

Indian Rocks Beach (off Rte. 8 south of Clearwater Beach) attracts mostly couples.

Maximo Park Beach (34th St. and Pinellas Point Dr. S, Madeira Beach) is on Boca Ciega Bay. There is no lifeguard, but there is a picnic area with grills, tables, shelters, and a boat ramp.

North Shore Beach (901 North Shore Dr. NE, Belleair Beach) charges $1 admission and has a pool, beach umbrellas, cabanas, windbreaks, and lounges.

Pass-A-Grille Beach, the southern part of St. Pete Beach, has park-ing meters, a snack bar, rest rooms, and showers.

St. Petersburg Municipal Beach (11260 Gulf Blvd.) is a free beach on Treasure Island. There are dressing rooms, metered parking, and a snack bar.

Tarpon Springs has two public beaches: **Howard Park Beach** (Sunset Dr.), where a lifeguard is on duty daily 8:30–6 Easter through La-bor Day, and **Sunset Beach** (Gulf Rd.), where there is similar life-guard coverage as well as rest rooms, picnic tables, grills, and a boat ramp.

Participant Sports

Biking Bicycles can be rented at the **Beach Cyclist** (7517 Blindpass Rd., St. Petersburg, tel. 813/367–5001) and **D & S Bicycle Shop** (12073 Semi-nole Blvd., Largo, tel. 813/393–0300).

Boating and Fishing **Florida Charter** (1740 Liebman La., St. Petersburg, tel. 813/347–7245) has powerboats and sailboats for rent, bareboat or captained. **Florida Deep Sea Fishing** (Corey Landing, St. Petersburg Beach, tel. 813/360–2082) runs party boats. You can take sailing lessons and rent boats at **M & M Beach Service & Boat Rental** (5300 Gulf Blvd., St. Petersburg Beach, tel. 813/360–8295).

Golf Courses open to the public include **Clearwater Golf Park** (Clearwa-ter, tel. 813/447–5272), **Dunedin Country Club** (Dunedin, tel. 813/733–7836), **Innisbrook Hilton Resort** (Tarpon Springs, tel. 813/942–2000), **Largo Golf Course** (Largo, tel. 813/587–6724), **Mangrove Bay Golf Course** (St. Petersburg, tel. 813/893–7797), and **Twin Brooks Golf Course** (St. Petersburg, tel. 813/893–7445).

Tennis Tennis facilities can be found at **Dunedin Community Center** (Pinehurst and Michigan Sts., Dunedin, tel. 813/737–3950) and **McMullen Park** (1000 Edenville Ave., Clearwater, tel. 813/462–6144).

Spectator Sports

Baseball The season comes early to Florida with the annual convergence of the Grapefruit League—major-league teams that offer exhibitions in March and April during their spring training camps. For informa-tion on all the teams, call 904/488–0990. The teams that play in this area are the **Baltimore Orioles** and **St. Louis Cardinals** (Al Lang Sta-dium, 1st St. and 2nd Ave., St. Petersburg, tel. 813/822–3384), **Phil-adelphia Phillies** (Jack Russell Stadium, Seminole St. and Greenwood Ave., Clearwater, tel. 813/442–8496), and **Toronto Blue Jays** (Grant Field, 373 Douglas Ave., north of Rte. 88, Dunedin, tel. 813/733–9302).

The Arts and Nightlife

The Arts

Ruth Eckerd Hall (1111 McMullen Booth Rd., Clearwater, tel. 813/791–7400) plays host to many national performers of ballet, drama, and music—pop, classical, or jazz. The **St. Petersburg Concert Ballet** (tel. 813/892–5767) performs periodically throughout the year, mostly at the Bayfront Center in St. Petersburg.

Nightlife

Carlie's (5641 49th St., St. Petersburg, tel. 813/527–5214) is hopping on Friday and Saturday nights, with plenty of dancing. At the popular **Cha Cha Coconuts** (City Pier, St. Petersburg, tel. 813/822–6655), jazz musicians perform several nights a week. **Coliseum Ballroom** (535 4th Ave. N, St. Petersburg, tel. 813/892–5202) offers ballroom dancing Wednesday and Saturday nights. **Harp & Thistle** (650 Corey Ave., St. Petersburg Beach, tel. 813/360–4104) presents live Irish music Wednesday through Saturday. **Hurricane Lounge** (807 Gulf Way, Pass-A-Grille Beach, tel. 813/360–9558) is a nice place to watch the sun go down while listening to light jazz. **Joyland Country Night Club** (11225 U.S. 19, St. Petersburg, tel. 813/573–1919) is very busy on weekends. **Ron Bennington's Comedy Scene** (Rodeway Inn, 401 U.S. 19 S, Clearwater, tel. 813/799–1181) is a barrel of laughs on weekends, as comedians vie for the greatest applause.

The Manatee Coast

⑯ About 60 miles north of St. Petersburg, in the town of **Weeki Wachee,** you'll find **Weeki Wachee Spring.** Here, an underwater theater presents mermaid shows, a nature trail threads through the subtropical wilderness, and a jungle boat cruises to view local wildlife. Allow at least four hours to see everything. *U.S. 19 and Rte. 50, tel. 904/596–2062. Admission: $14.95 adults, $10.95 children 3–11. Open daily 9:30–5:30.*

★ ⑰ About 15 miles farther north on U.S. 19 (90 minutes north of Tampa) you come to **Homosassa Springs** and another of Florida's natural wonders: **Homosassa Springs State Wildlife Park.** Turn left on Route 490-A and follow the signs. Here you may see manatees, but the main attraction is the "Spring of 10,000 Fish," a clear spring with many species of fish. A walk along the park's paths will lead you to alligator, other reptile, and exotic bird shows. Jungle boat cruises on the Homosassa River are available across Fish Bowl Drive from the entrance. *1 mi west of U.S. 19 on Fish Bowl Dr., tel. 904/628–2311. Admission: $6.95 adults, $3.95 children 3–11. Open daily 9–5:30.*

⑱ A great place to stop for a picnic is the **Yulee Sugar Mill State Historic Site,** just a short drive farther from Homosassa Springs on Route 490-A. It's on the site of a ruined sugar plantation built by the state's first U.S. senator. *Rte. 490-A, tel. 904/795–3817. Admission free. Open daily sunrise–sunset.*

★ ⑲ Go north on U.S. 19 to the town of **Crystal River,** and turn left on Paradise Point Road. On Kings Bay, next to the Port Paradise Resort is the office of the **Crystal River Wildlife Refuge,** a U.S. Fish and Wildlife Service sanctuary for manatees. Wide stretches of the river are designated for people to watch and swim with the sea cows. The main spring feeds crystal-clear water into the river at 72° year-round, and during winter months manatees congregate around the spring. In the warmer months, when manatees scatter, the main spring is still a fun place for a swim. Though it's accessible only by boat, the refuge provides neither tours nor boat rentals. For these, contact marinas in town. *1502 S.E. Kings Bay Dr., tel. 904/563–2088. Admission free. Open daily 9–4; office open weekdays 7:30–4.*

Budget Lodging
$$

Plantation Inn & Golf Resort. Set on the banks of Kings Bay, this recently remodeled two-story plantation-style resort sits on 175 acres near several nature preserves and rivers. Pets are permitted. *9301 W. Fort Island Trail, Crystal River 34423, tel. 904/795–4211 or*

800/632–6262, fax 904/795–1368. 136 rooms. Facilities: restaurant, lounge, pools, saunas, golf, tennis, dive shop, boating, fishing. AE, DC, MC, V.

$$ **Riverside Inn.** A rustic little place, this inn boasts an intimate location beside the Homosassa River and across from Monkey Island—residence of six such mammals. Though it comes complete with its own restaurant (The Yard Arm) and lounge (Ship's Lounge), the Riverside is also within walking distance of three local restaurants, and two others are accessible by boat. Rent bicycles to get a feel for the lovely surroundings. *Box 258, Homosassa Springs 32687, tel. 904/628–2474, fax 904/628–5208. 76 rooms. Facilities: restaurant, lounge, pool, tennis courts, bicycles. AE, MC, V.*

$$ **Riverside Inn Downtown.** This is a simple motor inn that features queen-size beds in most rooms. It accepts pets and has a playground for the kids; children 14 and under stay for free. *U.S. 19 at Rte. 490A W, Homosassa Springs 34448, tel. 904/628–4311, fax 904/628–4311. 104 rooms. Facilities: restaurant, lounge, pool, tennis courts, playground. AE, D, DC, MC, V.*

$ **Best Western Crystal River Resort.** This cinder-block roadside motel is close to Kings Bay and its manatee population. There's a marina within steps of the motel, from which dive boats depart for scuba and snorkeling excursions. The only rooms that have water views are 114 and 128. *614 N.W. U.S. 19, Crystal River 34428, tel. 904/ 795–3171, fax 904/795–3179. 96 rooms, 18 efficiencies. Facilities: restaurant, lounge, pool. AE, DC, MC, V.*

$ **Homosassa River Retreat.** Located right on the banks of the Homosassa River, with two boat docks and nearby boat and pontoon rentals, this resort of one- and two-bedroom cottages with kitchens is well situated for outdoor adventuring. Washer and dryer are across the street. *10605 Hall's River Rd., Homosassa Springs 32646, tel. 904/628–7072. 9 cottages. Facilities: docks, laundry. MC, V.*

Budget Dining **Charlie's Fish House Restaurant.** This popular, no-frills seafood spot
$ features locally caught fish, oysters, crab claws, and lobster. *224 U.S. 19 N, Crystal River, tel. 904/795–3949. No reservations. Dress: casual. MC, V.*

Tour 2: South of Tampa Bay

Across Tampa Bay, the two cities of Bradenton and Sarasota maintain their independence from the Tampa–St. Pete urban area. They have their own airport, their own cultural institutions, and their own barrier islands. One Sarasota publication headline reads "A Bonanza of Beaches," and it's true—there are long stretches of white sand, turquoise water, gentle surf, and plenty of sun. Route 789, which connects most of the islands (except Siesta and Casey keys), makes a scenic drive, past miles of blue-green water, beaches, and waterfront homes.

Arriving and The area's airport, just north of Sarasota, is **Sarasota–Bradenton**
Departing (tel. 941/359–5200). It is served by American, Continental, Delta,
By Plane Northwest, TWA, United, and USAir. **Airport Shuttle** (tel. 941/355–9645) and **West Coast Executive Sedan** (tel. 941/359–8600) deliver to most parts of the county. An average cab fare is $12–$25. The cheapest forms of transportation, however, are **Sarasota County Rapid Transit** (SCAT) (tel. 941/951–5850) and **Manatee County Area Transit** (tel. 941/749–7116), which run into Sarasota or Bradenton for $1.50.

By Bus **Greyhound Lines** (tel. 800/231–2222) stops in Sarasota (575 N. Washington St., tel. 941/955–5735).

By Car The quickest route for most motorists is I–75, which skirts the eastern edges of both Sarasota and Bradenton. It stretches down from

Tampa and continues on to Fort Myers and ultimately Fort Lauderdale, on the east coast.

Getting
Around
By Bus

Bus service is provided by **Manatee County Area Transit** (tel. 941/749–7116) in the Bradenton area and **Sarasota County Area Transit** (SCAT) (tel. 941/951–5850) around Sarasota. The fare on both systems is $1.50 adults, 75¢ senior citizens.

By Car

The Tamiami Trail (U.S. 41) and its stop-and-go traffic run north–south through the region's coastal towns, from Bradenton through Sarasota and on to Venice. In Bradenton, Route 64 goes east–west through town, connecting I–75 with Anna Maria Island. From there, Route 789 travels the length of the barrier islands—down Anna Maria Island and Longboat Key and onto Lido Key—before swinging east across the Ringling Causeway, which connects back to the mainland at Sarasota. To reach Siesta Key from Sarasota, cross on either the Route 758 or Route 72 causeway.

Bradenton

Manatee Chamber of Commerce (Box 321, Bradenton 34206, tel. 941/748–3411).

Numbers in the margin correspond to points of interest on the Bradenton/Sarasota map.

Bradenton, on the southern bank of the Manatee River, is a nice area in which to catch your breath and slow down, especially if you are coming from the theme parks in Orlando or the fast pace of the Tampa area. Casual and laid-back, Bradenton tends to be less pricey than other coastal communities, and with a little detective work, you can get acquainted with the history of Old Florida.

On the north side of the Manatee River, take U.S 301 about 3 miles east of U.S. 41, turn left onto Ellenton–Gillette Road, and take the
㉒ first right to the **Gamble Plantation and Confederate Memorial.** Built in 1850, the mansion is the only pre–Civil War plantation house in south Florida, and some of the original furnishings are on display. Here the Confederate secretary of state took refuge when the Confederacy fell to Union forces. *3708 Patten Ave., Ellenton, tel. 941/723–4536. Admission: $2 adults, $1 children 6–12. Open Thurs.–Mon. 8–5; tours at 9:30, 10:30, 1, 2, 3, 4.*

Head south on U.S. 41, cross the river into **Bradenton,** and take
㉑ Route 64 east for a mile to **Manatee Village Historical Park,** consisting of an 1860 courthouse, 1887 church, 1903 general store and museum, and 1912 settler's home. The Old Manatee Cemetery, which dates back to 1850, contains the graves of early Manatee County settlers. *Rte. 64, tel. 941/749–7165. Admission free. Open Sept.–June, weekdays 9–4:30, Sun. 2–5; July–Aug., weekdays 9–4:30. Appointments necessary to tour cemetery.*

To the west on Route 64, in the center of the city, and only a few
㉒ blocks from the Manatee River, the **South Florida Museum** exhibits artifacts of Florida history, including displays of Native American culture and an excellent collection of Civil War memorabilia. The museum is also home to Snooty, the oldest living manatee in captivity. Snooty likes to shake hands and perform other tricks at feeding time in his viewing pool in the Manatee Education and Resource Center. At the Bishop Planetarium, a domed theater, you can see star shows and special-effects laser-light displays. *201 10th St., tel. 941/746–4132 for museum or 941/746–4131 for planetarium. Admission: $5.50 adults, $3.50 children and students. Open Tues.–Sat. 10–5, Sun. noon–6; star show Tues.–Sun. at 1:30, 3 PM.*

★ **㉓** Continue west on Route 64 to 75th Street Northwest, turn north, and drive to the **De Soto National Memorial.** Hernando de Soto, one of the first Spanish explorers, set foot in Florida in 1539 near what is

Bradenton/Sarasota

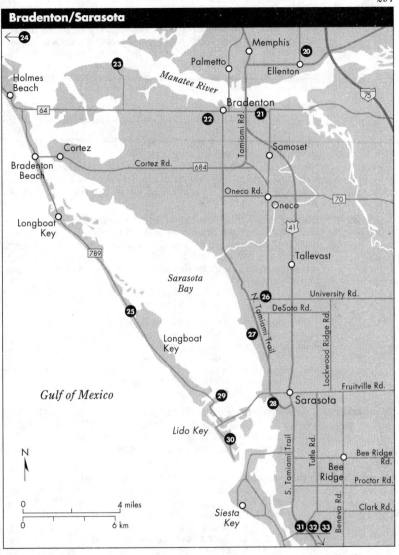

Bellm's Cars & Music of Yesterday, **26**

De Soto National Memorial, **23**

Egmont Key, **24**

Gamble Plantation and Confederate Memorial, **20**

Historic Spanish Point, **31**

Manatee Village Historical Park, **21**

Marie Selby Botanical Gardens, **28**

Mote Marine Aquarium, **29**

Myakka River State Park, **33**

Oscar Sherer State Recreation Area, **32**

Ringling Museums, **25**

Sarasota Jungle Gardens, **27**

South Florida Museum, **22**

South Lido Park, **30**

now Bradenton. Here, in the high season (late-December–early April), park employees dressed in 16th-century costumes demonstrate various period weapons and show how the European explorers prepared and preserved food for their journeys over the untamed land. Films, demonstrations, and a short nature trail are available on the grounds. *75th St. NW, tel. 941/792–0458. Admission free. Open daily 8–5:30.*

㉔ Egmont Key lies just off the northern tip of Anna Maria Island, Bradenton's barrier island to the west. On it are **Fort Dade,** a military installation built in 1900 during the Spanish-American War, and Florida's sixth-brightest lighthouse. The primary inhabitant of the 2-mile-long island is the threatened gopher tortoise. The only way to get here is by the 54-foot excursion boat *Miss Cortez* (tel. 941/ 794–1223), which leaves three times a week from Cortez, on the mainland. The fare is $14 adults, $8 children. Shellers, in particular, will find the trip rewarding.

Budget Lodging **Duncan House.** This late-1800s Victorian house was barged to the Gulf from downtown Bradenton in the 1940s. It's across the street $$ from the beach and is quite moderately priced even in high season. Upstairs are two apartments, each with a living room, bedroom, kitchen, and bath. Downstairs are two more rooms. All are charmingly decorated with antiques. This is a no-smoking property. *1703 Gulf Dr., Bradenton Beach 34217, tel. 941/778–6858. 2 apts., 2 rooms. AE, MC, V.*

Splurge **Harrington House.** The lowest on-season rate is $119, but off-season rooms start at $79 at this three-story house built on the beach in 1925. The gourmet breakfast, part of the package, might consist of orange waffles or French toast stuffed with strawberry and apricot preserves and cream cheese. The house is no-smoking, and children are not welcome. *5626 Gulf Dr., Holmes Beach 34217, tel. 941/778– 5444. 11 rooms. Facilities: breakfast room, pool. MC, V.*

Camping **Lake Manatee State Recreation Area** (Rte. 64, 15 mi east of Bradenton, tel. 941/741–3028) costs $6 per night in the off-season and $9 in winter, plus tax and extra amenities charges. On site are 60 camping spots, separated by vegetation, as well as facilities for swimming and fishing.

Budget Dining **Crab Trap.** Rustic decor, ultrafresh seafood, gator tail, and wild pig $$ are among the trademarks of this restaurant. *U.S. 19 at Terra Ceia Bridge, Palmetto, tel. 941/722–6255; 4814 Memphis Rd., Ellenton, tel. 941/729–7777. No reservations. Dress: casual. D, MC, V.*

$$ **Sand Bar.** This popular spot, busy year-round, offers lunchtime bargains—a local catch or house special for $5–$10. Dinner entrées range from $12 to $20 in the dining room, but you can get sandwiches and burgers on the outdoor deck for very low prices. *100 Spring Ave., Anna Maria Island, tel. 941/778–0444. Reservations accepted for dining room. Dress: casual. AE, D, DC, MC, V.*

$ **The Anchorage.** What used to be the well-known Fast Eddie's restaurant, on the tip of Anna Maria Island, now offers live entertainment. There's a swing band on Tuesday night, and '60s and '70s oldies are on tap Friday and Saturday nights. *101 S. Bay Blvd., Anna Maria Island, tel. 941/778–9611. Reservations accepted. Dress: casual. MC, V.*

Shopping for Bargains Shopping in the Bradenton area tends to be touristy, with souvenir shops on every street corner hawking T-shirts and beach attire. A big attraction is the **Red Barn** (1707 1st St. E) flea market, with the requisite big red barn. It operates during the week, but the number of vendors increases to about 1,000 on weekends. Some stores open Tuesday–Sunday 10–4, whereas others sell on Wednesday, Saturday, and Sunday 8–4.

Beaches Take Manatee Avenue (Route 64) west from downtown Bradenton to the **Palma Sola Causeway,** which crosses over to Anna Maria Island. Along the causeway, there's a long, sandy beach fronting Palma Sola Bay, equipped with boat ramps, a dock, and picnic tables. When you reach **Anna Maria Island,** you'll have four other public beaches to choose among. **Anna Maria Bayfront Park,** at the north end of the municipal pier, is a secluded beach fronting the Intracoastal Waterway and the Gulf of Mexico. Facilities include picnic grounds, a playground, rest rooms, showers, and lifeguards. At mid-island, in the town of Holmes Beach, is **Manatee County Beach,** popular with all ages. It has picnic facilities, a snack bar, showers, rest rooms, and lifeguards. **Cortez Beach** (Gulf Blvd., Bradenton Beach) is for those who like their beaches without facilities—nothing but sand, water, and trees. At the island's southern end is **Coquina Beach,** big with singles and families. Facilities here include a picnic area, boat ramp, playground, refreshment stand, rest rooms, showers, and lifeguards.

Participant Sports
Biking **Bicycle Center** (2610 Cortez Rd., tel. 941/756–5480) is a source for rental bikes. You can also ask here for suggestions of good cycling routes.

Fishing Bring your fishing gear to the downtown Memorial Pier, or cast from the beach. There are boat ramps at Manatee Avenue West on Palma Sola Bay, Anna Maria Sound, and Coquina Beach.

Golf Several courses in Manatee County are open to the public, including **Buffalo Creek** (Palmetto, tel. 941/776–2611) and **Manatee County Golf Course** (tel. 941/792–6773).

Spectator Sports
Baseball In March and April, take in a spring training exhibition game of the **Pittsburgh Pirates** at McKechnie Field (17th Ave. W and 9th St., tel. 941/747–3031).

Sarasota

Sarasota Chamber of Commerce (1819 Main St., Suite 240, Sarasota 34236, tel. 941/955–8187). Sarasota Convention and Visitors Bureau (655 N. Tamiami Trail, Sarasota 34236, tel. 941/957–1877 or 800/522–9799).

Long ago, circus tycoon John Ringling found Sarasota an ideal spot to bring his clowns and performers to train and recuperate during the winter. Along Sarasota Bay, Ringling also built himself a fancy home, patterned after the Palace of the Doges in Venice, Italy. Today, the **Ringling Museums** include that mansion, as well as his art ★ 25 museum (with a world-renowned collection of Rubens paintings and 17th-century tapestries) and a museum of circus memorabilia. *½ mi south of Sarasota-Bradenton Airport on Rte. 789, tel. 941/355–5101. Admission (good for mansion and museums): $8.50 ages 13 and over, $7.50 senior citizens. Open daily 10–5:30.*

26 Across the road, **Bellm's Cars & Music of Yesterday** displays 175 restored antique automobiles, including Rolls-Royces, Pierce Arrows, and Auburns, and 2,000 old-time music makers, such as hurdy-gurdies, calliopes, and 1,200 music boxes. *5500 N. Tamiami Trail, tel. 941/355–6228. Admission: $7.50 adults under 89, $3.75 children 6–12. Open Mon.–Sat. 8:30–6, Sun. 9:30–6.*

27 Head south on U.S. 41 about 1½ miles to **Sarasota Jungle Gardens.** It'll take you a couple of hours to stroll through this 10-acre spread of tropical plants. Also on site are a petting zoo, a shell and butterfly museum, and shows featuring snakes, turtles, and alligators. *3701 Bayshore Rd., tel. 941/355–5305. Admission: $8 adults, $4 children 3–12. Open daily 9–5; shows at 10, noon, 2, 4.*

Farther south, just off U.S. 41, near the Island Park yacht basin, are 28 the **Marie Selby Botanical Gardens.** Here you can stroll through a world-class display of orchids, see air plants and colorful bromeliads, and wander through 14 garden areas along Sarasota Bay. There is also a small museum of botany and art in a gracious restored mansion. *800 S. Palm Ave., tel. 941/366–5730. Admission: $6 adults, $3 children 6–11. Open daily 10–5; closed Dec. 25.*

Budget Lodging **La Rue Motel Apartments.** Being on the mainland makes the rates affordable, but Gulf lovers will like its location close to a causeway and only 10 minutes from Siesta Key's beautiful beaches. Units are simply furnished but very well maintained, and the mostly British management is welcoming and helpful. Apartments with full kitchens and efficiencies with small refrigerators and two-burner stoves are available at very modest weekly rates. Off-season, rates are truly a bargain. *1710 Stickney Point Rd., 34231, tel. 941/921–7957. 19 rooms, 2 efficiencies, 2 apartments. Facilities: pool. AE, D, MC, V.*

Budget Dining **Trolley Station.** Not surprisingly, this popular spot looks and feels a lot like a trolley station, inside and out. Long benches frame the entrance, the cashier sits behind an old-fashioned ticket counter, and people line up for dinner the way they probably used to for the trolley. The lunch and dinner menu will satisfy almost everyone, from picky eaters to penny watchers. It ranges from salads and the salad or baked potato bar to roast beef, fish, chicken, and pasta dishes, all at remarkably low prices. A bar and lounge area is large and comfortable. *1941 Stickney Point Rd., tel. 941/923–2721. No reservations. Dress: casual. AE, MC, V.*

Splurge **Marina Jack.** Eat in the restaurant overlooking Sarasota Bay or take a dinner cruise on the *Marina Jack II.* The paddle wheeler heads out Wednesday through Sunday for two romantic hours that include entertainment. Menus in both places emphasize fresh seafood. Entrées on land and sea average around $15, but there is also a $6 per person charge to ride the boat. *2 Marina Plaza, tel. 941/365–4232. Reservations advised. Dress: casual but neat. MC, V.*

Shopping for Bargains Summertime can be a bonanza of bargains at clearance sales. **Gulf Gate Mall** (S. Tamiami Trail) includes food courts, an arcade, some upscale clothing boutiques, a discount bookstore, and Terry Shulman's discount drugstore, offering wonderful opportunities for bargain hunters. **Sarasota Quay** (U.S. 41 at 3rd St.), right on the bay, is a fun place to browse amid the shops and restaurants. Some customers arrive by boat. Romantics can soak up the sunlit fountain, moonlit piazza, and lots of free views.

Participant Sports **Biking** You can rent bikes at **Mr. CB's** (1249 Stickney Point Rd., tel. 941/349–4400) and **Pedal N Wheels** (Merchants Pointe Shopping Center, 2881 Clark Rd., tel. 941/922–0481).

Golf **Bobby Jones Golf Course** (Circus Blvd., tel. 941/955–8097) is a public course that also has tennis facilities.

Tennis Some of the Sarasota area's many county and municipal parks have tennis courts, including the **Bobby Jones Golf Course** (*see above*). Fees are sometimes charged. **Arlington Park and Recreation Center** (2650 Waldemere St., tel. 941/366–0466) has lighted tennis courts and complete recreational facilities. **Bee Ridge Park** (4430 S. Lockwood Ridge Rd., tel. 941/924–4738) has courts.

Water Sports **Don and Mike's Boat and Jet Ski Rental** (520 Blackburn Point Rd., tel. 941/966–4000) has water skis, Jet Skis, pontoon boats, and instruction for all. **O'Leary's Sarasota Sailing School** (near Marina Jack's, at U.S. 41 and the bay front, tel. 941/953–7505) rents 19- to 39-foot sailboats and offers sailing lessons at all levels.

Spectator Sports **Baseball** "Take Me out to the Ball Game" is a familiar tune heard in March and April as the **Chicago White Sox** play their spring exhibition baseball games at Ed Smith Stadium (2700 12th St., tel. 941/954–7699).

The Arts and Nightlife

The Arts

The **Van Wezel Performing Arts Hall** (777 N. Tamiami Trail, tel. 941/953–3366) is easy to find—just look for the purple shell rising along the bay front. It offers some 200 performances each year, including Broadway plays, ballet, jazz, rock concerts, symphonies, children's shows, and ice-skating.

Theater thrives in Sarasota. The **Asolo Center for the Performing Arts** (5555 N. Tamiami Trail, tel. 941/351–8000) is a $10 million facility that offers productions nearly year-round. **Florida Studio Theatre** (1241 N. Palm Ave., tel. 941/366–9796) is a small professional theater that presents contemporary dramas, comedies, and musicals. **Golden Apple Dinner Theatre** (25 N. Pineapple Ave., tel. 941/366–5454) combines a buffet dinner with musicals and comedies. A long-established community theater, the **Players of Sarasota** (U.S. 41 and 9th St., tel. 941/365–2494) has launched such performers as Montgomery Clift, Polly Holiday, and Pee-Wee Herman. The troupe performs comedies, thrillers, and musicals.

Music, too, is alive and well. **Florida West Coast Symphony Center** (709 N. Tamiami Trail, tel. 941/953–4252) consists of a number of area groups that perform in Manatee and Sarasota counties regularly: the Florida West Coast Symphony, Florida String Quartet, Florida Brass Quintet, Florida Wind Quintet, and New Artists String Quartet. The **Sarasota Concert Band** (Van Wezel Performing Arts Hall, 777 N. Tamiami Trail, tel. 941/955–6660) includes 50 players, many of whom are full-time musicians. The group performs monthly concerts. The **Sarasota Opera** (61 N. Pineapple Ave., tel. 941/953–7030) performs February through March in a historic theater downtown. Internationally known artists sing the principal roles, supported by a professional apprentice chorus—24 young singers studying with the company.

The **Sarasota Film Society** operates year-round, showing foreign and nonmainstream films daily at 2, 5:45, and 8 at the Burns Court Cinema (506 Burns La., tel. 941/388–2441).

Nightlife

In Extremis (Sarasota Quay, tel. 941/954–2008) features laser-light shows and disco and alternative high-energy music. At the **306th Bomb Group** (8301 N. Tamiami Trail, tel. 941/355–8591), decorated with World War II gear, a DJ spins Top-40 tunes for a generally over-25 clientele.

Longboat, Lido, and Siesta Keys

Longboat Key Chamber of Commerce (5360 Gulf of Mexico Dr., Suite 107, Longboat Key 34228, tel. 941/383–2466).

Across the water from Sarasota lie the barrier islands of Longboat, Lido, and Siesta keys, with shops, hotels, condominiums, houses, and the big attraction—beaches. Longboat stretches down from Anna Maria Island and connects to Lido Key. Siesta Key, the next island south, is separated from Lido by the waters of Big Pass and must be reached by car from the mainland.

29 At the north end of Lido Key, just before the bridge to Longboat Key, turn right at the sign for City Island and the **Mote Marine Aquarium,** which displays sharks, rays, and other marine creatures native to the area. A huge outdoor shark tank lets you see its inhabitants from above and below the water's surface, and a neat touch tank lets you handle rays, guitar fish, horseshoe crabs, and sea urchins. *1600 City Island Park, tel. 941/388–2451. Admission: $6 adults, $4 children 4–17. Open daily 10–5.*

30 At the opposite (south) end of the key, past the public beach, you'll come to **South Lido Park.** Here you can try your luck at fishing, take a dip in the waters of the bay or Gulf of Mexico, roam the paths of the 130-acre park, or picnic as the sun sets through the Australian pines into the Gulf. *Ben Franklin Dr. Admission free. Open daily 8–sunset.*

Budget
Lodging
$$

Gulf Beach Resort Motel. The stylized pink sign, enclosed in teal arching waves, gives new arrivals their first—and accurate—impression of this kitschy cinder-block, beachfront palace. Guests—a number of them young Europeans—sign in, meet others, and return year after year to reacquaint with old friends. The management is one of the draws here, and you can have a choice of rooms, each furnished differently. The best—both with sea views—are a modern two-bedroom, done in white, and the one-bedroom below it. Some rooms have balconies, screened-in patios, or small private gardens with lime trees. All have kitchens, private baths, and basic cable TV. It's a 1-mile walk from St. Armand's Circle, through one of Florida's typical '50s neighborhoods. Daily, weekly, or monthly (September–January) rates are available. *930 Ben Franklin Dr., Lido Key 34236, tel. 941/388–2127, 800/232–2489 in U.S., or 800/331–2489 in Canada, fax 941/388–1312. 49 rooms. Facilities: pool, shuffleboard. MC, V.*

$$

Surfrider Beach Apartments. This lodging is nicely maintained, and, best of all, it's right on Crescent Beach, yet rates are much lower than those at nearby luxury hotels. Rooms are simply decorated and a bit small but are a bargain considering the location. There are also beachfront cottages and apartments that rent for as low as $115 in season. *6400 Midnight Pass Rd., Siesta Key 34242, tel. 941/349–2121. 21 units. Facilities: restaurant, pool. AE, D, MC, V.*

$$

Toscany on Lido Key. Management is helpful and friendly at this bargain of a place, a mile from St. Armand's Circle and across the street from the beach. (Summer rates begin at $39 for a double room; winter rates begin at $66.) The simply decorated neat units are arranged around a landscaped courtyard with a heated pool and shuffleboard courts nearby. Standard rooms have two double beds and a small refrigerator. Efficiencies have a full kitchen. *129 Taft Dr., Lido Key 33426, tel. 941/388–5525. 24 rooms. Facilities: pool, shuffleboard, laundry. MC, V.*

Splurge

Half Moon Beach Club. On season the lowest-priced double is $175, but off-season rates come down as low as $145. Conveniently located just minutes from St. Armand's Circle, this horseshoe-shape hotel offers Lido Key's finest accommodations. Elegance begins with the alabaster-lit lobby and continues as you pass through the glass doors to the hotel's centerpiece, a tropical garden surrounding the pool. Walk past the pool, the tiki huts, and yogurt bar to the spacious beach deck where you can enjoy a cool drink. Continue on to the wide beach where, to the left, the sand meets the forest. Decorated in pink pastels, every asymmetrical room and suite is unique; four have direct Gulf views. Rooms on the inside of the horseshoe overlook the pool and garden. *2050 Ben Franklin Dr., Lido Key 34236, tel. 941/388–3694 or 800/358–3245, fax 941/388–1938. 75 rooms, 12 suites. Facilities: restaurant, bar, pool, beach. AE, DC, MC, V.*

Budget Dining
$$

Ophelia's on the Bay. Sample mussel soup, eggplant crepes, chicken pot pie, or cioppino, among other dishes, at this waterfront restaurant. *9105 Midnight Pass Rd., Siesta Key, tel. 941/349–2212. Reservations advised. Dress: casual. AE, D, DC, MC, V.*

$

Old Salty Dog. On the waterside at New Pass, by the bridge to Longboat Key, is a laid-back, casual eatery and bar with indoor-outdoor dining and boat dockage. The NO SHIRT, NO SHOES, NO SERVICE sign is missing here; bare feet and bathing suits are welcome. The menu includes the now-famous Salty Dog—dipped in beer batter, deep fried, and delicious—and dog bites, deep-fried hot-dog morsels served on a bed of fries. Sandwiches, soups, munchies, and burgers are also on the menu, as well as 26 brands of beer from around the world. The most expensive item is a pint (about 40) of peel-and-eat shrimp at $10. *1601*

Ken Thompson Dr., City Island, tel. 941/388-4311. No reservations. Dress: casual. No credit cards.

$ **Old Salty Dog.** Though it has the same owners as the Old Salty Dog on City Island (*see above*), this saline canine is completely different. Located in Siesta Village, a shopping mall on Siesta Key, the casual restaurant is billed as the Sarasota area's only English pub. It specializes in traditional English fish-and-chips. *5023 Ocean Blvd., Siesta Key, tel. 941/349-0158. No reservations. Dress: casual. No credit cards.*

$ **Wildflower.** Vegetarian and fish dishes are available in this friendly café. *5218 Ocean Blvd., Siesta Key, tel. 941/349-1758. No reservations. Dress: casual. MC, V.*

Shopping for Bargains
Budget watchers won't find much to buy on Lido Key's **St. Armand's Circle,** but it's a great place to window-shop. The circle is lined with a huge number of exclusive restaurants and upscale boutiques.

Beaches
At the northern tip of Longboat Key, **Greer Island Beach** is accessible by boat or via North Shore Boulevard. The secluded peninsula has a wide beach and excellent shelling but no facilities.

On Lido Key, in addition to **South Lido Park** (*see above*), there's **Lido Beach** (Ben Franklin Dr.), a public beach with showers, a swimming pool, a souvenir shop, and a playground. From it you can walk to **North Lido Beach,** a secluded ½-mile stretch of white sand bordered by Australian pines at the north end of the key.

On Siesta Key, **Siesta Beach** (Beach Rd.), located mid-island, is the widest and most popular beach in the county. It's part of a 40-acre park that also contains nature trails, a concession stand, soccer and softball fields, picnicking facilities, play equipment, rest rooms, and tennis and volleyball courts. **Crescent Beach** (Midnight Pass Rd.) is famous for its sand, and here, at the Point of Rocks, snorkelers may find underwater wonders. Tranquil **Turtle Beach** (Midnight Pass Rd.), farther south, comprises only 14 acres, but its facilities include boat ramps, horseshoe pits, picnic areas, playgrounds, a recreation building, rest rooms, and a volleyball court. By walking across Midnight Pass to Casey Key, you reach **Palmer Pointe South,** which has 24 acres of white sandy beach but no facilities.

Nightlife
The Patio (Columbia Restaurant, St. Armand's Circle, Lido Key, tel. 941/388-3987) is a casual lounge with live music Tuesday through Saturday.

Osprey

③ At Osprey, between Sarasota and Venice, you'll find **Historic Spanish Point,** comprising a group of pioneer homestead buildings from the late 1800s, a prehistoric Indian mound and middens dating from 2150 BC, and the 1911–1918 gardens of the estate of the wealthy Mrs. Potter Palmer. This is a pleasant place to spend an afternoon. *500 Tamiami Trail, tel. 941/966-5214. Admission: $5 adults, $3 children 6–12. Open Mon.–Sat. 9–5, Sun. noon–5.*

㉜ **Oscar Scherer State Recreation Area,** just south of Osprey across U.S. 41N, is a 462-acre natural area of pine and scrub flatwoods on the banks of a small tidal creek. Boating, fishing, campgrounds, nature trails, a picnic area, and a swimming pond are all available. *1943 S. Tamiami Trail, tel. 941/483-5956. Admission: $3.25 per vehicle with up to 8 people. Open daily sunrise–sunset.*

Beaches
A causeway leads from Osprey to the barrier island of Casey Key. At its south end, **North Jetty Park** (Albee Rd.) is considered one of the best surfing beaches on Florida's west coast because of the way the jetties affect wave action.

Venice

Venice Area Chamber of Commerce (257 N. Tamiami Trail, Venice 34285–1908, tel. 941/488–2236).

The winter headquarters of the Ringling Brothers Circus, Venice is crisscrossed with even more canals than the city for which it was named. Venice beaches are quite good for shell collecting, but they're best known for their wealth of sharks' teeth and fossils.

Budget Lodging
$$ **Days Inn.** Located on the main business route through town, this recently renovated motor inn has comfortable rooms—and it's only 10 minutes from the beach. Pets are allowed. *1710 S. Tamiami Trail (U.S. 41), 34293, tel. 941/493–4558, fax 941/493–1593. 72 rooms. Facilities: restaurant, lounge, pool. AE, MC, V.*

$$ **Veranda Inn–Venice.** A landscaped pool is the focal point of this small but spacious inn. All rooms look out on the pool and courtyard. *625 S. Tamiami Trail (U.S. 41), 34285, tel. 941/484–9559, fax 941/484–8235. 38 rooms. Facilities: restaurant, pool. AE, DC, MC, V.*

Budget Dining
$$ **Sharky's on the Pier.** Gaze out on the beach and sparkling waters while dining on grilled fresh seafood. *1600 S. Harbor Dr., tel. 941/488–1456. Reservations advised. Dress: casual. MC, V.*

Beaches Much of **Casperson Beach** (Harbor Dr., south of Venice Airport) has been left in its natural state—a wild, windswept, and picturesque site. Considered a fine shelling beach, it's also a good place to find sharks' teeth. Amenities include picnic tables, a nature trail, and rest rooms. **Venice Beach** (west end of Venice Ave.), site of a reef of fossilized material ¼ mile offshore, is a favorite spot for local divers.

Participant Sports
Biking For rental bikes and information on the best places in the area to ride, try **Bicycles International** (1744 Tamiami Trail S, tel. 941/497–1590).

Golf **Bird Bay Executive Golf Course** (tel. 941/485–9333) and **Plantation Golf & Country Club** (tel. 941/493–2000) both welcome visiting golfers when space permits.

The Arts **Theatre Works** (1247 1st St., tel. 941/952–9170) presents professional, non-Equity productions at the Palm Tree Playhouse. **Venice Little Theatre** (Tampa and Nokomis Aves., tel. 941/488–1115) is a community theater offering comedies, musicals, and a few dramas during its October–May season.

Myakka River State Park

③ **Myakka River State Park** is a wonderful 29,000-acre wildlife and bird sanctuary with nature trails, canoeing, and picnic grounds. *The Gator Gal*, a large airboat, conducts four one-hour tours daily. Tickets are sold on a first-come, first-served basis each morning; it's best to arrive around 9 and definitely before noon to have a good chance of getting them. Another option is to rent a canoe, paddles, and life vests and see the park under your own power. *15 mi southeast of Sarasota on Rte. 72, tel. 941/361–6511. Admission: $3 per vehicle; tours: $6 adults, $3 children 6–12; canoes: $6 an hr, $18 for half day, $25 a day. Open daily 8–sunset.*

9 Southwest Florida

Updated by
Pamela
Acheson

The southwestern Florida coast is often called "Florida's Florida" because its natural subtropical environment has made it a favorite vacation spot for Floridians as well as for visitors from across the United States and abroad. There's lots to do in this small corner of the state, and though most of it has to do with beaches and water, there are a number of distinctly different travel destinations.

Fort Myers, a small and pretty inland city built along the Caloosa-hatchee River, was the winter home of Thomas Edison and Henry Ford. Off the coast to the west, more than 100 barrier islands range in length from just a few feet to more than 20 miles. Here you'll find Sanibel and Captiva, two thoughtfully developed resort islands. Sanibel is known for its world-class shelling, fine fishing, luxury hotels and restaurants (at the south end of the island), and wildlife refuge.

Once a small fishing village, Naples has grown into a thriving and sophisticated town, which many liken to a smaller Palm Beach. There are a number of fine restaurants and several upscale shopping complexes, including the gracious, tree-lined 3rd Street South area. Unlike Palm Beach, the Naples area offers easy access to its many miles of sun-drenched white beach.

East of Naples stretches the wilderness of the Big Cypress National Preserve, and a half hour south is Marco Island, with several large resorts and good beaches, restaurants, and shops. Still farther southeast on U.S. 41 is Everglades City, the western gateway to Everglades National Park (*see* Chapter 3, the Everglades).

Though resorts in Naples and on the popular Sanibel, Captiva, and Marco islands can be pricey, you can still find quite inexpensive lodgings away from the beach and then head to the shore just for the day. For this reason, you'll get much more out of this vacation spot if you have a car.

Southwest Florida Basics

Budget Lodging

In general, the farther away from the beach, the less expensive the room. In beachfront hotels, the most expensive rooms are those with waterfront views. The area's many apartment-motels, some on the beach and some just a block or two away, can offer great savings for families and groups. You can take advantage of weekly rates and save dining costs by cooking some of your own meals.

Seasonal rates change almost monthly. Rates are highest mid-December–mid-April, when they are almost double what you'd pay in summer.

Budget Dining

In southwest Florida, fresh fish and other seafood reign supreme, especially the succulent claw of the native stone crab, in season from October 15 through May 15. It's usually served with drawn butter or a tangy mustard sauce. Many restaurants offer early-bird menus with seating before 6 PM.

Bargain Shopping

Since the main reason for coming to this area is usually to loll on the beach, shopping may not be a top priority for you, but if it is, there's a wide range available, from tacky tourist shops hawking shell-encrusted souvenirs to the sophisticated and expensive stores of Olde Naples.

Beaches

The best beaches in the region are those on Sanibel and Captiva islands and the mainland Gulf beaches in the Naples area.

Sports and the Outdoors

Biking Cycling is a popular pastime, especially on Boca Grande and Sanibel Island, which have dedicated bike paths.

Fishing Tarpon, kingfish, speckled trout, snapper, grouper, sea trout, snook, sheepshead, and shark are among the species to be found in coastal waters. You can charter your own boat or join a group on a party boat for full- or half-day outings.

The Arts and Nightlife

Naples, with its Philharmonic Center for the Arts, is the region's cultural capital. Bars, discos, and other nightspots cluster in Fort Myers and Naples.

Festivals

In March, the annual **Shrimpfest** brings distinctive shrimp boats from as far away as Texas to the Fort Myers Beach dock. Shrimp feasts are the order of the day, as are a parade and a Queen's Ball. In Naples, the **Tropicool** festival, celebrating the end of the winter season, comes the first two weeks of May. Events include the Great Dock Canoe Race, from the Dock restaurant at the City Dock, and the Taste of Collier food fair in Olde Naples. **Swamp Buggy Mania** (tel. 941/774–2701) accompanies Naples's Swamp Buggy Races, held at Rattlesnake-Hammock Road and Route 951 in March, May, and October. In July, **Saddle Up!**, Florida's oldest rodeo (since 1928), features bareback riding, calf roping, and steer wrestling at the Arcadia Rodeo Arena (tel. 800/749–7633). From mid-July to mid-August is **Dance and Music Everywhere: The New Arts Festival** (tel. 941/332–6736), in Fort Myers. Music and dance concerts and presentations, which feature students, instructors, and professional groups from around the world, are offered nearly every day. The **Annual Summer Jazz on the Gulf** series runs June through September at the Naples Beach Hotel & Golf Club (tel. 941/261–2222).

Tour 1: Fort Myers and North

Fort Myers gets its nickname, the City of Palms, from the hundreds of towering royal palms that inventor Thomas Edison had planted along the main residential street, McGregor Boulevard, on which his winter estate stood. Edison's idea caught on, and there are now more than 2,000 royal palms on McGregor Boulevard alone, with countless more throughout the city. Other parts of the area hold allure for boaters, beachers, and backcountry explorers.

Arriving and Departing
By Plane

The Fort Myers/Naples area's airport is **Southwest Florida International Airport** (tel. 941/768–1000), about 12 miles southwest of Fort Myers. It is served by **Air Canada** (tel. 800/776–3000), **American** (tel. 800/433–7300), **Canadian Holidays** (tel. 800/282–4751), **Continental** (tel. 800/525–0280), **Delta** (tel. 800/221–1212), **Northwest** (tel. 800/225–2525), **TWA** (tel. 800/221–2000), **United** (tel. 800/241–6522), and **USAir** (tel. 800/428–4322).

A taxi ride from the airport to downtown Fort Myers costs about $30. Other transportation companies include **Aristocrat Super Mini-Van Service** (tel. 941/275–7228), **Personal Touch Limousines** (tel. 941/549–3643).

By Bus

Greyhound Lines (tel. 800/231–2222) has service to Fort Myers (2275 Cleveland Ave., tel. 941/334–5660). The fare for the 1½-hour trip from Naples to Fort Myers is $7.50 one-way.

By Car

I–75 and U.S. 41 run the length of the region. Once you cross the border into Florida from Georgia, it should take about five hours to reach Fort Myers.

Getting Around
By Bus

Affordable local transportation is provided by the **Lee County Transit System** (tel. 941/275–8726), which serves most of the county for a $1 flat fare.

By Car

I–75 and U.S. 41 are the main north–south thoroughfares in the region, from Port Charlotte and Punta Gorda down through Fort Myers. U.S. 41, also known as the Tamiami Trail, goes through downtown Fort Myers, where it is also called Cleveland Avenue. McGregor Boulevard (Route 867) is Fort Myers's premier road. Lined with thousands of royal palm trees and many large old houses, it passes what were the winter homes of Thomas Edison and Henry Ford.

Several east–west roads provide access to points away from the two major arteries. Pine Island–Bayshore Road (Route 78) leads from North Fort Myers through northern Cape Coral onto Pine Island. Route 74 stretches east from Punta Gorda to Babcock and Palmdale. From downtown Fort Myers, head east on Route 80, and take Route 31 north to Babcock or Route 29 northeast toward Palmdale.

Guided Tours

Classic Flight (tel. 941/939–7411) flies an open cockpit biplane for sightseeing tours of the Fort Myers area, leaving from the Fort Myers Jet Center (501 Danley Rd.).

Everglades Jungle Cruises (tel. 941/334–7474) explores the Caloosahatchee and Orange rivers of Lee County. From mid-November through mid-April, the *Capt. J.P.*, a stern paddle wheeler, conducts a variety of tours along the Caloosahatchee, departing from the Fort Myers Yacht Basin. Brunch, lunch, and dinner cruises are available, and a smaller boat takes manatee-watching trips. Also based at the yacht basin, *Quest* (tel. 941/334–0670) is a 34-foot classic sloop that runs two-hour morning and afternoon sails and sunset and moonlight champagne cruises. Call for reservations.

King Fisher Cruise Lines (tel. 941/639–0969) has half-day, full-day, Sunday brunch, and sunset cruises in Charlotte Harbor, Peace River, and the Intracoastal Waterway. Boats depart from Fishermen's Village, Punta Gorda.

Fort Myers

Lee County Visitor and Convention Bureau (2180 W. 1st St., Fort Myers 33901, tel. 941/338–3500). Greater Fort Myers Chamber of Commerce (2310 Edwards Dr., Box 9289, Fort Myers 33902, tel. 941/332–3624).

Though most people come to Lee County for the beaches, if you're in the mood for sightseeing, head for downtown Fort Myers. Drive ★ along palm-lined **McGregor Boulevard** from the Gulf into town; the most scenic stretch is north of College Parkway.

★ The city's premier attraction is **Thomas Edison's Winter Home,** containing a laboratory, botanical gardens, and a museum. A remarkable showpiece, the house was donated to the city by Edison's widow. As a result, the laboratory is just as Edison left it, not merely a reconstruction of how he might have left it. The property straddles McGregor Boulevard about a mile west of U.S. 41. The inventor spent his winters on the 14-acre estate, developing the phonograph and teletype, experimenting with rubber, and planting some 600 species of plants from those collected throughout the world. Next door is **Mangoes,** the winter home of the inventor's longtime friend, automaker Henry Ford. *2350 McGregor Blvd., tel. 941/334–3614. Combined admission to Edison home and Mangoes: $10 adults, $5 children 6–12. Tours Mon.–Sat. 9–4, Sun. noon–4; closed Thanksgiving, Dec. 25.*

A few blocks east, just off Dr. Martin Luther King Jr. Boulevard, is the **Fort Myers Historical Museum,** housed in a restored railroad depot. Displays depict the area's history dating back to 1200 BC, with special exhibits about boats and fishing and a collection of Ethel Cooper Glass. *2300 Peck St., tel. 941/332–5955. Admission: $2.50 adults, $1 children. Open Tues.–Sat. 9–4:30.*

Head northwest to Edwards Drive, which borders the Caloosahatchee River. The **Fort Myers Yacht Basin** has tour boats that offer sightseeing and luncheon cruises on the river (*see* Guided Tours, *above*). Alongside Edwards Drive, a string of shuffleboard courts weather heavy use on all but the hottest days, and adjacent to the courts is the Harborside Convention Center complex.

Park and walk a block in from the river to 1st Street, which runs through the heart of downtown Fort Myers. Stroll past the shops and have lunch at one of several eateries, including **Casa De Guerrero** (2225 1st St., tel. 813/332–4674) and **April's** (2269 1st St., tel. 941/337–4004).

Getting away from downtown, the **Nature Center and Planetarium of Lee County** offers frequently changing exhibits on wildlife, fossils, and Florida's native animals and habitats. Rustic boardwalks lead through subtropical wetlands, an aviary, and a Seminole Indian village. There are snake and alligator demonstrations several times

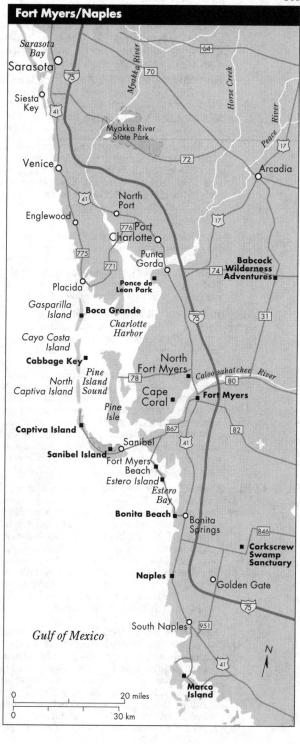

Fort Myers/Naples

Sarasota Bay
Sarasota
I-75
41
Siesta Key
41

Myakka River
70
64
Horse Creek
Peace River
17

Myakka River State Park
72
Arcadia
17

Venice
41

North Port
776
Port Charlotte
17

Englewood
775

Punta Gorda
74
Babcock Wilderness Adventures

Placida
771
Ponce de Leon Park
I-75
31

Gasparilla Island
Boca Grande
Charlotte Harbor

Cayo Costa Island
Cabbage Key

North Fort Myers
Caloosahatchee River
80

North Captiva Island
Pine Island Sound
78
Cape Coral
Fort Myers

Pine Isle
867
82

Captiva Island
Sanibel
41

Sanibel Island
Fort Myers Beach
Estero Island

Estero Bay

Bonita Beach
Bonita Springs
846
Corkscrew Swamp Sanctuary

Naples
Golden Gate

Gulf of Mexico

South Naples
951
I-75

N

41

Marco Island

0 — 20 miles
0 — 30 km

daily. The planetarium offers star shows, laser-light shows, and Cinema-360 films. *3450 Ortiz Ave., tel. 941/275–3435. Nature center admission: $3 adults, $1.50 children 3–11; planetarium admission: $3 adults, $2 children under 12. Nature center open Mon.–Sat. 9–5, Sun. 11–5; planetarium open Thurs.–Sun. 9–5.*

Sun Harvest Citrus offers free guided tours of its citrus-packing house from November through May. Visitors learn the history of the Florida citrus industry while watching fruit get squeezed into juice at a rate of 500 gallons per hour. *Six Mile Cypress and Metro Pkwys., tel. 800/743–1480. Tours Mon.–Sat. at 10, 1, 3.*

ECHO (Educational Concerns for Hunger Organization) is a small, active nonprofit group striving to solve the world's hunger problems. The group offers tours of its 5-acre demonstration farm, which feature collections of tropical food plants, simulated rain forests, and fish farming. *17430 Durrance Rd., North Fort Myers, tel. 941/543–3246. Admission free. Tours Tues., Fri., Sat. at 10 AM or by appointment.*

Eden Vineyards Winery and Park opened to the public in 1989 and claims to be the southernmost bonded winery in the United States. The family-owned vineyard offers tours, tastings, picnics, and tram rides. *10.2 mi east of I–75 on Rte. 80, tel. 941/728–9463. Admission: $2.50 ages 13 and over; complimentary tasting. Reservations needed for groups of 10 or more. Open daily 11–5 (last tour 3:30).*

Budget Lodging

$$ **Best Western Robert E. Lee Motor Inn.** On the other side of the Caloosahatchee River but only a mile from downtown Fort Myers and the Edison home, this motel has spacious rooms, with patios or balconies overlooking the river. *6611 U.S. 41 N, North Fort Myers 33903, tel. 941/997–5511 or 800/528–1234, fax 941/656–6962. 108 rooms. Facilities: lounge, pool, dock. AE, DC, MC, V.*

$$ **Comfort Suites.** This two-story motel is about 5 miles from downtown, but it's close to the airport and the price is right. Rooms are adequately furnished, and, because all rooms have a refrigerator, microwave, and coffeemaker, you can save money by doing your own light cooking. Rooms also have VCRs, and there's a video rental library on the premises. *13651 Indian Paint La., 33912, tel. 941/768–0005, fax 941/768–5458. 65 rooms. Facilities: lounge, pool, exercise room. AE, DC, MC, V.*

Budget Dining

$$ ★ **Prawnbroker Restaurant and Fish Market.** Its ads urge you to scratch and sniff. There is no odor, says the ad, because fresh fish does not have one. What there is is an abundance of reasonably priced seafood seemingly just plucked from Gulf waters, plus some selections for landlubbers. This place is almost always crowded, for good reasons. *13451 McGregor Blvd., tel. 941/489–2226. Reservations accepted. Dress: casual. AE, MC, V. No lunch.*

$$ **The Veranda.** Within a sprawling turn-of-the-century home is served an imaginative assortment of American regional cuisine. This is a popular place for business and government bigwigs. *2122 2nd St., tel. 941/332–2065. Reservations accepted. Dress: casual. AE, DC, MC, V.*

$ ★ **Mel's Diner.** During peak hours you have to wait for a table, but it's worth it at this '50s-style diner, which serves real mashed potatoes, homemade soups, spicy chili, and blue-plate specials. For dessert, try the popular mile-high pie. *4820 Cleveland Ave., tel. 941/275–7850. No reservations. Dress: casual. No credit cards.*

$ **Mill Bakery, Eatery, and Brewery.** Homemade beer is just one of the draws at this popular spot. People flock here to dine on freshly baked breads, pizzas, deli-style stacked sandwiches, and prime rib. *11491 S. Cleveland Ave., tel. 941/939–2739. No reservations. Dress: casual. AE, MC, V.*

$ **Woody's Bar-B-Q.** A no-frills barbecue pit, Woody's features chicken, ribs, and beef in copious amounts at bargain-basement prices.

13101 N. Cleveland Ave. (U.S. 41), North Fort Myers, tel. 941/997–1424. No reservations. Dress: casual. AE, MC, V.

¢ **Ballengers.** With a Florida-style metal roof outside and bright beach murals inside, this seafood restaurant is busy year-round. It offers many specials, including such fresh Gulf fish as pompano and grouper, and in the summer, you can order all-you-can-eat peel-and-eat shrimp for $9.95. On Sundays, there's a breakfast buffet in summer and a champagne brunch in winter, both special treats. *Summerlin Rd. and San Carlos Blvd., tel. 941/466–2626. Reservations accepted. Dress: casual but neat. AE, MC, V.*

¢ **Miami Connection.** If you hunger for choice chopped liver, lean but
★ tender corned beef, and a chewy bagel, this kosher-style deli can fill the bill. The sandwiches are huge. It is, as the local restaurant critic aptly said, "the real McCohen." *11506 Cleveland Ave., tel. 941/936–3811. No reservations. Dress: casual. No credit cards. No dinner.*

Shopping for Historic downtown **1st Street** has been renovated and features
Bargains charming restaurants and stores as well as street musicians and artists. **Sanibel Factory Outlets** (McGregor Blvd. and Summerlin Rd.) has 35 brand-name outlets, including Dexter, Van Heusen, Maidenform, and Corning/Revere. Though it's somewhat tacky and strictly for tourists, the **Shell Factory** (2787 N. Tamiami Trail, North Fort Myers, tel. 941/995–2141) claims to have the world's largest display of seashells and coral. Just east of Fort Myers, **Fleamasters Fleamarket** (1¼ mi west of I–75 [Exit 23] on Rte. 82) features covered walkways and hundreds of vendors selling new and used items. It's open Friday–Sunday 8–4.

Participant The best choice for cycling in the area is the path along Summerlin
Sports Road. For rentals, try **Trikes & Bikes & Mowers** (3224 Fowler St.,
Biking tel. 941/936–4301).

Boating For sailing lessons or bareboat or captained sail cruises, contact **Fort Myers Yacht Charters** (Port Sanibel Yacht Club, South Fort Myers, tel. 941/466–1800) or **Southwest Florida Yachts** (3444 Marinatown La. NW, tel. 941/656–1339 or 800/262–7939).

Canoeing **Estero River Tackle and Canoe Outfitters** (20991 Tamiami Trail S, Estero, tel. 941/992–4050) has canoes and equipment for use on the meandering Estero River.

Fishing Party-boat outfits in the area include **Deebold's Marina** (1071 San Carlos Blvd., tel. 941/466–3525).

Golf Area courses include **Cypress Pines Country Club** (Lehigh Acres, tel. 941/369–8216), **Eastwood Golf Club** (tel. 941/275–4848), **Fort Myers Country Club** (tel. 941/936–2457), **Lochmoor Country Club** (North Fort Myers, tel. 941/995–0501), **Oxbow** (La Belle, tel. 941/334–3903), and **Wildcat Run** (Estero, tel. 941/936–7222).

Tennis The **Lochmoor Country Club** (3911 Orange Grove Blvd., North Fort Myers, tel. 941/995–0501) has courts.

Spectator Major-league teams offer exhibitions in this area in March and
Sports April, during their spring-training sojourns. For information call
Baseball 904/488–8347 or contact the individual teams: **Boston Red Sox** (2201 Edison Ave., tel. 941/334–4700) and **Minnesota Twins** (Lee County Sports Complex, 1410 Six Mile Cypress Pkwy., tel. 941/768–4278).

The Arts and The **Barbara B. Mann Performing Arts Hall** (8099 College Pkwy.
Nightlife SW, tel. 941/481–4849) hosts plays, concerts, musicals, and dance
The Arts programs. The **Broadway Palm Dinner Theater** (1380 Colonial Blvd., tel. 941/278–4422) serves up a buffet dinner along with some of Broadway's best comedies and musicals. Call for schedules for both.

Nightlife **Crystal Pistol Saloon** (Parkway Square Shopping Mall, tel. 941/482–7900) has country dancing every night but Sunday. Beginner lessons are Monday and Thursday, advanced lessons are Wednesday, and open dancing is Tuesday, Friday, and Saturday. **Edison's Electric**

Lounge (Holiday Inn, 13051 Bell Tower Dr., tel. 941/482–2900) plays Top-40 tunes, usually with live bands, every night but Monday. **Flashback's Bar and Grill** (2855 Colonial Blvd., tel. 941/275–4487) has country-dancing lessons Tuesday and Wednesday 7:30–8:30, followed by open dancing. Musicians play nightly at **Upstairs at Peter's** (2224 Bay St., tel. 941/332–2228). The music is usually blues, but once a week or so it's jazz.

Cape Coral

Seven miles from Fort Myers by water and 8½ miles by land, Cape Coral lies on the north bank of the Caloosahatchee River. Although it is still a popular retirement center, it's drawing an increasing number of younger residents, who are attracted by the area's affordability. Cape Coral makes a good base for vacationers, too, and has a few of its own family-oriented attractions.

Children's Science Center, a "please do touch" center, has rotating exhibits that include mazes, optical tricks, mind benders, dinosaurs, and brain twisters. *2915 Pine Island Rd., tel. 941/997–0012. Admission: $4 adults, $2 children 3–16. Open weekdays 9:30–4:30, Sat. and some Sun. noon–5.*

Sun Splash Family Waterpark features more than two dozen wet and dry attractions. *400 Santa Barbara Blvd., tel. 941/574–0557. Admission: $8.50 visitors over 48 inches, $6.50 children 3 and over but under 48 inches. Open mid-Mar.–May, Wed.–Fri. 11–5, weekends 10–5; June–Aug., Sun.–Wed. and Fri. 10–6, Thurs. and Sat. 10–9; Aug.–mid-Oct., weekends 10–5.*

Budget Lodging
$$ **Cape Coral Golf & Tennis Resort.** Oriented toward golf and tennis enthusiasts, this resort offers good value. The main clubhouse houses a reception area and the restaurant, whereas the 100 comfortably furnished rooms are in a nearby white two-story, motel-like building. Understated decor reflects the sporty atmosphere. *4003 Palm Tree Blvd., 33904, tel. 941/542–3191, fax 941/542–4694. 100 rooms. Facilities: restaurant, lounge, pool, driving range, golf, tennis, baby-sitting. AE, DC, MC, V.*

$$ **Quality Inn.** Conveniently located in downtown Cape Coral near parks, beaches, restaurants, and malls, this motel offers no-smoking and wheelchair-accessible rooms with complimentary breakfast and newspaper. Pets are permitted. *1538 Cape Coral Pkwy., 33904, tel. 941/542–2121, fax 941/542–6319. 146 rooms. Facilities: pool. AE, DC, MC, V.*

Budget Dining
$$ **Cape Crab House.** Crabs are served Maryland-style—with mallet and pliers and heaped on a tablecloth of newspaper—or in the more refined atmosphere of a second dining room with linen tablecloths and a piano player. Although entrées go as high as $29.95, there is much to choose from in the $12–$15 range. *Coralwood Mall, Del Prado Blvd., tel. 941/574–2722. Reservations accepted. Dress: casual. AE, MC, V.*

$ **Siam Hut.** Thai music pings and twangs in the background while the dishes do the same to your taste buds. Get it fiery hot or extra mild. Specialties are *pad thai* (a mixture of noodles, crushed peanuts, chicken, shrimp, egg, bean sprouts, and scallions) and crispy Siam rolls (spring rolls stuffed with ground chicken, bean thread, and vegetables). *1873 Del Prado Blvd., Coral Pointe Shopping Center, tel. 941/772–3131. No reservations. Dress: casual. AE, MC, V.*

Golf **Cape Coral Golf & Tennis Resort** (4003 Palm Tree Blvd., tel. 941/542–7879) has a good 18-hole course, with lots of sand traps and affordable greens fees.

Punta Gorda and Port Charlotte

Charlotte County Chamber of Commerce (2702 Tamiami Trail, Port Charlotte 33950, tel. 941/627-2222).

Port Charlotte and Punta Gorda are both boating centers bordering Charlotte Harbor, the inlet formed where the Peace and Myakka rivers begin to empty into the Gulf. If you're not a boater yourself, you can still enjoy watching the activity at Punta Gorda's **Burnt Store Marina.**

The **Museum of Charlotte County** features many animal specimens from Africa and North America, plus dolls and shells. A variety of programs entertain and educate the kids. *260 W. Retta Esplanade, Punta Gorda, tel. 941/639-3777. Donations welcome. Open weekdays 8-5, Sat. 10-3.*

Budget Lodging $$ **Days Inn of Port Charlotte.** This modern mid-rise motel on Charlotte County's major business route is between Fort Myers and Sarasota and offers free coffee in the lobby, as well as a refrigerator in every room. *1941 Tamiami Trail, Port Charlotte 33948, tel. 941/627-8900, fax 941/743-8503. 126 rooms. Facilities: pool. AE, DC, MC, V.*

Budget Dining $$ **Salty's Harborside.** Although seafood is the specialty here, including some of the freshest mahimahi and grouper around, you'll also find grilled filet mignon, rosemary chicken, and various salads on the menu. The dining room looks out on Burnt Store Marina and Charlotte Harbor. There's a great seafood buffet every Wednesday evening for $15.95; entrées on other nights of the week run anywhere from $7 to $23. *Burnt Store Marina, Burnt Store Rd., Punta Gorda, tel. 941/639-3650. Reservations advised. Dress: casual. AE, DC, MC, V.*

$ **Olive Garden.** Like its sister restaurants elsewhere, this Olive Garden features everything from all the soup and salad you can eat for $4.95 to sandwiches, hamburgers, pastas, and veal and chicken dishes, most of which are priced in the $4–$12 range. Sunday brunch is a feast. *1341 Tamiami Trail, Port Charlotte, tel. 941/625-8807. No reservations. Dress: casual. AE, DC, MC, V.*

Beaches **Englewood Beach,** near the Charlotte-Sarasota county line, is popular with teenagers, although beachgoers of all ages frequent it. In addition to a wide and shell-littered beach, there are barbecue grills, picnic facilities, boat ramps, a fishing pier, and a playground.

Participant Sports **Fishing** If you're interested in going out on a party boat, get in contact with **King Fisher Charter** (Fishermen's Village, Punta Gorda, tel. 941/639-0969).

Golf Area links include **Burnt Store Marina Resort** (Punta Gorda, tel. 941/332-7334), **Deep Creek Golf Club** (Charlotte Harbor, tel. 941/625-6911), and **Sable Trace Golf and Country Club** (North Port, tel. 941/426-2804).

Tennis Visitors can play at **Port Charlotte Tennis Club** (22400 Gleneagles Terr., Port Charlotte, tel. 941/625-7222).

Spectator Sports **Baseball** Catch an exhibition game of the **Texas Rangers,** who have their spring-training base at Charlotte County Stadium (Rte. 776, Port Charlotte, tel. 941/625-9500).

Inland to Old Florida

To the north and east of Fort Myers, off Routes 31 and 74, are areas that still look much as they did centuries ago. One of the best examples is **Babcock Wilderness Adventures,** where 90-minute swamp buggy excursions take you through the Telegraph Cypress Swamp on the 90,000-acre Babcock Crescent B Ranch. Among the inhabitants you are likely to see are turkey, deer, bobcats, alligators, cows, and a herd of bison. Check local newspapers for great discount coupons. Reservations are a must. *Rte. 31, northeast of Fort Myers, tel. 941/489–3911. Admission: $15.95 adults, $7.95 children. 4 tours daily, weather permitting; closed Mon. May–Dec. and Sun.*

Due east is **Palmdale,** a speck of a town whose claim to dubious fame takes the form of two singular attractions, both on U.S. 27. You know you're approaching the **Cypress Knee Museum** when you see spindly hand-carved signs with such sayings as LADY, IF HE WON'T STOP, HIT HIM ON HEAD WITH A SHOE. In the museum are thousands of cypress knees—the knotty, gnarled protuberances that sprout mysteriously from the bases of some cypress trees and grow to resemble all manner of persons and things. Specimens resemble dogs, bears, ballet dancers' feet, an anteater, Joseph Stalin, and Franklin D. Roosevelt. There's also a beautiful, ¼-mile walk into a cypress swamp. *¼ mi north of Rte. 29 on U.S. 27, tel. 941/675–2951. Donations welcome. Open daily 8–sunset.*

Just over 3 miles southeast on U.S. 27, **Gatorama**'s 1,000 alligators and assorted crocodiles await visitors, smiling toothily. Visitors who want to take a good long gander at gators can get their fill here, where a variety of species and sizes cohabit. It's also a commercial gator farm, so you'll see how the "mink" of the leather trade is raised for profit. *3 mi south of Rte. 29 on U.S. 27, tel. 941/675–0623. Admission: $4.50 adults, $2.50 children 2–11. Open daily 8–6.*

Canoeing With several locations throughout Florida, **Canoe Outpost** (Rte. 7, Arcadia, tel. 941/494–1215) conducts all-day and overnight canoe trips; camping equipment is included. Up the Peace River, about 25 miles northeast of Fort Myers, **Canoe Safari** (3020 N.W. Rte. 661, Arcadia, tel. 941/494–7865) operates half- and full-day trips, plus overnighters including camping equipment.

Tour 2: The Barrier Islands

Most vacationers who come to Lee County spend their time on the beach, and some of the best places to do just that are on the many barrier islands along the county's Gulf shore. Estero Island contains Fort Myers Beach, a laid-back beach community favored by young singles and those who want to stay on the Gulf without paying the higher prices of resorty Sanibel or Captiva, a few miles farther off the coast. You won't be able to see most of Sanibel's houses, which are shielded by tall Australian pines, but the beaches and tranquil Gulf waters are readily accessible. There are also some smaller islands that deserve at least a day's exploration.

Arriving and The nearest airport is **Southwest Florida International Airport** (*see*
Departing Arriving and Departing by Plane *in* Tour 1, *above*), from which you
By Plane can take transportation, such as **Sanibel Island Limousine** (tel. 941/427–8888), to the islands. A taxi ride from the airport to Sanibel and Captiva costs about $30.

By Boat You have to take a boat to visit Cabbage Key. You can take a ferry from Pine Island or an all-day, afternoon, or dinner cruise from **South Seas Plantation** (Captiva, tel. 941/472–5111) or **Fishermen's Village** (Punta Gorda, tel. 941/639–0969).

By Car McGregor Boulevard (Route 867) runs southwest from Fort Myers over the Sanibel Causeway (round-trip toll $3) to Sanibel and Captiva. To reach Fort Myers Beach from Fort Myers, take San Carlos Boulevard southwest off of McGregor Boulevard or Summerlin Road to the causeway to Estero Island. To get to Boca Grande from U.S. 41 in Murdock (in northern Port Charlotte), head southwest on Route 776, then south on Route 771 into Placida, where a causeway (toll $3.25) runs out to the island.

Guided Tours **Boca Grande Seaplane Service** (tel. 941/964–0234) operates sight-seeing tours in the Charlotte Harbor area, leaving from 4th and Bayou streets, Boca Grande.

Adventure Sailing Charters (tel. 941/472–7532) offers captained, half- and full-day sailing cruises and sunset cruises for groups of six or fewer. Boats leave from South Seas Plantation on Captiva.

In Fort Myers Beach, the tall ship *Island Rover* (tel. 941/765–7447), a 72-foot schooner, takes morning, afternoon, and sunset sails in the Gulf of Mexico, leaving from Gulf Star Marina. Also on Estero Island, **Jammin' Sailboat Cruises** (tel. 941/463–3520) offers day and sunset cruises; call for reservations.

Gasparilla Island (Boca Grande)

Before roads to southwest Florida were even talked about, the wealthy boarded trains to get to the Gasparilla Inn, built in 1912 in Boca Grande, on Gasparilla Island. While condominiums and other forms of modern sprawl are creeping up on Gasparilla, much of Boca Grande looks as it has for a century or more. The mood is set by the old Florida homes, many made of wood, with wide, inviting verandas and wicker rocking chairs. Gasparilla's old railroad bed is now dedicated to bicycles—an easy and pleasant way to see the island. The island's general sleepy ambience is disrupted only in the spring, when tarpon fishermen descend with a vengeance on Boca Grande Pass, considered among the best tarpon-fishing spots in the world.

Cabbage Key

Cabbage Key sits at Marker 60 on the Intracoastal Waterway. Atop an ancient Calusa Indian shell mound on Cabbage Key is the friendly six-room **Cabbage Key Inn,** built by novelist and playwright Mary Roberts Rinehart in 1938. Now the inn also offers several guest cottages, a marina, and a dining room that is papered in thousands of dollar bills, signed and posted by patrons over the years.

Sanibel and Captiva Islands

Sanibel–Captiva Chamber of Commerce (Causeway Rd., Sanibel 33957, tel. 941/472–1080).

Sanibel and Captiva islands are a 3-mile toll causeway away from the mainland, but the trip is worth it, especially for avid shell collectors and nature enthusiasts. Sanibel's beaches are rated among the best shelling grounds in the world. For the choicest pickings, get there as the tide is going out or just after a storm.

At the southern end of **Sanibel Island** is **Old Lighthouse Beach,** where a historic wooden lighthouse still stands. There's ample parking and lots of Gulf-front beach space.

★ Heading north on Sanibel, on the way to Captiva, explore the **J. N. "Ding" Darling National Wildlife Refuge**—by car, foot, bicycle, canoe, or a specially designed open-air tram with a naturalist on board. The 5,030-acre refuge, which occupies about a third of the island, is home to raccoons, otters, alligators, and numerous exotic birds, such as roseate spoonbills, egrets, ospreys, and herons. Footpaths, winding canoe trails, and the 5-mile, dirt Wildlife Drive wander through sea grape, wax and salt myrtles, red mangrove, sabal palms, and other flora native to Florida. An observation tower along the road is a prime bird-watching site, especially in the early morning and just before dusk. *Refuge: tel. 941/472–1100. Admission: $4 per car or $15 for a duck stamp (which covers all national wildlife refuges), $1 for pedestrians and bicyclists. Wildlife Drive open Sat. and Mon.–Thurs. 7–5:45. Visitor center open daily 9–5. Tram: Tar-*

pon Bay Recreation Center, tel. 941/472–8900. Fare: $6.75 adults, $3.50 children. Runs daily.

★ An additional treat on the island is the new **Bailey-Matthews Shell Museum,** which opened in spring 1995. The centerpiece, a 6-foot revolving globe, shows visitors where in the world the museum's shells are found. More than a million shells are in the museum's archives, as are thousands of 35-millimeter slides. *3075 Sanibel–Captiva Rd., tel. 941/395–2233. Admission: $3. Open Tues.–Sun. 10–4.*

Captiva Island is mostly privately developed. The road follows the west shore along the beach and travels through the South Seas Plantation to a pretty and popular beach on the northern tip.

Budget Lodging
$$
★
Beachview Cottages. These little cottages, painted light gray, house efficiencies and one- and two-bedroom apartments. Though quite modest, they have an appealing beachy quality and are right on a great shelling beach. Efficiencies are $100 in season and $80 off-season; a two-bedroom duplex is a bargain for this area at $150 off-season. Units are on the small side but do have kitchens, and screened-in porches are a nice touch. There's even a sundeck on the beach. *3325 W. Gulf Dr., Sanibel Island 33957, tel. 941/472–1202. 22 units. Facilities: grills, pool, beach. D, MC, V.*

Splurge
'Tween Waters Inn. Situated at the narrowest part of beautiful Captiva Island, this turn-of-the-century resort offers both Gulf- and bay-front accommodations and still retains much of its original architectural charm. Choose from cottages, apartments, and motel rooms. In the summer a one-room cottage in the middle of the complex, with a queen-size bed and private bath but no water view, may be had for $85. It's worth a splurge in season—when cottages begin at $145 per night. Also on the property are a full-service marina with boat rentals and three restaurants, including the Old Captiva House and the Canoe Club, a waterfront pizzeria. *Box 249, Captiva Island 33924, tel. 941/472–5161 or 800/223–5865. 125 units. Facilities: 3 restaurants, lounge, pool, 3 lighted tennis courts, boating. D, MC, V.*

Budget Dining
$$
Lighthouse Cafe. Near Sanibel's historic lighthouse, this café is an ideal stop after a bike ride or for late sleepers, since breakfast is served all day. Luncheon and dinner menus are also available, however. The ocean frittata, an open-face omelet with seafood, is a favorite; served until 3 PM, it's only $5.95. *362 Periwinkle Way S, Sanibel Island, tel. 941/472–0303. No reservations. Dress: casual. MC, V. Closed 3–5 PM.*

$$
★
McT's Shrimphouse and Tavern. McT's is lively and informal and features a host of fresh seafood specialties, including numerous oyster and mussel appetizers, shrimp prepared all kinds of ways, and all-you-can-eat shrimp and crab. Landlubbers will enjoy the black bean soup, prime rib, and blackened chicken. There's always a dessert du jour, but most people end up choosing the Sanibel mud pie, a delicious concoction of Oreo cookies and other sinful items. *1523 Periwinkle Way, Sanibel Island, tel. 941/472–3161. No reservations. Dress: casual. AE, DC, MC, V.*

$
Grandma Dot's. Located at the Sanibel Marina, this seaside saloon features a menu of fresh seafood, grilled chicken breasts, sandwiches, and burgers. There is also a children's menu. Open seven days a week from 11:30 until 8, Grandma Dot's attracts a crowd at lunchtime. *634 N. Yachtsman Dr., Sanibel Island, tel. 941/472–8138. No reservations. Dress: casual. MC, V.*

Beaches
Bowman's Beach is mainly a family beach on Sanibel's northwest end. **Gulfside Park,** off Casa Ybel Road, is a lesser-known and less-populated beach, ideal for those who seek solitude and do not require facilities.

Participant Sports	Sanibel Island's well-maintained and extensive bike path runs throughout the island but away from traffic, providing a safe route and time to reflect on the waterways and wildlife you'll encounter. Rent bikes at **Finnimore's Cycle Shop** (2353 Periwinkle Way, Sanibel, tel. 941/472–5577), **Tarpon Bay Marina** (900 Tarpon Bay Rd., Sanibel, tel. 941/472–8900), or **Jim's Bike & Scooter Rental** (11534 Andy Rosse La., Captiva, tel. 941/472–1296).
Biking	
Boating	**Boat House of Sanibel** (Sanibel Marina, tel. 941/472–2531) rents powerboats.
Canoeing	**Tarpon Bay Marina** (*see* Biking, *above*) has canoes and equipment for exploring the waters of Sanibel's J. N. "Ding" Darling National Wildlife Refuge.
Golf and Tennis	A premier resort for these sports is the **Dunes** (949 Sand Castle Rd., Sanibel Island, tel. 941/472–2535 for golf or 941/472–3522 for tennis).

Estero Island (Fort Myers Beach)

Estero Island, otherwise known as Fort Myers Beach, is actually 18 miles from downtown Fort Myers. The big draw is, not surprisingly, the beach, which is frequented by families and young singles. It can be reached by numerous public accesses and is for the most part lined with houses, condominiums, and hotels, so you're never far from civilization. The shore slopes gradually into the usually tranquil and warm Gulf waters, providing a safe swimming area for children.

The marina at the north end of the island is the starting point for much boating activity, including sunset cruises, sightseeing cruises, and deep-sea fishing. Route 865 runs down the center of Estero Island and then leads across a small causeway to the **Carl E. Johnson Recreation Area,** consisting of two islands (connected by yet another causeway) that are entirely reserved for recreation. Here you'll find areas for boating, beaching, and fishing.

Budget Lodging $$	**Mariner's Lodge.** It's a mile and a half to the beach, but this two-story harborside lodging yields nice views of sailboats docked at the marina. Rooms are average in size but well kept, and the prices are a bargain; 18 of the units have small kitchens, so you can do your own cooking. *17990 San Carlos Blvd., 33931, tel. 941/466–9700. 34 rooms. Facilities: pool, playground. MC, V.*
Camping	**Indian Creek Park** (17340 San Carlos Blvd., tel. 941/466–6060), close to the Gulf beaches, has some spots for RVs, but pop-up campers and tents are not allowed. Daily rates for lake-view spaces are $25 for two adults (no credit cards); weekly and monthly rates are also available.
Budget Dining $$	**Mucky Duck.** There are two restaurants by this name—one a waterfront spot on Captiva Island, the other a slightly more formal restaurant in Fort Myers Beach. Both are moderately priced—though it is possible to eat here for less than $20—and both concentrate on fresh, well-prepared seafood. The bacon-wrapped barbecued shrimp is a popular dish. *2500 Estero Blvd., tel. 941/463–5519; Andy Rosse La., Captiva, tel. 941/472–3434. Reservations for large parties only. Dress: casual. MC, V.*
$$ ★	**Snug Harbor.** You can watch boats coming and going whether you sit inside or out at this dockside restaurant set on stilts above the water. The secret of its success is the absolutely fresh seafood, courtesy of the restaurant's private fishing fleet. This place is a favorite of year-round residents and seasonal visitors alike. The most expensive entrée is $21, the cheapest is $9.95, and there are many for about $15. *645 San Carlos Blvd., tel. 941/463–4343. No reservations. Dress: casual. MC, V.*

¢ **Dusseldorfs on the Beach.** Good inexpensive homemade specials are the draw here. In fact, the highest priced item on the menu is $6.59, not counting a specialty German beer for $7.10, including the stein, which you keep. There are 127 other brands of beer to choose from as well as such unabashedly German dishes as sausage and sauerkraut, Reuben sandwiches, and a German-style pizza. Happy hours, live entertainment, and dancing make this a fun spot for hanging out on the beach; the outdoor porch, bright with flower boxes, is a pleasant place to sit in winter. *1113 Estero Blvd., tel. 941/463–5251. No reservations. Dress: casual. MC, V.*

Beaches **Lynn Hall Memorial Park** (Estero Blvd.) is in the more commercial northern part of Fort Myers Beach. Singles and teens can be found playing in the gentle surf or sunning and socializing on shore. A number of nightspots and restaurants are within easy walking distance, and a free fishing pier adjoins the public beach. Facilities include picnic tables, barbecue grills, playground equipment, and a bathhouse with rest rooms. The beach is open 7 AM–10 PM; lifeguards are on duty 10 AM–5:45 PM.

Participant For those interested in fishing or just boating, **Getaway Bait and**
Sports **Boat Rental** (1091 San Carlos Blvd., tel. 941/466–3200) rents motor-
Fishing boats and fishing equipment and sells bait.

Golf Golf can be had at **Bay Beach Club Executive Golf Course** (tel. 941/463–2064).

Tennis **Bay Beach Racquet Club** (120 Lenell St., tel. 941/463–4473) has courts.

Tour 3: Naples Area

Naples is a mix of old world and new wealth. Here you can still appreciate the magnificent natural beauty of a bygone era while taking in some of the most lush tropical landscaping on earth. Shoppers can make serious inroads in their disposable cash along 3rd Street South and 5th Avenue South in Olde Naples, and the number of golf courses per capita here is the highest in the world. Culture is alive, too: A 1,200-seat performing arts hall attracts world-class performers, and the town is the west-coast home of the Miami City Ballet.

Naples is also the centerpiece of a fertile agricultural area. Much of the U.S. winter vegetable crop is grown here, and there are an increasing number of citrus groves. Roadside fruit and vegetable stands sell this bounty everywhere—excellent produce at affordable prices.

In general, however, Naples is not the most affordable destination in southwest Florida, so you may want to stay elsewhere and just drive over for a day. If you want to stay here, try to come in summer, during the off-season, when hotel rates drop considerably. Though the weather will be hot, proximity to the beach should make it quite bearable.

Arriving and **Southwest Florida International Airport** (*see* Arriving and Depart-
Departing ing by Plane *in* Tour 1, *above*) is 25 miles north of Naples, and cab
By Plane fare into town is about $60. The **Naples Airport** (tel. 941/643–6875), a small facility just east of downtown Naples, is served by **American Eagle** (tel. 800/433–7300), **Comair** (tel. 800/282–3424), and **USAir Express** (tel. 800/428–4322). Commercial shuttle service between this airport and Naples is generally $10–$25 per person. Call **Naples Taxi** (tel. 941/643–2148) or, to get to nearby Marco Island, try **Marco Transportation, Inc.** (tel. 941/394–2257).

By Bus **Greyhound Lines** (tel. 800/231–2222) has service to Naples (2669 Davis Blvd., tel. 941/774–5660). The fare for the 1½-hour trip from Fort Myers to Naples is $7.50 one-way.

By Car I–75 spans the region from north to south. It should take about six hours to reach Naples from the Georgia border, about an hour from Fort Myers. Alligator Alley, a section of I–75, is a two-lane toll road (75¢ at each end) that runs from Fort Lauderdale through the Everglades to Naples, bringing travelers from the east coast. Count on two hours between Naples and Fort Lauderdale.

Getting The Tamiami Trail (U.S. 41) goes through downtown Naples, where Around it's called 9th Avenue. Bonita Springs is about 15 miles north of Na- By Car ples via either I–75 or U.S. 41. To reach Marco Island, take U.S. 41 south from Naples for 7 miles to Belle Meade, where Route 951 heads southwest to the island's causeway.

Guided Tours **Naples Trolley Tours** (tel. 941/262–7300) offers five 1¾-hour narrated tours daily, covering more than 100 points of interest. Tickets are $9 for adults and $4 for children under 12, and you can get off and reboard at no extra cost throughout the day. **Dalis Charter** (tel. 941/262–4545) conducts half-day fishing and sightseeing trips. The boat is docked at Old Marine Market Place at Tin City (1200 5th Ave. S).

Naples

Naples Area Chamber of Commerce (3620 N. Tamiami Trail, Naples 33940, tel. 941/262–6141).

★ To get a feel for what this part of Florida was like before civil engineers began draining the swamps, stop at the **Corkscrew Swamp Sanctuary,** northeast of Naples. The National Audubon Society manages the 11,000-acre tract to help protect 500-year-old trees and endangered birds, such as wood storks, which often nest high in the bald cypress. Visitors taking the 1¾-mile self-guided tour along the boardwalk may glimpse alligators, graceful wading birds, and unusual air plants that cling to the sides of trees. *16 mi east of I–75 on Rte. 846, tel. 941/657–3771. Admission: $6.50 adults, $3 children 6–18. Open Dec.–Apr., daily 7–5; May–Nov., daily 8–5.*

From Corkscrew Swamp Sanctuary, take Route 846 back to I–75 and head south toward the center of Naples. At the next exit, take Pine Ridge Road (Route 896) west to the **Teddy Bear Museum of Naples.** Built by oil heiress and area resident Frances Pew Hayes, the $2 million museum houses more than 1,500 teddy bears. *2511 Pine Ridge Rd., tel. 941/598–2711. Admission: $5 adults, $3 students and senior citizens, $2 children 4–12. Open Wed.–Sat. 10–5, Sun. 1–5.*

For some real wildlife, head for **Jungle Larry's Zoological Park.** Continue west on Pine Ridge Road to U.S. 41. Turn left and drive south, past Golden Gate Parkway (Route 886), until you see the big sign on the left for Jungle Larry's. Originally a botanical garden planted in the early 1900s, the 52-acre junglelike park now houses exotic wildlife. For a safari, take the boat ride out to the island where the primates live. Kids will enjoy the petting zoo. *1590 Goodlette Rd., tel. 941/262–5409. Admission: $10.95 adults, $6.95 children 3–15. Open Dec.–Apr., daily 9:30–5:30; May–Nov., Tues.–Sun. 9:30–5:30.*

If you're ready for a little shopping, take U.S. 41 south, cross Central Avenue, and turn right on 5th Avenue South, which is lined with upscale shops. Next turn left onto 3rd Street South, and at 12th Avenue South, you reach the beginning of the shopping area called ★ **Olde Naples** (and perhaps the end of your rope). It's not as confusing as it sounds, however. Downtown Naples is laid out in a grid, with streets running north–south and avenues running east–west. Tree-lined streets and promenades make this an attractive place to get out of your car and walk around.

Naples covers a large area. Much of it runs down a peninsula, cut off from the rest of the mainland by Naples Bay. First-time visitors mistakenly look for the city docks along the Gulf, but the docks, along with a marina, shops, and restaurants, are clustered along Naples's bay shore at the east end of 12th Avenue South.

Merriman's Wharf (1200 5th Ave. S, tel. 941/261–1811), in the Old Marine Market Place, is a good bet for a drink or a seafood lunch—either along the dock or indoors in air-conditioned comfort.

Antique-car enthusiasts should head to the **Collier Automotive Museum,** where you can see 75 antique and classic sports cars, including Gary Cooper's 1935 Duesenberg SSJ. Sometimes a traveling exhibit of Rolls-Royces comes to visit. *2500 S. Horseshoe Dr., Collier Park of Commerce, off Airport-Pulling Rd., tel. 941/643–5252. Admission: $6 adults, $3 children 5–12. Open Dec.–Apr., daily 10–5; May–Nov., Tues.–Sat. 10–5.*

The T-shape **Naples Fishing Pier** (12th Ave. S), extending 600 feet into the Gulf (and not to be confused with the bay-side city docks), is said to be the most photographed pier anywhere. It's a perfect spot for viewing spectacular sunsets as well as pelicans diving for their dinner. Bait, a snack bar, rest rooms, and showers are available.

Budget Lodging

$$ **Comfort Inn.** One of the more attractive chain motels along busy U.S. 41, this four-floor, pink-and-white stucco lodging on the banks of the Gordon River is centrally located—a 20-minute walk from the beaches. Rooms are clean, and a bountiful breakfast (everything but bacon and eggs) is served every morning in a bright lounge. *1221 5th Ave. S, 33940, tel. 941/649–5800 or 800/221–2222, fax 941/649–0523. 100 rooms. Facilities: lounge, pool. AE, D, DC, MC, V.*

$$
★ **Stoney's Courtyard Inn.** A long-established Naples institution, Stoney's has a great location—2 miles from downtown and within walking distance of the beach. Cheerfully managed, clean, and with good-size rooms, it centers on a landscaped courtyard. For the area, it's a real bargain. *2630 N. Tamiami Trail, 33940, tel. 941/261–3870 or 800/432–3870. 72 rooms, 4 suites. Facilities: pool. AE, D, MC, V.*

Budget Dining

$$ **Chef's Garden.** A focus on new American cuisine has consistently won this restaurant awards over the past decade. House favorites include grilled portobello mushrooms, veal tenderloin, roast duck, seared filet mignon, and whiskey-marinated grilled chicken. Lighter lunch fare includes black bean soup, chicken and grape salad, and spinach and fresh mango salad with toasted cashews and honey vinaigrette. The less formal Truffles bistro, upstairs, features creative sandwiches, pastas, and salads, plus tasty pastries to take out or eat in. *1300 3rd St. S, tel. 941/262–5500. Reservations advised. Jacket required during winter season. AE, D, DC, MC, V.*

$
★ **Busghetti Ristorante.** Despite the cutesy name and the very affordable prices, this eatery serves excellent Italian cuisine in an appealing, upscale setting. The menu includes a wide range of pastas, from traditional lasagna to "busghetti" with everything from gorgonzola to ratatouille. There are also many veal, steak, chicken, and seafood selections and a good wine list. (This is a younger sister to the Lakeside Inn's Busghetti Ristorante, an old Marco Island favorite.) *1181 3rd St. S, tel. 941/263–3667. Reservations accepted. Dress: casual but neat. AE, MC, V.*

$ **Carrabba's.** New to Naples but immediately popular is this dimly lit Italian spot whose atmosphere suggests a pricey menu. Just the opposite is true, however, as almost all entrées are $8–$14. Pizzas and pastas, such as fettuccine Alfredo and rigatoni with sweet peppers and sausage, hover at the low end, whereas sautéed shrimp with garlic butter and quail with *pancetta* (thinly sliced Italian bacon) and sage are on the high side. *4320 N. Tamiami Trail, tel. 941/643–7727. No reservations. Dress: casual. AE, MC, V. No lunch.*

$ **Old Naples Pub.** From Robinson Court, walk up a few stairs to this comfortable pub, where from 11 AM to midnight (kitchen closes at 11:30) you can sample from 20 kinds of beer and the not-so-traditional pub menu. It encompasses fish-and-chips, burgers, bratwurst, pizza, and light salads as well as a good selection of snacks: nachos, fries smothered in chili, and cheese-stuffed, deep-fried jalapeños. There's piano entertainment Monday through Saturday. *255 13th Ave. S, tel. 941/649–8200. No reservations. Dress: casual. AE, MC, V.*

¢ **Backstage Tap & Grill.** Spotlights hang overhead and playbills and posters cover the walls, adding to the backstage theme at this restaurant in the Waterside Shops at Pelican Bay. As at a New York theater district deli, there are jars of fresh, fat dill pickles set out on every table. The popular Steak 'n' Chips sirloin center cut, at $9.95, is the most expensive item offered. Most items are in the $3.50–$5.95 range. Choose from overstuffed club sandwiches, Caesar salad topped with grilled chicken or tuna, brats, quiche, and chili. *5535 N. Tamiami Trail, tel. 941/598–1300. Reservations advised. Dress: casual. AE, MC, V.*

Splurge **Cafe Chablis.** Sunday brunch at this Registry Resort eatery is sim-
★ ply outstanding. Table after table is laden with exquisitely prepared selections. At one you can choose waffles with fresh berries, cover French toast with tasty syrups, or order an omelet with anything in it. At another you'll find platters and platters of beautifully arranged, thinly sliced meats and triangles of imported cheeses; bowls of crisp greens and an array of fresh vegetables to create your own salad; baskets of irresistible breads; and plates of cold, fresh shrimp and crab legs. If you can, save room for a visit to the dessert table, covered with all kinds of fresh berries, miniature tarts, multilayered cakes, and flaky pastries filled with treats. It could be the best and most elegant brunch ever. Guests dress up for it, although very neat casual attire is acceptable. *475 Seagate Dr., tel. 941/597–3232. Reservations required. Dress: casual but neat. AE, DC, MC, V.*

Shopping for The largest shopping area is **Olde Naples,** with more than 100 shops
Bargains and a number of restaurants. Here shoppers stroll along broad, tree-lined walkways in an eight-block area bordered by Broad Avenue on the north and 4th Street South on the east. **Old Marine Market Place at Tin City** (1200 5th Ave. S), in a collection of former fishing shacks along Naples Bay, has 40 boutiques, artisans' studios, and souvenir shops offering everything from scrimshaw to Haitian art. The **Village on Venetian Bay** (Gulf Shore Blvd.) has more than 50 upscale shops built over the bay. The **Waterside Shops** (Pelican Bay) are built around an interior courtyard with a series of waterways. Anchored by a Saks Fifth Avenue boutique and Jacobson's Department Store, Waterside houses 50 shops and several eating places. **Coral Isle Factory Outlet Stores** (1920 Isle of Capri Rd.) offer discounts on such brand items as Bass shoes, Cannon sheets and towels, Mikasa crystal, and Dansk housewares.

Beaches **Clam Pass** (Seagate Dr.) is one of Naples's newest beach accesses. A 3,000-foot boardwalk winds through tropical mangroves to the beach.

Delnor-Wiggins Pass State Recreation Area (west end of 111th Ave. N, North Naples) is a well-maintained park of more than 100 acres. Along with sandy beaches, there are lifeguards, barbecue grills, picnic tables, a boat ramp, observation tower, rest rooms with wheelchair access, lots of parking, bathhouses, and showers. Fishing is best in Wiggins Pass at the north end of the park. Florida residents pay $1 for the driver and 50¢ per passenger, whereas out-of-state drivers pay $2, plus $1 per passenger. Boat launching costs $1. No alcohol is allowed.

Lowdermilk Park (Gulf Shore Blvd.) has more than 1,000 feet of beach, volleyball courts, a playground, rest rooms, showers, a pavilion, vending machines, and picnic tables. No alcoholic beverages or fires are permitted.

Participant Sports

Biking For rentals and tips on where to go for the best bicycling in the area, try the **Bicycle Shop** (813 Vanderbilt Beach Rd., tel. 941/566-3646).

Boating and Fishing **Deep Sea Charter Fishing** (Boat Haven, tel. 941/263-8171) operates party boats. **Port-O-Call** (550 Port-O-Call Way, tel. 941/774-0479) rents 16- to 25-foot powerboats. In addition, there are a number of small rental concessions at the **city docks.**

Golf Golfers can choose from **Hibiscus Country Club** (tel. 941/774-0088), **Lely Flamingo Island Club** (tel. 941/793-2223), and **Naples Beach Hotel & Golf Club** (tel. 941/261-2222).

Tennis You'll find courts at **Cambier Park** (775 8th Ave. S, tel. 941/434-4690) and **Forest Hills Racquet Club** (100 Forest Hills Blvd., tel. 941/774-2442).

The Arts and Nightlife

The Arts Naples is the cultural capital of this stretch of the coast. The **Naples Philharmonic Center for the Arts** (5833 Pelican Bay Blvd., tel. 941/597-1111) has two theaters and two art galleries offering a variety of plays, concerts, and exhibits year-round. It's home to the 80-piece Naples Philharmonic, which presents both classical and pop concerts. Halfway between U.S. 41 and I-75, the **Naples Dinner Theatre** (Immokalee Rd., tel. 941/597-6031) features professional companies performing mostly musicals and comedies, October-August; admission includes a candlelight buffet prepared by a French chef. The **Naples Players** (399 Goodlette Rd., tel. 941/263-7990) has winter and summer seasons; winter shows often sell out well in advance.

Nightlife The extremely casual **Backstage Tap & Grill** (*see* Budget Dining, *above*) has great jazz a few nights each week in addition to cheap eats. **Chef's Garden** (1300 3rd St. S, tel. 941/262-5500) is a quiet spot for jazz once or twice a week. Stop at the **Silver Dollar Saloon** (Gulf Gate Shopping Plaza, tel. 941/775-7011) for open country dancing and lessons Wednesday through Sunday evenings. **Witch's Brew** (4836 N. Tamiami Trail, tel. 941/261-4261) is a lively location for nightly entertainment. There's a happy hour weekdays 4-6 PM and an excellent menu featuring Continental cuisine. The upstairs lounge at Witch's Brew's sister restaurant, **Seawitch** (179 Commerce St., Vanderbilt Beach, tel. 941/566-1514), overlooks Vanderbilt Bay and is a relaxing spot for casual dining. Bands play Top-40 music here Tuesday through Sunday nights.

Bonita Springs and Bonita Beach

As you might expect, **Bonita Beach** lies on the Gulf and draws people mostly for the beach and water. Though the **Carl E. Johnson Recreation Area** (*see* Estero Island *in* Tour 2, *above*) lies on Lovers Key, the island south of Fort Myers Beach, the park entrance is here. Catch a tram to the island (tram fare and park admission: $1.50 adults, 75¢ children) for some shelling, bird-watching, fishing, canoeing, or just walking in an unspoiled setting. There are rest rooms, picnic tables, a snack bar, and showers.

Bonita Springs is inland and boasts the **Everglades Wonder Gardens,** which captures the flavor of untamed Florida with its exhibit of native wildlife and natural surroundings. *U.S. 41, tel. 941/992-2591. Admission: $8 adults, $4 children 3-12. Open daily 9-5.*

Beaches **Bonita Springs Public Beach** is 10 minutes from the I-75 exit at Bonita Beach Road, on the southern end of Bonita Beach. There are picnic tables, free parking, and nearby refreshment stands and shopping.

Participant Sports

Biking One source in the area for bicycle rentals and information is **Pop's Bicycles** (3685 Bonita Beach Rd., Bonita Springs, tel. 941/947-4442).

Golf **Pelican's Nest Golf Course** (Bonita Springs, tel. 941/947–4600) accommodates visitors.

Spectator You can watch dog racing year-round at the **Naples–Fort Myers Grey-**
Sports **hound Track** (10601 Bonita Beach Rd., Bonita Springs, tel. 941/992–
Dog Racing 2411).

Marco Island

South of Naples, the resort of Marco Island is linked to the mainland by a short causeway. High-rise condominiums and hotels line much of the waterfront, but many natural areas have been preserved, including the tiny fishing village of **Goodland,** at the south end of the island, where old Florida lives on.

Budget **Lakeside Inn.** Though it will never win any architectural awards and
Lodging it's not on the beach (it's about a mile away), this longtime inn is one
$$ of Marco Island's best values and does overlook a small lake. Com-
★ fortably furnished efficiencies and one-bedroom suites have kitch-
ens but are on the cozy side. An excellent, affordable Italian
restaurant, Busghetti Ristorante, is on the premises. *155 1st Ave.,*
33937, tel. 941/394–1161. 26 efficiencies, 12 suites. Facilities: res-
taurant, lake, pool, fishing. AE, MC, V.

Splurge **Marco Beach Hilton.** With fewer than 300 rooms and wisely appor-
★ tioned public areas, the Hilton is smaller than the other big-name
resorts in the area, and facilities tend to be a little less crowded. All
of the rooms in this 11-story beachfront hotel have private balconies
with unobstructed Gulf views, a sitting area, wet bar, and refrigera-
tor. Furnishings are cheerful and unobtrusive—the same can be
said about the staff. Though the lowest rate in season is $209, off-
season prices go down to $110! *560 S. Collier Blvd., 33937, tel. 941/*
394–5000 or 800/443–4550, fax 941/394–5251. 295 rooms. Facilities:
restaurant, lounges, pool, tennis, exercise room, beach,
windsurfing, boating. AE, D, DC, MC, V.

Budget Dining **Island Cafe.** This small, intimate European-style café specializes in
$$ seafood and Continental cuisine. Pompano is prepared in a multitude
★ of ways. *918 N. Collier Blvd., tel. 941/394–7578. Reservations ac-*
cepted. Dress: casual but neat. MC, V. No lunch.
$$ **Marco Lodge Waterfront Restaurant & Lounge.** Built in 1869, this is
Marco's oldest landmark. The tin-roofed, wood building is on the wa-
terfront; boats (up to 35 feet) tie up dockside, and you can dine on a
wide veranda overlooking the water. Fresh local seafood and Cajun
entrées are featured. One specialty is a wood bowl of blue crabs in
rich garlic butter. *1 Papaya St., Goodland, tel. 941/642–7227. Res-*
ervations advised. Dress: casual. AE, DC, MC, V.

Beaches **Tigertail Beach** is at the end of Hernando Drive, on the southwest-
ern side of the island. Singles and families congregate here. Facili-
ties include parking, a concession stand, a picnic area, sailboat
rentals, volleyball, rest rooms, and showers.

Participant Biking around the island is a great way to enjoy your surroundings.
Sports Rentals are available at **Scootertown** (855 Bald Eagle Dr., tel. 941/
Biking 394–8400).

Boating and For sailing lessons or bareboat or captained sail cruises, contact
Fishing **Marco Island Sea Excursions** (1281 Jamaica Rd., tel. 941/642–6400).
Sunshine Tours (tel. 941/642–5415) operates fishing charter boats.

10 The Panhandle

By Ann Hughes

Northwest Florida resident Ann Hughes is a former editor of Indiana Business *magazine and a contributing editor to other travel and trade publications.*

Northwest Florida is often called the "other Florida." It's much more like the Deep South than it is like the rest of the state. Magnolias, live oaks, and loblolly pines flourish here instead of palm trees, and houses in the historic districts of its older cities, such as Pensacola and Tallahassee, have colonnaded porticos and wrought-iron lace rather than the pink-stucco walls and red-tile roofs of south Florida. But there's another more significant difference: Its low season is during the winter, when most people are paying through the nose to visit south Florida. At this time of year, room rates in the Panhandle are one of the nation's best tourist bargains. In October and November, for example, a three-bedroom apartment with a fully equipped kitchen in an ocean-side high-rise may rent for 25% of what it would in summer. When high season winds down in south Florida, May through September, it picks up here, and prices tend to go up—but they're still nothing compared with high-season rates in the posh resort areas farther down the peninsula. Discount airfares are sometimes available into Pensacola, the region's major airport; otherwise you might have to pay top dollar for a commuter flight into one of the lesser air terminals.

The region has other sobriquets. This little green corner of Florida that snuggles up to Alabama is also known as the Emerald Coast (even the water sparkles green). Because its uncrowded state parks, unpretentious lifestyle, and fabulous beaches are still relatively undiscovered, it's also called "Florida's best-kept secret." It's a land of superlatives: It has the biggest military installation in the Western Hemisphere (Eglin Air Force Base), arguably the oldest settlement in the state (Pensacola, claiming a founding date of 1559), and the most prolific fishing village in the world (Destin). Thanks to restrictions against commercial development imposed by Eglin AFB and the Gulf Islands National Seashore, the Emerald Coast has been able to maintain several hundred linear miles of unspoiled beaches. A 1994 study by the University of Maryland's Laboratory for Coastal Research named Grayton Beach, St. Andrews State Recreation Area, St. Joseph Peninsula State Park, and St. George Island among the top 10 beaches in the United States.

The result is that the Panhandle is an ideal tourist destination. It has resorts that out-glitz the Gold Coast's and campgrounds where possums invite themselves to lunch. History lovers can have a field day wandering in Pensacola, visiting an archaeological dig, or stepping back to the era of tintypes and gaslight in downtown DeFuniak Springs. For sports enthusiasts, there's a different golf course or tennis court for each day of the week, and for those who decide to spend time with nature, there's a world of hunting, canoeing, biking, and hiking. And anything that happens on water happens here: surfing, scuba diving, and plenty of fishing, whether from a deep-sea charter boat or the end of a pier. If you're a senior citizen touring on a retiree's tight budget and aren't looking for a lot of swinging nightlife, you can feel the sun on your back and the warm sand on your feet, people-watch from a bench in a mall, or just sit on a veranda gazing out at the Gulf and the orange sun sinking slowly in the west.

Panhandle Basics

Budget Lodging

Though accommodations here run the gamut, budget-conscious travelers can get the best deal from popular-priced franchise motels without restaurants. As a rule of thumb, the closer you are to the water, the more you can expect to pay. Because tourism is its economic mainstay, Destin has the widest range of options, including several modest Gulf-side motels. For a family group or senior citizens on an extended stay, a condominium rental with kitchen facilities can be the cheapest way to go. Most accept walk-ins, but to avoid any unpleasant surprises, make a reservation through a property management service, such as **Abbott Realty Services, Inc.** (35000 Emerald Coast Pkwy., Destin 32541, tel. 904/837–4853 or 800/336–4853) or **Emerald Coast Vacation Rentals** (621 U.S. 98E, Destin 32541, tel. 904/837–6100).

Budget Dining

Year-round, restaurant prices are reasonable here, though they're slightly lower in Eglin Air Force Base's sphere of influence than they are in the areas dominated by the beaches. Be on the lookout in newspapers and on billboards for dining discounts. Especially during the off-season, many eating establishments promote two-for-one meal deals and early-bird specials to drum up business. When the sun goes down, the restaurant tab goes up, so it sometimes pays to eat heavy at noon (most places offer square-meal luncheon specials) and light at night. And for those who elect to eat in instead of out, all the major supermarket chains have deli departments where you can pick up the essentials for a picnic or a simple room-cooked supper.

Several outstanding restaurants in the Panhandle specialize in exotic ethnic cuisine, but to be on the safe side, stick with seafood, simply because it's so fresh and because most local chefs know how to cook it right.

Bargain Shopping

The sizable cities of Pensacola, Fort Walton Beach, Panama City, and Tallahassee have enclosed malls aimed to local folks rather than to visitors, but there are a handful of factory outlets, with merchandise as much as 70% off regular price, that do cater to tourists.

Beaches

If surf and sand are your raisons d'être, make your vacation headquarters in Destin or Panama City, where beach-lolling is the prime activity and there are lots of ancillary facilities, from video arcades and minigolf to souvenir shops. If you prefer your beach undeveloped, try the Gulf Islands National Seashore (tel. 904/934–2600), near Pensacola. It has 10 unspoiled miles of white, sugary sand, and just about all of it's free.

Sports and the Outdoors

Opportunities for all kinds of sports abound in this area. Base a golfing vacation in Fort Walton Beach, which is equidistant from courses near Pensacola and Destin. If you want a more strenuous, outdoorsy sport that enables you to explore deep into the backwoods and backwaters, such as canoeing or hiking, Milton or Crestview might be your best headquarters.

Biking   The terrain in the Panhandle is generally flat to rolling, making for good bicycling. **Emerald Coast Cyclists** (tel. 904/864–7166) is a ride and activity hot line.

Boating   The Emerald Coast is accessible to yacht captains and sailors from the Intracoastal Waterway, which turns inland at Apalachicola and runs through the bays around Panama City, along Choctawhatchee Bay, and into Santa Rosa Sound.

Fishing   Northwest Florida's catches range from pompano, snapper, marlin, and grouper in the salt water of the Gulf of Mexico to bass, catfish, and bluegill in the freshwater of the region's rivers and streams.

Hiking   Serious hikers should give first consideration to Florida's state parks, many of which, such as **Blackwater River State Park** and **Fred Gannon Rocky Bayou, Falling Waters,** and **Grayton Beach state recreation areas,** maintain trails specifically for jogging and hiking. You can obtain additional information on the park of your choice through the **Florida Department of Natural Resources** (3900 Commonwealth Blvd., Tallahassee 32399-3000, tel. 904/488–9872).

The Arts and Nightlife

There are several first-rate community theaters in the Panhandle, but their presentations aren't all that frequent. The same holds true for the Panhandle's symphonies and ballet companies. The **Northwest Florida Ballet** (101 S.E. Chicago Ave., Fort Walton Beach, tel. 904/664–7787), for example, has a repertoire of the classics and performs in communities throughout the Panhandle. Northwest Florida's nightlife falls on the scale somewhere between uptown Manhattan supper clubs and Las Vegas–style dinner shows. There are hot spots pitched specifically to night owls, but some of the family restaurants also take on a different character when the sun goes down.

Festivals

Crestview's **Old Spanish Trail Festival,** the first weekend in May, is essentially a street carnival with a local historical twist. In June, the landing of a pirate ship kicks off the **Billy Bowlegs Festival** in Fort Walton Beach, and a treasure hunt and a Surrender of the City ceremony initiate the two-week-long **Fiesta of Five Flags** celebration in Pensacola. A monthlong event in October, the **Destin Fishing Rodeo** offers anglers a chance to compete for more than $100,000 in cash and prizes. Also in October, the **Boggy Bayou Mullet Festival** draws more than 100,000 people to Niceville and Valparaiso for big-name entertainment and a seafood extravaganza.

Tour 1: Pensacola Area

A combination of big-city amenities and small-town charm makes Pensacola a city that stands on its own. It's the focal point of a metro area with something for every taste, from ultrasophisticated resorts with golf courses and gourmet restaurants to unspoiled beaches where sugar-white sand crunches underfoot like snow on a subzero night.

Since its founding Pensacola has come under the control of five nations, earning this fine, old southern city its nickname: the City of Five Flags. Spanish conquistadors, under the command of Don Tristan de Luna, made landfall on the shores of Pensacola Bay in 1559, but, discouraged by a succession of destructive tropical storms and dissension in the ranks, de Luna abandoned the settlement two years after its founding. In 1698, the Spanish once again established a fort at the site, and during the early 18th century, control jockeyed back and forth between the Spanish, the French, and the British. Finally, in 1819, Pensacola passed into U.S. hands, though during the Civil War it was governed by the Confederate States of America.

Arriving and Departing
By Plane A new, state-of-the-art terminal opened in 1991 at the **Pensacola Regional Airport,** which is served by **American Eagle** (tel. 800/433–7300), **ASA–The Delta Connection** and **Comair** (tel. 800/282–3424), **Continental** (tel. 800/525–0280), **Delta** (tel. 800/221–1212), **Northwest Airlink** (tel. 800/225–2525), and **USAir** and **USAir Express** (tel. 800/428–4322). A trip from the airport via **Yellow Cab** (tel. 904/433–1143) costs about $9 to downtown and $17 to Pensacola Beach. Several lodging properties offer complimentary shuttle service to and from the airport.

By Bus **Greyhound Lines** (tel. 800/231–2222) provides intercity service to Pensacola (505 W. Burgess Rd., tel. 904/476–4800). Buses to Fort Walton Beach and points east depart several times daily, and one-way fares are $9 to Fort Walton Beach, $19.50 to Panama City, $10 to Crestview, $15.50 to DeFuniak Springs, and $36 to Tallahassee.

By Car East–west routes into Pensacola are I–10, U.S. 90 (Mobile Highway), and U.S. 98. The best way to access it from the north is via U.S. 29 (Pensacola Boulevard/Palafox Highway); if you're on I–65, take the Flomaton exit to U.S. 29. To reach downtown from I–10, take I–110 to Exit 4.

By Train **Amtrak** (tel. 800/872–7245) serves Pensacola (980 E. Heinburg St.) on its Los Angeles to Jacksonville route.

Getting Around
By Bus **Escambia County Area Transit** (1515 Fairfield Dr., tel. 904/436–9383) provides bus service throughout the city. The fare to any part of town is $1, plus 10¢ for a transfer.

Guided Tours **Right This Way, Pensacola** (Box 18647, Pensacola 32523, tel. 904/432–4079 or 800/688–8253) tailors tours to individual interests, by reservation.

Pensacola

Pensacola Convention & Visitor Information Center (1401 E. Gregory St., Pensacola 32501, tel. 904/434–1234 or 800/874–1234).

Historic Pensacola consists of three distinct districts—Seville, Palafox, and North Hill—though they are easy to explore as a unit. Stroll down streets mapped out by the British and renamed by the Spanish, such as Cervantes, Palafox, Intendencia, and Tarragona. You can pick up maps of self-guided tours at the Pensacola Convention & Visitor Information Center (*see above*), located at the foot of the Three-Mile Bridge over Pensacola Bay. Be warned, though, that

The Panhandle

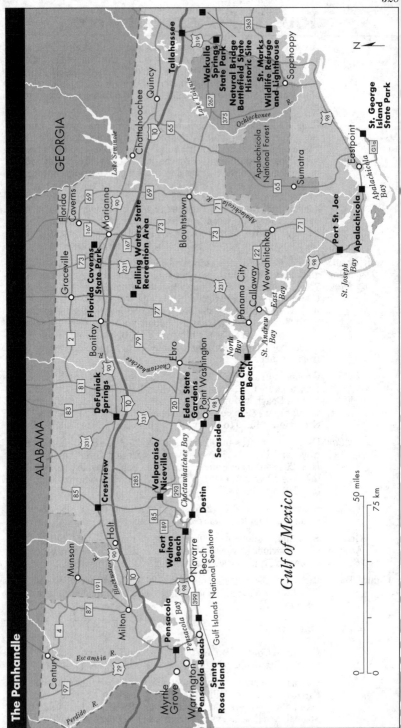

GEORGIA

ALABAMA

Gulf of Mexico

Century

Myrtle Grove
Warrington
Pensacola
Pensacola Beach
Santa Rosa Island
Gulf Islands National Seashore

Milton
Munson
Holt
Navarre Beach
Fort Walton Beach
Valparaiso/Niceville
Crestview
Destin

DeFuniak Springs
Bonifay
Graceville
Florida Caverns
Marianna
Falling Waters State Recreation Area
Florida Caverns State Park

Eden State Gardens
Point Washington
Seaside
Ebro
Blountstown

Panama City Beach
Panama City
Callaway
Wewahitchka
St. Andrew Bay
North Bay
East Bay

Port St. Joe
Apalachicola
St. Joseph Bay
Apalachicola Bay
Eastpoint
St. George Island State Park

Sumatra
Apalachicola National Forest

Chattahoochee
Quincy
Tallahassee
Wakulla Springs State Park
Natural Bridge Battlefield State Historic Site
St. Marks Wildlife Refuge and Lighthouse
Sopchoppy

Lake Seminole
Lake Talquin
Ochlockonee R.
Apalachicola R.
Choctawhatchee R.
Choctawhatchee Bay
Blackwater R.
Escambia R.
Perdido R.
Pensacola Bay

N

50 miles
75 km

it's best to stick to the beaten path; Pensacola is a port town and can get rough around the edges, especially at night.

As you approach from the east, the first historic district you reach is **Seville**—the site of Pensacola's first permanent Spanish colonial settlement. Its center is Seville Square, a live oak–shaded park bounded by Alcaniz, Adams, Zaragoza, and Government streets. Park your car and roam these brick streets past honeymoon cottages and bay-front homes. Many of the buildings have been restored and converted into restaurants, commercial offices, and shops where you can buy anything from wind socks to designer clothes.

★ Continue west to Palafox Street, the main stem of the **Palafox Historic District.** This was the commercial and government hub of old Pensacola. On Palafox Place, note the Spanish Renaissance–style Saenger Theater, Pensacola's old movie palace, and the Bear Block, a former wholesale grocery with wrought-iron balconies that are a legacy from Pensacola's Creole past. Nearby, on Palafox between Government and Zaragoza streets, is a statue of Andrew Jackson that commemorates the formal transfer of Florida from Spain to the United States in 1821.

Palafox Street also funnels into the **North Hill Preservation District,** where Pensacola's affluent families, many made rich during the turn-of-the-century timber boom, built their homes on ground where British and Spanish fortresses once stood. To this day residents occasionally unearth cannonballs while digging in their gardens. North Hill occupies 50 blocks that consist of more than 500 homes in Queen Anne, neoclassical, Tudor revival, and Mediterranean architectural styles. Take a drive through this community, but remember that these are private residences not open to the public. Places of general interest in the district include the 1902 Spanish mission–style Christ Episcopal Church; Lee Square, where a 50-foot-high obelisk stands as Pensacola's tribute to the Old Confederacy; and Fort George, an undeveloped parcel of land at the site of the largest of three forts built by the British in 1778.

From the North Hill district, go south on Palafox Street to Zaragoza Street to reach the **Historic Pensacola Village,** a cluster of museums between Adams and Tarragona. The **Museum of Industry,** housed in a late-19th-century warehouse, hosts permanent exhibits dedicated to the lumber, maritime, and shipping industries—once mainstays of Pensacola's economy. A reproduction of a 19th-century streetscape is displayed in the **Museum of Commerce,** and the city's historical archives are kept in the **Pensacola Historical Museum**— what was once Old Christ Church, one of Florida's oldest churches. Also in the village are the **Julee Cottage Museum of Black History, Dorr House, Lavalle House,** and **Quina House.** *Historic Pensacola Village, tel. 904/444–8905. Admission free. Open Mon.–Sat. 10–4. Pensacola Historical Museum, tel. 904/433–1559. Admission: $2 adults, $1.50 senior citizens and military, $1 children 4–16. Open Mon.–Sat. 9–4:30.*

In the days of the horse-drawn paddy wagon, the two-story Mission-revival building housing the **Pensacola Museum of Art** served as the city jail. *407 S. Jefferson St., tel. 904/432–5682. Admission free. Open Tues.–Fri. 10–5, Sat. 10–4, Sun. 1–4.*

Pensacola's old City Hall, built in 1908, has been refurbished and re-opened as the **T. T. Wentworth, Jr., Florida State Museum.** The Wentworth displays some 150,000 artifacts ranging from Civil War weaponry to bottle caps. Representing more than 80 years of collecting, the assemblage is worth $5 million. *333 S. Jefferson St., tel. 904/444–8905. Admission: $5.50 adults, $2.25 children 4–16. Open Mon.–Sat. 10–4.*

From the port, take Palafox Street to U.S. 98 (Garden Street) to reach the **Pensacola Naval Air Station** (tel. 904/452–2311). Established in 1914, it is the nation's oldest such facility. On display in the **National Museum of Naval Aviation** (tel. 904/452–9304) are more than 100 aircraft that have played an important role in naval aviation history. Among them are the NC-4, which in 1919 became the first plane to cross the Atlantic by air; the famous World War II fighter, the F6F *Hellcat*; and the *Skylab Command Module*. Thirty-minute films on aeronautical topics are shown June–August. Call for details.

The National Park Service–protected **Fort Barrancas,** established during the Civil War, is also located at the NAS. Nearby are picnic tables and a ½-mile woodland nature trail. *Navy Blvd., tel. 904/455–5167. Admission free. Open Oct.–Apr., Wed.–Sun. 10:30–4; May–Sept., daily 9:30–5.*

Budget Lodging
$$

New World Inn. This is Pensacola's little hotel, where celebrities who visit the city are likely to stay. Photos of dozens of the inn's famous guests (Lucille Ball, Shirley Jones, Charles Kuralt) hang behind the front desk in the lobby. The exquisite furnishings in the guest rooms take their inspiration from the five periods of Pensacola's past: French or Spanish provincial, early American, antebellum, and Queen Anne. The baths are handsomely appointed with brass fixtures and outfitted with oversize towels. *600 S. Palafox St., 32501, tel. 904/432–4111, fax 904/435–8939. 14 rooms, 2 suites. Facilities: restaurant, lounge. AE, DC, MC, V.*

$

Ramada Inn North. All the guest rooms at this hotel have been renovated. Suites have game tables and entertainment centers; some have whirlpools. This Ramada is conveniently located close to the airport. *6550 Pensacola Blvd., 32505, tel. 904/477–0711 or 800/272–6232, fax 904/477–0711, ext. 602. 106 rooms. Facilities: restaurant, lounge, pool, airport shuttle. AE, D, DC, MC, V.*

¢

Days Inn. If you arrive without a car, consider this generic motel in the midst of downtown Pensacola. From here, you can walk to museums, theaters, and the historic districts. Several suites have been especially designed for those traveling with children. *710 N. Palafox St., 32501, tel. 904/438–4922 or 800/325–2525. 156 rooms. Facilities: restaurant, pool. AE, DC, MC, V.*

Budget Dining
$$
★

Jamie's. Dining here is like spending the evening in the antiques-filled parlor of a fine, old southern home. If a visit to Florida has you oystered and shrimped out, try the fresh fillet of grilled Norwegian salmon, served on a bed of spinach and topped with soy sauce and an orange glacé. The wine list boasts more than 200 labels. *424 E. Zaragoza St., tel. 904/434–2911. Reservations advised. Dress: casual. AE, MC, V. Closed Sun. No lunch Mon.*

$

McGuire's Irish Pub. Drink beer brewed right on the premises in copper and oaken casks, and eat your corned beef and cabbage while an Irish tenor croons in the background. Located in an old firehouse, the pub is replete with antiques, moose heads, Irish Tiffany lamps, and Erin-go-bragh memorabilia. More than 98,000 dollar bills signed and dated by the pub's patrons flutter from the ceiling. McGuire's also has a House Mug Club with more than 5,000 personalized mugs. The waitresses are chatty and aim to please. Menu items run from kosher-style sandwiches to chili con carne to pecan pie. *600 E. Gregory St., tel. 904/433–6789. No reservations. Dress: casual. AE, D, DC, MC, V.*

$

Mesquite Charlie's. Stop by for the best gol' darn steaks east (or west) of the Mississippi. You can watch 'em broil over mesquite charcoal in a pit just inside the door. Got a hankerin' for sumpin' else? Try baby back ribs barbecued with a tangy house sauce. No neckties allowed—"We cut 'em off." There's a special menu for little cowpokes. *5901 N. W St., tel 905/434–0498. Reservations advised. Dress: casual. AE, MC, V. No lunch.*

$ **Napoleon Bakery.** This local spot is French-y, right down to the accents of the wait staff. Mingle with workaday Pensacolans over a Continental breakfast of just-baked pastries or a lunch of quiche, croissants, and, of course, napoleons served tearoom-style with fresh-brewed, aromatic coffees. *101 S. Jefferson St., tel. 904/434–9701. No reservations. Dress: casual. MC, V. Closed Sun. No dinner.*

$ **Perry's Seafood House & Gazebo Oyster Bar.** This vintage 1858 house, known locally as "the big red house," was a residence, a tollhouse, and a fraternity house before Perry purchased it in 1968 and turned it into a restaurant. Native fish are broiled with Perry's secret sauce and garlic butter, or baked and topped with garlic sauce and lemon juice. The menu varies depending on weather conditions, fishing-boat schedules, and the catch of the day. *2140 S. Barrancas Ave., tel. 904/434–2995. No reservations. Dress: casual. AE, DC, MC, V. Closed Mon.*

Shopping for Bargains **Cordova Mall** (511 N. 9th Ave.), anchored by four department stores, has specialty shops and a food court with 20 fast-food outlets. **Harbourtown Shopping Village** (913 Gulf Breeze Pkwy., Gulf Breeze) has trendy shops and the ambience of a wharf-side New England village.

Fishing If your idea of fishing is dropping a line off the end of a pier, try the **Old Pensacola Bay Bridge.** Bait and tackle are available at **Penny's Sporting Goods** (1800 Pace Blvd., tel. 904/438–9633).

The Arts and Nightlife **The Arts** The **Saenger Theatre** (118 S. Palafox St., tel. 904/444–7686) books top-name entertainment and Broadway touring shows and hosts an annual five-concert series by the **Pensacola Symphony Orchestra** (tel. 904/435–2533). The **Pensacola Little Theatre** (186 N. Palafox St., tel. 904/432–8621) presents plays and musicals during a season that runs from fall through spring.

Nightlife After dark, **McGuire's Irish Pub** (*see* Budget Dining, *above*) welcomes anyone of legal drinking age, particularly those of Irish descent. If you don't like crowds, stay away from McGuire's on Friday night and nights when Notre Dame games are televised. **Mesquite Charlie's** (*see* Budget Dining, *above*) offers good ol' country music and all the trappings of a Wild West saloon. **Seville Quarter** (130 E. Government St., tel. 904/434–6211) has seven fabulous bars featuring music from disco to Dixieland; it's Pensacola's equivalent to the New Orleans French Quarter.

Santa Rosa Island

Back on U.S. 98, head south over the 3-mile-long Pensacola Bay Bridge to Santa Rosa Island, a spit of duneland jutting into the Gulf of Mexico and part of the Gulf Islands National Seashore. This barrier island offers more than seascapes and water sports: It's also a must-see for bird-watchers. Since 1971 more than 280 species of birds, from the common loon to the majestic osprey, have been spotted here. Two caveats for visitors: "Leave nothing behind but your footprints," and "Don't pick the sea oats" (natural grasses that help keep the dunes intact). At the island's western tip is **Fort Pickens National Park,** which has a museum, nature exhibits, aquariums, and a large campground. Fort Pickens's most famous resident was imprisoned Apache Indian chief Geronimo, who was reportedly fairly well liked by his captors. *Ranger station at Ft. Pickens Rd., tel. 904/934–2635. Admission: $4 per car. Open daily 8:30–sunset.*

To the east along Route 399 is **Navarre Beach,** a small, relaxed community without the traffic and congestion common to most resort areas.

Budget Lodging
$$

Holiday Inn/Pensacola Beach. Inside, the lobby is simple, with potted plants, floral arrangements, and a coral-color decor. Outside, there's 1,500 feet of private beach. From the ninth-floor Penthouse Lounge, you can watch the goings-on in the Gulf, especially when the setting sun turns the western sky to lavender and orange. *165 Ft. Pickens Rd., Pensacola Beach 32561, tel. 904/932–5361 or 800/ 465–4329, fax 904/932–7121. 150 rooms. Facilities: restaurant, lounge, pool, tennis courts, game room. AE, D, DC, MC, V.*

Beaches

Pensacola Beach (tel. 904/932–2258) is the first place you'll come to after crossing the Bob Sikes Bridge from Gulf Breeze. Beachcombers and sunbathers, sailboarders and sailors keep things going at a fever pitch in and out of the water. Ten miles east is the **Santa Rosa Day Use Area,** another popular beach.

Participant Sports
Biking

Often touted as one of the best bike routes in the country, Route 399 between Pensacola Beach and Navarre Beach enables you to pedal for 18 miles without losing sight of the water. Biking on the crystal sand itself is tough, however.

Fishing

For fishing off a dock, try the **Navarre Fishing Pier** (8577 Gulf Blvd., Navarre Beach, tel. 904/939–5658), which offers everything you need for an outing, including a restaurant, bait and tackle shop, and beach chairs and umbrellas for rent. If you'd prefer trolling offshore in the deep-blue waters of the Gulf of Mexico, consider a deep-sea fishing charter. Though $350 for half a day aboard a charter boat sounds steep, most boats carry several passengers, which reduces the price per person considerably if you're traveling with a group. You can arrange for fishing charters at **Lafitte Cove Marina** (1010 Ft. Pickens Rd., Pensacola Beach, tel. 904/932–9241) and at the **Moorings Marina** (655 Pensacola Beach Blvd., Pensacola Beach, tel. 904/ 932–0305).

Tour 2: Choctawhatchee Bay

The communities clustered at the western end of Choctawhatchee Bay are all a little different. Fort Walton Beach, site of Eglin Air Force Base, is the largest urban area on the Emerald Coast. Though the military is the town's main source of income, tourism runs a close second. Destin, Fort Walton Beach's neighbor, is known worldwide as a fishing center. The twin cities of Valparaiso and Niceville, across the bay, are much sleepier, but since the 1993 opening of the Mid-Bay Bridge, which linked them to the beaches of South Walton County, the cities have come into their own as reasonably priced vacation destinations.

Arriving and Departing
By Plane

Fort Walton Beach/Eglin AFB Airport/Okaloosa County Air Terminal is served by American Eagle, ASA–The Delta Connection, **Northwest** (tel. 800/225–2525), and USAir Express. A ride from the Fort Walton Beach airport via **Checker Cab** (tel. 904/244–4491) costs $10 to Fort Walton Beach, Niceville, or Valparaiso and $18 to Destin. **A-1 Taxi** (tel. 904/678–2424) charges $12 to Fort Walton Beach and $20 to Destin.

By Bus

Greyhound Lines (tel. 800/231–2222) has connections from Fort Walton Beach (101 S.E. Perry St., tel. 904/243–1940) to Pensacola and Panama City. There is no direct service to Destin.

By Car

U.S. 98 is the direct east–west route into Fort Walton Beach and Destin. From I–10, you can pick up Route 85 at the Crestview exit and head south to Valparaiso, Niceville, and Route 123, a bypass to Fort Walton Beach that reconnects with Route 85. If you're coming from the east on I–10, take U.S. 331 south to U.S. 98, and head west to Destin.

Getting Destin is less than 10 miles east of Fort Walton Beach on U.S. 98.
Around Valparaiso and Niceville lie 12 miles inland from Fort Walton Beach
By Car via Route 85. From Destin, go east to Route 293, north over the
bridge, and west on Route 20.

Fort Walton Beach

Fort Walton Beach Chamber of Commerce (34 S.E. Miracle Strip Pkwy., Fort Walton Beach 32548, tel. 904/244–8191).

Fort Walton Beach dates from the Civil War. Patriots loyal to the Confederate cause organized Walton's Guard (named in honor of Colonel George Walton, one-time acting territorial governor of West Florida) and made camp on Santa Rosa Sound, later known as Camp Walton. In 1940, fewer than 90 people lived in Fort Walton Beach, but within a decade the city became a boom town, thanks to New Deal money for new roads and bridges and the development of Eglin Field during World War II. Today, Greater Fort Walton Beach has more than 78,000 residents.

Dominating Fort Walton Beach, huge **Eglin Air Force Base** (Rte. 85, tel. 904/882–3931) encompasses 728 square miles of land; it has 10 auxiliary fields (including Hurlburt and Duke fields) and a total of 21 runways. Jimmie Doolittle's Tokyo Raiders trained here, as did the Son Tay Raiders, a group that made a daring attempt to rescue American POWs from a North Vietnamese prison camp in 1970. Group tours of the base are given by special arrangement.

★ Just outside Eglin's main gate is the **Air Force Armament Museum,** with an uncluttered display of more than 5,000 articles of Air Force armament from World Wars I and II and the Korean and Vietnam wars. Included are uniforms, engines, weapons, aircraft, and flight simulators; larger craft such as transport planes and swept-wing jets are exhibited on the grounds outside the museum. A 32-minute movie about Eglin's history and its role in the development of armament is presented continuously throughout the day. *Rte. 85, Eglin Air Force Base, tel. 904/882–4062. Admission free. Open daily 9:30– 4:30; closed Thanksgiving, Dec. 25, Jan. 1.*

Kids especially enjoy the **Indian Temple Mound Museum,** on U.S. 98, where they can learn all about the prehistoric peoples who inhabited northwest Florida as long as 10,000 years ago. The funerary masks and weaponry on display are particularly fascinating. The museum is adjacent to the 600-year-old **National Historic Landmark Temple Mound,** a large earthwork built over salt water. *139 Miracle Strip Pkwy., tel. 904/243–6521. Admission: $2 adults, $1 children 5–17. Open Sept.–May, weekdays 11–4, Sat. 9–4; June–Aug., Mon.–Sat. 9–4.*

A 2-mile jaunt east on U.S. 98 will bring you to the **Gulfarium**—a great way to spend a few hours when bad weather drives you off the beach. The Gulfarium's main attraction is its "Living Sea" presentation, a 60,000-gallon tank that simulates conditions on the ocean bottom. There are performances by trained porpoises; sea lion shows; and marine life exhibits featuring seals, otters, and penguins. There's also an extensive gift shop where you can buy anything from conch shells and sand-dollar earrings to children's beach toys. *U.S. 98E, tel. 904/244–5169. Admission: $12 adults, $10 senior citizens, $8 children 4–11. Open May 15–Sept. 15, daily 9–6; Sept. 16–May 14, daily 9–4.*

Budget **Ramada Beach Resort.** The lobby and entrance present a slick look:
Lodging black marble and disco lights—and some locals feel it's too much like
$$ the Las Vegas strip. Activity here centers on a pool with a five-story grotto and a swim-through waterfall and on the 800-foot private beach. *U.S. 98E, 32548, tel. 904/243–9161, 800/874–8962, or 800/ 272–6232, fax 904/243–2391. 454 rooms. Facilities: 3 restaurants, 2*

lounges, pools, tennis courts, exercise room, beach. *AE, D, DC, MC, V.*

$$ Sheraton Inn. A sweeping driveway through an avenue of palms leading to a canopied entrance could beguile you into believing this resort is too rich for your blood. While not cut-rate, it's reasonable, considering what you get—sandy beaches, a courtyard with a Disneyland-like grotto, a spiffy lobby, and refined guest rooms that are constantly being brought up to snuff. Without leaving the property, you can enjoy dinner, dancing, and a moonlit walk beside the Gulf. *1325 Miracle Strip Pkwy., 32548, tel. 904/243–8116 or 800/874–8104, fax 904/244–3064. 154 rooms. Facilities: restaurant, lounge, pool, beach. AE, D, DC, MC, V.*

$ Aloha Village. Set among palm trees, this stucco-and-tile beachside motel, oriented to families and snowbirds, offers all the amenities the big places do, except for food and beverage service. Not to worry, though—its Okaloosa Island location is conveniently near restaurants and bars as well as all points of interest on the Fort Walton Beach amusement menu. Still, it's secluded enough to have a getaway feel. Though minisuites cost more than standard rooms, they have all-electric kitchens that let you make up the difference with savings on your food bill. When accompanied by their parents, youngsters 12 and under stay free. *866 Santa Rosa Blvd., 32548, tel. 904/243–3114 or 800/548–8552. 118 rooms. Facilities: pool, beach. AE, D, DC, MC, V.*

Budget Dining **Seagull.** In addition to an unobstructed view of Brooks Bridge and **$$** the sound, this waterside restaurant has a 400-foot dock for its **★** cruise-minded customers. Dimly lit and decorated with pictures from Fort Walton in the 1940s, it's a comfortable place to dine. Choose between no-frills steak and prime rib or fancier fare, such as fillet of snapper topped with almonds and Dijon mustard sauce. Things liven up a bit when the family business clears out and one of two bands starts playing soft-rock music. *U.S. 98E, by the Brooks Bridge, tel. 904/243–3413. Reservations accepted. Dress: casual. AE, D, DC, MC, V. No lunch.*

$ The Sound. Lean back and watch the action on Santa Rosa Sound from any seat in the house in this easygoing establishment where wood paneling and rattan fixtures make a happy marriage. The grouper del Rio (sauced with Dijon mayonnaise and topped with bread crumbs and Parmesan cheese) is touted, as is the prime rib. Let your appetite determine whether you order a junior or senior cut. A children's menu is available at lunch and dinner. Cap off an evening meal with a wedge of Key lime pie; then move over to the adjacent lounge for live jazz and blues. *108 S.W. Miracle Strip Pkwy., tel. 904/243–7772. Reservations accepted. Dress: casual. AE, D, DC, MC, V.*

$ Staff's. Sip a Tropical Depression or a rum-laced Squall Line while you wait to be served from a menu that's in the centerfold of a tabloid-size newspaper filled with snippets of local history, early photographs, and family memorabilia. Since 1931, people have been coming to this garage turned eatery for steaks broiled as you like them and such seafood dishes as freshly caught Florida lobster (steamed or broiled and stuffed) and char-grilled amberjack. The grand finale is a trip to the delectable dessert bar; try a generous wedge of cherry cheesecake. *24 S.E. Miracle Strip Pkwy, tel. 904/243–3482. Reservations accepted. Dress: casual. AE, D, MC, V.*

Shopping for There are four department stores in the **Santa Rosa Mall** (300 Mary **Bargains** Esther Cut-Off, Mary Esther), as well as 118 other shops and 15 bistro-style eateries. Manufacturer-owned and -operated stores in the **Manufacturer's Outlet Centers** (127 and 225 Miracle Strip Pkwy.) sell brand-name merchandise at low factory-to-you prices. You can get a discount on women's wear with such designer labels as Oleg

Cassini and Givenchy at **Designer's Merchandise for Ladies** (104 S.E. Perry St., tel. 904/244–9006).

Beaches **Eglin Reservation Beach** is situated on 5 miles of undeveloped military land, about 3 miles west of the Brooks Bridge. It's a favorite haunt of local teenagers and young singles.

John C. Beasley State Park is a seaside playground on Okaloosa Island, along U.S. 98 on the way to Destin. A boardwalk leads to the beach, where you'll find covered picnic tables, changing rooms, and freshwater showers. Lifeguards are on duty during the summer.

Participant Routes through Eglin AFB Reservation present cyclists with a few
Sports challenges; to ride there, you'll need a $3 permit, which may be ob-
Biking tained at the **Jackson Guard** (Rte. 85N, Niceville, tel. 904/882–4164). Rentals are available from **Bob's Schwinn Cycling & Fitness Center** (426 Mary Esther Cutoff, Mary Esther, tel. 904/243–5856).

Fishing The 1,261-foot **Okaloosa Island Pier** (1030 Miracle Strip Pkwy., tel. 904/244–1023) is lighted for night fishing and has rental gear available. Get your bait, tackle, and a fishing license at **Stewart's Outdoor Sports** (4 Eglin Pkwy., tel. 904/243–9443).

Golf **Fort Walton Beach Municipal Golf Course** (Rte. 189, tel. 904/862–3314) has 36 holes and is one of the state's finest public courses.

The Arts and **Okaloosa Symphony Orchestra** (tel. 904/244–3308) performs a series
Nightlife of concerts featuring guest artists at Rita Schaeffer Hall (38 S.W.
The Arts Robinwood Dr.). **Stage Crafters Community Theatre** (U.S. 98W, tel. 904/243–1102) stages four first-rate amateur productions a year at the Fort Walton Beach Civic Auditorium.

Nightlife Catch the action at **Cash's Faux Pas Lounge** (106 Santa Rosa Blvd., tel. 904/244–2274), where anything goes.

Destin

Destin Chamber of Commerce (1021 U.S. 98E, Destin 32541, tel. 904/837–6241 or 904/837–0087).

Destin lies on the other side of the strait that connects Choctawhatchee Bay with the Gulf of Mexico. It takes its name from its founder, Leonard A. Destin, a New London, Connecticut, sea captain who settled his family here sometime in the 1830s. For the next 100 years, Destin remained a sleepy little fishing village until the strait, or East Pass, was bridged in 1935. Then, recreational anglers discovered its white sands, blue-green waters, and the abundance of some of the most sought-after sport fish in the world. But you don't have to be the rod-and-reel type to love Destin. There's plenty to entertain the sand-pail set as well as senior citizens, and there are many gourmet restaurants.

Destin didn't get its nickname, "The World's Luckiest Fishing Village," in a public-relations campaign—it earned it. Beginners as well as dyed-in-the-wool fisherfolk will think they have died and gone to heaven here. Freshwater lakes and rivers teem with panfish, bass, and catfish; the brackish waters of Choctawhatchee Bay produce flounder, speckled trout, and redfish; and the salt water yields snapper, bluefish, tarpon, cobia, grouper, and marlin. More billfish are hauled in around Destin each year than in all other Gulf fishing ports combined.

Destin Fishing Museum has a dry aquarium, where lighting and sound effects create the sensation of being underwater. You can get the feeling of walking on a sandy bottom that's broken by coral reef and dotted with sponges. It's a good place for the marine enthusiast to get an overview of aquatic life in the Gulf of Mexico. *35 U.S. 98E, tel. 904/654–1011. Admission: $1 ages over 12. Open Tues.–Sat. noon–4, Sun. 1–4.*

To get an idea of the rampaging growth that's occurred in the Destin area, visit the **Old Destin Post Office Museum.** This tiny facility, a working post office until 1954, was adequate to serve the community's needs until that time. Its display of old photographs and office machines reflects the fishing-hamlet ambience of Old Destin. *Stahlman Ave., tel. 904/837–8572. Admission free. Open Wed. 1:30–4:30.*

Just off U.S. 98 about 8 miles east of Destin is the **Museum of the Sea and Indian.** Cassette players let you set your own pace at this funky tourist attraction, a Destin fixture for more than 30 years. It began with arrowheads and seashells from a private collection and has since been augmented with child-pleasing stuffed whales, killer sharks, and alligators. A haunted house and live zoo add to the fun. *4801 Beach Hwy., tel. 904/837–6625. Admission: $3.75 adults, $3.45 senior citizens, $2 children 5–16. Open May–Aug., daily 8–7; Sept.–Apr., daily 9–4.*

Budget Lodging

$$ **Holiday Inn.** Stay here, and you can lounge on the Gulf's sugar-white sands, get to a variety of golf courses with comparative ease, and walk to some of Destin's amusement-park attractions. Vaulted-ceiling common areas, jazzed up with skylights and greenery, are spacious and eye-pleasing. Although the standard motel appointments don't vary much from room to room, prices do, depending on the view. If you're content to overlook the parking lot instead of the Gulf, you can save $20 a night. *U.S. 98E, 32541, tel. 904/837–6181 or 800/465–4329, fax 904/837–1523. 230 rooms. Facilities: restaurant, lounge, 2 pools, exercise room, game room. AE, D, DC, MC, V.*

$$ **Summer Breeze.** White picket fences and porches or patios outside each unit make this condominium complex look like a summer place out of the Gay '90s. One-bedroom suites have fully equipped kitchens and can sleep up to six people in queen-size beds, sleeper sofas, or bunks. It's halfway between Destin and Sandestin and is across from a roadside park, which gives it a private and secluded feel. *2384 Old Hwy. 98, 32541, tel. 904/837–4853, 800/874–8914, or 800/336–4853, fax 904/837–5390. 36 units. Facilities: grill, pool, hot tub. AE, D, MC, V.*

$ **Village Inn of Destin.** This property, only minutes from the Gulf, was built in 1983 with families in mind. A variety of amenities, including entertainment, are provided to occupy each member of the family in some way. Rooms have serviceable dressers and queen- or king-size beds. *215 U.S. 98E, 32541, tel. 904/837–7413, fax 904/654–3394. 100 rooms. Facilities: pool. AE, D, DC, MC, V.*

Budget Dining

$$ **★** **Marina Cafe.** A harbor-view setting, impeccable service, and uptown ambience have earned this establishment a reputation as one of the finest dining experiences on the Emerald Coast. The decor's oceanic motif is expressed in shades of aqua, green, and sand accented with marine tapestries and sea sculptures. An up-to-the-minute menu gives diners a choice of classic Creole, Italian, or Pacific Rim cuisine. Try a regional specialty, such as the award-winning black pepper–crusted yellowfin tuna with braised spinach and spicy soy sauce, or grilled jumbo Gulf shrimp with Oriental vegetables and a topping of fiery-hot habanero-pepper sauce. The wine list is extensive. *404 U.S. 98E, tel. 904/837–7960. Reservations advised. Dress: casual but neat. AE, D, DC, MC, V. No lunch.*

$ **Captain Dave's on the Gulf.** This beachfront restaurant comprises three dining rooms: a glass-domed central room overlooking the Gulf; a sports room filled with bats, helmets, jerseys, autographed baseballs, and photographs of professional athletes; and a more intimate dining area with dim lights and potted plants. The hearty menu offers such seafood entrées as fillet of snapper sprinkled with crabmeat and covered with shrimp sauce and Parmesan cheese as well as a medley of broiled seafood served with celery, onions, bell peppers, and tomatoes and topped with black olives and mozzarella cheese. Children's plates are available. Dancing and live entertainment are featured in the downstairs lounge. *3796 Old Hwy. 98, tel. 904/837–2627. No reservations. Dress: casual. AE, MC, V. No lunch.*

$ **Flamingo Cafe.** This café serves up two different atmospheres. The black, white, and pink color scheme, with waiters and waitresses dressed in tuxedos with pink bow ties, screams nouveau, whereas the panoramic view of Destin harbor seen from every seat in the house, or from a table on the full-length porch outside, lends an airy, seaside feel. Chef's specialties include oysters *Bienville* (with shrimp, crabmeat, and Romano and Cheddar cheese topping) and triggerfish Napoleon (grilled, with marinated vegetables and pasta and topped with Louisiana crawfish cream). *14 U.S. 98E, tel. 904/837–0961. Reservations accepted. Dress: casual. AE, D, DC, MC, V.*

$ **Harbor Docks.** An unimposing gray clapboard building in front fans out into a series of dining areas behind, all within the sights and sounds of the fishing boats and Jet Skis in Destin Harbor. Chargrilled, sautéed, or poached fish include such regional favorites as snapper, cobia, and triggerfish, fresh from the restaurant's own wholesale market. Cap off a meal with a wedge of Key lime pie. *538 U.S. 98E, tel. 904/837–2506. Reservations accepted for large groups. Dress: casual. AE, D, DC, MC, V.*

Shopping for Bargains The **Market at Sandestin** (5494 U.S. 98E) is an elegant minimall with 28 upscale shops that peddle such wares as gourmet chocolates and designer clothes. Though the stuff tends to be pricey, shopkeepers are reluctant to carry over their high-fashion inventory, so at the end of the season, you can find good buys in the marked-down merchandise. **Silver Sands Factory Stores** (5021 U.S. 98E) is an upscale shopping center featuring more than 50 fashion-forward stores that offer goods at as much as 70% off retail.

Beaches **Crystal Beach Wayside Park** (tel. 904/837–6447) is a Gulf-side sanctuary located just 5 miles east of Destin and protected on each side by undeveloped state-owned land. **Henderson Beach State Recreation Area** (tel. 904/837–7550), just off U.S. 98 at the eastern edge of Destin, is a stretch of white sandy duneland that offers such improvements as two bathhouses with outdoor showers, six boardwalks, picnic tables, shelter houses, and grills.

Participant Sports
Boating You can rent powerboats for fishing, skiing, and snorkeling at **Baytowne Marina at Sandestin** (9300 U.S. 98W, Sandestin, tel. 904/267–7777). **Friendship Charter Sailing** (404 U.S. 98, tel. 904/837–2694) provides sailing instruction as well as rentals.

Fishing Though there's some fishing activity year-round, the season revs up big-time with the cobia run in March and slacks off around the middle of November. You can spend just about any amount on fishing—from renting a rowboat with an outboard motor to splurging on a deep-sea charter. When planning for the latter, be advised that rates are usually quoted by the day (about $550) or half day (about $350). Most boats carry several people, making the per-person cost lighter than it sounds. This is an immensely popular pastime, so there are boat charters aplenty. Among them are **Miller's Charter Services/***Barbi-Anne* (off U.S. 98 on the docks next to A.J.'s Restaurant, tel. 904/837–6059) and **East Pass Charters** (East Pass Marina, U.S. 98E, tel. 904/654–2022). Party boats that carry as many as 100 passengers at $35–$40 per head are the cheapest deep-sea option. Everything from a half-day fishing excursion to a dinner cruise is offered. Fishing lessons and fish storage are provided aboard the charter boat *Emmanuel* (U.S. 98E, tel. 904/837–6313), an ultranew, air-conditioned catamaran captained by Ben Marler, a descendent of one of Destin's pioneer families.

If all of the above sounds like it takes too much energy, consider casting a line from the 3,000-foot-long **Destin Catwalk,** along the East Pass Bridge. It's lighted for night fishing and has rental gear available. Get your bait and tackle at the **Ships Chandler** (329 U.S. 98E, tel. 904/837–9306).

Golf **Indian Bayou Golf & Country Club** (Airport Rd. off U.S. 98, tel. 904/837–6192), with 27 holes, and **Sandestin Beach Resort** (9300 U.S. 98W, tel. 904/267–8211), with 63 holes, offer Destin's best golf.

Tennis **Destin Racquet & Fitness Center** (995 Airport Rd., tel. 904/837–7300) boasts six Rubico courts. **Sandestin Resort** (9300 U.S. 98W, tel. 904/267–7110), one of the nation's five-star tennis resorts, has 14 courts with grass, hard, or Rubico surfaces.

Nightlife **Nightown** (140 Palmetto St., tel. 904/837–6448) has a dance floor with laser lights and a New Orleans–style bar with a live band.

Valparaiso/Niceville

Niceville/Valparaiso/Bay Area Chamber of Commerce (170 John Sims Pkwy., tel. 904/678–2323).

On the northern side of Choctawhatchee Bay are the twin cities of Valparaiso and Niceville, both relatively young towns, having been granted their charters in 1921 and 1938, respectively. Niceville evolved from a tiny fishing hamlet called Boggy, whose sandy-bottom bays were rich in mullet. Valparaiso was founded by an entrepreneurial Chicagoan named John B. Perrine, who envisioned it as an ideal city by the sea, or "vale of paradise." Together, the cities have maintained an uncomplicated and serene existence, more or less untouched by the tourist trade farther south. However, with improved access to the Gulf, they have become bona fide alternatives to the higher-priced waterside communities.

In **Valparaiso,** you can take a step back in time among 8,000-year-old stone tools and early 20th-century iron pots and kettles at the **Heritage Museum.** A rarity on display here is a steam-powered, belt-driven cotton gin. The museum also maintains a reference library of genealogical and historical research materials and official Civil War records. *115 Westview Ave., tel. 904/678–2615. Admission free. Open Tues.–Sat. 11–4.*

East of **Niceville,** off Route 20 on Rocky Bayou, are 50 excellent picnic areas, nature trails, boat ramps, and uncrowded campsites with electrical and water hookups in the **Fred Gannon Rocky Bayou State Recreation Area.** It's quiet and secluded, yet easy to find, and a great venue for serious bikers. *Rte. 20, tel. 904/833–9144. Admission: $2 per vehicle for day use; campsites $8.48 ($10.60 with electricity). Open daily 8–sunset.*

Budget Lodging $$ ★ **Bluewater Bay Resort.** This upscale residential resort is carved out of 1,800 acres of pines and oaks on the shores of Choctawhatchee Bay. It's still woodsy around the edges, but showcase homes are surrounded by tenderly manicured gardens. Rentals run the gamut from motel rooms to villas (some with fireplaces and fully equipped kitchens) and patio homes. Check-out information in the rental units is translated into German for the benefit of the international visitors who flock to this golf course–rich region. *1950 Bluewater Blvd., Niceville 32578, tel. 904/897–3613 or 800/874–2128, fax 904/897–2424. 106 units. Facilities: restaurant, lounge, 3 pools, 36 holes of golf, 19 tennis courts, beach, playground. AE, D, DC, MC, V.*

Budget Dining ¢ **Giuseppi's Wharf.** Grouper Parmesan and Cajun fries earned this waterfront steak and seafood house a reputation as a great best-for-less eatery. Arrive by land or sea, and dine inside at tables spread with back-to-basics oilcloth or on the deck next to the pleasure craft in the yacht basin. If you want anything harder than beer or wine, imbibe before you come. *821 Bayshore Dr., Niceville, tel. 904/678–4229. Reservations accepted. Dress: casual. AE, MC, V.*

¢ **Nicometo's.** Wedged between a jeweler's shop and a sporting-goods store, this shopping-plaza restaurant dishes up steamed shrimp that makes even the most blasé of diners sit up and take notice. Fried shrimp and char-grilled grouper also go over big with the regulars, but the only concession to red-meat eaters is a New York strip. The decor in the dimly lit main dining room is plain and simple, consisting of fishing trophies and advertising memorabilia. If you prefer a little jazzier setting, pick a table in the sports bar, where you can throw darts or watch TV while you wait. *1027 John Sims Pkwy., Niceville, tel. 904/678–5072. Reservations accepted. Dress: casual. MC, V.*

Tour 3: Down the Gulf Coast

In the relatively new, planned community of Seaside, houses with Victorian fretwork, white picket fences, and captain's walks make visitors feel as though they have been magic-carpeted to Cape May or Cape Cod. Upscale vacationers come to soak up the re-created quaintness. Not too far away, Panama City Beach is filled with shoulder-to-shoulder condominiums, motels, and amusement parks that make it seem like one big carnival ground. Visitors are largely families and students on spring break. The common denominator is sugar-white sand and blue-green water, which make up the gentle arc that is the Gulf coast.

Arriving and Departing
By Plane **Panama City–Bay County Airport** is served by ASA–The Delta Connection, Delta, Northwest Airlink, and USAir Express. **Yellow Cab** (tel. 904/763–4691) charges about $15–$27 to the beach area, depending on where your hotel is. **DeLuxe Coach Limo Service** (tel. 904/763–0211) provides van service to downtown Panama City for $6.50 and to Panama City Beach for $11.50–$14.25.

By Bus **Greyhound Lines** (tel. 800/231–2222) serves Panama City (917 Harrison Ave., tel. 904/785–7861) from Pensacola and Fort Walton Beach. One-way fares are $19.50 and $12, respectively, and round-trip fares are simply double the one-way price. There is also service to Tallahassee three times daily for $19.50 one-way.

By Car U.S. 98 runs east to Panama City, 29 miles from Fort Walton Beach and 22 miles from Destin. Coming from the north, take U.S. 231 directly into Panama City.

Getting Around
By Car U.S. 98 runs along the coast, connecting the towns in this region. Seaside is off the highway on Route 30A. Back on U.S. 98, head southeast to Panama City Beach and to Panama City proper, 5 miles farther east. Port St. Joe is about 40 miles southeast of Panama City Beach, and Apalachicola is 22 miles past that.

Grayton Beach and Seaside

Walton County Information Center (U.S. 331 at U.S. 98, Santa Rosa Beach 32459, tel. 904/267–3511).

★ Off U.S. 98 on Route 30A, **Grayton Beach State Recreation Area** (tel. 904/231–4210) is one of the most scenic spots along the Gulf coast, with blue-green waters, white-sand beaches, salt marshes, and swimming, snorkeling, and campground facilities.

Just east of here is the architectural award–winning village of **Seaside,** the brainchild of Robert Davis, who dictated certain elements that he felt would promote a neighborly, old-fashioned lifestyle. Built on small lots, no house is more than ¼ mile from the center of town, so residents get about most easily on foot. Building didn't start until 1981, so there isn't enough moss in the brick sidewalks yet for Seaside to have the "historic district" look, but pastel paint jobs, latticework, and rockers on the front porches make this architectural-social experiment a visual stunner.

★ Three miles inland, **Eden State Gardens** contain an antebellum mansion set amid an arcade of moss-draped live oaks. Furnishings in the spacious rooms date from several periods as far back as the 17th century. The surrounding gardens are beautiful year-round, but they're nothing short of spectacular in mid-March when the azaleas and dogwoods are in full bloom. *Rte. 395 just north of U.S. 98, Point Washington, tel. 904/231–4214. Admission to gardens free; mansion tour: $1.50 adults, 50¢ children 12 and under. Open daily 8–sunset; hourly mansion tours Thurs.–Mon. 9–4.*

Budget Dining
$
★
Bud & Alley's. This roadside restaurant grows its own herbs—rosemary, thyme, basil, fennel, and mint. The inside room has a down-to-earth feel, with hardwood floors, ceiling fans, and six-foot windows looking out onto the garden. There is also a screened-in porch area with a view of the Gulf. The Gorgonzola salad with sweet peppers is a delightful introduction to one of the entrées, perhaps the seared duck breast with caramelized garlic, wild mushrooms, and cabernet sauce. *Rte. 30A, tel. 904/231–5900. Reservations accepted for dinner. Dress: casual. MC, V. Closed Tues. Sept.–May.*

Panama City Beach

Panama City Beach Convention & Visitor Bureau (12015 W. Front Beach Rd., Panama City Beach 32407, tel. 904/233–6503 or 800/722–3224).

Panama City Beach is known mainly for the Miracle Strip, lined with a plethora of video-game arcades, miniature golf courses, public beaches, sidewalk cafés, souvenir shops, and shopping centers but the town also has a natural beauty that excuses its overcommercialization. The incredible white sands, navigable waterways and plentiful marine life that attracted Spanish conquistadors make it a vacation spot with mass appeal, especially good for families.

A number of new, glitzy resorts have sprung up, trying to emulate the French Riviera. Their prices never dip down into the affordable range, not even during the winter months when activity on the beach slows. Luckily, a raft of older properties have rates that are always manageable, but there's also a lot of tacky, low-budget stuff places that make you realize why this area is often called the "Redneck Riviera." If you're thinking of booking a room in a rock-bottom priced property, ask the room clerk to let you see it first.

At the eastern tip of Panama City Beach is the **St. Andrews State Recreation Area** (tel. 904/233–5140), Florida's most visited park. It comprises 1,038 acres of beaches, pinewoods, and marshes and offers complete camping facilities as well as ample opportunities to swim, pier fish, or hike the dunes along clearly marked nature trails. An artificial reef creates a calm, shallow play area that is perfect for young children. You can board a ferry to **Shell Island**—a barrier island in the Gulf of Mexico that offers some of the best shelling north of Sanibel Island.

Budget Lodging
$–$$
Gulfside Beach Resort. A mile of beachfront is awash with hotels Howard Johnson, Comfort Inn, Sands, Barefoot Beach Inn. These older properties target the family and convention trade. *9450 S Thomas Dr., 32408, tel. 904/234–3484 or 800/874–6613, fax 904/233–4369. 627 units. Facilities: restaurant, lounge, 4 pools. AE, D, DC MC, V.*

Splurge
Marriott's Bay Point Resort. Sheer elegance is the hallmark of this pink stucco jewel on the shores of Grand Lagoon. Wing chairs, camelback sofas, and Oriental-pattern carpets in the common areas re

create the ambience of an English manor house, which is sustained by the Queen Anne furnishings in the guest rooms. Gulf view or golf view—take your pick. Kitchen-equipped villas are a mere tee-shot away from the hotel. *4200 Marriott Dr., 32408, tel. 904/234–3307 or 800/874–7105, fax 904/233–1308. 355 rooms, suites, or villas. Facilities: 5 restaurants, lounges, indoor pool, 5 outdoor pools, hot tub, 2 golf courses, 12 lighted tennis courts, boating, fishing. AE, D, DC, MC, V.*

Budget Dining
$–$$

Capt. Anderson's. Come early to watch the boats unload the catch of the day, and be among the first to line up for one of the 600 seats in this noted restaurant. The atmosphere is nautical, with tables made of hatch covers. The Greek specialties aren't limited to feta cheese and shriveled olives; charcoal-broiled fish and steaks have a prominent place on the menu, too. *5551 N. Lagoon Dr., tel. 904/234–2225. No reservations. Dress: casual. AE, D, DC, MC, V. Closed Nov.–Jan., Sun. May–Sept. No lunch.*

$ **Boar's Head.** An exterior that looks like an oversize thatched-roof cottage sets the mood for dining in this ever-popular ersatz-rustic restaurant and tavern. Prime rib has been the number-one people-pleaser since the house opened in 1978, but broiled shrimp with crabmeat and vegetable stuffing, and native seafood sprinkled with spices and blackened in a white-hot skillet are popular, too. For starters, try escargot in mushroom caps or a shrimp bisque. There's a special menu for the junior appetite. *17290 Front Beach Rd., tel. 904/234–6628. No reservations. Dress: casual. AE, D, DC, MC, V. No lunch.*

¢ **Montego Bay.** Queue up with vacationers and natives for a table at any one of the five restaurants in this local chain. Service is swift and the food is good. Some dishes, such as red beans and rice or oysters on the half shell, are no surprise. Others, such as shrimp rolled in coconut and served with a honey mustard and orange marmalade sauce, or steak doused with Kentucky bourbon and presented with a bourbon marinade, are real treats. *4920 Thomas Dr., tel. 904/234–8686; 9949 Thomas Dr., tel. 904/235–3585; The Shoppes at Edgewater, tel. 904/233–6033; 17118 Front Beach Rd., tel. 904/233–2900; 1931 N. Cove Blvd., tel. 904/872–0098. No reservations. Dress: casual. AE, D, MC, V.*

Shopping for
Bargains

You can find great buys, as much as 70% off regular price, at **Manufacturers Outlet Center** (105 W. 23rd St., Panama City). **Panama City Mall** (U.S. 231 and Rte. 77, Panama City) has a mix of more than 100 franchise shops and national chain stores.

Participant
Sports
Diving

Panama City Beach is a great area for divers, who can investigate the wreckage of sunken tanker ships, tugboats, and cargo vessels. For snorkelers and beginning divers, the jetties of St. Andrews State Recreation Area, where there is no boat traffic, are safe. Wreck dives are offered by **Diver's Den** (3120 Thomas Dr., tel. 904/234–8717) and **Panama City Dive Center** (4823 Thomas Dr., tel. 904/235–3390).

Fishing

Fishing is permitted off the **city pier,** where the charge is $2 adults, $1.50 children, or $1 observer. *Capt. Anderson's* (Captain Anderson Pier, 5550 N. Lagoon Dr., tel. 904/234–3435) is a party boat that's been a fixture on the waterfront for years.

Golf

Water, water everywhere and island fairways make the Lagoon Legend, at **Marriott's Bay Point Resort** (*see* Budget Lodging, *above*), northwest Florida's answer to the Blue Monster at Doral. Bruce Devlin and Bob von Hagge designed this one to punish the big boys; its complement, the Club Meadows course, is kinder and gentler.

Tennis

Marriott's Bay Point Resort (*see* Budget Lodging, *above*) has a tennis center with 12 Har-Tru clay courts.

Nightlife   **Pineapple Willie's** (9900 S. Thomas Dr., tel. 904/235–0928) brings together the best elements of a discotheque and a Wild West saloon
and caters to the 25–40 crowd. If you feel overwhelmed by the live
entertainment, you can escape to the serenity of a seaside deck.

Port St. Joe and Apalachicola

*Apalachicola Chamber of Commerce (128 Market St., Apalachicola
32320, tel. 904/653–9419).*

Port St. Joe is the spot where Florida's first constitution was drafted
in 1838. Most of the old town, including the original hall, is gone—
wiped out by hurricanes—but the exhibits in the **Constitution Convention State Museum** recall the event. There are also provisions for
camping and picnicking in a small park surrounding the museum.
*200 Island Memorial Way, tel. 904/229–8029. Admission: $1 ages
over 6. Open Thurs.–Mon. 9–noon and 1–5.*

Apalachicola is the state's most important oyster fishery. Drive by
the Raney House, circa 1850; Trinity Episcopal Church, built from
prefabricated parts in 1838; and the **John Gorrie State Museum,** honoring the physician who is credited with inventing ice-making and
air-conditioning. Exhibits of Apalachicola history are displayed
here as well. *Ave. C and 6th St., tel. 904/653–9347. Admission: $1
ages over 6. Open Thurs.–Mon. 9–5.*

St. George Island State Park can be reached by a causeway from
Eastpoint, east of Apalachicola. You can drive toward the sea along
the narrow spit of land with its dunes, sea oats, and abundant bird
life. *Tel. 904/927–2111. Admission: $3.25 per vehicle with up to 8
people. Open 8–sunset.*

Tour 4: Lower Alabama

Locals labeled this inland region Lower Alabama, and the name fits.
It's even more like the Deep South than the rest of the Panhandle,
and it tends to be quite a bit less expensive, too.

Arriving and   **Greyhound Lines** (tel. 800/231–2222) has stations in Crestview
Departing   (James Lee Blvd., tel. 904/682–6922) and DeFuniak Springs (5 W
By Bus   Nelson Ave., tel. 904/892–5566).

By Car   I–10, which is paralleled by U.S. 90 for much of the way, connects
the region to Alabama in the west and Tallahassee and Jacksonville
in the east. From the Fort Walton Beach area to Crestview, follow
Route 85 for 15 miles north of Niceville, just past the junction with
I–10. To reach DeFuniak Springs from the coast, take U.S. 331 for
25 miles north of U.S. 98. From Panama City, Falling Waters is
about an hour's drive north on Route 77, and Florida Caverns State
Park is two hours northeast via U.S. 231 and Route 167.

By Train   **Amtrak** (tel. 800/872–7245) trains on the Los Angeles to Jacksonville route stop in Crestview (101 N. Main St.) and Chipley (101 S
7th St.).

Crestview

*Crestview Area Chamber of Commerce (502 S. Main St., Crestview
32536, tel. 904/682–3213).*

When the Louisville & Nashville Railroad Company completed a
line through northwest Florida in 1882, surveyors dubbed the area
Crestview because, at 235 feet above sea level, it's quite high by
Florida standards. There's been a settlement of sorts here since the
days of the conquistadors, when it was a crossroads on the Old Spanish Trail. Crestview is the sort of small town where the mayor rides
shotgun with the police patrol on a Saturday night and folks enjoy

the simpler pleasures, such as roller-skating and playing softball. But it is not without its cultural attributes. The **Robert L. F. Sikes Public Library** and its research center, housed in an imposing Greek Revival building, boasts more than 44,000 volumes as well as the private papers of its eponym, a former U.S. congressman.

Take U.S. 90 about 12 miles west to the **Blackwater River State Park** (Holt, tel. 904/623–2363). Don't be fooled by the river's dark color— the result of tannic acid that leaches into it from the cypress trees along its banks. This is regarded as one of the cleanest rivers in the country. Its shallow waters offer the best canoeing in the area and the largest, whitest sandbars. In the surrounding Blackwater River State Forest, you can take in the scenic beauty of magnolias and cedars.

Budget Lodging
$

Crestview Holiday Inn. Within this simple sandstone stucco motel is typical Florida decor: shell-shape ceramic lamps, seashell-print bedspreads, and oceanic art on the walls. It's right on the main drag and is the "in" place for local wedding receptions and high-school proms. *Rte. 85 and I–10, Box 1355, 32536, tel. 904/682–6111, fax 904/689–1189. 120 rooms. Facilities: restaurant, lounge, pool. AE, D, DC, MC, V.*

Budget Dining
¢

McLain's Family Restaurant. Assorted Wal-Mart art on the walls, piped-in country-and-western music, and a fireplace with a raised hearth give this mom-and-pop establishment a folksy feel that carries right over to the menu. The owners offer an all-you-can-eat buffet three times a day, always with a poached or broiled entrée to please the diet-conscious. All steaks are hand-cut, just as they are in big-city chophouses. On weekends, McLain's lays on a seafood buffet that draws customers from as far away as Alabama. *2680 S. Rte. 85, tel. 904/682–5286. Reservations accepted. Dress: casual. AE, D, MC, V.*

Canoeing

Blackwater River State Park and the river for which it was named are a canoeist's dream. Veterans will enjoy the special challenges of a paddle up Sweetwater/Juniper Creek, whose sandbars and cliffs call for maneuvering and technical skill. The gentler currents in the sheltered marshes and inlets are less intimidating. **Blackwater Canoe Rental** (U.S. 90E, Milton, tel. 904/623–0235) provides complete round-trip service; you are met at the end point of your trip, transported upstream, and launched on your way. When you have made it back to your car, you simply beach your canoe and leave, without having to wait or load the gear yourself. **Adventures Unlimited** (12 mi north of Milton on Rte. 87, tel. 904/623–6197) also rents canoes.

DeFuniak Springs

Walton County Chamber of Commerce (200 W. Circle Dr., DeFuniak Springs 32433, tel. 904/892–3191).

DeFuniak Springs, 2 miles north of I–10, is another small town that brags about its culture. It was the site of the Knox Hill Academy, founded in 1848 and for more than half a century the only institution of higher learning in northwest Florida. When the railroad came in 1882, the town was named to flatter a then-prominent railroad official, Frederick de Funiak. In 1885, it was chosen as the location for the New York Chautauqua educational society's winter assembly. The Chautauqua programs were discontinued in 1928, but DeFuniak Springs attempts to revive them, in spirit at least, with a county-wide Chautauqua Festival every May.

Another legacy from the Chautauqua era is the **Walton–DeFuniak Public Library**, by all accounts Florida's oldest library continuously operating in its original building. This tiny facility, measuring 16 feet by 24 feet, opened in 1887 to make reading material available to the Chautauqua crowd. Added to and expanded over the years, at present it contains nearly 30,000 volumes, including rare books, many of which are older than the structure itself. The collection has grown to include antique musical instruments and an impressive display of European armor. *100 Circle Dr., tel. 904/892–3624. Open Mon. 9–7; Tues., Wed., Fri. 9–6; Sat. 9–3.*

Chautauqua Winery opened in 1989, but already its award-winning wines have earned raves from oenophiles nationwide. You can take a free tour of the winery to see how ancient art blends with modern technology; then retreat to the tasting room. *I–10 and U.S. 331, tel. 904/892–5887. Admission free. Open Mon.–Sat. 9–5, Sun. noon–5.*

Falling Waters State Recreation Area

One of Florida's most recognized geological features is the **Falling Waters Sink,** a 100-foot-deep cylindrical pit that provides the background for a waterfall. There's an observation deck for viewing this natural phenomenon. *Rte. 77A, Chipley, tel. 904/638–6130. Admission: $3.25 per vehicle with up to 8 people. Open daily 8–sunset.*

Florida Caverns State Park

At the 1,783-acre park, take a ranger-led spelunking tour to see an array of stalactites, stalagmites, and "waterfalls" of solid rock. The park also has hiking trails, campsites, and areas for swimming and canoeing on the Chipola River. *Rte. 167, Marianna, tel. 904/482–9598. Admission to park: $3.25 per vehicle with up to 8 people; to caverns: $4 adults, $2 children 3–12. Open daily 8–sunset; cavern tours daily 9–4.*

Tour 5: Tallahassee Area

I–10 rolls east over the timid beginnings of the Appalachian foothills and through thick pines into the state capital, Tallahassee, with its canopies of ancient oaks and spring bowers of azaleas. Among the best canopied roads are St. Augustine, Miccosukee, Meridian, Old Bainbridge, and Centerville, which are still dotted with country stores and antebellum plantation houses.

Arriving and Departing

By Plane **Tallahassee Regional Airport** is served by **Air South** (tel. 800/247–7688), American Eagle, ASA–The Delta Connection, **Continental Express** (tel. 800/523–3278), Delta, and USAir. **City Taxi** (tel. 904/893–4111) and **Yellow Cab** (tel. 904/222–3070) travel to downtown for about $12. Some Tallahassee hotels provide free shuttle service.

By Bus The one-way fare on **Greyhound Lines** (tel. 800/231–2222) from the Tallahassee depot (112 Tennessee St., tel. 904/222–4240) is $36 to Pensacola, $27.50 to Crestview, $23 to DeFuniak Springs, and $19.50 to Panama City.

By Car East and west routes through Tallahassee are I–10 and U.S. 90. Coming from the south, take U.S. 19 to U.S. 27. From the north, U.S. 19 to U.S. 319 is the best route.

By Train **Amtrak** (tel. 800/872–7245) trains stop in Tallahassee (918 Railroad Ave.) on the route between Pensacola and Jacksonville.

Getting Around

By Bus and Trolley The **Taltran** (tel. 904/891–5200) system provides bus service throughout Tallahassee's city limits.

The downtown Capitol complex is compact enough for walking, but it's also served by a free, continuous shuttle trolley.

Tallahassee

Tallahassee Area Convention and Visitors Bureau (200 W. College Ave., Tallahassee 32302, tel. 904/413–9200 or 800/628–2866).

★ Part of the downtown **Capitol complex,** the **New Capitol** is a modern skyscraper that looms up 22 stories directly behind the low-rise Old Capitol. On a clear day, you can catch a panoramic view of Tallahassee and its surrounding countryside from the top floor. *Duvall St., tel. 904/488–6167. Admission free. Hourly tours daily 9–3.*

The centerpiece of the Capitol complex is the **Old Capitol,** a pre–Civil War structure that has been added to, and subtracted from, several times over the years. A recent renovation has restored its jaunty red-and-white-striped awnings and combination gas-electric lights to make it look much as it did in 1902. *Monroe St. and Apalachee Pkwy., tel. 904/487–1902. Admission free. Self-guided and guided tours weekdays 9–4:30, Sat. 10–4:30, Sun. noon–4:30.*

Across the street is the 1833 **Union Bank Building**—Florida's oldest bank building. Since the bank closed in 1843, the building has played many roles, from ballet school to bakery. It's been restored to what is thought to be its original appearance. *Monroe St. and Apalachee Pkwy., tel. 904/487–3803. Admission free. Open Tues.–Fri. 10–1, weekends by appointment.*

Two blocks west of the New Capitol is the **Museum of Florida History.** Here, the long, intriguing story of the state's past—from mastodons to space shuttles—is told in lucid and entertaining ways. *500 S. Bronough St., tel. 904/488–1484. Admission free. Open weekdays 9–4:30, Sat. 10–4:30, Sun. noon–4:30.*

Allow at least four hours for the 8-mile **Downtown Tallahassee Historic Trail,** a walking tour originally mapped and documented by an eagle scout as part of a merit-badge project. It has since become a Tallahassee sightseeing staple. The starting point is the Old Capitol, where you can pick up maps and descriptive brochures. You'll walk through the **Park Avenue** and **Calhoun Street historic districts,** which will take you back in time to Territorial days and the era of Reconstruction. Landmark churches and cemeteries dot the trail as do houses that are outstanding examples of Greek Revival, Italianate, and prairie-style architecture. Some of the houses are open to the public, such as the **Brokaw-McDougall House** (329 N. Meridian St., tel 904/488–3901), which is a superb example of the Greek Revival and Italianate styles, and the **Meginnis-Monroe House** (125 N. Gadsden St., tel. 904/222–8800), which served as a field hospital during the Civil War and is now an art gallery.

The **Tallahassee Museum of History and Natural Science** features a collection of old cars and carriages, a red caboose, nature trails, a snake exhibit, and a restored plantation house. *3945 Museum Dr., tel. 904/576–1636. Admission: $5 adults, $4 senior citizens, $3 children 4–15. Open Mon.–Sat. 9–5, Sun. 12:30–5.*

Housed in a former Carnegie library on the campus of Florida A&M University, the **Black Archives** is one of the United States's most extensive collections of African-American artifacts. Included in the exhibits are a 500-piece Ethiopian cross collection and memorabilia of noteworthy black Americans. *Martin Luther King Blvd., tel. 904/599–3020. Admission free. Open weekdays 9–4.*

Artifacts, heirlooms, and documents that chronicle Florida's agricultural history, its turpentine industry, and its rural heritage are housed in the **Florida Agricultural Museum.** Included in the exhibits are 19th-century farm implements, vintage saddles, and an old steam engine. Animal lovers take note: Endangered domestic-animal species are pastured on the museum grounds. *3125 Conner Blvd., tel. 904/487–4428. Admission free. Open weekdays 9–4.*

San Luis Archaeological and Historic Site focuses on the archaeology of 17th-century Spanish mission and Apalachee Indian town sites. In its heyday, in 1675, the Apalachee village here had a population of at least 1,400. Threatened by Creek Indians and British forces in 1704, the locals burned the village and fled. *2020 W. Mission Rd., tel. 904/487–3711. Admission free. Open weekdays 9–4:30, Sat. 10–4:30, Sun. noon–4:30; 1-hr guided tours weekdays at noon, Sat. at 11 and 3, Sun. at 2.*

Just north of Tallahassee off U.S. 27 is **Lake Jackson Mounds State Archaeological Site,** a resource bass fishermen hold in reverence. For sightseers, Indian mounds and the ruins of an early 19th-century plantation built by Colonel Robert Butler, adjutant to General Andrew Jackson during the siege of New Orleans, are found along the shores of the lake. *Indian Mound Rd., tel. 904/562–0042. Admission free. Open daily 8–sunset.*

Five miles north of town on U.S. 319 are the magnificent **Maclay State Gardens.** In springtime the grounds are afire with azaleas, dogwoods, and other showy or rare annuals, trees, and shrubs. Allow at least half a day for wandering the paths past the reflecting pool, into the tiny walled garden, and around the lakes and woodlands. The Maclay residence, furnished as it was in the 1920s; picnic grounds; and swimming and boating facilities are open to the public. *3540 Thomasville Rd., tel. 904/487–4556. Admission: $3.25 per vehicle with up to 8 people. Open daily 8–sunset.*

Budget Lodging

$$ **Holiday Inn Capitol Plaza.** Bustling and upscale, the hotel hosts heavy hitters from the worlds of politics and media, who can walk from here to the Capitol. *101 S. Adams St., 32301, tel. 904/224–5000 or 800/465–4329, fax 904/224–5000. 246 rooms. Facilities: restaurant, bar, lounge, pool. AE, D, DC, MC, V.*

$$ **Ramada Inn Tallahassee.** Surrounded by 13 parklike acres, this property is a distance from the city's hub, but it offers shuttle service to both the airport and downtown as well as a lively comedy club on the premises. Rooms are decorated with blond-wood traditional furniture and a background of splashy, abstract murals. *2900 N. Monroe St., 32303, tel. 904/386–1027 or 800/272–6232. 198 rooms. Facilities: restaurant, lounge, pool. AE, D, DC, MC, V.*

$$ **Shoney's Inn.** The quiet courtyard with its own pool and the darkly welcoming cantina (where a complimentary Continental breakfast is served) convey the look of old Spain. Rooms are furnished in heavy Mediterranean style. *2801 N. Monroe St., 32303, tel. 904/386–8286 or 800/222–2222, fax 904/422–1074. 112 rooms. Facilities: cantina, pool. AE, D, DC, MC, V.*

¢ **Days Inn Downtown.** With 24-hour food service and refrigerators and microwaves in selected rooms, this inn is an improvement over the usual budget motel. Close to the Capitol complex, it's a favorite of state legislators as well as tourists who want to do the city on foot. *722 Apalachee Pkwy., 32301, tel. 904/224–2181 or 800/325–2525, fax 904/224–2181, ext. 213. 100 rooms. Facilities: restaurant, pool. AE, D, DC, MC, V.*

Budget Dining

$ **Anthony's.** This is the locals' choice for uncompromising Italian classics. Try one of the Italian-style grouper or salmon dishes. *1950 Thomasville Rd., tel. 904/224–1447. Reservations advised. Dress: casual. AE, MC, V.*

$ ★ **Barnacle Bill's.** The seafood selection is whale-size and it's steamed to succulent perfection before your eyes, with fresh vegetables on the side. This popular hangout is famous for pasta dishes and home-smoked fish, too. Choose from complete weight-loss menus and daily chalkboard specials. Children eat for free on Sunday. The full menu is available for carryout. *1830 N. Monroe St., tel. 904/385–8734. Reservations advised for large groups. Dress: casual. AE, MC, V.*

$ **Nicholson's Farmhouse.** The name says a lot about this friendly, informal country place with an outside kitchen and grill. Hand-cut steaks and chops are specialties of the house. *From U.S. 27 take Rte. 12 toward Quincy and follow signs, tel. 904/539–5931. Reservations* *advised on weekends. Dress: casual. AE, D, MC, V. BYOB. Closed Sun., Mon.*

The Arts and Nightlife
The Arts

Broadway touring shows, top-name entertainers, and concert artists are booked into the **Tallahassee-Leon County Civic Center** (505 W. Pensacola St., tel. 904/487–1691).

Florida State University annually hosts 350 concerts and recitals given by its **School of Music** (tel. 904/644–4774) as well as performances of the **Tallahassee Symphony Orchestra** (tel. 904/224–0461) from October to April. Near Tallahassee, the **Monticello Opera House** (U.S. 90E, tel. 904/997–4242) presents operas in a restored gaslight-era playhouse.

Nightlife

On Friday and Saturday nights, stop by **Andrew's Upstairs** (228 S. Adams St., tel. 904/222–3446) to hear contemporary jazz and reggae.

South to the Gulf

In 1865, Confederate soldiers stood firm against a Yankee advance on St. Marks. The Rebs held, saving Tallahassee—the only Southern capital east of the Mississippi that never fell to the Union. The **Natural Bridge Battlefield State Historic Site,** about 10 miles southeast of the capital off U.S. 363, marks the victory and is a good place for a hike and a picnic. *Natural Bridge Rd. (Rte. 354), Woodville, tel. 904/922–6007. Admission free. Open daily 8–sunset.*

★ **Wakulla Springs State Park,** about 15 miles south of Tallahassee on Route 61, has one of the deepest springs in the world. The wilderness remains relatively untouched, retaining the wild and exotic look it had in the 1930s, when Tarzan movies were made here. Take a glass-bottom boat deep into the lush, jungle-lined waterways to catch glimpses of alligators, snakes, nesting limpkin, and other waterfowl. More than 154 bird species can be spotted, as well as raccoons, gray squirrels, and an encyclopedia of southern flora. *1 Springs Dr., Wakulla Springs, tel. 904/922–3632. Admission: $3.25 per car; boat tour: $4.50 adults, $2.25 children under 13. Open daily 8–sunset; 4 tours daily 9:15–4:30.*

Still farther south, about 25 miles from Tallahassee off Route 363, is the **St. Marks Wildlife Refuge and Lighthouse,** where the once-powerful Fort San Marcos de Apalache was built in 1639. Stones salvaged from the fort were used in the lighthouse, which is still in operation. There are exhibits at the visitor center. *Rte. 59, St. Marks, tel. 904/925–6121. Admission: $4 per car. Refuge open sunrise–sunset; visitor center open weekdays 8–4:15, weekends 10–5.*

Spreading west of Tallahassee and north of Apalachicola is the **Apalachicola National Forest,** where you can camp, hike, picnic, fish, or swim.

Budget Dining
$

Wakulla Springs Lodge. This restaurant on the grounds of Wakulla Springs State Park serves three meals a day in a sunny, spartan room that, like the wilderness around it, seems little changed from the 1930s. Shrimp, fried or broiled, and southern fried chicken are some of the traditional dishes that have made this dining room famous. Schedule lunch here to sample the renowned bean soup, home-baked muffins, and a slab of pie. *1 Springs Dr., Wakulla Springs, tel. 904/224–5950. Reservations required for parties of 8 or more. Dress: casual. MC, V.*

11 Northeast Florida

Updated by
Pamela
Acheson

In northeastern Florida you'll find some of the oldest settlements in the state—indeed in all of the United States—though this region didn't get much attention from outsiders until Union Army troops came through here during the Civil War. Their rapturous accounts of the mild climate, pristine beaches, and lush vegetation captured the imagination of folks up north. First came the speculators and the curiosity seekers; the advent of the railroads brought more permanent settlers and the first wave of winter vacationers; and finally, with the invention of the automobile, came the full rush of snowbirds, seasonal residents escaping from harsh northern winters. They still come, to sop up the sun on the beaches that stretch all along the Atlantic coastline; to tee 'em up in this year-round golfer's paradise; to bass fish and bird-watch in the forests and parks; and to party in the dance clubs and barrooms of Daytona (which has the dubious honor of replacing Fort Lauderdale as the destination of choice for spring break).

This region of Florida is an area of remarkable diversity. Towering, tortured live oaks; plantations; and antebellum-style architecture feel like the Old South. The mossy marshes of Silver Springs and the St. Johns River look as untouched and junglelike today as they did generations ago. Horse farms around Ocala resemble Kentucky's bluegrass country or the hunt clubs of Virginia. St. Augustine is a showcase of early U.S. history, and Jacksonville is a young but sophisticated metropolis. Yet these are all but light diversions from northeastern Florida's primary draw: its absolutely sensational beaches. From the Georgia border straight down through Cocoa, long and slender barrier islands hug the coast. Along the entire eastern side of each of these islands runs a broad band of spectacular sand. Except in the most populated areas, development has been modest, and the beaches are lined with funky, appealing little towns.

Northeast Florida Basics

Budget Lodging

Accommodations range from splashy beachfront resorts and glitzy condominiums to cozy inns and bed-and-breakfasts nestled in historic districts. You can expect to pay top dollar for accommodations in downtown Jacksonville's high-rise luxury hotels, but you might be able to save on transportation costs because so much is accessible from these properties by public transportation or on foot. At the beaches, fancy resorts command fancy prices, but there are also many simple places to stay that are remarkably inexpensive.

The rule of thumb is, the closer you are to the center of activity or a beachfront in the coastal resorts, the more you'll pay. You'll save a few dollars if you stay across from the beach rather than on it, and you'll save even more if you select a place with a kitchenette or refrigerator and microwave and fix your own food. Bear in mind as well that lodging prices are reduced by as much as half during the off-season.

Budget Dining

The northeast coast is edged by the Atlantic Ocean and is laced with waterways, which means that seafood is prominently featured. In coastal towns, the catches often come straight from the restaurant's own fleet. Shrimp, oysters, snapper, and grouper are especially popular. As they are everywhere else, prices are influenced by the surrounding real estate, so expect to pay more in metro areas than in smaller towns. In the Jacksonville area, the closer you get to the beaches the more likely you are to find chicken-dinner places and seafood shacks where the atmosphere is unpretentious and prices are right.

Bargain Shopping

Prices in northeast Florida's shopping malls aren't perceptibly lower than they are anywhere else, but you usually can get good buys in the manufacturers' outlet stores, which depend heavily on the tourist trade. Because tourism is the state's largest industry, the area is awash with souvenir shops. Souvenirs unique to northeast Florida include citrus fruits, gems and minerals from De Land, beach and surf-theme merchandise from along the coast, and auto-racing items from Daytona Beach.

Beaches

Beaches in northeastern Florida are luxuriously long. Some consist of hard-packed white sand, whereas others have a more sugary texture and are white or blond in color. Although all have surf, much of it is gentle, and there are many safe areas for swimming. Bear in mind that the very fragile dunes, held in place by the sea grasses, are responsible for protecting the shore from the sea. A single afternoon of roughhousing can destroy a dune forever.

The area's most densely developed beaches, with rows of high-rise condominiums and hotels, are those in Daytona and Cocoa. Elsewhere coastal towns are still mostly small and laid-back, and beaches are crowded only on summer weekends.

Sports and the Outdoors

A lot of people move to Florida solely for its plethora of golf courses. Some of the highest-priced rounds of golf are played here, but there are also a multitude of championship municipal and semiprivate courses for the economy-minded. Similarly, though the area has several resorts that focus on tennis, there are many racquet clubs open to the public, too, where you can play for a reasonable fee. With the ocean, the St. Johns River, and several large inland lakes nearby, almost anything you can do on water you can do here. Serious freshwater fishing and canoeing go on in the De Land area. Several state parks, such as Little Talbot Island, have bicycle trails, and O'Leno and Payne's Creek state parks are recommended for backpacking. **Suwannee Country Tours** (White Springs, tel. 904/397–2347), run by the Florida Council of American Youth Hostels, organizes bicycle and canoe trips on some of the state's most unspoiled and unique roads and waters. Stay overnight in country inns, picnic in ghost towns, eat at country churches, and explore forgotten sites.

The Arts and Nightlife

Tastes in northeast Florida run from honky-tonk to highbrow. Top-name entertainers and Broadway productions are booked into the larger cities, such as Jacksonville and Daytona Beach, as are artists and musical ensembles with appeal to the longhairs. Something cultural is always going on in the university cities; concerts and recitals in De Land, for example, showcase some of Stetson University's outstanding faculty and student musical talent.

Festivals

The first two weeks in February are **Speed Weeks** in Daytona Beach, culminating in the **Daytona 500**, the world's biggest and most lucrative event in stock-car racing. In July, the **Greater Jacksonville Kingfish Tournament** draws more than 50,000 from all over the United States for four days of offshore fishing and a chance to win more than $250,000 in cash and merchandise. More than 150,000 people pack Jacksonville during the second week of October for the **Jacksonville Jazz Festival,** which amounts to the world's largest free jam session.

Tour 1: Jacksonville Area

Gleaming glass office towers cast reflections in the St. Johns River, giving the impression that Jacksonville is a young town, when, in fact, it is one of the oldest cities in Florida. In terms of square miles (730), it's the largest city in the United States. Modern-day Jacksonville began to emerge when the railroads came through in the Gay '90s, and by the end of World War I, more than 110 trains and 20,000 passengers daily went through its terminal, a Parthenon-like specimen of Greek revival architecture that's been adapted for reuse as the Prime F. Osborn III Convention Center.

Jacksonville and its outlying areas are an underrated tourist destination and well worth a stop. You'll find appealing downtown riverside areas with restaurants and shops; handsome, well-established residential neighborhoods; a thriving arts scene; and some of the best beaches in the state. Remnants of the Old South flavor the city, though it also maintains the sense of subtropical paradise for which Florida is famous.

For an interesting excursion in the area, take the ferry to Mayport, and follow the Buccaneer Trail (Route A1A) along the Atlantic coast. The trail passes through marshlands and beaches to the 300-year-old seaport town of Fernandina Beach and then into Fort Clinch State Park, with its massive brick fortress. Sometimes called the First Coast, this area was colonized by the Spanish in the mid-16th century. French Huguenots organized the United States's first Protestant colony at Fort Caroline on the St. Johns River, and

Northeast Florida

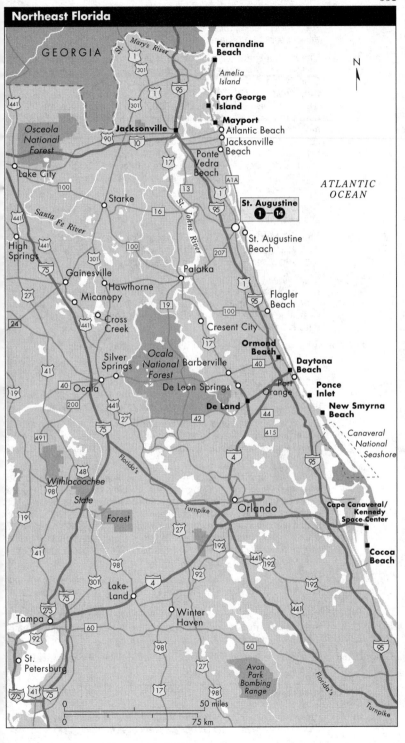

Kingsley Plantation was a reception center and training ground of sorts for slaves on their way from Africa and the Caribbean to work on southern plantations.

Arriving and Departing
By Plane
The main airport for the region is **Jacksonville International.** It is served by **American** and **American Eagle** (tel. 800/433–7300), **Comair** (tel. 800/354–9822), **Continental** (tel. 800/525–0280), **Delta** (tel. 800/221–1212), **TWA** (tel. 800/221–2000), **United** (tel. 800/241–6522), and **USAir** (tel. 800/428–4322). Vans from the Jacksonville airport to area hotels cost $16 per person. Taxi fare is about $20 to downtown, $40 to the beaches and Amelia Island. Among the limousine services, which must be booked in advance, is **AAA Limousine Service** (tel. 904/751–4800 or 800/780–1705), which charges $25 for one to four people going downtown ($8 for each additional person) and $39 for one to four people going to the Jacksonville beaches or Amelia Island.

By Bus
Greyhound Lines (tel. 800/231–2222) stops in Jacksonville (10 N. Pearl St., tel. 904/356–9976).

By Car
The chief interstates are I–95, which runs north–south along the east coast and right through downtown Jacksonville, and I–10, which originates in Jacksonville and runs across all of northern Florida.

Route 13 runs through tiny hamlets along the east side of the St. Johns River, from Jacksonville to East Palatka. U.S. 17 travels the west side of the river, passing through Green Cove Springs and Palatka.

By Train
Amtrak (tel. 800/872–7245) trains connecting the Northeast Corridor to Tampa and Miami stop regularly at Jacksonville's Clifford Lane Station (3570 Clifford La.), whereas trains on the western route from Los Angeles and New Orleans arrive on Mondays, Wednesdays, and Fridays. The Jacksonville station is off the beaten path and may require an expensive cab ride to your lodging.

Getting Around
By Car
Jacksonville's various beach towns are about a half hour's drive from downtown, via Routes 10 and 202 or U.S. 90. The quickest route from Jacksonville to Amelia Island is I–95 north to Route A1A east.

If you want to drive as close to the Atlantic as possible and are not in a hurry, stick with A1A. It runs along the barrier islands, changing its name several times along the way. Where there are no bridges between islands, cars must return to the mainland via causeways; some are low and have drawbridges that open for boat traffic on the inland waterway, causing unexpected delays. The Buccaneer Trail, which overlaps part of Route A1A, goes from St. Augustine north through Mayport, where a ferry is part of the state highway system, to Fort Clinch State Park.

By Water Taxi
Connecting the banks of the St. Johns River, the **Bass Marine Water Taxi** (tel. 904/730–8685) runs from 11 to 10 daily (except during rainy or other bad weather) between several locations, including Riverwalk and Jacksonville Landing. The one-way trip takes about five minutes. Round-trip fare is $3 adults, $2 senior citizens and children 3–12; one-way is $1.50.

Guided Tours
City tours of Jacksonville are offered by **Jacksonville Historical Society Tours** (tel. 904/396–6307).

Jacksonville

Jacksonville and Its Beaches Convention & Visitors Bureau (6 E. Bay St., Suite 200, Jacksonville 32202, tel. 904/353–9736).

Because Jacksonville was settled along both sides of the St. Johns River, many attractions are on or near a riverbank. On the map the twists of the river and its estuaries resemble the cardiovascular system on an anatomical chart. It helps to plan your trip carefully. Some attractions can be reached by water taxi (*see* Getting Around, *above*), a handy alternative to driving back and forth across the bridges, but a car is generally necessary.

At **Jacksonville's Museum of Science and History,** exhibits range from those on pre-Columbian history and the ecology and history of the St. Johns River to the Maple Leaf Civil War Collection and the hands-on Kidspace section. There are also excellent special exhibits. Devote a half day to this museum, and don't miss the popular 3-D laser shows in the Alexander Brest Planetarium. Located downtown on the south bank, the museum can be reached by water taxi from Jacksonville Landing. *1025 Museum Circle, tel. 904/396–7062. Admission: $5 adults, $3 senior citizens and children over 4. Open weekdays 10–5, Sat. 10–6, Sun. 1–6.*

Also on the south side of the river, though not on the water taxi route, the **Jacksonville Art Museum** brings together contemporary and classic arts. Especially noteworthy are the Koger collection of Asian porcelains, works by Pablo Picasso, and the pre-Columbian collection of rare artifacts. Special exhibits, film and lecture series, and workshops make this destination worthy of more than one visit. *4160 Boulevard Center Dr., tel. 904/398–8336. Admission free. Open Tues., Wed., Fri. 10–4; Thurs. 10–10; weekends 1–5.*

The **Cummer Gallery of Art,** situated on the northwest side of the river, amid leafy formal gardens, occupies a former baron's estate home. The permanent collection, in 10 galleries, depicts 4,000 years of changing styles. The more than 2,000 items include one of the nation's largest troves of early Meissen porcelain as well as the works of some impressive Old Masters. *829 Riverside Ave., tel. 904/356–6857. Admission: $3 adults, $2 senior citizens, $1 students and children. Open Tues.–Fri. 10–4, Sat. noon–5, Sun. 2–5.*

The **Alexander Brest Museum,** located on the river's east bank, on the campus of Jacksonville University, has a small but important collection of Steuben glass, Boehm porcelain, ivories, and pre-Columbian artifacts. The home of composer Frederick Delius is also on the campus and is open for tours, upon request. *2800 University Blvd. N, tel. 904/744–3950, ext. 3371. Admission free. Open weekdays 9–4:30, Sat. noon–5; closed school holidays.*

Take a free tour of the **Anheuser-Busch Brewery** (111 Busch Dr., tel. 904/751–8118) and see first-hand how beer is made. There's a gift shop and a hospitality room, where visitors can sample the product, compliments of the house.

Jacksonville Zoo is best known for its white rhinos and an outstanding collection of rare waterfowl. On a 7-acre veld, you can see 10 species of African birds and animals. *Hecksher Dr. E, off I–95, Jacksonville, tel. 904/757–4462. Admission: $4 adults, $3 senior citizens, $2.50 children 3–12. Open daily 9–5.*

Budget Lodging
$$

Comfort Suites Hotel. Located in Baymeadows and central to some currently "in" restaurants, nightclubs, and shops, this all-suites hotel is an unbeatable value. Suites, which are decorated in breezy, radiant Florida hues, include refrigerators, remote control TVs, and sleeper sofas. Microwaves and VCRs come with master suites. Daily Continental breakfast and cocktail hour during the week are included in rates. *8333 Dix Ellis Trail, 32256, tel. 904/739–1155, fax 904/731–0752. 128 suites. Facilities: pool, spa, laundry. AE, DC, MC, V.*

$$ **House on Cherry St.** This early 20th-century treasure is furnished with pewter, Oriental rugs, woven coverlets, and other remnants of a rich past. Carol Anderson welcomes her guests to her riverside home with wine and hors d'oeuvres and serves full breakfast every morning. Walk to the parks and gardens of the chic Avondale district. *1844 Cherry St., 32205, tel. 904/384–1999. 4 rooms. Facilities: bicycles. MC, V.*

Budget Dining
$$

Cafe on the Square. This 1920 building, the oldest on San Marco Square, is an unpretentious place for an after-theater meal, tête-à-tête dining, or Sunday brunch. Dine indoors or out, and choose from a menu ranging from steak sandwiches to quiche, marinated chicken, and pasta—all with a Continental flair. *1974 San Marco Blvd., tel. 904/399–4848. Reservations accepted. Dress: casual. AE, MC, V. Closed Sun. No lunch.*

$ **Crawdaddy's.** Take it Cajun or cool. This riverfront fish shack, just off I–10 at I–95, is the place for seafood, jambalaya, and country chicken. Lunch is a sumptuous buffet, and there's a very popular Sunday brunch. Dig into the house specialty, catfish—all you can eat—then dance to a fe-do-do beat. *1643 Prudential Dr., tel. 904/396–3546. Reservations accepted. Dress: casual. AE, D, DC, MC, V.*

$ **River City Brewing Company.** This popular new brew pub overlooks the river on the city's south bank. Take one of the daily brewery tours; then choose from at least six daily homemade beer specials, or sample them all. Sandwiches and salads are featured at lunch, while dinner entrées include shrimp, fresh fish, grilled steaks, and pasta dishes. (Lunch prices are a bargain, and although some dinner entrées are expensive, many are less than $15.) Sunday brunch is accompanied by live jazz. *835 Museum Circle Dr., Southbank Riverwalk, tel. 904/398–2299. Reservations accepted. Dress: casual. AE, MC, V.*

$ **Silver Spoon.** In the second floor of Jacksonville Landing, on the water side, this popular spot serves meals nonstop from 11 AM to 11 PM (Sunday to 10, Friday and Saturday to midnight). Tables overlook the river, but people head here as much for excellent, reasonably priced food as for the great views. Choose from heaping salads, giant bowls of soup, gourmet pizzas, chicken pot pies, hamburgers, pasta dishes, sandwiches, and grilled fish and steaks. *Jacksonville Landing, 2 Independent Dr., tel. 904/353–4503. No reservations. Dress: casual. AE, MC, V.*

Shopping for
Bargains

For a huge group of specialty shops and a number of restaurants, roam around the downtown **Jacksonville Landing** (at the Main Street Bridge), on the north side of the river. **Riverdale/Avondale Shopping Center** (Riverside Ave.), in the heart of historic Avondale, has two blocks chock-full of art galleries, restaurants, and boutiques. Stop at the **San Marco Shopping Center** (San Marco Blvd.), and wander through interesting stores and restaurants in 1920s Mediterranean revival–style buildings.

Participant
Sports
Golf

The **Baymeadows Golf Club** (7981 Baymeadows Circle W, tel. 904/731–5701) touts itself as the best golf value in northeast Florida, and it may well be. For $24 on Monday and Tuesday and $28 Wednesday through Friday (greens fees and cart), you can play a superbly maintained layout designed by Desmond Muirhead and Gene Sarazen. Four sets of tees ensure playability for golfers of all skill levels. At **Ravines Golf & Country Club** (2932 Ravines Rd., Middleburg, tel. 904/282–7888), trees, rolling terrain, and deep gorges present golfers with a different set of problems from those usually encountered at typical Florida courses, where water hazards create the interest.

Spectator
Sports
Dog Racing

Greyhounds race year-round, with seasons split among three tracks: **Jacksonville Kennel Club** (1440 N. McDuff Ave., tel. 904/646–0001), May–September; **Orange Park Kennel Club** (½ mi south of I–295 on U.S. 17, tel. 904/646–0001), November–April; and **St. Johns Greyhound Park** (7 mi south of I–95 on U.S. 1, tel. 904/646–0001), March–April.

Football The blockbuster event in northeast Florida is Jacksonville's **Gator Bowl** (tel. 904/396–1800) on New Year's Day. The **Jacksonville Jaguars** (tel. 904/633–6000), a new NFL franchise, play their inaugural season in 1995.

The Arts and *First Coast Entertainer* and *Folio Weekly*, distributed free through-
Nightlife out the Jacksonville area, carry weekly arts and entertainment cal-
The Arts endars. Obtain tickets to theatrical, musical, and sporting events through **Ticketmaster** (255 E. Robinson St., tel. 904/353–3309).

Broadway touring shows, top-name entertainers, and other major events are booked at the **Florida Theater Performing Arts Center** (128 E. Forsyth St., tel. 904/355–5661) and the **Jacksonville Civic Auditorium** (300 W. Water St., tel. 904/630–0701). The **Alhambra Dinner Theater** (12000 Beach Blvd., tel. 904/641–1212) offers professional theater and complete menus that change with each play. The **Jacksonville Symphony Orchestra** (tel. 904/354–5479) presents a variety of concerts around town.

Nightlife **Cafe on the Square** (*see* Budget Dining, *above*) has live local blues, jazz, and rock bands Tuesday through Saturday. At **Club 5** (1028 Park Ave., tel. 904/356–5555), there's alternative high-energy-techno and disco-dance music nightly. **River City Brewing Company** (*see* Budget Dining, *above*) has live local jazz or blues bands Friday and Saturday nights and Sunday at brunch.

Jacksonville Beach and Other Beach Towns

Atlantic Beach is a favored surfing area. Around the popular Sea Turtle Inn, you'll find catamaran rentals and instruction. Five areas have lifeguards on duty in the summer 10–6.

The other of the area's best surfing sites is neighboring **Neptune Beach.** It's more residential and offers easy access to quieter beaches than Jacksonville Beach, just to the south.

Jacksonville Beach is the liveliest of the long line of area beaches. Young people flock to the beach, where there are all sorts of games to play as well as concessions, rental shops, and a fishing pier.

Ponte Vedra Beach, where the PGA, Tournament Players Club, and American Tennis Professionals are now based, has been popular with golfers since 1922, when the National Lead Company built a nine-hole course for its workers.

Budget **Sea Turtle Inn.** Every room in this inn has a view of the Atlantic. Let
Lodging the staff arrange special outings for you: golf, deep-sea fishing, or a
$$ visit to a Nautilus fitness center. You'll be welcomed each evening with a complimentary cocktail reception, and in the morning you'll be awakened with hot coffee and a newspaper. *1 Ocean Blvd., Atlantic Beach 32233, tel. 904/249–7402, fax 904/241–7439. 198 rooms. Facilities: restaurant, bar, lounge, pool, airport shuttle. AE, D, DC, MC, V.*

Budget Dining **Homestead.** A down-home place with several dining rooms, a huge
$ fireplace, and country cooking, this restaurant specializes in skillet-fried chicken, which comes with rice and gravy. Chicken and dumplings, deep-fried chicken gizzards, buttermilk biscuits, and strawberry shortcake also draw in the locals. *1712 Beach Blvd., Jacksonville Beach, tel. 904/249–5240. Reservations accepted for parties of 6 or more. Dress: casual. AE, D, MC, V. No lunch.*

$ **Ragtime.** A New Orleans theme threads through everything from
★ the Sunday jazz brunch to the beignets. It's loud, crowded, and alive with a sophisticated young bunch. If you aren't into Creole and Cajun classics, have a simple po'boy sandwich or fish sizzled on the grill. *207 Atlantic Blvd., Atlantic Beach, tel. 904/241–7877. No reservations. Dress: casual. AE, DC, MC, V.*

¢ **Ward's Landing.** The Harley-Davidsons parked on the asphalt and the sleek sport boats tied up at the dock say it all about the diversity of the crowd that comes to savor the steak and seafood specialties at this fish camp. The action revs up to a fever pitch on Sunday afternoons. *15 S. Roscoe, Palm Valley, tel. 904/285-9444. Reservations required for parties of 6 or more. Dress: casual. AE, MC, V.*

Participant Sports

Golf Top-flight courses that you can arrange to play on include **Ponte Vedra Inn & Club** (200 Ponte Vedra Blvd., Ponte Vedra Beach, tel. 904/285-1111 or 800/234-7842), with 36 holes, and the **Tournament Players Club** (Marriott at Sawgrass, 110 TPC Blvd., Ponte Vedra Beach, tel. 904/273-3235 or 800/457-4653), with 18 holes (99 total holes at the resort) and home of the PGA Tour. The **Jacksonville Beach Public Golf Course** (605 S. Penman Rd., Jacksonville Beach, tel. 904/249-8600) is open every day of the year. A round of golf is modestly priced at $25 per person including cart, and you can walk for $14.50.

Tennis Resorts especially well known for their tennis programs include the **Marriott at Sawgrass** (Ponte Vedra Beach, tel. 904/285-7777) and the **Ponte Vedra Inn & Club** (Ponte Vedra Beach, tel. 904/285-3856). The **Huguenot Tennis Center** (S. 16th Ave. and 3rd St., Jacksonville Beach, tel. 904/249-9407) has six hard-surface courts, a pro shop, and locker rooms, and courts cost just $3 per person per hour.

Water Sports Most of the local surf shops on the beaches rent surfboards for $10-$20 a day, but most require deposits of $50-$150, which are refundable. Sailboard rentals run about $35 a day.

Spectator Sports

Golf The Tournament Players Championship is a March event at the **Tournament Players Club** (near Sawgrass in Ponte Vedra Beach, tel. 904/273-3382 or 800/404-7887).

Nightlife **Ragtime Taproom Brewery** (207 Atlantic Blvd., Atlantic Beach, tel. 904/241-7877) resonates with live local jazz and blues bands Thursday through Sunday.

Mayport Loop

Dating back more than 300 years, **Mayport** is one of the oldest fishing villages in the United States. Today it's home to a large commercial shrimp-boat fleet and is the Navy's fourth-largest home port. The surrounding area has an interesting group of sights, arranged in a circle, which make for a nice drive. Where you start will depend on where you're staying, but however you go, consider taking the fun **ferry** ride between Fort George Island and Mayport, at the mouth of the St. Johns River (A1A follows the ferry route). *3 mi east of Rte. A1A, tel. 904/246-2922. Fare: $2.50 per car, 50¢ pedestrians. Runs daily 6:20 AM–10 PM, every ½ hr.*

From Mayport, travel south on A1A to Route 10. Drive west for about 2 miles to Girven Road, and follow signs to the **Fort Caroline National Monument** (about 8 miles). The original fort was built in the 1560s by French Huguenots, who were later slaughtered by the Spanish in the first major clash between European powers for control of what would become the United States. A replica maintains the memory of a brief French presence in this area. Today, it's a sunny place to picnic (bring your own food and drink), stretch your legs, and explore a small museum. *12713 Fort Caroline Rd., tel. 904/641-7111. Admission free. Museum open daily 9–5; closed Dec. 25.*

Take Fort Caroline Road west to Route 9A; travel north on it for 3 miles, crossing the N.B. Broward Bridge (known locally as Dames Point Bridge); take the first exit (Route 105/Heckscher Drive); and drive northeast for about 12 miles to **Fort George Island,** where signs
★ will lead you to the **Kingsley Plantation.** Built by an eccentric slave trader, the Kingsley dates to 1792 and is the oldest remaining plan-

tation in the state. Slave quarters, as well as the modest Kingsley home, are open to the public. *Tel. 904/251–3537. Admission free. Open daily 9–5; guided tours Thurs.–Mon. at 9:30, 11, 1:30, 3.*

To finish the loop north of Mayport, drive northeast from the plantation for about 5 miles on A1A to the **Talbot Island State Parks.** Here you'll find 17 miles of gorgeous beaches, sand dunes, and golden marshes that hum with birds and bugs. Come to picnic, fish, swim, snorkel, or camp. *Tel. 904/251–2320. Admission: $3.25 per vehicle with up to 8 people. Open daily 8–sunset.*

Beaches **Kathryn Abbey Hanna Park,** near Mayport, is the Jacksonville area's showplace park, drawing families and singles alike. It offers beaches, showers, and snack bars that operate April–Labor Day.

Amelia Island/Fernandina Beach

Amelia Island–Fernandina Beach Chamber of Commerce (102 Centre St., Amelia Island 32034, tel. 904/261–3248).

The town of Fernandina Beach lies north of Jacksonville on Amelia Island, across the border from St. Marys, Georgia. Once an important political and commercial stronghold, now a quaint haven for in-the-know tourists, Fernandina Beach offers a wide range of accommodations from bed-and-breakfasts to the elegant Ritz-Carlton Amelia Island (*see* Budget Lodging, *below*).

The town's **historic district** contains 50 blocks of historically registered homes, including some of the nation's finest examples of Queen Anne, Victorian, and Italianate mansions, which date back to the haven's glory days in the mid-19th century. Begin your self-guided walking or driving tour with a visit to the **old railroad depot** (102 Centre St., tel. 904/261–3248), originally a stopping point on the first cross-state railroad and now home to the chamber of commerce.

Follow Centre Street (which turns into Atlantic Avenue) east for about eight blocks to **St. Peter's Episcopal Church.** Founded in 1859, the church once served as a school for freed slaves. Continuing on Atlantic Avenue, you will reach the bridge. From here you can see the **Amelia Lighthouse,** built in 1839. It's a great background for photos, but the inside is not open to the public.

★ A mile north of town is **Fort Clinch State Park,** home to one of the country's best-preserved and most complete brick forts. Ft. Clinch protected against further British intrusion after the War of 1812 and was occupied in 1863 by the Confederacy; a year later it was retaken by the North. During the Spanish-American War, it was reactivated for a brief time but for the most part was not used. Today the park offers camping, nature trails, carriage rides, swimming, surf fishing, picnicking, and living-history reenactments showing life in the garrison at the time of the Civil War. *Tel. 904/261–4212. Admission: $3.25 per vehicle with up to 8 people. Open daily 8–sunset.*

Budget **1735 House.** Flower-filled window boxes grace the exterior of this
Lodging charming New England–style inn. Ocean-view suites are furnished
$$ with captain's bunks covered with Hudson Bay blankets, wicker furniture, and 19th-century sea chests. There is also a romantic two-bedroom suite in a replica of a lighthouse. *584 S. Fletcher Ave., 32034, tel. 904/261–5878. 5 suites. Facilities: beach. AE, MC, V.*

Splurge **Ritz-Carlton Amelia Island.** Considered by many to be the finest re-
★ sort in Florida, this hotel woos guests with its stylish elegance, superb comfort, and excellent service, plus one of the prettiest and most pristine beaches on Florida's east coast. All units in the eight-story building have balconies and ocean views. Suites and rooms are very spacious and predictably luxurious, with wall-to-wall carpet-

ing, comfortable chairs, and king-size or two double beds. All have a separate dressing and closet area plus oversize marble baths. The top-floor Ritz-Carlton Club has a private lounge with complimentary beverages and an ever-changing array of culinary delights. Public areas are exquisitely maintained, grounds are beautifully manicured, and fine cuisine can be had at a choice of restaurants, including the award-winning Grill (*see below*). This is the only Ritz-Carlton with an on-site golf course. *4750 Amelia Island Pkwy., 32034, tel. 904/277–1100. 449 rooms. Facilities: 3 restaurants, 3 bars, indoor and outdoor pools, 18-hole golf course, 9 tennis courts (5 lighted), fitness center, beach, bicycles. AE, D, DC, MC, V.*

Budget Dining
$–$$
★

O'Kane's Irish Pub. Stop here for authentic Irish fare: shepherd's pie, steak and Guinness pie, corned beef and cabbage, or fish-and-chips. Also on the menu are sandwiches, ribs, and pasta and an amazing soup that's served in a bowl of sourdough bread. You eat the whole thing! This is one of the few bars in the United States that still prepares Irish coffee the way they do in Ireland—with very cold, barely whipped heavy cream floated on top. *318 Centre St., tel. 904/ 261–1000. Reservations accepted. Dress: casual. AE, MC, V.*

¢

Palace Saloon. The state's oldest continuously operating watering hole, this saloon still sports swinging doors that look like they're straight out of Dodge City. Stop in for a cold drink and a bowl of boiled shrimp. The menu is limited, but the place is unpretentious, comfortable, and as genuine as a silver dollar. *117 Centre St., tel. 904/261–6320. No reservations. Dress: casual but neat. MC, V.*

Splurge
★

The Grill. Hotel restaurants can be less than great, but this quietly elegant dining room in the Ritz-Carlton Amelia Island is truly outstanding. Chef Matthew Medure has created an exhilarating and unusual menu, and, thanks to his talent, it works. Dine on grilled bison tenderloin with stewed Vidalia onions in a tuna sauce or salmon escallop with angel hair pasta in tomato-basil oil. Appetizers include wild-mushroom ragout, oyster and mussel bisque, and an exceptional grilled foie gras. The daring can choose the Adventurous Guest menu, a multicourse meal created for you on the spot by the chef. *4750 Amelia Island Pkwy., tel. 904/277–1100. Reservations required. Dress: jacket required for men, dress or pantsuit required for women. AE, D, MC, V. No lunch.*

Shopping for Bargains

Historic Downtown Fernandina is geared to the tourist trade, so don't expect to find bargain-basement merchandise. **Palmetto Walk,** north of Amelia Island Plantation, is even more trendy, but both shopping districts will get you into the spirit of things and are worth checking out for an unexpected price break.

Golf and Tennis

With 45 holes of golf and plenty of courts, **Amelia Island Plantation** (3000 First Coast Hwy., Amelia Island 32034, tel. 904/261–6161 or 800/874–6878 for golf or 904/277–5145 for tennis) is favored by golf and tennis enthusiasts. Each year it's the site of the nationally televised WTA Championships.

Tour 2: St. Augustine Area

The first U.S. site marked for settlement by European explorers, St. Augustine traces its existence back to 1513, when it was founded on Easter Sunday by Ponce de León. The 61-year-old Spaniard's quest for a Fountain of Youth was precipitated by his infatuation with a teenage girl. A Fountain of Youth Memorial Park marks the spot where de León began his search for his anti-aging elixir, and a bubbling fountain just a few paces away offers sips of what is alleged to be the "youthfulness water." There are those who contend that little has changed in St. Augustine since de León's time. In Old St. Augustine, residents still work at traditional handcrafts, such as jewelry-making and metal-working. Much of this old city's charm stems from the restored 16th-century buildings that line its streets.

Once you've visited the historic sites, however, you haven't exhausted this area's charms. There are beaches and gardens and more contemporary attractions to whet the explorer's appetite.

Arriving and Departing
By Bus

Greyhound Lines (tel. 800/231–2222) stops in St. Augustine (100 Malaga St., tel. 904/829–6401); a one-way fare from Jacksonville is $9.

By Car

To reach St. Augustine, take U.S. 1 south from Jacksonville or Route A1A south from Jacksonville Beach, a drive that takes about 45 minutes.

St. Augustine

St. Augustine Visitor Information Center (10 Castillo Dr., St. Augustine 32084, tel. 904/825–1000).

Numbers in the margin correspond to points of interest on the St. Augustine map.

Upon arrival, head straight for the Visitor Information Center (*see above*), where you'll find loads of brochures, maps, and information about the nation's oldest city. There's lots to see, and you may want to choose the sights you are most interested in from the many described below.

★ ❶ The massive **Castillo de San Marcos National Monument** looks every century of its 300 years. Park rangers provide an introductory narration, after which you're on your own. This is a wonderful fort to explore, complete with moat, turrets, and 16-foot-thick walls. The fort was constructed of coquina, a soft limestone made of broken shells and coral, and it took 25 years to build. Garrison rooms depict the life of the era, and special artillery demonstrations are held periodically on the gun deck. *1 Castillo Dr., tel. 904/829–6506. Admission: $2 ages 16–62. Open Mar.–Nov., daily 9–6; Dec.–Feb., daily 9–5:15.*

❷ The **City Gate,** at the top of St. George Street, is a relic from the days when the Castillo's moat ran westward to the river and the Cubo Defense Line (defensive wall) protected the settlement against approaches from the north. Today it is the entrance to the city's popular restored area.

❸ The **Oldest Wooden Schoolhouse** (14 St. George St.) is a tiny, 18th-century structure that, because it was the closest structure to the city gate, served as a guardhouse and sentry shelter during the Seminole Wars.

❹ Stop by the **Museum Theatre** to see *Dream of an Empire,* about St. Augustine's founding. There are nine showings daily. *5 Cordova St., tel. 904/824–0339. Admission: $3 adults, $1.50 children under 15. Open daily 9–5.*

❺ The **Spanish Quarter** is a state-operated, living-history village with eight sites; you can wander through the narrow streets at your own pace. Along your way you may see a Colonial soldier's wife cooking over an open fire; a blacksmith building his shop (a historic reconstruction); and craftspeople busy at candle dipping, spinning, weaving, and cabinet-making. They are all making reproductions that will be used within the restored area. *Entrance at Triay House, 29 St. George St., tel. 904/825–6830. Admission: $5 adults, $3.75 senior citizens, $2.50 students 6–18, $10 family ticket. Open daily 9–5.*

❻ The **Basilica Cathedral of St. Augustine** has parish records dating back to 1594, the oldest written records in the country. Following a fire in 1887, extensive changes were made to the current structure,

Basilica Cathedral of
St. Augustine, **6**

Castillo de San Marcos
National Monument, **1**

City Gate, **2**

Flagler College, **11**

Flagler Memorial
Presbyterian
Church, **12**

Fountain of Youth, **14**

Lightner Museum, **10**

Mission of Nombre
de Dios, **13**

Museum Theatre, **4**

Oldest House, **9**

Oldest Store
Museum, **8**

Oldest Wooden
Schoolhouse, **3**

Spanish Quarter, **5**

Ximenez-Fatio
House, **7**

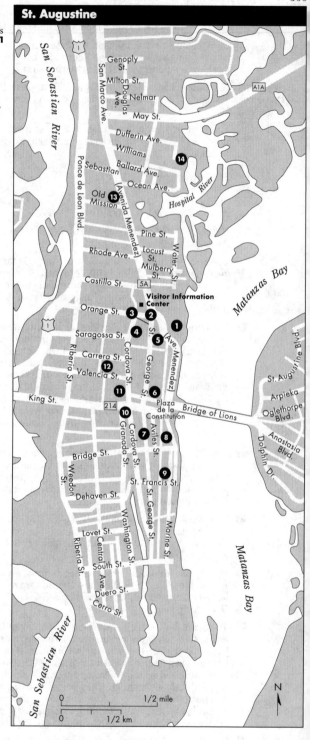

which dates from 1797. It was remodeled in the mid-1960s. *40 Cathedral Pl., tel. 904/824–2806. Donations welcome. Open weekdays 5:30–5, weekends 5:30–7.*

Plaza de la Constitution, at St. George Street and Cathedral Place, is the central area of the original settlement. It was laid out in 1598 by decree of King Philip II, and little has changed since. At its center there is a monument to the Spanish constitution of 1812; at the east end is a public market dating from Early American days. Just beyond is a statue of Juan Ponce de León.

❼ The **Ximenez-Fatio House** was built in 1797, and it became a boarding house for tourists in 1885. *20 Aviles St., tel. 904/829–3575. Admission free. Open Mar.–Aug., Sun.–Thurs. 1–4.*

❽ The **Oldest Store Museum** re-creates a turn-of-the-century general store. There are high-button shoes, lace-up corsets, patent drugs, and confectionery specialties. *4 Artillery La., tel. 904/829–9729. Admission: $3.50 adults, $3 senior citizens, $1.50 children 6–12. Open Mon.–Sat. 9–5, Sun. noon–5.*

❾ Operated by the Historical Society, the **Oldest House** reflects much of the city's history through its changes and additions, from the coquina walls built soon after the town was burned in 1702 to the house's enlargement during the British occupation. *14 St. Francis St., tel. 904/824–2872. Admission: $5 adults, $4.50 senior citizens, $2.50 students, $10 family ticket. Open daily 9–5.*

★ ❿ The **Lightner Museum** is housed in one of two posh hotels built in 1888 by Henry Flagler, who wanted to turn Florida into an American Riviera. The museum contains a collection of ornate antique music boxes (demonstrations daily at 11 and 2), and the Lightner Antique Mall perches on three levels of what was the hotel's grandiose indoor pool. *75 King St., tel. 904/824–2874. Admission to museum: $4 adults, $1 students over 12. Museum open daily 9–5; mall open Tues.–Sun. 10–4.*

⓫ Across from the Lightner Museum, **Flagler College** (78 King St.) occupies the second of Flagler's hotels. The riveting structure is replete with towers, turrets, and arcades decorated by Louis Comfort Tiffany. The front courtyard is open to the public.

⓬ Behind Flagler College, the **Flagler Memorial Presbyterian Church,** which Flagler built in 1889, is a splendid Venetian Renaissance structure. The dome towers more than 100 feet, and it is topped by a 20-foot Greek cross. *Valencia and Sevilla Sts. Open weekdays 8:30–4:30.*

⓭ North of the historic district are a few more sights. Head up San Marco Avenue to Old Mission Road to see the **Mission of Nombre de Dios,** which commemorates the site where America's first Christian mass was celebrated. A 208-foot stainless-steel cross marks the spot where the mission's first cross was planted. *San Marco Ave. and Old Mission Rd., tel. 904/824–2809. Donations requested. Open mid-Feb.–Nov., daily 7 AM–8 PM; Dec.–mid-Feb., daily 8–6.*

⓮ From San Marco Avenue, head east on Dufferin Avenue to the **Fountain of Youth,** which salutes Ponce de León. In the complex there is a springhouse, an explorer's globe, a planetarium, and a Native American village. *155 Magnolia Ave., tel. 904/829–3168. Admission: $4 adults, $3 senior citizens, $1.50 children 6–12. Open daily 9–5.*

Budget **Carriage Way Bed and Breakfast.** A Victorian mansion grandly re-
Lodging stored in 1984, this B&B is within walking distance of restaurants
$$ and historic sites. Innkeepers Diane and Bill Johnson see to such
★ welcoming touches as fresh flowers and home-baked breads. A full breakfast is included in the rate. Special-occasion breakfasts, flowers, picnic lunches, romantic dinners, or a simple family supper can

be arranged with advance notice. *70 Cuna St., 32084, tel. 904/829–2467. 9 rooms. Facilities: bicycles. D, MC, V.*

$$ **Kenwood Inn.** For more than a century this stately Victorian inn has
★ been welcoming wayfarers, and the Constant family continues the tradition. Located in the heart of the historic district, the inn is within walking distance of restaurants and sightseeing. A Continental breakfast of home-baked cakes and breads is included. There's a walled-in courtyard and a fish pond. *38 Marine St., 32084, tel. 904/824–2116. 10 rooms, 4 suites. Facilities: pool. D, MC, V.*

$$ **Southern Wind Inns.** Built in 1916 by Henry Flagler, this inn is divided between two buildings a block and a half from each other. The East Inn, for adults only, is decorated with antiques. A full breakfast is served in its formal dining room or on the verandas. The West Inn, for families, has roomy suites for less than $100. Each suite has a refrigerator and microwave and can accommodate three to six people. Breakfast for West Inn residents is served in their rooms, though adults are also welcome to eat at the East Inn. *18 Cordova St. and 34 Saragossa St., 32084, tel. 904/825–3623. 13 rooms. Facilities: bicycles. D, MC, V.*

$$ **Victorian House.** This tiny inn was built in 1890 and has just four rooms and four suites. Walls are delicately hand-stenciled, pine plank floors are dotted with hand-hooked rugs, and there are many period antiques. Continental breakfast is served daily. *11 Cadiz St., 32084, tel. 904/824–5214. 8 units. Facilities: bicycles. AE, D, MC, V.*

$ **St. Francis Inn.** If only the walls could whisper, this late-18th-century house would tell tales of slave uprisings, buried doubloons, and Confederate spies. The inn, which has been a guest house since 1845, now offers rooms, suites, an apartment, and a cottage. Furnishings are a mix of antiques and just plain old. Rates include Continental breakfast. *279 St. George St., 32084, tel. 904/824–6068. 16 units. Facilities: pool, bicycles. MC, V.*

Budget Dining **Columbia.** An heir to the cherished reputation of the original Co-
$$ lumbia, founded in Tampa in 1905, this one serves time-honored Cuban and Spanish dishes including arroz con pollo, filet *salteado* (with a spicy sauce), shrimp and scallops Marbella, and a fragrant, flagrant paella. The Fiesta Brunch on Sunday is a bountiful array of everything from a grand steamship round to cheeses and cold meats to Belgian waffles. Although some entrées run more than $20, there are also some at $10 and portions are large. *98 St. George St., tel. 904/824–3341 or 800/227–1905 in FL. Reservations advised for dinner. Dress: casual but neat. AE, D, MC, V.*

$$ **La Parisienne.** Tiny and attentive, pleasantly lusty in its approach to
★ honest bistro cuisine, this little place is a true find—and weekend brunches are available, too. Save room for the pastries at this excellent, very French restaurant. *60 Hypolita St., tel. 904/829–0055. Reservations required for dinner. Dress: casual but neat. AE, MC, V. Closed Mon.*

$$ **Le Pavilion.** The Swiss chef's Continental approach spills over from France to Germany with a wow of a schnitzel with spätzle. Hearty soups and good breads make a budget meal, or you can splurge on the rack of lamb or escargot. *45 San Marco Ave., tel. 904/824–6202. Reservations advised, required for parties of 6 or more. Dress: casual but neat. AE, D, DC, MC, V.*

$$ **Raintree.** The oldest home in this part of the city, this building has been lovingly restored and is worth a visit even though the food is generally not outstanding. The buttery breads and pastries are baked on the premises. Try the brandied pepper steak or the Maine lobster special. The Raintree's madrigal and champagne dinners are especially fun. The wine list is impressive, and there are two dozen beers to choose from. Courtesy pickup is available from any lodging in the city. *102 San Marco Ave., tel. 904/824–7211. Reservations accepted. Dress: casual but neat. AE, DC, MC, V. No lunch.*

$$ **Santa Maria.** This ramshackle landmark, run by the same family since the 1950s, perches over the water beside the colorful city marina. Seafood is the focus, but there are also steaks, chicken, prime rib, and a children's menu. Have drinks first in the salty lounge or feed the fish from the open-air porch. *135 Avenida Menendez, tel. 904/829–6578. No reservations. Dress: casual. AE, DC, MC, V.*

$ **Zaharias.** The room is big, busy, and buzzing with openhanded hospitality. Serve yourself from an enormous buffet instead of, or in addition to, ordering from the menu. Greek and Italian specialties include homemade pizza, a big gyro dinner served with a side order of spaghetti, shish kebab, steaks, seafood, and sandwiches. *3945 Rte. A1A S, tel. 904/471–4799. Reservations accepted. Dress: casual. AE, MC, V.*

Beaches If you and your feet tire of historic sites, escape to any of St. Augustine's 43 miles of wide, white, level Atlantic Ocean beaches. **St. Augustine Beach,** where young people gravitate, and the family-oriented **Anastasia State Recreation Area,** both on Anastasia Island, across the Bridge of Lions, are accessible via Route A1A.

Golf Two local places to play are **Ponce de Leon Golf and Conference Resort** (4000 U.S. 1N, tel. 904/824–2821), 18 holes, and **Sheraton Palm Coast** (300 Clubhouse Dr., Palm Coast, tel. 904/445–3000), 90 holes.

Nightlife **Scarlett O'Hara's** (70 Hypolita St., tel. 904/824–6535) has live blues, jazz, or reggae bands nightly. **Trade Winds** (124 Charlotte St., tel. 904/829–9336) showcases live bands most nights; call for a schedule. Crowds head to **White Lion** (20 Cuna St., tel. 904/829–2388) for a variety of live music on weekends. Call to find out who's playing and the type of music being played.

South of St. Augustine

Marineland, one of the first of such attractions in the United States, is still a magic place. Dolphins grin, sea lions bark, and seals slither seductively to everyone's delight. *South of St. Augustine on Rte. A1A, Marineland, tel. 904/471–1111 or 800/824–4218 in FL. Admission: $12 adults, $9 students 12–18, $7 children 3–11. Open daily 9–5:30; shows held continuously.*

Two miles farther south, off A1A, is **Washington Oaks State Gardens,** a preserve with 389 acres hugging the shores of the Atlantic Ocean and Mantanzas River. The craggy, boulder-strewn beach on the Atlantic side is a bird-watcher's paradise; flocks of shorebirds come to feed in the pools here when the tide is out. Along the riverbanks are ornamental gardens where the landscape is less rugged. *6400 N. Ocean Blvd., Palm Coast, tel. 904/445–3161. Admission: $3.25 per vehicle with up to 8 people. Open daily 8–sunset.*

Inland, **Ravine State Gardens** is about 25 miles southwest of St. Augustine and 55 miles south of Jacksonville. Begun during the Depression as a WPA project, it blossomed into one of the area's great azalea showplaces. Any month is a good time to hike the shady glens here, but the gardens are nothing short of spectacular in February and March when the azaleas are in full bloom. *Off Twig St., from U.S. 17 S, Palatka, tel. 904/329–3721. Admission: $3.25 per vehicle with up to 8 people. Open daily 8–sunset.*

Tour 3: Daytona Area

Daytona Beach, home of the Daytona 500, the biggest stock-car event in the world, has been a magnet for racing fans since 1902, when the sport was founded near here on the hard-packed sands of Ormond Beach. To pay homage to that tradition, Daytona is one of the few places left that still allows driving on the beach, just one of the things that attracts spring breakers here in droves. The invasion only lasts for a couple of weeks in March; during the calm after the storm, a more sedate sort of tourist traffic settles in, consisting of senior citizens and families with kids.

Daytona Beach was first developed with elaborate beach cottages for affluent northerners who came by rail. Then came tourist camps and tourist courts, which lured car travelers with billboards up and down the East Coast. The boom continued into the '60s, when franchise motels began to appear, and into the '80s, with the construction of high-rise hotels. Some of the old stuff was torn out to make way for the new, but many existing facilities were renovated and updated. The result is a wonderful mixture of small family-owned motels and quaint bed-and-breakfast inns along with glitzy condos and posh resorts.

In the '30s, a promotional brochure touted Daytona's "all-season rates" and its "reasonableness." It still makes good on that boast. Throughout Daytona the emphasis is on family, so if you're traveling with children, be sure to check whether the property you're interested in lets them stay free: Many do.

Unlike the string of beach communities that sprang up along the railroads sometime around the turn of the century, New Smyrna Beach goes back a ways. Indian mounds hereabouts date to pre-Columbian times. New Smyrna also was the site of an 18th-century British colony organized by a Scottish physician, Dr. Andrew Turnbull, which was nearly three times larger than the settlement at Jamestown. (It gets its name from the Turkish birthplace of Turnbull's wife.) Believing that Mediterranean peoples would flourish in Florida, Turnbull rounded up eight shiploads of Greeks, Corsicans, and Minorcans and transported them to New Smyrna in 1768 with the promise of 50 acres of land to each family head in exchange for eight years of indentured servitude. Nine years later, however, the multicultural colony had dwindled from the original 1,500 to fewer than 600, and it was dissolved in 1777. Today, New Smyrna Beach has a large retiree population. Like Daytona Beach, it's reasonably priced, but it moves at a slower pace than its neighbor. It's known primarily for its 7-mile-long white-sand beach, its national seashore, and its art center.

Arriving and Departing
By Plane

Daytona Beach International Airport is served by American, Continental, Delta, and USAir. Taxi fare to beach hotels is about $10–$12; cab companies include **Yellow Cab** (tel. 904/252–5536), **Checker Cab** (tel. 904/255–8421), and **AAA Cab** (tel. 904/253–2522). **DOTS Transit Service** (tel. 904/257–5411) has scheduled service connecting the Daytona Beach airport to Orlando International Airport, the Sheraton Palm Coast area, De Land, De Land's Amtrak station, Sanford, and Deltona; fares are $26 one-way and $46 round-trip between the Daytona and Orlando airports, $20 one-way and $36 round-trip from the Orlando airport to De Land or Deltona.

By Bus

Greyhound Lines (tel. 800/231–2222) buses stop in Daytona Beach (138 S. Ridgewood Rd., tel. 904/255–7076) and De Land (E. Ohio Ave., tel. 904/734–2747). The one-way fare to Daytona Beach is $15 from Jacksonville and $11 from St. Augustine; between Daytona Beach and De Land, it's $5.50.

By Car

From north and south, take I–95 into Daytona or the more local U.S. 1 (called the Dixie Highway here). From Tampa, Orlando, and other points to the southwest, take I–4.

By Train

Amtrak (tel. 800/872–7245) serves the Daytona Beach area via De Land (Old New York Ave., tel. 904/829–6401), which is 30 minutes inland. Trains traveling from Tampa and the Northeast Corridor stop there.

Getting Daytona Beach has an excellent bus network, **Votran** (tel. 904/756–
Around 7496), which serves the beach area, airport, shopping malls, and ma-
By Bus jor arteries. Exact fare (75¢) is required.

By Car Route A1A connects towns along the coast, whereas U.S. 1 runs
parallel down the mainland side of the Intracoastal Waterway. To
reach New Smyrna Beach, 15 miles south of Daytona, take U.S. 1
and then pick up A1A to reach the ocean. U.S. 92 (International
Speedway Boulevard) runs east–west from De Land straight
through Daytona to the beach.

Daytona Beach and Ormond Beach

Like most of coastal Florida, Daytona sprang up around the water,
so its waterfront offers views of historic homes between expanses of
natural marsh. As you venture along the Intracoastal Waterway,
take note of the different names assigned to the passage. In the Daytona area, it's called the Halifax River, though it is not actually a river but a tidal waterway that flows between the mainland and the
barrier islands.

A good place to begin touring the Daytona environs is **Ormond
Beach** and **Tomoka State Park.** From I–95, take Exit 88 (Route 40)
east, cross the Old Dixie Highway (U.S. 1), turn left at North Beach
Street, and drive for 2 miles. The park is the site of a Timucuan Indian settlement discovered in 1605 by Spanish explorer Alvaro Mexia.
Wooded campsites, bicycle and walking paths, and guided canoe
tours on the Tomoka and Halifax rivers are the main attractions.
*2099 N. Beach St., tel. 904/676–4050. Admission: June–Dec., $8 per
day; Jan.–May, $15 per day; electricity, $2 per day. Open daily 8–
sunset.*

Continue east on Route 40 to the water. Auto racing was born on this
hard-packed beach back in 1902, when R.E. Olds and Alexander
Winton staged the first race. **Birthplace of Speed Antique Car Show
and Swap Meet** is an annual event, attracting enthusiasts from
across the nation.

Follow Route 40 across the causeway, and at the far end, turn right
on Riverside Drive to see the **Casements,** the restored winter retreat of John D. Rockefeller, now serving as a cultural center and
museum. The estate and its formal gardens host an annual lineup of
special events and exhibits. Tours of the estate also are offered. *25
Riverside Dr., tel. 904/673–4701. Donations welcome. Open Mon.–
Thurs. 9–9, Fri. 9–5, Sat. 9–noon.*

Go one block east to the **Ormond Memorial Art Museum and Gardens,** where you can walk through lush tropical gardens, past
fishponds and fountains. Inside are historical displays and exhibits
by Florida artists. *78 E. Granada Blvd., tel. 904/677–1857. Admission free. Open Tues.–Fri. 11–4; weekends noon–4.*

★ One more block to the east, the **Birthplace of Speed Museum** is devoted to the most exciting moments in America's long love affair
with the automobile. The museum exhibits a replica of the Stanley
Steamer, old Model T and Model A Fords, and a wealth of auto-racing memorabilia. *160 E. Granada Blvd., tel. 904/676–3216. Admission: $1 adults, 50¢ children under 12. Open Tues.–Sat. 1–5.*

To reach (and drive on) the famous beaches of Daytona, follow A1A
several miles south to the beginning of **Daytona Beach,** and follow
signs to beach ramps, which occur frequently for the next 10 miles.
During spring break, race weeks, and summer holidays, expect
heavy traffic along this strip of garishly painted beach motels and
tacky souvenir shops.

Cross over to the mainland on East International Speedway Boulevard, and turn south on Beach Street. At the **Halifax Historical Soci-**

ety **Museum,** photographs, Native American artifacts, and memorabilia from the early days of beach automobile racing are on display. There is also a postcard exhibit and a video that details the history of the city, and you can shop for gifts and antiques. *252 S. Beach St., tel. 904/255–6976. Admission: $2 adults, 50¢ children 12 and under. Open Tues.–Sat. 10–4.*

Now head back up Beach Street to International Speedway Boulevard (also known as Volusia Avenue), and drive west. Just past Nova Road look for signs for the **Southeast Museum of Photography.** One of only 12 photography museums in the country, it contains historical and contemporary exhibits that change throughout the year. *1200 International Speedway Blvd., tel. 904/254–4475. Admission free. Open Tues. 10–3 and 5–7, Wed.–Fri. 10–3, Sun. 1–4.*

Return to Nova Road and turn south, following signs to Museum Boulevard and the **Museum of Arts and Sciences.** This competent little museum has two blockbuster features: One is a large collection of pre-Castro Cuban art; the other is a complete and eye-popping skeleton of a giant sloth, 13 feet long and 130,000 years old. The sloth remains—found near here—are the most complete skeleton of its kind ever found in North America. *1040 Museum Blvd., tel. 904/255–0285. Admission: $3 adults, $1 children and students; members free Fri. Open Tues.–Fri. 9–4, weekends noon–5.*

If you've got children with you, you might want to stop at **Castle Adventure,** a slick update of an old-style family fun park, where you can play miniature golf, wander through a giant maze, and explore waterfalls, caves, and lush tropical landscaping. *200 Hagen Terr., off U.S. 92, tel. 904/238–3887. Admission: $7 adults, $6 children and senior citizens; golf or maze alone: $5.50 adults, $3.50 children and senior citizens. Open daily 10–10.*

Budget Lodging

$$ **Howard Johnson Hotel.** Straight out of the glamour films of the 1930s, this 14-story hotel on the beach is an oldie that has been brought back to the splendor of its Deco years. Kitchenette suites are available. There's live entertainment and dancing in the lounge. *600 N. Atlantic Ave., Daytona Beach 32118, tel. 904/255–4471 or 800/767–4471, fax 904/253–7543. 324 rooms. Facilities: restaurant, lounge, pool. AE, D, DC, MC, V.*

$$ **Perry's Ocean-Edge.** Long regarded as a family resort, Perry's is famous for its free homemade doughnuts and coffee—a breakfast ritual. Served in the lush solarium, it's a good way to get acquainted with other guests. The hotel's 700 feet of oceanfront lawns stretch along the beach. Three-quarters of the rooms are efficiencies, and most have great ocean views. For something to do, you can choose from several pools, including an indoor one; a wide beach; and a putting green. *2209 S. Atlantic Ave., Daytona Beach 32118, tel. 904/255–0581, 800/447–0002 outside FL, or 800/342–0102 in FL, fax 904/258–7315. 204 rooms. Facilities: café, indoor pool, 2 outdoor pools, beach, putting green, beach, game room. AE, D, DC, MC, V.*

$ **Aladdin Inn.** An onion-dome-shape pool carries out the Turkish theme at this high-rise, where Las Vegas–type glitz is tempered by the sands and palms of the Atlantic Coast. Most of the airy and spacious rooms have refrigerators; ocean-side units have balconies overlooking the surf. Thanks to the building's unique shape and placement, the sundeck is in business year-round. *2323 S. Atlantic Ave., Daytona Beach Shores 32118, tel. 904/255–0476 or 800/874–7517, fax 904/255–3376. 118 rooms. Facilities: 2 pools, shuffleboard, game room, laundry. AE, D, DC, MC, V.*

$ **Mainsail Motel.** Right on the beach, this four-story building has a nautical theme—windows in the corridors are portholes, for example. Rooms are quite large and well maintained. Most have at least a glimpse of the ocean, and some have truly excellent ocean views. On top of that, management is quite friendly and helpful. *281 S. Atlan* tic Beach St., Ormond Beach 32176, tel. 904/677–2131. Facilities: 2 pools, sauna, exercise room, beach. AE, D, MC, V.

Splurge **Captain's Quarters Inn.** It may look like just another mid-rise hotel,
★ but inside, this is a home away from home and quite a bargain off-season, when units drop from $145 to $75. An antique desk, Victorian love seat, and tropical greenery grace the lobby of this beachfront, all-suite inn, and fresh-baked goodies and coffee are served in the Galley, which overlooks the ocean and resembles Grandma's kitchen with a few extra tables and chairs. Each guest suite features rich oak furnishings, a complete kitchen, and private balcony. Penthouse suites have fireplaces. *3711 S. Atlantic Ave., Daytona Beach Shores 32127, tel. 904/767–3119, fax 904/760–7712. 25 suites. Facilities: pool. AE, D, MC, V.*

Budget Dining **Anna's Trattoria.** White table linens and flowers set the scene for de-
$$ lightful Italian fare. Choose from two pages of delicious pasta items:
★ spaghetti with Italian sausage and onions, angel hair with fresh chopped tomatoes and garlic, and spinach ravioli. There are also many veal and chicken dishes. *304 Seabreeze Blvd., Daytona Beach, tel. 904/239–9624. Reservations accepted. Dress: casual. AE, MC, V. Closed Mon.*

$$ **Cafe Frappe.** This cozy second-floor restaurant across from a park
★ cooks up such unusual appetizers as a papaya and Brie quesadilla and ravioli stuffed with goat cheese and sun-dried tomatoes. Entrées include beef tenderloin sautéed with herbs and peppers, shrimp in an Asiago-Romano cream sauce, and fresh salmon. *174 N. Beach St., Daytona Beach, tel. 904/254–7999. Reservations advised. Dress: casual but neat. AE, DC, MC, V. No dinner Sun.–Mon., no lunch weekends.*

$ **Aunt Catfish's on the River.** This popular place on the southwest bank of the Intracoastal (off U.S. 1, just before you cross the Port Orange Causeway), just south of Daytona, is crowded day and night. Locals and visitors flock here for the great salad bar, the hot cinnamon rolls and hush puppies that come with any entrée, the southern-style chicken, and the freshly cooked seafood—fried shrimp, fried catfish, and crab cakes are specialties. People stand in line outside for the buffet-style Sunday brunch. *4009 Halifax Dr., Port Orange, tel 904/767–4768. No reservations. Dress: casual. AE, MC, V.*

$ **Mangiere Ristorante.** Dine on the terrace overlooking the Halifax
★ River or in the spacious dining rooms decorated with delightful early 20th-century black-and-white photographs of Italian families. The food is delicious, the ambience and service are excellent, and the cost is next to nothing. There are eight pasta dishes and two chicken dishes that come with copious amounts of bread and salad for $6.95 or less. A grilled steak, the most expensive entrée, is $15. Portions are giant, and what you can't eat, you can take home in a doggy bag big enough for a Great Dane! What's called a "half" order is more than enough for one, but the recommended way to eat is to share a "full" order family-style, which makes this place an exceptional bargain. *125 Basin St., Daytona Beach, tel. 904/248–8400. No reservations. Dress: casual. AE, D, MC, V.*

Shopping for Brand-name items are sold at discount prices at the **Daytona Beach**
Bargains **Outlet Mall** (2400 S. Ridgewood Ave., South Daytona). Daytona's **Flea Market** (I–4 at U.S. 92) is one of the South's largest.

Participant There are two marked canoe trails in the Daytona area, all part of a
Sports state recreational canoe-trail system administered by the Florida
Canoeing Department of Natural Resources. The Tomoka River trail starts on Route 40, 1 mile west of I–95, and runs for 13 miles. The 13-mile-long Bulow Creek trail originates at the Bulow Plantation Ruins State Historic Site, north of Ormond Beach.

Diving Scuba equipment, trips, refills, and lessons are available from **Adventure Diving** (3127 S. Ridgewood Ave., South Daytona, tel. 904/788–8050).

Fishing Deep-sea fishing charters are provided by **Critter Fleet Marina** (Daytona Beach, tel. 904/767–7676 or 800/338–0850 in FL).

Golf **Indigo Lakes Golf Club** (312 Indigo Dr., Daytona Beach, tel. 904 254–3607) and **Spruce Creek Golf & Country Club** (1900 Country Club Dr., Daytona Beach, tel. 904/756–6114) each have 18 holes.

Water Sports Most larger beachfront hotels rent water-sports equipment, such as sailboards, surfboards, and boogie boards, as does **Salty Dog** (700 Broadway, Daytona Beach, tel. 904/258–0457).

Spectator The massive **Daytona International Speedway** (U.S. 92, Daytona
Sports Beach, tel. 904/254–2700 for racing schedules) is home to year-round
Auto Racing auto and motorcycle racing, including the annual Daytona 500 in February and Pepsi 400 in July. Twenty-minute narrated tours of the historic track are offered daily 9–5 except on race days, and an interactive auto-racing museum, built by and adjacent to the speed way, is planned for 1996.

Dog Racing You can bet on the greyhounds every night but Sunday year-round at the **Daytona Beach Kennel Club** (U.S. 92, near the International Speedway, Daytona Beach, tel. 904/252–6484).

Jai Alai The speediest of sports, jai alai is played seasonally at the **Daytona Beach Jai-Alai Fronton** (International Speedway Blvd., Daytona Beach, tel. 904/255–0504).

The Arts and Broadway touring shows, top-name entertainers, and other major
Nightlife events are booked at the **Ocean Center** (101 N. Atlantic Ave., Dayto
The Arts na Beach, tel. 904/254–4545 or 800/858–6444 in FL). **Peabody Auditorium** (600 Auditorium Blvd., Daytona Beach, tel. 904/255–1314) is used for many concerts and programs throughout the year.

Seaside Music Theater (Box 2835, Daytona Beach, tel. 904/252–3394) presents professional musicals in two venues, January–March and June–August.

Nightlife **Razzles** (640 N. Grandview St., Daytona Beach, tel. 904/257–6236) is the hottest spot in town. DJs spin high-energy dance music from early evening until the early morning hours.

Ponce Inlet

Sleepy Ponce Inlet is about 13 miles south of Daytona on Route A1A at the end of the barrier island. Here you'll find a small marina, a few bars, and informal restaurants specializing in very fresh fish. Boardwalks traverse delicate dunes and provide easy access to the beach, which has been damaged recently by some bad storms. It's frequented by locals and visitors who are familiar with the area. A manicured drive winds through low-growing shrubs and windblown scrub oaks to parking and picnic areas.

Marking this prime spot is the bright red, century-old **Ponce de León Lighthouse,** now a historic monument and museum with a little gift shop. *Tel. 904/761–1821. Admission: $4 adults, $1 children under 11. Open daily 10–5.*

Fishing For deep-sea fishing, contact **Sunny Day Charters** (tel. 904/788–3469).

New Smyrna Beach

New Smyrna Beach Chamber of Commerce (115 Canal St., New Smyrna Beach 32168, tel. 904/428–2449).

Also relatively sleepy is the town of **New Smyrna Beach,** a seashore retreat where the seagulls still outnumber the people and the only castles in sight are the ones you build in the sand.

The **Atlantic Center for the Arts**, off U.S. 1 (Dixie Freeway), has gallery exhibits that change every two months. Works by internationally known artists are featured and represent sculpture, mixed media, video, drawings, prints, and paintings. During the year, there are intensive, three-week workshops run by visual, literary, and performing master artists. Past masters have included Edward Albee, James Dickey, and Beverly Pepper. *1414 Art Center Ave., tel. 904/ 427–6975. Admission free. Open weekdays 9–5, Sun. 2–5.*

Head south to Route 44 and east across the high causeway; then turn left on Peninsula Avenue. Just before the Coast Guard station, a sign indicates the entrance to the **Smyrna Dunes Park** and its beautiful views across the inlet. Here, at the northern tip of this barrier island, 1½ miles of boardwalks crisscross sand dunes and delicate dune vegetation as they lead to beaches and a fishing jetty. Botanical signs identify the flora, and many birds can be spotted. There are picnic tables and an information center. *N. Peninsula Ave. Admission free. Open daily 7–sunset.*

Head back down Peninsula Avenue to Flagler Avenue, where you'll find a number of restaurants, a historic hotel, and stores selling antiques, clothes, gifts, books, and pottery. Drive east to the end of Flagler, and you'll find yourself right smack on the beach. Park your car on the sand and go for a swim. The beach is wide, especially at low tide, and not very crowded, except on summer weekends.

★ Drive south on the beach to the 27th Avenue exit, and turn left on A1A. About 10 miles later you'll reach the **Canaveral National Seashore,** a remarkable 57,000-acre park with 24 miles of undeveloped coastline; miles of grassy, wind-swept dunes; and a virtually empty beach. But be warned: It's against the law to walk on the dunes or pick the sea grass. Stop at any of the six parking areas and follow the wooden walkways to the beach. Ranger-led weekly programs range from canoe trips to sea turtle talks. Call for a schedule. *South end of Rte. A1A, tel. 904/428–3384. Admission free. Open sunrise–sunset.*

Remote **Playalinda Beach,** at the southern end of the national seashore (tel. 407/267–1110), is the longest stretch of undeveloped coast on Florida's Atlantic Seaboard; hundreds of giant sea turtles come ashore here from May to August to lay their eggs. The extreme northern area is favored by nude sun worshippers. There are no lifeguards, but park rangers patrol. Take Exit 80 from I–95, follow Route 406 east across the Indian River, then Route 402 east for 12 more miles.

Budget Lodging

$$ **Coastal Waters Inn.** This three-story beachfront hotel has one- and two-bedroom suites with kitchens as well as standard rooms. Some have excellent ocean views. Furnishings are spare but adequate, and the beach is just a few steps away. *3509 S. Atlantic Ave., 32169, tel. 904/428–3800. 40 units. Facilities: pool. AE, D, MC, V.*

$$ **Holiday Inn Hotel Suites.** Families tend to like these comfortable suites, which sleep four, six, or eight people. Bedrooms are raised and set behind the living room, which opens out to a balcony and a spectacular view of the ocean. The furnishings are contemporary, and each unit has a full kitchen. *1401 S. Atlantic Ave., 32169, tel. 904/426–0020. 102 suites. Facilities: restaurant, bar, pool. AE, MC, V.*

$$ **Riverview Hotel.** A landmark since 1886, this former bridge-tender's home is set back from the Intracoastal at the edge of the North Causeway, which to this day has an operating drawbridge. Rooms open out to plant-filled verandas and balconies, and views look either through trees to the Intracoastal or onto the private courtyard and pretty pool. Each room is furnished differently with charming antique touches, such as an old washbasin, a quilt, or a rocking chair. A complimentary Continental breakfast is served in your room. The inn is near many interesting shops. *103 Flagler Ave.,*

32169, tel. 904/428–5858 or 800/945–7416, fax 904/423–8927. 18 rooms. Facilities: restaurant, pool, bicycles. AE, D, DC, MC, V.

Budget Dining
$$ **Skyline.** Watch private airplanes land and take off at the New Smyrna Beach airport as you dine on secretly seasoned Tony Barbera steaks, veal, shrimp, chicken, and fish. Service can be overbearing here and prices are high for the area, but the fresh fish is usually excellent. *2004 N. Dixie Fwy., tel. 904/428–5325. Reservations advised. Dress: casual but neat. AE, MC, V. No lunch.*

$ **Norwood's Seafood Restaurant.** Crowds head day and night to this casual New Smyrna Beach landmark, which has been open almost 50 years. Fresh local fish and shrimp are the specialties here, but you can also order grilled filet mignon, grilled or blackened chicken breast, jambalaya, and pasta. The mashed potatoes and onion rings are outstanding. Prices are incredibly low, and the wine list is extraordinarily extensive. Wines can also be purchased over the counter by the bottle or case. *400 E. 2nd Ave., tel. 904/428–4621. No reservations. Dress: casual. AE, MC, V.*

$ **Teddy's.** You wouldn't expect to find a New York–style Greek coffee shop in a small Florida town, but here's a great one. The menu runs the gamut from homemade soups to sandwiches, hamburgers, fresh salads, and steaks plus gyros, Greek salads, and an absolutely superb spinach pie. Early risers flock here for French toast, blueberry pancakes, and western omelets (available with Eggbeaters). *812 3rd Ave., tel. 904/428–0443. No reservations. Dress: casual. No credit cards. No dinner mid-Apr.–mid-Dec.*

Participant Sports
Biking Riverside Drive, where New Smyrna Beach's turn-of-the-century homes line the Intracoastal Waterway, is a good bicycle path, not to mention a picturesque thruway.

Canoeing You can pick up the Spruce Creek trail 10 miles west of New Smyrna Beach at the Moody Bridge (1 mi south of the Port Orange exit on I–95); from there you can paddle 5 miles upstream and 9 miles downstream. Canaveral National Seashore (*see above*) also has good canoeing.

Golf Play a round of golf for $18.50 a person at the **New Smyrna Beach Municipal Golf Club** (1000 Wayne Ave., tel. 904/424–2190). It's one of the only public courses routed by eminent architect Donald Ross who has designed more than 600 courses at some of the country's most prestigious private clubs.

De Land

De Land Chamber of Commerce (336 N. Woodland Blvd., De Land 32720, tel. 904/734–4331).

The gateway to the hill and lake region, as the topographers call the country surrounding Ocala, is the little town of **De Land,** home of **Stetson University.** The **Gillespie Museum of Minerals,** on the stately campus, houses one of the largest private collections of gems and minerals in the world. *Michigan and Amelia Aves., tel. 904/822–7330. Admission free. Open weekdays 9–noon and 1–4.*

Drive 4 miles south on U.S. 17/92, toward Orange City, and follow signs to **Blue Spring State Park,** a great place to spot manatees. February is the top month for sightings, but the creatures begin to head here in November, as soon as the water gets cold enough (below 68°F). The park, once a river port where paddle wheelers stopped to take on cargoes of oranges, also contains a historic homestead that is open to the public. Park facilities include camping, picnicking, and hiking. *2100 W. French Ave., Orange City, tel. 904/775–3663. Admission: $3.25 per vehicle with up to 8 people. Open 8–sunset.*

Budget Lodging

$$
De Land Country Inn. This home, replete with spacious verandas and glowing hardwoods, was built in 1903 and is furnished in an eclectic blend of restored antiques and reproductions. Hosts Raisa and Bill Lilley serve a complimentary Continental breakfast to start your day. *228 W. Howry Ave., 32720, tel. 904/736–4244. 5 rooms. Facilities: pool. AE, MC, V.*

$$
Holiday Inn De Land. Picture a snazzy, big-city hotel in a little college town, run by friendly, small-town folks with city savvy. An enormous painting by nationally known local artist Fred Messersmith dominates the plush lobby. Rooms are done in subdued colors and styles; prestige suites have housed the likes of Tom Cruise and New Kids on the Block. Tennis and golf privileges at the De Land Country Club are offered. *350 International Speedway Blvd. (U.S. 92), 32724, tel. 904/738–5200 or 800/826–3233, fax 904/734–7552. 150 rooms. Facilities: restaurant, bar, pool, nightclub. AE, D, MC, V.*

$
University Inn. For years this has been the choice of business travelers and visitors to the university. Located on campus, and across from the popular Holiday House restaurant, this motel is in a convenient location; has clean, comfortable rooms; and offers a Continental breakfast each morning. Some rooms have kitchenettes. *644 N. Woodland Blvd., 32720, tel. 904/734–5711 or 800/345–8991, fax 904/734–5716. 60 rooms. Facilities: pool. AE, D, DC, MC, V.*

Budget Dining

$$
Pondo's. You lose almost half a century as you step into what was once a romantic hideaway for young pilots who trained in De Land during the war. The owner-chef specializes in whimsical veal dishes, but he also does fish, beef, and chicken—always with fresh vegetables, a platter-size salad, and oven-baked breads. The old-fashioned bar is *Cheers*-y, and a pianist entertains. *1915 Old New York Ave., tel. 904/734–1995. Reservations advised. Dress: casual but neat. AE, MC, V.*

$
Karlings Inn. A sort of Bavarian Brigadoon, set beside a forgotten highway near De Leon Springs, this restaurant is decorated like a Black Forest inn. Karl Caeners personally oversees the preparation of the sauerbraten, red cabbage, succulent roast duckling, sumptuous soups, and tender schnitzels. Ask to see the dessert tray. On Sundays, the restaurant closes at 7. *4640 N. U.S. 17, tel. 904/985–5535. Reservations advised. Dress: casual but neat. AE, MC, V. Closed Mon. No lunch Tues.–Sat.*

$
Original Holiday House. This, the original of what has become a small chain of buffet restaurants in Florida, is enormously popular with senior citizens, families, and college students. Patrons can choose from three categories: salads only, salads and vegetables only, or the full buffet. *704 N. Woodland Blvd., tel. 904/734–6319. No reservations. Dress: casual but neat. MC, V.*

Participant Sports

Boating and Fishing
The fishing in these parts is about as good as you can get, but you have to know the St. Johns River and its associated lakes. Several freshwater fishing guides work out of De Land, but their per diem can be steep, so your best bet is to pick up a fishing map at a tackle shop or the chamber of commerce and go it alone. If you do want a guide, one of the savviest about St. Johns River bass is **Bob Stonewater** (tel. 904/736–7120). He'll tow his boat to whichever launch ramp is best for the day's fishing and meet you there.

Rental boats and motors for fishing the St. Johns are available from **Blair's Jungle Den Fish Camp** (near Astor, tel. 904/749–2264), **Highland Park Fish Camp** (tel. 904/734–2334), **South Moon Fishing Camp** (near Astor, tel. 904/749–2383), and **Tropical Apartments & Marina** (tel. 904/734–3080). Pontoon boats, houseboats, and bass boats are available from **Hontoon Landing Marina** (tel. 904/734–2474 or 800/248–2474 in FL).

Diving
In addition to ocean diving, northeast Florida offers a wide range of cave diving and snorkeling over spring "boils." For information

about spring and freshwater diving and scuba instruction, try **Dive Tour Inc.** (1403 E. New York Ave., tel. 904/736–0571).

Skydiving Anybody who wants to jump out of an airplane when it's thousands of feet up in the air can do so with the help of **Skydive De Land** (tel. 904/738–3539), open daily 8–sunset.

Tour 4: Cocoa Beach

This area, sometimes called the Space Coast, is best known for the Kennedy Space Center, where NASA has launched many a rocket over the decades. Space shuttle launches and landings still take place here. Beyond the center, though, the coast is much like elsewhere in northeast Florida.

Arriving and Cocoa Beach is about 1½ hours down the coast from Daytona on I-
Departing 95, slightly longer if you take the more scenic U.S. 1. From Orlando,
By Car about an hour's drive away, you can take the wonderfully picturesque Beeline Expressway (Route 528), with a toll of up to $2.45 per car.

Cocoa Beach

Cocoa Beach Area Chamber of Commerce (400 Fortenberry Rd., Merritt Island 32952, tel. 407/459–2200).

★ For those who are at all interested in space travel and its lore, **Spaceport USA** is perhaps the best entertainment bargain in Florida. There are two narrated bus tours: One passes by some of NASA's office and assembly buildings, including current launch facilities and the space-shuttle launching and landing sites. The other goes to Cape Canaveral Air Force Station, where early launch pads and unmanned rockets that were later adapted for manned use illuminate the history of the early space program. Even more dramatic is the IMAX film *The Dream Is Alive*, shown hourly in the Galaxy Theater. Projected onto a 5½-story screen, this overwhelming 40-minute film, shot mostly by the astronauts, takes you from astronaut training, through a thundering shuttle launch, and into the cabins where the astronauts live while in space. (A second film, *Destiny in Space*, is also worth seeing.) *Kennedy Space Center, tel. 407/452–2121 or 800/432–2153. Admission free; bus tours: $7 adults, $4 children 3–11; IMAX film: $4 adults, $2 children 3–11. Open daily 9–sunset; last tour 2 hrs before dark; closed Dec. 25, certain launch dates (call ahead).*

At the entrance to Spaceport USA, one block east of U.S. 1, is the **United States Astronaut Hall of Fame** museum. Here you can view videotapes of historical moments in the space program. *Tel. 407/269–6100. Admission: $6.95 adults, $4.95 children 3–11. Open mid-Aug.–May, daily 9–5; June–mid-Aug., daily 9–7; closed Dec. 25.*

After leaving the space center, as you go toward Cocoa Beach southbound on A1A, the first traffic light you reach marks the entrance to **Port Canaveral,** a once-bustling commercial fishing area where cruise ships and charter and party fishing boats now dock. A few miles farther south on A1A is **Cocoa Beach** proper. **Ron Jon Surf Shop** (4151 N. Atlantic Ave., tel. 407/799–8840) is a local attraction in its own right—a castle that's purple, pink, and glittery as an amusement park, plunked right down in the middle of the beach community. In downtown Cocoa Beach, cobblestoned walkways wind through **Olde Cocoa Village,** a cluster of restored turn-of-the-century buildings now occupied by restaurants and specialty shops purveying pottery, macramé, leather and silver craft, afghans, fine art, and clothing.

Take Route 520 to U.S. 1 and Michigan Avenue, then turn west, and follow the signs to the **Brevard Museum of History and Natural Science.** Don't overlook the hands-on discovery rooms and the Taylor Collection of Victorian-era memorabilia. The museum's nature center has 22 acres of trails encompassing three distinct ecosystems—sand pine hills, lake lands, and marshlands. *2201 Michigan Ave., tel. 407/632–1830. Admission: $3 adults, $1.50 senior citizens and students over 3. Open Tues.–Sat. 10–4, Sun. 1–4.*

Budget Lodging

$$ **Pelican Landing Resort on the Ocean.** This two-story beachfront motel is friendly and warm. Units have ocean views and fully equipped kitchens; one even has a screened porch. Boardwalks to the beach, picnic tables, and a gas grill round out the amenities. *1201 S. Atlantic Ave., 32931, tel. 407/783–7197. 11 units. Facilities: grill, picnic area, beach. D, MC, V.*

$$ **Wakulla Motel.** This motel has the best occupancy rate on the beach. Rooms are bright and decorated in tropical prints. The completely furnished five-room suites, designed to sleep six, are great for families; they include two bedrooms, living room, dining room, and fully equipped kitchen. The grounds are landscaped with tropical vegetation. *3550 N. Atlantic Ave., 32931, tel. 407/783–2230. 116 suites. Facilities: grills, 2 pools, shuffleboard. AE, D, DC, MC, V.*

Budget Dining

$$ **Pier House Restaurant.** In this elegant establishment in a shopping, dining, and entertainment complex on Cocoa Beach Pier, you can enjoy fresh fish in a room with floor-to-ceiling windows that overlook the ocean. Try the mahimahi or the grouper, which you can order broiled, blackened, grilled, or fried. *401 Meade Ave., tel. 407/783–7549. Reservations advised. Dress: casual but neat. AE, DC, MC, V. No lunch.*

$ ★ **Herbie K's.** This diner is a 1950s rock-and-roll landmark. The jukebox plays the '50s, and dancing servers dress, walk, and talk the '50s. You'll see saddle shoes and revisit expressions such as "daddy-o" and "doll-face." Famous for its burgers, Herbie K's also serves home-style blue plate dinners and old-fashioned ice-cream desserts. It's great for families. *2080 N. Rte. A1A, tel. 407/783–6740. Reservations not needed. Dress: casual. AE, D, DC, MC, V.*

$ **Lone Cabbage Fish Camp.** The natural habitat of wildlife and local characters, this one-of-a-kind spot sits on the St. Johns River 9 miles north of Cocoa city limits on Route 520 and 4 miles west of I–95. The catfish, frogs' legs, turtle, country ham, and alligator on the menu make the drive well worthwhile. You can also fish from a dock here, buy bait, or rent a canoe for a trip on the St. Johns, making for a fun family outing. *8199 Rte. 520, Cocoa, tel. 407/632–4199. Dress: casual. No credit cards.*

Index

NOTES

NOTES

NOTES

NOTES

NOTES

NOTES

NOTES

NOTES

NOTES

Fodor's Travel Publications

Available at bookstores everywhere, or call 1–800–533–6478, 24 hours a day.

Gold Guides

U.S.

Alaska
Arizona
Boston
California
Cape Cod, Martha's Vineyard, Nantucket
The Carolinas & the Georgia Coast
Chicago
Colorado

Florida
Hawaii
Las Vegas, Reno, Tahoe
Los Angeles
Maine, Vermont, New Hampshire
Maui
Miami & the Keys
New England

New Orleans
New York City
Pacific North Coast
Philadelphia & the Pennsylvania Dutch Country
The Rockies
San Diego
San Francisco

Santa Fe, Taos, Albuquerque
Seattle & Vancouver
The South
U.S. & British Virgin Islands
USA
Virginia & Maryland
Waikiki
Washington, D.C.

Foreign

Australia & New Zealand
Austria
The Bahamas
Barbados
Bermuda
Brazil
Budapest
Canada
Cancún, Cozumel, Yucatán Peninsula
Caribbean
China
Costa Rica, Belize, Guatemala
The Czech Republic & Slovakia
Eastern Europe

Egypt
Europe
Florence, Tuscany & Umbria
France
Germany
Great Britain
Greece
Hong Kong
India
Ireland
Israel
Italy
Japan
Kenya & Tanzania
Korea
London

Madrid & Barcelona
Mexico
Montréal & Québec City
Morocco
Moscow, St. Petersburg, Kiev
The Netherlands, Belgium & Luxembourg
New Zealand
Norway
Nova Scotia, New Brunswick, Prince Edward Island
Paris
Portugal

Provence & the Riviera
Scandinavia
Scotland
Singapore
South America
South Pacific
Southeast Asia
Spain
Sweden
Switzerland
Thailand
Tokyo
Toronto
Turkey
Vienna & the Danube

Fodor's Special-Interest Guides

Branson
Caribbean Ports of Call
The Complete Guide to America's National Parks
Condé Nast Traveler Caribbean Resort and Cruise Ship Finder
Cruises and Ports of Call

Fodor's London Companion
France by Train
Halliday's New England Food Explorer
Healthy Escapes
Italy by Train

Kodak Guide to Shooting Great Travel Pictures
Shadow Traffic's New York Shortcuts and Traffic Tips
Sunday in New York
Sunday in San Francisco
Walt Disney World, Universal Studios and Orlando

Walt Disney World for Adults
Where Should We Take the Kids? California
Where Should We Take the Kids? Northeast

Special Series

Affordables

Caribbean

Europe

Florida

France

Germany

Great Britain

Italy

London

Paris

Fodor's Bed & Breakfasts and Country Inns

America's Best B&Bs

California's Best B&Bs

Canada's Great Country Inns

Cottages, B&Bs and Country Inns of England and Wales

The Mid-Atlantic's Best B&Bs

New England's Best B&Bs

The Pacific Northwest's Best B&Bs

The South's Best B&Bs

The Southwest's Best B&Bs

The Upper Great Lakes' Best B&Bs

The Berkeley Guides

California

Central America

Eastern Europe

Europe

France

Germany & Austria

Great Britain & Ireland

Italy

London

Mexico

Pacific Northwest & Alaska

Paris

San Francisco

Compass American Guides

Arizona

Canada

Chicago

Colorado

Hawaii

Hollywood

Las Vegas

Maine

Manhattan

Montana

New Mexico

New Orleans

Oregon

San Francisco

South Carolina

South Dakota

Texas

Utah

Virginia

Washington

Wine Country

Wisconsin

Wyoming

Fodor's Español

California

Caribe Occidental

Caribe Oriental

Gran Bretaña

Londres

Mexico

Nueva York

Paris

Fodor's Exploring Guides

Australia

Boston & New England

Britain

California

Caribbean

China

Florence & Tuscany

Florida

France

Germany

Ireland

Italy

London

Mexico

Moscow & St. Petersburg

New York City

Paris

Prague

Provence

Rome

San Francisco

Scotland

Singapore & Malaysia

Spain

Thailand

Turkey

Venice

Fodor's Flashmaps

Boston

New York

San Francisco

Washington, D.C.

Fodor's Pocket Guides

Acapulco

Atlanta

Barbados

Jamaica

London

New York City

Paris

Prague

Puerto Rico

Rome

San Francisco

Washington, D.C.

Rivages Guides

Bed and Breakfasts of Character and Charm in France

Hotels and Country Inns of Character and Charm in France

Hotels and Country Inns of Character and Charm in Italy

Short Escapes

Country Getaways in Britain

Country Getaways in France

Country Getaways Near New York City

Fodor's Sports

Golf Digest's Best Places to Play

Skiing USA

USA Today The Complete Four Sport Stadium Guide

Fodor's Vacation Planners

Great American Learning Vacations

Great American Sports & Adventure Vacations

Great American Vacations

National Parks and Seashores of the East

National Parks of the West

What's hot, where it's hot!

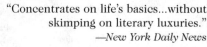

Wet 'n Wild®

$3 OFF

Present this coupon and save $3.00 off the regular all-day adult or child admission price. Coupon good for up to six people. Not to be used in conjunction with any other discounted offer or afternoon pricing.

Expires 12/31/96.

Wet 'n Wild®

$3 OFF

Present this coupon and save $3.00 off the regular all-day adult or child admission price. Coupon good for up to six people. Not to be used in conjunction with any other discounted offer or afternoon pricing.

Expires 12/31/96.

$3⁰⁰ OFF

All-Day Studio Pass

Regular admission price $37⁰⁰ (plus tax)

RIDE THE MOVIES!®

At Universal Studios Florida® you'll find yourself "in the movies" at every turn! So get ready to ride the blockbusters like E.T.®, Back to the Future®...The Ride℠, Earthquake® and more as you see how movie magic is recreated at THE #1 MOVIE STUDIO AND THEME PARK IN THE WORLD!

20% OFF

Food and beverages purchased for your party (up to six) at Studio Stars Restaurant or Finnegan's Pub.

Present Coupon to your server when ordering. Tax and gratuity not included. This coupon has no cash value and is not valid with other specials or discounts. Valid through 12/31/96.

$3⁰⁰ OFF
All-Day Studio Pass

$3.00 discount valid through 12/31/96. Coupon valid for up to 6 people and must be presented at the time of purchase. This offer has no cash value and is not valid with any other special discounts. Subject to change without notice. Parking fee not included.

6183920001990

DINE HOLLYWOOD-STYLE

Be a part of the scene at the Studio Stars Restaurant (across from Ghostbusters®) or drop into Finnegan's Pub for Irish spirits, ales and entertainment. Your 20% discount is good for a party of six! Remember to present this coupon when ordering.